Microsoft® Windows®
Registry Guide,
Second Edition

Jerry Honeycutt

PUBLISHED BY
Microsoft Press
A Division of Microsoft Corporation
One Microsoft Way
Redmond, Washington 98052-6399

Library of Congress Control Number: 2005923733
Printed and bound in the United States of America.

1 2 3 4 5 6 7 8 9   QWT   9 8 7 6 5

Distributed in Canada by H.B. Fenn and Company Ltd. A CIP catalogue record for this book is available from the British Library.

Microsoft Press books are available through booksellers and distributors worldwide. For further information about international editions, contact your local Microsoft Corporation office or contact Microsoft Press International directly at fax (425) 936-7329. Visit our Web site at www.microsoft.com/learning/. Send comments to *rkinput@microsoft.com.*

Microsoft, Active Directory, Authenticode, DirectX, FrontPage, Hotmail, InfoPath, IntelliMirror, JScript, Microsoft Press, MSDN, MS-DOS, MSN, NetMeeting, OneNote, Outlook, PhotoDraw, PowerPoint, Tahoma, Visio, Visual Basic, Visual InterDev, Win32, Windows, Windows Media, Windows NT, and Windows Server are either registered trademarks or trademarks of Microsoft Corporation in the United States and/or other countries. Other product and company names mentioned herein may be the trademarks of their respective owners.

The example companies, organizations, products, domain names, e-mail addresses, logos, people, places, and events depicted herein are fictitious. No association with any real company, organization, product, domain name, e-mail address, logo, person, place, or event is intended or should be inferred.

This book expresses the author's views and opinions. The information contained in this book is provided without any express, statutory, or implied warranties. Neither the authors, Microsoft Corporation, nor its resellers, or distributors will be held liable for any damages caused or alleged to be caused either directly or indirectly by this book.

Acquisitions Editor: Martin DelRe
Project Editor: Denise Bankaitis
Technical Editor: Bob Hogan
Copy Editor: Maria Gargiulo
Production: Elizabeth Hansford
Indexer: Julie Hatley

Body Part No. X11-06983

For Roelof Kroes

Contents at a Glance

Contents

Part IV   Appendixes

A   File Associations 455

B   Network Settings 467

C   Per-User Settings 485

Acknowledgments

Never let authors tell you that they wrote their books all by themselves. Creating a book out of an author's gibberish takes a lot of work from a lot of people with a lot of different skills. Some crack the whip, and others are artisans. They all deserve credit.

I'd like to thank my acquisitions editor, Martin DelRe, who gave me the opportunity to update this book for the second edition. Next, I'm indebted to my project editors Maureen Zimmerman and Denise Bankaitis. Maureen got this edition started, and Denise saw it through to the finish line. They had the responsibility for managing the overall process. If only I could have a manager like Denise working on every book I write....

A number of other people have my admiration as well. The copy editor, Maria Gargiulo, had the unenviable job of correcting my disregard for the rules of grammar. The technical editor, Bob Hogan, reviewed the facts contained in this book. To everyone else involved in the production of this book, I thank you for all your hard work.

Last but not least, I have to extend special accolades to Ralph Ramos. Ralph proofread and tested this book's manuscripts independently. Ralph also converted the settings and scripts contained in this book into the files you find on the companion CD. At a time when depending on other people to get things done is becoming risky, I always know that I can depend on Ralph to deliver. Ralph is a smart fellow who has a strong understanding of the real world, and I'm pretty sure that you'll be hearing much more from Ralph in the future.

Introduction

The registry is the heart and soul of Microsoft Windows XP and Microsoft Windows Server 2003. In my other registry books, I said the same thing about the registry in every version of Windows since Windows 95, and by the time you're finished reading this book, I hope you'll agree. The registry contains the configuration data that makes the operating system work; enables developers to organize configuration data in ways that are impossible using other mechanisms, such as INI files; and is behind just about every feature that you think is great in Windows. More importantly, it enables you to customize Windows in ways that you can't through the user interface.

Windows and every application that runs on Microsoft's latest desktop operating systems do absolutely nothing without consulting the registry first. When you double-click a file, Windows consults the registry to figure out what to do with that file. When you install a device, Windows assigns resources to the device based on information in the registry and then stores the device's configuration in the registry. When you run an application such as Microsoft Office Word 2003, the application looks up your preferences in the registry. If you were to monitor the registry during a normal session, you'd see that it serves up thousands of values within minutes.

In this book, you will learn how to customize the registry, but you must also learn how to maintain it. You must learn how to back up the registry so you can restore it if things go awry. You must also learn the best practices for editing the registry safely.

The registry is an invaluable tool for the IT professional who is deploying, managing, and supporting Windows. Did you know that most policies in Group Policy and system policies are really settings in the registry? Does that give you any ideas? Did you know that scripting registry edits is one of the best ways to deploy settings to users? This book teaches you about policies, scripting, and much more. For example, you will learn how to deploy registry settings during Windows and Microsoft Office 2003 Editions installations. Some deployment problems can be solved only by using the registry, so I describe the most common IT workarounds, too. For example, I show you how to prevent Windows from creating the Microsoft Outlook Express icon on the desktop when a user logs on to the computer for the first time.

This Book Is Different—Really

This book contains information that you're not going to find in any other book about the Windows registry. You'll learn how to find the places where Windows and other programs store settings in the registry. You'll learn how to write scripts to edit the registry. You'll discover registry hacks that are both unique and useful. And you'll read about my personal experiences with the registry and what I consider best practices. For example, in Chapter 2, "Using Registry Editor," you'll learn how I quickly document my changes to the registry—right inside the registry itself.

That's all information for power users, but more than half of this book is for IT professionals. Whether you're a desktop engineer, a deployment engineer, or a support technician, you'll learn techniques that will make your job easier. A lot of this book focuses on how the registry affects Windows and Office deployment. You'll learn about creating and deploying effective default user profiles. You'll learn how to deploy settings with Windows and Office. You'll even learn how to build your own Windows Installer package files expressly for managing settings in the registry. The best part is that just about every tool that I suggest in this book is either free or very inexpensive.

Power Users First, Then IT Professionals

Even the most focused IT professional is a power user at heart, so this book presents information for power users first. Here are the first six chapters, which make up Part I, "Registry Overview":

- **Chapter 1, "Learning the Basics."**   This chapter gives an overview of the registry. It includes common terminology and an explanation of how Windows organizes the registry. You'll learn important concepts, such as the different types of data that you can store in the registry and the difference between little-endian and big-endian storage of double-word values. What exactly is a GUID, anyway? You'll find out here.

- **Chapter 2, "Using Registry Editor."**   Registry Editor is your window into the registry, so this chapter teaches you how to use it effectively.

- **Chapter 3, "Backing Up the Registry."**   Backing up the registry protects your settings. This chapter shows quick and easy ways to back up settings, as well as ways to back up the entire registry.

- **Chapter 4, "Hacking the Registry."**   This chapter is a power user's dream come true because it describes some of the greatest hacks for Windows, such as how to customize Windows Explorer.

- **Chapter 5, "Mapping Tweak UI."** Microsoft now has an updated version of Tweak UI, and this chapter describes it in detail. You not only learn how to use Tweak UI—you'll learn exactly where in the registry Tweak UI stores each setting so that you can use your own scripts to apply these settings.

- **Chapter 6, "Configuring Servers."** This chapter describes some common registry customizations for Windows Server 2003.

Part II, "Registry in Management," contains information useful to both power users and IT professionals. In this section, you'll learn how to manage the registry and how to use the registry as a management tool.

- **Chapter 7, "Using Registry-Based Policy."** This chapter focuses on Group Policy and system policies. You'll learn the differences between them and how each policy can be used to manage computers and users. Also—and this is important—you'll learn how to build your own policy templates for Group Policy.

- **Chapter 8, "Configuring Windows Security."** Windows secures settings in the registry. This chapter shows you how to manage the registry's security. It also shows you how to selectively poke holes in the registry's security so that you can deploy and run legacy applications on Windows. Last, this chapter describes how to customize new security features in Windows XP Service Pack 2 (SP2).

- **Chapter 9, "Troubleshooting Problems."** Things sometimes go wrong. This chapter shows you how to recover if they do.

- **Chapter 10, "Finding Registry Settings."** Finding the location where Windows stores a setting in the registry is easy, as long as you know which tools to use. I'll give you a hint: Word 2003 is the second-best registry tool. You'll also learn about tools that you can use to remotely monitor the registry.

- **Chapter 11, "Scripting Registry Changes."** A plethora of methods for customizing registry edits are available to you. This chapter teaches the best of them, including REG files, INF files, and Microsoft Windows Installer (MSI) package files. It also describes tools such as Console Registry Tool for Windows, which comes free with Windows. This is useful for editing the registry from batch files.

Part III, "Registry in Deployment," is primarily for IT professionals. This part of the book helps you use the registry to deploy Windows and Office more effectively. It includes the following chapters:

- **Chapter 12, "Deploying User Profiles."** Default user profiles are an effective way to deploy default settings to users. This chapter describes not only default user profiles, but mandatory and roaming user profiles as well. This chapter is unique because it describes a useful process for building profiles that ensures that they'll work for all users in your organization.

- **Chapter 13, "Mapping Windows Installer."** Windows Installer is a relatively new service that provides a better way to install applications. This chapter describes how Windows Installer interacts with the registry. It will also help you clean up the registry when things go wrong with Windows Installer–based applications.

- **Chapter 14, "Deploying with Answer Files."** This chapter shows you how to script a Windows installation and how to add registry settings.

- **Chapter 15, "Cloning Disks with Sysprep."** Many companies that previously maintained up to 50 Windows 2000 disk images now can use a single Windows XP disk image. They do this by generalizing their disk images so that they work on the widest possible variety of hardware. That's the topic of this chapter. This chapter also shows how Sysprep interacts with the registry.

- **Chapter 16, "Configuring Windows PE."** This chapter describes how to create and customize Windows Preinstallation Environment (Windows PE) CD images.

- **Chapter 17, "Deploying Office 2003 Settings."** A big part of an Office 2003 Editions deployment project is deploying user settings. This chapter describes a variety of ways to do just that. You'll learn about tools that come with the *Microsoft Office 2003 Editions Resource Kit*, for example, as well as techniques for using them.

- **Chapter 18, "Fixing Common IT Problems."** This is a special chapter that addresses the comments and questions that I frequently receive from IT professionals. How should you handle coexistence issues between Microsoft Access 97 and Access 2003? That's just one of many IT issues that you can address by using the registry.

Part IV, "Appendixes," is a reference that describes the contents of the registry. In the few pages available in this book, I can't possibly describe every registry value. But Part IV describes some of the most interesting settings. These appendixes describe the relationships between different portions of the registry, including how a variety of registry keys and values interact.

Some Terminology

Most of the terminology that I use in this book is fairly standard by now, but to avoid confusion, I'll take a moment to describe how I use some of it.

Rather than give you hardcoded paths, I instead use the standard environment variables that represent those paths. That way, when you read the instructions, you'll be able to apply them to your scenario regardless of whether you're using a dual-boot configuration and regardless of where on your computer user profiles exist: C:\Documents and Settings or C:\Winnt\Profiles. Additionally, on your computer, the folder that contains the Windows system files might be in a different location depending on whether you upgraded to Windows, installed a clean copy of the operating system, or customized the installation path in an answer file. Thus, I use the following environment variables throughout this book. (You can see these environment variables by typing **set** in a command prompt window.)

- *%UserProfile%* represents the current user profile folder. Thus, if you log on to the computer as **Jerry** and your profile folders are in C:\Documents and Settings, you'd translate *%UserProfile%* to C:\Documents and Settings\Jerry.

- *%SystemDrive%* is the drive that contains the Windows system files. That's usually drive C, but if you installed Windows on a different drive, perhaps in a dual-boot configuration, it could be drive D, E, and so on.

- *%SystemRoot%* is the folder containing Windows. In a clean installation, this is usually C:\Windows, but if you upgraded from Windows NT or Windows 2000, it's probably C:\Winnt.

In addition to environment variables, I also use abbreviations for the various root keys in the registry. HKEY_CLASSES_ROOT and HKEY_LOCAL_MACHINE are unwieldy, for example, and cause lines of text to wrap in odd places. To make the book more readable, I use the following abbreviations:

HKCR	HKEY_CLASSES_ROOT
HKCU	HKEY_CURRENT_USER
HKLM	HKEY_LOCAL_MACHINE
HKU	HKEY_USERS
HKCC	HKEY_CURRENT_CONFIG

Why I Love Windows XP

Before we move on to the rest of the book, I thought I'd share with you why I love Windows XP so much. Windows XP makes all my tasks much easier; it even made it easier to write this book than it was to write any other book I've ever written.

For example, one of my favorite features in Windows XP is Remote Desktop. Before I got Windows XP, I either had to have several computers sitting on my desk for testing instructions, digging around in the registry, taking screen shots, and so on, or I had to walk back and forth between my lab and my office, which was a major productivity drain. For this book, I configured Remote Desktop on each Windows XP–based computer in my lab so that I could connect to them from my production computer. That way, I could have two or three Remote Desktop connections open, each with a different test scenario running. Remote Desktop reduced by a huge amount the time it took to write this book. It also reduced the number of times that I was tempted to experiment on my production computer (which could result in a day of lost work if I corrupted the computer's configuration). Remote Desktop alone was worth the cost of Windows XP.

And did I mention wireless networking? Windows XP enables me to get out of my office—in which I have 10 or so computers running, with the fan and hard drive noise that that entails. Thanks to wireless networking, which Windows XP makes very easy to configure, I could find a quiet place in my house to work while I was writing this book. No fans. No noise. And even when I was working in the bedroom, I could still connect to the computers in my lab.

Regarding the registry itself, there are a few changes that struck me right away. First, Microsoft got rid of the dueling registry editors. Windows 2000 had two editors: Regedit and Regedt32. Both had strengths and weakness, and you had no choice but to flip back and forth between the two. Windows XP and Windows Server 2003 combine both editors into a single registry editor. Another new feature is Console Registry Tool for Windows (Reg). Windows XP and Windows Server 2003 include this tool by default, whereas in Windows 2000, you had to install it from the support tools. This makes it a more viable tool for scripting registry edits using batch files. And it's free!

Sample Files and Scripts

This book describes a large number of settings. It also includes numerous scripts. To make it easier to use these settings, I've provided on the companion CD the REG files that implement them. You also find sample scripts from this book on the companion CD in the RegistryGuideTools folder.

> **Note**   The tools on the CD are designed to be used on Windows Server 2003 or Windows XP (or as specified in the documentation of the tool).

Resource Kit Support Policy

Microsoft does not support the tools supplied on this book's companion CD. Microsoft does not guarantee the performance of the tools or any bug fixes for these tools. However, Microsoft Press provides a way for customers who purchase *Microsoft Windows Registry Guide, Second Edition* to report any problems with the software and to receive feedback for such issues. To report any issues or problems, send an e-mail message to *rkinput@microsoft.com*.

Microsoft Press also provides corrections for books and companion CDs through the World Wide Web at *http://www.microsoft.com/learning/support/*. To connect directly to the Microsoft Knowledge Base and enter a query regarding a question or issue you have, go to *http://support.microsoft.com*. For issues related to the Microsoft Windows family of operating systems, refer to the support information included with your product.

Final Note

I hope that this book makes your Windows XP and Windows Server 2003 experience even better. I also hope that it will make you more productive and more effective.

If you have any comments or questions, please feel free to send them my way at *jerry@honeycutt.com*. I answer my e-mail. You can also visit my Web site, *http://www.honeycutt.com*, to download the samples that you see in this book. You'll also find mailing lists that you can join as well as additional articles that I've written about Windows, the registry, and various deployment topics.

System Requirements

The system requirements for using this book and the files on the companion CD are simple: these files work on any computer running Windows XP or Windows Server 2003. For more detailed information about whether any individual file works on Windows XP, Windows Server 2003, or both, see the help file on this book's companion CD.

The following system configuration is recommended for the best viewing experience with Microsoft Press eBooks:

- Microsoft Windows Server 2003, Windows 2000, or Windows XP
- Pentium II (or similar) with 266-megahertz (MHz) or higher processor
- 64 megabytes (MB) of RAM
- 800 x 600 display settings with high-color (16-bit)
- Microsoft Internet Explorer 5.5 or later
- Adobe Acrobat or Acrobat Reader

Part I
Registry Overview

Working with the registry is daunting if you know little about it. Thus, in Part I, you master the basic information you need to successfully leverage the registry. For example, you learn about the contents of the registry and the types of data that you find in it. You also learn how to back up and restore the registry and how to edit the registry using Registry Editor.

Part I is for information technology (IT) professionals and power users. Aside from teaching the basics, such as how to back up the registry, it describes how to configure settings in the registry to customize Microsoft Windows XP and Microsoft Windows Server 2003. Many of the settings you learn about in this part aren't available through the user interface. This part also describes one of the most popular downloads on the Internet: Tweak UI. Instead of showing you how to use this simple program, however, it describes where the program stores each of its settings in the registry.

Don't skip Part I; read it from beginning to end. With the basics mastered, and a sense of what you can do with the registry, you'll be better prepared to tackle the rest of this book.

Chapter 1
Learning the Basics

The registry has a subtle but important role in Microsoft Windows XP and Microsoft Windows Server 2003 (both referred to throughout this book as Windows). On one hand, the registry is passive—it's just a big collection of settings sitting on your hard disk, and you probably don't think much about it while you're editing a document, browsing the Internet, or searching for a file. On the other hand, it plays a key role in all those activities. The registry settings determine how Windows appears and behaves. They even control applications running on your computer. This gives the registry great potential as a tool for power users or IT professionals, enabling them to customize settings that aren't available in the user interface.

This chapter introduces the registry. First you learn about the registry's role and how it fits into your computing world. Then some important terminology is explained, and you learn how Windows organizes the registry. Next you learn about the tools used to edit the registry. And finally, you see how Windows stores the registry on the hard disk. Throughout this chapter, you'll find information that is useful even outside of a discussion of the registry. For example, you learn about the two different architectures for storing numbers in memory; IT professionals run into these architectures outside the registry as much as they do inside it.

This is all basic information, but don't skip this chapter. Read it once, and you'll be ready for the rest of this book.

Heart and Soul of Windows

Windows stores configuration data in the registry. The registry is a hierarchical data-base, which can be described as a central repository for configuration data (Microsoft's terminology) or as a configuration database (my terminology). A hierar-chical database's characteristics make it ideally suited for storing configuration data. If you lay out the database in a diagram, like the one shown in Figure 1-1, it looks like an outline or an organization chart. This allows settings to be referenced using paths, similar to file paths in Windows. For example, in Figure 1-1, the path A\G\M references the shaded box. Each setting is an ordered pair that associates a value's name with its data. The registry's hierarchical organization makes all settings easy to reference.

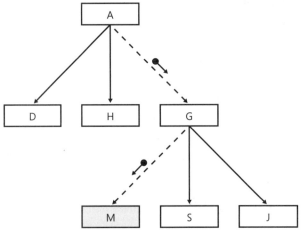

Figure 1-1   The registry is a hierarchical database that contains most Windows settings.

You can do nothing in Windows that doesn't access the registry. I use a tool to moni-tor registry access and often leave it running while clicking around the operating sys-tem's user interface. I almost never see this monitor idle. With every click, Windows consults the registry. Every time I launch a program, the operating system consults the registry. Every application that I use looks for its settings in the registry. The reg-istry is certainly the center of attention.

I've written other books about the registry, and in them, I call the registry *the operating system's heart and soul.* Aside from being a central place to store settings, the registry by its very nature allows complex relationships among different parts of Windows, appli-cations, and the user interface. For example, when you right-click different types of files, you see different shortcut menus. Settings in the registry make this type of con-text-sensitive user interface possible. The settings for each user who logs on to Win-dows are separate from those of other users—again, because of the registry. The ability of Windows to use different configurations for laptop computers depending on whether they're docked or undocked is due in large part to the registry. Even Plug and Play depends on the registry.

For Power Users

So the registry is important, but what good does it do power users to learn about it? First, being a technology enthusiast implies that you like to dabble in technology to learn more about it. What better way to learn more about Windows than to figure out how and where it stores settings? This is analogous to tearing apart your VCR to learn how it works. If you've ever wondered why the operating system behaves in a certain way, the answer can often be found by consulting the registry.

Mastering the registry has concrete advantages for power users, too. Because it is the operating system's configuration database, backing up your settings is a bit easier than it would be without the registry. And unlike in the old days when settings were stored in initialization (INI) files, you always know where to begin looking when you need to find a value. But the biggest advantage of mastering the registry is more exciting and very real: you can customize Windows and the applications that run on it in ways that aren't otherwise possible. Windows has thousands of settings that you'll never see in any dialog box, but that you might want to customize. For example, you can redirect your Favorites folder to a different location, improve your Internet connection's performance, and add commands to any type of file's shortcut menu. Chapter 4, "Hacking the Registry," details many different customization possibilities.

For IT Professionals

IT professionals rely on the registry because it enables most of the management features they use. Large portions of this book focus on those features and how they use the registry.

Policy management is one such feature. IT professionals use policies to configure computer and user settings to a standard, and users can't change those settings. For example, I use policies to configure users' screen savers to lock the desktop after 15 minutes of idle time. This secures the computers if users walk away from their desks without logging off of Windows. Policy management is a great boon to every IT organization because it can lower costs and boost user productivity.

IT professionals can also manage the registry's security so that users can run legacy applications in their restricted accounts instead of logging on to their computers as the administrator (a bad idea in any enterprise environment). You can manage the registry's security directly or by using a tool such as the Security Configuration And Analysis console to automate the process. (For more information on configuring security, see Chapter 8, "Configuring Windows Security.")

IT professionals can also use a combination of scripts with the registry to automate customizations. One IT professional with whom I worked recently wrote scripts that cleaned up and configured users' computers after installing Windows on them. You can address most needs with a good script.

An indirect but important benefit of the registry for IT professionals is application compatibility. Microsoft defines standards for the locations in which different types of settings belong in the registry. The company has standards for file associations, Plug and Play configuration data, printer settings, application settings, and much more. Applications that follow these standards are more likely to work well with the operating system, as well as other applications, because they're all looking for the same settings in the same places. In fact, most applications that work well in Windows 2000 will also work well in Windows XP and Windows Server 2003, given that the overall structure of the registry doesn't change much between the operating systems.

The registry enables too many other management features for IT professionals to neglect mastering it. (See Figure 1-2.) Some of those features include the following:

- Deployment customization
- Folder redirection
- Hardware profiles
- Offline files
- Performance monitoring
- Roaming user profiles
- Windows Management Instrumentation (WMI)

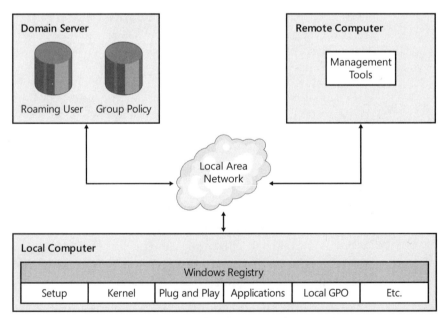

Figure 1-2   The registry enables local and remote administration.

Brief History of the Registry

MS-DOS got its configuration data from Config.sys and Autoexec.bat. The primary purpose of Config.sys was to load device drivers, and the primary purpose of Autoexec.bat was to run programs, set environment variables, and more, to prepare MS-DOS for use. Every application that ran on MS-DOS was responsible for managing its own settings. Neither of these configuration files is useful in Windows.

Windows 3.0 somewhat alleviated the limitations of Autoexec.bat and Config.sys by providing INI files for storing settings. INI files, which you've probably seen, are text files that contain one or more sections with one or more settings in each section. The main problems with INI files are that they provide no hierarchy, storing binary values in them is cumbersome (although not impossible), and they provide no standard for storing similar types of settings. INI files also cause other subtle problems, all related to the configuration file's inability to build complex relationships between applications and the operating system. One big problem for early versions of Windows was the sheer number of INI files that floated around on the average computer. Every application had its own INI files.

Windows 3.1 introduced the registry as a tool for storing OLE (object linking and embedding) settings, and Windows 95 and Microsoft Windows NT 3.5 expanded the registry into the configuration database that Windows XP and Windows Server 2003 use now. Even though INI files are no longer necessary because applications now have a far better way to store settings, you'll always find a handful of INI files, including Win.ini, on any computer.

A few years ago, people were more interested in the history of the registry than they are now. The registry has been around since before 1995, and everyone pretty much takes it for granted these days, so I won't waste any more book pages on its lineage. The history lesson is over; now you're living in the present.

Registry Warnings and Myths

For all of its benefits, the registry is a great paradox. On one hand, it's the central place for all of the Windows configuration data. It's the keystone. On the other hand, the fact that the registry is so critical also makes it one of the operating system's weaknesses. Take out the keystone, and the arch crumbles. If the registry fails, Windows fails. Fortunately, total failure is less likely than my winning the lottery before you finish this book, and partial failure that doesn't prevent you from starting the computer is often easily overcome.

The registry's keystone role is one of the reasons for its mythic stature. Microsoft doesn't say much about it. You don't find Registry Editor on the Start menu. You find very little information about the registry in Help. Microsoft doesn't provide white papers that help users unlock its secrets. And why should they? Do you really want the average user tampering with the registry? The dearth of information coming from Microsoft led to home-grown registry Web sites and FAQs, which are still somewhat popular. These factors have contributed to the myth of the registry as a magical configuration tool.

I want to debunk that myth. Don't get me wrong: there is a lot of power packed into the registry. But there is no magic, and there's nothing to fear. Simply put, the registry is nothing more than your computer's settings. After you're used to working in the registry, doing so no longer gives you chills of excitement; it barely gets a yawn.

The warnings you see in most documents that contain instructions for editing the registry are definitely overblown, particularly for readers of this book, who are either power users or IT professionals. (I wouldn't say that if the book were for novice or intermediate users.) You can do very little damage to the registry that you can't undo, assuming you take the straightforward precautions of backing up settings before you change them and backing up your computer on a regular basis. Failing those steps, you can fix problems by using one of the many troubleshooting tools you learn about in this book. Chapter 9, "Troubleshooting Problems," contains a lot of troubleshooting help. Use a bit of common sense, and you'll do just fine.

Must-Know Concepts

Learning the concepts in the following sections is important to your satisfaction with this book. These are the things you must know to work efficiently with the registry. For example, the registry is filled with hexadecimal numbers, and if you don't understand hexadecimal, they're not going to make sense to you. If you're a programmer, you can probably skip these sections; otherwise, *don't*.

The following sections walk you through the most important of these concepts, beginning with security and globally unique identifiers (GUIDs). You learn how to read hexadecimal numbers, convert them to binary and decimal notation, and use them as bit masks. You learn the difference between Unicode and ANSI character encoding. You even learn how Intel-based computers store numbers in memory. All these topics are significant to your ability to use the registry as a tool.

Security Identifiers

Computer accounts, user accounts, groups, and other security-related objects are *security principles*. *Security Identifiers* (SIDs) uniquely identify security principles. Each time Windows and Active Directory create a security principle, they generate a SID for it. The Windows Local Security Authority (LSA) generates SIDs for local security principles and then stores them in the local security database. The Domain Security Authority generates SIDs for domain security principles and then stores them in Active Directory. SIDs are unique within their scope. Every local security principle's SID is unique on the computer, and every domain security principle's SID is unique within any domain in the enterprise. What's more, Windows and Active Directory never reuse a SID, even if they delete the security principle to which that SID belonged. Thus, if you delete an account and then add it back, the account gets a new SID.

The important thing to remember is that every account has a SID. It's like having a passport number that uniquely identifies you to immigration. You can refer to an account by its name or by its SID, but in practice you seldom use the SID because its format is cumbersome. You frequently see accounts' SIDs in the registry, though, and that's why you're learning about them here.

An example of a SID is `s-1-5-21-2857422465-1465058494-1690550294-500`. A SID always begins with `s-`. The next number identifies the SID's version—in this case, version 1. The next number indicates the identifier authority and is usually `5`, which is NT Authority. The string of numbers up to `500` is the domain identifier, and the rest of the SID is a relative identifier, which is the account or group. This is a very rough overview of the SID format, which is much more complex than this brief example characterizes. If you want to learn more about SIDs, see *http://msdn.microsoft.com/library/ default.asp?url=/library/en-us/secauthz/security/security_identifiers.asp.*

Some SIDs, such as `s-1-5-18`, are shorter than the one in the previous example. These are *well-known SIDs,* and they are the same on every computer and in every domain. They are interesting because they pop up over and over again in the registry and in other places. Table 1-1 describes the SIDs well known by Windows. I've italicized the names of SIDs that are of particular relevance to you while you're reading this book. The placeholder *domain* is the SID's domain identifier.

Table 1-1   Well-Known SIDs

SID	User or Group Name
s-1-0	Null Authority
s-1-0-0	Nobody
s-1-1	World Authority
s-1-1-0	*Everyone*
s-1-2	Local Authority
s-1-2-0	Local
s-1-3	Creator
s-1-3-0	Creator Owner
s-1-3-1	Creator Group
s-1-3-2	Creator Owner Server
s-1-3-3	Creator Owner Group

Table 1-1   Well-Known SIDs

SID	User or Group Name
S-1-4	Nonunique Authority
S-1-5	NT Authority
S-1-5-1	Dialup
S-1-5-2	Network
S-1-5-3	Batch
S-1-5-4	Interactive
S-1-5-5-*X-Y*	Logon Session
S-1-5-6	Service
S-1-5-7	Anonymous
S-1-5-8	Proxy
S-1-5-9	Enterprise Domain Controllers
S-1-5-10	Self
S-1-5-11	Authenticated Users
S-1-5-12	Restricted
S-1-5-13	Terminal Service User
S-1-5-14	Remote Interactive Logon
S-1-5-18	*LocalSystem* or *System*
S-1-5-19	*LocalService*
S-1-5-20	*NetworkService*
S-1-5-*domain*-500	*Administrator*
S-1-5-*domain*-501	*Guest*
S-1-5-*domain*-502	krbtgt
S-1-5-*domain*-512	Domain Admins
S-1-5-*domain*-513	Domain Users
S-1-5-*domain*-514	Domain Guests
S-1-5-*domain*-515	Domain Computers
S-1-5-*domain*-516	Domain Controllers
S-1-5-*domain*-517	Cert Publishers
S-1-5-*root domain*-518	Schema Admins
S-1-5-*root domain*-519	Enterprise Admins
S-1-5-*root domain*-520	Group Policy Creator Owners
S-1-5-*domain*-553	RAS and IAS Servers
S-1-5-32-544	*Administrators*
S-1-5-32-545	*Users*

Table 1-1 Well-Known SIDs

SID	User or Group Name
S-1-5-32-546	*Guests*
S-1-5-32-547	*Power Users*
S-1-5-32-548	Account Operators
S-1-5-32-549	Server Operators
S-1-5-32-550	Print Operators
S-1-5-32-551	Backup Operators
S-1-5-32-552	Replicator
S-1-5-32-554	Pre-Windows 2000 Compatible Access
S-1-5-32-555	*Remote Desktop Users*
S-1-5-32-556	Network Configuration Operators
S-1-6	Site Server Authority
S-1-7	Internet Site Authority
S-1-8	Exchange Authority
S-1-9	Resource Manager Authority

Globally Unique Identifiers

Globally unique identifiers are better known as *GUIDs* (pronounced *goo ids*). They are numbers that uniquely identify objects such as computers, program components, and devices. These objects often have names, but their GUIDs remain unique even if two of the objects have the same name or if their names change. In other words, an object's GUID is similar to a security principle's SID. You will see GUIDs scattered all over the registry, so you should become familiar with them.

All GUIDs have the same interesting format. They're 16-byte hexadecimal numbers in groups of 8, 4, 4, 4, and 12 digits (0 through 9 and A through F). A dash divides each group of digits, and curly brackets enclose the whole number. An example of a real GUID is {645FF040-5081-101B-9F08-00AA002F954E}, which represents the Recycle Bin object that you see on the desktop. The GUID {127A89AD-C4E3-D411-BDC8-001083FDCE08} belongs to one of the computers in my lab.

Programmers often use the Microsoft tool Guidgen.exe to create GUIDs, but Windows generates them, too. Regardless of the source, Microsoft guarantees that GUIDs are globally unique—hence their name. No matter how many times Guidgen.exe or Windows generates a GUID, the result is always unique. That's what makes GUIDs perfect for identifying objects like computers and devices.

Hexadecimal Notation

Ninety-nine percent of the data you see in the registry is in hexadecimal notation. Computers use hexadecimal rather than decimal notation for a good reason, which you'll learn in a bit. You must learn how to read and convert hexadecimal numbers in order to use the registry as an effective tool. And that's the focus of this section.

Binary and decimal notations don't interchange well. You probably learned decimal notation as a child. In this notation, 734 is $7 \times 10^2 + 3 \times 10^1 + 4 \times 10^0$, which is $7 \times 100 + 3 \times 10 + 4 \times 1$. Easy enough, right? The digits are 0 through 9, and because you multiply each digit right to left by increasing powers of 10 (10^0, 10^1, 10^2, and so on), this notation is called *base 10*. The problem is that decimal notation doesn't translate well into the computer's system of ones and zeros. Binary notation does. In this notation, 1011 is $1 \times 2^3 + 0 \times 2^2 + 1 \times 2^1 + 1 \times 2^0$ or $1 \times 8 + 0 \times 4 + 1 \times 2 + 1 \times 1$ or 11. The digits are 0 and 1, and because you multiply each digit right to left by increasing powers of 2 (2^0, 2^1, 2^2, and so on), this notation is called *base 2*. Converting a binary number to a decimal number is a lot of work, and binary numbers are too cumbersome for people to read and write.

That brings us to hexadecimal notation. Hexadecimal notation is *base 16,* and because you can evenly divide 16 by 2, converting between binary and hexadecimal is straightforward. The digits are 0 through 9 and A through F. Table 1-2 shows the decimal equivalent of each digit. In hexadecimal, A09C is $10 \times 16^3 + 0 \times 16^2 + 9 \times 16^1 + 12 \times 16^0$ or $10 \times 4096 + 0 \times 256 + 9 \times 16 + 12 \times 1$, or 41,116 in decimal notation. As in the other examples, you multiply each hexadecimal digit right to left by increasing powers of 16 (16^0, 16^1, 16^2, and so on).

Table 1-2   **Hexadecimal Digits**

Binary	Hexadecimal	Decimal
0000	0	0
0001	1	1
0010	2	2
0011	3	3
0100	4	4
0101	5	5
0110	6	6
0111	7	7
1000	8	8
1001	9	9
1010	A	10
1011	B	11
1100	C	12

Table 1-2   **Hexadecimal Digits**

Binary	Hexadecimal	Decimal
1101	D	13
1110	E	14
1111	F	15

Converting between binary and hexadecimal notations might be straightforward, but it is also time consuming, so Table 1-2 offers a solution. When converting from binary to hexadecimal, use Table 1-2 to look up each group of four digits from left to right, and jot down its hexadecimal equivalent. For example, to convert 01101010 to hexadecimal, look up 0110 to get 6, and then look up 1010 to get A, so that you end up with the hexadecimal number 6A. If the number of digits in the binary number isn't evenly divisible by 4, just pad the left side with zeros. To convert hexadecimal numbers to binary, use Table 1-2 to look up each hexadecimal digit from left to right, and jot down its binary equivalent. For example, to convert 1F from hexadecimal to binary, look up 1 to get 0001, look up F to get 1111, and string them together to get 00011111.

One last problem: Is 12 a decimal number or a hexadecimal number? You don't have enough information to know for sure. The solution is to always use the prefix 0x at the beginning of hexadecimal numbers. Then 0x12 is a hexadecimal number, whereas 12 is a decimal number. This is the standard format for hexadecimal numbers, and it's the format that Microsoft uses in its documentation and in all the tools you'll use in this book.

> **Tip**   If converting binary, hexadecimal, and decimal numbers is too much work for you, as it certainly is for me, use the Windows Calculator. Click Start, All Programs, Accessories, and Calculator. Make sure you change to scientific view by clicking Scientific on the View menu. In the top left part of Calculator's window, you see four buttons: Hex, Dec, Oct, and Bin. Click the button corresponding to the notation in which you want to input a number, type the number, and then click the button corresponding to the notation to which you want to convert the number. You can also use Registry Editor to toggle between decimal and hexadecimal notations when editing certain types of values.

Bits and Bit Masks

You now understand binary and hexadecimal notations, and now you need to know about bit masks. In the registry, Windows sometimes groups settings together in one number. Each bit within that number is a different setting. Thus, you can store eight settings in a byte, 16 settings in a word, and so on. In this book and elsewhere, you'll see instructions that tell you that a setting's bit mask is 0x20, which simply means that you turn on that setting by enabling the bits that 0x20 represents. This will make more sense as you read on.

You count a binary number's bits from right to left, starting with 0. The number in Figure 1-3 is 0x26. The top part shows the binary equivalent, and the second part shows each bit's number. The bit on the far right is bit 0. In this example, bits 1, 2, and 5 are 1, whereas the remaining bits are 0. If you saw instructions that told you to turn on bit 7, you'd change the number to 10100110. When dealing with bits, a binary 1 is the same thing as "yes" or "true," and a binary 0 is the same thing as "no" or "false." In other words, they are *Boolean values.*

Many times, instructions you read won't give you an exact bit number, so you have to do some math. Often, all you'll see is a bit mask, and you'll have to figure out which bits the mask actually represents. For example, to turn on bit 0x40 in the number 0x43, convert both numbers to binary, figure out which bits the mask represents, change those bits to ones in the number, and then convert the number back to hexadecimal. Using Calculator in scientific view is the easiest way to perform these steps. You'd follow the same steps to turn off the setting, except that you'd change the target bits to 0. After a while, you get pretty good at figuring out which bits a mask represents. Moving from right to left, each bit's mask is 0x01, 0x02, 0x04, 0x08, 0x10, 0x20, 0x40, and 0x80. The bottom part of Figure 1-3 illustrates this.

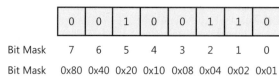

0	0	1	0	0	1	1	0

Bit Mask   7   6   5   4   3   2   1   0

Bit Mask   0x80 0x40 0x20 0x10 0x08 0x04 0x02 0x01

Figure 1-3   You count bits moving from right to left.

> **Note**   Turning bit masks on and off is even easier if you use bitwise math. To turn on a bit mask in a number, OR the two numbers together. To turn a bit mask off in a number, reverse the bits in the mask, and then AND it together with the number: *number* AND NOT *mask*. Using Calculator in scientific view supports all these operations. AND, OR, and NOT are Boolean logic operations. To learn more about these operations, visit the following Web site. *http://www.techweb.com/encyclopedia /defineterm.jhtml?term=boolean+logic&x=47&y=11*

Little-Endian and Big-Endian

In a hexadecimal number such as 0x0102, the 0x01 is the most significant byte, and the 0x02 is the least significant. The leftmost bytes are more significant because you multiply these digits by a higher power of 16. The rightmost digits are less significant, so the digits become more significant as you move from right to left.

Programs store numbers in memory in two ways: big-endian or little-endian. When a program stores a number using big-endian (*big end first*) storage, it stores the most significant bytes in memory first, followed by the less significant bytes. When stored in memory using big-endian storage, the number 0x01020304 is 0x01 0x02 0x03 0x04. It makes sense, doesn't it? However, Intel-based processors use the little-endian (*little end first*) architecture, which means they store the least significant bytes first, followed by the more significant bytes. Thus, the number 0x01020304 is 0x04 0x03 0x02 0x01 in memory.

Although most of the tools you'll use display all numbers—little-endian or big-endian—correctly, you'll have to pay careful attention when you're looking at numbers in binary values, because the tools won't automatically reverse the order of the bytes for you. Thus, if you see the number 0x34 0x77 in a binary value, you'll have to remember to reverse the order of bytes to get the result 0x7734.

ANSI and Unicode Encoding

The first prominent character-encoding scheme (how a computer represents text) was ASCII, and it's still in use today. In ASCII character encoding, each character is eight bits, or a single byte. Because ASCII was for western languages, its use was limited in European countries and regions whose languages contained characters that weren't included in the 256 characters that ASCII supported. To get around this limitation, the International Standards Organization (ISO) created a new character-encoding standard called Latin-1, which included European characters left out of the ASCII set. Microsoft enhanced Latin-1 and called this new standard ANSI. But ANSI is still an 8-bit character encoding that can represent only 256 unique characters. Many languages have thousands of symbols, particularly Asian languages such as Chinese, Korean, and Japanese.

To overcome the limitations of an 8-bit character-encoding standard, Microsoft, partnering with companies such as Apple Computer, Inc., and IBM, created the non-profit consortium Unicode, Inc., to define a new character-encoding standard for international character sets. The work done at Unicode merged with work already in progress at ISO, and the result was the Unicode standard for character encoding. Unicode is a 16-bit encoding standard, which provides for 65,536 unique characters—more than enough to represent all of the world's languages. It even supports arcane languages, such as Sanskrit and Egyptian hieroglyphs, and includes punctuation marks, mathematical symbols, and graphical symbols.

Unicode is the character encoding that is native to Windows, but Windows also supports ANSI. Internally, the operating system represents object names, paths, and file names as 16-bit Unicode characters. It also usually stores data in the registry using Unicode. If a program stores the text *Jerry* using ANSI, it looks like 0x4A 0x65 0x72 0x72 0x79 in memory. However, if the program stores the same string using Unicode, it looks like 0x4A 0x00 0x65 0x00 0x72 0x00 0x72 0x00 0x79 0x00 in memory. Why? Because Unicode text is 16-bit numbers, which Windows stores in little-endian format. (See "Little-Endian and Big-Endian" earlier in this chapter.) Thus, it writes the *J* into memory as 0x004A (with the bytes reversed), followed by the *e* as 0x0065, and then the remaining characters as 0x0072, 0x0072, and 0x0079.

Null and Empty Strings

If you've written programs using a language such as C, the concept of *null* isn't foreign to you. Null is 0x00, or the null character. Windows terminates strings with the null character so that programs know where strings end.

In the registry, a similar concept is that a value can have null data, meaning that it contains no data at all. It's empty. Usually, when you're looking at the null value in the registry, you see the text *(value not set)*. This is different from a value that contains an empty string–text that's zero characters in length, or "". The following values are not the same:

- Null
- ""

Registry Structure

The structure of the Windows registry is very similar to the structure of the Windows file system. Figure 1-4 compares Registry Editor, the tool you use to edit the registry, and Windows Explorer. (You learn how to use Registry Editor in Chapter 2, "Using Registry Editor.") In the editor's left pane, which is called the *key pane,* you see the registry's hierarchy, just as in Windows Explorer you see the file system's hierarchy in the left pane. Each folder in the key pane is a registry *key.* In the editor's right pane, which is called the *value pane,* you see a key's *values,* just as in Windows Explorer's right pane you see a folder's contents.

Take a look at Figure 1-4. In Windows Explorer, you see each of the computer's disks under My Computer. Likewise, in Registry Editor, you see each of the registry's *root keys* under My Computer. Although you see the full name of each root key in Registry Editor, the standard abbreviations that you see in Table 1-3 are easier to type and read.

Table 1-3   Root Keys

Name	Abbreviation
HKEY_CLASSES_ROOT	HKCR
HKEY_CURRENT_USER	HKCU
HKEY_LOCAL_MACHINE	HKLM
HKEY_USERS	HKU
HKEY_CURRENT_CONFIG	HKCC

Keys and folders

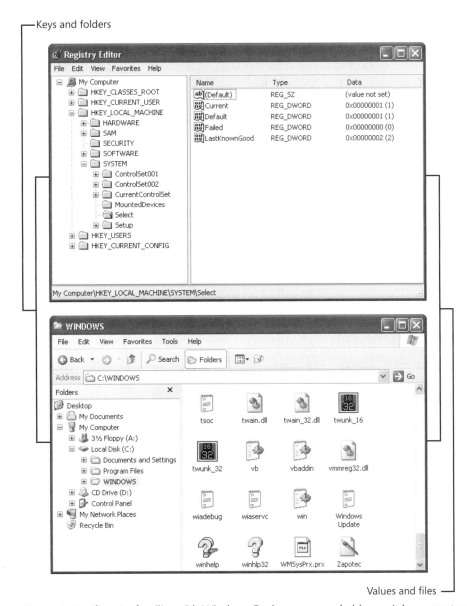

Values and files

Figure 1-4 If you're familiar with Windows Explorer, you probably won't have any trouble understanding the registry's structure, which is similar to that of the file system.

Keys

Keys are so similar to folders that they have the same naming rules. (Registry Editor even uses the same icon for keys that Windows Explorer uses for folders.) You can nest one or more keys within another key as long as the names are unique within each key. A key's name is limited to 512 ANSI or 256 Unicode characters, and you can use any

ASCII character in the name other than a backslash (\), asterisk (*), and question mark (?). In addition, Windows reserves all names that begin with a period for its own use.

The similarities between the registry and file system continue with paths. The path C:\Windows\System32\Sol.exe refers to a file called Sol.exe on drive C in a subfolder of \Windows called System32. The path `HKCU\Control Panel\Desktop\Wallpaper` refers to a value called `Wallpaper` in the root key `HKCU` in a subkey of `Control Panel` called `Desktop`. This notation is a *fully qualified path*. I often refer to a key and all its subkeys as a *branch*.

> **Note**   I usually use the term *key*, but occasionally I use *subkey* to indicate a parent-child relationship between one key and another. Thus, when you see, for example, text that describes the key `Software` and its subkey `Microsoft`, it indicates that `Microsoft` is a child key under `Software`.

The last thing to discuss in this section is the concept of *linked keys*. Windows stores hardware profiles in `HKLM\SYSTEM\CurrentControlSet\Hardware Profiles\`. Each hardware profile is a subkey *nnnn*, where *nnnn* is an incremental number beginning with `0000`. The subkey `Current` is a link to whichever key is the current hardware profile, and root key `HKCC` is a link to `Current`. It all sounds terribly convoluted until you see the relationship illustrated in Figure 1-5. To continue the file system analogy, think of links as aliases or shortcuts.

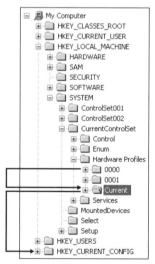

Figure 1-5   When one key is linked to another, as in this example, the same subkeys and values appear in both places.

Values

Each key contains one or more values. In my analogy with Windows Explorer, values are similar to files. A value's *name* is similar to a file's name. A value's *type* is similar to a file's extension, which indicates its type. A value's *data* is similar to the file's actual contents. Click a key in Registry Editor's key pane, and the program shows the key's values in the value pane. In the value pane, you see three columns, which correspond to the three parts of a value:

- **Name.**   Every value has a name. The same rules for naming keys apply to values: up to 512 ANSI or 256 Unicode characters except for the backslash (\), asterisk (*), and question mark (?), with Windows reserving all names that begin with a period. Within each key, value names must be unique, but different keys can have values with the same name.

- **Type.**   Each value's type determines the type of data that it contains. For example, a REG_DWORD value contains a double-word number, and a REG_SZ value contains a string. The section "Types," later in this chapter, describes the different types of data that Windows supports in the registry.

- **Data.**   Each value can be empty, or null, or it can contain data. A value's data can be a maximum of 32,767 bytes, but the practical limit is 2 kilobytes (KB). The data usually corresponds to the type, except that binary values can contain strings, double-words, or anything else.

Every key contains at least one value, and that's the default value. When you look at the registry through Registry Editor, you see the default value as (Default). The default value is almost always a string, but some programs can change it to other types. In most cases, the default value is null, and Registry Editor displays its data as (value not set). When instructions require that you change a key's default value, they usually say so explicitly: "Set the key's default value."

Note   When looking at a key's fully qualified path, you have to figure out whether the path includes a value or not. Usually, the text is clear about whether the path is to a key or includes a value, but sometimes it isn't. For example, does HKCR\txtfile \EditFlags refer to a key or a value? In this case, it refers to a value, and I prefer to use explicit language, such as "the value HKCR\txtfile\EditFlags," to make the reference clear. Sometimes, paths that don't include a value name end with a backslash (\). If there is no backslash, pay particular attention to the context to make sure you know whether the path is just a key or includes a value. Sometimes a bit of common sense is all you need.

Types

Windows supports the following types of data in the registry. As you look through this list, realize that REG_BINARY, REG_DWORD, and REG_SZ account for the vast majority of all the settings in the registry.

- **REG_BINARY.**   Binary data. Registry Editor displays binary data in hexadecimal notation, and you enter binary data using hexadecimal notation. An example of a REG_BINARY value is 0x02 0xFE 0xA9 0x38 0x92 0x38 0xAB 0xD9.

- **REG_DWORD.**   Double-word values (32 bits). Many values are REG_DWORD values used as Boolean flags (0 or 1, true or false, yes or no). You also see time stored in REG_DWORD values in milliseconds (1000 is 1 second). 32-bit unsigned numbers range from 0 to 4,294,967,295, and 32-bit signed numbers range from 2,147,483,648 to 2,147,483,647. You can view and edit these values in decimal or hexadecimal notation. Examples of REG_DWORD values are 0xFE020001 and 0x10010001.

- **REG_DWORD_BIG_ENDIAN.**   Double-word values with the most significant bytes stored first in memory. The order of the bytes is the opposite of the order in which REG_DWORD stores them. For example, the number 0x01020304 is stored in memory as 0x01 0x02 0x03 0x04. You don't see this data type much on Intel-based architectures.

- **REG_DWORD_LITTLE_ENDIAN.**   Double-word values with the least significant bytes stored first in memory (reverse-byte order). This type is the same as REG_DWORD, and because Intel-based architectures store numbers in memory in this format, it is the most common number format in Windows. For example, the number 0x01020304 is stored in memory as 0x04 0x03 0x02 0x01. Registry Editor doesn't offer the ability to create REG_DWORD_LITTLE_ENDIAN values, because this value type is identical to REG_DWORD in the registry.

- **REG_EXPAND_SZ.**   Variable-length text. A value of this type can include environment variables, and the program using the value expands those variables before using it. For example, a REG_EXPAND_SZ value that contains %USERPRO-FILE%\Favorites might be expanded to C:\Documents and Settings\Jerry\Favorites before the program uses it. The registry application programming interface (API) relies on the calling program to expand the environment variables in REG_EXPAND_SZ strings, so the registry value is useless if the program doesn't expand them. See Chapter 12, "Deploying User Profiles," to learn how to use this type of value to fix some interesting problems.

- **REG_FULL_RESOURCE_DESCRIPTOR.** Resource lists for a device or device driver. This data type is important to Plug and Play, but it doesn't figure much in your work with the registry. Registry Editor doesn't provide a way to create this type of value, but it does allow you to display it. See HKLM\HARDWARE\DESCRIPTION \Description for examples of this data type.

- **REG_LINK.** A link. You can't create REG_LINK values.

- **REG_MULTI_SZ.** Binary values that contain lists of strings. Registry Editor displays one string on each line and allows you to edit these lists. In the registry, a null character (0x00) separates each string, and two null characters end the list.

- **REG_NONE.** Values with no defined type.

- **REG_QWORD.** Quadruple-word values (64 bits). This type is similar to REG_DWORD but contains 64 bits instead of 32 bits. The only version of Windows XP that supports this type of value is Windows XP Professional x64 Edition. You can view and edit these values in decimal or hexadecimal notation. An example of a REG_QWORD value is 0xFE02000110010001.

- **REG_QWORD_BIG_ENDIAN.** Quadruple-word values with the most significant bytes stored first in memory. The order of the bytes is the opposite of the order in which REG_QWORD stores them. See REG_DWORD_BIG_ENDIAN for more information about this value type.

- **REG_QWORD_LITTLE_ENDIAN.** Quadruple-word values with the least significant bytes stored first in memory (reverse-byte order). This type is the same as REG_QWORD. See REG_DWORD_LITTLE_ENDIAN for more information. Registry Editor doesn't offer the ability to create REG_QWORD_LITTLE_ENDIAN values, because this value type is identical to REG_QWORD in the registry.

- **REG_RESOURCE_LIST.** List of REG_FULL_RESOURCE_DESCRIPTOR values. Registry Editor allows you to view, but not edit, this type of value.

- **REG_RESOURCE_REQUIREMENTS_LIST.** List of resources that a device requires. Registry Editor allows you to view but not edit this type of value.

- **REG_SZ.** Fixed-length text. Other than REG_DWORD values, REG_SZ values are the most common types of data in the registry. An example of a REG_SZ value is Microsoft Windows XP or Jerry Honeycutt. Each string ends with a null character. Programs don't expand environment variables in REG_SZ values.

Data in Binary Values

Of all the values in the registry, binary values are the least straightforward. When an application reads a binary value from the registry, deciphering its meaning is up to that program. This means that applications can store data in binary values using their own data structures, and those data structures mean nothing to you or any other program. Also, applications often store REG_DWORD and REG_SZ data in REG_BINARY values, which makes finding and deciphering them difficult, as you learn in Chapter 10, "Finding Registry Settings." In fact, some programs use REG_DWORD and 4-byte REG_BINARY values interchangeably; thus, keeping in mind that Intel-based computers use little-endian architecture, the binary value 0x01 0x02 0x03 0x04 and the REG_DWORD value 0x04030201 mean exactly the same thing.

Now it gets more complicated. The registry actually stores all values as binary values. The registry API identifies each type of value by a number, which programmers refer to as a *constant*, and which I tend to think of as the *type number*. You'll notice this type number mostly when you export keys to REG files—something you learn how to do in Chapter 2. For example, when you export a REG_MULTI_SZ value to a REG file, Registry Editor writes a binary value with the type number 7. Normally, the type number associated with each value type doesn't matter because you refer to the values by their names, but there are times when the information in Table 1-4 will be useful.

Table 1-4   Value Types

Number	Type
0	REG_NONE
1	REG_SZ
2	REG_EXPAND_SZ
3	REG_BINARY
4	REG_DWORD
4	REG_DWORD_LITTLE_ENDIAN
5	REG_DWORD_BIG_ENDIAN
6	REG_LINK
7	REG_MULTI_SZ
8	REG_RESOURCE_LIST

Registry Organization

Part IV, "Appendixes," describes the contents of the registry in detail. Until you get there, the following overview makes it easier to get around in the registry.

Of the five root keys you learned about earlier, HKLM and HKU are more important than the others. These are the only root keys that Windows actually stores on disk. The other root keys are links to subkeys in HKLM or HKU. HKCU is a link to a subkey in HKU. HKCR and HKCC are links to subkeys in HKLM. Figure 1-6 illustrates this relationship between root keys and their links to subkeys.

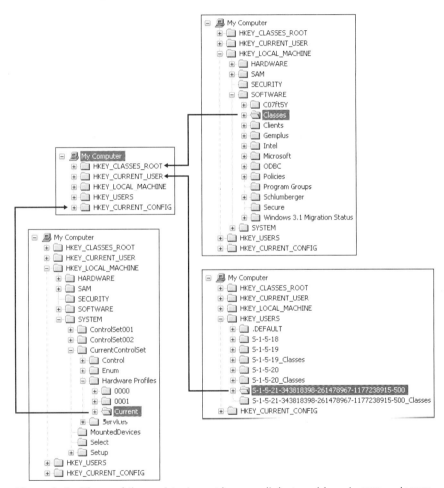

Figure 1-6   Three of the registry's root keys are links to subkeys in HKU and HKLM.

Throughout this book, you'll see the terms *per-user* and *per-computer,* which indicate whether a setting applies to the user or the computer. Per-user settings are user specific—for example, whether or not a user prefers to display Windows Explorer's status bar. Per-computer settings apply to the computer and every user who logs on to the computer—for example, network configuration. Per-user settings are in HKCU, and per-computer settings are in HKLM. In Chapter 12, "Deploying User Profiles," you learn how Windows keeps one user's settings separate from every other user's settings.

HKEY_USERS

HKU contains at least three subkeys:

- .DEFAULT contains the per-user settings that Windows uses to display the desktop before any user logs on to the computer. This isn't the same thing as a default user profile, which Windows uses to create settings for users the first time they log on to the computer.

- *SID*, where *SID* is the security identifier of the *console user* (the user sitting at the keyboard), contains per-user settings. HKCU is linked to this key. This key contains settings such as the user's desktop preferences and Control Panel settings.

- *SID*_classes, where *SID* is the security identifier of the console user, contains per-user class registrations and file associations. Windows merges the contents of keys HKLM\SOFTWARE\Classes and HKU*SID*_classes into HKCR.

> **Note** HKU\.DEFAULT is not the default user profile. For more information on default user profiles, see Chapter 12, "Deploying User Profiles."

You'll usually see other SIDs in HKU, including the following. (See Table 1-1 for a refresher.)

- S-1-5-18 is the well-known SID for the LocalSystem account. Windows loads this account's profile when a program or service runs in the LocalSystem account.

- S-1-5-19 is the well-known SID for the LocalService account. Service Control Manager uses this account to run local services that don't need to run as the LocalSystem account.

- S-1-5-20 is the well-known SID for the NetworkService account. Service Control Manager uses this account to run network services that don't need to run as the LocalSystem account.

You can ignore these SIDs when working in HKU.

Any other subkeys in HKU belong to secondary users. For example, if you use the Windows Runas command to run a program as a different user, the operating system loads that user account's settings into HKU. This feature, which runs under the

Secondary Logon service, enables users to run programs with elevated privileges without requiring them to actually log on to a new session with a different account. For example, if I'm logged on to a computer using the account Jerry, which is in the Power Users group, but I need to perform a task requiring administrative privileges, I hold down the SHIFT key on my keyboard, right-click the program's shortcut, click Run As, and then type the Administrator account's name and password. The program then runs in the context of the Administrator account and, in this case, HKU contains settings for both the Jerry and Administrator accounts. This technique helps prevent human error as well as opportunistic viruses.

Figure 1-7 shows a typical HKU and describes each of its subkeys. You'll see on your computer the same default and service account settings that you see in the figure. The remaining subkeys and their SIDs will be different, depending on the SID of the console user account and whether other accounts have logged on to Windows.

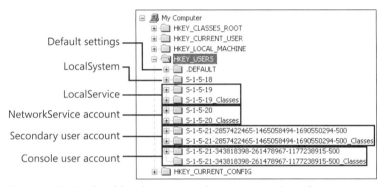

Figure 1-7 Each subkey in HKU contains an account's settings.

HKEY_CURRENT_USER

HKCU contains the console user's per-user settings. This root key is a link to HKU*SID*, where *SID* is the console user's security identifier. This branch includes environment variables, desktop settings, network connections, printers, and application preferences. Here's a snapshot of some of this root key's subkeys:

- **AppEvents.** Associates sounds with events. For example, it associates sounds with opening menus, minimizing windows, and logging off of Windows.

- **Console.** Stores data for the console subsystem, which hosts all character-mode applications, including the MS-DOS command prompt. In addition, the `Console` key can contain subkeys for custom command windows.

- **Control Panel.** Contains accessibility, regional, and desktop appearance settings. You configure most of these settings in Control Panel. However, this key contains a handful of useful settings that have no user interface; you can configure them only through the registry.

- **Environment.** Stores environment variables that users have set. Each value associates an environment variable with the string that Windows substitutes for the variable. The default values for these entries are in the user's profile.

- **Identities.** Contains one subkey for each identity in Microsoft Outlook Express. Outlook Express uses identities to allow multiple users to share a single mail client. With the Windows support for user profiles, one user's settings are separate from other users' settings, so this key is seldom necessary to use.

- **Keyboard Layout.** Contains information about the installed keyboard layouts.

- **Network.** Stores information about mapped network drives. Each subkey in `Network` is a mapped drive to which Windows connects each time the user logs on to the computer. The subkeys' names are the drive letters to which the drives are mapped. Each drive's key contains settings used to reconnect the drive.

- **Printers.** Stores user preferences for printers.

- **Software.** Contains per-user application settings. Windows stores much of its own configuration in this key, too. Microsoft has standardized its organization so that programs store settings in `HKCU\Software\`*Vendor*`\`*Program*`\`*Version*`\`. The variable *Vendor* is the name of the program's publisher, the variable *Program* is the name of the program, and the variable *Version* is the program's version number. Often, as is the case with Windows, *Version* is simply `CurrentVersion`.

- **Volatile Environment.** Contains environment variables that were defined when the user logged on to Windows.

Other subkeys you see in `HKCU` are usually legacy leftovers or uninteresting. They include `UNICODE Program Groups`, `SessionInformation`, and `Windows 3.1 Migration Status`.

HKEY_LOCAL_MACHINE

`HKLM` contains per-computer settings, which means the settings in this branch apply to the computer's configuration and affect every user who logs on to it. Settings range from device driver configurations to Windows settings. `HKLM` contains the following subkeys. (Notice that these subkeys are capitalized; I'll explain why later in this chapter.)

- **HARDWARE.** Stores data describing the hardware that Windows detects as it starts. The operating system creates this key each time it starts, and it includes information about devices and the device drivers and resources associated with them. This key contains information that IT professionals find useful during a network inventory.

- **SAM.** Contains the Windows local security database, the Security Accounts Manager (SAM). Windows stores local users and groups in `SAM`. This key's access control list (ACL) prevents even administrators from viewing it. `SAM` is a link to the key `HKLM\SECURITY\SAM`.

- **SECURITY.**   Contains the Windows local security database in the subkey SAM, as well as other security settings. This key's ACL prevents even administrators from viewing it, unless they take ownership of it.

- **SOFTWARE.**   Contains per-computer application settings. Windows stores settings in this key, too. Microsoft standardized this key's organization so that programs store settings in HKLM\SOFTWARE*Vendor**Program**Version*\. *Vendor* is the name of the program's publisher, *Program* is the name of the program, and *Version* is the program's version number. Often, as is the case with Windows, *Version* is CurrentVersion. HKCR is a link to the key HKLM\SOFTWARE\Classes.

- **SYSTEM.**   Contains control sets, one of which is current. The remaining sets are available for use by Windows. Each subkey is a control set named ControlSet-*nnn*, where *nnn* is an incremental number beginning with 001. The operating system maintains at least two control sets to ensure that it can always start properly. These sets contain device driver and service configurations. HKLM\SYSTEM\CurrentControlSet is a link to ControlSet*nnn*, and the key HKLM\SYSTEM\Select indicates which ControlSet*nnn* is in use.

HKEY_CLASSES_ROOT

HKCR contains two types of settings. The first type is file associations that associate different file types with the programs that can open, print, and edit them. The second type is class registrations for Component Object Model (COM) objects. This root key is one of the most interesting in the registry to customize, because it enables you to change a lot of the operating system's behavior. This root key is also the largest in the registry, accounting for the vast majority of the space that the registry consumes.

Before Windows 2000, HKCR was a link to the key HKLM\SOFTWARE\Classes, but this root key is more complicated now. To derive HKCR, the operating system merges two keys: HKLM\SOFTWARE\Classes, which contains default file associations and class registrations, and HKCU\Software\Classes, which contains per-user file associations and class registrations. HKCU\Software\Classes is really a link to HKU*SID*_Classes, which you learned about in the "HKEY_USERS" section in this chapter. If the same value appears in both branches, the value in HKCU\Software\Classes has higher precedence and wins over the value in HKLM\SOFTWARE\Classes. This new merge algorithm has several benefits:

- Programs can register per-computer *and* per-user program file associations and program classes. (One user can have file associations that other users who share the computer don't have.) This is probably the biggest benefit of the merge.

- Users who share a single computer can use two different programs to edit the same type of file without affecting each other.

- Because per-user file associations and class registrations are in the users' pro-files, they follow users from computer to computer when using roaming user profiles.

- IT professionals can limit access to HKLM\SOFTWARE\Classes without preventing users from changing HKCU\Software\Classes, allowing for greater security in the registry without crippling users' ability to change associations.

Create a new key in the root of HKCR, and Windows actually creates it in HKLM\SOFT-WARE\Classes. Windows doesn't provide a user interface other than Registry Editor to add class registrations to HKCU\Software\Classes, because the intention is to allow programs to register per-user program classes. When you edit an existing program class, the change is reflected in HKLM or HKCU, depending on where the program class already exists. If the program class exists in both places, Windows updates only the version in HKCU.

Note   HKCR is significant enough that it has its own appendix. Appendix A, "File Associations," describes this root key in detail. You learn how it associates file extensions with file types, how Windows registers COM objects, and which subkeys are the most interesting to customize.

HKEY_CURRENT_CONFIG

HKCC is a link to configuration data for the current hardware profile, the key HKLM\SYS-TEM\CurrentControlSet\Hardware Profiles\Current. In turn, Current is a link to the key HKLM\SYSTEM\CurrentControlSet\Hardware Profiles*nnnn*, where *nnnn* is an incremental number beginning with 0000. For more information, see Appendix D, "Per-Computer Settings."

Registry Management Tools

Hundreds of third-party and shareware registry tools are available. You learn about many of them throughout this book. The following list introduces some of the tools I use most often:

- **Microsoft Registry Editor.**   You learn about Registry Editor in Chapter 2, "Using Registry Editor." This is the primary tool you use to edit settings in the registry.

- **Microsoft Console Registry Tool for Windows (Reg.exe).**   This command-line registry tool supports most of the capabilities of Registry Editor. This tool is significant because it allows you to script registry edits in batch files. For more information about Reg.exe, see Chapter 11, "Scripting Registry Changes."

- **Microsoft WinDiff.**   This tool comes with the Windows Support Tools, which you install from \Support\Tools on the Windows installation CD. It's the best program I've found for comparing files, a useful technique for tracking down settings in the registry. For more information about using this tool, see Chapter 10, "Finding Registry Settings."

- **Microsoft Word 2003.**   This application might not seem like a registry management tool, but when WinDiff isn't available, I use Word to compare files so I can figure out where a program stores a setting in the registry. I also use Word to edit scripts so that I can take advantage of its built-in version control and revision-tracking features.

If you used the *Microsoft Windows 2000 Resource Kit* tools to manage Windows, you probably noticed the absence of tools from the *Microsoft Windows XP Resource Kit*. The *Microsoft Windows XP Resource Kit* CD contains only a copy of the kit's documentation. This is partially because Windows XP includes many of these tools, as do the Windows Support Tools. (These are on your Windows XP installation CD in \Support \Tools.) Most of the *Microsoft Windows 2000 Resource Kit* tools still work well in Windows XP, and you can download many of them from Microsoft's Web site at *http://www.microsoft.com/windows2000/techinfo/reskit/tools/default.asp*.

> **Note**   If you're looking for a particular tool not discussed in this book, you can find it easily. Navigate to the ZDNet Downloads site at *http://downloads-zdnet.com.com* in Microsoft Internet Explorer, and then search for *registry* in the Windows category. The result is a list of hundreds of registry tools with a wide variety of special features, such as search and replace. Make sure that any program you download works with Windows XP and Windows Server 2003, though.

Registry Hive Files

In Registry Editor, you see the registry's logical structure. This is how Windows presents the registry to you and to the programs that use it, regardless of how the operating system actually organizes it on disk, which is much more complicated.

Physically, Windows organizes the registry in *hives* (registry branches stored in unique files), each of which is in a binary file called a *hive file*. For each hive file, Windows creates additional supporting files that contain backup copies of each hive's data. These backups allow the operating system to repair the hive during the installation and boot processes if something goes terribly wrong. You find hives in only two root keys: HKLM and HKU. (All other root keys are links to keys within those two.) The hive and supporting files for all hives other than those in HKU are in %SystemRoot% \System32\config. Hive files for HKU are in users' profile folders. Hive files don't have a file name extension, but their supporting files do, as described in Table 1-5.

Table 1-5   Hive File Name Extensions

Extension	Description
None	Hive file.
.alt	Not used in Windows XP or Windows Server 2003. In Windows 2000, System.alt is a backup copy of the System hive file.
.log	Transaction log of changes to a hive.
.sav	Copy of a hive file made at the end of the text-mode phase of the Windows setup program.

> **Note**   The Windows setup program has two phases: text-mode and graphics-mode. The setup program copies each hive file to a SAV (.sav) file at the end of the text-mode phase so that it can recover the Windows setup process if the graphics-mode phase fails. If the graphics-mode phase does fail, the setup program repeats that phase after restoring the hive file from the SAV file.

Hives in HKLM

Table 1-6 shows the relationship between each registry hive and its hive file. Notice that the name of each hive is capitalized in the registry, which is sometimes a useful reminder while you're editing. Notice in this table that each hive in the first column comes from the files in the second column. Thus, Windows loads the hive HKLM\SOFTWARE from the hive file Software, which is in %SystemRoot%\System32\config. It loads the hive HKLM\SYSTEM from the hive file System, which is in the same location. To see the hive files that Windows has loaded, see HKLM\SYSTEM\CurrentControlSet\Control\hivelist\.

Table 1-6   Hive Files

Hive	Hive, Supporting Files
HKLM\SAM	SAM, SAM.LOG
HKLM\SECURITY	SECURITY, SECURITY.LOG
HKLM\SOFTWARE	Software, Software.log, Software.sav
HKLM\SYSTEM	System, System.log, System.sav

Did you notice that you don't find a hive file for HKLM\HARDWARE in Table 1-6? That's because this hive is dynamic. Windows builds it each time the operating system boots, and it doesn't save the hive as a hive file when it shuts down.

Note   Other files in %SystemRoot%\System32\config seem conspicuously out of place. AppEvent.Evt, SecEvent.Evt, and SysEvent.Evt are the Windows event logs—Application, Security, and System, respectively. You can see in the registry where Windows stores each event log by looking at the subkeys of HKLM\SYSTEM\CurrentControlSet \Services\Eventlog. Userdiff is a file that Windows uses to convert user profiles from earlier versions of Windows (notably versions of Microsoft Windows NT) so that Windows can use them. Finally, the file Netlogon.ftl contains the names of available domains in the drop-down list box in the Welcome to Windows dialog box.

Hives in HKU

Each subkey in HKU is also a hive. For example, HKU\.DEFAULT is a hive, and its hive file is %SystemRoot%\System32\config\default. The remaining subkeys come from two different sources, though. The hive HKU*SID* is in the hive file %UserProfile% \NTUSER.DAT, while the hive HKU*SID*_Classes is in the hive file %UserProfile% \Local Settings\Application Data\Microsoft\Windows\UsrClass.dat.

Each time a new user logs on to Windows, the operating system uses the default user profile to create a new profile for that user. The profile contains a new NTUSER.DAT hive file, which is the user profile hive. You learn much more about user profiles and how to deploy them in Chapter 12, "Deploying User Profiles."

To see which profiles Windows has loaded and the hive file that corresponds to each hive, see the key HKLM\SOFTWARE\Microsoft\Windows NT\CurrentVersion\ProfileList. This key contains one subkey for each profile that the operating system has ever loaded, past and present. The subkey's name is the name of the hive in HKU, and the value ProfileImagePath contains the path to the hive file, which is always NTUSER.DAT. ProfileList does not mention the *SID*_Classes hives, however; it contains only user profile hives.

Note   Windows 2000 limited the size of the registry, but Windows XP and Windows Server 2003 do not. This means that the operating system no longer limits the amount of space that the registry hives consume in memory or on the hard disk. Microsoft made an architectural change to the way Windows maps the registry into memory, eliminating the need for the size limit you might have struggled with in Windows 2000.

Chapter 2
Using Registry Editor

Registry Editor is the tool you use to edit the registry directly. You change the registry every time you log on to the computer, and you also do it indirectly through Control Panel or the Run dialog box, which updates the registry's list of programs that you've run recently. With Registry Editor, you affect settings without the help of a user interface. That makes Registry Editor one of the operating system's most powerful and dangerous tools. On one hand, you can customize Microsoft Windows XP and Windows Server 2003 in ways that aren't possible through the user interface. On the other hand, no other tool is double-checking the settings you change.

Every version of Windows since 3.1 has had a registry editor. The editor in Windows 95 can search the registry and has an interface that is simple to use. Microsoft Windows NT 4.0 has an archaic editor that can't search and is more difficult to use than the editor in Windows 95 is, but it has capabilities unique to a secure operating system, such as the ability to set permissions on keys and edit more advanced data types such as REG_MULTI_SZ. Windows 2000 provides both editors, requiring you to switch back and forth to use each editor's unique abilities. Now, with Windows XP and Windows Server 2003, you get the best features of both editors in a single program.

Registry Editor in Windows XP and Windows Server 2003 (both referred to in this chapter as Windows unless otherwise noted) is the tool you learn about in this chapter. It's the basis for just about every set of instructions you see in this book. It is also the basis for many solutions you find in the Microsoft Knowledge Base, solutions that people post to UseNet, and so on. This chapter contains more than just instructions for how to use the editor, though. You'll find useful information that comes from my own experience using this program, such as how to search better and how to quickly back up settings before changing them, which will hopefully give you a great experience with the single most powerful tool in Windows.

Regedit Has Improved

Regedit in more recent versions of Windows makes several improvements over the version in Windows 2000:

- Access the features of both Regedit and Regedt32.exe (the second registry editor in Windows 2000) in a single editor. You no longer have to flip back and forth between both registry editors to complete most tasks.

- Search for keys, values, and data faster.

- Add the keys you use most frequently to the Favorites menu, and then access them just by clicking their names on the menu.

- Return to the last key that you selected the next time you run Regedit.

- Export any portion of the registry to a text file that's much easier to read than anything earlier versions of either registry editor provided.

Additionally, Windows has made substantial improvements to the registry itself. First, Windows supports much larger registries than earlier versions of Windows did; the registry is now limited only by the amount of disk space available. Second, the registry is faster in Windows XP and Windows Server 2003 than in earlier versions of Windows. Windows keeps related keys and values closer together in the database, preventing page faults that degenerate into disk swapping. Last, Windows reduces fragmentation by allocating space for large values in 16 KB chunks. All in all, it is significantly faster to query the registry in recent versions of Windows than it was in Windows 2000.

Running Regedit

You won't find a shortcut to Registry Editor (Regedit) on the Start menu. You don't *want* to find a shortcut to Regedit on the Start menu. Imagine what life as an IT professional or a power user who supports friends and relatives would be like if Microsoft advertised this program to every Windows user on the planet. That's one reason why you find so little documentation about Regedit in Help or elsewhere. That's also why Windows provides policies that you can use to limit access to Regedit. IT professionals and power users have great need for Regedit, however—it's often the only way to fix a problem or customize certain settings. For example, I recently used a program that changed critical settings while it was running and then restored them when the program shut down. Unfortunately, the program crashed without restoring the settings, and the only way I could get them back to their original values was to edit the registry. Sometimes, it's the only tool for the job.

Note Regedit and Registry Editor are terms that mean the same thing. Regedit.exe is the name of Registry Editor's program file. "Regedit" is easier to type, say, and read, so I will use this term for Registry Editor throughout the remainder of this book.

Regedit is in %SystemRoot%, C:\Windows on most computers. Click Start, click Run, and type **regedit** to run Regedit. You don't have to type the path. If you want to start Regedit even more quickly, drag Regedit.exe to your Quick Launch toolbar or to the Start button to add it to the top of your Start menu.

IT professionals can prevent users from running Regedit. They can set the `Disable registry editing tools` policy in Group Policy, local or otherwise. When users try to run Regedit, they see an error message that says, "Registry Editing has been disabled by your administrator." Although it's probably not a good idea to prevent the setup program from installing Regedit.exe, you can set the Regedit.exe file's permissions to prevent users from running it, or better yet, you can use Software Restriction Policies to prevent users from running Regedit.exe, regardless of the file's permissions or the users' rights.

Note For more information about Group Policy and Software Restriction Policies, see Chapter 18, "Fixing Common IT Problems." To learn the best way to deploy file and registry permissions, see Chapter 8, "Configuring Windows Security."

Note Administrators shouldn't rely on any of these methods to secure the registry completely. These simple barriers don't stop determined users from gaining access to the registry. For instance, users can download shareware registry editors, most of which don't honor the `Disable registry editing tools` policy. Shareware registry editors also circumvent Software Restriction Policies and permissions that you apply to Regedit.exe. In reality, determined users will always find a way to access the registry, so part of the solution must be a corporate IT policy that you clearly communicate to users.

Regedit

With all its power, Regedit is still a simple program with a straightforward user interface. Its few menus are simple. It has a status bar that displays the name of the current key. Its window contains two panes, split by a divider that you can drag left or right to change the size of both panes. (If you double-click the divider, the column will automatically resize so the longest value is displayed.) On the left is the key pane; on the right is the value pane. As discussed in Chapter 1, "Learning the Basics," the key pane displays the registry's keys and subkeys, analogous to folders and subfolders in Windows Explorer. This is the registry's hierarchy. The value pane displays the settings that each key contains. Click a key in the key pane, and you see that key's values in the value pane. Again, this is so similar to Windows Explorer that if you know how to use one, you probably can easily use the other. Figure 2-1 is a snapshot of Regedit.

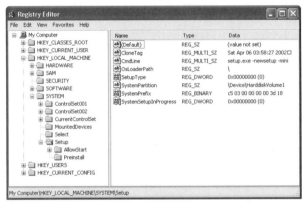

Figure 2-1   Regedit is much easier to use when you maximize its window, which helps you see the full names of subkeys and each value's data in its entirety.

Regedit saves its settings every time you close it. The next time you start Regedit, the window will open to its last position, and the window and panes will be the same size. The columns will also be the same size. Regedit reselects the last key that you selected. Sometimes, though, you won't want Regedit to use these settings—when, for example, you're writing a book about the registry and are capturing screens. Chapter 11, "Scripting Registry Changes," shows you how to prevent Regedit from highlighting the last key: you create a script that automatically removes the key `HKCU\Soft-ware\Microsoft\Windows\CurrentVersion\Applets\Regedit`. (You can't just remove this key using Regedit, though, because Regedit creates this key each time you close it, and it will use the current settings to do so.)

The following sections describe each pane in more detail, including special tips for working on each side of Regedit's window.

Key Pane

The key pane displays the registry's hierarchy. It is organized much like an outline, with each key's child keys, or subkeys, indented immediately below it. At the top, you see My Computer, which represents the local computer. When you connect to another computer's registry over the network, you see that computer's name at the top level of the key pane, too. Immediately under My Computer, you see each of the local registry's root keys. Following each root key are its subkeys. The term *branch* refers to a key and all its subkeys.

Click the plus sign (+) next to a key to expand that branch. Click the minus sign (−) next to a key to collapse that branch. Click any key to see its values in the value pane.

You can use the mouse to explore the registry, but using the keyboard is much more efficient when you know the keyboard shortcuts that are available. Table 2-1 describes the keyboard shortcuts that you can use. Of all the shortcuts available, I use the RIGHT ARROW and LEFT ARROW keys the most. These are quick ways to move around the registry while expanding and collapsing entire branches at the same time. The other shortcut I find most helpful is CTRL+F, which quickly opens the Find dialog box.

Table 2-1   Keyboard Shortcuts

Key	Description
Searching	
CTRL+F	Opens the Find dialog box
F3	Repeats the last search
Browsing	
Keypad +	Expands the selected branch
Keypad −	Collapses the selected branch
Keypad *	Expands all the selected branch's subkeys
UP ARROW	Selects the previous key
DOWN ARROW	Selects the next key
LEFT ARROW	Collapses the selected branch if it's not collapsed; otherwise, selects the parent key
RIGHT ARROW	Expands the selected branch if it's not already expanded; otherwise, selects the key's first subkey
HOME	Selects My Computer
END	Selects the last key that's visible in the key pane
PAGE UP	Moves up one page in the key pane
PAGE DOWN	Moves down one page in the key pane
TAB	Moves between the key and value panes
F6	Moves between the key and value panes
Other	
DELETE	Deletes the selected branch or value
F1	Opens Regedit's Help
F2	Renames the selected key or value
F5	Refreshes the key and value panes
F10	Gives focus to Regedit's menu bar
SHIFT+F10	Opens the shortcut menu for the selected key or value
ALT+F4	Closes Regedit

As you learned in Chapter 1, "Learning the Basics," Windows stores different parts of the registry in different hive files (files containing portions of the registry). Regedit displays all the hive files together to show a single, unified registry. In Regedit, you can see when a branch is its own hive because its name is capitalized. For example, all the subkeys under HKLM are hives, so their names are capitalized. You find each subkey's hive file in %SystemRoot%\System32\config. Notice in Figure 2-1 that all the sub-keys under HKLM are capitalized, because they are also hives. You find most of those hive files in %UserProfile%\NTUSER.DAT. When you change a value in Regedit, Windows updates the appropriate hive file. While you're editing, you don't really care which hive file a particular setting belongs to, though. Refer back to Chapter 1 if you need a refresher on how Windows stores the registry on disk.

Value Pane

The value pane displays the selected key's values. In this pane, you see three columns: Name, Type, and Data. You can change the size of each column by dragging the dividers left or right. I typically use about half the pane to display the Name and Type columns and the remainder of the pane to display the Data column. Each row contains a single value. The first value in the value pane is always (Default), which is the key's default REG_SZ value.

For more information about default values, see Chapter 1, "Learning the Basics."

The value pane displays the name, type, and data for each value. The Name column contains the value's name. Next to the name, you see one of the icons in Table 2-2 that indicates the value's type: string or binary. The Type column indicates the type of data in that value. Unlike earlier versions of Regedit, the current version properly displays all the different data types that Windows supports in the registry, and you can edit most of them. That includes not only REG_SZ, REG_DWORD, and REG_BINARY, but also REG_EXPAND_SZ, REG_MULTI_SZ, and so on. The Data column displays the value's contents. You'll easily recognize REG_DWORD and REG_SZ values in this column, but REG_BINARY and other types of values are much more difficult to view in their entirety. To get a better glimpse of binary values, click the View menu, and then click Display Binary Data.

Table 2-2   Binary and String Icons

Icon	Description
🔲	Binary values, including REG_DWORD and REG_BINARY
🔲	String values, including REG_SZ and REG_MULTI_SZ

Searching for Data

You're going to spend a lot of time searching the registry. I promise. This is particularly true if you're an IT professional responsible for helping users, deploying Windows, and so on. This is even true if you're a power user trying to figure out why a program is doing something that you don't particularly like. For instance, you might want to figure out why a program runs every time you start Windows. If you don't already know about the registry's Run key, you'd have to search the registry for the program's file name. I spend a lot of time locating programs' settings in the registry and I do that by searching for their names and file names.

You can search key names, value names, and string data in the registry. You can also search for partial matches (searching for *Windows* matches both *C:\Windows* and *Windows XP*) or require full matches. The first hit can take a long time to show up, so be patient. It takes even longer if you're searching a remote computer's registry. After Regedit finds a hit, it selects the key or value it found. If Regedit searches to the end of the registry without a match, it displays a message that says, "Finished searching through the registry." Here's how to search using Registry Editor:

1. On the Edit menu, click Find.

2. In the Find dialog box, shown in Figure 2-2, type the text you want to find in the Find What box.

3. To find keys whose names contain the text, select the Keys check box. To find values whose names contain the text, select the Values check box. To find REG_SZ values whose data contains the text, select the Data check box.

4. Click Find Next.

5. Press F3 to repeat your search if necessary.

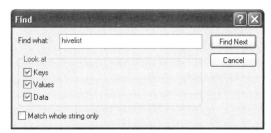

Figure 2-2   Use fewer characters and partial matches to get more hits. Use more characters or require full matches to get fewer hits.

You can significantly cut down the time it takes to search the registry by narrowing the focus to keys, values, or data. For example, if you know that you want to search only for values that contain certain characters in their names, limit your search to value names. If you know that you're searching for data, limit your search to value data. In the Find dialog box, shown in Figure 2-2, clear the Keys, Values, or Data check boxes to prevent Regedit from searching those areas. Selecting the Match Whole String Only check box won't improve turnaround time, but it will reduce the number of hits you receive and, because you don't have to look at as many hits, make searching quicker. Select this check box only if you're 100 percent certain about the name or data for which you're searching; otherwise, you won't find it.

Searching Incrementally

Incremental searching makes finding subkeys and values in long lists much faster. It's a timesaver when you're trying to find a subkey in HKCR, because searching takes too long and paging down the long list is boring. Here's how it works: select in either pane the first item in a long list, and then start typing the item you want to find. Regedit selects the first item that matches what you've typed so far. So if you click the first subkey under HKCR and then type **wm**, Regedit selects wmafile. Type **d** (without delaying too long or the incremental search will restart), and Regedit selects WMDFile. You get the idea. Keep in mind that it won't find keys or values that are collapsed. That is, incremental searching only finds keys that you can see by scrolling the key pane up or down.

Searching in Binary Values

Regedit can't search for REG_DWORD or binary values. It searches only for key names, value names, or string values. This means that you can't use Regedit to find numeric values in REG_DWORD or REG_BINARY values, and you certainly can't find text that Windows stores as REG_BINARY values, which is very common.

The solution is straightforward, though. Export the branch that you want to search to a REG file (i.e., Text.reg). (See "Exporting Settings to Files," later in this chapter, to learn how to create a REG file.) Then open the REG file in Notepad, and search for the number or binary string you want to find. You have to know how Regedit formats values in REG files in order to find them, however. Chapter 11, "Scripting Registry Changes," describes the format of REG files in detail. For now, you need to know what the different types of values look like in a REG file, which is what Table 2-3 describes. For example, if you want to find the word *Jerry* in a REG_BINARY value, you'd convert its letters to their Unicode values, a task that's easy if you know that a capital *A* has a hex value of 0x0041, a lowercase *a* has a hex value of 0x0061, and the number 0 has a hex value of 0x0030. Thus, *Jerry* as a binary string is 0x4A 0x00 0x65 0x00 0x72 0x00 0x72 0x00 0x79 0x00. (If you're not familiar with reverse byte notation and Unicode, see Chapter 1, "Learning the Basics.") To find binary strings that contain the word *Jerry* in a REG file, search for 4a,00,65,00,72,00,72,00,79.

Table 2-3   REG File Data Formats

Type	In Regedit	In REG files
REG_SZ	Microsoft Windows XP	"Microsoft Windows XP"
REG_DWORD	0x00000009	dword:00000009
REG_BINARY	0xC2 0x00 0x02 0x9E 0x00 0x00 0x3D	hex:c2,00,02,9e,00,00,3d

Table 2-3 contains only REG_SZ, REG_DWORD, and REG_BINARY examples. That's because Regedit uses a variation of REG_BINARY to represent all other value types. In a REG file, for instance, a REG_MULTI_SZ looks like
hex(7):4a,00,65,00,72,00,72,00,79,00,00,00. Chapter 11 describes the format of every value type and what they look like in REG files.

Bookmarking Favorite Keys

Regedit adopts one of Microsoft Internet Explorer's most useful features: Favorites. This enables you to bookmark the subkeys that you edit most frequently and to return to them quickly. Clicking a subkey on the Favorites menu is certainly a better alternative to clicking your way through the key pane or, worse yet, trying to remember where Windows stores the Run key in the registry. Adding a key to Favorites is easy, and after you add it, you can click its name on the Favorites menu (as shown in Figure 2-3) and go straight to that key.

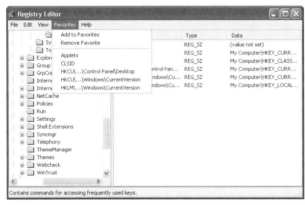

Figure 2-3   Bookmark your most-used keys to return to them quickly.

To add a key to Favorites, click it, and then click Favorites, Add To Favorites. In the Add To Favorites dialog box, type a descriptive name for your shortcut. I typically name shortcuts with the root key and last couple of subkeys, such as HKCU\...\Windows \CurrentVersion, so that I can quickly tell whether the shortcut is in HKCU or HKLM (as they have similar structures). Using the full name, such as HKCU\Software \Microsoft\Windows\CurrentVersion, isn't practical, because it makes the menu too wide.

You might like to have some help starting your Favorites list. Thus, the following list shows you what I typically put on mine:

- HKCR\CLSID
- HKCU\Control Panel\Desktop
- HKCU\Software\Microsoft\Active Setup\Installed Components

- `HKCU\Software\Microsoft\Internet Explorer`

- `HKCU\Software\Microsoft\Windows\CurrentVersion`

- `HKCU\Software\Microsoft\Windows\CurrentVersion\Explorer`

- `HKCU\Software\Policies`

- `HKLM\SOFTWARE\Microsoft\Active Setup\Installed Components`

- `HKLM\SOFTWARE\Microsoft\Windows\CurrentVersion`

- `HKLM\SOFTWARE\Microsoft\Windows\CurrentVersion\Explorer`

- `HKLM\SOFTWARE\Policies`

- `HKLM\SYSTEM\CurrentControlSet\Control`

Removing a key from Favorites is also easy. On the Favorites menu, click Remove Favorite, and then click the names of the keys you want to remove. If you want to rename keys in Favorites, you can edit the key `HKCU\Software\Microsoft\Windows\CurrentVersion\Applets\Regedit\Favorites` and rename shortcuts or change their targets.

> **Tip**   Regedit displays keys in the order that you added them; it doesn't sort them alphabetically. If you want this list to be in alphabetical order, export `HKCU\Software\Microsoft\Windows\CurrentVersion\Applets\Regedit\Favorites` to a REG file. Edit the REG file to sort the keys in alphabetical order or any other order that you prefer, and then import the REG file back into the registry after removing the `Favorites` key. The Favorites menu is resorted. Save this REG file, too, so you can use your favorites elsewhere.

Using Better Techniques

After a while, you'll know enough about the registry in Windows to search much more quickly. You'll know where to begin and end your searches so that you don't waste your time searching parts of the registry where you're not going to find what you want. To limit your search, click a subkey near where you want to begin, and then search. As you repeat your search by pressing F3, keep an eye on the status bar and notice the key that contains the current hit. After you've gone past the branch that you think should contain the value, quit searching.

Here's an example of focusing a search. When you build a default user profile, which is covered in Chapter 12, "Deploying User Profiles," you'll check it for references to the current user profile folder, which you don't want to deploy to desktops throughout the organization. To narrow your search to that profile, you'll select its first key in the registry and then search for the path, deciding along the way what to do with any references to your search that you find. After you're out of that profile, though, quit searching so that you don't waste your time and accidentally change values you don't intend to change.

Other examples of focusing searches to find data faster are:

- Limiting your search to HKCR when you want to find values related to file associations. For that matter, do an incremental search to speed things up.

- Looking only in the branches HKCU\Software and HKLM\SOFTWARE to find programs' settings. And if you know the names of the vendor and program, you can go straight to the key that contains its settings because you know that programs store their settings in HKCU and HKLM in the branch Software*Company**Program* *Version*.

- Searching HKCU if you know you're searching for per-user settings, and searching HKLM if you know you're searching for per-machine settings.

- Searching the branch HKLM\System if you're looking for device driver and service settings.

Shareware Search Tools

A variety of shareware tools are available for searching the registry. They are far more advanced than Regedit and designed specifically to make digging around the registry easier and quicker. You can download evaluation versions of these tools at any shareware site. Try *http://www.zdnet.com/downloads* or *http://www.tucows.com*. Here are some of the most popular:

- Registry Crawler from 4Developers at *http://www.4developers.com*

- Registry Toolkit from Funduc Software at *http://www.funduc.com*

- Resplendent Registrar from Resplendence at *http://www.resplendence.com*

- Registry Detective from PC Magazine at *http://www.pcmagazine.com*

Registry Crawler is my personal favorite, but the other tools also get good results. Registry Crawler not only searches the registry faster than Regedit does but also has features that make the task easier. You can access the tool quickly from the system tray. It presents a list of matches that you see all at once, rather than bouncing around from hit to hit, and you can export the results to a REG file. It also enables you to search the registries of multiple computers at one time if you have access to them over a network. Its most powerful feature is its search-and-replace capability, however, which enables you to replace all instances of a value with another.

Editing the Registry

In Regedit, assuming that a key's or a value's permissions don't prevent it, you can add, delete, and rename keys and values. You can also change most values.

As you'd suspect, there's more than one way to do just about anything in Regedit. You'll find three different ways to change a value: through the main menu, through the shortcut menu, or with a keyboard shortcut. Use whichever method is right for you, but I prefer keyboard shortcuts because I deplore touching the mouse without a reason. You can edit any value by selecting it and pressing ENTER.

The following sections describe the features that Regedit provides for editing the registry. These are the basic steps that you'll rely on throughout this book.

Changing Values

I promise that 99.999 percent of the time, when working with Regedit, you will double-click a value to change it. There are other ways you can change a value, however. One way is to click Edit, Modify. Another way is to right-click the value, and then click Modify on the shortcut menu.

Regedit displays a different editor depending on the value's type. For example, Regedit opens the Edit String dialog box when you edit a REG_SZ value. It displays the Edit DWORD Value dialog box when you edit a REG_DWORD value. Unlike the version of Regedit that comes with Windows 2000, the version in Windows XP and Windows Server 2003 doesn't make you use the Edit Binary Value dialog box for values such as REG_MULTI_SZ. This version has dialog boxes for almost all the value types that Windows supports. The following graphics show what the different editors look like, with a description of each.

You use the Edit String dialog box to edit REG_SZ and REG_EXPAND_SZ values. Enclosing the value in quotation marks isn't necessary unless you intend to include the quotation marks in your value. You can copy values from this dialog box to the Clipboard and then paste them into scripts and documents.

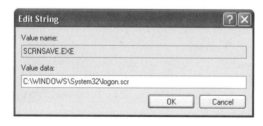

You use the Edit DWORD Value dialog box to edit REG_DWORD values. By default, you're editing a hexadecimal value, but you won't include any prefixes such as 0x in the value; you just type the hexadecimal digits. Select the Decimal option to edit the value as a decimal number. Notice that Regedit displays REG_DWORD values in the Value Data box using both hexadecimal and decimal notations.

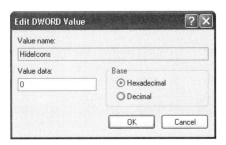

You use the Edit Binary Value dialog box to edit REG_BINARY values. The first column of numbers in this dialog box is the offset, starting from zero. The second column of numbers contains the binary string in hexadecimal notation. The last column shows the text representation of the binary string. You can edit either the second or third column. You can type hexadecimal digits in the second column or plain text in the third.

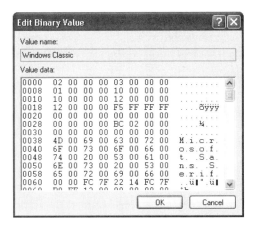

You use the Edit Multi-String dialog box to edit REG_MULTI_SZ values. Each string is on its own line with no blank lines.

To change a value, click Edit, Modify, and then type the value's new data into the Value Data box. When you change a value using Regedit, the editor immediately applies that change to the registry, but that doesn't mean Windows or other programs have incorporated the change. In fact, no changes are incorporated until the program or operating system has a reason to load or reload that value from the registry. For example, if you change the Windows Explorer settings in the registry, open windows won't reflect those changes—you must close and reopen those windows. If you customize Microsoft Office 2003 Editions, you must shut down and restart it before it'll recognize your changes. Settings that Windows loads are applied only when you log on to the operating system, and per-user settings, such as the location of shell folders like Favorites, require you to log off and back on to Windows for your changes to be reflected. Likewise, settings in HKLM and per-machine settings often require you to restart the computer for Windows to recognize those changes because the operating system loads those settings only as it starts.

Chances are good that you're going to make mistakes. Unless you have access to a test lab, you're likely to experiment on your production computer. (Read "production" as "essential.") An alternative is to use Microsoft Virtual PC for testing. If things get unmanageable, don't panic, and by all means, don't make things worse by restarting your computer over and over again or editing away at the registry until there's nothing left. Instead, see Chapter 3, "Backing up the Registry," to learn how to easily recover your recent working configuration.

More Info   For more information on Virtual PC, see *http://www.microsoft.com /virtualpc*.

Clipboard Tricks

If you're writing scripts, documentation, or deployment plans, you'll be typing a lot of key names and values. This is an error-prone and painful process, and it's one that you can do much more easily using the Clipboard.

For example, instead of trying to type a fully qualified key name, flipping back and forth between Regedit and your text editor, and trying to remember each subkey in the branch, just copy the key name to the Clipboard and then paste it into your document: in the key pane, right-click a key, and then click Copy Key Name.

You can copy value names and data to the Clipboard, too. Value names don't tend to be long, but using the Clipboard is the only way to ensure you have the value's data correct. In the value pane, right-click the value whose name you want to copy to the Clipboard, and click Rename. Press CTRL+C to copy the name to the Clipboard, and then press ESC so that you don't accidentally change the name. If you prefer a less risky way to copy a value's name, edit the value, select the value's name, and then press CTRL+C to copy it to the Clipboard.

Copying a value's data to the Clipboard is useful and easy: edit the value, select the value's data, and then press CTRL+C to copy it to the Clipboard. This is a great way to back up data before changing it. Before changing a value, copy its data to the Clipboard, create a new value of the same type, and then paste the data from the Clipboard into the new value. For example, if I wanted to change a REG_SZ value called Stubpath, I'd copy its data to the Clipboard and then paste that data into a new REG_SZ value called StubpathBackup. Then, if the change didn't work out, I could restore the original value and repair the problem that I created with my edits.

Adding Keys or Values

You would create keys and values only if you were instructed to do so—that is, if you know adding the value will have some effect. For example, the Microsoft Knowledge Base often instructs you to add a value that fixes a certain problem. Throughout this book, you learn about values you can add to the registry that customize Windows. Otherwise, adding a value that no program reads does not accomplish anything. If you want to add something to the registry, take a look at some of the tips in Chapter 4, "Hacking the Registry," or Chapter 18, "Fixing Common IT Problems."

To create a new key, first click the key under which you want to create a subkey; click Edit, New, and Key; and then type a name for the new key. When you create a new key, Regedit names it `New Key` #N, where *N* is an incremental number beginning with 1, and then selects the name so you can change it.

Creating a new value is similar:

1. In the Key pane, click the key in which you want to add a value.

2. On the Edit menu, click New, and then click the type of value you want to create: String Value, Binary Value, DWORD Value, Multi-String Value, or Expandable String Value.

3. Type a name for the new value.

Regedit names the new value `New Value` #N and then selects it so you can type a new name. Windows requires all names contained in a key to be unique. No two subkeys can have the same name, and no two values can have the same name. That's why Regedit names new values `New Value #1`, `New Value #2`, and so on. The default data for binary values is null, or no value whatsoever. The default value for strings is the empty string. The default value for `REG_DWORD` values is 0. After you create a new value, you edit it to change its value from the default.

Deleting Keys or Values

Click the key or value that you want to delete, and then click Edit, Delete. I don't delete settings often, but there are a few recurring circumstances in which it's necessary. The first is when I want to reset a program's settings. For example, to reset Regedit's view settings, you must remove the value that contains them. You can delete most programs' settings by deleting the settings from the registry. You just have to know where to look: the branch `Software\`*Company*`\`*Program*`\`*Version*, under `HKCU` and `HKLM`. Although deleting a program's values works well for programs that re-create missing settings, it's not a solution for programs that don't work when their settings are missing.

Another circumstance in which I delete settings is when I want to tidy up the registry a bit. Often, the registry contains references to files that don't exist (*orphan settings*) or settings that just shouldn't be in the registry anymore, particularly after their program has been removed. With a little thought and a little luck, you can clean these settings out of the registry. Chapter 9, "Troubleshooting Problems," is a helpful resource for either scenario.

Tip   There's a better, safer way to remove keys and values than just deleting them. You can rename settings you want to remove, which hides them from any code that's looking for them. Just add your initials to the beginning of the key or value's name. For example, I can hide a value called Session by renaming it JH-Session. Then if something goes terribly wrong (and it happens from time to time when digging around in the registry), I can remove the current version of Session and give the old version its original name.

Renaming Keys or Values

In Regedit, you can't click a selected file to rename it as you can do in Windows Explorer. Instead, you click the key or value that you want to rename and then click Rename on the Edit menu. You can also click the key or value you want to rename and then press F2.

In the section "Deleting Keys or Values," you learned that one of the main reasons I rename keys and values is to hide them from Windows and other programs instead of permanently deleting them. Then, only after I'm happy with the result, I permanently remove the item. Sometimes I don't even bother to do that, as renamed keys serve as good documentation for the changes I make in the registry. To rename a key or a value, select the key, click Edit, Rename, and type a new name.

Printing the Registry

Regedit has a feature that prints all or part of the registry. I confess that I've never printed anything in the registry; I just haven't found a good reason to do it. You can certainly print subkeys as a backup before making changes, but I tend to use hive files for that purpose, and this doesn't require me to retype keys, values, and data to restore the old settings. You might not get much use out of the print feature, but this chapter wouldn't be complete without describing how to use it. To print all or part of the registry, follow these steps:

1. Click the key you want to print, keeping in mind that you're going to print every subkey and value under it.

2. On the File menu, click Print to display the Print dialog box, shown in Figure 2-4.

3. Do one of the following:

   ❑   To print the entire registry, select All.

   ❑   To print the selected branch, select Selected Branch.

4. Click Print.

Figure 2-4   The format of Regedit's printer output is the same as the format that Regedit uses when exporting portions of the registry to a text file.

Listing 2-1 shows you what Regedit's printer output looks like. As you see, it's not very useful except maybe as a temporary way to remember values. Still, Microsoft greatly improved Regedit's printer output for Windows. Regedit now prints REG_DWORD values so they look like REG_DWORD values, rather than printing them as binary values in little-endian format. (See Chapter 1, "Learning the Basics.") Regedit also prints binary values along with their ASCII-equivalent text. Finally, this version of Regedit actually prints each value's type so that you don't have to flip through pages to figure it out.

Listing 2-1   Sample Printer Output

```
Key Name:          HKEY_LOCAL_MACHINE\SYSTEM\Setup
Class Name:        <NO CLASS>
Last Write Time:   1/2/2002 - 1:16 AM
Value 0
  Name:            SetupType
  Type:            REG_DWORD
  Data:            0x0
Value 1
  Name:            SystemSetupInProgress
  Type:            REG_DWORD
  Data:            0x0
Value 2
  Name:            CmdLine
  Type:            REG_SZ
  Data:
Value 3
  Name:            SystemPrefix
  Type:            REG_BINARY
  Data:
00000000    cd 03 00 00 00 80 3c d2 - Í.....<Ò
```

```
Value 4
  Name:              SystemPartition
  Type:              REG_SZ
  Data:              \Device\HarddiskVolume1
Value 5
  Name:              OsLoaderPath
  Type:              REG_SZ
  Data:              \
```

Exporting Settings to Files

Exporting all or part of the registry is something that IT professionals and power users do often. By *exporting*, I mean copying portions of the registry to another file, typically a REG file, though hive files are more useful. This is a great way to back up settings so you can easily restore them later, if necessary. It's also a good way to share settings with other users or computers. I often create REG files for settings I prefer so that I can change those settings simply by importing a REG file rather than clicking my way through the Windows user interface—one double-click replaces a hundred clicks.

In the IT world, exporting settings to REG files has practical purposes, too. The first is deployment. REG files are the simplest and often the only way to deploy some settings with Windows. You can deploy REG files through your Windows answer file, for example, as you will learn in Chapter 14, "Deploying with Answer Files." It's also a convenient way to deploy settings from an intranet or help desk. REG files are also an easy way to add settings to your Office 2003 Editions deployment. You can do this through the Custom Installation Wizard found in the *Microsoft Office 2003 Editions Resource Kit*. Chapter 17, "Deploying Office 2003 Settings," describes how to add REG files to an Office 2003 Editions installation.

Regedit exports settings to four different types of files: registration, Win9x/NT4 registration, hive files, and text files. The differences between the four are significant, and you learn about them later in this chapter. Follow these steps to export branches of the registry to files:

1.   Click the key at the top of the branch you want to export.

2.   On the File menu, click Export to display the Export Registry File dialog box, shown in Figure 2-5.

3.   In the File Name box, type a name for the file you're creating.

4.   Select one of the following options, depending on the export range you want:

     ❑   To back up the entire registry, select the All option.

     ❑   To back up the selected branch, select the Selected Branch option.

5. In the Save As Type drop-down list, click the type of file you want to create: Registration Files (*.reg), Registry Hive Files (*.*), Text Files (*.txt), or Win9x/NT4 Registration Files (*.reg).

6. Click Save.

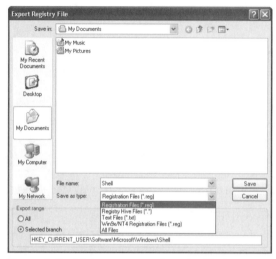

Figure 2-5   Make sure you select the file format you want to use, regardless of the file extension you type in the File Name box.

Importing a file into the registry is similar to opening a file. Click File, Import; in the Files Of Type drop-down list, click the type of file that you're importing; then, in the File Name box, type the path and name of the file you're importing. The following sections describe each of the file types that you see in the Save As Type and Files Of Type drop-down lists. Each type is a different file format and is thus suited to different purposes than the other types are.

Registration Files

Registration files are version 5 (Unicode) REG files—plain text files that look similar to INI files. Each section name represents a key, and each item in a section represents a value. Listing 2-2 is a sample of a version 5 REG file:

Listing 2-2   Sample Version 5 REG File

```
Windows Registry Editor Version 5.00

[HKEY_CURRENT_USER\Sample]
"String"="Jerry Honeycutt"
"Binary"=hex:01,02,03,04,05,06,07,08
"DWORD"=dword:00004377
"Expandable String"=hex(2):25,00,55,00,53,00,45,00,52,00,00,00
"MultiString"=hex(7):48,00,65,00,6c,00,6c,00,6f,00,00,00,00,00

[HKEY_CURRENT_USER\Sample\Subkey]
```

The most important thing to know about version 5 REG files is that they are Unicode, and some programs can't handle Unicode REG files properly. And because these files are Unicode, each character in the `REG_EXPAND_SZ` and `REG_MULTI_SZ` values is two bytes wide. In Listing 2-2, you'll notice this in the values called `Expandable String` and `Multistring`. For example, the letter A is `0x0041`, not `0x41`. For more information about Unicode-encoded text, see Chapter 1, "Learning the Basics." Windows 2000, Windows XP, and Windows Server 2003 are the only Microsoft operating systems that support version 5 REG files.

Earlier in this section, you learned how to import REG files using Regedit. You can also double-click a REG file to merge it into the registry. Regedit will prompt you to merge the settings that the file contains into the registry and, after you click Yes, it will tell you when it's finished. If you're deploying a REG file to users, however, you don't want them to see the message or answer the prompt, so you'll use Regedit's `/s` command-line option to run the program quietly. For example, use the command line `regedit settings.reg /s` from batch files, scripts, answer files, or even from the Custom Installation Wizard found in the *Microsoft Office 2003 Editions Resource Kit*. For more information about creating and deploying REG files, see the following chapters:

- Chapter 11, "Scripting Registry Changes," describes the format of each value type in REG files and shows you how to build them manually.

- Chapter 14, "Deploying with Answer Files," describes how to deploy REG files as part of your Windows answer file—a great way to deploy user settings.

- Chapter 17, "Deploying Office 2003 Settings," describes how to deploy REG files as part of your Office 2003 customizations.

Caution   Don't import a REG file created in one version of Windows into another version—at least not without thinking about it carefully. For example, exporting hardware settings from the Windows NT 4.0 registry and importing them into the Windows XP or Windows Server 2003 registry will likely wreak havoc on either operating system. Some settings are fine to share across Windows versions, however, such as file associations in HKCR and some programs' settings. Use common sense.

Win9x/NT4 Registration Files

Win9x/NT4 registration files are version 4 (ANSI) REG files, which Windows 95, Windows 98, Windows Me, and Windows NT 4.0 support. Listing 2-3 is a version 4 ANSI REG file. The settings are the same as those in the version 5 Unicode REG file that you saw in the preceding section:

Listing 2-3   Sample Version 4 REG File

```
REGEDIT4

[HKEY_CURRENT_USER\Sample]
"String"="Jerry Honeycutt"
"Binary"=hex:01,02,03,04,05,06,07,08
"DWORD"=dword:00004377
"Expandable String"=hex(2):25,55,53,45,52,00
"MultiString"=hex(7):48,65,6c,6c,6f,00,00

[HKEY_CURRENT_USER\Sample\Subkey]
```

Instead of Unicode text, version 4 files are ANSI text files. That means that each character is a single byte wide. The letter A is 0x41. You notice the difference between this and the earlier Unicode REG file in the Expandable String and MultiString values. Characters in the REG_EXPAND_SZ and REG_MULTI_SZ values are single bytes, which is more intuitive for most people. This is the file format that's compatible with programs expecting ANSI REG files, and it has the added benefit of being compatible with earlier versions of Regedit.

Hive Files

Hive files are binary files that contain portions of the registry. As you recall from Chapter 1, "Learning the Basics," Windows stores different parts of the registry in different hive files. Regedit displays all these hives together in one logical unit. Hive files are useful tools, though. You can export branches to hive files that can then be imported to another computer or by another user. They're great backups.

Exported hive files have purposes similar to those of REG files. Hive files have most of the advantages of REG files, except that you can't view and edit them in a text editor. Also, they can't target individual settings. The advantage that hive files have over REG files is that you can load and edit them in Regedit without actually replacing your own settings. The section "Working with Hive Files," later in this chapter, describes how to load hive files.

> ## Choosing Between REG and Hive Files
>
> Regedit exports branches to four different file formats. Each format has strengths and weaknesses that make it appropriate for some tasks and useless for others. This section should help you choose the right format each time.
>
> Exporting to hive files is my choice most of the time. I like hive files because they're much more accurate than either type of REG file. They are the same format as the Windows working hive files, so they represent settings in exactly the same way. Also, when you import a hive file, Regedit deletes the branch it's replacing before importing the settings. In other words, the editor removes any settings that exist in the working registry but do not exist in the hive file you're importing. When restoring keys from a backup after an unsuccessful registry edit, this is exactly the behavior you want. Hive files have another strength that makes them my choice most of the time: you can load them as new hives and view their contents without affecting other parts of the registry. The only drawback to this is that you can't view them in Notepad.
>
> Although hive files are usually my choice, there are a few scenarios that require me to use REG files. The first is when I'm working with programs that don't understand hive files. For example, the Custom Installation Wizard found in *Microsoft Office 2003 Editions Resource Kit* can read REG files but not hive files. The second scenario is when I'm exporting settings to different versions of Windows. Windows 98 doesn't provide a way to load hive files. Finally, and importantly, when I'm trying to track down a setting in the registry by comparing snapshots, comparing two hive files isn't feasible, but comparing two REG files is easy using Microsoft Word 2002.

Text Files

You can export keys to text files, but you can't import keys back into the registry. If you're curious about what an exported text file looks like, take a look at the sample printer output in the "Printing the Registry" section earlier in this chapter. Exported text files and printer output are one and the same. Regedit makes exported text files more readable than REG files are, which can help you interpret settings better, but that's about the only use of text files.

Working with Hive Files

There are two scenarios in which working with hive files is an important part of an IT professional's job. The first is when creating a default user profile, which you learn how to do in Chapter 12, "Deploying User Profiles." The other is troubleshooting. You can take a hive file from a computer or user profile that's not working properly, repair it on another computer, and then replace it on the original computer.

Loading a hive file is different from *importing* a hive file. When you import a hive file, which you learned how to do in the previous section, you actually replace settings in the registry. In other words, you load the hive file over existing settings. When you load a hive file, you create a whole new branch in the registry that doesn't overlap or replace any other branch. This enables you to edit the settings in a hive file without changing your own settings. Here's how to load a hive file into the registry:

1. In the key pane, click either HKU or HKLM.

2. On the File menu, click Load Hive.

3. In the File Name box, type the path and file name of the hive file you're loading, and then click Open.

4. In the Key Name box, shown in Figure 2-6, type the name you want to assign to the hive.

The name you give to the key is arbitrary. Use any name that helps you identify the hive file that you're loading. All you're doing in this step is creating a root key in which to load the hive file.

Figure 2-6   Type a name that describes what the hive file contains.

When you're finished editing settings in the hive file, you must unload it before doing anything else with it, such as copying it to a removable disk. That's because Windows locks the file until you unload it. Unloading a hive file is easy: click the key into which you loaded the hive, which you specified in step 4, and then click Unload Hive on the File menu. If you get an error message when you try to copy the hive file or profile folder that contains a hive file, you probably forgot to unload it from the registry.

Command-Line Alternative

Windows comes with a great command-line alternative to Regedit. Anything you can do with Regedit, you can also do with Console Registry Tool for Windows, otherwise known as Reg.exe. And this tool is installed by default with Windows XP and Windows Server 2003, unlike earlier versions of Windows, which required you to get the tool from the resource kits.

What's so great about a command-line registry editor? You can use it to script registry changes. For example, you can write a batch file that automatically backs up a portion of the registry. Imagine a batch file that extracts hardware information from a computer and dumps it onto a network share. That's a quick inventory system. Recently, I used Reg.exe to extract the GUID from every computer on a network so that I could configure them as managed computers in Active Directory. (See Chapter 1, "Learning the Basics.")This was a huge timesaver.

Chapter 11, "Scripting Registry Changes," describes Console Registry Tool for Windows in great detail. For more information, you can also type **Reg.exe** at the Windows command prompt.

Getting Beyond Basics

This chapter described Regedit's essential features. These are the basics that you must know to perform routine tasks such as changing registry values. What you didn't learn in this chapter are some of the more advanced tasks that an IT professional or power user needs in order to truly master Windows. From this point forward, it's time to get past the basics and branch out into other parts of this book. Learn more about Regedit in the following chapters:

- Chapter 3, "Backing Up the Registry," describes how to use Regedit as a troubleshooting tool. You also learn how to protect the registry.

- Chapter 8, "Configuring Windows Security," describes how to set subkeys' permissions using Regedit. You also learn how to secure remote registry editing to prevent users from gaining access to other users' registries.

- Chapter 12, "Deploying User Profiles," shows you how to use Regedit to edit the settings in a user profile so you can deploy those settings to hundreds or even thousands of desktops throughout the organization.

Chapter 3
Backing Up the Registry

Mistakes happen—whether they are due to your own silly errors or to users' meddling with the registry when they shouldn't. Nothing can happen that warrants a lot of anxiety, however. Ninety-nine times out of 100, the tools you learn about in this chapter can prevent or overcome any registry error. Because I know how to use these tools, there's been only one time when I broke a computer so badly that I gave up and reinstalled Microsoft Windows XP. The sad part was that after spending hours reinstalling the operating system and incumbent applications, I discovered an easy fix for the problem.

Not only do most of these tools back up and protect the registry, they're also features that push the reliability of Windows XP and Microsoft Windows Server 2003 (Windows) far beyond the levels present in earlier versions of Windows. System Restore ensures that you can roll back the configuration of Windows XP to an earlier state, which the operating system saves automatically. Other features that make Windows more stable include Device Driver Rollback, Error Reporting, and Windows Driver Protection. See *http://www.microsoft.com/technet/prodtechnol/winxppro/plan/rlbwinxp.mspx* for the "Reliability Improvements in Windows XP Professional" white paper.

In this chapter, I show you many ways to restore a configuration, but you won't need all of them. Pick one or two techniques that work for you, and stick with them. In particular, decide which of the methods you're going to use to protect the registry while editing it. I prefer to save keys to hive files before making changes to the registry, but you might prefer to make backup copies of individual values. Also, you definitely need to know about System Restore in Windows XP. Chapter 9, "Troubleshooting Problems," describes advanced troubleshooting tools that you turn to only when things are so dire that you have no other choice.

Many of these tools require advance preparation. For example, to restore a backup copy of the registry, you must have made a backup. Read this chapter first in preparation for problems that hopefully won't occur.

Editing the Registry Safely

It's easy to forget about backing up values before making what seem to be simple changes. But how do you know that a simple change isn't going to be the one that causes a major error? You don't—so you should back up values before changing or deleting them. There are both easy and difficult ways to do this; I'm going to show you the easy ways.

You'll learn three techniques in this section. The first is making backup copies of values, which you can quickly restore in the registry. Backups also document the changes you make. The second is exporting the part of the registry in which you're working to a REG file. I don't like this method for reasons that I'll explain later, but a REG file has the advantage of being readable, and this is the method that most people use. The third method, and my first choice when making significant changes, is exporting branches to hive files. This method is the most accurate way to back up and restore parts of the registry. Using any of these methods, you'll be able to recover from most pitfalls.

> **Tip**   If these techniques fail, or if you're planning on major changes to the registry, move on to the techniques described later in this chapter. System Restore can get you out of trouble most of the time; it fails only when Windows XP no longer even starts properly. (System Restore is only available in Windows XP.) In that case, you're left with Automated System Recovery and Recovery Console, which are tools you learn about in Chapter 9, "Troubleshooting Problems." But first try starting Windows XP in Safe Mode and then running System Restore. Do you find yourself making the same changes over and over again? I tend to customize the same settings every time I install Windows or every time I log on to a computer and get a new user profile. You don't have to worry about backing up the values you're changing if you write a script to change them automatically. Test the script carefully so you can apply it with assurance that it works properly. Chapter 11, "Scripting Registry Changes," shows you how to write these scripts. Test them *again* every time you change them, too.

Copying Single Values

The easiest way to leave a way out if things go wrong is to make backup copies of values before changing them.

Here's how to do it: rename the original value to something like *Initials_Name*, where *Initials* is your initials, and *Name* is the value's original name. Add a date if you think you're going to change the value often. Then use the original name and type to add a new value with new data. Alternatively, use a new name to create a new value of the same type as that of the value you're changing. Copy the original value's data to the Clipboard, and then paste it into the new value. You're ready to change the value, and if you don't like the result, you can restore the original value with little effort. Figure 3-1 shows backup settings in the key HKCU\Control Panel\Desktop.

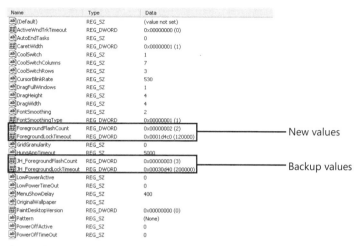

Figure 3-1 Backing up values in the registry is like having a built-in revision-tracking feature.

Likewise, instead of deleting a value, which you can recover only by memory because Registry Editor (Regedit) does not have an Undo feature, you can rename the value to hide it from any program that's looking for it. The effect is the same, and you can always restore the value by restoring its name. Although you can't easily back up entire branches before changing settings in them, you can hide entire branches to make it seem like they no longer exist. This is a safe way to remove a program's settings from the registry so that the program might be able to re-create them, for example. This *is* your Undo feature.

Printing portions of the registry isn't an alternative to creating backups of them. You would have to restore each and every value manually from the information on the printout, and the format isn't easily readable. If you want just a quick snapshot of a value before you change it, take a screen shot instead: press ALT+PRTSCN, and then paste the screenshot into Microsoft Paint. Print or save your screenshot for future reference.

Backing Up to REG Files

If you'd rather have a more tangible backup, one with which you can restore an entire branch, export that branch to a REG file. In Regedit, click the top-level key in the branch you're editing. Then, on the File menu, click Export, type the name of the REG file to which you want to export the branch's settings, and then click Save. Your settings are safely saved, and you can edit that branch knowing that restoring the original values will be easy. Don't export the entire registry—this takes a very long time. Back up only the branch in which you're working.

Restoring your backup REG file is easy, too. On Regedit's File menu, click Import; type the name of the REG file that contains your settings; and then click Open. You can also double-click the file to import it. I mentioned earlier that I don't like using REG files to back up settings. This is because when you import a REG file, Regedit merges the REG file's settings into the registry rather than replacing them. That means that Regedit replaces or creates any value that the REG file contains, but values that the REG file doesn't contain aren't removed from the registry. This creates a problem if you add values to the registry while editing it, because importing the REG file doesn't remove them. See Table 3-1 for a summary of the merge process.

Table 3-1   Merging REG Files

Value Exists in REG File?	Value Exists in Registry?	Action
No	No	None.
No	Yes	Regedit doesn't remove or change the value in the registry.
Yes	No	Regedit adds the value.
Yes	Yes	Regedit changes the value.

> **Note**   Most of the techniques you'll learn about in this chapter work remotely, too. You can back up and restore keys for other users. If your computer fails while logging on to Windows, you can access the computer over the network and restore that computer's settings using Regedit. On the File menu, click Connect Network Registry, and type the name of the computer containing the registry you want to open. Not only can you edit the remote computer's registry, but you can also export hive files from it and import hive files into it.

Backing Up to Hive Files

Hive files are better than REG files are for backing up the registry. When you import a hive file containing a key, Regedit completely replaces the current key and all of its subkeys with the contents of the hive file. That means that Regedit removes any value you added since backing up the registry to a hive file. This is a far more accurate way to back up branches before editing them.

Exporting branches to hive files is similar to exporting them to REG files; you just pick a different file type. On Regedit's File menu, click Export. In the Save As Type list, click Registry Hive Files, type the name of the new hive file, and then click Save. Reverse the process to restore your settings: click File, Import; in the Save As Type list, click Registry Hive Files; type the name of the hive file to which you backed up your settings; and then click Open. You can use any file extension you like, but I prefer to give hive files the *.dat* extension. The *.hiv* extension is also common for hive files.

Don't confuse exporting and importing hive files with loading and unloading them. When you import a hive file, you're making changes to working parts of the registry. When you load a hive file, you're creating a whole new branch that Windows doesn't use. It doesn't read or change those settings, but they're visible in Regedit, so you can examine them. Unloading the hive file just unlinks the file from the registry. You can unload only hive files you've manually loaded, not hive files Windows loaded.

Whereas importing a hive file is a great way to restore an entire branch, loading a hive file is a good method of restoring settings precisely or just checking an original value. First load the file into the registry: click either HKLM or HKU in Regedit; on the File menu, click Load; type the name of the hive file that contains your settings; and then click Open. When Regedit prompts you for a key name, type any name that will help you identify the hive. You'll then see that hive file under the root key into which you loaded it. Figure 3-2 is an example of loading a hive file that contains a backup copy of the key HKU\Control Panel\Desktop. Examine the setting in the hive file you loaded, or even copy the backup setting, and then paste it over the current value. Don't forget to unload the hive, or you won't be able to remove the file later (Windows doesn't automatically unload hive files when you quit Regedit).

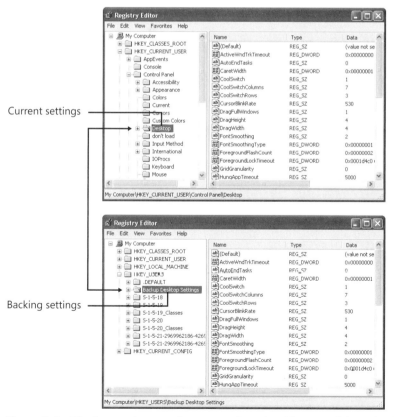

Figure 3-2   The key Backup Desktop Settings is a hive containing a backup copy of HKCU\Control Panel\Desktop\ that I've loaded into the registry.

Now that you will hopefully use hive files to back up settings before changing them, I'm going to introduce you to the ultimate way to back up registry settings: Console Registry Tool for Windows (Reg.exe). This command-line tool comes with Windows and provides most of Regedit's features, plus some other features. You learn its full use in Chapter 11, "Scripting Registry Changes." You can use it to save keys to hive files. You can also use it to restore, load, and unload hive files. With Reg.exe, saving a hive file is the same as exporting, and restoring a hive file is the same as importing. The best part is one of the tool's unique features: the ability to copy one key to another key, creating a quick backup copy of a key right there in the registry. For example, I can copy `HKCU\Control Panel\Desktop\` to `HKCU\Control Panel\JH_Backup\` with a single command. Table 3-2 describes the Reg.exe command lines for each of these features. See Chapter 11 for a full explanation of all the different options.

Table 3-2   Backing Up the Registry with Reg.exe

Command Line	Description
REG SAVE *keyname filename*	Save the branch starting with the key *keyname* to the hive file called *filename*. *Keyname* begins with one of the root key abbreviations, HKCR, HKLM, HKCU, HKU, or HKCC.
REG RESTORE *keyname filename*	Restore the hive file *filename* to the key *keyname*, replacing all of its contents. *Keyname* begins with one of the root key abbreviations, HKCR, HKLM, HKCU, HKU, or HKCC.
REG LOAD *keyname filename*	Load the hive file *filename* to a new temporary branch beginning with the key *keyname*. *Keyname* begins with one of the root key abbreviations, HKCR, HKLM, HKCU, HKU, or HKCC.
REG UNLOAD *keyname*	Unload the hive file in the temporary branch beginning with the key *keyname*. *Keyname* begins with one of the root key abbreviations, HKCR, HKLM, HKCU, HKU, or HKCC.
REG COPY *keyname1 keyname2* [/s]	Copy the values in the key *keyname1* to the key *keyname2*, creating *keyname2* if it doesn't already exist. *Keyname1* and *keyname2* begin with one of the root key abbreviations, HKCR, HKLM, HKCU, HKU, or HKCC. The option /s copies the entire branch, not just the values in *keyname1*.

Using System Restore

System Restore returns your computer to a previous state without losing recent personal information, such as documents, history lists, favorites, or e-mail. System Restore is only available in Windows XP. It monitors the computer and many applications for changes and creates restore points. I call these restore points *snapshots*, but they're really instructions for undoing recent changes. You restore these snapshots when your configuration isn't working. By default, Windows XP creates restore points daily and when significant events such as installing an application or device driver occur. System Restore is ideal for serious work in the registry because you can create your own restore points any time you like. You can also change the snapshot schedule or even script System Restore, as I'll show you.

System Restore creates different types of restore points:

- **Initial system checkpoints.**   System Restore creates initial system checkpoints when Windows XP starts for the first time. Restoring to this point returns Windows XP and programs to their states immediately after installing Windows XP.

- **System checkpoints.**   System Restore creates restore points regularly, whether or not the system changes. By default, it creates system checkpoints every 24 hours. If you turn the computer off for more than 24 hours, System Restore will create a system checkpoint the next time you start Windows XP.

- **Installation checkpoints.**   System Restore creates installation checkpoints when you install programs that use current installer technologies, so you can restore the computer to the state it was in before you installed the programs. To reverse the changes made by other programs, restore the most recent checkpoint.

- **Automatic update checkpoints.**   System Restore creates a restore point before updating Windows XP by using Automatic Update or Windows Update.

- **Manual checkpoints.**   You can use System Restore or a script to create your own restore points; I'll show you how later in this chapter. Create manual checkpoints before making significant changes to the registry.

- **Restore operation checkpoints.**   System Restore creates restore operation checkpoints each time you restore a checkpoint. You use restore operation checkpoints to undo a restoration if you don't like the results.

- **Unsigned device driver checkpoints.**   System Restore creates a restore point when you install an unsigned device driver. If installing the device driver interferes with your computer's stability, you can restore the computer to the state it was in before you installed the device driver.

- **Backup utility recovery checkpoints.**   System Restore creates a restore point before you use the Backup utility to perform a recovery. You can restore the computer if the recovery leaves your computer in a questionable state.

> **Note**   You must still use Add Or Remove Programs to uninstall programs, even if you restore to a point prior to program installation. Removing the program and then restoring the checkpoint is the best sequence.

System Restore requires at least 200 megabytes (MB) of available disk space. If 200 MB of space isn't available, Windows XP disables System Restore. By default, Windows XP allocates 12 percent of the hard disk's size (or 400 MB on hard disks that are smaller than 4 gigabytes), which is the most that Windows XP can allocate to System

Restore. You can otherwise configure the amount of disk space System Restore consumes, though. On the System Restore tab of the System Properties dialog box, drag the slider left or right to adjust the amount of disk space it uses. To open System Properties, click Start, Control Panel, Performance And Maintenance, and then click System. However, don't reduce the amount—doing so limits the number of restore points that System Restore can maintain at one time.

Taking Configuration Snapshots

Here's how to create a restore point using System Restore:

1. Start System Restore in one of the following ways:

   ❑ Click System Restore in Help and Support Center.

   ❑ Click Start, All Programs, Accessories, System Tools, System Restore.

   ❑ Run %SystemRoot%\System32\Restore\rstrui.exe.

2. Select the Create A Restore Point option, and then click Next.

3. In the Restore Point Description box, type a descriptive name for the restore point, and then click Create. (System Restore adds the date and time to the name of the restore point.)

To restore a checkpoint, follow these steps:

1. Start System Restore using one of the three methods in the previous procedure.

2. Select the Restore My Computer To an Earlier Time option, and then click Next.

3. Select the restore point that you want to restore, and then click Next.

   System Restore maintains up to 90 days of restore points, given enough disk space, so you can move backward and forward in the calendar to see the restore points created on each day. In the calendar, shown in Figure 3-3, bold dates are those that contain restore points.

4. Click a date, and then click the restore point in the list.

5. Click Next again, and Windows XP restarts so it can restore your configuration to the restore point you selected.

Sometimes, if your configuration is too unstable, you won't be able to start Windows XP normally. That leaves you with Safe Mode. (See Chapter 9, "Troubleshooting Problems.") In Safe Mode, you can't create restore points, but you can restore ones that have already been created. Thus, if Windows XP doesn't start normally, start it in Safe Mode, restore to an earlier configuration, and then restart the computer.

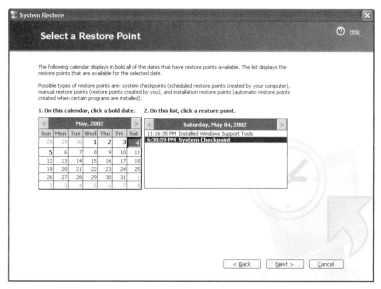

Figure 3-3   Before continuing, make sure you save your documents and close any programs that are running. System Restore restarts your computer.

Looking Inside System Restore

Many of the files and folders System Restore uses are super hidden, so you won't see them unless you display system and hidden files. In Windows Explorer, click Tools, Folder Options. On the Folder Options dialog box's View tab, select the Show Hidden Files And Folders option, and then clear the Hide Protected Operating System Files check box. System Restore's program files are in %SystemRoot%\System32\Restore. Aside from the program file Rstrui.exe, you'll find the super-hidden file Filelist.xml, which lists the files and settings that System Restore monitors. Double-click this file to view the XML in Internet Explorer. It excludes a few legacy configuration files—for example, Win.ini, System.ini, Autoexec.bat, and Config.sys. It excludes a few folders, too, most of which aren't important to the operating system's stability. What's inter-esting is the list of file extensions that it includes. System Restore protects everything from EXE and DLL files to VBS and VXD (virtual device driver) files. If a file matches one of the included file extensions and it's not in a folder that Filelist.xml excludes, System Restore monitors it. It also monitors the per-user hive files listed in the key `HKLM\SOFTWARE\Microsoft\Windows NT\CurrentVersion\ProfileList`.

The actual restore points are in each volume's System Volume Information folder. This folder is also super hidden, so you'll need to select the Show Hidden Files And Folders option and then clear the Hide Protected Operating System Files check box to see it. To open it, you'll have to add your user account to the folder's ACL. I don't recom-mend you do this on a production computer, however, because you risk corrupting the file system. If you have a lab computer, go for it; otherwise, I'll describe this folder for you.

Each System Volume Information folder contains a subfolder called _restore*GUID*, where *GUID* is the computer's GUID. (See Chapter 1, "Learning the Basics.") For example, my computer has _restore{4545302B-EA51-4100-A7E2-C7A37551AA83}. Beneath that folder is one folder for each restore point, called RP*N*, where *N* is an incremental number beginning with 1. RP*N* contains backup copies of changed and deleted files. In fact, I opened my latest restore point folder, deleted a program file, and watched as System Restore added it to the restore point. It also backs up files that change so it can restore those. System Restore changes the file names, so you won't find missing files or documents in there. This folder also contains a list of the changes that System Restore must apply to the computer to restore the checkpoint, including instructions for restoring backup files.

The \snapshot subfolder is in RP*N*, which contains backup copies of the registry's hive files. If you have access to System Volume Information, you can load these hive files in Regedit, examine them, or even recover settings from them. If you really need settings from these hive files, you're better off restoring them using System Restore. You can see System Volume Information in Figure 3-4; hopefully that will satisfy your curiosity enough to keep you out of it. The following is a list of the registry hive files you find in \snapshot:

- _REGISTRY_MACHINE_SAM

- _REGISTRY_MACHINE_SECURITY

- _REGISTRY_MACHINE_SOFTWARE

- _REGISTRY_MACHINE_SYSTEM

- _REGISTRY_USER_.DEFAULT

- _REGISTRY_USER_NTUSER_SID

- _REGISTRY_USER_USRCLASS_SID

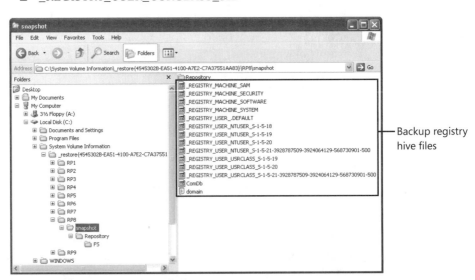

Figure 3-4   System Restore backs up all the hive files so it can restore them if necessary.

Managing System Restore

System Restore has sparse management options. You can change how much disk space it uses, which I've already covered, and you can even disable it altogether. There's only one good time to disable System Restore, and that's when you install Windows XP on sluggish computers. System Restore consumes a small slice of your computer's resources as it monitors the file system for changes, and disabling it can recover those resources. To disable System Restore, click Start, Control Panel, Performance And Maintenance, and then click System to open the System Properties dialog box. On the System Restore tab, select the Turn Off System Restore check box. But unless the computer is painfully slow, leave System Restore alone.

Two policies for managing System Restore are available to IT professionals. The first is `Turn off System Restore`, which disables System Restore altogether. I know some administrators who haven't embraced System Restore yet, and they're disabling it in their organizations. Their concern is the amount of disk space it uses, the small performance penalty for using it, and the potential for restoring unwanted code such as viruses. If you don't want users to be able to configure System Restore, enable the `Turn off Configuration` policy, which locks the user interface so users can't change System Restore's configuration. Users can still create their own restore points, however. Both of these policies are per-computer administrative settings available in the Group Policy console under `Computer Configuration\Administrative Templates\ System\System Restore`.

System Restore has a few other settings for which it doesn't provide a user interface or policy. These are mostly settings in the registry that control System Restore's schedule. You can build your own administrative template for these, however, which you learn about in Chapter 7, "Using Registry-Based Policy." Chapter 7 also shows you how to enable policies.

Customizing System Restore

`HKLM\Software\Microsoft\Windows NT\CurrentVersion\SystemRestore` is the key where you find all of System Restore's settings. Unless otherwise noted, all the settings in the following list are `REG_DWORD` values:

- `CompressionBurst.` This value specifies, in seconds, the idle time compression—that is, the amount of time it takes to compress data after the computer becomes idle. System Restore can compress data for the amount of time specified, and then it must stop until after the next time the computer becomes idle.

- `DiskPercent and DSMax.` Together, these values specify how much disk space System Restore uses. System Restore uses the greater of the two values. Thus, for hard disks smaller than 4 gigabytes (GB), System Restore uses 400 MB, which is the default value of `DSMax`. For hard disks larger than 4 GB, System Restore uses 12 percent, which is the default value of `DiskPercent`.

- **DSMin.**   This value specifies the minimum amount of free disk space that System Restore requires during the installation process. This value also specifies the minimum amount of disk space that System Restore needs in order to be reactivated and resume the creation of restore points after Windows XP has disabled System Restore due to low disk space.

- **RestoreStatus.**   This value indicates whether the last restore operation failed (**0x00**), succeeded (**0x01**), or was interrupted (**0x02**).

- **RPGlobalInterval.**   This value specifies the amount of time in seconds that System Restore waits between creating system checkpoints. The default value is 24 hours (86,400 seconds), or **0x15180**.

- **RPLifeInterval.**   This value specifies the time in seconds that System Restore keeps restore points before removing them from the computer. The default value is **0x76A700**, or 90 days (7,776,000 seconds).

- **RPSessionInterval.**   This value specifies, in seconds, the amount of time that System Restore waits before it creates the system checkpoints while the computer is turned on. The default value is zero, disabling this feature. You can change this value to **0xE10** to create a restore point every hour that the computer is in use. On a computer that you customize often, such as a lab computer, you might create a restore point every hour.

- **ThawInterval.**   This value specifies, in seconds, the amount of time that System Restore waits before it reactivates itself after adequate disk space becomes available. Start the System Restore user interface, and it reactivates immediately.

It isn't useful to customize the remaining settings you find in **SystemRestore**, and Microsoft warns in no uncertain terms that you shouldn't change them. However, you can disable System Restore by setting **DisableSR** to **0x01**, and doing so doesn't remove existing restore points as when you disable System Restore in the user interface. Editing the remaining settings can do bad things to your computer's performance, so limit yourself to the settings I described in this section.

Scripting System Restore

You can script System Restore using Windows Scripting Host (WSH) and Windows Management Instrumentation (WMI). Chapter 11, "Scripting Registry Changes," describes in detail how to script registry edits. But perhaps you want to write scripts to automate System Restore specifically. Using these scripts gives you more control over the creation of restore points than did the registry settings in the previous section.

Scripting System Restore relies on WMI and Srclient.dll, which is the System Restore client DLL. The account in which you run these scripts must have administrative privileges to prevent them from being used by members of the Users or Power Users groups. In the Scheduled Tasks folder, you can schedule these scripts to run with elevated privileges, though. The following listing shows a script that automatically creates a restore point: it creates a System Restore object using WMI and then creates a restore point by calling the method `CreateRestorePoint()`. The first parameter is the name of the restore point; you should use a descriptive name that begins with a verb, such as *Installed* or *Changed*.

```
Set SRP = GetObject("winmgmts:\\.\root\default:Systemrestore")
CSRP = SRP.CreateRestorePoint("Hacked the registry", 0, 100)
```

In addition to creating restore points, you can restore checkpoints using scripts. You can also configure System Restore, enable and disable it, or iterate through the list of restore points on the computer. For more information about System Restore's WMI classes, see *http://msdn.microsoft.com/library/en-us/sr/sr/system_restore_wmi_classes.asp*, which is the MSDN documentation for System Restore.

Backing Up the Registry Regularly

Backup Utility has come a long way since the original version that shipped with the earliest versions of Windows. Microsoft licenses Backup Utility from VERITAS Software Corporation (*http://www.veritas.com*), and it's a modified edition of the company's Backup Exec. Users of the Windows 2000 backup program are already familiar with this version. The user interfaces of the two versions are almost identical, and the steps for backing up a computer are almost the same. As with the earlier version of this utility, you can back up to a file, tape, or other removable media. Enterprise users will likely have tape changers to automate a full backup schedule, including tape swapping. Backup-to-disk is another popular option for option due to the growth of storage servers.

Windows makes a few significant enhancements. The first is Shadow Copy. A volume shadow copy is an exact copy of the contents of a hard disk, including open files, at any given point in time. Users can continue to access files on the hard disk while Backup Utility backs them up during a volume shadow copy. In this way, it correctly copies files that change during the backup process. Shadow Copy ensures that programs can continue to write to files on the volume, open files aren't omitted from the backup, and backing up the system doesn't lock users out.

To open Backup Utility, click Start, All Programs, Accessories, System Tools, and then Backup. I prefer to use the mouse as little as possible, so I just click Start, Run, and type **ntbackup** in the Run dialog box. Backup Utility has a robust set of command-line options you can use to script the backup process; you can learn more about those options in Backup Utility's Help. That's the hard way to use Backup Utility's command-line options. The easy way is to schedule a job using Backup Utility, configure options in its user interface, and then copy its command line syntax from the backup job's entry listed in the Scheduled Tasks folder. Why spend an hour getting the command line just right when Backup Utility can do that for you?

Note   To back up a computer's file and folders, users must be in the Administrators or Backup Operators groups. If they aren't in either of those groups, they must have at least Read permission on each file and folder they want to back up using Backup Utility. Alternatively, you can grant users the Back Up Files And Directories and the Restore Files And Directories user rights.

Backing Up Using Symantec Ghost

I'm a big fan of Symantec Ghost Corporate Edition, which you can learn more about at *http://www.symantec.com*. It's the tool I prefer for deploying Windows in big environments. It's also useful as a backup utility, and you can use the Personal Edition of Ghost to back up a single computer.

The backup strategy for my home-office network uses both Ghost and Windows' Backup Utility. Backup Utility is better at protecting documents than it is at protecting entire configurations. To restore a computer from a backup tape, you first have to install Windows on the computer, and honestly, it takes as much time to reinstall everything from the very beginning as it takes to restore a good backup. That's why I prefer to protect my configurations using Ghost. After installing Windows and all of my applications on a computer, I create an image of the computer's disk on the server. I update that image any time I make a significant change to the computer, such as after I install new applications. If the computer fails, I can use a Ghost boot disk to start the computer and restore the disk image, and the computer is running again. The process takes less than 15 minutes, whereas restoring the computer using Backup Utility can take a few hours.

I protect important documents and other important files using Backup Utility. Documents, images, and many other files change often enough that it's impractical to use Ghost to protect them. Thus, I schedule Backup Utility to run each day so that I can restore any of my documents if something goes wrong.

I take this approach one step further by completely separating my configuration from my data. I use Folder Redirection to move users' My Documents folders from their local user profiles to a central location on the network. I back up all users' documents each time I back up their redirected folders that are located on the server. For the most part, then, each computer's configuration is completely replaceable. I can restore its current disk image and log on to Windows, and the computer is back to where it was before it failed.

Planning a Backup Strategy

If you're an IT professional in a large enterprise, you already have a backup strategy. Many small and home-based businesses go without backup strategies or backing up their computers at all, and that's a shame. Unproductive downtime probably hurts small businesses more than it hurts huge enterprises, but it can be easily avoided. Whether you back up your computers using Backup Utility, Symantec Ghost, or any other method, just do it, and do it often.

The first part of a good strategy is rotation—that is, keeping backups around for a period of time so you can restore any one of them later. For example, you might back up computers once a week and keep each backup set for a month. You'll always have the four most recent backups available. I use tapes and like to keep one set of tapes offsite in case of a disaster. (I also store tapes in a fireproof safe, but you never know about fireproof safes until you try them.) Use a rotation that works for you; on my server, I use the one shown in Figure 3-5. (Backing up individual computers isn't necessary because I store anything I want to save on the server.) I don't change my daily backup tapes because one tape holds a full week's worth of changes. That's why I can get away with having only nine sets of tapes. With more users, you might change tapes daily. Here's a summary of what you see in Figure 3-5:

- **Monthly.**   Move the most recent full-backup tape offsite (tape 5).

- **Weekly.**   Back up the entire server to tape (tapes 1 through 4).

- **Daily.**   Back up changed files to tape and mark those files as archived (tapes 6 through 9). The backup set includes system information, users' home folders, documents, mail folders, roaming user profiles, and more.

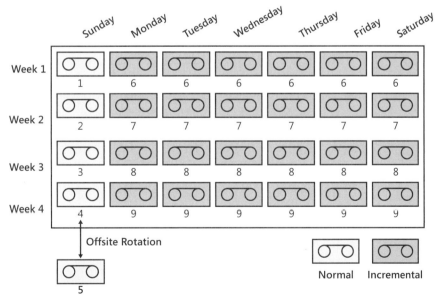

Figure 3-5   Normal backup tapes contain all the server's files; incremental backup tapes contain only files that changed since the last normal or incremental backup.

The second part of a good strategy is automation. You'll never stick to your backup plan if you don't automate it. Backup Utility integrates with Scheduled Tasks to schedule backup jobs through its own user interface, so this is easy. You can schedule your own backup jobs in Scheduled Tasks, but the command-line options are a bit intense, so I'd stick to the user interface. If your backup jobs require multiple tapes, as mine usually do, you'll have to be around to swap tapes. Large organizations will want to consider investing in a robotic tape changer or library, if they haven't already invested in large-scale backup technology.

Backing Up System State Data

In Backup Utility, you don't see an option to back up the registry. Furthermore, if you try to back up the hive files in %SystemRoot%\System32\config, you'll fail. Instead, you back up the Windows *system state data*. System state data is the combination of the following system components:

- Registry
- COM+ Class Registration database
- Boot files, including the system files
- System files that are under Windows File Protection

A server's system state data might include additional components, including Active Directory data, SYSVOL, Certificate Services database, and more, depending on the role of the server.

To back up the registry, you have to copy all the system state data. Likewise, in order to restore the registry, you have to restore all the system state data. This makes Backup Utility less than ideal for backing up the registry if that's all you're really trying to accomplish. To back up Windows system state data, select the System State check box in Backup Or Restore Wizard, shown in Figure 3-6, or click Only Backup The System State Data in Backup Wizard. (Note that they are two different wizards.) You can also select the System State check box on Backup Utility's Backup tab.

Backup Utility doesn't back up and restore everything on the computer. The key `HKLM\SYSTEM\CurrentControlSet\Control\BackupRestore` contains two interesting subkeys. The first subkey, `FilesNotToBackup`, contains a list of files and folders that Backup Utility skips. Each value contains a path to skip, and those values often contain wildcards. The second subkey, `KeysNotToRestore`, contains a list of keys not to restore to the computer. Likewise, each value contains a key to skip, and you see wildcards in many of the values. You'll find few surprises in either subkey. For example, Backup Utility doesn't back up System Restore's restore points because \System Volume Information_restore*GUID** is in `FilesNotToBackup`. It doesn't restore Plug and Play information, either, because `CurrentControlSet\Enum\` is in `KeysNotToRe-store`. For a complete list of the files and subkeys listed in these subkeys, visit *http://support.microsoft.com/default.aspx?scid=kb;en-us;233427.*

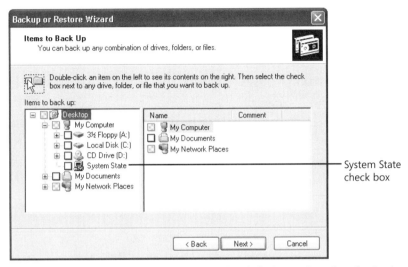

System State check box

Figure 3-6   Backup Or Restore Wizard is the default user interface for Backup Utility. If you'd rather use the classic user interface, click Advanced Mode on the first page.

Restoring System State Data

Restoring system state data from a backup is similar to backing up the system state data in the first place. If you backed up only system state data, just restore the entire backup. Otherwise, click System State in Backup Or Restore Wizard or on Backup Utility's Restore And Manage Media tab. If you restore the files to the original location, you'll restore your computer's settings, protected system files, boot files, and so on. This is the quick approach to restoring system state data from a backup.

However, the precise approach is sometimes more appropriate. Restore the files to an alternate location. Backup Utility tells you that it won't restore all system state data to alternate locations, but don't worry; it does restore the registry hive files. Figure 3-7 shows you the contents of system state data as well as how Backup Utility restores the registry to an alternate location. When you restore system state data to a folder, the registry hive files are in the subfolder \Registry. You can load these hive files in Regedit and then copy settings from them to the working registry.

You don't always have to restore a backup to get the backup copy of the registry. If the most recent backup contains the settings you want to restore, you'll be happy to know that Backup Utility copies the hive files to %SystemRoot%\Repair. Don't try replacing the hive files in %SystemRoot%\System32\config with the backup copies you find in

%SystemRoot%\Repair—you can't because they're in use by Windows. You can load the backup hive files by using Regedit to borrow settings from them, or you can start Recovery Console and then copy the backup hive files to %SystemRoot%\System32\ Config. It's worth pointing out that System Restore does a far better job of restoring your settings than you can.

Figure 3-7　Restoring system state data to an alternate location is the best choice if you want to restore a limited number of files or settings.

Backing Up User Settings

Backup Utility puts per-computer settings in system state data, but it doesn't back up per-user settings from users' profile folders. Those settings are in each profile folder's NTUSER.DAT file. Don't forget the per-user class registrations that Windows stores in %UserProfile%\Local Settings\Application Data\Microsoft\Windows\UsrClass.dat. You have to pick these up manually either by selecting them in Backup or Restore Wizard or by using another means of backing up users' settings, such as backing up roaming user profiles. Windows does a great job of protecting per-computer settings and fixing them when they aren't functioning properly, but it doesn't do as good of a job with per-user settings. In my experience, after users' settings are completely fouled, the support call lasts too long, and users don't always leave the experience happy.

Backing up user profiles from each computer isn't practical on a large network. You can use System Restore to fix users' profiles because it backs up settings from the profiles in the key HKLM\SOFTWARE\Microsoft\Windows NT\CurrentVersion\ProfileList. You can take a more proactive approach, however. One solution is implementing roaming user profiles. Assuming they're compatible with your environment—roaming user profiles don't work well in mixed environments or when hardware configurations vary wildly from one computer to the next—the central storage of roaming user profiles makes it possible to back up users' settings as part of the server's normal backup routine. Even if users don't log on to multiple computers, roaming user profiles might be worth implementing just for this capability alone. Restoring a user's profile consists of logging the user off of Windows, restoring the user's profile folder to the server, and then logging the user back on to Windows.

Note   Chapter 12, "Deploying User Profiles," gives this subject more attention. You learn how to deploy different types of user profiles, back them up, and more. You also learn about the many improvements that Windows makes to roaming user profiles, which just might make them more feasible in your organization.

Chapter 4
Hacking the Registry

This chapter covers hacking the registry to make Microsoft Windows XP and Windows Server 2003 (both referred to throughout as Windows) look and feel the way that you want them to. Rather than showing you how Windows organizes the registry, which is covered in Part IV, "Appendixes," I'll show you the hacks that immediately change the way you use Windows. To make these customizations easier, I've included scripts for many of them. Download these and new scripts at *http://www.honeycutt.com.*

I use the term *hack* loosely. These aren't security hacks or hacks that give you more features than you're supposed to have. By no means am I helping you hack product activation. Rather, these are hacks that help you customize the operating system in ways that you can't do through its user interface. For example, this chapter helps you customize the shortcut menus and the icons you see in the user interface and change how Windows works. It even describes how you can log on to Windows automatically, bypassing the Log On To Windows dialog box. You can find some of these hacks on various Web sites and FAQs, but hopefully, I'm giving you many new ones that you won't find anywhere else.

These hacks are for power users. If you're looking for customizations aimed at IT professionals, see Chapter 18, "Fixing Common IT Problems," which has customizations that help IT professionals deploy Windows and solve particular IT problems. Though the chapter you're reading now is aimed at end users, IT professionals might also find that its customizations are a good fit for their enterprise users, and professionals can deploy those customizations in a variety of ways, including for default user profiles, policies, and scripts. For example, IT professionals frequently ask me how to simulate IntelliMirror features, like Folder Redirection, without using policies, and the first hack in this chapter shows you how to do exactly that.

Redirecting Special Folders

The My Documents, My Pictures, and Favorites folders, among many others, are examples of special folders. Table 4-1 shows the special folders—and their default paths—that Windows creates when creating a new profile. The first column contains each folder's internal name as Windows and other programs know it. The second column contains each folder's default path, which almost always starts with %UserProfile%, making these folders part of each user's profile folder. Chapter 12, "Deploying User Profiles," describes user profile folders in depth.

Users might want to redirect special folders for a variety of reasons, but in two scenarios in particular. The first is when you want to redirect the My Documents folder to a different volume. For example, users might redirect My Documents to drive D so they can reinstall Windows on drive C without losing their documents. The second scenario is when users have a network and want to access their documents from more than one computer. In that case, they can redirect both their My Documents and Favorites folders to a network location so they can access them from anywhere. IT professionals also frequently want to redirect My Documents to a network location, which makes backing up users' documents easier. This can be done with the IntelliMirror feature Folder Redirection. IT professionals can't use IntelliMirror features without Active Directory, but they can simulate Folder Redirection. Chapter 18, "Fixing Common IT Problems," shows how to simulate Folder Redirection in that scenario.

Microsoft does not recommend that you use the techniques described in this section in a business-computing environment, particularly if that environment includes Active Directory and Group Policy. (Group Policy provides policies for redirecting folders.) In environments that don't include Active Directory, these techniques remain valuable; however, you must test them in a lab environment before deploying them in a production environment.

Table 4-1 **Special Folders**

Name	Default Path
AppData	%UserProfile%\Application Data
Cache	%UserProfile%\Local Settings\Temporary Internet Files
Cookies	%UserProfile%\Cookies
Desktop	%UserProfile%\Desktop
Favorites	%UserProfile%\Favorites
History	%UserProfile%\Local Settings\History
Local AppData	%UserProfile%\Local Settings\Application Data
Local Settings	%UserProfile%\Local Settings
My Pictures	%UserProfile%\My Documents\My Pictures
NetHood	%UserProfile%\NetHood
Personal	%UserProfile%\My Documents
PrintHood	%UserProfile%\PrintHood
Programs	%UserProfile%\Start Menu\Programs
Recent	%UserProfile%\Recent
SendTo	%UserProfile%\SendTo
Start Menu	%UserProfile%\Start Menu
Startup	%UserProfile%\Start Menu\Programs\Startup
Templates	%UserProfile%\Templates

HKCU\Software\Microsoft\Windows\CurrentVersion\Explorer\User Shell Folders.
Each value in this key is a special folder, as shown in Table 4-1. Because these are
REG_EXPAND_SZ values, you can use environment variables in them. Use %UserProfile%
in a path to direct the folder to a location inside users' profile folders, or use
%UserName% in a path to include users' names. To redirect users' Favorites folders
to the network, set the value Favorites, which you can look up in Table 4-1, to
*Server**Share*\%UserName%\Favorites, where *Server**Share* is the server and share
containing the folders. The next time the user logs on, Windows updates a second
key, HKCU\Software\Microsoft\Windows\CurrentVersion\Explorer\Shell Folders,
with the paths from User Shell Folders, so you don't have to update it. In fact,
Microsoft's documentation says Windows doesn't use Shell Folders.

The following listing shows you how to redirect special folders automatically. Save this
listing to the text file Redirect.inf and replace the string PERSONAL with the location to
which you want to redirect the My Documents folder. (Use environment variables
so the script works for all users.) Perform the same steps for the strings FAVORITES,
PICTURES, and APPDATA. To configure these settings, right-click Redirect.inf, and then
click Install. Chapter 11, "Scripting Registry Changes," shows you other ways to
deploy these settings. You can uninstall this script using Add Or Remove Programs.

Listing 4-1   Redirect.inf

```
[Version]
Signature=$CHICAGO$

[DefaultInstall]
AddReg=Reg.Settings
AddReg=Reg.Uninstall
CopyFiles=Inf.Copy

[DefaultUninstall]
DelReg=Reg.Settings
DelReg=Reg.Uninstall
DelFiles=Inf.Copy

[Reg.Settings]
HKCU,Software\Microsoft\Windows\CurrentVersion\Explorer\
\User Shell Folders,AppData,0x20000,"%APPDATA%"
HKCU,Software\Microsoft\Windows\CurrentVersion\Explorer\
\User Shell Folders,Personal,0x20000,"%PERSONAL%"
HKCU,Software\Microsoft\Windows\CurrentVersion\Explorer\
\User Shell Folders,My Pictures,0x20000,"%PICTURES%"
HKCU,Software\Microsoft\Windows\CurrentVersion\Explorer\User Shell \
Folders,favorites,0x20000,"%FAVORITES%"

[Reg.Uninstall]
HKCU,Software\Microsoft\Windows\CurrentVersion\Uninstall\%NAME%
HKCU,Software\Microsoft\Windows\CurrentVersion\Uninstall\
\%NAME%,DisplayName,,"%NAME%"
HKCU,Software\Microsoft\Windows\CurrentVersion\Uninstall\%NAME%,UninstallString\
,,"Rundll32.exe setupapi.dll,InstallHinfSection DefaultUninstall 132"\
" %53%\Application Data\Custom\Redirect.inf"

[Inf.Copy]
Redirect.inf

[DestinationDirs]
Inf.Copy=53,Application Data\Custom

[SourceDisksNames]
55=%DISKNAME%

[SourceDisksFiles]
Redirect.inf=55

[Strings]
NAME        = "Jerry's Redirect Folders"
APPDATA     = "\\Server\Folders\%UserName%\Application Data"
PERSONAL    = "\\Server\Folders\%UserName%\My Documents"
PICTURES    = "\\Server\Folders\%UserName%\My Documents\My Pictures"
FAVORITES   = "\\Server\Folders\%UserName%\Favorites"
DISKNAME    = "Setup Files"
```

Note The special folders in this section are per-user and exist within users profile folders. Windows also lists per-computer special folders in HKLM. Exan of per-computer folders include Common AppData, Common Desktop, and Common Documents. It's not as useful to customize per-computer folders; however, the same rules apply. Change the location of the folder in User Shell Folders; Windows automatically updates Shell Folders.

Customizing Shell Folders

Some folders you see in Windows Explorer, Control Panel, or on the desktop don't actually exist on the file system. They're objects based on classes registered in the key HKCR\CLSID. Some folders and files that do exist on the file system (the History and Briefcase folders for example) have special capabilities that come from objects based on classes registered in HKCR\CLSID. A class is essentially a template for creating something real, like an object in the user interface, and CLSID is the location where those classes are registered so Windows knows about them.

Third-party programs might register additional classes, and you can easily spot interesting ones in HKCR\CLSID because they have the subkey ShellFolder and the value Attributes in that subkey. Appendix A, "File Associations," describes the value Attributes and how to understand each bit in it. Figure 4-1 shows what this subkey and value look like in the registry. Class registrations containing the value LocalizedString are likely candidates for customization because they contain this value only if objects based on that class appear in the user interface. These classes have a variety of purposes, and you'll use them frequently to hack Windows.

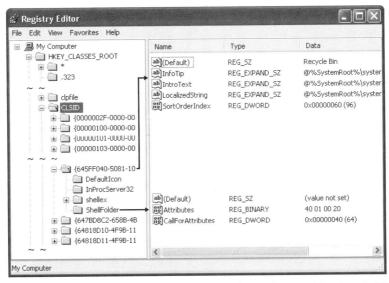

Figure 4-1 You can find interesting object classes by searching for ShellFolder subkeys that contain the value Attributes. Look for LocalizedString, too.

Table 4-2 lists the classes registered in HKCR\CLSID that I find the most interesting. I divided this table into four sections. The first is shell folders. These are special-purpose folders, such as My Computer and My Network Places. The second section is Control Panel folders—for example, Administrative Tools and Scheduled Tasks. The third section is Control Panel icons. The fourth section lists other interesting classes, such as the Run dialog box. Objects created from classes in the first two sections are folders. Objects created from classes in the last two sections are usually dialog boxes, but sometimes they add capabilities to files and folders, as Briefcase does. The first column is the class's name, and the second column is the class's GUID, or *class identifier*. I've italicized those that aren't useful for hacking but that you run into frequently while hacking the registry.

Table 4-2   Special Object Classes

Object	Class Identifier
Shell folders	
ActiveX Cache	{88C6C381-2E85-11D0-94DE-444553540000}
Computer Search Results	{1F4DE370-D627-11D1-BA4F-00A0C91EEDBA}
History	{FF393560-C2A7-11CF-BFF4-444553540000}
Internet Explorer	{871C5380-42A0-1069-A2EA-08002B30309D}
My Computer	{20D04FE0-3AEA-1069-A2D8-08002B30309D}
My Documents	{450D8FBA-AD25-11D0-98A8-0800361B1103}
My Network Places	{208D2C60-3AEA-1069-A2D7-08002B30309D}
Offline Files	{AFDB1F70-2A4C-11D2-9039-00C04F8EEB3E}
Programs	{7BE9D83C-A729-4D97-B5A7-1B7313C39E0A}
Recycle Bin	{645FF040-5081-101B-9F08-00AA002F954E}
Search Results	{E17D4FC0-5564-11D1-83F2-00A0C90DC849}
Shared Documents	{59031A47-3F72-44A7-89C5-5595FE6B30EE}
Start Menu	{48E7CAAB-B918-4E58-A94D-505519C795DC}
Temporary Internet Files	{7BD29E00-76C1-11CF-9DD0-00A0C9034933}
Web	{BDEADF00-C265-11D0-BCED-00A0C90AB50F}
Control Panel folders	
Administrative Tools	{D20EA4E1-3957-11D2-A40B-0C5020524153}
Fonts	{D20EA4E1-3957-11D2-A40B-0C5020524152}
Network Connections	{7007ACC7-3202-11D1-AAD2-00805FC1270E}
Printers and Faxes	{2227A280-3AEA-1069-A2DE-08002B30309D}
Scanners and Cameras	{E211B736-43FD-11D1-9EFB-0000F8757FCD}
Scheduled Tasks	{D6277990-4C6A-11CF-8D87-00AA0060F5BF}
Control Panel icons	
Folder Options	{6DFD7C5C-2451-11D3-A299-00C04F8EF6AF}
Taskbar and Start Menu	{0DF44EAA-FF21-4412-828E-260A8728E7F1}
User Accounts	{7A9D77BD-5403-11D2-8785-2E0420524153}

Table 4-2   **Special Object Classes**

Object	Class Identifier
Other classes	
Add Network Places	{D4480A50-BA28-11D1-8E75-00C04FA31A86}
Briefcase	{85BBD920-42A0-1069-A2E4-08002B30309D}
E-mail	{2559A1F5-21D7-11D4-BDAF-00C04F60B9F0}
Help and Support	{2559A1F1-21D7-11D4-BDAF-00C04F60B9F0}
Internet	{2559A1F4-21D7-11D4-BDAF-00C04F60B9F0}
Network Setup Wizard	{2728520D-1EC8-4C68-A551-316B684C4EA7}
Run	{2559A1F3-21D7-11D4-BDAF-00C04F60B9F0}
Search	{2559A1F0-21D7-11D4-BDAF-00C04F60B9F0}
Windows Security	{2559A1F2-21D7-11D4-BDAF-00C04F60B9F0}

You can do a lot when armed with the information in Table 4-2. You can customize which folders you see in My Computer, for example. You can rename the icons you see on the desktop and even configure which icons appear on the desktop at all. For example, administrators might put the Administrative Tools folder on their desktops for quicker access. See the upcoming sections for information about the different ways I've found to use these classes.

Renaming Desktop Icons

On the desktop, you can rename the My Computer, My Network Places, My Documents, and Internet Explorer icons. Assuming you see these icons on your desktop, right-click them, and then click Rename. No Rename command is available for other icons, like the Recycle Bin.

You rename an icon without a Rename command by editing its class registration. Change the value of `LocalizedString`. Here's an example: in Table 4-2, you see that the Recycle Bin's class ID is {645FF040-5081-101B-9F08-00AA002F954E}. To rename the Recycle Bin icon "Trash Can," set the value of `LocalizedString` in the key `HKCR\CLSID\{645FF040-5081-101B-9F08-00AA002F954E}` to `Trash Can`. Then click the desktop, and press F5 to refresh its contents. The value `LocalizedString` usually contains something like `@%SystemRoot%\system32\SHELL32.dll,-8964`, which means that Windows uses the string with the ID 8964 from the file Shell32.dll. Just replace all that with the new name.

Tip   `LocalizedString` is a REG_EXPAND_SZ value, so you can use environment variables in it. For example, set `LocalizedString` to %UserName%'s Garbage, and the user Jerry sees "Jerry's Garbage" below the icon. You can do this for other icons as well. My Computer's class ID is {20D04FE0-3AEA-1069-A2D8-08002B30309D}. Change `LocalizedString` in HKCR\CLSID\{20D04FE0-3AEA-1069-A2D8-08002B30309D} to %UserName%'s Computer, and the user Jerry sees "Jerry's Computer" instead of My Computer; the user Sally sees "Sally's Computer."

In some class registrations, you don't see the value `LocalizedString`. The absence of this value indicates that Microsoft didn't intend to display the names of those objects in the user interface. To rename a class that doesn't contain this value, change the default value of `HKCR\CLSID\`*classID*, or better yet, add `LocalizedString` to it. When Windows looks for an object's name, it looks first for `LocalizedString` and then for the class registration's default value.

Using Custom Icon Images

Each class registration you see in Table 4-2 contains the subkey `DefaultIcon`. This subkey's default value is the icon that Windows uses when it displays objects based on that class. For example, the default value of `DefaultIcon` in `HKCR\CLSID\{20D04FE0-3AEA-1069-A2D8-08002B30309D}` is the icon that Windows displays when it creates the My Computer object in the user interface, such as in Windows Explorer or on the desktop.

To use a different icon, change the default value of `DefaultIcon`. You can use the path and file name of an icon file, which has the *.ico* extension, or you can use a resource path. A resource path is either *Name,Index* or *Name,-resID*. *Name* is the path and name of the file containing the icon, which is usually a DLL or EXE file. Most of the icons that Windows uses come from %SystemRoot%\System32\Shell32.dll. *Index* is the index number of the icon, beginning with 0, and *resID* is the resource identifier (resource ID) of the icon. Programmers assign resource IDs to resources that they store in program files, such as icons, strings, and dialog boxes.

> **Tip**   My favorite tool for finding icons in program files is PE Explorer from Heaven Tools. You can download an evaluation copy from the Web site at *http://www.heaventools.com*. This tool can even extract all of the icons from DLL and EXE files so that you can use them individually.

Adding Desktop Icons

Windows now has a much cleaner desktop than earlier versions of Windows did. By default, you see only the Recycle Bin icon. You can add the typical icons, though. On the Display Properties dialog box, click the Desktop tab, and then click Customize Desktop. In the Desktop Items dialog box, choose the icons that you want to display on the desktop. You can add the My Documents, My Computer, My Network Places, and Internet Explorer icons. To open the Display Properties dialog box, right-click the desktop, and then click Properties.

If the icon you want to add isn't one of those four choices, or if you want to script these changes, or if you want to add icons to other special folders, you must edit the registry. All the hacks you learn about in this section are in the branch

SOFTWARE\Microsoft\Windows\CurrentVersion\Explorer. Change this branch in HKLM to affect all users; change it in HKCU to affect an individual user. Figure 4-2 shows the contents of this branch.

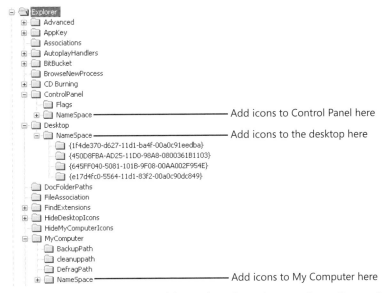

Figure 4-2   The NameSpace subkeys of Explorer\ControlPanel, Explorer\Desktop, and Explorer\MyComputer determine the contents of each corresponding folder.

You add icons to Control Panel or the desktop, for example, by editing the subkeys indicated in Table 4-3. Create a new subkey in NameSpace, and name it with the class ID of the object you want to add. For example, to add to the desktop an icon that opens the Run dialog box, add a new subkey called {2559A1F3-21D7-11D4-BDAF-00C04F60B9F0} to Desktop\Namespace. (See Table 4-2.) Then refresh the desktop by clicking it and pressing F5. As shown in Figure 4-3, you can add folders to My Computer, too. In this case, I added the Administrative Tools and Network Connections folders to My Computer. The only objects that are good to place in My Computer are folder objects, so pick class IDs from the first two sections of Table 4-1. Add class IDs from the second and third sections of the table, and you'll see only those objects in the right pane of Windows Explorer. Objects based on classes in the second and third sections of Table 4-1 are good choices for Control Panel.

Table 4-3   NameSpace Subkeys

Folder	Subkey
Control Panel	ControlPanel\NameSpace
Desktop	Desktop\NameSpace
My Computer	MyComputer\NameSpace
My Network Places	NetworkNeighborhood\NameSpace
Remote Computer	RemoteComputer\NameSpace

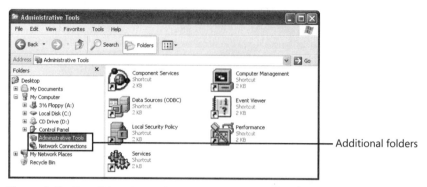

Figure 4-3   By editing the registry, you can reorganize the contents of Windows Explorer.

Hiding Desktop Icons

In earlier versions of Windows, you removed icons from the desktop by removing their subkeys from the key NameSpace. This often caused problems, especially when removing the Network Neighborhood icon from the desktop.

Windows makes a special provision for hiding desktop icons. You remove icons from the desktop or from My Computer by editing in HKLM or HKCU the branch SOFTWARE\ Microsoft\Windows\CurrentVersion\Explorer. To hide icons in My Computer, add a REG_DWORD value to HideMyComputerIcons. The name will be the class ID of the icon you want to hide. Then set the value to 0x01. Refresh Windows Explorer to see your changes.

Hiding desktop icons is a bit more complicated. In HideDesktopIcons, you see two subkeys: ClassicStartMenu and NewStartPanel. The first subkey determines which icons to hide when Windows is using the classic Start menu. The second determines which icons to hide when Windows is using the new Start menu. Add a REG_DWORD value named for the icon's class ID to either subkey to hide it in that view. Set the value to 0x01. For example, to hide the Recycle Bin icon when the new Start menu is in use, create a REG_DWORD value called {645FF040-5081-101B-9F08-00AA002F954E} in the subkey HideDesktopIcons\NewStartPanel, and then set it to 0x01. Click the desktop, and then press F5 to refresh.

> **Tip**   When adding a class ID to HideMyComputerIcons or HideDesktopIcons, use the default value of that subkey to remind you which icon you're hiding. Windows doesn't use this subkey's default value, so using the icon's name in it will help you figure out which subkey to remove in order to show that icon. For example, you can add notes to the default value of the HideDesktopIcons key to indicate which values belong to the different icons.

Reorganizing Control Panel

The Control Panel in Windows XP includes a category view that divides specific tasks and Control Panel icons into different categories. You can include a Control Panel icon in a particular category by adding a REG_DWORD value for it in the key HKLM\ Software\Microsoft\Windows\CurrentVersion\Control Panel\Extended Properties\ {305CA226-D286-468e-B848-2B2E8E697B74} 2. (The 2 is part of the key's name.) Most of the Control Panel icons already have values in this key, so all you have to do is assign a category ID to each one. The following list describes the available category IDs:

- **0x00000000.** Other Control Panel Options. (Any tool that does not specify a category ID is placed in this category.)
- **0x00000001.** Appearance and Themes.
- **0x00000002.** Printers and Other Hardware.
- **0x00000003.** Network and Internet Connections.
- **0x00000004.** Sounds, Speech, and Audio Devices.
- **0x00000005.** Performance and Maintenance.
- **0x00000006.** Date, Time, Language, and Regional Options.
- **0x00000007.** Accessibility Options.
- **0xFFFFFFFF.** This indicates not to put the tool in any category, and is for special tools that only start directly, such as Add Or Remove Programs.

For example, to put the System Control Panel tool in the Appearance and Themes category, set %SystemRoot%\System32\sysdm.cpl to 0x01. For Control Panel tools that are implemented as shell namespace extensions (for example, Fonts and Scheduled Tasks), the category ID is specified in the registry under the CLSID entry. For example, the category setting for the Administrative Tools folder is in HKCR\CLSID\{D20EA4E1-3957-11D2-A40B-0C5020524153}. It's the REG_DWORD value {305CA226-D286-468e-B848-2B2E8E697B74} 2, which is set to 0x05 by default.

> **Note** Windows doesn't provide a method for creating new categories or adding tasks to existing categories.

Customizing File Associations

File associations control the following aspects of how Windows treats files:

- Which icon Windows displays for a file

- Which application launches when users double-click files

- How Windows Explorer displays particular types of files

- Which commands appear on files' shortcut menus

- Other features, such as what displays in InfoTips

Appendix A, "File Associations," describes file associations in detail. In that chapter, you also learn how to customize file associations using methods that only programmers know—until now. Because Appendix A gives a full discussion of file associations and the root key that contains them, HKCR, I'm not going to duplicate that material here. I thought you'd have more fun with some specific file association customizations that I like, such as adding Tweak UI to the My Computer shortcut menu or opening a command prompt window at a particular folder.

File Associations in the Registry

Appendix A, "File Associations," is the place to go to learn about file associations in HKCR, but this section will help you use the hacks you see in this chapter. Look at Figure 4-4, which shows how Windows chooses what to display on a file's shortcut menu.

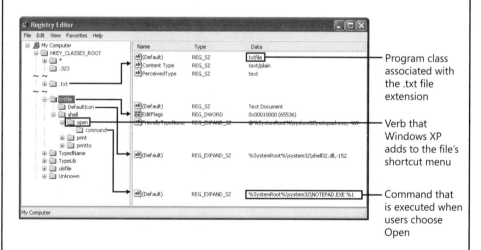

Figure 4-4   A file extension key's default value indicates the program class with which it's associated. The program class's shell subkey contains commands you see on the shortcut menu.

In Figure 4-4, you see the keys that Windows consults when you right-click a text file and then click Open. First, the operating system looks up the file extension in HKCR. The default value, shown in Figure 4-4, indicates that the program class associated with the *.txt* file extension is txtfile. So the operating system looks in HKCR\txtfile for the subkey shell to find the commands that it adds to the shortcut menu. For example, as shown in Figure 4-4, Windows adds Open to the shortcut menu, and when users choose Open, it runs the command in the command subkey.

The command in the command subkey is usually *"program" options "%1"*, where *program* is the path and file name of the program you want to run. If you're using a script and you change the default value of command to REG_EXPAND_SZ, you can use environment variables like %SystemRoot% in it. Otherwise, use an explicit path. You use the %1 as a placeholder for the target file. Windows will add the path and name of the target file to the end of the command by default, but you don't want to leave this up to chance. Also, always enclose %1 in quotation marks in case the target path and file name include spaces.

You often see this same shell subkey in class registrations, too. For example, the class registration for My Computer contains a command for managing the computer. The class registration for Recycle Bin contains commands for emptying and exploring its contents.

Running Programs from My Computer

I like any customization that makes things easier. There are some programs that I use over and over again, and I want an easy place from which to run them. The Quick Launch toolbar is a good place, as is the list of frequently used programs on the Start menu. I also want a place where I can put system-oriented commands, though, so I put those on My Computer's shortcut menu. Then I can display the My Computer icon on the desktop and they're one mouse-click away. You learned how to show the icon in the section "Hiding Desktop Icons."

To add commands to My Computer's shortcut menu, edit its class registration, which is in HKCR\CLSID\{20D04FE0-3AEA-1069-A2D8-08002B30309D}. Add the command to this key's shell subkey. For example, after installing Microsoft Tweak UI, which you learn about in Chapter 5, "Mapping Tweak UI," I like to add to My Computer's shortcut menu a command that opens Tweak UI. So I add the branch tweak\command to My Computer's class registration. I set the default value of tweak to Tweak UI, the menu item text, and the default value of command to C:\Windows\System32\Tweakui.exe, the path and file name of Tweak UI. After customizing the class registration for My Computer, starting Tweak UI is fast: right-click My Computer, and then click Tweak UI.

The following INF file automates this setting. First, install Tweak UI. Then save this script to the file Tweakui.inf, right-click the file, and then click Install. (Again, you can download these sample scripts from *http://www.honeycutt.com.*) See Chapter 11, "Scripting Registry Changes," for other ways to script this hack. You can uninstall these settings in Add Or Remove Programs.

Listing 4-2   Tweakui.inf

```
[Version]
Signature=$CHICAGO$

[DefaultInstall]
AddReg=Reg.Settings
AddReg=Reg.Uninstall
CopyFiles=Inf.Copy

[DefaultUninstall]
DelReg=Reg.Settings
DelReg=Reg.Uninstall
DelFiles=Inf.Copy

[Reg.Settings]
HKCR,CLSID\{20D04FE0-3AEA-1069-A2D8-08002B30309D}\shell\tweak
HKCR,CLSID\{20D04FE0-3AEA-1069-A2D8-08002B30309D}\shell\tweak,,,"%MENUITEM%"
HKCR,CLSID\{20D04FE0-3AEA-1069-A2D8-08002B30309D}\shell\tweak\command\
,,0x20000,"%SYSTEMROOT%\System32\Tweakui.exe"

[Reg.Uninstall]
HKLM,Software\Microsoft\Windows\CurrentVersion\Uninstall\%NAME%
HKLM,Software\Microsoft\Windows\CurrentVersion\Uninstall\%NAME%,DisplayName\
,,"%NAME%"
HKLM,Software\Microsoft\Windows\CurrentVersion\Uninstall\%NAME%,UninstallString\
,,"Rundll32.exe setupapi.dll,InstallHinfSection DefaultUninstall 132"\
" %17%\Tweakui.inf"
[Inf.Copy]
Tweakui.inf

[DestinationDirs]
Inf.Copy=17

[SourceDisksNames]
55=%DISKNAME%

[SourceDisksFiles]
Tweakui.inf=55

[Strings]
NAME     = "Jerry's Tweak UI Shortcut"
MENUITEM = "Tweak UI"
DISKNAME = "Setup Files"
```

You can add any command to any shortcut menu, and that command doesn't have to edit, print, or do anything at all with the menu's target. My Computer is a good place to put system-oriented commands like Tweak UI, but you could also put them on the shortcut menu of another object, such as Recycle Bin, if you don't display the My Computer icon on the desktop.

Opening Command Prompts at Targeted Folders

Another favorite customization, and the one I probably use the most, enables me to quickly open a command prompt window with the targeted folder set as the current working directory. I add the command `C:\WINDOWS\System32\cmd.exe /k cd "%1"` to the `Directory` and `Drive` program classes. Then I right-click a folder and click CMD Prompt Here to open a command prompt with that folder set as the current working directory. This saves a lot of time. Here are the settings to add to `HKCR\Directory` and `HKCR\Drive`.

- In `HKCR\Directory\shell`, create the subkey `cmdhere`.
- In `HKCR\Directory\shell\cmdhere`, set the default value to `CMD Prompt Here`. This is the text you'll see on the shortcut menu.
- In `HKCR\Directory\shell\cmdhere`, create the subkey `command`.
- In `HKCR\Directory\shell\cmdhere\command`, set the default value to `C:\Windows\System32\cmd.exe /k cd "%1"`.

The following script automatically adds this command to the `Directory` and `Drive` program classes. Save it to the text file Cmdhere.inf, right-click it, and then click Install. To understand how this script works, see Chapter 11, "Scripting Registry Changes." Remove these settings using Add Or Remove Programs.

Listing 4-3   Cmdhere.inf

```
[Version]
Signature=$CHICAGO$

[DefaultInstall]
AddReg=Reg.Settings
AddReg=Reg.Uninstall
CopyFiles=Inf.Copy

[DefaultUninstall]
DelReg=Reg.Settings
DelReg=Reg.Uninstall
DelFiles=Inf.Copy

[Reg.Settings]
HKCR,Directory\Shell\Cmdhere
HKCR,Directory\Shell\Cmdhere,,,"%MENUITEM%"
```

```
HKCR,Directory\Shell\Cmdhere\command,,,"%11%\cmd.exe /k cd ""%1"""
HKCR,Drive\Shell\Cmdhere
HKCR,Drive\Shell\Cmdhere,,,"%MENUITEM%"
HKCR,Drive\Shell\Cmdhere\command,,,"%11%\cmd.exe /k cd ""%1"""

[Reg.Uninstall]
HKLM,Software\Microsoft\Windows\CurrentVersion\Uninstall\%NAME%
HKLM,Software\Microsoft\Windows\CurrentVersion\Uninstall\%NAME%,DisplayName\
,,"%NAME%"
HKLM,Software\Microsoft\Windows\CurrentVersion\Uninstall\%NAME%,UninstallString\
,,"Rundll32.exe setupapi.dll,InstallHinfSection DefaultUninstall 132 "\
"%17%\Cmdhere.inf"

[Inf.Copy]
Cmdhere.inf

[DestinationDirs]
Inf.Copy=17

[SourceDisksNames]
55=%DISKNAME%

[SourceDisksFiles]
Cmdhere.inf=55

[Strings]
NAME     = "Jerry's CMD Prompt Here"
MENUITEM = "CMD &Prompt Here"
DISKNAME = "Setup Files"
```

Rooting Windows Explorer at a Targeted Folder

This customization opens Windows Explorer without all the usual clutter, so you can focus on a single folder. Add the command `Explorer.exe /e,/root,/idlist,%I` to the `Folder` program class's `shell` subkey. Then right-click any folder, choose the command you added, and another Windows Explorer window opens with that folder rooted at the top of the left pane. Here are the settings you add to the `Folder` program class to target Windows Explorer at a particular folder:

- In `HKCR\Folder\shell`, create the subkey `fromhere`.

- In `HKCR\Folder\shell\fromhere`, set the default value to `Explore from Here`. This is the text you'll see on the shortcut menu.

- In `HKCR\Folder\shell\fromhere`, create the subkey `command`.

- In `HKCR\Folder\shell\fromhere\command`, set the default value to `Explorer.exe /e,/root,/idlist,%I`.

The following script automatically adds this command to the `Folder` program class. Save it to the text file Fromhere.inf, right-click it, and then click Install. To understand how this script works, see Chapter 11, "Scripting Registry Changes." Remove these settings using Add Or Remove Programs.

Listing 4-4   Fromhere.inf

```
[version]
Signature=$CHICAGO$

[DefaultInstall]
AddReg=Reg.Settings
AddReg=Reg.Uninstall
CopyFiles=Inf.Copy

[DefaultUninstall]
DelReg=Reg.Settings
DelReg=Reg.Uninstall
DelFiles=Inf.Copy

[Reg.Settings]
HKCR,Folder\shell\fromhere
HKCR,Folder\shell\fromhere,,,"%MENUITEM%"
HKCR,Folder\shell\fromhere\command,,,"explorer.exe /e,/root,/idlist,%I"

[Reg.Uninstall]
HKLM,Software\Microsoft\Windows\CurrentVersion\Uninstall\%NAME%
HKLM,Software\Microsoft\Windows\CurrentVersion\Uninstall\%NAME%\
,DisplayName,,"%NAME%"
HKLM,Software\Microsoft\Windows\CurrentVersion\Uninstall\%NAME%\
,UninstallString,,"Rundll32.exe setupapi.dll,InstallHinfSection DefaultUninstall 132 "\
"%17%\Fromhere.inf"

[Inf.Copy]
Fromhere.inf

[DestinationDirs]
Inf.Copy=17

[SourceDisksNames]
55=%DISKNAME%

[SourceDisksFiles]
Fromhere.inf=55

[Strings]
NAME     = "Jerry's Explore from Here"
MENUITEM = "Explore from &Here"
DISKNAME = "Setup Files"
```

Adding InfoTips to Program Classes

InfoTips are the balloons that users see when the mouse pointer hovers over an object. I like InfoTips; you might not. Position the mouse pointer over an object in the user interface, and Windows displays the InfoTip associated with it in a small yellow box. For documents, the InfoTip typically includes the type of document, the date of its last modification, its size, and more. You can customize InfoTips to display further information, though.

Windows uses the REG_SZ value InfoTip to display InfoTips. The operating system uses this value, which it finds in the class registration or the program class to which the object belongs. For example, if you position the mouse pointer over a file with the *.doc* file extension, Windows looks in the associated program class `wordpad.Document.1` for the value `InfoTip`. If it doesn't find the value there, it uses the value `InfoTip` that it finds in `HKCR\*`. The default value of that is `prop:Type;DocAuthor;DocTitle;DocSubject;DocComments;Write;Size`.

Thus, you can customize individual classes or create an InfoTip that applies to all classes. If you want a specific object or file type, add the `REG_SZ` value `InfoTip` to that specific class registration or program class. Otherwise, customize the value `InfoTip` in `HKCR\*` to see that tip for all file classes.

So what does all that mean? The notation **prop:***name* indicates to Windows that it should use the document property *name* in the InfoTip. Thus, the value you just saw means that Windows should display the document properties Type, DocAuthor, DocTitle, DocSubject, DocComments, Write, and Size in the InfoTip. You can also set `InfoTip` to the exact string that you want Windows to display when users position the mouse pointer over objects of that particular class. For example, you can set `InfoTip` for the `txtfile` program class to `This is a text file`, and Windows displays that text when users position the mouse pointer over text files. Windows ignores any property in the InfoTip that the document doesn't define, and InfoTips can be up to six lines long. Available properties depend on each individual program class. The following list shows just some of the document properties that you can add to an InfoTip:

■ Access	■ DocCategory	■ Owner
■ Album	■ DocComments	■ ProductName
■ Artist	■ DocPages	■ ProductVersion
■ Attributes	■ DocSubject	■ Protected
■ Bit Rate	■ DocTitle	■ Size
■ CameraModel	■ Duration	■ Status
■ Company	■ FileDescription	■ Track
■ Copyright	■ FileVersion	■ Type
■ Create	■ Genre	■ WhenTaken
■ Dimensions	■ LinkTarget	■ Write
■ DocAuthor	■ Name	■ Year

Note   A related value is `TileInfo`. The contents of this value are the same as the contents of `InfoTip`. Windows displays `TileInfo` next to icons in Tile view. You're limited to two lines, however, so make good use of the space you have. I usually prefer to display more useful information in the default value of TileInfo, such as a file's attributes. Thus, I like to set the value `HKCR\*\TileInfo` to `prop:Type;Attributes`, because it is more useful to me. Although you don't have to log off and back on to Windows to see changes you make to `InfoTip`, you do have to log off of Windows to see changes you make to `TileInfo`.

Customizing Folders with Desktop.ini

This chapter shows you how to customize files and other objects you see in the user interface, but customizing individual folders is useful, too. For example, there might be a folder in My Documents that you want to stand out from others.

You do that by creating the file Desktop.ini in the folder. There are numerous ways to customize folders by using this file, but the two most interesting are setting unique icons for folders and displaying InfoTips when users position the mouse pointer over them. In this sample Desktop.ini file, the value `IconFile` points to the file containing the icon that I want Windows Explorer to display for the folder. The value `IconIndex` is the index number of the icon, starting with 0, which is the first icon in the file. If you use an icon file instead of a DLL or EXE file, put the path of the file in `IconFile`, and set `IconIndex` to 0. `InfoTip` is the text that I want Windows Explorer to display when I position the mouse pointer over the folder.

```
[.ShellClassInfo]
IconFile=C:\Windows\Regedit.exe
IconIndex=0
InfoTip="Manuscripts for my latest registry book."
```

Set the Desktop.ini file's Hidden And System attribute by typing the command **attrib +s +h** *filename* in the Run dialog box. You set the folder's System attribute by typing the command **attrib +s** *foldername* in the Run dialog box. Figure 4-5 shows what the folder Registry Book looks like after you add this Desktop.ini file to it and set the file and folder's attributes. Now, whenever I position the mouse pointer over the folder, I am reminded of the important task at hand.

Figure 4-5   When I hold the mouse pointer over the Registry Book folder, I see the text "Manuscripts for my latest registry book."

Adding File Templates

I'm sure you know about the New menu. Right-click within any folder, click New, and choose one of the templates available to create a new, empty file; then double-click the new file to edit it. By default, Windows provides the following templates: Briefcase, Bitmap Image, Wordpad Document, Rich Text Document, Text Document, Wave Sound, and Compressed (Zipped Folder). You can add templates, though, making the chore of starting new files quicker and easier.

Adding new templates is a two-step process:

1. In the file extension key HKCR\.*ext*, create the ShellNew subkey.

2. Add one of the following four values to the ShellNew subkey to define how Windows creates new files of the .*ext* type:

   ❑ **NullFile.** This is an empty REG_SZ value. Windows creates a zero-length file. Make sure that the associated program can handle empty files.

   ❑ **FileName.** This is a REG_SZ value that contains the name of a template file. By default, Windows looks in %UserProfile%\Templates for this file, but you can include an explicit path.

   ❑ **Data.** This is a REG_BINARY value containing a binary stream of data that Windows uses to create the new file.

   ❑ **Command.** This is a REG_SZ value. Windows executes the command in this value, passing it the path and name of the file it's to create.

For example, the template for the .*txt* file extension creates a null file. Double-click the file to edit it in Notepad. If you'd rather create the file and open it in Notepad automatically, remove the value NullFile from the key HKCR\.txt\ShellNew. Then add the value Command, and set it to Notepad.exe "%1". When you create a new text file using the New menu, Notepad starts and prompts you to choose whether you want it to create the new file. Ideally, any application you launch using the Command value would have a command-line option to suppress the prompt, but as most don't, you have no choice but to answer it.

Preventing Messenger from Running

Believe it or not, some people don't like Windows Messenger, and they tire of the program's constant nagging to sign up for a Passport. Windows doesn't provide a user interface to remove Windows Messenger permanently. (See Chapter 18, "Fixing Common IT Problems," for a simple way to uninstall it.) But you can prevent it from running. In Windows Messenger, click Tools, Options. On the Preferences tab of the

Options dialog box, clear the Run This Program When Windows Starts check box. The problem with this setting is that the program still runs when other programs start. Clearing this check box removes the command that starts Windows Messenger from the key HKCU\Software\Microsoft\Windows\CurrentVersion\Run.

The most fail-proof solution is to set the policy that prevents Windows Messenger from ever running. You can set this policy using Group Policy editor to edit the local Group Policy Object. (See Chapter 7, "Using Registry-Based Policy.") You can also set the policy directly. To do that, create the REG_DWORD value PreventRun in HKLM\SOFTWARE\Policies\Microsoft\Messenger\Client, and set it to 0x01. This setting affects all users who log on to the computer. When they try to run Windows Messenger, they don't see an error message: it just doesn't run. Chapter 18, "Fixing Common IT Problems," describes an alternative method. The chapter shows you how to edit Sysoc.inf to prevent the installation of Windows Messenger and other optional components.

Personalizing the Start Menu

Windows has a nice new Start menu, which you can customize more thoroughly than you could with the Start menu in any earlier version of Windows. Open the Taskbar And Start Menu Properties dialog box by right-clicking the taskbar and clicking Properties. On the Start Menu tab, select either the Start Menu option or the Classic Start Menu option to choose which version of the Start menu to use, and then click Customize. The Customize Start Menu dialog box appears; you use this box to customize how Windows displays the Start menu.

You can customize the Start menu using other methods, too. For example, you can use Tweak UI to control which programs appear in the frequently used programs list, and to customize which icons you see on the Start menu. You learn how to use Tweak UI in Chapter 5, "Mapping Tweak UI." In addition, Windows has dozens of policies that control the Start menu's behavior. Those policies aren't useful as hacks, however, because it's difficult to script and deploy policies to users in the Users and Power Users groups. Members of neither group can change settings in the Policies branch of the registry.

The following sections describe the most useful Start menu hacks. First you learn how to configure what does and does not appear on the Start menu. Then you learn how to prevent some programs from appearing on the frequently used programs list. You also learn how to restore the Start menu's sort order when it's not in alphabetical order.

Configuring the Menu's Contents

Even though you can completely customize the Start menu in the user interface, power users and IT professionals will likely want to script Start menu customizations. Power users don't want to reconfigure the Start menu every time they install Windows. IT professionals can use scripts to deploy these settings or configure them automatically when creating default user profiles. (See Chapter 12, "Deploying User Profiles.")

If you want to script these settings, you need to know where to find them in the registry. All these settings are in the same place: HKCU\Software\Microsoft\Windows\CurrentVersion\Explorer\Advanced. Table 4-4 describes which values you can add to this key. You see two sections in this table. The first section, "Classic Start Menu," contains values that affect the classic Start menu. The second section, "New Start Menu," contains values that affect the new Start menu, also known as the Start panel. Most of these settings are REG_DWORD values, but some are REG_SZ values. If the possible data for any of the settings in Table 4-4 includes 0x01, 0x02, and so on, that setting is a REG_DWORD value. If the possible data includes NO or YES, it's a REG_SZ value.

Table 4-4   Start Menu Settings

Name	Data
Classic Start Menu	
StartMenuAdminTools	0x00–Hide Administrative Tools
	0x01–Display Administrative Tools
CascadeControlPanel	NO–Display Control Panel as link
	YES–Display Control Panel as menu
CascadeMyDocuments	NO–Display My Documents as link
	YES–Display My Documents as menu
CascadeMyPictures	NO–Display My Pictures as link
	YES–Display My Pictures as menu
CascadePrinters	NO–Display Printers as link
	YES–Display Printers as menu
IntelliMenus	0x00–Don't use personalized menus
	0x01–Use Personalized Menus
CascadeNetworkConnections	NO–Display Network Connections as link
	YES–Display Network Connections as menu
Start_LargeMFUIcons	0x00–Show small icons in Start menu
	0x01–Show large icons in Start menu

Table 4-4   **Start Menu Settings**

Name	Data
StartMenuChange	0x00–Disable dragging and dropping
	0x01–Enable dragging and dropping
StartMenuFavorites	0x00—Hide Favorites
	0x01–Display Favorites
StartMenuLogoff	0x00–Hide Log Off
	0x01–Display Log Off
StartMenuRun	0x00–Hide Run command
	0x01–Display Run command
StartMenuScrollPrograms	NO–Don't scroll Programs menu
	YES–Scroll Programs menu
New Start Menu	
Start_ShowControlPanel	0x00–Hide Control Panel
	0x01–Show Control Panel as link
	0x02–Show Control Panel as menu
Start_EnableDragDrop	0x00–Disable dragging and dropping
	0x01–Enable dragging and dropping
StartMenuFavorites	0x00–Hide Favorites menu
	0x01–Show Favorites menu
Start_ShowMyComputer	0x00–Hide My Computer
	0x01–Show My Computer as link
	0x02–Show My Computer as menu
Start_ShowMyDocs	0x00–Hide My Documents
	0x01–Show My Documents as link
	0x02–Show My Documents as menu
Start_ShowMyMusic	0x00–Hide My Music
	0x01–Show My Music as link
	0x02–Show My Music as menu
Start_ShowMyPics	0x00–Hide My Pictures
	0x01–Show My Pictures as link
	0x02–Show My Pictures as menu
Start_ShowNetConn	0x00–Hide Network Connections
	0x01–Show Network Connections as link
	0x02–Show Network Connections as menu

Table 4-4   **Start Menu Settings**

Name	Data
Start_AdminToolsTemp	0x00–Hide Administrative Tools
	0x01–Show on All Programs menu
	0x02–Show on All Programs menu and Start menu
Start_ShowHelp	0x00–Hide Help and Support
	0x01–Show Help and Support
Start_ShowNetPlaces	0x00–Hide My Network Places
	0x01–Show My Network Places
Start_ShowOEMLink	0x00–Hide Manufacturer Link
	0x01–Show Manufacturer Link
Start_ShowPrinters	0x00–Hide Printers and Faxes
	0x01–Show Printers and Faxes
Start_ShowRun	0x00–Hide Run command
	0x01–Show Run command
Start_ShowSearch	0x00–Hide Search command
	0x01–Show Search command
Start_ScrollPrograms	0x00–Don't scroll Programs menu
	0x01–Scroll Programs menu

Trimming the Frequently Used Programs List

Each time you run a program, Windows adds it to the list of frequently used programs you see on the Start menu. (See Figure 4-6). However, you might not want every program you open to appear in this list. For example, I don't want to see Notepad in this list, nor do I want to see Command Prompt. By customizing HKCR\Applications, you can choose which programs do and don't appear in this list.

HKCR\Applications contains subkeys for a variety of programs that Windows knows about. The name of each subkey is the name of the program file. Thus, you see the subkeys notepad.exe and explorer.exe in HKCR\Applications. If you want to customize another program, add its subkey to this key. For example, to customize whether Command Prompt appears in the list of frequently used programs, add the subkey cmd.exe to HKCR\Applications. Then, to keep the program off of the list, add the REG_SZ value NoStartPage to it.

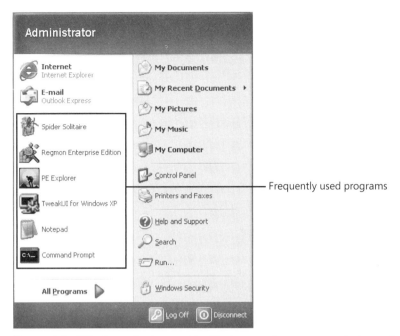

Figure 4-6   Windows displays on the Start menu the programs that you frequently use.

Restoring the Sort Order

Unless you disable dragging and dropping on the Start menu (see Table 4-4), users can sort the All Programs menu. Windows also sometimes adds new shortcuts to the bottom of the All Programs menu. In either case, finding the program that you want to run is difficult when the sort order of the Start menu gets disorganized.

HKCU\Software\Microsoft\Windows\CurrentVersion\Explorer\MenuOrder contains the sort orders of the Favorites menu and the Start menu. The subkey Favorites contains the sort order of the Favorites menu. The subkey Start Menu contains the sort order of the classic Start menu, and the subkey Start Menu2 contains the sort order of the new Start menu. Deciphering the contents of these three keys is almost impossible, but you can remove any of them to re-sort the corresponding menu in alphabetical order. For example, to restore the All Programs menu to alphabetical order, remove the subkey Start Menu2. To restore the Favorites menu in both Windows Explorer and Microsoft Internet Explorer, remove the subkey Favorites.

I like to keep a script handy to automatically remove MenuOrder. The following listing is an example. Save this listing to the text file Resort.inf, right-click it, and then click Install. This script is different from the others you've seen in this chapter because you can't uninstall it; its changes are permanent.

Listing 4-5   Resort.inf

```
[Version]
Signature=$CHICAGO$

[DefaultInstall]
DelReg=Reg.Settings

[Reg.Settings]
HKCU,Software\Microsoft\Windows\CurrentVersion\Explorer\MenuOrder
```

> **Tip**   You've sorted the Start menu just the way you wanted it—wouldn't it be dandy if you could transfer that sort order to another computer? You're in luck. Export the key MenuOrder to a REG file, and then import that REG file to the computer on which you want to use that sort order.

Disabling Windows Tour

Not everyone likes the Windows XP Tour balloon that relentlessly pops up in the task bar after a clean installation of Windows. You can prevent this balloon from appearing at all by setting the REG_DWORD value RunCount in the key HKLM\SOFTWARE\Microsoft\Windows\CurrentVersion\Applets\Tour to 0x00.

Creating Program Aliases

I'll bet you didn't know that you can create aliases for your favorite programs' paths and file names. For example, you can create an alias called *ed.exe* to run TextPad—my favorite text editor from Helios (http://www.textpad.com).

The key HKLM\SOFTWARE\Microsoft\Windows\CurrentVersion\App Paths contains these aliases. For each alias, create a subkey and name it the alias you want to create. Then, set the subkey's default value to the full path and file name of the program you want to launch when you run the alias. Using my previous example, create a subkey called **ed.exe** and set its default value to C:\Program Files\TextPad 4\TextPad.exe. Then, you can launch the path and file name by simply typing the alias in the Run dialog box and pressing ENTER.

Customizing Internet Explorer

Windows comes with Internet Explorer 6. IT professionals can customize Internet Explorer in a number of ways using the Internet Explorer Administration Kit (IEAK). For more information about IEAK and to download it see *http://www.microsoft.com/windows/ieak/default.mspx*. It also comes with the Office 2003 Editions Resource Kit. You can do the following with the kit:

- Tailor Internet Explorer and other Internet components to fit the needs of your enterprise or users. For example, you can customize the Links bar and the Favorites menu to promote your intranet or to provide helpful information.

- Configure and deploy settings without ever touching desktops.

- Customize the setup program so that it requires little or no user interaction.

- Control which settings users can change, so that IT professionals can ensure that security, connection, and important settings meet corporate standards.

The following sections describe a few of my favorite customizations for Internet Explorer, including extending its shortcut menus, changing the toolbar's background, and adding search URLs to it.

Extending the Shortcut Menus

Right-click a Web page and Internet Explorer displays a shortcut menu. You can customize this shortcut menu by adding commands to it that you link to scripts in an HTML file. For example, you can add to the shortcut menu a command that opens the current Web page in a new window or highlights the selected text on it.

`HKCU\Software\Microsoft\Internet Explorer\MenuExt` is where Internet Explorer looks for extensions. Add this key if it doesn't exist, and then add a subkey for each command that you want to add. Finally, set that subkey's default value to the path and name of the HTML file containing the script that carries out the command. For example, to add the command Magnify to the shortcut menu that runs a script in an HTML file C:\Windows\Web\Magnify.htm, add the subkey `Magnify`, and set its default value to `C:\Windows\Web\Magnify.htm`. When you choose this command on Internet Explorer's shortcut menu, it executes the script contained in the file. Then you need to create Magnify.htm. The following listing comprises the contents of Magnify.htm. The property `external.menuArguments` contains the window object in which you executed the command. Because you have access to the window object, you can do almost anything in that window, such as reformatting its contents.

Listing 4-6   Magnify.htm

```
<HTML>
<SCRIPT LANGUAGE="JavaScript" defer>
var objWin = external.menuArguments;
var objDoc = objWin.document;
var objSel = objDoc.selection;
var objRange = objSel.createRange();
objRange.execCommand( "FontSize", 0, "+2" );
</SCRIPT>
</HTML>
```

You can also configure the shortcut menus to which Internet Explorer adds your command. In the subkey you created for the extension, add the REG_DWORD value Contexts, and apply to it the bit masks shown in Table 4-5. For example, to limit the previous example so that Internet Explorer displays it only for text selections, add the REG_DWORD value Contexts to Magnify, and set it to 0x10.

Table 4-5   Internet Explorer Menu Extensions

Bit Mask	Menu
0x01	Default
0x02	Image
0x04	Control
0x08	Table
0x10	Text Selection
0x11	Anchor
0x12	Unknown

> **Note**   If you're interested in learning more about extending Internet Explorer, you should check out Microsoft's documentation for extending the browser, at *http:// msdn.microsoft.com/workshop/browser/ext/overview/overview.asp*. This requires proficiency with writing scripts and HTML, though.

Changing the Toolbar Background

You can customize the background you see on Internet Explorer's toolbar. It's just a bitmap. To change the background, create a REG_SZ value called BackBitmap in HKCU\Software\Microsoft\Internet Explorer\Toolbar. Set this value to the path and name of the bitmap file you want to see in the toolbar's background. Internet Explorer tiles the bitmap horizontally and vertically to fill the toolbar.

Customizing Search URLs

Using search URLs is a convenient way to use different Internet search engines. For example, you might have a search URL called *news* that searches Google Groups. Type **news Jerry Honeycutt** in the address bar to automatically search Google Groups for all UseNet articles that contain the words "Jerry" and "Honeycutt."

You create search URLs in `HKCU\Software\Microsoft\Internet Explorer\SearchURL`. If you don't see this subkey, create it. Then add a subkey for each search prefix you want to use. To use the example I just gave, create the subkey `news`. Set the default value of the prefix's subkey to the URL of the search engine. Use `%s` as a placeholder for the search string. Internet Explorer replaces the `%s` with any text you type to the right of the prefix. Continue the example, and set it to `http://groups.google.com/ groups?q=%s&hl=en`.

Add the `REG_SZ` values shown in Table 4-6 to the prefix key you created. These values describe substitutions for special characters in your search string, including a space, percent sign (%), ampersand (&), and plus sign (+). These characters have special meaning when submitting forms to Web sites, so you must substitute a plus sign for a space, for example, or %26 for an ampersand. Thus, the browser translates the string *Ben & Jerry* to *Ben+%26+Jerry*.

Deriving the URL that you must use is easy. Open the search engine that you want to add to Internet Explorer's search URLs, and then search for something. When the browser displays the results, copy the URL from the address bar, replacing your search word with a `%s`. For example, after searching Google Groups for *sample*, the resulting URL is *http://groups.google.com/ groups?q=sample&hl=en*. Replace the word *sample* with `%s` to get `http://groups.google.com/ groups?q=%s&hl=en`.

Table 4-6   Values in Search URLs

Name	Data
<space>	+
%	%25
&	%26
+	%2B

This hack is so useful that I have a script that automatically creates search URLs for the search engines that I use most often. Copy the following listing to the file Search.inf, right-click it, and then click Install. You can remove this script and all its settings using Add Or Remove Programs. This script creates search URLs for the five search engines that I use most often. The search URL *news* searches Google Groups; *msn* searches MSN; *ms* searches Microsoft's Web site; *msdn* searches MSDN; and *technet* searches TechNet.

Listing 4-7   Search.inf

```
[Version]
Signature=$CHICAGO$

[DefaultInstall]
AddReg=Reg.Settings
AddReg=Reg.Uninstall
CopyFiles=Inf.Copy

[DefaultUninstall]
DelReg=Reg.Settings
DelReg=Reg.Uninstall
DelFiles=Inf.Copy

[Reg.Settings]
HKCU,Software\Microsoft\Internet Explorer\SearchURL

HKCU,Software\Microsoft\Internet Explorer\SearchURL\news,,0,"%GOOGLE%"
HKCU,Software\Microsoft\Internet Explorer\SearchURL\news," ",0,"+"
HKCU,Software\Microsoft\Internet Explorer\SearchURL\news,"%",0,"%25"
HKCU,Software\Microsoft\Internet Explorer\SearchURL\news,"&",0,"%26"
HKCU,Software\Microsoft\Internet Explorer\SearchURL\news,"+",0,"%2B"

HKCU,Software\Microsoft\Internet Explorer\SearchURL\msn,,0,"%MSN%"
HKCU,Software\Microsoft\Internet Explorer\SearchURL\msn," ",0,"+"
HKCU,Software\Microsoft\Internet Explorer\SearchURL\msn,"%",0,"%25"
HKCU,Software\Microsoft\Internet Explorer\SearchURL\msn,"&",0,"%26"
HKCU,Software\Microsoft\Internet Explorer\SearchURL\msn,"+",0,"%2B"

HKCU,Software\Microsoft\Internet Explorer\SearchURL\ms,,0,"%MICROSOFT%"
HKCU,Software\Microsoft\Internet Explorer\SearchURL\ms," ",0,"+"
HKCU,Software\Microsoft\Internet Explorer\SearchURL\ms,"%",0,"%25"
HKCU,Software\Microsoft\Internet Explorer\SearchURL\ms,"&",0,"%26"
HKCU,Software\Microsoft\Internet Explorer\SearchURL\ms,"+",0,"%2B"

HKCU,Software\Microsoft\Internet Explorer\SearchURL\msdn,,0,"%MSDN%"
HKCU,Software\Microsoft\Internet Explorer\SearchURL\msdn," ",0,"+"
HKCU,Software\Microsoft\Internet Explorer\SearchURL\msdn,"%",0,"%25"
HKCU,Software\Microsoft\Internet Explorer\SearchURL\msdn,"&",0,"%26"
HKCU,Software\Microsoft\Internet Explorer\SearchURL\msdn,"+",0,"%2B"

HKCU,Software\Microsoft\Internet Explorer\SearchURL\technet,,0,"%TECHNET%"
HKCU,Software\Microsoft\Internet Explorer\SearchURL\technet," ",0,"+"
HKCU,Software\Microsoft\Internet Explorer\SearchURL\technet,"%",0,"%25"
HKCU,Software\Microsoft\Internet Explorer\SearchURL\technet,"&",0,"%26"
HKCU,Software\Microsoft\Internet Explorer\SearchURL\technet,"+",0,"%2B"

[Reg.Uninstall]
HKCU,Software\Microsoft\Windows\CurrentVersion\Uninstall\%NAME%
HKCU,Software\Microsoft\Windows\CurrentVersion\Uninstall\%NAME%,DisplayName\
,,"%NAME%"
HKCU,Software\Microsoft\Windows\CurrentVersion\Uninstall\%NAME%,UninstallString\
,,"Rundll32.exe setupapi.dll,InstallHinfSection DefaultUninstall 132 "\
"%53%\Application Data\Custom\Search.inf"
```

```
[Inf.Copy]
Search.inf

[DestinationDirs]
Inf.Copy=53,Application Data\Custom

[SourceDisksNames]
55=%DISKNAME%

[SourceDisksFiles]
Search.inf=55

[Strings]
NAME    = "Jerry's IE Search URLs"
DISKNAME = "Setup Files"

; Search URLs

GOOGLE="http://groups.google.com/groups?q=%s&hl=en"
MSN="http://search.msn.com/pass/results.aspx?q=%s"
MICROSOFT="http://search.microsoft.com/search/results.aspx?qu=%s"
MSDN="http://search.microsoft.com/search/results.aspx?qu=%s&View=msdn"
TECHNET="http://search.microsoft.com/search/results.aspx?View=en-us&qu=%s"
```

Maximum Concurrent Downloads

By default, Internet Explorer allows you to download two files from a server at a time. If you're downloading numerous files, you have to wait for one of the files to finish downloading before you can start another. However, you can easily increase the number of files that Internet Explorer can download concurrently. Set the REG_DWORD values MaxConnectionsPer1_0Server and MaxConnectionsPerServer (create them if necessary) in the key HKCU\Software\Microsoft\Windows\CurrentVersion\Internet Settings to the maximum number of files that you want to download concurrently.

Clearing History Lists

So that you can quickly open documents and programs that you use frequently, Windows keeps history lists. These are MRU or "most recently used" lists. Table 4-7 shows you where in the registry the operating system stores these lists. Clear these lists by removing the keys associated with them. After removing the RecentDocs key, make sure to delete the contents of %UserProfile%\Recent, too.

The history list in Windows Search Assistant deserves a bit more attention. The key ACMru contains a variety of subkeys associated with the types of things for which you've searched. For example, if you search for files and folders, you'll see the subkey 5603, which contains a list of the different search strings. If you search the Internet using Search Assistant, you'll see the subkey 5001. You can remove each subkey individually to clear a specific type of query's history list, or you can remove the key ACMru to clear all of Search Assistant's history lists. Table 4-7 contains a list of the subkeys that I've found in ACMru.

Table 4-7   History Lists

Location	Subkey
Internet Explorer's address bar	HKCU\Software\Microsoft\Internet Explorer\TypedURLs
Run dialog box	HKCU\Software\Microsoft\Windows\CurrentVersion\Explorer\RunMRU
Documents menu	HKCU\Software\Microsoft\Windows\CurrentVersion\Explorer\RecentDocs
Common dialog boxes	HKCU\Software\Microsoft\Windows\CurrentVersion\Explorer\ComDlg32\LastVisitedMRU
Search Assistant	HKCU\Software\Microsoft\Search Assistant\ACMru The following are subkeys within ACMru: ■ 5001. Internet ■ 5603. Files and folders ■ 5604. Pictures, music, and video ■ 5647. Printers, computers, and people
Notification Icons	HKCU\Software\Microsoft\Windows\CurrentVersion\Explorer\TrayNotify\IconStreams HKCU\Software\Microsoft\Windows\CurrentVersion\Explorer\TrayNotify\PastIconsStream

Running Programs at Startup

The Run and RunOnce subkeys are useful for running programs automatically when the computer starts or when users log on to the computer. You learn about these keys in Chapter 18, "Fixing Common IT Problems." These keys are a handy way to deploy software that requires administrator privileges.

The Run and RunOnce keys are in two different locations. First, you see these subkeys in HKLM\SOFTWARE\Microsoft\Windows\CurrentVersion. Commands that appear in this branch run when any user logs on to the computer. You also see these subkeys in HKCU\Software\Microsoft\Windows\CurrentVersion. Commands in this branch run after a specific user logs on to Windows. Windows also treats commands in Run differently than commands in RunOnce:

- **Run.** Windows runs the commands in this subkey every time a user logs on to the computer.

- **RunOnce.** Windows runs the commands in this subkey once, and then removes the key from RunOnce after the command is completed successfully.

To add a command to Run or RunOnce in HKLM or HKCU, create a REG_SZ value that has an arbitrary but descriptive name. Put the command line you want to execute in the new value. For example, the Run key in HKCU has the value MSMSGS by default, and this value contains "C:\Program Files\Messenger\msmsgs.exe" /background, which runs Windows Messenger every time the user logs on to Windows. Although you might have occasion to add commands to the Run subkey, it's more common to remove commands from this subkey to prevent programs from running when you start or log on to Windows.

Controlling Registry Editor

Registry Editor (Regedit) has a few features that most users like, but some prefer to disable. The following sections show you how to customize these features. First, you customize the default action for REG files: in other words, you can control what Regedit does when a file with the *.reg* extension is double-clicked. Second, you prevent Regedit from saving its settings when you close it. By doing so, Regedit opens the window to the same size and position every time.

Default Action for REG Files

When you double-click a file with the *.reg* extension and click Yes when it prompts you to merge the file's settings, Regedit imports the file's settings into the registry. If you edit REG files frequently, this behavior might concern you because you might accidentally import a REG file when you meant to edit it. Conversely, if you frequently import REG files, you might want to prevent Regedit from prompting you to merge the file's settings into the registry. Here are steps for accomplishing both tasks:

- **Prevent Regedit from automatically importing REG files.** To do this, make the default action for REG files something other than opening the file, such as editing the file. To do that, set the default value of HKCR\regfile\shell to edit. The next time you double-click a REG file, it will open in Notepad.

- **Merge a REG file into the registry without prompting.** To do this, change the command line that Windows executes when you open the file. Set the default value of HKCR\regfile\shell\open\command to regedit.exe /s "%1".

Storing Window Position and Size

Each time you close Regedit, the program stores its view settings (window position and size, column sizes, last open key, and more) in the registry. The next time you run Regedit, it restores the window with those settings. Many users want Regedit to clear these settings, but Regedit doesn't provide an option to do that.

`HKCU\Software\Microsoft\Windows\CurrentVersion\Applets\Regedit` is the key in which Regedit stores these settings. Set the key's Access Control List (ACL) so that you can't write to it, and then Regedit can't store its last view settings there. You can either delete the values in this key so that Regedit uses defaults every time it starts, or customize them so that Regedit uses your custom settings every time it starts. In either case, set the key's ACL so that you can read—but not write—values:

1. In Regedit, click the key `Applets\Regedit`.

2. On the Edit menu, click Permissions.

3. Click Advanced, clear the check box that allows inheritable permissions, click Copy, and then click OK.

4. In the Group Or User Names list, select each account and group; then clear the Full Control check box.

> **More Info**   See Chapter 8, "Configuring Windows Security," for more information about configuring keys' ACLs. In particular, if you decide that you don't like this customization, and you don't already own the key, you'll have to take ownership of the key to gain full control of it again.

Logging On Automatically

Some users don't like having to log on to Windows. When they restart the computer, they want it to boot all the way to the desktop without stopping at the Log On To Windows dialog box along the way. Before I tell you that this is possible (oops), let me add that you should never skip the logon process if your computer is connected to a business network. Obvious security concerns are present when you allow anyone with access to your computer to have full access to all of its contents and the network.

You configure the ability to log on to Windows automatically in `HKLM\SOFTWARE\Microsoft\Windows NT\CurrentVersion\Winlogon`. First, you set the `REG_SZ` value `AutoAdminLogon` to 1, which turns on this feature. You may need to create the described keys. Just remember that this is a REG_SZ value and not a REG_DWORD value. Next, set the values DefaultUserName and DefaultPassword to the user name and password that you want to use for logging on to the operating system. Both are REG_SZ values. Last, set the REG_SZ value DefaultDomainName to the name of the domain that's authenticating your user name and password. Table 4-8 summarizes these values, which you create if they don't already exist.

Table 4-8   Values in Winlogon

Name	Type	Data
HKLM\SOFTWARE\Microsoft\Windows NT\CurrentVersion\Winlogon		
AutoAdminLogon	REG_SZ	0 | 1
DefaultUserName	REG_SZ	*Name*
DefaultDomainName	REG_SZ	*Domain*
DefaultPassword	REG_SZ	*Password*

Changing User Information

On a regular basis, people ask me questions about changing user information, the information you provided when you installed Windows. You can change it. Both of the following values are in the key HKLM\SOFTWARE\Microsoft\Windows NT\CurrentVersion:

- **RegisteredOrganization.**   The name of the organization
- **RegisteredOwner.**   The name of the user

Both are REG_SZ values. Changing the registered organization and owner names doesn't affect installed applications. However, applications that you install after changing these values are likely to pick up the new names.

Looking for More Hacks

This chapter just begins to discuss hacks. If I had the space, I could fill another 50 pages with great Windows hacks. But you do find good hacks in other chapters:

- Chapter 5, "Mapping Tweak UI," shows you where all the settings in Tweak UI are in the registry. Tweak UI makes the most popular hacks available in one sleek user interface, and this chapter documents the corresponding hacks.
- Chapter 10, "Finding Registry Settings," helps you discover your own hacks.

- Chapter 18, "Fixing Common IT Problems," contains hacks that apply to IT scenarios, such as deploying software or fixing IT-unfriendly behavior.

- Appendix A, "File Associations," describes HKCR in detail, including hacking it.

And don't forget the chapters in Part IV, "Appendixes." These chapters are the ultimate source for registry hacks because they document the most interesting settings found in the registry.

> **More Info**   Quite possibly the single largest and most usable source of registry hacks is published by WinGuides at *http://www.winguides.com/registry*. Download the Registry Guide, which is an HTML help file that's well organized and formatted. This guide contains hundreds, if not thousands, of useful settings that enable you to customize all versions of Windows. Another useful and popular Web site is Jerold Schulman's site at *http://www.jsiinc.com*. He has put significant energy into the thousands of IT tips and tricks on his Web site.

Chapter 5
Mapping Tweak UI

Microsoft Tweak UI is a must-have tool for anyone customizing Microsoft Windows XP or Windows Server 2003 (Windows). It allows users to customize settings that wouldn't be available in the operating system's user interface without editing the registry. Tweak UI started as a grassroots utility built by a handful of rebellious programmers and ended up one of the most popular downloads on the Internet. Microsoft has released versions of this tool for every version of Windows since Windows 95. Microsoft even included it on the Windows 98 CD. And now it's available for Windows XP and Windows Server 2003, and it includes even more customizations.

You can download Tweak UI from *http://www.microsoft.com/windowsxp/downloads/ powertoys/xppowertoys.mspx*. (Microsoft split apart the original Microsoft PowerToys programs—utilities for enhancing Windows.) The file you download is called Tweak-UiPowertoySetup.exe. Run this program to install Tweak UI on your computer. To run Tweak UI, click Start, All Programs, Powertoys for Windows XP, and then click Tweak UI. In the left pane, click a category, and then in the right pane, edit the settings you want to change. The program is mostly self-explanatory; you see a description of each setting at the bottom of the window. Pay attention to the bottom part of the window. It tells you whether the settings in that category are per-user or per-machine. In order for them to take effect, per-user settings sometimes require that you log off and back on to Windows. Per-machine settings affect every user who logs on to the computer.

This chapter isn't about *using* Tweak UI–that's too easy. Instead, I'll tell you where in the registry Tweak UI changes each setting. Information like this is powerful. You can script Tweak UI customizations. For example, power users can write a script for applying their favorite Tweak UI settings and then, simply by running the script, can apply all those settings to every computer that they use. The process is streamlined–compare one double-click with dozens of clicks and edits–and it helps with consistency too. IT professionals can write a script for deploying useful settings to users or can include those settings in default user profiles for new users. (See Chapter 12, "Deploying User Profiles.") Scripting these settings is amazingly easy, and you learn how to do that in Chapter 11, "Scripting Registry Changes."

The sections in this chapter correspond to the major categories in Tweak UI. (I skipped the About, Access Control, and Repair categories because they have little to do with the registry. You should look at all three, though. The About category contains useful tips for using Windows. The Access Control category can configure various ACLs. The Repair category can fix a variety of small problems, including those affecting icons, fonts, and folders.) Each section in this chapter contains a brief description of the settings in that category and how to change them in the registry. In most cases, each section contains a table that describes each setting's value name, value type, and value data. Each table contains subheadings that show the key for the values following it.

General

In the General category, the items in the Settings list are effects that you can enable or disable. In fact, the Settings list, shown in Figure 5-1, used to be called the Effects list in earlier versions of Tweak UI. Settings range from list box and window animations to menu fading. Disable these settings only on slower computers when you think disabling them can improve the computer's performance; otherwise, these settings make Windows look great.

Table 5-1 lists all the settings in the General category. One value needs a bit of explaining, though: UserPreferencesMask. The bits in this REG_BINARY value are various settings, which Chapter 4, "Hacking the Registry," and Appendix C, "Per-User Settings," describe in detail. To turn on a setting, set the appropriate bit to 1 in UserPreferencesMask. To turn off a setting, clear the corresponding bit. The number in the Data column tells you which bit to toggle. The easiest way to toggle the bit is to use Calculator in scientific view. Bitwise math is beyond most simple scripting techniques, including REG files. If you want to create a script to change the settings in UserPreferencesMask, use INF files or look to Windows Script Host (WSH). (See Chapter 11, "Scripting Registry Changes.")

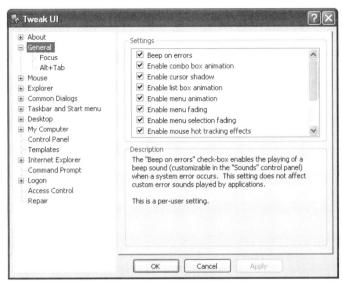

Figure 5-1   Many of these settings are in the Performance Options dialog box. Right-click My Computer, click Properties, and in the Performance section of the Advanced tab click Settings.

Tip   UserPreferencesMask is an example of a REG_DWORD value disguised as a REG_BINARY value. When you see a 32-bit binary value, it's likely that it's really a double-word value. In that case, you can safely replace the value with a REG_DWORD value. Don't forget that Windows uses the little-endian architecture, though, so it stores double-word values in reverse-byte order. In other words, you replace the REG_BINARY value 0x04 0x03 0x02 0x01 with the REG_DWORD 0x01020304. See Chapter 1, "Learning the Basics," for a refresher on little-endian architecture and bitwise math.

Table 5-1   Values in the General Category

Setting	Name	Type	Data
HKCU\Control Panel\Sound			
Beep on errors	Beep	REG_SZ	Yes | No
HKCU\Control Panel\Desktop			
Enable combo box animation	UserPreferencesMask	REG_BINARY	Bit 0x0004
Enable cursor shadow	UserPreferencesMask	REG_BINARY	Bit 0x2000
Enable list box animation	UserPreferencesMask	REG_BINARY	Bit 0x0008
Enable menu animation	UserPreferencesMask	REG_BINARY	Bit 0x0002
Enable menu fading	UserPreferencesMask	REG_BINARY	Bit 0x0200
Enable menu selection fading	UserPreferencesMask	REG_BINARY	Bit 0x0400

Table 5-1   Values in the General Category

Setting	Name	Type	Data
Enable mouse hot tracking effects	`UserPreferencesMask`	REG_BINARY	Bit 0x0080
Enable tooltip animation	`UserPreferencesMask`	REG_BINARY	Bit 0x0800
Enable tooltip fade	`UserPreferencesMask`	REG_BINARY	Bit 0x1000
Show Windows version on desktop	`PaintDesktopVersion`	REG_DWORD	0X00 | 0X01
HKCU\Control Panel\Desktop\WindowMetrics			
Enable Window Animation	`MinAnimate`	REG_SZ	0 | 1
HKLM\SOFTWARE\Microsoft\Windows\CurrentVersion\OptimalLayout			
Optimize hard disk when idle	`EnableAutoLayout`	REG_DWORD	0 | 1

Tracking Down Tweak UI Settings

Are you curious about how I tracked down all the Tweak UI program's settings? I used the techniques you learn about in Chapter 10, "Finding Registry Settings." The first technique uses a program from Winternals Software called Registry Monitor (Regmon), which monitors access to the registry. It reports every setting that Windows or other programs read or write.

The second technique, and the one that I used most, is to compare snapshots of the registry before and after making the change. Here's how that process worked for me while writing this chapter:

1. Export the branch of the registry that you suspect contains the setting to a REG file. If in doubt, export the entire registry. Name the file Before.reg.

2. Change the setting. In this case, change a setting in Tweak UI.

3. Export the same branch of the registry that you exported in step 1. Name the file After.reg.

4. Compare both files; the differences between them represent the changes in the registry.

The primary tool that I use for comparing REG files is Windiff, which comes with the Windows Support Tools and the Windows 2000 Resource Kit. If you don't have Windiff, you can use Microsoft Office Word 2003 just as effectively: open the first REG file in Word, and then, from the Tools menu, click Compare And Merge Documents to compare it with the second file.

Focus

When an application needs your attention—or when it simply wants to annoy you—it steals the focus from the application in which you're currently working. This leads to frustration as you flip back and forth between windows. The settings in the Focus category prevent that scenario; they get your attention by causing applications to flash their taskbar buttons rather than stealing focus from the application in the foreground.

Table 5-2 describes the settings in the Focus category. The default value for ForegroundLockTimeout is 0x00030D40, or 200000. This value is the time in milliseconds before Windows allows an application to steal the focus from the foreground application. To convert 200,000 to seconds, divide it by 1000 (200 seconds). You see the value ForegroundFlashCount in the table twice, because setting it to **0** causes the taskbar button to flash until you click it; otherwise, the taskbar button flashes the number of times you set in ForegroundFlashCount.

Table 5-2   **Values in the Focus Category**

Setting	Name	Type	Data
HKCU\Control Panel\Desktop			
Prevent applications from stealing focus	ForegroundLockTimeout	REG_DWORD	*N*
Flash taskbar button until I click on it	ForegroundFlashCount	REG_DWORD	0x00
Flash taskbar button *N* times	ForegroundFlashCount	REG_DWORD	*N*

ALT+TAB

The settings in the ALT+TAB category configure the number of rows and columns that you see when you press ALT+TAB. The REG_SZ value for the Rows setting is CoolSwitchRows. The REG_SZ value for the Columns setting is CoolSwitchColumns. Both values are in HKCU\Control Panel\Desktop. Be careful that you don't configure so many rows and columns that the window no longer fits on the screen. To take effect, this setting requires that you log off and back on to Windows.

Mouse

The settings in the Mouse category control the sensitivity of the mouse. Before adjusting these values manually, use Tweak UI to figure out what the best settings are for you. You can use the test icon, shown in Figure 5-2, to try different values.

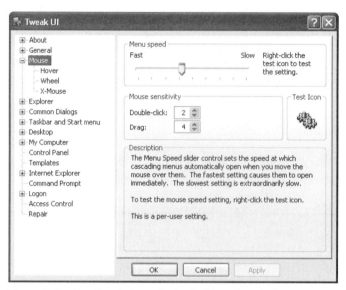

Figure 5-2   Use Tweak UI to find suitable values before trying to set mouse sensitivity values manually.

The first value in Table 5-3, `MenuShowDelay`, is the time in milliseconds that Windows waits before opening a menu to which you point. The default is **400**, or .4 seconds, but you can cut that number in half if you want menus to open faster. The values `DragHeight` and `DragWidth` are the settings that specify the distance (in number of pixels) that you must move the mouse with a button held down before Windows recognizes that you're dragging something. The default value is **4** pixels, and the height and width should be equal to each other. The last two values, `DoubleClickHeight` and `DoubleClickWidth`, are the settings that specify the maximum distance (in pixels) allowed between two mouse clicks before Windows recognizes that you're double-clicking something. The default value is **2**. These are REG_SZ values; Windows expects decimal rather than hexadecimal numbers.

Table 5-3   **Values in the Mouse Category**

Setting	Name	Type	Data
HKCU\Control Panel\Desktop			
Menu speed	`MenuShowDelay`	REG_SZ	0 to 65534
Drag	`DragHeight DragWidth`	REG_SZ	0 to *N*
HKCU\Control Panel\Mouse			
Double-click	`DoubleClickHeight DoubleClickWidth`	REG_SZ	0 to *N*

Hover

The settings in the Hover category are similar to the settings in the Mouse category. They control the size of the area in pixels and the time in milliseconds that the mouse pointer must remain in one spot before Windows recognizes that the mouse is hovering over something. Table 5-4 describes the values for this category. The default sensitivity is 2, and you should keep the height and width equal to each other. The default hover time is 400. Cut that number in half to select objects more quickly when you point to them. If you don't see these values in the registry, create them.

Table 5-4   Values in the Hover Category

Setting	Name	Type	Data
HKCU\Control Panel\Mouse			
Hover sensitivity	`MouseHoverWidth MouseHoverHeight`	REG_SZ	0 to N
Hover time (ms)	`MouseHoverTime`	REG_SZ	0 to N

Wheel

The setting in the Wheel category controls the mouse wheel. The value `WheelScrollLines` is the only value in Table 5-5. That's because the three different options in this category relate to the different data you can assign to this value. The default is 3, which enables the mouse wheel to scroll three lines at a time.

Table 5-5   Values in the Wheel Category

Setting	Name	Type	Data
HKCU\Control Panel\Desktop			
Use mouse wheel for scrolling	`WheelScrollLines`	REG_SZ	0
Scroll a page at a time	`WheelScrollLines`	REG_SZ	−1
Scroll N lines at a time	`WheelScrollLines`	REG_SZ	1 to N

X-Mouse

The settings in the X-Mouse category, as described in Table 5-6, used to be one of my favorite customizations. I liked the idea of windows popping to the foreground when I pointed at them. It gets annoying after a while, but it's a novelty you should try because you might like it. Here's more information on each of these settings:

- **Activation follows mouse (X-Mouse).**   Gives focus to any window to which you point but doesn't raise the window to the foreground unless you check the next option in this list

- **Autoraise when activating.**   Brings the window that has focus to the foreground

- **Activation delay (ms).**   Specifies the delay (in milliseconds) before Windows brings the window to which you pointed to the foreground

These settings in the value `UserPreferencesMask` are bits, which you learned about earlier in this chapter. The default value for `ActiveWndTrkTimeout` is 0, but 400 is a more reasonable delay. A higher timeout prevents windows from flipping between the foreground and background, making this feature much less annoying and more useful.

Table 5-6   Values in the X-Mouse Category

Setting	Name	Type	Data
HKCU\Control Panel\Desktop			
Activation follows mouse (X-Mouse)	`UserPreferencesMask`	`REG_BINARY`	`Bit 0x0001`
Autoraise when activating	`UserPreferencesMask`	`REG_BINARY`	`Bit 0x0040`
Activation delay (ms)	`ActiveWndTrkTimeout`	`REG_DWORD`	0 to *N*

Explorer

The settings in the Explorer category affect many different actions: you can customize the Start menu, enable smooth scrolling, and automatically clear the document history. Table 5-7 maps the settings in this category to their registry values. Create any keys and values that you don't see in the registry.

You'll notice that the setting Show Links On Favorites Menu is missing from Table 5-7. This is because that setting isn't in the registry. When you disable the Links menu, Tweak UI simply sets the Links folder's hidden attribute. Enable the folder, and Tweak UI clears the Links folder's hidden attribute. This is the only way to prevent Internet Explorer from displaying the Links folder on the Favorites menu.

> **Note**   Most of the settings in this category are policies, and you must pay attention to how the settings are phrased. For example, the Tweak UI setting Allow Help on Start Menu is positive. The corresponding value `NoSMHelp` is negative, which is true of most policies, as you will learn in Chapter 7, "Using Registry-Based Policy." Thus, to *enable* Help on the Start Menu, you must disable `NoSMHelp`. To *disable* Help on the Start Menu, you must enable `NoSMHelp`.

Table 5-7   Values in the Explorer Category

Setting	Name	Type	Data
HKCU\Control Panel\Desktop			
Enable smooth scrolling	`SmoothScroll`	`REG_DWORD`	`0x00	0x01`
HKCU\Software\Microsoft\Internet Explorer\Main			
Use Classic Search in Internet Explorer	`Use Search Asst`	`REG_SZ`	`Yes	No`

Table 5-7   Values in the Explorer Category

Setting	Name	Type	Data
HKCU\Software\Microsoft\Windows\CurrentVersion\Explorer			
Manipulate connected files as a unit	NoFileFolderConnection	REG_DWORD	0x00 | 0x01
Prefix "Shortcut to" on new shortcuts	Link	REG_DWORD	0x00 | 0x01
HKCU\Software\Microsoft\Windows\CurrentVersion\Explorer\Advanced			
Detect accidental double-clicks	UseDoubleClickTimer	REG_DWORD	0x00 | 0x01
Show "Encrypt" on context menu	EncryptionContextMenu	REG_DWORD	0x00 | 0x01
HKCU\Software\Microsoft\Windows\CurrentVersion\Explorer\AutoComplete			
Use Tab to navigate AutoComplete	Always Use Tab	REG_DWORD	0x00 | 0x01
HKCU\Software\Microsoft\Windows\CurrentVersion\Explorer\CabinetState			
Use Classic Search in Explorer	Use Search Asst	REG_SZ	Yes | No
HKCU\Software\Microsoft\Windows\CurrentVersion\Policies\Explorer			
Allow Help on Start Menu	NoSMHelp	REG_DWORD	0x00 | 0x01
Allow Logoff on Start Menu	NoLogoff	REG_DWORD	0x00 | 0x01
Allow Recent Documents on Start Menu	NoRecentDocsMenu	REG_DWORD	0x00 | 0x01
Allow Web content to be added to the desktop	NoActiveDesktop	REG_DWORD	0x00 | 0x01
Clear document history on exit	ClearRecentDocsOnExit	REG_DWORD	0x00 | 0x01
Enable Windows+X hotkeys	NoWinKeys	REG_DWORD	0x00 | 0x01
Lock Web content	NoActiveDesktopChanges	REG_DWORD	0x00 | 0x01
Maintain document history	NoRecentDocsHistory	REG_DWORD	0x00 | 0x01
Maintain network history	NoRecentDocsNetHood	REG_DWORD	0x00 | 0x01
Show My Documents on classic Start Menu	NoSMMyDocs	REG_DWORD	0x00 | 0x01
Show My Pictures on classic Start Menu	NoSMMyPictures	REG_DWORD	0x00 | 0x01
Show Network Connections on classic Start Menu	NoNetworkConnections	REG_DWORD	0x00 | 0x01
Use intuitive filename sorting	NoStrCmpLogical	REG_DWORD	0x00 | 0x01

Shortcut

When you create a shortcut, Windows adds an overlay to the original document's icon so you can easily identify it as a shortcut. The Shortcut category enables you to customize that overlay. You can choose not to add an overlay, to add a light arrow, to use the normal arrow, or to use a custom icon as the overlay. Table 5-8 shows the value and data that Tweak UI uses for shortcuts.

Table 5-8   Values in the Shortcut Category

Setting	Name	Type	Data
HKLM\SOFTWARE\Microsoft\Windows\CurrentVersion\Explorer\ShellIcons			
Arrow	29	REG_SZ	null
Light Arrow	29	REG_SZ	C:\WINDOWS\system32\TweakUI.exe,2
None	29	REG_SZ	C:\WINDOWS\system32\TweakUI.exe,3
Custom	29	REG_SZ	*filename,index*

HKLM\SOFTWARE\Microsoft\Windows\CurrentVersion\Explorer\ShellIcons is the key where you customize the shortcut overlay. Create this key if you don't see it in the registry. You add the REG_SZ value 29 and set it to *filename,index*, where *filename* is the name of the file containing the icon, and *index* is the index of that icon. For more information about using icons, see Chapter 4, "Hacking the Registry." Tweak UI removes 29 from ShellIcons if you choose the default arrow. It sets 29 to C:\WINDOWS\system32\TweakUI.exe,2 for a light arrow or to C:\WINDOWS\system32\TweakUI.exe,3 for no arrow.

Colors

Table 5-9 describes the values in the Colors category. Create any values that you don't see in the registry. HotTrackingColor is a string value, and Windows expects a Red Green Blue (an RGB) value in decimal notation. For example, white is 255 255 255. The operating system expects binary RGB values in hexadecimal for the remaining values. Windows uses each color as follows:

- **Hot-tracking.**   Windows displays file names in this color when you point to them and if you've enabled the single-click user interface.

- **Compressed files.**   Windows displays compressed files in this color.

- **Encrypted files.**   Windows displays encrypted files in this color.

Table 5-9   Values in the Colors Category

Setting	Name	Type	Data
HKCU\Control Panel\Colors			
Hot-tracking	HotTrackingColor	REG_SZ	*RRR GGG BBB*
HKCU\Software\Microsoft\Windows\CurrentVersion\Explorer			
Compressed files	AltColor	REG_BINARY	0x*RR* 0x*GG* 0x*BB* 0x00
Encrypted files	AltEncryptionColor	REG_BINARY	0x*RR* 0x*GG* 0x*BB* 0x00

Thumbnails

The Thumbnails category controls the quality of thumbnails in Windows Explorer. Table 5-10 describes the values for Image Quality and Size. Create values that you don't see in the registry. The default value for ThumbnailQuality is 0x5A. The default value for ThumbnailSize is 0x60. Keep in mind that higher quality and larger thumbnails require more disk space, which is not usually a problem, but they also take longer to display. Changing the quality does not affect thumbnails that already exist on the file system.

Table 5-10   Values in the Thumbnails Category

Setting	Name	Type	Data
HKCU\Software\Microsoft\Windows\CurrentVersion\Explorer			
Image Quality	ThumbnailQuality	REG_DWORD	0x32 0x64
Size (pixels)	ThumbnailSize	REG_DWORD	0x20 0xFF

Command Keys

If you have a keyboard with navigation keys, such as the Microsoft Internet Keyboard Pro (learn more about this keyboard at *http://www.microsoft.com/hardware*), you can customize them. For example, you can reassign the Calculator key to open your favorite calculator instead of the program that comes with Windows.

The key where you customize the keyboard navigation keys is HKCU\Software\ Microsoft\Windows\CurrentVersion\Explorer\AppKey. If you don't see this key, create it. Look up the keyboard key that you want to customize in Table 5-11, and then add the corresponding subkey to AppKey. Within that subkey, create the REG_SZ value ShellExecute, and set it to the path and file name of the program you want to execute by pressing that key. If you want to disable the keyboard navigation key, set it to an empty string. You can restore the original behavior by removing the subkey you added to AppKey. For example, to run PowerToy Calculator by pressing the Calculator key, add 18 to AppKey. Then create the REG_SZ value ShellExecute in 18, and set it to PowerCalc.exe.

Table 5-11   Subkeys for the Command Keys Category

Key	Subkey	Key	Subkey
Back (Internet browser)	1	New	29
Calculator	18	Open	30
Close	31	Paste	38
Copy	36	Print	33
Corrections	45	Raise microphone volume	26
Cut	37	Redo	35
Favorites	6	Refresh (Internet browser)	3
Find	28	Reply	39
Forward (Internet browser)	2	Save	32
Forward (mail)	40	Search	5
Help	27	Send	41
Lower microphone volume	25	Spelling checker	42
Mail	15	Stop (Internet browser)	4
Media	16	Toggle dictation and command/control	43
Mute microphone	24	Toggle microphone	44
Mute volume	8	Undo	34
My Computer	17	WebHome	7

Customizations

Windows Explorer remembers how you customize it. For example, you can customize the view for a particular folder, and Windows Explorer will remember and use that setting the next time that you open that folder. By default, Windows Explorer only remembers 400 customizations. You can reduce or increase that number, however. The Folders to Remember setting is the REG_DWORD setting Bag MRU Size in the keys HKCU\Software\Microsoft\Windows\Shell and HKCU\Software\Microsoft\Windows\ShellNoRoam.

Slide Show

The REG_DWORD value Timeout in the key HKCU\Software\Microsoft\Windows\CurrentVersion\Explorer\ShellImageView controls the amount of time that Windows Explorer displays each picture during a slide show. This is a per-user setting that requires you to log off and on to Windows for it to take effect.

Common Dialog Boxes

The common dialog boxes, such as the Save As dialog box, display the Places Bar on the left side. These are shortcuts to common folders, which make it much easier to get around. By default, you see the History, Documents, Desktop, Favorites, and My Network Places folders there. You can customize the folders that appear in the places bar by using the Common Dialogs category in Tweak UI.

First things first: Table 5-12 describes the settings that enable you to remove the Back button and history from common dialog boxes. You can also hide the Places Bar altogether by setting the value `NoPlacesBar` to `0x01`. Create this value if it doesn't exist.

Table 5-12   Values in the Common Dialogs Category

Setting	Name	Type	Data
HKCU\Software\Microsoft\Windows\CurrentVersion\Explorer\AutoComplete			
Enable AutoComplete	AutoComplete in File Dialog	REG_DWORD	0x00 | 0x01
HKCU\Software\Microsoft\Windows\CurrentVersion\Policies\comdlg32			
Remember previously used file names	NoFileMru	REG_DWORD	0x00 | 0x01
Show Back button on File Open/ Save dialog box	NoBackButton	REG_DWORD	0x00 | 0x01
	NoBackButton	REG_DWORD	0x00 | 0x01
Hide places bar	NoPlacesBar	REG_DWORD	0x00 | 0x01

Places Bar

Figure 5-3 shows the Places Bar category in Tweak UI. The Hide Places Bar option is described in Table 5-12.

Figure 5-3   Make network document folders easily accessible by adding them to the places bar.

Customizing the places bar by editing the registry is a bit more complicated. First you add to HKCU\Software\Microsoft\Windows\CurrentVersion\Policies\comdlg32\ the PlacesBar subkey. In PlacesBar, create the REG_DWORD values Place0, Place1, Place2, Place3, and Place4. These correspond to the five available buttons from top to bottom. The common dialog boxes will display only the buttons specified by these values; if there is a PlacesBar subkey with no values, an empty places bar will be displayed. Then, set PlacesN to one of the settings shown in Table 5-13. For example, to set the second button to My Music, create the REG_DWORD value Places1 in PlacesBar, and set it to 0x0D. You're not limited to the folders you see in Table 5-13, by the way. You can create the PlacesN value as a REG_SZ and then add the path of any folder. To restore the default places bar, remove the PlacesBar subkey, and remove the NoPlacesBar value.

Table 5-13   Folders for the Places Bar

Folder	Value	Folder	Value
Desktop	0x00	Network Neighborhood	0x12
Favorites	0x06	History	0x22
My Documents	0x05	My Pictures	0x27
My Music	0x0D	Recent Documents	0x08
My Computer	0x11		

Taskbar and Start Menu

Table 5-14 describes the settings in the Taskbar category. Most notably, you can disable balloon tips by setting the REG_DWORD value EnableBalloonTips to 0x00. Create this value if it doesn't already exist.

Table 5-14   Values in the Taskbar Category

Setting	Name	Type	Data
HKCU\Software\Microsoft\Windows\CurrentVersion\Explorer\Advanced			
Enable balloon tips	EnableBalloonTips	REG_DWORD	0x00 | 0x01
HKCU\Software\Microsoft\Windows\CurrentVersion\Policies\Explorer			
Warn when low on disk space	NoLowDiskSpaceChecks	REG_DWORD	0x00 | 0x01
Show name on Start menu	NoUserNameInStartMenu	REG_DWORD	0x00 | 0x01
Show taskbar notification icons	NoTrayItemsDisplay	REG_DWORD	0x00 | 0x01

Grouping

The settings in the Grouping category, as described in Table 5-15, enable you to control how buttons are grouped on the taskbar. Using the `TaskbarGroupSize` value, which you should create if it doesn't already exist, you determine the applications that Windows collapses into groups first:

- **Group least used applications first.** Windows groups least frequently used applications first, and groups more frequently used applications as necessary.

- **Group applications with the most windows first.** Windows groups applications that have the most open windows first, and groups applications with fewer open windows only as necessary.

- **Group any application with at least N windows.** Windows groups applications that have N windows open on the desktop.

Windows uses the same `REG_DWORD` value for all three cases. If you set `TaskbarGroup-Size` to 0x00, Windows uses least-used grouping. If you set it to 0x01, Windows uses most-windows grouping. If you set it to any other value, Windows groups any application that has that number of open windows.

Table 5-15   **Values in the Grouping Category**

Setting	Name	Type	Data
HKCU\Software\Microsoft\Windows\CurrentVersion\Explorer\Advanced			
Group least used applications first	TaskbarGroupSize	REG_DWORD	0x00
Group applications with the most windows first	TaskbarGroupSize	REG_DWORD	0x01
Group any application with at least N windows	TaskbarGroupSize	REG_DWORD	N

Start Menu

Windows displays the most frequently used programs on the bottom of the Start menu. This handy feature prevents you from having to hunt for applications that you use often. Some applications don't belong on this list, however. I tire of seeing Notepad on the Start menu just because I happened to use it to view a text file. I also don't like seeing Command Prompt on the Start menu every time I type **cmd** in the Run dialog box. The solution is to tell Windows which applications you don't want it to add to the Start menu. Do that in the key HKCU\Software\Classes\Applications.

In Table 5-16, look up the application that you want to keep off the Start menu's list of frequently used programs. If you don't find the program in Table 5-16, find the program's file name by looking in the Program Files folder or at the program's shortcut on the Start menu. Then add to `Applications` a subkey with the same name as the program's file name (but omit the path). Add the `REG_SZ` value `NoStartPage` to the program's subkey, and leave it blank. For example, to keep Notepad off the Start menu, create the subkey `Notepad.exe` in `HKCU\Software\Classes\Applications`, and add the value `NoStartPage`.

Table 5-16   Values in Windows Start Menu Category

Application	File Name	Application	File Name
Accessibility Wizard	`Accwiz.exe`	Narrator	`Narrator.exe`
Address book	`Wab.exe`	Notepad	`Notepad.exe`
Backup	`Ntbackup.exe`	On-Screen Keyboard	`Osk.exe`
Calculator	`Calc.exe`	Outlook Express	`Msimn.exe`
Character map	`Charmap.exe`	Paint	`Mspaint.exe`
Command prompt	`Cmd.exe`	Pinball	`Pinball.exe`
Data sources (ODBC)	`Odbcad32.exe`	Remote Assistance	`Rcimlby.exe`
Disk cleanup	`Cleanmgr.exe`	Remote Desktop Connection	`Mstsc.exe`
FreeCell	`Freecell.exe`	Solitaire	`Sol.exe`
Files and Settings Transfer Wizard	`Migwiz.exe`	Sound Recorder	`Sndrec32.exe`
Hearts	`Mshearts.exe`	Spider Solitaire	`Spider.exe`
HyperTerminal	`Hypertrm.exe`	System Information	`Msinfo32.exe`
Internet Backgammon	`Bckgzm.exe`	System Restore	`Rstrui.exe`
Internet Checkers	`Chkrzm.exe`	Tour Windows XP	`Tourstart.exe`
Internet Explorer	`Iexplore.exe`	Utility Manager	`Utilman.exe`
Internet Hearts	`Hrtzzm.exe`	Windows Media Player	`Wmplayer.exe`
Internet Reversi	`Rvsezm.exe`	Windows Messenger	`Msmsgs.exe`
Internet Spades	`Shvlzm.exe`	Windows Movie Maker	`Moviemk.exe`
Magnifier	`Magnify.exe`	Windows Update	`Wupdmgr.exe`
Minesweeper	`Winmine.exe`	WordPad	`wordpad.exe`
MSN Explorer	`Msn6.exe`		

Desktop

One of the most popular customizations for Windows 98 was to remove the icons from the desktop. That meant that users did not display the My Documents icon or the Network Neighborhood icon. Windows has caught up with users' tastes and now displays only the Recycle Bin icon on the desktop by default.

If you miss the good old days, you can add the icons back to the desktop. Use the Tweak UI Desktop category. Table 5-17 describes the values corresponding to each icon. Add each value to the subkey NewStartPanel, creating it if it doesn't exist, and set it to 0x00 to hide the icon or to 0x01 to display the icon.

Table 5-17   Values in the Desktop Category

Setting	Name	Type	Data
HKCU\Software\Microsoft\Windows\CurrentVersion\Explorer\HideDesktopIcons\ NewStartPanel			
Internet Explorer	{871C5380-42A0-1069-A2EA-08002B30309D}	REG_DWORD	0x00 | 0x01
My Computer	{20D04FE0-3AEA-1069-A2D8-08002B30309D}	REG_DWORD	0x00 | 0x01
My Documents	{450D8FBA-AD25-11D0-98A8-0800361B1103}	REG_DWORD	0x00 | 0x01
My Network Places	{208D2C60-3AEA-1069-A2D7-08002B30309D}	REG_DWORD	0x00 | 0x01
Recycle Bin	{645FF040-5081-101B-9F08-00AA002F954E}	REG_DWORD	0x00 | 0x01

First Icon

Using the First Icon category, choose the icon that you want to appear first on the desktop: My Documents or My Computer. Table 5-18 describes the settings you need to apply for either scenario.

Table 5-18   Values in the First Icon Category

Setting	Name	Type	Data
HKCR\CLSID\{450D8FBA-AD25-11D0-98A8-0800361B1103}			
My Documents	SortOrderIndex	REG_DWORD	0x48
My Computer	SortOrderIndex	REG_DWORD	0x54

My Computer

Use the My Computer category to determine which icons you see in My Computer. Table 5-19 describes the settings you must apply to show the Control Panel and Files Stored On This Computer icons in My Computer.

Table 5-19   **Values in the My Computer Category**

Setting	Name	Type	Data
HKCU\Software\Microsoft\Windows\CurrentVersion\Explorer\HideMyComputerIcons			
Control Panel	{21EC2020-3AEA-1069-A2DD-08002B30309D}	REG_DWORD	0x00 | 0x01
HKCU\Software\Microsoft\Windows\CurrentVersion\Policies\Explorer			
Files Stored On This Computer	NoSharedDocuments	REG_DWORD	0x00 | 0x01

Drives

Windows can hide drive letters. You hide them by setting NoDrives in the key HKCU\Software\Microsoft\Windows\CurrentVersion\Policies\Explorer, but it's easier using the Tweak UI category Drives. The trick is figuring out the value to put in the REG_BINARY value NoDrives.

Each bit in NoDrives, right to left, corresponds to the drive letters A through Z. To hide drive A, turn on the first bit. To hide drive B, turn on the second bit. Turn on the bit representing each drive that you want to hide. This math is easier if you use Calculator in scientific view. Also, see Chapter 1, "Learning the Basics," for some tips on doing bitwise math.

> **Note**   Hiding drive letters in Windows doesn't prevent users from accessing those drives through other means, including a command prompt window. This setting hides only those drives in Windows Explorer, the common dialog boxes, and Windows applications. Thus, you can't rely on this as a security measure.

Special Folders

Windows users have special folders, such as the My Documents, My Pictures, and Favorites folders, in their user profiles. The default location for these folders is in %UserProfile%, but you can redirect them to any location, including a location on the network. That's the purpose of the Tweak UI category Special Folders.

The key where you find each of these special folders is HKCU\Software\Microsoft\Windows\CurrentVersion\Explorer\User Shell Folders. You learn about them in detail in Chapter 4, "Hacking the Registry," and in Appendix C, "Per-User Settings." In Table 5-20, look up the folder you want to redirect. Then in User Shell Folders, change the value shown in the Folder drop-down list to the folder's new location. I suggest that you use environment variables, particularly when referencing folders in %UserProfile% or %SystemRoot%. The next time you log on to Windows,

Windows updates `HKCU\Software\Microsoft\Windows\CurrentVersion\Explorer\Shell Folders\` to reflect your changes. After relocating a shell folder, you must manually move your files and folders from the old location to the new location.

> **Tip**   I always relocate the My Documents, My Pictures, and Favorites folders to a network location. Doing so ensures that I always have access to my documents and Internet shortcuts from any computer on the network. I use Group Policy to automatically redirect the My Documents and My Pictures folders so I don't have to think about it. I use a script to relocate the Favorites folder on each computer that I use, however, because Group Policy doesn't support redirecting Favorites folders. Using a script makes redirecting Favorites easy, but still not automatic.

Table 5-20   Values in the Special Folders Category

Folder	Value	Default Path
CD Burning	`CD Burning`	`%UserProfile%\Local Settings\Application Data\Microsoft\CD Burning`
Desktop	`Desktop`	`%UserProfile%\Desktop`
Document templates	`Templates`	`%UserProfile%\Templates`
Favorites	`Favorites`	`%UserProfile%\Favorites`
My Documents	`Personal`	`%UserProfile%\My Documents`
Programs	`Programs`	`%UserProfile%\Start Menu\Programs`
Send To	`SendTo`	`%UserProfile%\SendTo`
Start Menu	`Start Menu`	`%UserProfile%\Start Menu`
Startup	`Startup`	`%UserProfile%\Start Menu\Programs\Startup`

The value for the Installation Path setting is not in HKCU. It's the REG_SZ value `SourcePath` in `HKLM\SOFTWARE\Microsoft\Windows\CurrentVersion\Setup`. Likewise, the values for the Shared Music, Shared Pictures, and Shared Video folders are in `HKLM\SOFTWARE\Microsoft\Windows\CurrentVersion\Explorer\Shell Folders`. They are the REG_SZ values `CommonMusic`, `CommonPictures`, and `CommonVideo`, respectively.

AutoPlay

All the action in the AutoPlay category is in its subcategories: Drives, Types, and Handlers. In the Drives category, you can prevent specific drives from playing media automatically when you insert them. You use the value `NoDriveAutoRun`, which is a REG_BINARY value, just like the `NoDrives` value you learned about earlier. For each drive that you want to stop from playing media automatically, set the bit, right to left, which corresponds to the drive letters A through Z. `NoDriveAutoRun` is in the key `HKCU\Software\Microsoft\Windows\CurrentVersion\Policies\Explorer`.

The next subcategory is Types, which controls Autoplay for specific types of media. In this category, you can control whether CDs, DVDs, and removable drives automatically play when you insert disks. Table 5-21 describes the values that correlate to the settings you see in this category. Just like you did with the value UserPreferencesMask, you must toggle the bit shown in the Data column. To prevent CD drives from automatically playing, for example, set bit 0x20 in the REG_DWORD value NoDriveTypeAutoRun.

Table 5-21   Values in Autoplay Drive Types

Setting	Name	Type	Data
HKCU\Software\Microsoft\Windows\CurrentVersion\Policies\Explorer			
Enable Autoplay for CD and DVD drives	NoDriveTypeAutoRun	REG_DWORD	Bit 0x20
Enable Autoplay for removable drives	NoDriveTypeAutoRun	REG_DWORD	Bit 0x04

The last subcategory is Handlers. When Windows detects that you've inserted a CD, DVD, or removable disk, it automatically runs the program that it associates with the type of content on that disk. You use the Autoplay Handlers list to control which programs are used with different types of content. This setting is much easier to configure in Tweak UI than manually, but we'll try it, anyway.

The key where you find these associations is HKLM\SOFTWARE\Microsoft\Windows\CurrentVersion\Explorer\AutoplayHandlers\EventHandlers. In Table 5-22, look up the type of content you want to customize. Then open the subkey shown in the Subkey column for EventHandlers. In that subkey, add any combination of the following handlers as an empty REG_SZ value, if they don't already exist:

- MSCDBurningOnArrival
- MSGenericVolumeArrival
- MSOpenFolder
- MSPlayCDAudioOnArrival
- MSPlayDVDMovieOnArrival
- MSPlayMediaOnArrival
- MSPlayMusicFilesOnArrival
- MSPlayVideoFilesOnArrival
- MSPrintPicturesOnArrival
- MSPromptEachTime
- MSPromptEachTimeNoContent
- MSShowPicturesOnArrival

- `MSRipCDAudioOnArrival`

- `MSTakeNoAction`

- `MSVideoCameraArrival`

- `MSWiaEventHandler`

- `MSWMDMHandler`

- `MSWMPBurningOnArrival`

Table 5-22   Values in Autoplay Handlers

Media	Subkey	Media	Subkey
Generic	`GenericVolumeArrival`	Music files	`PlayMusicFilesOnArrival`
Blank CD-R	`HandleCDBurningOnArrival`	Video files	`PlayVideoFilesOnArrival`
Mixed content	`MixedContentOnArrival`	Digital images	`ShowPicturesOnArrival`
CD audio	`PlayCDAudioOnArrival`	Video camera	`VideoCameraArrival`
DVD	`PlayDVDMovieOnArrival`		

Drive Letters

The Drive Letters category allows you to configure how Windows Explorer displays drive letters in relation to the volume label. Set the REG_DWORD value `ShowDriveLetters-First` in HKLM\SOFTWARE\Microsoft\Windows\CurrentVersion\Explorer to one of the following values:

- **0x00.** Show all drive letters after the label

- **0x01.** Show all drive letters before the label

- **0x02.** Show network drive letters before the label, and show local drive letters after the label

- **0x04.** Never show drive letters

Control Panel

The Control Panel category enables you to hide specific icons in Control Panel. Create a REG_SZ value in the key HKCU\Control Panel\don't load, with a file extension of *.cpl* for the icon you want to hide. Set the value to **Yes** to display the icon or to **No** to hide the icon. Table 5-23 shows the file names of the .cpl files that come with Windows. For example, to hide the Internet Options icon, add the REG_SZ value `Inetcpl.cpl` to don't load, and set its value to **No**.

Table 5-23   **Values in Control Panel**

File Name	Description	File Name	Description
Access.cpl	Accessibility Options	Mmsys.cpl	Sounds and Audio Devices Properties
Appwiz.cpl	Add Or Remove Programs	Keymgrr.cpl	Stored Usernames and Passwords
Desk.cpl	Display	Nwc.cpl	Client Service for NetWare
Hdwwiz.cpl	Add Hardware	Odbccp32.cpl	Data Sources (ODBC)
Inetcpl.cpl	Internet Options	Powercfg.cpl	Power Options
Intl.cpl	Regional and Language Options	Sysdm.cpl	System
Joy.cpl	Game Controllers	Telephon.cpl	Phone and Modem Options
Main.cpl	Mouse and Keyboard	Timedate.cpl	Date and Time

Templates

Use the Templates category to customize the templates that you see when you right-click the desktop or the unused space in a folder window, and then click New. Chapter 4, "Hacking the Registry," and Appendix A, "File Associations," describe how to build customized templates. Table 5-24 describes the values that Tweak UI uses for each of the default templates in Windows. Note that if you disable any of the templates shown in Table 5-24, Tweak UI hides the `ShellNew` key by renaming it to `ShellNew-` (adding a dash).

Table 5-24   **Values in Document Templates**

Setting	Name	Type	Data
HKCR			
Bitmap Image	`HKCR\.bmp\` `ShellNew \NullFile`	REG_SZ	`""`
Briefcase	`HKCR\.bfc\` `ShellNew \Command`	REG_EXPAND_SZ	`%SystemRoot%\system32` `\rundll32.exe %System-` `Root% \system32\syncui.` `dll,Briefcase_Create` `%2!d! %1`
Compressed (zipped) folder	`HKCR\.zip` `\CompressedFolder` `\ShellNew\Data`	REG_BINARY	`0x50 0x4B 0x05 0x06` `0x00 0x00 0x00 0x00` `0x00 0x00 0x00 0x00` `0x00 0x00 0x00 0x00` `0x00 0x00 0x00 0x00` `0x00 0x00`
Rich Text Document	`HKCR\.rtf\` `ShellNew \Data`	REG_SZ	`{\rtf1}`

Table 5-24   Values in Document Templates

Setting	Name	Type	Data
Text Document	HKCR\.txt\ ShellNew \NullFile	REG_SZ	" "
Wave Sound	HKCR\.wav\ ShellNew \FileName	REG_SZ	sndrec.wav
WordPad Document	HKCR\.doc \WordPad.Document. 1 \ShellNew\ NullFile	REG_SZ	" "

Internet Explorer

The two settings you see in the Internet Explorer category, the Autocorrect Backslashes to Slashes setting and the Include Path Search in Address Bar setting, are in the key HKCU\Software\Microsoft\Windows\CurrentVersion\Explorer\ Band\Address. The first is the REG_DWORD value AutoCorrect. The second is the REG_DWORD value Use PATH. The following sections describe the settings in the subcategories beneath Internet Explorer.

Toolbar Background

Table 5-25 describes the settings that Tweak UI establishes when you customize Internet Explorer and Windows Explorer toolbars with a bitmap image. These settings are in the Internet Explorer category.

Table 5-25   Values in the Internet Explorer Category

Setting	Name	Type	Data
HKCU\Software\Microsoft\Internet Explorer\Toolbar			
Use custom background for Internet Explorer toolbar	BackBitmapIE5	REG_SZ	*Filename*
Use custom background for Windows Explorer toolbar	BackBitmapShell	REG_SZ	*Filename*

Search

This is my favorite customization. Tweak UI's Search category enables you to add search URLs to Internet Explorer so that you can use search engines from the browser's address bar. For example, add the prefix news and set its URL to http:// groups.google.com/groups?q=%s&hl=en; then you can quickly search Google Groups for *Windows XP* by typing **news Windows XP** in the address bar. Figure 5-4 shows a search URL.

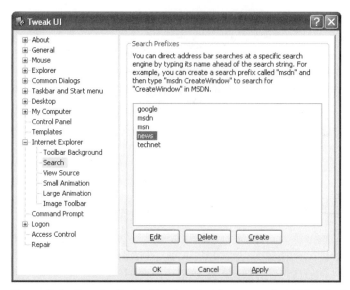

Figure 5-4   You don't need to download any search add-ins for Internet Explorer when using your favorite search engines is this easy.

Add the subkey `SearchURL` to `HKCU\Software\Microsoft\Internet Explorer`. Then add a subkey for each search prefix that you want to use. To use the example I just gave you, create the subkey `news`. Set the default value of the prefix's subkey, `news` in this example, to the URL of the search engine. Use the `%s` as a placeholder for the search string. Internet Explorer replaces the `%s` with any text you type to the right of the prefix. Continuing the Google Groups example, you'd set the default value to `http://groups.google.com/groups?q=%s&hl=en`.

Add the `REG_SZ` values shown in Table 5-26 to the prefix key you created. The purpose of these values is to describe what to substitute for special characters in your search string, including a space, percent sign (%), ampersand (&), and plus sign (+). These characters have special meaning when submitting forms to Web sites, so you must substitute a plus sign for a space, for example, or %26 for an ampersand. Thus, the browser translates the search string *Windows XP Bits & Pieces* to *Windows+XP+Bits+%26+Pieces*.

The only question left now is where to get the URL. That's easy. Open the search engine that you want to add to Internet Explorer's search URLs, and then search for something—anything. When the browser displays the results, copy the URL from the address bar, replacing your search word with a `%s`. For example, when searching Google Groups for *honeycutt*, the results are in a Web page with the URL *http://groups.google.com/groups?q=honeycutt&hl=en*. Replace the search word *honeycutt* with a `%s` to get `http://groups.google.com/groups?q=%s&hl=en`.

> **Note**   Searching from the address bar doesn't work properly with the original Windows XP Release to Manufacturing (RTM) bits. You must update the operating system using Windows Update or the latest service pack from Microsoft.

Table 5-26   Values in Search

Name	Data
<space>	+
%	%25
&	%26
+	%2B

> **Note**   If this customization doesn't work, you should suspect that your browser has been taken over by other programs (maybe spyware). Make sure you see the REG_SZ value {CFBFAE00-17A6-11D0-99CB-00C04FD64497} in HKCU\Software\Microsoft\ Internet Explorer\URLSearchHooks. The value's data is empty.

View Source

Use the View Source category in Tweak UI to change the program in which Internet Explorer displays a Web page's source. Set the default value of the key HKLM\SOFTWARE\ Microsoft\Internet Explorer\View Source Editor\Editor Name to the path and file name of the program that you want to use. Create this value if it doesn't already exist.

Small Animation

The small-animation icon is the icon you see in the top right corner of the Internet Explorer toolbar. The icon is animated when the browser is busy, and it's static when the browser isn't busy. Using the Small Animation category of Tweak UI, you can easily customize this animation. Tweak UI stores this animated bitmap in the key HKCU\Software\Microsoft\Internet Explorer\Toolbar. It's a REG_EXPAND_SZ value called SmBrandBitMap. The static bitmap is in the REG_EXPAND_SZ value SmallBitmap. The value contains the path and name of the animated bitmap file. The Frame Height setting is in the REG_DWORD value SmBrandHeight, and the Restart Frame settings is in the REG_DWORD value SmBrandLeadIn.

Large Animation

The large-animation icon is the big version of the same icon that you learned about in the previous section. The icon is animated when the browser is busy, and it's static when the browser isn't busy. Using the Large Animation category of Tweak UI, you can easily customize this animation. Tweak UI stores this animated bitmap in the key HKCU\Software\Microsoft\Internet Explorer\Toolbar. It's a REG_EXPAND_SZ value called BrandBitMap. The static bitmap is in the REG_EXPAND_SZ value BigBitMap. The value contains the path and name of the animated bitmap file. The Frame Height setting is in the REG_DWORD value BrandHeight, and the Restart Frame setting is in the REG_DWORD value BrandLeadIn.

Image Toolbar

The image toolbar is the little toolbar that you see when you hover the mouse pointer over an image on a Web page. For example, it enables you to expand an image that the browser isn't displaying at 100 percent. By default, however, Internet Explorer only displays the image toolbar for images that are larger than 200 pixels. And you can change this size. The setting is in the REG_DWORD value Image_Filter in the key HKCU\Software\Microsoft\Internet Explorer\Main.

Command Prompt

If you're a command-line junkie like me, you'll appreciate file name and directory completion. The command prompt window supports both of these features, but you have to enable them first. Table 5-27 describes the settings in the Command Prompt category in Tweak UI. Set the value CompletionChar to the keystroke that you want to use for file name completion, and set the value PathCompletionChar to the keystroke that you want to use for directory completion. You can use the same keystroke for both values. The value you use for *key* is the ASCII key code. Thus, TAB is 0x09. The value WordDelimiters is a string of characters that delimit words on the command line when you press CTRL+RIGHT ARROW or CTRL+LEFT ARROW. Create these values if they don't exist.

Table 5-27   Values in the Command Prompt Category

Setting	Name	Type	Data
HKCU\Software\Microsoft\Command Processor			
File name completion	CompletionChar	REG_DWORD	*key*
Directory completion	PathCompletionChar	REG_DWORD	*key*
HKCU\Console			
Word separators	WordDelimiters	REG_SZ	*Separators*
Enable selection coloring	EnableColorSelection	REG_DWORD	0x00	0x01

Logon

In the Logon category, you toggle Autoexec.bat parsing by setting the REG_SZ value ParseAutoexec in the key HKLM\Software\Microsoft\Windows NT\CurrentVersion\Winlogon to 0 or 1. Set ParseAutoexec to 0 to prevent Windows from parsing Autoexec.bat for environment variables. Otherwise, set ParseAutoexec to 1, and Windows will parse it for environment variables.

There are three other settings in the same key. The Keep RAS Connections After Logoff setting is in the REG_SZ value KeepRasConnections. The Show Additional Domain Information at Logon setting is in the REG_DWORD value DCacheShowDnsNames. Last, the Show Full DNS Domain Names at Logon setting is in the REG_DWORD value DCacheShowDomainTags.

Autologon

The last useful category in Tweak UI is Autologon, and it enables you to automatically log on to Windows without providing your name, domain, or password. Table 5-28 describes the values that you must set to log on to the computer automatically. *Name* is the user name, and *Domain* is the domain name. To enable Autologon, you must set the REG_SZ value AutoAdminLogon to 1. Last, set the value REG_SZ value DefaultPassword in the subkey Winlogon to the password that you want to use to log on to the computer automatically. You don't see this value in Tweak UI because it stores the password differently.

> **Note**   This setting is useful for IT professionals deploying software. It's one way to install applications that require administrative access to the computer, which users in most enterprises don't have. Chapter 18, "Fixing Common IT Problems," discusses this setting in detail.

Table 5-28   Values in the Autologon Category

Setting	Name	Type	Data
HKLM\SOFTWARE\Microsoft\Windows NT\CurrentVersion\Winlogon			
Log on automatically at system startup	AutoAdminLogon	REG_SZ	0 | 1
User name	DefaultUserName	REG_SZ	*Name*
Domain	DefaultDomainName	REG_SZ	*Domain*

Settings

The Settings category allows you to copy current desktop settings from your current user profile (the profile you're using while logged on to the computer and using Tweak UI) to the .DEFAULT user profile, which is the user profile that Windows uses when it displays the logon dialog box.

Screen Saver

Configuring the screen saver to lock the desktop is always a good idea. It prevents other people from accessing your computer when you walk away from your desk. As a convenience, though, Windows gives you a grace period from the time the screen saver starts to the time it actually locks the desktop. By default, this grace period is five seconds. You can change it to any value, however. This setting is in the key HKLM\SOFTWARE\Microsoft\Windows NT\CurrentVersion\Winlogon. It's REG_SZ value ScreenSaverGracePeriod. You simply set this string value to the number of seconds you want to use for a grace period.

Chapter 6

Configuring Servers

In Chapter 4, "Hacking the Registry," you found a variety of registry hacks for customizing Microsoft Windows XP and Windows Server 2003. For example, you might want to customize file associations on a server, personalize the Start menu, or keep your servers' history lists clear.

This chapter focuses more on customizing Windows Server 2003 than on customizing Windows XP. It describes *server hacks* that you can use to customize servers. For example, you can optimize the Server service by editing the registry, you can configure Kerberos troubleshooting, and more.

Server Customizations

This section contains two useful server customizations. First, it describes how to add comments to server announcements, making it easier for users to discern the purpose of each server they see in My Network Places. Second, it describes how you can optimize the Server service to favor memory usage, network throughput, or a balance of both.

Adding Comments to Server Announcements

Windows broadcasts the contents of the `REG_SZ` value `srvcomment` in server announcements. This value is in `HKLM\SYSTEM\CurrentControlSet\Services\LanmanServer\Parameters`. If you set this value to a description of the server, such as "Marketing file server," users will see that description in Windows Explorer when they're browsing My Network Places.

143

Optimizing the Server Service

You can manually optimize the Server service, customizing it to favor memory usage, network throughput, or both. To do so, create the REG_DWORD value Size, if it doesn't already exist, in the key HKLM\SYSTEM\CurrentControlSet\Services\lanmanserver. Set this to one of the values described in the following list:

- **0x01.**   Minimize memory usage
- **0x02.**   Balance memory and network throughput
- **0x03.**   Maximize network throughput

Authentication

The following sections contain customizations that help you troubleshoot and optimize authentication. The section "Configuring Kerberos" describes how to configure Kerberos for troubleshooting. The section "Disabling Global Catalog Requirement" describes how to remove the requirement of having a Global Catalog server at remote sites. Finally, the section "Enabling Verbose Winlogon Messages" describes how you can get more information from Winlogon for troubleshooting.

Configuring Kerberos

Kerberos is an authentication mechanism that is used to verify user or host identity. Kerberos is the preferred authentication method for services in Windows Server 2003. If you are running Windows Server 2003, you can modify Kerberos parameters to help troubleshoot Kerberos authentication issues or to test the Kerberos protocol. After you finish troubleshooting or testing the Kerberos protocol, remove any registry entries that you added. Otherwise, your computer's performance might be affected.

Table 6-1 describes the values you can configure in the key HKLM\SYSTEM\CurrentControlSet\Control\Lsa\Kerberos\Parameters and that are REG_DWORD values.

Table 6-1 `Control\Lsa\Kerberos\Parameters`

Name	Value	Description
SkewTime	5 (minutes)	This value is the maximum time difference that is permitted between the client computer and the server that accepts Kerberos authentication. In Windows Server 2003 checked build version, the default SkewTime value is two hours. A checked build version—also known as a debug version—of the Windows operating system is used in production and testing environments. This kind of build helps trace the cause of problems in system software by turning on many debugging checks in the operating system code and in the system drivers. These debugging checks help the checked build identify internal inconsistencies as soon as they occur. A checked build has many compiler optimizations turned off and is larger and runs more slowly than an end-user version of Windows does. An end-user version of Windows is also known as a free build version or a retail-build version. In a free build version, debugging information is removed, and Windows is built with full compiler optimizations. A free build version is also faster and uses less memory than a checked build version does.
LogLevel	0	This value indicates whether events are logged in the system event log. If this value is set to any non-zero value, all Kerberos-related events are logged in the system event log.
MaxPacketSize	1465 (bytes)	This value is the maximum User Datagram Protocol (UDP) packet size. If the packet size exceeds this value, TCP is used.
StartupTime	120 (seconds)	This value is the time that Windows waits for the Key Distribution Center (KDC) to start before Windows gives up.
KdcWaitTime	10 (seconds)	This value is the time Windows waits for a response from a KDC.
KdcBackoffTime	10 (seconds)	This value is the time between successive calls to the KDC if the previous call failed.

Table 6-1 `Control\Lsa\Kerberos\Parameters`

Name	Value	Description
KdcSendRetries	3	This value is the number of times that a client will try to contact a KDC.
DefaultEncryption-Type	23 (decimal) or 0x17 (hexadecimal)	This value indicates the default encryption type for pre-authentication.
FarKdcTimeout	10 (minutes)	This is the time-out value that is used to invalidate a domain controller from a different site in the domain controller cache.
NearKdcTimeout	30 (minutes)	This is the time-out value that is used to invalidate a domain controller in the same site in the domain controller cache.
StronglyEncrypt-Datagram	FALSE	This value contains a flag that indicates whether to use 128-bit encryption, as opposed to weaker encryption, for datagram packets.
MaxReferralCount	6	This value is the number of KDC referrals that a client pursues before the client gives up.
KerbDebugLevel	1 (for Windows Server 2003 checked build version), 0 (for Windows Server free build version)	This value indicates whether debug logging is on (1) or off (0).
MaxTokenSize	12000 (Decimal)	This value is the maximum value of the Kerberos token. Microsoft recommends that you set this value to less than 65535.
SpnCacheTimeout	15 (minutes)	This value is the lifetime of the Service Principal Names (SPN) cache entries. On domain controllers, the SPN cache is disabled.
S4UCacheTimeout	15 (minutes)	This value is the lifetime of the S4U negative cache entries that are used to restrict the number of S4U proxy requests from a particular computer.
S4UTicketLifetime	15 (minutes)	This value is the lifetime of tickets that are obtained by S4U proxy requests.
RetryPdc	0 (false) Possible values: 0 (false) or any non-zero value (true)	This value indicates whether the client will contact the primary domain controller for Authentication Service Requests (AS_REQ) if the client receives a password expiration error.

Table 6-1   `Control\Lsa\Kerberos\Parameters`

Name	Value	Description
RequestOptions	Any RFC 1510 value	This value indicates whether there are additional options that must be sent as KDC options in Ticket Granting Service requests (TGS_REQ).
ClientIpAddress	0 Possible values: 0 (false) or any non-zero value (true). (This setting is 0 because of Dynamic Host Configuration Protocol and network address translation issues.)	This value indicates whether a client IP address will be added in AS_REQ to force the Caddr field to contain IP addresses in all tickets.
TgtRenewalTime	600 (seconds)	This value is the time that Kerberos waits before it tries to renew a Ticket Granting Ticket (TGT) before the ticket expires.
AllowTgtSessionKey	0 Possible values: 0 (false) or any non-zero value (true)	This value indicates whether session keys are exported with initial or with cross realm TGT authentication. The default value is false for security reasons.

Table 6-2 describes the values that you can configure in the key HKLM\SYSTEM\ CurrentControlSet\Services\Kdc. (Create the subkey Kdc if it doesn't exist.)

Table 6-2   `Services\Kdc`

Name	Value	Description
KdcUseClientAddresses	0 Possible values: 0 (false) or any non-zero value (true)	This value indicates whether IP addresses will be added in the Ticket Granting Service Reply (TGS_REP).
KdcDontCheckAddresses	0 Possible values: 0 (false) or any non-zero value (true)	This value indicates whether IP addresses for the TGS_REQ and the TGT Caddr field will be checked.
NewConnectionTimeout	50 (seconds)	This value is the time that an initial TCP endpoint connection will be kept open to receive data before it disconnects.

Table 6-2 `Services\Kdc`

Name	Value	Description
MaxDatagramReplySize	1465 (decimal, bytes)	This value is the maximum UDP packet size in TGS_REP and Authentication Service Reply (AS_REP) messages. If the packet size exceeds this value, the KDC returns a KRB_ERR_RESPONSE_TOO_BIG message that requests that the client switch to TCP.
KdcExtraLogLevel	2 Possible values: 1 (decimal) or 0x1 (hexadecimal): Audit SPN unknown errors. 2 (decimal) or 0x2 (hexadecimal): Log PKINIT errors. (PKINIT is an Internet Engineering Task Force [IETF] Internet draft for "Public Key Cryptography for Initial Authentication in Kerberos.") 4 (decimal) or 0x4 (hexadecimal): Log all KDC errors.	This value indicates what information the KDC will write to event logs and to audits.
KdcDebugLevel	1 (for checked build), 0 (for free build)	This value indicates whether debug logging is on (1) or off (0). If the value is set to 0x10000000 (hexadecimal) or 268435456 (decimal), specific file or line information will be returned in the data field of KERB_ERRORS as PKERB_EXT_ERROR errors during a KDC processing failure.

Disabling Global Catalog Requirement

Placement of Global Catalog servers in remote sites is usually desired to improve performance of user logon time, searches, and other actions requiring communication with Global Catalog servers, and to reduce wide area network (WAN) traffic. However, to reduce administrative intervention, hardware requirements, and other related overhead, you might not always want to locate a Global Catalog server at a remote site. This is especially relevant in environments that have a large number of sites that could experience substantially increased hardware costs when the size of the sites might not justify that hardware and administration. The problem is that logons require the domain controller authenticating the user to contact a Global Catalog server to determine whether the user is a member of any universal groups. If the remote office does not have a Global Catalog server and a Global Catalog server cannot be contacted (for various reasons), then the user's logon request might fail (based on the rules stated earlier).

Windows Server 2003 offers an alternative to universal group caching. When this is enabled for a site, users who log on while a Global Catalog server is online can continue to do so if the Global Catalog server is inaccessible at the next logon.

To eliminate the need for a Global Catalog server at a site and to avoid potential denial of user logon requests, enable logons when a Global Catalog server is not available. You must configure this setting on the domain controller that performs the user authentication. To do that, add the REG_DWORD value IgnoreGCFailures to HKLM\SYSTEM\CurrentControlSet\Control\Lsa. Set this value to 0x01. After changing this value, you must restart the domain controller.

> **Caution**   The universal groups setting causes potential security vulnerabilities. Universal groups should not be used because if a user is a member of a universal group and the group is denied access to a resource, the key turns off enumeration of universal groups. The result is that the universal group SID is not added to the user's token, and the user could have access to the resource.

Enabling Verbose Winlogon Messages

You can configure Windows so that you receive verbose startup, shutdown, logon, and logoff status messages. Verbose status messages might be helpful when you are troubleshooting slow startup, shutdown, logon, or logoff behavior. To enable verbose status messages, create the REG_DWORD value verbosestatus in the key HLKM\SOFTWARE\Microsoft\Windows\CurrentVersion\Policies\System. Set this value to 0x01. Note that Windows doesn't display status messages if the value DisableStatusMessages exists in the key HKLM\SOFTWARE\Microsoft\Windows\CurrentVersion\Policies\System.

Internet Information Services

The following sections describe how to customize Internet Information Services (IIS) 6.0. The section "Configuring Http.sys" describes settings for customizing Http.sys. The section "Using Incremental Site ID Numbers" describes customizing IIS to use incremental site identification numbers.

Configuring Http.sys

In Windows Server 2003, Http.sys is the kernel mode driver that handles HTTP requests. Several registry values can be configured according to specific requirements. Table 6-3 describes the settings that you can configure in the key `HKLM\System\CurrentControlSet\Services\HTTP\Parameters`. All of these values are `REG_DWORD` values.

Caution Microsoft considers customizing the values `MaxConnections`, `MaxEndpoints`, `MaxFieldLength`, `MaxRequestBytes`, `UrlSegmentMaxCount`, `UriMaxUriBytes`, `UriScavengerPeriod`, and `UrlSegmentMaxLength` to be very risky. Test your changes in a safe environment before introducing them into a production environment.

Table 6-3 Http.sys Parameters

Name	Value	Range	Description
AllowRestricted-Chars	0	Boolean	If the value is non-zero, Http.sys accepts hex-escaped chars in request URLs that decode to U+0000–U+001F and U+007F–U+009F ranges.
EnableNonUTF8	1	Boolean	If the value is 0, Http.sys accepts only UTF-8-encoded URLs. If non-zero, Http.sys also accepts ANSI- or DBCS-encoded URLs in requests.
FavorUTF8	1	Boolean	If the value is non-zero, Http.sys always tries to decode a URL as UTF-8 first; if that conversion fails and EnableNonUTF8 is non-zero, Http.sys then tries to decode the URL as ANSI or DBCS. If the value is 0 (and EnableNonUTF8 is non-zero), Http.sys tries to decode the URL as ANSI or DBCS; if that is not successful, it tries a UTF-8 conversion.

Table 6-3   **Http.sys Parameters**

Name	Value	Range	Description
MaxConnections	MAX_ULONG	1024–2031616 (connections)	This value overrides the MaxConnections calculation in the driver. This is primarily a function of memory.
MaxEndpoits	0	0–1024	This value represents the maximum number of current end point objects that are permitted. The default value of zero implies that the maximum is computed from available memory.
MaxFieldLength	16384	64–65534 (bytes)	This value sets an upper limit for each header. See MaxRequestBytes.
MaxRequestBytes	16384	256–16777216 (bytes)	This value determines the upper limit for the total size of the Request line and the headers.
MaxFieldLength	16384	64–65534 (bytes)	This value sets an upper limit for each header.
PercentUAllowed	1	Boolean	If the value is non-zero, Http.sys accepts the %uNNNN notation in request URLs.
UrlSegment-MaxCount	255	0–16383 (segments)	This value represents the maximum number of URL path segments. If the value is 0, the count is bounded by the maximum value of a ULONG.
UriEnableCache	1	Boolean	If the value is non-zero, the Http.sys response and fragment cache is enabled.
UriMaxUriBytes	262144 (bytes)	4096–16777216 (bytes)	Any response that is greater than this value is not cached in the kernel response cache.

Table 6-3   Http.sys Parameters

Name	Value	Range	Description
UriScavenger-Period	120 (seconds)	10–0xFFFFFFFF (seconds)	This value determines the frequency of the cache scavenger. Any response or fragment that has not been accessed in the number of seconds equal to the value of UriScavengerPeriod is flushed.
UrlSegment-MaxLength	260	0–32766 (chars)	This value represents the maximum number of characters in a URL path segment (the area between the slashes in the URL). If zero, it is the length that is bounded by the maximum value of a ULONG.

Using Incremental Site ID Numbers

When you create a new Web site through the Internet Information Services (IIS) Manager in IIS 6.0, an identification number for that site is automatically generated and stored in the metabase. The identification number is based on the name of the Web site. In earlier versions of IIS, the Web site identification numbers were incremental. The new design ensures that all IIS 6.0 servers in a Web farm have a good chance of generating the same site identification numbers for sites with the same name. To use incremental site identification numbers, set the REG_DWORD value IncrementalSiteIDCreation to 0x01 in the key HKLM\SOFTWARE\Microsoft\InetMgr\Parameters. Create the value if it does not already exist.

Network Connections

This section contains two network customizations for Windows Server 2003. The section "Enabling IP Forwarding" shows you how to turn on IP forwarding in Windows Server 2003. The section "Changing MTU Settings" describes how you can optimize PPP and VPN connections by changing the MTU sizes in the registry.

Enabling IP Forwarding

By default, TCP/IP forwarding is disabled in Windows Server 2003. To enable IP forwarding, add the REG_DWORD value IPEnableRouter to the key HKLM\SYSTEM\CurrentControlSet\Services\Tcpip\Parameters. Set this value to 0x01. This enables IP forwarding on all network adapters installed on the server.

Changing MTU Settings

This section describes how to change the default maximum transfer unit (MTU) size settings for Point-to-Point Protocol (PPP) connections or for virtual private network (VPN) connections. Windows uses a fixed MTU size of 1500 bytes for all PPP connections and a fixed MTU size of 1400 bytes for all VPN connections. These are the default settings for PPP clients, for VPN clients, for PPP servers, and for VPN servers that are running Routing and Remote Access.

PPP connections are connections such as modem connections and Integrated Services Digital Network (ISDN) connections, or direct cable connections over null serial cable or parallel cable. VPN connections are Point-to-Point Tunneling Protocol (PPTP) connections or Layer 2 Tunneling Protocol (L2TP) connections.

Note   Use the methods discussed here to edit the registry to modify the MTU size settings. If you experience any problems or any performance-related issues after you modify the MTU size settings, remove the registry keys that you added.

To change the MTU settings for PPP and VPN connections, add the REG_DWORD values ProtocolType, PPPProtocolType, and ProtocolMTU, as well as TunnelMTU, to HKLM\SYSTEM\CurrentControlSet\Services\Ndiswan\Parameters\Protocols\0. (Create this subkey if it doesn't already exist.) Table 6-4 describes what settings to put in each value. ProtocolType and PPPProtocolType are required values. You can add either ProtocolMTU, TunnelMTU, or both.

Table 6-4   MTU Settings for PPP

Name	Setting	Description
ProtocolType	0x800	Set the protocol type.
PPPProtocolType	0x21	Set the tunnel protocol type.
ProtocolMTU	*Size*	Replace *Size* with the size of the MTU that you want to use for PPP connections.
TunnelMTU	*Size*	Replace *Size* with the size of the MTU that you want to use for VPN connections.

Shutdown Event Tracker

Shutdown Event Tracker is a feature of Windows Server 2003 that provides a way for IT professionals to track why users restart or shut down their computers. The feature captures the reasons users give for restarts and shutdowns to help create a comprehensive picture of an organization's system environment. It does not document why users choose other options, such as Log off or Hibernate. In Windows Server 2003,

Shutdown Event Tracker is enabled by default, and its tracking is a routine part of the computer shutdown process. This section describes the registry settings that you can use to configure the feature.

> **More Info**   For more information about the tools you can use with Shutdown Event Tracker, see *http://www.microsoft.com/resources/documentation/WindowsServ/2003/all/techref/en-us/Default.asp?url=/Resources/Documentation/windowsserv/2003/all/techref/en-us/w2k3tr_set_tools.asp.*

Shutdown Event Tracker interacts with the registry in the following ways:

- The expected shutdown dialog box reads custom shutdown reasons from the registry.

- Remote Shutdown (Shutdown.exe) reads custom shutdown reasons from the registry. It also writes bulk annotations to the registry and deletes keys from the registry.

- Custom Reason Editor (CustReasonEdit.exe) writes custom shutdown reasons to the registry.

- The unexpected shutdown dialog box reads from the registry to determine if the previous shutdown was unexpected.

- The Event Log service writes the Shutdown Event Tracker heartbeat to the registry and then deletes it just before a normal shutdown occurs. Upon restarting, it verifies whether the heartbeat is present and, if so, writes the DirtyShutdown key to the registry. Heartbeat is a time stamp interval, written once a minute, that indicates that Shutdown Event Tracker is still enabled.

The following list describes the values that Shutdown Event Tracker uses. (Unless otherwise noted, these values are in HKLM\SOFTWARE\Microsoft\Windows\CurrentVersion\Reliability.)

- **BugcheckString.**   This value contains the bug check string information that is used to fill in the unexpected shutdown dialog box comment field (which appears at logon after an unexpected shutdown) if the previous shutdown was caused by a system failure (also know as a system crash).

- **DirtyShutdown.**   This value is set during event log startup. It indicates whether a previous shutdown was expected.

- **LastAliveStamp.**   This value is cleared during shutdown. It indicates the date and time of the previous unexpected shutdown if it is present during startup.

■ **ReliabilityGUID.**   This value enables a GUID to be written to the system state data file in order to uniquely identify the computer this file came from. It is not possible to physically identify the computer using this GUID, but it is possible to see how many different computers sent files and how many distinct reports were submitted by each computer. If the GUID is deleted from the registry, a new GUID is generated when a new system state data (*.xml*) file is created in the %SystemRoot%\System32\LogFiles\Shutdown\ directory at the time of an unplanned shutdown.

■ **ShutdownIgnorePredefinedReasons.**   This value prevents the predefined or built-in shutdown reasons from being displayed. If at least one custom reason is defined in the registry and this key is set to `0x01`, the built-in reasons are not displayed.

■ **TimeStampInterval.**   This value defines how often `LastAliveStamp` (or heart-beat) is written to the registry. By default, it is written every minute in Windows Server 2003.

■ **UserDefined.**   This subkey contains custom reasons stored as values. To add custom reasons, the user must define one value for each reason. Each reason has a major and minor code that uniquely identifies the reason.

> **More Info**   For more information about Custom Reason Editor, see the *Microsoft Windows Resource Kit* Tools Read Me.

■ **ShutdownReasonUI.**   Shutdown Event Tracker references the Group Policy key for this value first. If the Group Policy key is not present, then this key can be configured as `0x00` (off) or `0x01` (on). If the Group Policy key is not present and this key is invalid or missing, then Shutdown Event Tracker is off.

> **Note**   You can use Group Policy to manage Shutdown Event Tracker. Its Group Policy settings are in Computer Configuration\Administrative Templates\System.

Part II
Registry in Management

Managing the registry is easier when you are armed with the right tools. This part describes those tools. You learn about registry-based policies and how to use them to manage settings in the registry. You learn how to track down registry settings and write scripts to change them. You also learn about registry security.

Whereas the first part of this book was for both power users and IT professionals, this part is aimed more toward IT professionals. Power users can still benefit from giving this part a thorough read, though, because some of the better customizations are actually policies, and customizing Microsoft Windows XP and Windows Server 2003 is better done through scripts. Still, I give this part an IT slant because these customizations are valuable IT tools.

Chapter 7

Using Registry-Based Policy

IT professionals use Group Policy to manage users' desktop environments. First introduced in Microsoft Windows 2000, Group Policy enables you to dramatically reduce the cost of deploying and managing desktops. This involves deploying standard desktop configurations rather than wasting money to support individual users. Using Group Policy in this way enforces corporate standards and configures users' computers, freeing them from this task and enabling them to do their jobs. For example, you enhance productivity by configuring users' applications, data, and settings so that they follow users regardless of where users log on to the network. Windows XP and Microsoft Windows Server 2003 (Windows) extend Group Policy with new settings, new features, and significant improvements.

In this chapter, I focus on local registry-based policies. Group Policy in the enterprise is a big subject, and one that requires familiarity with Active Directory. At the end of this chapter, however, you'll find a list of more resources that are useful for learning more about both Active Directory and Group Policy. Rather than teaching you about sites, domains, and organizational units (OUs), which are peripherally related to the Windows registry, I show you how to implement registry-based policies in a local Group Policy object. This information directly applies to network Group Policy. Because of the focus of this book—more or less quick and easy tricks for the IT professional—I also show you how to define your own policies and even deploy Windows policies on networks that aren't based on Active Directory, including Microsoft Windows NT and Novell Netware.

Whether you're an IT professional or a power user, this chapter is for you. If you're an IT professional, I assume that you understand the key Active Directory and Group Policy concepts. If you're not an IT professional, I don't anticipate that you will try to use this information in an enterprise environment, so this information is fairly complete. For example, power users often define local policies to customize their computers, and this doesn't require a lot of information about Active Directory or policy inheritance. In fact, some of the most popular and interesting customizations are available in Group Policy already, so you don't need to hack the registry at all.

Editing Local Policies

Policies are different from preferences, and comparing the two helps you better understand how Windows uses policies. Users set preferences, such as their desktop wallpaper, and they can change preferences any time. Administrators set policies, such as the location of the My Documents folder, and these policies take precedence over the equivalent user preference. Windows stores policies in the registry separately from user preferences. If a policy exists, the operating system uses the setting specified by that policy. If a policy doesn't exist, the operating system uses the user's preference. In the absence of a user preference, the operating system uses a default setting. The important thing to know is that a policy does not change the equivalent user preference, and if they coexist, then the policy takes precedence. Also, if the administrator removes the policy, the user's preference is once again used. In other words, Group Policy does not *tattoo* the registry. (See the sidebar "Tattoos on the Registry," later in this chapter.) Table 7-1 summarizes this behavior.

Table 7-1   Policies Compared to Preferences

Policy defined?	Preference defined?	Behavior
No	No	Default
No	Yes	Preference configures
Yes	No	Policy configures
Yes	Yes	Policy configures, ignoring the preference

Windows combines policies together in a *Group Policy Object* (GPO). In Active Directory, there are multiple GPOs, which apply to users and computers, depending on where they are in the directory. In Windows, you have only one GPO, and that's the *local GPO*. Settings in this GPO apply to the local computer and to every user who logs on to it. Because the local GPO is the first GPO that Windows applies when it starts and when users log on to it, *network GPOs* can overwrite settings in it. For example, if you define a local policy that enables you to install Windows Installer–based (.msi) programs with elevated privileges, but the network administrator sets a network policy that disallows that, then the network policy takes precedence, and you won't be able to install these programs unless you're a local administrator for that computer. If there is no network policy to prevent it, you can install Windows Installer–based programs regardless of the group in which your account is a member.

> **Note**   If you edit a policy setting without using Group Policy Editor (such as by using Registry Editor), you won't see that policy setting in the Group Policy Editor. You must manually change or remove the setting.

GPOs include settings for both computer configurations and user configurations, so GPOs contain branches for each:

- **Computer Configuration.**   These are per-computer policy settings that specify operating system behavior, desktop behavior, security settings, computer startup and shutdown scripts, computer-assigned applications, and application settings. Windows applies per-computer policies both when the operating system starts and at regular intervals.

- **User Configuration.**   These are per-user policy settings that specify operating system behavior, desktop settings, security settings, assigned and published applications, folder redirection settings, user logon and logoff scripts, and application settings. Windows applies per-user policies both when the user logs on to the computer and at regular intervals.

You edit the local GPO using Group Policy Editor, shown in Figure 7-1. To open Group Policy Editor, type **gpedit.msc** in the Run dialog box. The left and right panes that you see in the editor are similar to those in Registry Editor (Regedit), so I won't explain how to use them here. Immediately under Local Computer Policy, you see Computer Configuration and User Configuration. Computer Configuration contains per-computer policies, and User Configuration contains per-user policies. Registry-based policies, this chapter's focus, are in Administrative Templates under both branches.

Typing **gpedit.msc** in the Run dialog box is the quickest way to load the local computer's GPO, but you can create your own console in Microsoft Management Console (MMC) to edit a remote computer's GPO. Editing local policies on a remote computer is useful if your organization isn't using Active Directory, but it's too cumbersome to use as a general management tool, so I'd use it only in relevant scenarios:

1. In the Run dialog box, type **mmc**, and press ENTER.

2. On the File menu, click Add/Remove Snap-In.

3. In the Add/Remove Snap-In dialog box, on the Standalone tab, click Add.

4. In the Add Standalone Snap-in dialog box, select Group Policy Object Editor, and then click Add.

5. In the Select Group Policy Object dialog box, click Browse. In the Browse For A Group Policy Object dialog box, on the Computers tab, select the Another Computer option, type the remote computer's name in the space provided, and then click OK.

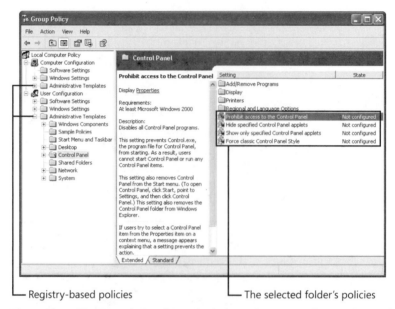

— Registry-based policies   — The selected folder's policies

Figure 7-1 The Extended and Standard view tabs are new for Windows. Click the Extended view tab to display help for the selected policy setting.

> **Note** Windows doesn't allow you to specify security settings in a remote computer's local GPO. Thus, when you open Security Settings for a remote computer, you don't see these settings. However, even though you can't apply these settings to remote computers, you can include them in a disk image for deployment, which you learn more about in the section "Deploying Registry-Based Policy," later in this chapter.

Tattoos on the Registry

Group Policy and System Policy, policies used by versions of Windows earlier than Windows 2000, handle changes differently from each other. Windows automatically removes a GPO's settings from the registry when the GPO no longer applies to the user or computer. Also, Group Policy doesn't overwrite users' preferences. So if you delete a GPO from Active Directory, Windows removes that GPO's settings from the registry and reverts back to following users' preferences. Likewise, if you remove an individual policy from a GPO, Windows removes that setting from the registry and restores users' existing preferences. Group Policy doesn't make permanent, irreversible changes to the registry.

System Policy does make permanent, irreversible changes to the registry, though. In other words, it *tattoos* the registry. When you remove System Policy, all the policies that it contained remain in the registry. The only way to restore users' preferences, assuming that these policies don't overwrite their preferences, is to manually remove the policy from the registry or explicitly change the setting in System Policy. This is one of the scenarios you learn to grapple with in Chapter 18, "Fixing Common IT Problems." One of the nastier incarnations of this behavior can occur when you upgrade from an earlier version of Windows to Windows XP or Windows Server 2003. When you upgrade, policies in the registry are permanent, so you must manually remove them from the registry; Windows doesn't remove them automatically.

Group Policy Extensions

Group Policy has several extensions that you can use to configure GPOs. In fact, each of the different nodes that you see in Group Policy Editor is an extension. By default, the editor loads all the available extensions when you start it. Computer Configuration and User Configuration contain different extensions, and you see more extensions when you're editing a network GPO in Active Directory than you see when you're editing a local GPO. The following list summarizes some of the extensions that Group Policy provides in a local GPO. (Network GPOs provide more.)

- **Scripts.**   You can assign to users scripts that run when they log on to or log off Windows. You can assign to computers scripts that run when Windows starts and when it shuts down. You see this extension in the Windows Settings folder.

- **Security Settings.**   You can manage security settings, including password, audit, and lockout policies. You can also manage user rights and restrict the applications that users can run. You see this extension in the Windows Settings folder.

- **Administrative Templates.**   Group Policy creates a file containing registry settings that are written to HKCU or HKLM in the registry. Windows loads settings from this file as the operating system starts and when users log on to the computer. These are registry-based policies.

Registry-Based Policy

Registry-based policies and *administrative policies* are two names for the same thing. They're registry settings that overwrite users' preferences, and there are good reasons that users can't change them, which you'll learn about in this section. Other policies, including security settings, might or might not be registry settings. In Group Policy Editor, you find registry-based policies in the Administrative Templates folder under Computer Configuration and User Configuration.

Figure 7-2 shows the workflow of using registry-based policies. Administrators use Group Policy Editor, which you saw in Figure 7-1, to define policies. *Administrative templates*, files with the *.adm* extension, define the policies that administrators can set. Administrative templates and *policy templates* are the same thing, and you frequently see these referred to as *ADM files*. These templates describe the user interface for collecting settings from the administrator and the locations of these settings in the registry. When the administrator defines policies, the editor stores them in a file called Registry.pol. Windows loads the settings contained in Registry.pol when the operating system starts, when users log on, and at regular intervals. The next section, "Group Policy Storage," describes where in the registry Windows stores policies and where you find Registry.pol.

The following extensions work together to implement registry-based policy:

■ The Administrative Templates extension, which you use to edit policy settings. This extension is the Administrative Templates folder in Group Policy Editor. It creates the Registry.pol file based on settings that the administrator defines.

■ A built-in registry client-side extension (available only in Windows 2000 or later), which processes policies and creates their corresponding values in the registry. Although the client-side extension is responsible for reading settings from Registry.pol and writing them to the registry, Windows and other applications must look for and use these settings to give them meaning.

Windows comes with administrative templates that define all the policies that the operating system supports. If you want to use policies for an application, such as one in Microsoft Office 2003 Editions, you must load the administrative templates for it. In fact, the *Microsoft Office 2003 Editions Resource Kit* comes with many administrative templates that help IT professionals better manage the entire productivity suite. Windows provides the following administrative templates:

■ **System.adm.**   Core settings and primary template file, defining most of the settings that you see in Administrative Templates

■ **Wmplayer.adm.**   Windows Media settings

■ **Conf.adm.**   NetMeeting conferencing software

■ **Inetres.adm.**   Microsoft Internet Explorer

All registry-based policies are set to one of three states: Enabled, Disabled, or Not Configured. Figure 7-3 shows these settings on a sample policy. *Enabled* explicitly turns on the setting by adding the setting to the registry with a value of **0x01**. *Disabled* explicitly turns off the setting by adding the setting to the registry with a value of **0x00** (or removing the value altogether). The *Not Configured* option removes the setting from the registry altogether, which then yields to the user's preference. Many policies collect additional settings, as shown in the figure.

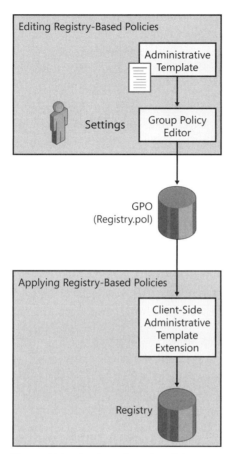

Figure 7-2   Registry-based policies start with administrative templates, which define the settings that are available and the location where they are stored in the registry.

Figure 7-3   Each policy has three states, Enabled, Disabled, or Not Configured, and some policies collect additional information.

When setting a policy, pay particular attention to the explanation to ensure that you get the result that you want. Some policies are positive, so enabling the policies turns on the features. Other policies are negative, however, so turning on those policies actually disables those features. To make things more confusing, outside of Windows, you frequently see policies that you have to enable, and then you have to turn the setting on or off. In other words, to turn on a setting, you have to enable the policy and then select or clear a second check box to turn the setting on or off. The Office 2003 Editions policy templates are notorious for this extra level of indirection. All this just illustrates that you have to pay close attention to the names of policies when setting them. Read their names out loud, prefixing the sentences with the words "enable" or "disable"—just to be sure.

Group Policy Storage

Where does Windows store policies in the registry and on the disk? The branch \Software\Policies is the preferred branch for storing registry-based policies. In HKLM, this branch contains per-computer policies, and in HKCU, this branch contains per-user policies. Another branch, inherited from earlier versions of Windows, is \Software\Microsoft\Windows\CurrentVersion\Policies. Policies in this branch tend to tattoo the registry, which means they make permanent changes to the registry; you must explicitly change these policies. Access control lists (ACLs) prevent users from changing these keys and thus the policies that they enforce. The Users and Power Users local groups do not have permission to change values in these keys, but an administrator can overwrite these keys directly to change the policy.

Now that we've covered the location of policies in the registry, we'll move on to covering their location in the file system. The local GPO is in %SystemRoot%\System32\GroupPolicy. This is a super-hidden folder. To show it in Windows Explorer, click Tools, Folder Options; on the View tab of the Folder Options dialog box, select the Show Hidden Files And Folders option, and then clear the Hide Protected Operating System Files check box. This folder contains the following subfolders and files. (Our focus is the file Registry.pol.)

- **\Adm.**   Contains all the ADM files for the local GPO.
- **\User.**   Includes the file Registry.pol, which contains registry-based policies for users. When users log on to the computer, Windows applies these to HKCU.
- **\User\Scripts.**   Contains the local GPO's per-user scripts. The scripts in \Logon run when users log on to Windows, and the scripts in \Logoff run when they log off the operating system.
- **\Machine.**   Includes Registry.pol, which contains registry-based policies for the computer. When Windows starts, it applies these settings to HKLM.

- **\Machine\Scripts.**   Contains the local GPO's per-computer scripts. The scripts in \Startup run when Windows starts, and the scripts in \Shutdown run when the operating system shuts down.

> **Tip**   You can copy the %SystemRoot%\System32\GroupPolicy folder from one computer to another to replicate the local policies it contains. Test before using this tip in a production environment.

If you're familiar with System Policy and the file Ntconfig.pol, you're probably wondering whether the files Registry.pol and Ntconfig.pol use similar formats. They don't. Both are binary files, but Registry.pol is much simpler. It contains a simple list of settings, including their value names, type, and data, in a binary format. Ntconfig.pol is actually a registry hive file that you can load and browse in Regedit. Unfortunately, you can't do the same with Registry.pol.

> **Note**   Domain GPOs are more complicated than local GPOs are. Active Directory stores policies in *Server*\Sysvol*Domain*\Policies, where *Server* is the name of the domain controller, Sysvol is a share name, and *Domain* is the name of the domain. Each GPO is in a subfolder, and the name of the subfolder is the GPO's GUID. (See Chapter 1, "Learning the Basics.") The structure of each GPO's subfolder is similar to the structure of the local GPO described in this chapter. In the domain GPO, though, the \User and \Machine folders have additional subfolders, and the various Group Policy extensions create these.

Extending Registry-Based Policy

You can extend registry-based policy by customizing existing administrative templates or by creating new ones. Windows provides administrative templates for its policies. Other applications, such as Office 2003 Editions, also provide templates. When you install the *Microsoft Office 2003 Editions Resource Kit*, it adds the Office 2003 Editions policy templates to %SystemRoot%\Inf. You should never customize these templates. You might want to create your own templates that extend registry-based policy, though.

First, the caveats: extending registry-based policy is generally something that developers do to give administrators more control over users' applications. Remember that a registry-based policy requires developers to add code that reads policies and enforces those settings to their applications. If developers added policies to their code, they almost certainly created policy templates for them, so you don't have to. On the other hand, if no code enforces a policy setting, creating an administrative template for it is useless. It almost sounds like extending registry-based policy is futile, right? But there are still times when it's useful, including times when it's extremely valuable:

- **Repairing broken policies.**   I don't run across broken policies often, but when I do, the only way to fix them is to create a custom template for them. For example, in the Windows XP beta, the screen saver policy stored the timeout period incorrectly in the registry. Creating a custom template was my simple fix to this.

- **Creating custom administrative templates.**   Windows supports hundreds of policies, as does Office 2003 Editions. Hunting for policies is sometimes frustrating. You can create a custom administrative template that assembles in one place all the policies you're deploying, making the job a bit easier. You can also rephrase the language of a policy with descriptions that are easier to understand.

- **Customizing Windows.**   Many of the registry settings that you can use to customize Windows have no user interface. You can build a user interface for them by creating an administrative template and then changing those settings with Group Policy Editor. For power users, this is a great reason to master this topic. This method goes against one of the primary features of Group Policy, however, because settings that you change outside the normal policy branches in the registry will tattoo the registry.

You can use any text editor to create an administrative template. Administrative templates have a language of their own, and you learn about that language in the remainder of this section. Group Policy Editor is very good at displaying intuitive error messages when a template file contains an error, giving you the line number, the erroneous keyword, and more information. In summary, here's how to use an administrative template:

1. Using the language that you learn about in this chapter, create an administrative template. The template file is a text file with the *.adm* extension.

2. Load the template file into Group Policy Editor as you learn to do later in this chapter in the section "Deploying Registry-Based Policy."

3. Edit the settings that the administrative template defines.

The following listing is a sample administrative template that doesn't do much, but does illustrate what a template file looks like. Figure 7-4 shows what this template looks like in Group Policy Editor. The figure's annotations show some of the keywords that are responsible for different portions of a policy. For example, the keyword EXPLAIN is responsible for displaying the policy's description that you see in the figure. Throughout the remainder of this section, you'll see dozens more examples that give you the building blocks for creating your own administrative templates. Take these building blocks and copy them into your file to get started right away.

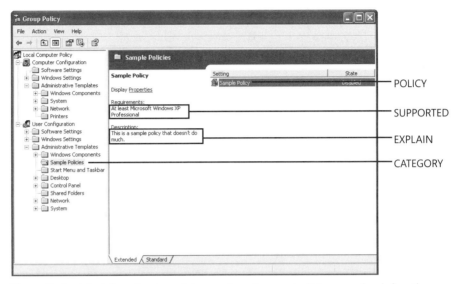

Figure 7-4   Administrative templates, such as the one in this example, define the user interface for collecting settings that the editor stores in the file Registry.pol.

Listing 7-1   example.adm

```
CLASS USER

CATEGORY "Sample Policies"
  #if version >= 4
    EXPLAIN "These are sample policies that don't do anything."
  #endif

  POLICY "Sample Policy"
    #if version >= 4
      SUPPORTED "At least Microsoft Windows XP Professional"
    #endif
    EXPLAIN "This is a sample policy that doesn't do much."
    KEYNAME "Software\Policies"
    VALUENAME Sample
    VALUEON NUMERIC 1
    VALUEOFF NUMERIC 0
  END POLICY

END CATEGORY
```

> **Note**   The statements #if and #endif enclose statements that work with only certain versions of System Policy or Group Policy. Using these statements, the developer can write one administrative template that works with different versions of Windows, including Windows NT, Windows 2000, Windows Server 2003, and Windows XP. System Policy in Windows NT is version 2. Windows 2000 is version 3. Windows XP Service Pack 1 (SP1) is version 4. Windows XP SP2 and Windows Server 2003 are version 5. Thus, to make sure that Group Policy Editor in Windows 2000 ignores keywords that only Windows XP supports, the developer encloses those keywords between #if version >= 4 and #endif. To ensure that only System Policy Editor in Windows NT sees a block of keywords, enclose them between #if version = 2 and #endif. These conditional statements show that Microsoft was thinking far into the future, even back in the old days.

Comments

Comments are useful and necessary for documenting the contents of your policy templates. There are two different ways to add comments to template files. First, you can precede the comment with a semicolon (;) or with two forward slashes (//). Second, you can place comments at the end of any valid line. You see examples of comments throughout this chapter; I've documented each example that uses them. Each line in the following example is a valid comment. I prefer using // for comments.

Listing 7-2   example.adm

```
; This is a comment
// This is also a comment
CLASS USER // Per-user settings
CLASS MACHINE; Per-computer settings
```

Strings

When creating a quick and easy template file that you'll only use once, don't feel badly about hard-coding strings, adding the string where you need it and then repeating the same string as often as necessary. The listing you saw earlier, in the section "Extending Registry-Based Policy," uses hard-coded strings. If you're using enterprise-class template files, or if you're managing the files over time, use string variables; this makes it easier to maintain template files that use the same strings more than once. More importantly, it makes localization of template files far easier and much less error-prone.

Define strings at the end of your template file in the [strings] section. The format of each string is name="string". You must enclose the string in double quotation marks. To use string variables in your template file, use the format !!name. Each time that Group Policy Editor sees !!name, it substitutes the string for the name. Incidentally, the !! makes it easy to search template files for strings—just search the file for the double exclamation marks. The following listing is an example of how strings and string variables are used in a template file:

Listing 7-3 example.adm

```
POLICY !!Sample                           // Defined in [strings] section
  SUPPORTED "At least Microsoft Windows XP" // Hard-coded string
  EXPLAIN !!Sample_Explain                 // Defined in [strings] section

...

[strings]
Sample="Sample Policy"
Sample_Explain="This sample policy doesn't do much of anything."
```

> **Note**   In this chapter, for clarity, I tend not to use string variables. Avoiding string variables prevents you from having to look up each string as you're wading through the listings. Keep in mind that you'll want to use string variables if you plan on localizing your files.

CLASS

The first entry in a template file is the keyword CLASS. It defines whether the policies following it are per-user or per-computer; that is, it specifies whether you see the policy in User Configuration or Computer Configuration. You can use multiple CLASS keywords in a template file. When the Windows client-side extensions process the file, they merge the settings defined in the CLASS USER sections and merge the settings defined in the CLASS MACHINE sections. Then they load the settings defined in the CLASS USER sections in HKCU and the settings defined in the CLASS MACHINE sections in HKLM.

Syntax

CLASS *Name*

Name	This must be MACHINE or USER. MACHINE specifies that the policies following the CLASS keyword are per-computer policies, and USER specifies that the policies following the keyword are per-user policies. This keyword persists until you change it using additional CLASS keywords.

Example

Listing 7-4 example.adm

```
CLASS MACHINE

// Policies here are per-computer policies

CLASS USER

// Policies here are per-user policies

CLASS MACHINE

// Policies here are per-computer policies
```

CATEGORY

After using the keyword CLASS to define whether your policy will appear under the Computer Settings branch or the User Settings branch of Group Policy Editor, use the keyword CATEGORY to create subfolders in that branch. The editor displays your settings in that folder. Just as you can create subkeys within keys in the registry, you can create subcategories within categories by nesting the keyword CATEGORY. Just keep in mind that all that the keyword CATEGORY does is create folders.

Categories can include zero or more policies. Categories that contain no policies usually contain one or more subcategories. You use the keyword KEYNAME, which you learn about in the next section, to define a registry key in which Group Policy Editor creates settings for that category. Using the keyword KEYNAME here is optional if you're defining the key elsewhere. You end a category with END CATEGORY.

Syntax

```
CATEGORY Name
   KEYNAME Subkey
   Policies


END CATEGORY
```

Name	This is the folder name that you want to see in Group Policy Editor. Use a string variable or a string enclosed in quotes.
Subkey	This is an optional subkey of HKLM or HKCU that you can use for the category. Do not include either root key in the path, though, because the preceding keyword, CLASS, specifies which of these root keys to use. If you specify a subkey, all subcategories, policies, and parts will use it unless they specifically provide subkeys of their own. Enclose in double quotes names that contain spaces.

Example

Listing 7-5   example.adm

```
CLASS USER // Settings are per-user in HKCU

CATEGORY "Desktop Settings"
  KEYNAME "Software\Policies\System"

  // Add policies for the Desktop Settings category here

  CATEGORY "Custom Application Settings"
    KEYNAME "Software\Policies\CustomApps"

    // Add policies for the custom applications subcategory here

  END CATEGORY
END CATEGORY
```

Keywords

The valid keywords you can use within a CATEGORY section are the following ones:

- CATEGORY
- END
- KEYNAME
- POLICY

KEYNAME

Use the keyword KEYNAME within a category to define which subkey of HKCU or HKLM (depending on the CLASS keyword) contains the value you're changing. Do not include a root key in the path because the keyword CLASS defines it. If the name contains spaces, you must enclose the string in double quotation marks. The example in the preceding section, "CATEGORY," shows how to use the keyword KEYNAME.

POLICY

Use the keyword POLICY to define a policy that the administrator can change. The policy editor displays the policy and its controls in a dialog box that the administrator uses to change the policy's state and settings. You can include multiple POLICY keywords in a single category, but you don't need to include the keyword KEYNAME before each keyword POLICY. The most recent keyword KEYNAME applies for each policy. You end a policy with END POLICY.

Each policy contains a VALUENAME keyword to associate a registry value with it. By default, the policy editor assumes it's a REG_DWORD value and stores 0x01 in it when you enable the policy. The policy editor also removes the value when you disable the policy. You must use the keywords VALUEON and VALUEOFF if you don't want the editor to remove the value when you disable the policy. You don't have to use any keywords other than VALUENAME to get this behavior. However, you can specify additional options, such as drop-down list boxes, check boxes, text boxes, and more, by including optional PART keywords. You see these controls in the bottom part of the policy's dialog box. (See Figure 7-3.)

Syntax

```
POLICY Name
[KEYNAME Subkey]
EXPLAIN Help
VALUENAME Value

   [Parts]

END POLICY
```

Name	This is the name of the policy as you want to see it in Group Policy Editor. Use a short, descriptive name.
Subkey	This is an optional subkey of HKLM or HKCU to use for the category. Do not include either root key in the path, though, because the preceding keyword CLASS specifies which of these root keys to use. If you specify a subkey, all subcategories, policies, and parts use it unless they specifically provide a subkey of their own. Enclose names that contain spaces in double quotes.
Help	This is the string that Group Policy Editor displays on the Explain tab and on the Extended tab of the policy's dialog box.
Value	This is the registry value to modify. Enabling the policy sets the REG_DWORD value to 0x01. Select the Not Configured option (disable the policy), and the policy editor removes the value from the registry. To specify values other than the default 0x01, use the keywords VALUEON and VALUEOFF directly following the keyword VALUENAME: VALUEON [NUMERIC] *Enabled* VALUEOFF [NUMERIC] *Disabled* When you use these keywords, the policy editor sets the registry value to *Enabled* when you enable the policy and sets the value to *Disabled* when you disable the policy. The default value type is REG_SZ, but you can change it to REG_DWORD by prefixing the value with the keyword NUMERIC. Regardless, setting the policy to Not Configured removes the value altogether.

Example

Listing 7-6   example.adm

```
CLASS MACHINE

CATEGORY "Disk Quotas"

  KEYNAME "Software\Policies\MS\DiskQuota"
  POLICY "Enable disk quotas"
    EXPLAIN "Enables and disables disk quotas management."
    VALUENAME "Enable"
    VALUEON NUMERIC 1
    VALUEOFF NUMERIC 0
  END POLICY

END CATEGORY
```

Keywords

The valid keywords within a POLICY section include the following:

- ACTIONLISTOFF

- ACTIONLISTON

- END

- KEYNAME

■ PART

■ VALUENAME

■ VALUEOFF

■ VALUEON

■ HELP

■ POLICY

Note Additional keywords are available for policies, but they are for developers creating policy extensions. For example, CLIENTEXT associates a client-side extension with a policy via the extension's GUID. I'm not covering these additional keywords because they don't fit our purposes here.

EXPLAIN

The keyword EXPLAIN provides help text for a specific policy. In Windows 2000, Windows XP, and Windows Server 2003, each policy's dialog box includes an Explain tab, which provides details about the policy settings. You also see this help text on the Extended tab of the editor's right pane in Windows XP and Windows Server 2003. Each policy you create for Windows 2000, Windows XP, and Windows Server 2003 should contain one EXPLAIN keyword followed by a full description of the policy and its settings. Although I don't show this in my examples (because I'm trying to keep them simple), you should enclose this keyword between #if version >=3 and #endif to prevent earlier versions of the policy editor from choking on these keywords, as shown in Listing 7-7.

Listing 7-7   example.adm

```
#if version >= 3
  EXPLAIN "Enables and disables disk quotas management."
#endif
```

VALUENAME

The keyword VALUENAME identifies the registry value that the policy editor modifies when you enable or disable the policy. The syntax is VALUENAME *Name*. You saw an example of this keyword earlier in this chapter in the section "POLICY." Unless you set the keywords VALUEON and VALUEOFF, described in the next section, the policy editor creates the policy as a REG_DWORD value:

■ **Enabled.**   Sets the value to 0x01

■ **Disabled.**   Removes the value

■ **Not Configured.**   Removes the value

The keywords VALUENAME, VALUEON, and VALUEOFF describe the value that enables and disables the policy. If you want to define additional settings that enable you to collect additional values to refine the policy, you must use the keyword PART. Settings in a PART section are in the bottom part of the policy's dialog box.

VALUEON and VALUEOFF

You can use the VALUEON and VALUEOFF keywords to write specific values based on the state of the policy. The section "POLICY" contains an example of how these keywords are used. The syntaxes are VALUEON [NUMERIC] *Enabled* and VALUEOFF [NUMERIC] *Disabled*. By default, the policy editor creates the value as a REG_SZ value; if you want the policy editor to create the value as a REG_DWORD value, prefix it with the NUMERIC keyword. The following are examples of both:

```
VALUEON 0          // Created as a REG_SZ value containing "0"
VALUEOFF NUMERIC 1 // Created as a REG_DWORD value containing 0x01
```

ACTIONLIST

The keyword ACTIONLIST enables you to group settings together. Think of it as a list of values that you want the policy editor to change when you change a policy. The following two variants of the keyword ACTIONLIST are the most commonly used ones:

- ■ **ACTIONLISTON.**   A list of values to change when the policy is enabled
- ■ **ACTIONLISTOFF.**   A list of values to change when the policy is disabled

Syntax

```
ACTIONLIST
  [KEYNAME subkey]
  VALUENAME value
  VALUE Data
END ACTIONLIST
```

Subkey	This is an optional subkey of HKLM or HKCU to use for the category. Do not include either root key in the path, though, because the preceding keyword CLASS specifies which of these root keys to use. If you specify a subkey, all subcategories, policies, and parts use it unless they specifically provide a subkey of their own. Enclose names that contain spaces in double quotes.
Value	This is the registry value to modify. Enabling the policy sets the REG_DWORD value to 0x01. Select the Not Configured option, and the policy editor removes the value from the registry. To specify values other than the default 0x00 and 0x01, use the keyword VALUE.
Data	This is the data to which you want to set the value. The default value type is REG_SZ, but you can change it to REG_DWORD by prefixing the value with the keyword NUMERIC. If you follow the keyword VALUE with the keyword DELETE (VALUE DELETE), policy editor removes the value from the registry. Regardless, setting the policy to Not Configured removes the value altogether.

Example

Listing 7-8   example.adm

```
POLICY "Sample Action List"
  EXPLAIN "This illustrates action lists"
  ACTIONLISTON
    VALUENAME Sample1 VALUE 1
    VALUENAME Sample2 VALUE 1
  END ACTIONLISTON

  ACTIONLISTOFF
    VALUENAME Sample1 VALUE 0
    VALUENAME Sample2 VALUE 0
  END ACTIONLISTOFF
END POLICY
```

PART

The keyword **PART** enables you to specify various options, including drop-down lists, text boxes, and check boxes, in the lower part of a policy's dialog box. Figure 7-5 shows an example of the settings that you want to collect in addition to enabling or disabling the policy. For simple policies that you only need to enable or disable, you won't need to use this keyword. In fact, only a relative handful of the policies in Windows use the keyword **PART** at all.

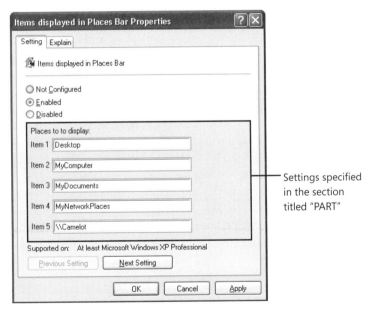

Figure 7-5   Use the PART keyword to collect additional data that further refines the policy.

You begin a part with the keyword **PART** and end it with **END PART**. The syntax of the keyword **PART** is **PART** *Name Type*. *Name* is the name of the part, and *Type* is the type of the part. Each policy can contain multiple **PART** keywords, and the policy editor displays them in the dialog box using the same order that they had in the administrative template. This section gives you the overall syntax of the keyword PART, and the sections following this one describe how to create the different types of parts.

Syntax

```
PART Name Type

   Keywords

   [KEYNAME Subkey]
   [DEFAULT Default]
   VALUENAME Name
END PART
```

Name	This specifies the name of the setting as you want to see it in the policy's dialog box. Enclose the name in double quotes if it contains spaces. This is the setting's prompt.
Type	This can be one of the following types: ■ **CHECKBOX.** Displays a check box. The REG_DWORD value is 0x01 if you select the check box or 0x00 if you clear it. ■ **COMBOBOX.** Displays a combo box. ■ **DROPDOWNLIST.** Displays a combo box with a drop-down list. The user can choose only one of the items in the list. ■ **EDITTEXT.** Displays a text box that accepts alphanumeric input. The value is either REG_SZ or REG_EXPAND_SZ. ■ **LISTBOX.** Displays a list box with Add and Remove buttons. This is the only type that can be used to manage multiple values in one key. ■ **NUMERIC.** Displays a text box with an optional spin box control that accepts a numeric value. The value is a REG_DWORD value. ■ **TEXT.** Displays a line of static text. It stores no data in the registry and is useful for adding help to the dialog box.
Keywords	This information is specific to each type of part. See the sections following this for more information about these keywords.
Subkey	This is an optional subkey of HKLM or HKCU to use for the category. Do not include either root key in the path, though, because the preceding keyword CLASS specifies which of these root keys to use. If you specify a subkey, all subcategories, policies, and parts use it unless they specifically provide a subkey of their own. Enclose names that contain spaces in double quotes.
Default	This is the default value for the part. When you enable the policy, the policy editor fills the control with the default value. Use a default value that's appropriate for the part's type.
Value	This is the registry value to modify. The value type and data depend entirely on the part's type.

Example

Listing 7-9   example.adm

```
POLICY "Sample Part"
  EXPLAIN "This illustrates parts"
  KEYNAME "Software\Policies"
  POLICY "Sample Policy"
    EXPLAIN "This is a sample policy including parts."
    VALUENAME "Sample"
    PART test EDITTEXT
      DEFAULT "This is the default text"
      VALUENAME Sample
    END PART
END POLICY
```

Keywords

The valid keywords within a PART section are the following ones:

- CHECKBOX

- COMBOBOX

- DROPDOWNLIST

- EDITTEXT

- END

- LISTBOX

- NUMERIC

- PART

- TEXT

CHECKBOX

The keyword CHECKBOX displays a check box. In the registry, it's a REG_SZ value. By default, the check box is cleared, and the settings it writes to the registry for each of its states are as follows:

- **Checked.**   Writes 1 to the REG_SZ value

- **Cleared.**   Writes 0 to the REG_SZ value

Include the keyword DEFCHECKED within the part if you want the check box selected by default. Otherwise, the check box is cleared by default.

Syntax

```
PART Name CHECKBOX
  DEFCHECKED
  VALUENAME Value
END PART
```

Name	This specifies the name of the setting as you want to see it in the policy's dialog box. Enclose the name in double quotes if it contains spaces. You see the name next to the check box.
Value	This is the registry value to modify. Enabling the policy sets the REG_SZ value to 1. Set the Not Configured option, and the policy editor removes the value from the registry. To specify values other than the default 0 and 1, use the keywords VALUEON and VALUEOFF following the keyword VALUENAME: VALUEON [NUMERIC] *Enabled* VALUEOFF [NUMERIC] *Disabled* When you use these keywords, the policy editor sets the registry value to *Enabled* when you enable the policy, and it sets the value to *Disabled* when you disable the policy. The default value type is REG_SZ, but you can change it to REG_DWORD by prefixing the value with the keyword NUMERIC. Regardless, setting the policy to Not Configured removes the value altogether. You can also use the keywords ACTIONLISTON and ACTIONLISTOFF to associate multiple values with a check box.

Example

Listing 7-10   example.adm

```
CLASS USER

CATEGORY "Sample Policies"
  EXPLAIN "These are sample policies that illustrate parts."

  POLICY "Sample Policy"
    SUPPORTED "At least Microsoft Windows XP Professional"

    EXPLAIN "This is a sample policy that illustrates a part."
    KEYNAME "Software\Policies"

    PART Sample1 CHECKBOX
      VALUENAME Sample1
    END PART

    PART Sample2 CHECKBOX
      DEFCHECKED
      VALUENAME Sample2
      VALUEON NUMERIC 11
      VALUEOFF NUMERIC 12
    END PART

  END POLICY

END CATEGORY
```

Keywords

The valid keywords within a CHECKBOX section include the following:

- ACTIONLISTOFF
- ACTIONLISTON
- DEFCHECKED
- END
- KEYNAME
- VALUENAME
- VALUEOFF
- VALUEON

COMBOBOX

The keyword COMBOBOX adds a combo box to the policy's dialog box. It has one additional keyword you must use: SUGGESTIONS. This creates a list of suggestions that the policy editor places in the drop-down list. Separate the items in this list with white space, and enclose items containing spaces in double quotation marks. End the list with the END SUGGESTIONS.

A few keywords modify the behavior of the combo box:

- **DEFAULT.** Specifies the default value of the combo box
- **EXPANDABLETEXT.** Creates the value as a REG_EXPAND_SZ value
- **MAXLENGTH.** Specifies the maximum length of the value
- **NOSORT.** Prevents the policy editor from sorting the list
- **REQUIRED.** Specifies that a value is required

Syntax

```
PART Name COMBOBOX
  SUGGESTIONS
    Suggestions
  END SUGGESTIONS
  [DEFAULT Default]
  [EXPANDABLETEXT]
  [MAXLENGTH Max]
  [NOSORT]
  [REQUIRED]
  VALUENAME Value
END PART
```

Name	This specifies the name of the setting as you want to see it in the policy's dialog box. Enclose the name in double quotation marks if it contains spaces. You see the name next to the combo box.
Suggestions	This is a list of items to put in the drop-down list. Separate each suggestion with white space (line feeds, tabs, and spaces, for example), and enclose any suggestion that includes a space in double quotes.
Default	This is the default value for the part. When you enable the policy, the policy editor fills the control with the default value. Use a default value that's appropriate for the part's type.
Max	This is the maximum length of the value's data.
Value	This is the registry value to modify. The policy editor creates this in the registry as a REG_SZ value and fills it with any text that you typed or selected in the combo box.

Example

Listing 7-11   example.adm

```
CLASS USER

CATEGORY "Sample Policies"
  EXPLAIN "These are sample policies that don't do anything but illustrate parts."

  POLICY "Sample Policy"
    SUPPORTED "At least Microsoft Windows XP Professional"

    EXPLAIN "This is a sample policy that illustrates creating a part."
    KEYNAME "Software\Policies"

    PART Sample COMBOBOX
      SUGGESTIONS
        Sample1 Sample2 "Another Sample"
      END SUGGESTIONS
      VALUENAME Sample
    END PART

  END POLICY

END CATEGORY
```

Keywords

The valid keywords within a COMBOBOX section are the following:

- DEFAULT

- END

- EXPANDABLETEXT

- KEYNAME

- MAXLENGTH

- ■ NOSORT

- ■ REQUIRED

- ■ SUGGESTIONS

- ■ VALUENAME

DROPDOWNLIST

The keyword DROPDOWNLIST adds a drop-down list to the policy's dialog box. It has one additional keyword that you must use, and that is ITEMLIST. This creates a list of items that the policy editor places in the drop-down list. Use the syntax NAME *Name* VALUE *Value* to define each item within the ITEMLIST section. Enclose items containing spaces within double quotation marks. End the list with the END ITEMLIST.

A few keywords modify the behavior of the drop-down list:

- ■ **DEFAULT.** Specifies the default value of the drop-down list

- ■ **EXPANDABLETEXT.** Creates the value as a REG_EXPAND_SZ value

- ■ **NOSORT.** Prevents the policy editor from sorting the list

- ■ **REQUIRED.** Specifies that a value is required

Syntax

```
PART Name DROPDOWNLIST
  ITEMLIST
    NAME Item VALUE Data
  END ITEMLIST
  [DEFAULT Default]
  [EXPANDABLETEXT]
  [NOSORT]
  [REQUIRED]
  VALUENAME Value
END PART
```

Name	This specifies the name of the setting as you want to see it in the policy's dialog box. Enclose the name in double quotes if it contains spaces. You see the name next to the drop-down list.
Item	This is the name of each item in the list. This is the text that you'll see in the drop-down list. This isn't the value that the policy editor stores in the registry, though.
Data	This is the data that you want the policy editor to store in the value when you select the associated item.
Default	This is the default value for the part. When you enable the policy, the policy editor fills the control with the default value. Use an item defined in ITEMLIST.
Value	This is the registry value to modify. The policy editor creates this in the registry as a REG_SZ value and fills it with the value of *Data* associated with the selected item.

Example

Listing 7-12   example.adm

```
CLASS USER

CATEGORY "Sample Policies"
  EXPLAIN "These are sample policies that illustrate parts."

  POLICY "Sample Policy"
    SUPPORTED "At least Microsoft Windows XP Professional"

    EXPLAIN "This is a sample policy that illustrates creating a part."
    KEYNAME "Software\Policies"

    PART Sample DROPDOWNLIST
      ITEMLIST
        NAME Sample1 VALUE 0
        NAME Sample2 VALUE 1
        NAME "Another Sample" VALUE 2
      END ITEMLIST
      VALUENAME Sample
    END PART

  END POLICY

END CATEGORY
```

Keywords

The valid keywords within a DROPDOWNLIST section are the following ones:

- DEFAULT

- END

- EXPANDABLETEXT

- KEYNAME

- NOSORT

- REQUIRED

- ITEMLIST

- VALUENAME

EDITTEXT

The keyword EDITTEXT enables you to enter alphanumeric text into a text box. Policy editor stores the text in a REG_SZ value. A few keywords modify the behavior of the text box:

- **DEFAULT.**   Specifies the default value of the text box

- **EXPANDABLETEXT.**   Creates the value as a REG_EXPAND_SZ value

- ■ **MAXLENGTH.** Specifies the maximum length of the value
- ■ **REQUIRED.** Specifies that a value is required

Syntax

```
PART Name EDITTEXT
  [DEFAULT Default]
  [EXPANDABLETEXT]
  [MAXLENGTH Max]
  [REQUIRED]
  VALUENAME Value
END PART
```

Name	This specifies the name of the setting as you want to see it in the policy's dialog box. Enclose the name in double quotes if it contains spaces. You see the name next to the text box.
Default	This is the default value for the part. When you enable the policy, the policy editor fills the control with the default value. Use a default value that's appropriate for the part's type.
Max	This is the maximum length of the value's data.
Value	This is the registry value to modify. The policy editor creates this in the registry as a REG_SZ value and fills it with any text that you typed.

Example

Listing 7-13   example.adm

```
CLASS USER

CATEGORY "Sample Policies"
  EXPLAIN "These are sample policies that illustrate parts."

  POLICY "Sample Policy"
    SUPPORTED "At least Microsoft Windows XP Professional"

    EXPLAIN "This is a sample policy that illustrates creating a part."
    KEYNAME "Software\Policies"

    PART Sample EDITTEXT
      VALUENAME Sample
    END PART

  END POLICY

END CATEGORY
```

Keywords

The valid keywords within an **EDITTEXT** section are the following ones:

- ■ DEFAULT

- ■ END

- EXPANDABLETEXT

- KEYNAME

- MAXLENGTH

- REQUIRED

- VALUENAME

LISTBOX

The keyword **LISTBOX** adds a list box with Add and Remove buttons to the policy's dialog box. This is the only type of part that you can use to manage multiple values in one key. You can't use the **VALUENAME** option with the **LISTBOX** part because the option doesn't associate just a single value with the list. Use the following options with the **LISTBOX** part type:

- **ADDITIVE.**   By default, the content of list boxes overwrites values already set in the registry. That means that the Windows client-side extensions remove values before setting them. When you use this keyword, the client-side extensions do not delete existing values before adding the values set in the list box.

- **EXPLICITVALUE.**   This keyword makes you specify the value name and data. The list box shows two columns: one for the name and one for the data. You can't use this keyword with the keyword **VALUEPREFIX**.

- **VALUEPREFIX.**   The prefix you specify determines value names. If you specify a prefix, the policy editor adds an incremental number to it. For example, a prefix of `Sample` generates the value names `Sample1`, `Sample2`, and so on. The prefix can be empty (""), causing the value names to be `1`, `2`, and so on.

By default, without using either the **EXPLICITVALUE** or **VALUEPREFIX** keywords, only one column appears in the list box. For each entry in the list, the policy editor creates a value using the entry's text for the value's name and data. For example, the entry `Sample` in the list box creates a value called `Sample` whose data is `Sample`. The default behavior is seldom a desirable result.

Syntax

```
PART Name LISTBOX
  [EXPANDABLETEXT]
  [NOSORT]
  [ADDITIVE]
  [EXPLICITVALUE | VALUEPREFIX Prefix]
END PART
```

Name	This specifies the name of the setting as you want to see it in the policy's dialog box. Enclose the name in double quotes if it contains spaces.
Prefix	This is the prefix to use for incremental names. If you specify a prefix, the policy editor adds an incremental number to it. For example, a prefix of `Sample` generates the value names `Sample1`, `Sample2`, and so on. The prefix can be empty (""), causing the value names to be 1, 2, and so on.

Example

Listing 7-14   example.adm

```
CLASS USER

CATEGORY "Sample Policies"
  EXPLAIN "These are sample policies that illustrate parts."

  POLICY "Sample Policy"
    SUPPORTED "At least Microsoft Windows XP Professional"

    EXPLAIN "This is a sample policy that illustrates creating a part."
    KEYNAME "Software\Policies"

    PART Sample LISTBOX
      EXPLICITVALUE
    END PART

  END POLICY

END CATEGORY
```

Keywords

The valid keywords within a **LISTBOX** section are the following ones:

- ADDITIVE

- END

- EXPANDABLETEXT

- EXPLICITVALUE

- KEYNAME

- NOSORT

- VALUEPREFIX

NUMERIC

The keyword NUMERIC enables you to enter alphanumeric text by using a spin box control that adjusts the number up and down. Group Policy Editor stores the number in a REG_DWORD value, but you can change the value's type to REG_SZ using the keyword TXTCONVERT. A few other keywords modify the behavior of the text box:

- **DEFAULT.**   Specifies the initial value of the text box.
- **MAX.**   Specifies the maximum value. The default is 9999.
- **MIN.**   Specifies the minimum value. The default is 0.
- **REQUIRED.**   Specifies that a value is required.
- **SPIN.**   Specifies the increment to use for the spin box control. The default value is 1, and using 0 removes the spinner control.
- **TXTCONVERT.**   Writes values as REG_SZ values rather than as REG_DWORD.

Syntax

```
PART Name NUMERIC
  [DEFAULT Default]
  [MAX Max]
  [MIN Min]
  [REQUIRED]
  [SPIN]
  [TXTCONVERT]
  VALUENAME Value
END PART
```

Name	This specifies the name of the setting as you want to see it in the policy's dialog box. Enclose the name in double quotes if it contains spaces. You see the name next to the text box.
Default	This is the default value for the part. When you enable the policy, the policy editor fills the control with the default value. Use a default value that's appropriate for the part's type.
Max	This is the maximum value. The default is 9999.
Min	This is the minimum value. The default is 0.
Value	This is the registry value to modify. The policy editor creates this in the registry as a REG_DWORD value, setting it to the value that you specify in the dialog box. To change the value's type to REG_SZ, use the keyword TXTCONVERT.

Example

Listing 7-15   example.adm
```
CLASS USER

CATEGORY "Sample Policies"
  EXPLAIN "These are sample policies that illustrate parts."
```

```
POLICY "Sample Policy"
  SUPPORTED "At least Microsoft Windows XP Professional"

  EXPLAIN "This is a sample policy that illustrates creating a part."
  KEYNAME "Software\Policies"

  PART Sample NUMERIC
    DEFAULT 11
    MIN 10
    MAX 20
    VALUENAME Sample
  END PART

END POLICY

END CATEGORY
```

Keywords

The valid keywords within a NUMERIC section are the following ones:

- DEFAULT

- END

- KEYNAME

- MAX

- MIN

- REQUIRED

- SPIN

- TXTCONVERT

- VALUENAME

TEXT

The keyword TEXT adds static text to the bottom part of the policy's dialog box.

Syntax

```
PART Text TEXT
END PART
```

Text	This is the text you want to add to the dialog box.

Example

Listing 7-16   example.adm

```
CLASS USER

CATEGORY "Sample Policies"
  EXPLAIN "These are sample policies that illustrate parts."

  POLICY "Sample Policy"
    SUPPORTED "At least Microsoft Windows XP Professional"

    EXPLAIN "This is a sample policy that illustrates creating a part."
    KEYNAME "Software\Policies"

    PART "This is sample text added to the dialog box." TEXT
    END PART

  END POLICY

END CATEGORY
```

Deploying Registry-Based Policy

Whether you create an administrative template or one provided by an application such as Office 2003 Editions, you must load it in the Administrative Templates extension in order to use it. You load template files into each GPO in which you want to use them. Because we're talking about the local GPO in this chapter, you only have to load template files once. If you used a template with Active Directory, you'd have to load it in each GPO in which you wanted to use it.

Here's how to load a template into the local GPO:

1. In the Group Policy Editor, under Computer Configuration or User Configuration, right-click Administrative Templates, and then click Add/Remove Templates.

2. In the Add/Remove Templates dialog box, click Add.

3. In the Policy Templates dialog box, type the path and file name of the administrative template that you want to load into the local GPO.

Windows Group Policy Improvements

Windows includes improved policy management, enabling IT professionals to adjust, manage, or simply turn off features that they don't want users to access. IT professionals can deploy any of the policy settings in Windows from Active Directory, too, without fear of altering their existing Windows 2000 configurations. Here's a brief list of the improvements that you find in Windows:

- Windows XP and Windows Server 2003 support most Windows 2000 policies.

- Windows XP and Windows Server 2003 add many new policy settings, which Windows 2000 ignores.

- Group Policy Editor uses a Web view to display useful information about policies for IT professionals to use in assessing and verifying settings.

- Group Policy Editor includes integrated help that makes learning and tracking down policies easier.

- Windows XP and Windows Server 2003 don't wait for the network to fully initialize before presenting the desktop, using cached credentials in the meantime, and allowing users to get to work faster. The operating system applies policies in the background when the network is ready.

These improvements are big advantages. However, you'll be happy to know that the overall process doesn't change much. You generally use the same tools in the same ways to configure and manage user settings. If you're already familiar with Windows 2000 Group Policy, you're equally familiar with Windows XP and Windows Server 2003 Group Policy.

Windows 2000 Server-Based Networks

The Windows XP policy templates are fully compatible with Microsoft Windows 2000 Server and its version of Active Directory. Windows Server 2003 includes the Windows XP administrative templates by default. You have to load them in each GPO in which you want to use them; the steps for doing that are the same as those you learned in the previous sections.

Note   You must update the administrative templates after deploying a Windows service pack. You can use the techniques described in this section to update existing administrative templates to the latest service pack.

You can avoid having to load the Windows XP administrative templates in each GPO by copying them to %SystemRoot%\Inf on the server. On a computer running Windows XP, just copy all the files with the *.adm* extension from %SystemRoot%\Inf to the same folder on the server. The server operating system automatically updates each GPO when you open it for editing. If you're uncomfortable with replacing your Windows 2000 administrative templates, you should continue loading the Windows XP templates into GPOs where you want to use them. I've replaced my Windows 2000 administrative templates with Windows XP administrative templates, however, and haven't had any problems.

Consider these best practices when using Windows XP administrative templates in Windows 2000 Server:

■ In a mixed environment, use Windows XP template files to administer your GPOs. Windows 2000 ignores Windows XP–specific settings.

■ Apply the same policy settings to both Windows XP and Windows 2000 to give roaming users a consistent experience.

■ Test interoperability of the various settings before deployment.

■ Configure policy settings only on client machines using GPOs. Do not try to create these registry values by using other methods.

Windows NT–Based Networks and Other Networks

Like Group Policy, System Policy configures and manages settings for groups of computers and groups of users. I assume you're familiar with System Policy Editor if you're facing this issue. Table 7-2 describes the differences between the two technologies. The policy file that System Policy Editor creates, usually Ntconfig.pol, contains the registry settings for all the users, groups, and computers that use those settings. To deploy this file on a network, put it in the NETLOGON share of the domain controller. Unlike in Group Policy, separate policy files aren't necessary.

Table 7-2   Group Policy Compared to System Policy

	Group Policy	System Policy
Tool	Group Policy Editor	System Policy Editor
Number of settings	620 registry-based settings	72 registry-based settings
Applied to	Users and computers in a specific Active Directory container, such as sites, domains, and organizational units (OUs)	Users and computers in a domain
Security	Secure	Not secure
Extensions	Microsoft Management Console (MMC) and administrative templates	Administrative templates
Persistence	Does not make permanent changes to the registry	Makes permanent changes to the registry, which you must manually remove
Usage	■ Implementing registry-based policy settings ■ Configuring security settings ■ Applying logon, logoff, startup, and shutdown scripts ■ Deploying and maintaining software ■ Optimizing and maintaining Internet Explorer	Implementing registry-based policy settings

Windows behaves differently depending on what kind of server authenticates the user and computer accounts. If an Active Directory–based server authenticates the account, Windows looks for Group Policy, not System Policy. If a Windows NT–based server authenticates the account, Windows looks for System Policy. (It uses the file Ntconfig.pol in the NETLOGON share.) You can use this to your advantage when you haven't deployed Active Directory but you still want to configure policies.

To configure System Policies, use System Policy Editor. You load the Windows policy templates into System Policy Editor before using them. Using System Policy, you can configure and deliver all the registry-based policies that these templates define. Note that Windows doesn't provide System Policy Editor, but Windows 2000 Server does. Also, you will find System Policy Editor in the *Microsoft Office 2003 Editions Resource Kit*, which you learn about in Chapter 17, "Deploying Office 2003 Settings." You create the Ntconfig.pol file, and drop it in the NETLOGON share. If Windows authenticates the account using that Windows NT–based server, it downloads and parses the policies from the Ntconfig.pol file it finds in the NETLOGON share.

If you're not using Active Directory or a Windows NT domain, you can still configure System Policy. You configure Windows to look for the Ntconfig.pol file in any share by specifying a path to the policy file. You must make this change on each individual computer, however, which makes it a labor-intensive process unless you configure it on your disk images. Set the `UpdateMode` `REG_DWORD` value to `0x02`, which changes Windows from automatic (`0x01`) to manual mode (`0x02`). (Set this value to `0x00` to turn off system policy.) Then set the `REG_SZ` value `NetworkPath` to the UNC path and name of the policy file that you want to use. These values are in the key `HKLM\SYSTEM\CurrentControlSet\Control\Update`. You might have to create them.

Customizing Windows

The key reason that power users want to create administrative templates is to customize settings that have no user interface. By creating an administrative template, you give those settings a user interface, preventing human error. The following listing is a sample administrative template that does just that: it defines a handful of custom settings that Tweak UI. contains. (See Chapter 5, "Mapping Tweak UI.") Figure 7-6 shows what this administrative template looks like in Group Policy Editor.

Listing 7-17   Tweakui.adm

```
CLASS USER

CATEGORY "Tweak UI Settings"
  EXPLAIN "These are settings from Tweak UI."

  CATEGORY "Mouse"
    EXPLAIN "Settings that customize the mouse."
```

```
POLICY "Menu Show Delay"
  EXPLAIN "Delay before Windows XP opens a menu when you point at it."
  KEYNAME "Control Panel\Desktop"
  PART "Menu Delay (milliseconds)" NUMERIC
    MIN 0
    MAX 65534
    DEFAULT 400
    TXTCONVERT
    VALUENAME MenuShowDelay
  END PART
END POLICY

POLICY "Drag Height and Width"
 EXPLAIN "Number of pixels the mouse moves before Windows XP thinks you're dragging
it."
  KEYNAME "Control Panel\Desktop"
  PART "Height" NUMERIC
    MIN 0
    MAX 16
    TXTCONVERT
    VALUENAME DragHeight
  END PART
  PART "Width" NUMERIC
    MIN 0
    MAX 16
    TXTCONVERT
    VALUENAME DragWidth
  END PART
END POLICY

END CATEGORY

CATEGORY "Taskbar"
  EXPLAIN "Settings that customize the taskbar."

  POLICY "Balloon Tips"
    EXPLAIN "Enable or disable balloon tips."
    KEYNAME Software\Microsoft\Windows\CurrentVersion\Explorer\Advanced
    VALUENAME EnableBalloonTips
    VALUEOFF NUMERIC 0
    VALUEON NUMERIC 1
  END POLICY

  POLICY "Taskbar Grouping"
    EXPLAIN "Control how buttons group on the taskbar."
    KEYNAME Software\Microsoft\Windows\CurrentVersion\Explorer\Advanced

    PART Grouping DROPDOWNLIST
      ITEMLIST
        NAME "Group least used applications first" VALUE 0
        NAME "Group applications with the mouse windows first" VALUE 1
        NAME "Group applications with at least 2 windows" VALUE 2
        NAME "Group applications with at least 3 windows" VALUE 3
        NAME "Group applications with at least 4 windows" VALUE 4
        NAME "Group applications with at least 5 windows" VALUE 5
        NAME "Group applications with at least 6 windows" VALUE 6
        NAME "Group applications with at least 7 windows" VALUE 7
```

```
        END ITEMLIST
        NOSORT
        VALUENAME TaskbarGroupSize
    END PART

  END POLICY

 END CATEGORY

END CATEGORY
```

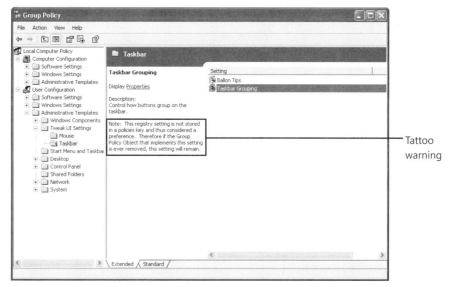

Figure 7-6   Notice the warning that the setting will tattoo the registry.

This administrative template does not contain proper policies. The settings aren't in an official policy branch in the registry, so Windows can't manage them. That means that if you remove the policy, the setting remains. The change is permanent. By default, Group Policy Editor does not display unmanaged settings because they tattoo the registry—a side effect that you don't normally want to happen. In this case, I'm consciously choosing to tattoo the registry in order to provide a user interface for user preferences that don't normally have a user interface. In Group Policy Editor, unmanaged settings have red icons rather than the normal blue icons. To display these settings, you must show unmanaged settings in Group Policy Editor:

1. In Group Policy Editor, under Computer Configuration or User Configuration, right-click Administrative Templates, point to View, and then click Filtering.

2. In the Filtering dialog box, clear the Only Show Policy Settings That Can Be Fully Managed check box.

Using the Group Policy Tools

The Group Policy tools in Windows contain a lot of improvements. The sections following this one describe each of these tools and how to use them. Some of these enhancements deserve special mention, though. First is Group Policy Update Tool (Gpupdate.exe). Group Policy refreshes policies every 90 minutes by default. In Windows 2000, if you changed a policy and wanted to see the results immediately, you had to use the commands `secedit /refreshpolicy user_policy` and `secedit /refreshpolicy machine_policy`. Gpupdate.exe replaces both of these commands in one command that's easy to use. You don't need to use this tool when updating the local GPO, though, because changes to the local GPO are instant.

Second is Resultant Set of Policy (RSoP). Windows includes new tools for seeing which policies the operating system is applying to the current user and computer and the location where they originated. One of the toughest parts of administering Group Policy on a large network is tracking down behaviors that result from combinations of GPOs that you didn't intend or didn't know were occurring. These tools help you track down these behaviors much faster than you could with Windows 2000, because they give you a snapshot of how the operating system is applying them and where they originated.

Gpresult

Group Policy Result Tool (Gpresult.exe) displays the effective policies and RSoP for the current user and computer. This section describes its command-line options.

Syntax

```
gpresult [/s Computer [/u Domain\User /p Password]] [/user TargetUserName] [/scope
{user|computer}] [/v] [/z]
```

/s *Computer*	This specifies the name or IP address of a remote computer. (Don't use backslashes.) It defaults to the local computer.
/u *Domain\User*	This runs the command with the account permissions of the user specified by *User* or *Domain\User*. The default is the permissions of the current console user.
/p *Password*	This specifies the password of the user account that the /u option specifies.
/user *TargetUserName*	This specifies the user name of the user for whom you want to display RSoP.
/scope {user|computer}	This displays either user or computer results. Valid values for the /scope option are user or computer. If you omit the /scope option, Gpresult.exe displays both user and computer settings.
/v	This specifies that the output will display verbose policy information.

/z	This specifies that the output will display all available information about Group Policy. Because this option produces more information than the /v option does, redirect output to a text file when you use the parameter `gpresult /z >c:\policy.txt`.
/?	This displays help.

Examples

```
gpresult /user jerry /scope computer
gpresult /s camelot /u honeycutt\administrator /p password /user jerry
gpresult /s camelot /u honeycutt\administrator /p password /user jerry /z
>c:\policy.txt
```

Gpupdate

Gpupdate.exe refreshes local and network policy settings, including registry-based settings. As I mentioned, this command replaces the obsolete command `secedit /refreshpolicy`.

Syntax

```
gpupdate [/target:{computer|user}] [/force] [/wait:value] [/logoff] [/boot] [/sync]
```

/target: {computer|user}	This processes only the computer settings or the current user settings. By default, both the computer and user settings are processed.
/force	This ignores all processing optimizations and reapplies all settings.
/wait:*value*	This is the number of seconds that policy processing waits to finish. The default is 600 seconds. A value of 0 means "don't wait," and a value of -1 means "wait forever."
/logoff	This logs the user off after the refresh has completed. This is required for those Group Policy client-side extensions, such as user Software Installation and Folder Redirection, that do not process on a background refresh cycle but do process when the user logs on. This option has no effect if there are no extensions called that require the user to log off.
/boot	This restarts the computer after the refresh is finished. This is required for those Group Policy client-side extensions, such as computer Software Installation, that do not process on a background refresh cycle but that do process when the computer starts up. This option has no effect if there are no extensions called that require the computer to be restarted.
/sync	This switch synchronously (in the background) applies the next boot or user logon policy.
/?	This displays help.

Examples

```
gpupdate
gpupdate /target:computer
gpupdate /force /wait:100
gpupdate /boot
```

Simulating Folder Redirection

IT professionals often ask me about Folder Redirection. Specifically, they want to know how to simulate this policy when they haven't yet deployed Active Directory. Active Directory is a requirement for this policy, after all.

Although you can't achieve automatic folder redirection without Active Directory, you can simulate it. Configure the key User Shell Folders to redirect My Documents and other folders to a network location. This key is in HKCU\Software\ Microsoft\Windows\CurrentVersion\Explorer and contains one value for each of the special folders that Windows supports. They are REG_EXPAND_SZ values, so you can use environment variables, such as %UserName% and %HomeShare%, in the path. This means that even on a Windows NT–based network, you can use redirected folders.

I suggest that you script this customization so that you can apply it uniformly. Chapter 4, "Hacking the Registry," describes the key User Shell Folders in great detail, and it also contains a sample script that automatically redirects folders. In a business environment, be careful to test this customization prior to deploying it to a production environment. In particular, make sure it works with the permissions of the network share to which you're redirecting the folders.

Help and Support Center

Although Help and Support Center's RSoP report is of limited use to IT professionals because you can't use it remotely, users can run it on their own computers to check policy settings. This tool provides a user-friendly, printable report of most policies in effect for the computer and console user. Figure 7-7 shows a sample of this report. Here's how to use this tool in Windows XP:

1. Click Start, and then click Help And Support.

2. Under Pick A Task, click Use Tools To View Your Computer Information And Diagnose Problems.

3. Click Advanced System Information, and then click View Group Policy Settings Applied.

Figure 7-7   Help and Support Center's RSoP report contains the same type of information as Gpresult.exe contains, but it's more readable and more suitable for printing.

Resultant Set of Policy

Although Help and Support Center's RSoP report isn't suitable for use by IT professionals, the RSoP snap-in is suitable because you can use it to view RSoP data for remote computers. You use this tool to predict how policies work for a specific user or computer, as well as for entire groups of users and computers. Sometimes, GPOs applied at different levels in Active Directory conflict with each other. Tracking down these conflicting settings is difficult without a tool like this snap-in.

The RSoP snap-in checks Software Installation for applications associated with the user or computer. It reports all other policy settings, too, including registry-based policies, redirected folders, Internet Explorer maintenance, security settings, and scripts. You've already seen two tools that report RSoP data: Gpresult.exe and Help and Support Center (Windows XP only). The RSoP snap-in is almost as easy to use. (Your account must be in the computer's local Administrators group to use this tool.)

1. Click Start, Run, and type **mmc**.

2. Click File, Add/Remove Snap-In, and then in the Add/Remove Snap-in dialog box, click Add.

3. In the Add Standalone Snap-In dialog box, select Resultant Set Of Policy, click Add, and then click Close.

4. In the Add/Remove Snap-In dialog box, click OK.

5. Right-click Resultant Set of Policy, and then select Generate RSoP Data.

6. In Resultant Set of Policy Wizard, click Next, and then click Next again.

7. On the Computer Selection page, select Another Computer, type the name of the computer that you want to inspect, and then click Next.

8. On the User Selection page, select the user for whom you want to display RSoP data, and then click Next.

9. Click Next, and then click Finish to close the wizard.

10. To view the results, expand the username node in the console.

Figure 7-8 shows the results. In this example, you see the password policies applied to the computer. You also see the GPO that's the source for each setting.

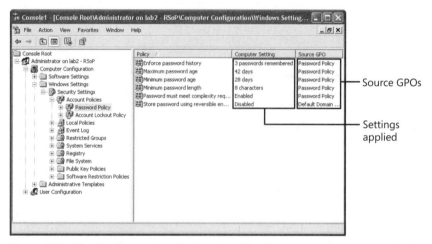

Figure 7-8   The RSoP snap-in is the best tool for figuring out the source of policy settings when multiple GPOs apply to a computer.

Using DesktopStandard PolicyMaker

Group Policy doesn't do everything that every IT professional needs it to do. In fact, even Microsoft folks will admit that there are holes in the coverage that Group Policy provides. That's why Microsoft made Group Policy extensible. To date, however, very few companies have extended Group Policy with useful tools that help you to better manage users and computers.

PolicyMaker from DesktopStandard (*http://www.desktopstandard.com*) is a new product that fills this void. If you've ever wished that your GPOs could do more, I recommend that you evaluate PolicyMaker. It seamlessly adds new features to every GPO you create, such as:

- **Network drive mappings.**   You can assign network drives. For example, you can create a GPO that maps drive M to the network share containing the accounting department's data files, and then assign that GPO to the accounting department's OU.

- **Shared printer connections.**   You can assign shared and TCP/IP printer connections. In a classroom environment, for example, you can assign GPOs to each classroom's OU that connects to the printer in that classroom.

- **Creating, changing, and removing shortcuts.**   You can create GPOs that add shortcuts to Internet Explorer, the Start menu, the Quick Launch toolbar, the desktop, and more. You can also use a GPO to remove shortcuts, such as those for distracting programs that are difficult to remove from Windows XP Professional. A practical application that I've found is using a GPO to update existing shortcuts. For example, you can add command-line options to existing shortcuts.

- **Configuring environment variables.**   You can create GPOs that define system and user environment variables. I've used GPOs to assign environment variables, and then relied on those environment variables in logon and other scripts. This approach makes scripts less sensitive to change.

- **Configuring registry settings.**   Instead of creating your own administrative templates for use with Group Policy, PolicyMaker allows you to add, change, or remove any setting in the registry. This is handy when no policy exists for a setting that you want to manage, but you know the location of the setting in the registry.

- **Copying and removing files.**   You can create a GPO that copies and removes files on the computer. For example, you can copy network shortcuts to the users' Nethood folders. You can create a GPO that automatically adds certain shortcuts to the SendTo folders.

- **Managing files and folders, even attributes.**   You can create GPOs that manage files and folders. For example, you can use a GPO to remove temporary folders. Another example is to create a GPO that changes the attribute of Internet Explorer's Links folder so that it doesn't show up on the Favorites menu. There are many practical applications for managing files and folders through a GPO, and PolicyMaker gives you numerous and flexible options for doing so.

- **Configuring Microsoft Office.**   You can almost completely configure Office by using a GPO. PolicyMaker even presents you with dialog boxes similar to those that Office presents, making it easier to configure Office in a GPO.

- **Building Outlook user profiles.**   You can use a GPO to create Outlook user profiles. This task has always been a tedious chore, but PolicyMaker makes it simple.

PolicyMaker is easy to install; installation usually takes just a few minutes. And because PolicyMaker fits seamlessly into Group Policy Editor, using PolicyMaker is straightforward for any IT professional with basic knowledge of using Group Policy Editor. The client-side extension supports Windows 2000, Windows XP Professional, and Windows Server 2003, and it supports reporting by using RSoP. ProfileMaker also supports all versions of Office and Outlook.

Note   DesktopStandard provides their PolicyMaker Registry Extension free of charge.

Finding More Resources

This chapter focused on local registry-based policies. This is a registry book, after all. If you're interested in learning more about Group Policy, Microsoft's Web site contains a plethora of good information. You don't even have to buy a book to learn more. Here's a list of resources that I found valuable when I was first learning about Group Policy:

- *http://www.microsoft.com/windows2000/techinfo/howitworks/management/grouppolwp.asp* This is the "Windows 2000 Group Policy" white paper, and it's the best starting point for understanding how to create GPOs and apply them to containers in Active Directory. This paper is long, but it's a worthy read.

- *http://www.microsoft.com/Windows2000/techinfo/howitworks/management/rbppaper.asp* This is the "Implementing Registry-Based Group Policy" white paper. The bulk of this paper is about creating administrative templates for Windows. It's the paper I used most when writing this chapter because it describes the syntax for each of the keywords that you can use in administrative templates.

- *http://www.microsoft.com/technet/prodtechnol/winxppro/maintain/mngwinxp.mspx* This is the "Managing Windows XP in a Windows 2000 Server Environment" white paper. It's a bit long, and all it really says is that Windows 2000 ignores Windows XP policies, and that you can copy the Windows XP administrative templates to %SystemRoot%\Inf on a Windows 2000–based server to use those templates for both Windows 2000 and Windows XP. Still, it's an interesting read because it goes into detail about the Group Policy improvements that Windows XP provides. Notice that this Web page includes a URL to a spreadsheet that lists all the policies. You can use it as a starting point for your own specification, recording which policies you're going to deploy.

Chapter 8
Configuring Windows Security

Security is not the most interesting registry-related topic, nor is it the most popular. It is one of the most important topics facing IT today, however.

There are hundreds of facets of security, but this chapter focuses on just one: the registry. You can change a key's access control list (ACL). You can audit keys. You can also take ownership of keys. You can't do any of these things with individual values, though, like you can with individual files. Power users generally won't care much about registry security, but IT professionals often have no choice.

Just because you can edit keys' ACLs doesn't mean you should, however. Changing your registry's security is not a good idea unless you have a specific reason to do so. At best, you will make a change that's irrelevant, but at worst, you could prevent Microsoft Windows XP and Windows Server 2003 (Windows) from working properly. So why am I including registry security in this book at all? There are cases in which IT professionals must change the registry's default permissions to deploy software. That is a totally different story than tinkering with your registry's security out of curiosity. For example, you might have an application that users can run only when they log on to the operating system as a member of the Administrators group. Ouch. In a corporate environment, you don't want to dump all your users in this group. The solution is to deploy Windows with custom permissions so that users can run those programs as a member of the Power Users or Users group. This is the most common scenario, and it's the primary focus of this chapter.

You have two methods of deploying custom permissions. First, you can do it manually. For the sake of completeness, I show you how to change a key's permissions in Registry Editor (Regedit). Second, you can build a security template, complete with custom registry permissions, and then apply that template to a computer manually. You wouldn't run around from desktop to desktop applying the template, though; you'd apply that template to your disk images before deployment. The second method is by using Group Policy. You create a Group Policy Object (GPO) and then import a security template into it to create a security policy for your network. Windows automatically applies the custom permissions in your template to the computer and user if that GPO is in scope. I don't talk about Group Policy a lot in this book, but the last section in Chapter 7, "Using Registry-Based Policy," points out a lot of good, free resources for learning more about it.

Windows XP Service Pack 2 (SP2) and Windows Server 2003 Service Pack 1 (SP1) provide a number of new security features. For example, the Windows Security Center helps users configure security for maximum protection. Windows Firewall prevents unwanted access to computers so that using the Internet and opening e-mail attachments are safer. This chapter doesn't discuss those features in detail; instead, it describes how to use the registry to customize these features. For more information about the security features in Windows XP SP2, see *http://www.microsoft.com/ windowsxp/sp2/default.mspx*. For more information about the security features in Windows Server 2003, see *http://www.microsoft.com/technet/prodtechnol/ windowsserver2003/servicepack/default.mspx*.

Setting Permissions for Keys

Registry security is similar to file system security except that you can set permissions for keys only, not values. Other than that, the dialog boxes look similar, the permissions are similar, and so on. If you don't understand basic security concepts, take a moment and review them in Help and Support Center before tinkering with permissions. I don't include the basic concepts in this chapter because I assume that you're an IT professional and already understand the basics of security.

If you have full control of or own a registry key, you can edit its permissions for users and groups in the key's ACL:

1. In Regedit, click the key with the ACL that you want to edit.

2. On the Edit menu, click Permissions. (See Figure 8-1.)

3. In the Group Or User Names list, click the user or the group for whom you want to edit permissions, and then select the check box in the Allow or Deny column to allow or deny the following permissions:

❑ **Full Control.** Grants the user or the group permission to open, edit, and take ownership of the key. This permission literally gives full control of the key.

❑ **Read.** Grants the user or the group permission to read the key's contents but not to save changes made to it. Read this as *read-only*.

❑ **Special Permissions.** Grants the user or the group a special combination of permissions. To grant special permissions, click Advanced. You learn more about this permission setting in the section "Assigning Special Permissions," later in this chapter.

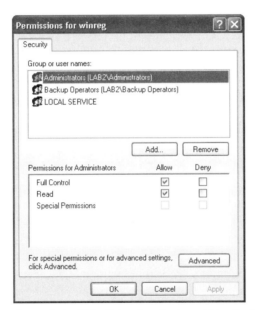

Figure 8-1 This dialog box is almost identical to the dialog box for file system security.

Sometimes the check boxes in the Permissions For *Name* area are shaded. You can't change them. The reason is that the key inherits that permission from the parent key. You can prevent a key from inheriting permissions, and you learn how to do that later in this chapter in the section "Assigning Special Permissions."

Tip OK, you had your fun. You tinkered with your registry's security and satisfied your curiosity; but now what? You can easily restore the original permissions by applying the Setup Security template. You learn how to apply this template in the section "Modifying a Computer's Configuration," later in this chapter.

Adding Users to ACLs

You can add users or groups to a key's existing ACL:

1. In Regedit, click the key with the ACL that you want to edit.

2. On the Edit menu, click Permissions, and then click Add.

3. In the Select Users, Computers, Or Groups dialog box, click Locations, and then click the computer, the domain, or the organizational unit in which you want to look for the user or the group that you want to add to the key's ACL.

4. In the Enter The Object Names To Select box, type the name of the user or the group that you want to add to the key's ACL, and then click OK.

5. In the Permissions For *Name* list, configure the permissions that you want to give the user or the group by selecting the Allow or Deny check box.

> **Tip**   In step 4, you type all or part of the user or the group name that you want to add to the key's ACL. If you don't know what the name is, you can search for it. First, if possible, narrow your search by choosing a location as I described in step 3. Then click Advanced, and click Find Now. Click the name of the user or the group that you want to add, and click OK. You can further narrow the results by clicking Object Types and then clearing the Built-In Security Principals check box.

The only real-world scenario I can think of for adding users to a key's ACL is allowing a group to access a computer's registry over the network, which you learn how to do in "Restricting Remote Registry Access," later in this chapter. Otherwise, adding a user or a group to a key's ACL is sometimes useful as a quick fix when an application can't access the settings it needs when users run it. Generally speaking, adding users or groups to a key's ACL does little harm, but if you're not careful, you can open holes in the security of Windows so wide that users and hackers can walk through them. And if the edit you're making will be required on more than one computer or user, consider deploying it as a security template. (See "Deploying Security Templates," later in this chapter.)

Removing Users from ACLs

Here's how to remove a user or a group from a key's ACL:

1. In Regedit, click the key with the ACL that you want to edit.

2. On the Edit menu, click Permissions.

3. Click the user or the group that you want to remove, and click Remove.

> **Caution**   Be wary of removing groups from keys' ACLs. Generally, the ACLs you see in Windows after installing it (Setup Security) are the bare minimum required for users to start and use the operating system. If you remove the Users or the Power Users group from a key, users in those groups can't read the key's values, and this is likely going to mangle the operating system or an application. If you dare remove the Administrators group from a key, you might not be able to manage the computer at all. Removing individual users from a key's ACL isn't necessarily a bad thing, however. Windows doesn't assign permissions to individual users, so those permissions might have gotten there by devious means. You should never remove users from their profile hives' ACLs, though. Doing so prevents them from accessing their own settings, of which they should have full control.

Assigning Special Permissions

Special permissions give you more granular control of a key's ACL than the basic Full Control and Read permissions. You can allow or deny users the ability to create subkeys, set values, read values, and so on. You can get very detailed. Here's how:

1. In Regedit, click the key with the ACL that you want to edit.

2. On the Edit menu, click Permissions.

3. In the Group Or User Names list, click the user or the group for whom you want to edit permissions. Add the user or the group if necessary. Then click Advanced.

4. Double-click the user or the group to whom you want to give special permissions. You see the Permission Entry For *Name* dialog box shown in Figure 8-2.

Figure 8-2   Special permissions give you finer control of a user or group's permissions to use a key, but assigning special permissions is generally unnecessary.

5. In the Apply Onto drop-down list, click one of the following:

❑ **This Key Only.**   Applies the permissions to the selected key only.

❑ **This Key And Subkeys.**   Applies the permissions to the selected key and all its subkeys. In other words, it applies them to the entire branch.

❑ **Subkeys Only.**   Applies the permissions to all the key's subkeys but not to the key itself.

6. In the Permissions list, select the Allow or Deny check box for each permission that you want to allow or deny:

❑ **Full Control.**   All the following permissions.

❑ **Query Value.**   Read a value from the key.

❑ **Set Value.**   Set a value in the key.

❑ **Create Subkey.**   Create subkeys in the key.

❑ **Enumerate Subkeys.**   Identify the key's subkeys.

❑ **Notify.**   Receive notification events from the key.

❑ **Create Link.**   Create symbolic links in the key.

❑ **Delete.**   Delete the key or its values.

❑ **Write DAC.**   Write the key's discretionary access control list.

❑ **Write Owner.**   Change the key's owner.

❑ **Read Control.**   Read the key's discretionary access control list.

A word about inheritance is necessary here. With inheritance enabled, subkeys inherit the permissions of their parent keys. In other words, if a key gives a group full control, all the key's subkeys also give that group full control. In fact, when you view the subkeys' ACLs, the Allow check box next to Full Control is shaded for that group because you can't change inherited permissions. There are a couple of actions that you can take to configure inheritance. First, you can prevent a subkey from inheriting its parent key's permissions: in the Advanced Security Settings For *Key* dialog box, clear the Inheritable Permission check box. Second, you can replace the ACLs of a key's subkeys, effectively resetting an entire branch to match a key's ACL: select the Replace Permission Entries On All Child Objects With Entries Shown Here That Apply To Child Objects check box.

Mapping Default Permissions

Understanding the registry's default permissions is useful if you're an IT professional deploying software. Knowing whether members of the Users group can change a particular setting helps you test applications prior to deployment and determine if the application works with default permissions. If you determine that an application does work properly with the default permissions, then it's ready to deploy. If you determine that an application doesn't work properly with the default permissions, you must either fix the program or change the offending key's permissions. The easiest way to do that, of course, is by using security templates.

First you must understand the three fundamental groups in Windows: Users, Power Users, and Administrators. Through these groups, Windows provides different levels of access depending on each group's needs:

- **Users.**   This group has the highest security because the default permissions given to it don't allow its members to change operating system data or other users' settings. Generally, users in this group can't change per-computer operating system and application settings. They can usually include programs certified for Windows that administrators deploy to their computers. Also, this group gives its members full control over everything in their user profiles, including their profile hives (HKCU). What frequently keeps IT professionals from assigning users to this group is that members can't usually run legacy applications. Rather than assign users to another group, deal with this problem by applying a compatible security template, which you learn how to do in the section titled "Deploying Security Templates," later in this chapter.

- **Power Users.**   This group provides backward compatibility for running programs that aren't certified for Windows. The default permissions give this group the ability to change many per-computer operating system and program settings. Generally, if you have legacy applications that users can't run as members of the Users group and you're not going to use security templates, adding those users to the Power Users group allows the applications to run. However, this group does have enough permissions to install most applications; members can't change operating system files or install services. The permissions given to the Power Users group is somewhere in the middle of the Users and Administrators groups. It's similar to the Users group in Microsoft Windows NT 4.0. And no, members of this group can't add themselves to the Administrators group.

- **Administrators.**   This group provides full control of the entire computer. Its members can change all operating system and application files. They can change all settings in the registry. Also, they can take ownership of keys and change a key's ACL. IT professionals are often tempted to add users to this group to avoid having trouble deploying applications that are otherwise difficult to install or run. Don't. Because users in this group can install anything they like or change any setting they like, viruses are free to do their damage and users are free to subject their configurations to the inevitable bout of human error. To secure your enterprise's desktops and reduce downtime, reserve this group for actual administrators. Even if you're an administrator, use your computer as a power user for the same reasons. Instead, when you need to perform an administrative task, use a secondary logon to start a program as Administrator: hold down the SHIFT key while you right-click the program's shortcut, click Run As, and then type the account name and password that you want to use to run the program.

Table 8-1 describes the registry's default permissions after a fresh installation of Windows. (These permissions don't apply to Windows Server 2003 domain controllers.) Keep in mind that the resulting permissions are different if you upgrade from an earlier version of Windows to Windows XP or Windows Server 2003. I got these permissions from the security template that you use to restore Windows to *out of box* security. I've focused on the Users and Power Users groups because these are the primary issue. In most of these cases, the Administrators group has full control, as do the Creator Owner and System built-in accounts. In most cases—but not all—each key's permissions replace all subkeys' permissions. This is through the magic of inheritance, which you learned about in the preceding section.

When you see the word *Special* in the Power Users column, it means the group has special permissions on that key (and subkeys in most cases), and that permissions is usually the ability to modify values. The Power Users group doesn't ever get the Full Control, Create Link, Change Permissions, or Take Ownership permission for any key in the registry, though. The interesting thing about this table is that Windows gives the Users group Read permission and the Power Users group special permissions for all of HKLM\SOFTWARE. The remaining entries in the table are exceptions to this rule that limit access to specific keys in HKLM\SOFTWARE.

Table 8-1 Default Windows Installation Registry Permissions

Branch	Users	Power Users
hklm\software	Read	Special
hklm\software\classes	Read	Special
hklm\software\classes\.hlp	Read	Read
hklm\software\classes\helpfile	Read	Read
hklm\software\microsoft\ads\providers\ldap\extensions	Read	Read
hklm\software\microsoft\ads\providers\nds	Read	Read
hklm\software\microsoft\ads\providers\nwcompat	Read	Read
hklm\software\microsoft\ads\providers\winnt	Read	Read
hklm\software\microsoft\command processor	Read	Read
hklm\software\microsoft\cryptography	Read	Read
hklm\software\microsoft\cryptography\calais	None	None
hklm\software\microsoft\driver signing	Read	Read
hklm\software\microsoft\enterprisecertificates	Read	Read
hklm\software\microsoft\msdtc	None	None

Table 8-1   **Default Windows Installation Registry Permissions**

Branch	Users	Power Users
hklm\software\microsoft\netdde	None	None
hklm\software\microsoft\non-driver signing	Read	Read
hklm\software\microsoft\ole	Read	Read
hklm\software\microsoft\protected storage system provider	None	None
hklm\software\microsoft\rpc	Read	Read
hklm\software\microsoft\secure	Read	Read
hklm\software\microsoft\systemcertificates	Read	Read
hklm\software\microsoft\upnp device host	Read	None
hklm\software\microsoft\windows nt\currentversion\ accessibility	Read	Read
hklm\software\microsoft\windows nt\currentversion\ aedebug	Read	Read
hklm\software\microsoft\windows nt\currentversion\ asr\commands	Read	Read
hklm\software\microsoft\windows nt\currentversion\ classes	Read	Read
hklm\software\microsoft\windows nt\currentversion\ drivers32	Read	Read
hklm\software\microsoft\windows nt\currentversion\efs	Read	Read
hklm\software\microsoft\windows nt\currentversion\ font drivers	Read	Read
hklm\software\microsoft\windows nt\currentversion\ fontmapper	Read	Read
hklm\software\microsoft\windows nt\currentversion\ image file execution options	Read	Read
hklm\software\microsoft\windows nt\currentversion\ inifilemapping	Read	Read
hklm\software\microsoft\windows nt\currentversion\ perflib	None	None
hklm\software\microsoft\windows nt\currentversion\ perflib\009	None	None
hklm\software\microsoft\windows nt\currentversion\ profilelist	Read	Read
hklm\software\microsoft\windows nt\currentversion\ secedit	Read	Read
hklm\software\microsoft\windows nt\currentversion\ setup\recoveryconsole	Read	Read
hklm\software\microsoft\windows nt\currentversion\ svchost	Read	Read

Table 8-1   Default Windows Installation Registry Permissions

Branch	Users	Power Users
hklm\software\microsoft\windows nt\currentversion\ terminal server\install\software\microsoft\windows\ currentversion\runonce	Read	Read
hklm\software\microsoft\windows nt\currentversion\ time zones	Read	Read
hklm\software\microsoft\windows nt\currentversion\ windows	Read	Read
hklm\software\microsoft\windows nt\currentversion\ winlogon	Read	Read
hklm\software\microsoft\windows\currentversion\ explorer\user shell folders	Read	Read
hklm\software\microsoft\windows\currentversion\ group policy	None	None
hklm\software\microsoft\windows\currentversion\ installer	None	None
hklm\software\microsoft\windows\currentversion\ policies	None	None
hklm\software\microsoft\windows\currentversion\ reliability	Read	Read
hklm\software\microsoft\windows\currentversion\ runonce	Read	Read
hklm\software\microsoft\windows\currentversion\ runonceex	Read	Read
hklm\software\microsoft\windows\currentversion\ telephony	Read	Special
hklm\software\policies	Read	Read
hklm\system	Read	Read
hklm\system\clone	None	None
hklm\system\controlset001	None	None
hklm\system\controlset001\services\dhcp\ configurations	Read	Read
hklm\system\controlset001\services\dhcp\parameters	Read	Read
hklm\system\controlset001\services\dhcp\ parameters\options	Read	Read
hklm\system\controlset001\services\dnscache\ parameters	Read	Read
hklm\system\controlset001\services\mrxdav\ encrypteddirectories	None	None
hklm\system\controlset001\services\netbt\parameters	Read	Read
hklm\system\controlset001\services\netbt\ parameters\interfaces	Read	Read

Table 8-1   **Default Windows Installation Registry Permissions**

Branch	Users	Power Users
hklm\system\controlset001\services\tcpip\linkage	Read	Read
hklm\system\controlset001\services\tcpip\parameters	Read	Read
hklm\system\controlset001\services\tcpip\parameters\adapters	Read	Read
hklm\system\controlset001\services\tcpip\parameters\interfaces	Read	Read
hklm\system\controlset002	None	None
hklm\system\controlset003	None	None
hklm\system\controlset004	None	None
hklm\system\controlset005	None	None
hklm\system\controlset006	None	None
hklm\system\controlset007	None	None
hklm\system\controlset008	None	None
hklm\system\controlset009	None	None
hklm\system\controlset010	None	None
hklm\system\currentcontrolset\control\class	None	None
hklm\system\currentcontrolset\control\keyboard layout	Read	Read
hklm\system\currentcontrolset\control\keyboard layouts	Read	Read
hklm\system\currentcontrolset\control\network	Read	Read
hklm\system\currentcontrolset\control\securepipeservers\winreg	None	None
hklm\system\currentcontrolset\control\session manager\executive	None	Special
hklm\system\currentcontrolset\control\timezoneinformation	None	Special
hklm\system\currentcontrolset\control\wmi\security	None	None
hklm\system\currentcontrolset\enum	None	None
hklm\system\currentcontrolset\hardware profiles	None	None
hklm\system\currentcontrolset\services\appmgmt\security	None	None
hklm\system\currentcontrolset\services\clipsrv\security	None	None
hklm\system\currentcontrolset\services\cryptsvc\security	None	None
hklm\system\currentcontrolset\services\dnscache	Read	Read
hklm\system\currentcontrolset\services\ersvc\security	None	None
hklm\system\currentcontrolset\services\eventlog\security	None	None

Table 8-1   Default Windows Installation Registry Permissions

Branch	Users	Power Users
hklm\system\currentcontrolset\services\irenum\ security	None	None
hklm\system\currentcontrolset\services\netbt	Read	Read
hklm\system\currentcontrolset\services\netdde\ security	None	None
hklm\system\currentcontrolset\services\netddedsdm\ security	None	None
hklm\system\currentcontrolset\services\remoteaccess	Read	Read
hklm\system\currentcontrolset\services\rpcss\security	None	None
hklm\system\currentcontrolset\services\samss\security	None	None
hklm\system\currentcontrolset\services\scarddrv\ security	None	None
hklm\system\currentcontrolset\services\scardsvr\ security	None	None
hklm\system\currentcontrolset\services\stisvc\ security	None	None
hklm\system\currentcontrolset\services\sysmonlog\ log queries	None	None
hklm\system\currentcontrolset\services\tapisrv\ security	None	None
hklm\system\currentcontrolset\services\tcpip	Read	Read
hklm\system\currentcontrolset\services\w32time\ security	None	None
hklm\system\currentcontrolset\services\wmi\security	None	None
hku\.default	Read	Read
hku\.default\software\microsoft\netdde	None	None
hku\.default\software\microsoft\protected storage system provider	None	None
hku\.default\software\microsoft\systemcertificates\ root\protectedroots	None	None

Figuring out which keys an application uses is part science but mostly art. Sometimes I simply open the program's binary file in a text editor and look for strings that look like keys. Most often, I use a tool such as Winternals Registry Monitor (Regmon), which you learn how to use in Chapter 10, "Finding Registry Settings," to monitor registry activity while I run the program I'm putting through its paces. Then I record the different keys that the program references and check to see whether the Users or Power Users groups have the required permissions for those keys. Last, well-behaved applications report errors when they can't read or write a value in the registry. I wouldn't count on this behavior, however, because ill-behaved programs just bounce along happily even after encountering a registry error.

Taking Ownership of Keys

By default, Windows assigns ownership to the HKLM and HKCU as follows:

- Administrators own each subkey in HKLM.
- Users own each subkey in their profile hives, HKCU.

If you have full control of a key (and administrators usually do), you can take ownership of it if you're not already the owner by following these steps:

1. In Regedit, click the key for which you want to take ownership.

2. On the Edit menu, click Permissions; then click Advanced.

3. On the Owner tab, select the new owner, and then click OK.

Auditing Registry Access

Auditing registry access is a great way to track down registry settings, and it's one of the methods that I discuss in Chapter 10, "Finding Registry Settings." It's also a reasonable way to monitor access to sensitive settings. The problem with auditing the registry is that you must either get very specific about which key you're auditing or pay a severe performance penalty by auditing too much of the registry. It's a fine line between getting the information you need and grinding the computer to a halt.

Auditing a key is a three-step process. First you must enable Audit Policy. You can do that on the network using Group Policy, but that seems silly considering the scope of the performance impact. If you're using auditing as a troubleshooting tool or to track down a setting, turn on Audit Policy locally. In Control Panel, in Classic view, open the Administrative Tools folder, and launch Local Security Policy. You won't find Local Security Policy on a domain controller. In the left pane, under Local Policies, click Audit Policy. In the right pane, double-click Audit Object Access, and then select the Success and Failure check boxes. After you've enabled Audit Policy, use Regedit to audit individual keys, as follows:

1. In Regedit, click the key that you want to audit.

2. On the Edit menu, click Permissions; then click Advanced.

3. On the Auditing tab, shown in Figure 8-3, click Add.

4. In the Select Users, Computers, Or Groups dialog box, click Locations, and then click the computer, the domain, or the organizational unit in which you want to look for the user or the group that you want to audit.

5. In the Enter The Object Names To Select box, type the name of the user or the group that you want to add to the key's audit list, and then click OK.

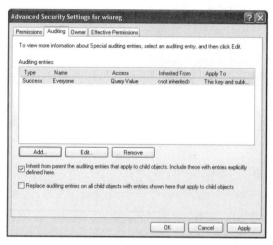

Figure 8-3   Audit keys sparingly because doing so can significantly impact performance.

6.   In the Auditing Entry For *Name* dialog box, in the Access list, select both the Successful and Failed check boxes next to the activities for which you want to audit successful and failed attempts. These correspond to the permissions you learned about in the section "Assigning Special Permissions" earlier in this chapter:

- ❏   Full Control
- ❏   Query Value
- ❏   Set Value
- ❏   Create Subkey
- ❏   Enumerate Subkeys
- ❏   Notify
- ❏   Create Link
- ❏   Delete
- ❏   Write DAC
- ❏   Write Owner
- ❏   Read Control

After enabling Audit Policy and auditing specific keys, check the results using Event Viewer. To open Event Viewer, in Control Panel, in Classic view, open the Administrative Tools folder, and launch Event Viewer. In Event Viewer's left pane, click Security. You see each entry in the right pane, and the most recent entries are at the top of the list. Double-click any entry to see more details. The Event Properties dialog box tells you what type of access Windows detected, the object type, and the process that accessed the key or the value. Chapter 10, "Finding Registry Settings," shows you how to use this information to figure out where Windows or a program stores certain settings in the registry.

Preventing Local Registry Access

Whenever I bring up registry security, the inevitable question is always how to prevent users from accessing the registry. You can't. Remember that the registry contains settings that the user must be able to read for Windows to work properly. Users also must have full control of their profile hives for the operating system and applications to save their preferences. You can't prevent access—nor do you want to prevent it. The best you should hope for is limiting users' ability to edit the registry using Regedit or other registry editors.

The most elegant way to prevent access to Regedit is by enabling the `Prevent access to registry editing tools` policy. When users start Regedit, all they see is an error message that says "Registry editing has been disabled by your administrator." The problem with this policy is that not all registry editors honor this policy. Nothing prevents a determined user from downloading a shareware registry editor, of which there are plenty, and using it. Another possibility is using Software Restriction Policies, which you can learn more about in Help and Support Center. Even this doesn't prevent users from running shareware registry editors unless you use Software Restriction Policies to completely restrict them to a short list of acceptable applications.

Restricting Remote Registry Access

Securing local access to the Windows registry is one thing; securing remote access is another. Windows gives members of the local Administrators and Backup Operators groups remote access to the registry. Because the Domain Admins group is a member of each computer's local Administrators group, all domain administrators can connect the registry of any computer that's joined to the domain. Also, Windows now limits remote access to the registry more than earlier versions of Windows.

There might be limited scenarios in which you want to open remote access to computers' registries. For example, in Active Directory, you might create an administrators group for each organizational unit and want to give it the ability to edit computers' registries if they belong to the organizational unit. To enable that group to remotely edit a computer's registry, add that group to the ACL of the key `HKLM\SYSTEM\CurrentControlSet\Control\SecurePipeServers\winreg`. The problem you're going to run into is that although adding a group to `winreg` allows remote access, each key's ACL still determines which keys the group can change. So to allow a remote user or group to change a setting on the computer, add that user or group to the local Users, Power Users, or Administrators group.

> **Caution**   Don't open each computer's registry to security threats by haphazardly adding groups to the winreg key's ACL. Doing so creates a hole large enough for many Trojan viruses to infect Windows and invites predators to hack away at your infrastructure. The best practice is to limit remote registry access to domain administrators.

Deploying Security Templates

You use security templates to create a security policy for your computer or network. Rather than using the techniques that you learned about in this chapter to hunt-and-peck security on a computer, security templates give you a single place to configure a range of security settings and then deploy those settings to numerous computers. It's a little used, often misunderstood tool that organizes many of the available security settings in one place to make managing security a far easier job. It saddens me when administrators tell me their security woes and yet they've never heard of security templates, which would deal with most of their problems admirably. Security templates are an IT professional's best friend. Interested yet? I hope so.

You use a variety of tools to create and apply templates. First you use security templates to create and edit templates. Then you use either the Security Configuration And Analysis or Group Policy console to apply templates. This section walks you through the process of using these tools, starting with creating the Microsoft Management Console (MMC) that you'll use to edit templates, and ending with deploying templates on a network.

To begin with, here's an explanation of the different security settings in a template. The following list shows the different categories of settings you see in a security template. Following each category is a description of the settings that you can define within it.

- **Account Policies.**   Password Policy, Account Lockout Policy, and Kerberos Policy
- **Local Policies.**   Audit Policy, User Rights Assignment, and Security Options
- **Event Log.**   Application, System, and Security Event Log settings
- **Restricted Groups.**   Membership of security-sensitive groups
- **System Services.**   Startup and permissions for system services
- **Registry.**   Permissions for registry keys (the topic of this section)
- **File System.**   Permissions for files and folders

Security templates are nothing more than text files that have the *.inf* extension. You can copy them, edit them, and so on. The file looks much like an INI file. You can create your own security templates from scratch, which I don't recommend because it's too much work with so much risk, or you can customize one of the predefined templates that come with Windows. Customizing a predefined template is definitely the way to go because most of the work is already done for you. Keep in mind that because only the Administrators group has permissions to change the default security template folder, %SystemRoot%\Security\Templates, only administrators can edit and apply security templates.

More Info   Regini.exe is a tool that ships with Windows that you can use to script changes to registry security. It's simple to use and sometimes useful for changing keys' ACLs from logon scripts. It is a legacy tool that's superseded by more robust security features in Windows, however. For more information about using Regini.exe, see *http://support.microsoft.com/kb/264584* and *http://support.microsoft.com/?kbid=237607*.

Creating a Security Management Console

To make your job easier, create an MMC that includes all the tools you'll need for editing, analyzing, and applying security templates:

1. Click Start, Run; then type **mmc**, and click OK.

2. On the File menu, click Add/Remove Snap-in.

3. In the Add/Remove Snap-in dialog box, click Add.

4. In the Add Standalone Snap-In dialog box, select Security Templates, and then click Add.

5. Select Security Configuration And Analysis, and click Add.

6. Click Close, and then click OK.

After creating your console, save it to a file for quick access. On the File menu, click Save. I like to name the file *Templates.msc*. MMC saves your file in your Administrative Tools folder. To open it again quickly, click Start, All Programs, Administrative Tools, and then Templates (or whatever you called it). Figure 8-4 shows the console that I created as described in this section.

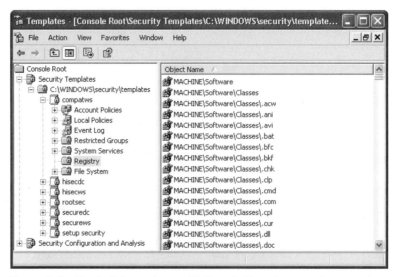

Figure 8-4   You build templates with SecurityTemplates, and you analyze and apply templates using Security Configuration And Analysis.

Choosing a Predefined Security Template

Windows comes with several predefined security templates. You almost never need to create a new template because you can usually just customize one of these predefined templates and save it to a different file. They provide starting points for applying security policies in different scenarios, whether those scenarios include one, one hundred, or thousands of computers. The following predefined security policies are in %SystemRoot%\Security\Templates by default:

- **Default security (Setup security.inf).**   This template contains the default security settings that setup applies when you install Windows. It includes file system and registry permissions, too. If you need information about the operating system's default permissions, you'll find that information here. You can use this template to restore a computer to the original Windows security settings by applying it with Security Configuration And Analysis, but don't deploy it using Group Policy.

- **Compatible (Compatws.inf).**   This template contains security settings that relax restrictions on the Users group enough to allow legacy applications to run. This is preferable to moving users from the Users group to the Power Users or, oh my, the Administrators groups. Specifically, this template changes the file system and registry permissions granted to the Users group so that they're consistent with legacy and other applications that aren't certified for Windows. This template also assumes that the administrator doesn't want users in the Power Users group, so it moves users from Power Users to the Users group. This template applies to workstations only, and you shouldn't apply it to servers.

- **DC Security (DC Security.inf).** This template is created when a server is promoted to a domain controller. It reflects file, registry, and system service default security settings. If you reapply this template, these settings are set to the default values. However, the template may overwrite permissions on new files, registry keys, and system services created by other programs.

- **Secure (Secure*.inf).** These templates tighten security settings that are least likely to affect application compatibility. Securedc.inf is for domain controllers, and Securews.inf is for workstations. It applies strong password, lockout, and audit settings, for example. It also limits the user of LAN Manager and Windows NT LAN Manager (NTLM) authentication protocols by configuring Windows to send only NTLM version 2 (NTLMv2) responses and configuring servers to refuse LAN Manager responses. Last, this template restricts anonymous users by preventing them from enumerating account names, enumerating shares, and translating Security Identifiers (SIDs). (See Chapter 1, "Learning the Basics.")Test this template carefully before deploying it.

- **Highly Secure (Hisec*.inf).** These templates are supersets of the previous templates, and they apply even more restrictions. Hisecdc.inf is for domain controllers, and Hisecws.inf is for workstations. For example, this template sets the levels of encryption and signing that Windows requires for authentication and for data moving over secure channels. It requires strong encrypting and signing. Last, it removes all members of the Power Users groups and makes sure that only the Domain Admins group and the local Administrator are members of the local Administrators group. Test these templates to ensure compatibility with your infrastructure and applications because only certified applications are likely to run after applying this template.

- **System root security (Rootsec.inf).** This template defines root permissions for the Windows file system. It contains no registry permissions. It does apply permissions for the root of %SystemDrive%. You can apply this template to a computer to restore these permissions to the root of the system drive or to apply the same permissions to additional volumes.

- **No Terminal Server user SID (Notssid.inf).** This template removes unnecessary Terminal Server SIDs from the file system and registry when running Terminal Server in application compatibility mode. If possible, run Terminal Server in full security mode instead, a mode in which the Terminal Server SID isn't used at all.

Most of these security templates are incremental. They modify the default or existing security settings if those settings are already configured on the computer. Other than the Setup Security template, they don't configure the default security settings before changing the computer's security configuration. Also, you can't use security templates to secure Windows when you use the FAT file system.

You can view these templates in your MMC. In the console's left pane, double-click a security template to open it. By default, the templates are under C:\Windows\Security\Templates, as shown under your console's Security Templates node. You can add a new path, however. Right-click Security Templates, and then click New Template Search Path. You'll see both the previous and new paths listed under Security Templates. If you want to remove a path from Security Templates, right-click it, and then click Delete.

Building a Custom Security Template

The hard way to create a custom security template is to start from scratch:

1. In Security Templates, right-click the folder in which you want to create the new template, and then click New Template.

2. In the Template Name box, type the name of the new template, and in the Description box, type a brief but useful description of your new template, and click OK.

3. In the left pane, double-click the new security template to open it. Select a security area, such as Registry, in the left pane, and configure that area's security settings in the right pane.

That's the hard way, and it's definitely not the way I recommend. First, it's too labor-intensive. Second, it's error-prone. The best way to create a security template is to start with one of the predefined templates, save it to a new file, and then edit it—carefully. Most of the times I've done this, I started with the Compatws.inf template file and customized it as necessary to give a legacy application enough room to work. Here's how:

1. In Security Templates, double-click C:\Windows\Security\Templates.

2. Right-click the predefined template that you want to customize, click Save As, type a new file name for the security template, and click Save.

3. In the left pane, double-click the new security template to open it. Select a security area, such as Registry, in the left pane, and configure that area's security settings in the right pane.

Because this is a registry book, I'll give you a little more detail about configuring registry security in a template. In the left pane of Security Templates, double-click your template, and then click Registry. You'll see a list of registry keys in the right pane. To add a key to the list, right-click Registry, and then click Add Key. Because the list already covers all of HKLM, add exceptions to the settings that the template defines for

HKLM\SOFTWARE and HKLM\SYSTEM. To edit a key's settings, double-click it, and then select one of the following options:

- **Configure This Key Then.**   After selecting this option, select one of the following:

  - ❑ **Propagate Inheritable Permissions To All Subkeys.**   The key's subkey inherits the key's security settings, assuming that the subkeys' security settings don't block inheritance. In case of a conflict, the subkey's explicit permissions overwrite the permissions that they inherit from the parent key.

  - ❑ **Replace Existing Permissions On All Subkeys With Inheritable Permissions.**   The key's permissions overwrite all its subkeys' permissions. In other words, each subkey's permissions will be identical to the parent key's permissions. If you select this option and apply the template, the change is permanent unless you change it by applying a different template to the registry.

- **Do Not Allow Permissions On This Key To Be Replaced.**   Select this option if you don't want to configure the key or its subkey's permissions.

To edit the actual permissions that you want the template to apply to a key, click Edit Security. You do this in the same Security For *Name* dialog box that you saw earlier in this chapter. You can add and remove groups. You can allow or deny permissions for different users and groups to perform various tasks. You can audit users' and groups' access to a key. You can also change ownership of a key. When you apply the template to a computer or deploy the template through Group Policy, the key receives the permissions that you define in this dialog box.

Analyzing a Computer's Configuration

With your custom template in hand, you can use it to analyze a computer's security configuration. Security Configuration And Analysis enables you to compare the current state of the computer's security configuration to the settings defined in the template. You can use this tool to make immediate changes to the computer's configuration, such as when troubleshooting a problem. You can also use it to track and ensure a certain level of security as part of your enterprise risk management program, detecting flaws in security as they occur over time.

Here's how to analyze a computer's security using Security Configuration And Analysis:

1. Right-click Security Configuration And Analysis, which you added to your console in the section titled "Creating a Security Management Console," earlier in this chapter, and then click Open Database.

2. In the Open Database dialog box, do one of the following:

   ❑ To create a new analysis database, type the name of your new database in the File Name box, and click Open (you don't have a database initially). Then in the Import Template dialog box, select a template and click Open.

   ❑ To open an existing analysis database, type the name of an existing database in the File Name box, and click Open.

3. Right-click Security Configuration And Analysis, click Analyze Computer Now, and then accept the default log file path or specify a new one.

Security Configuration And Analysis compares the computer's current security against the analysis database. If you import multiple templates into the database, which you can do by right-clicking Security Configuration And Analysis and then clicking Import Template, the tool merges the templates together to create one template. If it detects a conflict, the last template that you loaded has precedence (last in, first out). After Security Configuration And Analysis analyzes the computer, it displays results that you can browse. The organization of these results is the same as in security templates. The difference is that Security Configuration And Analysis displays the following indicators that show whether a current setting matches or is inconsistent with a setting defined in the template:

- **Red X.**   The setting is in the analysis database and on the computer, but the two versions don't match. The trick is to drill down through settings that have a red X next to them until you isolate the specific problem.

- **Green Check Mark.**   The setting is in the analysis database and on the computer, and the two match.

- **Question Mark.**   The setting is not in the analysis database and was not analyzed. This might also mean that the user who ran Security Configuration And Analysis didn't have the permissions necessary to do so.

- **Exclamation Point.**   The setting is in the analysis database but not on the computer. A registry key might exist in the database but not on the computer.

- **No Indicator.**   The setting is not in the database or on the computer.

What do you do with any discrepancies you find between the analysis database and the computer's settings? First you can update the database by double-clicking the troublesome registry setting and clicking Edit Security. (See Figure 8-5.) This updates the database but not the template, however. Also, it doesn't change the computer's settings. To do that, see the next section. You can also import a more appropriate template for that computer or an updated template into the database and then analyze it again. To avoid problems that result from merging templates, consider creating a new database if you use a new or updated template.

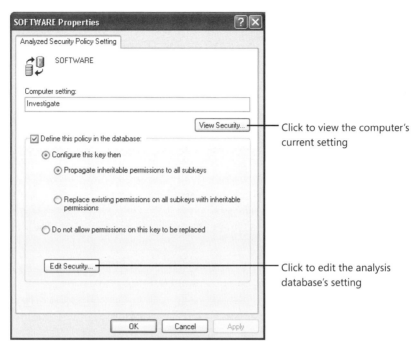

Figure 8-5   You can view and edit settings in the registry setting's Properties dialog box.

Modifying a Computer's Configuration

After you've created a security template and verified it by analyzing computers using Security Configuration And Analysis, you're ready to apply it to the computer:

1. Right-click Security Configuration And Analysis, and then click Open Database.

2. In the Open Database dialog box, do one of the following:

    ❑   To create a new database, type the name of your new database in the File Name box, and click Open. Then in the Import Template dialog box, click a template, and click Open.

    ❑   To open an existing database, type the name of an existing database in the File Name box, and click Open. If you modified a database without updating the template on which it's based, make sure you open the existing database.

3. Right-click Security Configuration And Analysis, click Configure Computer Now, and then accept the default log file path or specify a new one.

Deploying Security Templates on the Network

In the preceding section, "Modifying a Computer's Configuration," you learned how to apply a security template to a computer manually. This is fine for one-off scenarios, but it's not the way to deploy security templates to multiple computers on the network. To deploy templates on a network, use Group Policy: create a new GPO, and then edit it. In the Group Policy Editor, right-click Security Settings, and then click Import Policy. Click the template that you want to apply, and then click Open.

It's so simple, but I don't want to make light of this: deploying security templates on your network requires careful planning. You must first identify the templates that your network requires. Then you must identify which organizational units get which security templates. For example, if the sales department uses a legacy application that requires the Users group to have full control of certain registry keys, document and test the security template, and then import the template into a GPO that you assign to the sales department's organizational unit. Ideally, you'll account for security templates early in the deployment planning process. What really ends up happening, unless they planned carefully, is that IT professionals use security templates as a big fire hose to put out fires created by lack of foresight and planning.

Configuring New Security Features

New enhancements are available in Microsoft Windows XP SP2 for improving the manageability and visibility of key security capabilities in personal computers. New enhancements include the following:

- The new Windows Security Center feature tells you the status of three major security components: Windows Firewall, Automatic Updates, and Virus Protection.

- Windows Security Center indicates whether key security capabilities are turned on and up to date. Windows Security Center notifies you when updates are required or when you must take additional steps to help make your computer secure.

- You can manage Windows Security Center by using Active Directory Group Policy settings. By default, Windows Security Center is turned off in domain environments.

The following sections describe how you can configure Windows XP SP2 and Windows Server 2003 SP1 security features. These features include the new Windows Security Center (Windows XP) and Windows Firewall. The question I've been most frequently asked since the release of SP2 is how to configure these two features.

Security Center Alerts

The Windows Security Center displays alerts in popup balloons when the firewall, the virus scanner, or Automatic Updates is not configured properly or out of date. You see these alerts in the system tray. You can disable these alerts by using the registry. Table 8-2 describes the `REG_DWORD` values for each type of alert. You set these values in `HKLM\SOFTWARE\Microsoft\Security Center`. (Create the key and settings if they don't already exist.) For example, to prevent Windows Security Center from displaying alerts when the Windows Firewall is not enabled (a configuration that Microsoft recommends against), set `FirewallDisableNotify` to `0x01`.

Table 8-2   Security Center Settings

Name	Type	Values
`AntiVirusDisableNotify`	REG_DWORD	0x00—Disable AntiVirus alerts.
		0x01—Display AntiVirus alerts.
`AntiVirusOverride`	REG_DWORD	0x00—Windows Security Center monitors AntiVirus.
		0x01—Windows Security Center doesn't monitor AntiVirus.
`FirewallDisableNotify`	REG_DWORD	0x00—Disable firewall alerts.
		0x01—Display firewall alerts.
`FirewallOverride`	REG_DWORD	0x00—Windows Security Center monitors the firewall.
		0x01—Windows Security Center doesn't monitor the firewall.
`UpdatesDisableNotify`	REG_DWORD	0x00—Disable Automatic Update alerts.
		0x01—Display Automatic Update alerts.

Windows Firewall

Windows XP SP2 and Windows Server 2003 SP1 include the new Windows Firewall. Most companies and many enthusiasts will want to customize the Windows Firewall during installation. Microsoft provides three methods of doing so. The best way to manage Windows Firewall settings in a business environment is to use the new Windows Firewall Group Policy settings. This method requires the use of Active Directory with either Windows 2000 or Windows Server 2003 domain controllers. For more information, see *http://www.microsoft.com/technet/prodtechnol/winxppro/deploy/depfwset/wfsp2wgp.mspx*.

The following list describes methods that don't require Group Policy:

- **Unattended-setup answer file.**   The unattended-setup answer file (unattend.txt) for Windows XP SP2 has options to configure Windows Firewall settings when running an unattended setup of Windows XP SP2.

- **Netfw.inf.**   The Netfw.inf file for Windows XP SP2 can configure the Windows Firewall by specifying a set of registry settings equivalent to the options available from the Windows Firewall component in Control Panel and through Windows Firewall Group Policy settings when a user is performing an interactive setup of Windows XP SP2.

- **Netsh script.**   To configure computers running Windows XP with SP2 after SP2 has been installed, you can have your users run a script file, such as a .BAT or a .CMD file, that contains the series of Netsh.exe commands to configure the Windows Firewall operational mode, allowed programs, allowed ports, etc.

- **Custom configuration programs.**   To configure computers running Windows XP with SP2 after Windows XP SP2 has been installed, you can have your users run a custom configuration program that uses the new Windows Firewall configuration APIs to configure the Windows Firewall for operation mode, allowed programs, allowed ports, and other settings.

For more information about using these options, see *http://www.microsoft.com/technet/prodtechnol/winxppro/deploy/depfwset/wfsp2ngp.mspx*.

You can disable Windows Firewall by using the registry. The settings are in `HKLM\SOFTWARE\Policies\Microsoft\WindowsFirewall`. (Create the key and values if they don't already exist.) First, there are two subkeys: `DomainProfile` and `StandardProfile`. The settings in `DomainProfile` apply when the computer is currently connected to the domain. The settings in the `StandardProfile` apply when the computer isn't currently connected to the domain (a disconnected laptop computer, for example). Within each of those two subkeys, create the value `EnableFirewall`. Set this value to `0x00` to disable the firewall in that scenario, or set it to `0x01` to enable it.

Internet Explorer Privacy Settings

Microsoft Internet Explorer 6 added a Privacy tab to give users more control over cookies. There are different levels of privacy on the Internet zone, and they are stored in the registry at the same location as the security zones.

You can also add a site to allow or to block cookies based on the site, regardless of the privacy policy on the Web site. Those registry keys are stored in `HKCU\Software\Microsoft\Windows\CurrentVersion\Internet Settings\P3P\History`. In this key, you see the domains that have been added as a managed site. These domains are set to one of the following values:

- **0x00000005.**   Always Block
- **0x00000001.**   Always Allow

Internet Explorer Security Zones

Internet Explorer security zones settings are stored in HKLM\SOFTWARE\Microsoft\ Windows\CurrentVersion\Internet Settings and HKCU\SOFTWARE\Microsoft\Windows\ CurrentVersion\Internet Settings. By default, security zones settings are stored in HKCU. The settings for one user do not affect the settings for another. The Internet Settings key has the following subkeys:

- TemplatePolicies
- ZoneMap
- Zones

If the Security Zones: Use only machine settings setting in Group Policy is enabled, or if the Security_HKLM_only REG_DWORD value is present and has a value of 1 in HLKM\Software\Policies\Microsoft\Windows\CurrentVersion\Internet Settings, only local computer settings are used and all users have the same security settings. With the Security_HKLM_only policy enabled, HKLM values will be used by Internet Explorer, but the HKCU values will still be displayed in the zone settings on the Security tab in Internet Explorer. This is by design and there are no plans to change this functionality. If the Security Zones: Use only machine settings setting is not enabled in Group Policy, or if the Security_HKLM_only REG_DWORD value does not exist or is set to 0, computer settings are used along with user settings. However, only user settings appear in Internet Options. For example, when this REG_DWORD value does not exist or is set to 0, HKLM settings are read along with HKCU settings, but only HKCU settings appear in the Internet Options.

TemplatePolicies

The TemplatePolicies key determines the settings of the default security zone levels (Low, Medium Low, Medium, and High). You can change the security level settings from the default settings. However, you cannot add additional security levels. The keys contain values that determine the setting for the security zone. Each key contains a Description string value and a Display Name string value that determine the text that appears on the Security tab for each security level.

ZoneMap

The `ZoneMap` key contains the following keys:

- **`Domains.`**   The `Domains` key contains domains and protocols that have been added to change their behavior from the default behavior. When a domain is added, a key is added to the `Domains` key. Subdomains appear as keys under the domain where they belong. Each key that lists a domain contains a `REG_DWORD` with a value name of the affected protocol. The value of the `REG_DWORD` is the same as the numeric value of the security zone where the domain is added.

- **`ProtocolDefaults.`**   The `ProtocolDefaults` key specifies the default security zone that is used for a particular protocol (ftp, http, or https). To change the default setting, you can either add a protocol to a security zone by clicking Sites on the Security tab, or you can add a `REG_DWORD` value under the `Domains` key. The name of the `REG_DWORD` value must match the protocol name, and it must not contain any colons (:) or slashes (/).

  The `ProtocolDefaults` key also contains `REG_DWORD` values that specify the default security zones where a protocol is used. You cannot use the controls on the Security tab to change these values. This setting is used when a particular Web site does not fall in a security zone.

- **`Ranges.`**   The `Ranges` key contains ranges of TCP/IP addresses. Each TCP/IP range that you specify appears in an arbitrarily named key. This key contains a string value (`:Range`) that contains the specified TCP/IP range. For each protocol, a `REG_DWORD` value is added that contains the numeric value of the security zone for the specified IP range.

  When the Urlmon.dll file uses the MapUrlToZone public function to resolve a particular URL to a security zone, it uses one of the following methods:

  - ❑   If the URL contains a fully qualified domain name (FQDN), the `Domains` key is processed. In this method, an exact site match overwrites a random match.

  - ❑   If the URL contains an IP address, the `Ranges` key is processed. The IP address of the URL is compared to the `:Range` value that is contained in each of the arbitrarily named keys under the `Ranges` key.

> **Note**   Because arbitrarily named keys are processed in the order that they were added to the registry, this method might find a random match before it finds an exact match. If so, the URL might be executed in a different security zone than the zone where it is typically assigned. This behavior is by design.

Zones

The **zones** key contains keys that represent each security zone that is defined for the computer. By default, the following five zones are defined (numbered zero through four):

- 0. My Computer
- 1. Local Intranet Zone
- 2. Trusted Sites Zone
- 3. Internet Zone
- 4. Restricted Sites Zone

> **Note**   By default, My Computer does not appear in the Zone box on the Security tab.

Each of these keys contains the following REG_DWORD values that represent corresponding settings on the custom Security tab:

- 1001. Download signed ActiveX controls
- 1004. Download unsigned ActiveX controls
- 1200. Run ActiveX controls and plug-ins

  Run ActiveX controls and plug-ins (1200) has an extra setting named `Administrator approved`. When this setting is turned on, the REG_DWORD value is `0x00010000`, and `HKCU\Software\Policies\Microsoft\Windows\CurrentVersion\Internet Settings\AllowedControls` is checked for a list of approved controls.

- 1201. Initialize and script ActiveX controls not marked as safe
- 1206. Allow scripting of Internet Explorer Webbrowser control
- 1400. Active scripting
- 1402. Scripting of Java applets
- 1405. Script ActiveX controls marked as safe for scripting
- 1406. Access data sources across domains
- 1407. Allow paste operations via script
- 1601. Submit non-encrypted form data

- 1604. Font download

- 1605. Run Java

- 1606. Userdata persistence

- 1607. Navigate sub-frames across different domains

- 1608. Allow META REFRESH

- 1609. Display mixed content

- 1800. Installation of desktop items

- 1802. Drag and drop or copy and paste files

- 1803. File Download

    There is no prompt setting for File Download (1803) because it is either allowed or not allowed.

- 1804. Launching programs and files in an IFRAME

- 1805. Launching programs and files in webview

- 1806. Launching applications and unsafe files

- 1807. Reserved

- 1808. Reserved

- 1809. Use Pop-up Blocker

- 1A00. Logon

    Logon setting (1A00) may have any one of the following values:

    - 0x00000000. Automatically logon with current username and password

    - 0x00010000. Prompt for user name and password

    - 0x00020000. Automatic logon only in the Intranet zone

    - 0x00030000. Anonymous logon

- 1A02. Allow persistent cookies that are stored on your computer

- 1A03. Allow per-session cookies (not stored)

- 1A04. Don't prompt for client certificate selection when no certificates or only one certificate exists

- 1A05. Allow 3rd party persistent cookies

- 1A06. Allow 3rd party session cookies

- 1A10. Privacy Settings

  Privacy Settings (1A10) is used by the Privacy tab slider. The `REG_DWORD` values are in the following list:

  - ❑ 00000003. Block All Cookies

  - ❑ 00000001. High

  - ❑ 00000001. Medium High

  - ❑ 00000001. Medium

  - ❑ 00000001. Low

- 00000000. Accept All Cookies

- 1C00. Java permissions

  The Java Permissions setting (1C00) has the following five possible `REG_BINARY` values (binary):

  - ❑ 00 00 00 00. Disable Java

  - ❑ 00 00 01 00. High safety

  - ❑ 00 00 02 00. Medium safety

  - ❑ 00 00 03 00. Low safety

  - ❑ 00 00 80 00. Custom

- 1E05. Software channel permissions

  Software channel permissions (1E05) has three different values:

  - ❑ 00010000. High

  - ❑ 00020000. Medium

  - ❑ 00030000. Low

- 1F00. Reserved

- 2000. Binary and script behaviors

- 2001. Run .NET components signed with Authenticode

- 2004. Run .NET components not signed with Authenticode

- 2100. Open files based on content, not file extension

- 2101. Web sites in less privileged Web content zone can navigate into this zone

- 2102. Allow script-initiated windows without size or position constraints

- 2200. Automatic prompting for file downloads

- 2201. Automatic prompting for ActiveX controls

- 2300. Allow Web pages to use restricted protocols for active content

- {AEBA21FA-782A-4A90-978D-B72164C80120}First Party Cookie

- {A8A88C49-5EB2-4990-A1A2-0876022C854F}Third Party Cookie

Unless stated otherwise, each REG_DWORD value is equal to zero, one, or three. Typically, a setting of zero sets a specific action as permitted, a setting of one causes a prompt to appear, and a setting of three does not allow the specific action.

Each security zone also contains the Description string value and the Display Name string value. The text of these values appears on the Security tab when you click a zone in the Zone box. There is also an Icon string value that sets the icon that appears for each zone. Except for the My Computer zone, each zone contains a CurrentLevel, a MinLevel, and a RecommendedLevel REG_DWORD value. The MinLevel value sets the lowest setting that can be used before you receive a warning message, CurrentLevel is the current setting for the zone, and RecommendedLevel is the recommended level for the zone. The following list describes the settings for these values:

- **0x00010000.** Low Security

- **0x00010500.** Medium Low Security

- **0x00011000.** Medium Security

- **0x00012000.** High Security

The Flags REG_DWORD value determines the ability of the user to modify the security zone's properties. To determine the Flags value, add the numbers of the appropriate settings together. The following Flags values are available:

- 1. Allow changes to custom settings

- 2. Allow users to add Web sites to this zone

- 4. Require verified Web sites (https protocol)

- 8. Include Web sites that bypass the proxy server

- 16. Include Web sites not listed in other zones

- 32. Do not show security zone in Internet Properties (default setting for My Computer)

- 64. Show the Requires Server Verification dialog box

- 128. Treat Universal Naming Connections (UNCs) as intranet connections

Chapter 9

Troubleshooting Problems

In Chapter 3, "Backing Up the Registry," I said that mistakes happen. They do. If you didn't heed the advice that I gave in that chapter and back up the registry before making changes, or if something went wrong that just wasn't within your control, there are tools that you can use to troubleshoot and repair the registry.

This chapter describes those tools. It starts with some simple ways to repair an application's settings; it describes tools from third-party companies that you can use to find problems; and it ends with a description of the Windows Advanced Options Menu, Windows Recovery Console, and Automated System Recovery (ASR).

Fixing Corrupt Settings

Even if you've followed my advice to this point, you're going to run into problems. Sometimes a simple change to the registry has effects that can't be fixed by restoring a backup copy of a value. Microsoft Windows XP and Windows Server 2003 (Windows) and most applications are incredibly resilient, though, so fixing a problem is a simple matter of telling it, "*Heal thyself.*"

The quickest way to fix a corrupt setting is to remove the offending value and allow the program to re-create it using a default. (Windows and most programs re-create missing settings, which is what makes this method work in most cases.) This method is tantamount to uninstalling and reinstalling an application. The difficult part is figuring out which value contains the troublesome setting. Chapter 10, "Finding Registry Settings," helps you track down settings. For example, if your mouse pointer bounces around the screen in convulsive fits, remove the key HKCU\Control Panel\Mouse. When you log off and back on to Windows, the mouse settings are re-created. The operating system won't re-create everything you delete, though—particularly file associations in HKCR. So before you try this troubleshooting technique, back up any setting that you are going to delete.

There are also ways to fix those settings that Windows or other programs don't re-create. If you used the Files And Settings Transfer Wizard to transfer your settings from an earlier version of Windows to Windows XP, you can reapply your old settings to your current configuration. IT professionals use the User State Migration Tool for the same purpose. Of course, there must be copies of the original user state data for this to be possible. Chapter 12, "Deploying User Profiles," describes this tool. Other options for repairing settings are described later in this chapter.

Managing Settings to Avoid Problems

IT professionals avoid most problems with settings by properly managing the settings. The first and most important practice is not to place users into the local Administrators group. I understand the reasons why you might do this, such as legacy applications that won't otherwise run properly, or users who can't change settings because their accounts are in the local Power Users or local Users groups. You can successfully deal with all these issues by using tools such as security templates, which you learn about in Chapter 8, "Configuring Windows Security." Moving users from the local Administrators group to the Power Users or Users group is not difficult and can save professionals a lot of frustration—and their companies a lot of money.

Policies are another good way to manage settings. Policies accomplish two goals: first they configure settings for the user if, for example, he or she doesn't know the appropriate values. Policies also configure settings according to IT policy, and users can't change these settings. Moving users out of the local Administrators group saves your company money by reducing lost downtime and deviations from corporate standards, but policies actually help you recover money from your IT investment. Chapter 7, "Using Registry-Based Policy," describes exactly how to use policies and how they benefit IT.

In the Windows registry, you can also set keys' permissions to prevent users from changing those settings. This might sound like a great idea, but managing settings at that level of detail is so cumbersome that it is almost impossible to maintain. If you need to manage a key's ACL, use security templates instead. Security templates are much easier to deploy and maintain across the board, and you learn how to use them in Chapter 8.

Allowing Windows to Fix Errors

Perhaps you can't find a setting in the registry, or removing that setting from the registry doesn't fix the problem. In that case, use Control Panel, where you can fix many per-user settings and a few per-computer settings. These settings include the configuration of all your input and output devices, particularly the pointing device, keyboard, display, and printer. They also include accessibility and regional options.

When a device just doesn't work, your best bet is often to remove it and have Windows redetect the device. In my experience, this fixes a vast number of problems. You remove a device by using Device Manager and restarting the computer, and then Windows redetects it. If the operating system doesn't redetect the device, use the Add Hardware Wizard to detect it. You start the Add Hardware Wizard from Control Panel. Removing a device directly from the registry isn't a good idea because Windows scatters devices' settings, and the linkages are difficult to remove accurately. Follow these instructions to reinstall a device:

1.   Open Device Manager.

     To open Device Manager, right-click My Computer, click Properties, and then select the Hardware tab. On the Hardware tab, click Device Manager.

2.   Navigate to the device that you want to remove, select it, and then click Uninstall on the Action menu.

> **Tip**   Sysprep.exe is a Microsoft tool and is used to prepare a disk containing Windows for duplication and deployment; it can also be used to set things straight when your configuration is seriously out of order. When you restart a computer after running Sysprep, the Mini-Setup Wizard configures the computer for use. It detects the computer's hardware, configures the network connections, and optionally joins the computer to a business network. Chapter 15, "Cloning Disks with Sysprep," describes Sysprep in more detail. To use Sysprep to repair a broken configuration and redetect your computer's hardware, run `sysprep –activated –pnp –quiet – reseal`. If you want to fully automate the Mini-Setup Wizard, create the file Sysprep.inf, which you learn about in Chapter 15. This is a radical step—you'll lose the local Administrator user profile and a good number of per-computer settings—but it might give your configuration the refresh that it needs.

Repairing an Application's Settings

Predictability is a good thing when it comes to program settings. And most programs organize their settings in the registry in the same way. Per-user settings are in HKCU\Software*Company**Program**Version*\, and per-computer settings are in the same branch of HKLM. *Company* is the name of the application's publisher, *Program* is the name of the application, and *Version* is an optional version number. (Some people omit the version number, which isn't strictly by the standards but is common nonetheless.) Figure 9-1 shows where the TechSmith (*http://www.techsmith.com*) product SnagIt version 5 stores its settings. (This happens to be the program that I use to capture screenshots.)

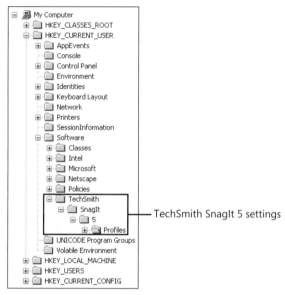

Figure 9-1 showing registry tree with "TechSmith SnagIt 5 settings" pointing to TechSmith > SnagIt > 5 > Profiles.

Figure 9-1 TechSmith SnagIt is the best screen capture tool, and it works well with Windows.

Well-designed applications re-create settings that they're missing. To reset the program's per-user settings, remove HKCU\Software*Company**Program*\. You typically don't want to remove the program's per-computer settings because doing so is likely to adversely affect most applications. You can hide the program's per-computer settings to test the scenario first, just to be safe.

Windows Installer–based applications are easier to reset because Windows Installer has repair functionality built right into it. Microsoft Office 2003 Editions are examples of a Windows Installer–based application. To learn more about Windows Installer–based applications, see Chapter 13, "Mapping Windows Installer." For now, I will describe the three different ways that you can make Windows Installer restore an application's original settings:

- On the application's Help menu, click Detect And Repair.

- In Control Panel, click Add Or Remove Programs. Click the application that you want to repair, and then click Change. To repair the application, follow the instructions that you see on the screen.

- In the Run dialog box, type **msiexec /f[u][m]** *package*, where *package* is the path and file name of the application's package file, which has the *.msi* file extension. Use /fu to repair per-user settings and /fm to repair per-computer settings. IT professionals like this command because it's the best way to repair settings without visiting the user's desk.

The last repair method for Windows Installer–based applications, particularly for Office 2003 Editions, is Profile Wizard. Chapter 17, "Deploying Office 2003 Settings," describes how to use this tool to deploy settings with Office 2003 Editions. Basically, you install and configure Office 2003 on a sample computer, capture Office 2003 Editions settings to an Office Profile Settings (OPS) file using the Office Profile Wizard, and then deploy the OPS file with your Office 2003 Editions customizations. IT professionals should think of that OPS file as a help desk tool and save it for later use. After users' phone time is up (we both know there's a limit to how long you want calls to last), and before you apply new disk images to their computers, reapply the OPS file to restore their settings. The command that you're running on their computers is `proflwiz /r filename /q`, where *filename* is the name of the OPS file that contains Office 2003 Editions per-user settings.

Removing Programs from the Registry

As I said earlier, predictability makes troubleshooting settings in the Windows registry possible. Predictability also makes removing programs' settings possible, but it does not make it easy. Some programs don't uninstall correctly, and you're left with no choice but to manually remove their settings from the registry. For example, if an uninstall program doesn't finish properly, it might fail to remove the entry from the list of programs in Add Or Remove Programs, or it might orphan a file association, causing you to see an error message about Windows not finding a program when you double-click a file.

You can invest in a third-party tool to look for and remove the program's settings, or you can do it manually. Even though it's somewhat difficult, you can remove most programs' settings successfully. Doing so is more art than science, but here are the general steps involved in the process:

1. List the EXE and DLL files in the application's folder.

   You install most programs in %SystemDrive%\Program Files*Program*, where *Program* is the name of the program. List the EXE and DLL files in that folder and all of its subfolders.

2. Remove keys and values that contain the application's installation folder.

   Search the registry for each of the application's folders and subfolders. For example, if an application installed in *C:\Program Files\Example* has two subfolders, *Binary* and *Templates*, search the registry for *C:\Program Files\Example*, *C:\Program Files\Example\Binary*, and *C:\Program Files\Example\Templates*. To avoid interfering with other programs that might require the settings that you will remove, choose those keys and values carefully.

3. Remove keys and values that contain the program's name.

   Search the registry for different versions of the program's name. For example, if the application is *Jerry's House of Horrors*, search for *Jerry's*, *Jerry's House*, and *House of Horrors*. Use any combinations that you think you'll find in the registry. Choose carefully the keys and values that you remove so that you don't break other applications that might also use those settings.

4. Remove keys and values that contain the EXE and DLL files you recorded.

   You recorded a list of EXE and DLL files in step 1. Search the registry for each of these program files. Search for the complete file name, including the extension, and remove the key or value only if the path matches the program's installation folder. As with the other steps, use caution here.

Removing Windows Installer–based applications manually is much more difficult because they knit themselves into the registry much more tightly than do programs that are packaged using other technologies. Chapter 13, "Mapping Windows Installer," is your best resource for figuring out these settings, but you still shouldn't remove them manually. Chapter 13 describes a tool called Msizap.exe that removes almost all traces of a program's Windows Installer data from the registry. This tool comes with the Windows Support Tools, and the command line is `msizap T! package`, where *package* is the path and file name of the package file from which you installed the application. Msicuu.exe is similar; you also learn about it in Chapter 13. After using either tool, use the instructions that you read earlier in this section to remove any remaining settings.

Msizap.exe Saves the Day

Msizap.exe has saved me on more than one occasion. In one case, I was upgrading a customer's deployment servers with the latest version of Symantec Ghost Corporate Edition. My plan was to upgrade to the latest version in place.

Nothing ever goes as planned, eh? Ghost's Windows Installer data was corrupt on one particular server, and I was certain that the customer wasn't going to believe me when I said, "I didn't do it." Because of the corrupt data, I couldn't upgrade to the newer version of Ghost. And my heart sank when I found out that I couldn't remove the earlier version, either.

I almost swapped servers, but I remembered Msizap.exe and thought I'd give it a try. Sure enough, Msizap.exe removed enough of Ghost's Windows Installer data from the registry that I was able to install the new version. I credit this handy utility with saving me a lot of work and a lot of explaining. You learn more about Msizap.exe in Chapter 13, "Mapping Windows Installer." Keep this tool nearby.

Using Another Computer's Settings

If all other methods fail, and you're desperate to repair settings, you can borrow settings from another computer. The only time that I recommend doing this is when the settings are simple and contained within a small key. For example, restoring a file association or a small program's settings from another computer is straightforward enough, but borrowing a device's settings from another computer just isn't a good idea. There's no reason to believe that Windows will store the exact same settings for the exact same device on two different computers.

When borrowing settings from another computer, you can use either REG files or hive files. I prefer hive files because importing them completely replaces the key that they contain. First connect to the remote computer's registry, and export the settings to a hive file. Regedit stores the hive file in a folder on your local computer so you don't have to copy it from the remote computer. Import the hive file to replace your old settings with the settings in the hive file. This is useful for IT professionals in a supporting role, too. You can borrow the key from one remote computer and then connect to another remote computer to restore the settings to the second computer's registry. For example, you can copy a file association from one remote computer to another remote computer.

Recovering from Disasters

Until this point, I've assumed in everything I've explained that you can start Windows. If you can't, your recovery options are a bit more limited and a lot more dramatic. If you have the money, I'd invest in Winternals Administrator's Pak, which you can learn more about at *http://www.winternals.com*. This is a set of advanced troubleshooting tools that I use to recover configurations that are almost ready for the trash bin. I'll tell you more about these tools in Chapter 10, "Finding Registry Settings," because I use them to track down programs' settings in the registry (which will be discussed later in this book).

It's fortunate that these types of problems don't occur as often as they once did. The reliability improvements in Windows mean that I don't have to recover nearly as many configurations as I did with Windows 98 or Microsoft Windows NT 4.0. The tools now available in Windows are similar to the ones that came with Windows 2000. The Windows Advanced Options Menu (the boot menu) offers a variety of modes in which you can start Windows, including safe mode. The Windows Recovery Console is a limited command window environment with which you can fix certain classes of problems. And ASR, which is the last resort, minimally reinstalls Windows on the computer. I'll present these in the order in which you should use each option.

> **Note**   Don't wait until after a failure to master the advanced troubleshooting tools. Practice with them in a lab environment. Make them your own by scoping out their advantages and disadvantages well in advance of any problems. Master these tools now, and you'll enjoy that feeling you get from fixing a user's computer and walking away saying "No worries" after just a few minutes of work.

Windows Advanced Options Menu

Windows gives you a number of options for starting the computer. Safe mode is the most common example. In safe mode, Windows uses default settings for the minimum set of device drivers required to start the operating system. When you can't start Windows normally, you can usually start it in safe mode and then either repair the problem or use System Restore to restore a checkpoint. You can also remove programs by using Add Or Remove Programs to uninstall cranky devices.

To start safe mode or one of the other modes, you have to display the Windows Advanced Options Menu. First restart the computer. When you see the Please Select The Operating System To Start message, press F8. (If you don't see this message, you can start pressing F8 as soon as the computer starts.) Then select one of the following options from the menu:

- **Safe Mode.**   Uses basic files and drivers (mouse, monitor, keyboard, mass storage, basic video, and default system services without network connections) to start Windows. If Windows doesn't start when you use safe mode, you might need to use the Windows Recovery Console to repair Windows.

- **Safe Mode With Networking.**   Starts Windows by using basic files and drivers, as described in the preceding item, but includes network connections.

- **Safe Mode With Command Prompt.**   Uses basic files and drivers to start Windows. After logging on to the operating system, you see a command prompt instead of the graphical user interface.

- **Enable Boot Logging.**   Starts Windows and logs all the device drivers and services that the operating system attempts to load. The log file is Ntbtlog.txt and is in the %SystemRoot% folder. Safe Mode, Safe Mode With Networking, and Safe Mode With Command Prompt add to the log a list of all the drivers and services that Windows loaded. The log is useful for determining which device driver or service is preventing Windows from starting properly.

- **Enable VGA Mode.**   Uses the basic VGA driver to start Windows. This mode is useful after installing a new device driver for the video card when it's preventing Windows from starting properly. Windows always uses the basic VGA driver when you start in Safe Mode, Safe Mode With Networking, or Safe Mode With Command Prompt.

- **Last Known Good Configuration.**   Uses the registry hive files and device drivers that Windows saved after the last successful logon. Any changes made since the last successful logon are lost. Only use Last Known Good Configuration when the problem is in the configuration because it doesn't solve problems caused by corrupt or missing files.

- **Directory Service Restore Mode.**   Restores the SYSVOL directory and the Active Directory directory service on a server. This option is irrelevant to Windows.

- **Debugging Mode.**   Starts Windows and sends debugging information to another computer through a serial cable.

> **Note**   If you're unable to start Windows using the graphical user interface, you can usually start it using Safe Mode with Command Prompt. To run System Restore, which you're likely to do if you want to restore an earlier restore point, run the command %SystemRoot%\System32\Restore\rstrui.exe. System Restore is only available in Windows XP, however.

Windows Recovery Console

If Safe Mode doesn't start your computer, try the Windows Recovery Console. It offers commands that help fix varieties of system-related problems. You can enable or disable services; format disks; read and write files on a local NTFS volume; and perform a number of other administrative tasks. Notably, you can copy files from a floppy disk or CD to %SystemRoot% in order to replace broken system files. The Windows Recovery Console is useful only if you're already familiar with a command prompt, and you must log on to the computer as an administrator to use it.

You start the Windows Recovery Console in one of the following two ways:

- **From the Windows CD.**   Use the Windows CD to boot the computer, and the setup program gives you the option of starting the Windows Recovery Console.

- **From the list of operating systems when the computer boots.**   First you must install the Windows Recovery Console on the computer by typing **D:\i386\winnt32.exe /cmdcons** in the Run dialog box, where *D* is the drive containing the Windows CD. Restart the computer, and in the list of operating systems, choose Microsoft Windows Recovery Console.

The Windows Recovery Console has numerous commands, but it's missing many of the commands that a command prompt provides. To see a list of commands and how to use them, type **help** at the Windows Recovery Console command prompt. Here's a brief overview of each of them:

- **Attrib**   Changes the attributes of a file or directory
- **Batch**   Executes the commands specified in the text file

- **Bootcfg**   Boot file (boot.ini) configuration and recovery
- **ChDir (Cd)**   Displays the name of the current directory or changes the current directory
- **Chkdsk**   Checks a disk and displays a status report
- **Cls**   Clears the screen
- **Copy**   Copies a single file to another location
- **Delete (Del)**   Deletes one or more files
- **Dir**   Displays a list of files and subdirectories in a directory
- **Disable**   Disables a system service or a device driver
- **Diskpart**   Manages partitions on your hard disks
- **Enable**   Starts or enables a system service or a device driver
- **Exit**   Exits the Windows Recovery Console and restarts your computer
- **Expand**   Extracts a file from a compressed file
- **Fixboot**   Writes a new partition boot sector onto the specified partition
- **Fixmbr**   Repairs the master boot record of the specified disk
- **Format**   Formats a disk
- **Help**   Displays a list of the commands that you can use in the Windows Recovery Console
- **Listsvc**   Lists the services and drivers available on the computer
- **Logon**   Logs on to a Windows installation
- **Map**   Displays the drive letter mappings
- **Mkdir (Md)**   Creates a directory
- **More**   Displays a text file
- **Rename (Ren)**   Renames a single file
- **Rmdir (Rd)**   Deletes a directory
- **Set**   Displays and sets environment variables

Policies that you can enable to add more capabilities to the Windows Recovery Console are new for Windows. The policies `Recovery console: Allow automatic administrative logon` and `Recovery console: Allow floppy copy and access to all drives and folders` are per-computer administrative policies in `\Windows Settings\Security Settings\Local Policies\Security Options`. Enable `Recovery console: Allow automatic administrative logon` to automatically log on to the Windows Recovery Console as Administrator. Set `Recovery console: Allow floppy` copy and access to all drives and folders to allow access to all of the computer's drives and folders. (By default, Windows Recovery Console limits access to %System-Root%.) After you enable this policy, you configure the Windows Recovery Console by setting environment variables: type **set** *variable* = *true* | *false* at the command prompt. (You must include a space on each side of the equal sign.) Table 9-1 shows the default environment settings. To see the current settings, type **set**.

Table 9-1 **Windows Recovery Console Environment Settings**

Setting	Default	Description
AllowWildCards	False	Enable wildcards for some commands.
AllowAllPaths	False	Allow access to all files and folders.
AllowRemovableMedia	False	Allow file copying to removable media.
NoCopyPrompt	False	Don't prompt to overwrite existing files.

Note You can't log on to the Windows Recovery Console if you installed Windows from a disk image prepared with Sysprep. (See Chapter 15, "Cloning Disks with Sysprep.") This is due to changes that Sysprep makes in the way that Windows stores password keys in the registry. These changes aren't compatible with the Windows Recovery Console. Microsoft publishes a fix for this problem in the Knowledge Base. Look for article 308402, "'The Password Is Not Valid' Error Message Appears When You Log On to Recovery Console in Windows XP," and download the files that it lists. This problem will not exist on Windows XP systems with Service Pack 1 (SP1) or later.

Automated System Recovery

Create Automated System Recovery (ASR) backups frequently as part of your overall strategy. It's a last resort for system recovery, useful only if you've already tried using the other options that I've described in this chapter, including Safe Mode, Last Known Good Configuration, and the Windows Recovery Console.

ASR is a two-part process. The first part is to back up the computer using Automated System Recovery Preparation Wizard, which is accessible within the Backup Utility. The wizard backs up system state data, services, and all operating system components. It also creates a file that contains information about the backup data, disk configurations, and how to restore the computer. ASR does not back up or restore data files or programs. It only backs up the files necessary to start the computer in the event of failure. Here's how to prepare for ASR:

1. Run Backup Utility. Click Start, All Programs, Accessories, System Tools, and then Backup.

2. If you see Backup or Restore Wizard, click Advanced Mode; otherwise, move on to the next step.

3. On the Welcome tab, click Automated System Recovery Wizard to start the wizard, and then follow the instructions that you see on the screen to back up the computer and create an ASR disk.

The second part of the process is to restore the computer. When booting the computer from the Windows CD, when prompted by the setup program, you press F2 to use ASR. ASR reads the disk configurations from the file that it created earlier and restores all disk signatures, volumes, and disks containing operating system files. (It tries to restore all the computer's disks but might not be able to do so successfully.) ASR then installs Windows minimally and restores the backup created by Automated System Recovery Preparation Wizard. The whole process is similar to reinstalling Windows manually and then restoring your own backup, but it's automated.

Administrator's Pak

Winternals Administrator's Pak contains tools that do much more than the Windows Recovery Console and ASR do. You can also buy these tools individually if the price of the entire pak is a bit high.

The first tool is ERD Commander. Using this tool, you can start computers directly from a CD in an environment similar to Windows. The environment gives you full access to all the computer's volumes. It's similar to a graphical version of the Windows Recovery Console. You can even reset a forgotten administrator password, edit the registry, and copy files from the computer to the network. If this tool is your last resort for fixing a downed computer, you're in good hands.

Disk Commander is another tool in the kit that enables you to recover files from dead volumes. After scanning a volume, it presents in a user interface similar to Windows Explorer the files it found, so you can copy them to a safe place.

Remote Recover is the last tool that I'm featuring here, but there are more in the Administrator's Pak. Use this tool to repair failed computers across a network; that is, it gives you access to a remote computer's disks as if you installed those disks on your computer. You have to boot the remote computer, though, and Remote Recover gives you two options. The first is to start the remote computer using a bootable floppy disk. The second, and the one I like best, is a PXE-based disk image that you can start remotely or add to a RIS (Remote Installation Services) server.

You can learn more about these notable tools by visiting the Winternals Web site at *www.winternals.com*. The wunderkind duo of Mark Russinovich and Bryce Cogswell, Winternals Software's founders, have developed these and other tools to such a high level of reliability that I often bet my job on them.

Diagnosing Registry Corruption

If, after you try the other techniques that this chapter describes, your computer does not start, the registry hive files might be corrupt. The error messages might vary. They can include any of the following:

- Windows could not start because the following file is missing or corrupt: \WINDOWS\SYSTEM32\CONFIG\SYSTEM.ced.

- Windows could not start because the following file is missing or corrupt: \WINDOWS\SYSTEM32\CONFIG\SYSTEM.

- Windows could not start because the following file is missing or corrupt: \WINDOWS\SYSTEM32\CONFIG\SOFTWARE.

- System hive error.

- Stop 0xc0000218 (0xe11a30e8, 0x00000000, 0x000000000, 0x00000000) UNKNOWN_HARD_ERROR.

- Stop: 0xc0000218 {Registry File Failure} The registry cannot load the hive (file): \SystemRoot\System32\Config\CorruptHive or its log or alternate. It is corrupt, absent, or not writable.

There are many reasons why a registry hive might be corrupt. Most likely, the corruption is introduced when the computer is shut down, and you cannot track the cause because the computer is unloading processes and drivers during shutdown. Sometimes, it is difficult to find the cause of registry corruption. The following sections describe three possible causes for the problem. To troubleshoot registry corruption, follow these steps:

1. Back up the registry.

   One tool that you can use to back up registry hives is the Windows Recovery Console. For additional information about how to back up, edit, and restore the registry, see Chapter 3, "Backing Up the Registry."

2. Check the hardware, the disk, the firmware drivers, and the basic input/output system (BIOS). To do this, follow these steps. These steps might require downtime for the computer.

   a. Make sure that the CPU is not being over-clocked.

   b. Make sure that system event logs do not contain event ID 9, event ID 11, or event ID 15 (or any combination of these events). These events might indicate hardware problems that must be addressed.

   c. On the disk that contains the registry hive files, run the Chkdsk command-line command with the /r switch. This command helps to verify that the area of the disk that contains the registry hive files is not involved with the problem.

   d. Apply the latest firmware revisions to disk controllers, and use the matching driver versions. Make sure that the drivers are signed drivers and that you have the appropriate firmware revisions installed.

   e. Make sure that you apply the latest BIOS updates to the computer.

3. After you complete step 2, you might not see any change in behavior. To stop the corruption from occurring, try to close all running processes before you shut down the computer. You might be able to narrow the scope to a single process that is involved. Even if you identify the process, you might not be able to prevent a component from being unloaded before the registry hive is written to. However, if you make sure that you stop the process before shutdown, you might be able to prevent registry hive corruption.

4. After you complete step 3, if you do not see any change in behavior, compare the registry hives. Capture a non-corrupted registry hive and a corrupted registry hive, and then use comparison tools such as WinDiff to compare the two. For more information about using WinDiff, see Chapter 10, "Finding Registry Settings."

5. Determine which registry hive section is growing. If it appears that the problem is a registry hive that is growing too large, you might be able to determine which section is growing and to trace this back to a process that is writing to the hive.

Power Failure

A power failure or some other unexpected shutdown event might cause a corrupted registry hive. To determine whether this is the cause of the issue, look for event ID 6008 entries. Event ID 6008 entries indicate that there was an unexpected shutdown. In this case, some process might have been in the process of modifying part of the registry hive, and the computer lost power before that change could be completed. This leaves the registry hive in an inconsistent state. On restart, when the operating system tries to load the registry hive, it might find data in that registry hive that it cannot interpret, and you might receive one of the earlier error messages.

File Corruption and Faulty Hardware

You must determine whether only the registry hives are corrupted or whether other files (system and data) are also corrupted. If corruption is not limited to registry hives, the corruption might result from faulty hardware. This hardware might include anything that is involved in writing to a disk, such as the following components:

- The random access memory (RAM)
- The cache
- The processor
- The disk controller

If you suspect faulty hardware, the hardware vendor must thoroughly investigate the condition of all computer components.

The Registry Is Written To at Shutdown

If one or two registry hives consistently become corrupted for what seems like no reason, the problem probably occurs at shutdown and is not discovered until you try to load the registry hive at the next restart. In this scenario, the registry hive is written to disk when you shut down the computer, and this process might stop the computer or a component in the computer before the writing is completed.

Repairing a Corrupt Registry

When you try to start or restart your Windows XP–based computer, you might receive one of the following error messages if your registry is corrupt:

- Windows XP could not start because the following file is missing or corrupt: \WINDOWS\SYSTEM32\CONFIG\SYSTEM

- Windows XP could not start because the following file is missing or corrupt: \WINDOWS\SYSTEM32\CONFIG\SOFTWARE

- Stop: c0000218 {Registry File Failure} The registry cannot load the hive (file): \SystemRoot\System32\Config\SOFTWARE or its log or alternate

The steps that this section describes use the Windows Recovery Console and System Restore. This section also lists all the required steps in specific order to ensure that the process is fully completed. When you finish this procedure, the system returns to a state very close to its original state before the problem occurred. If you have ever run NTBackup and completed a system state backup, you do not have to follow the procedures in steps 2 and 3; you can go directly to step 4.

 Warning   Do not use the procedure that is described in this section if your computer has an OEM-installed operating system. The system hive on OEM installations creates passwords and user accounts that did not exist previously. If you use the procedure that is described in this section, you might not be able to log back into the Windows Recovery Console to restore the original registry hives.

Step 1

In step 1, you start the Windows Recovery Console, create a temporary folder, back up the existing registry files to a new location, delete the registry files at their existing location, and then copy the registry files from the repair folder to the System32\ Config folder. When you have finished this procedure, a registry is created that you can use to start Windows XP. This registry was created and saved during the initial setup of Windows XP. Therefore any changes that occurred after the Setup program was finished are lost.

To complete step 1, follow these instructions:

1. Insert the Windows XP startup disk into the floppy disk drive, or insert the Windows XP CD-ROM into the CD-ROM drive, and then restart the computer. If prompted to do so, press a key to boot the computer from the CD-ROM drive.

2. When the Welcome To Setup screen appears, press R to start the Recovery Console.

3. If you have a dual-boot or multiple-boot computer, select the installation that you want to access from the Windows Recovery Console.

4. When you are prompted to do so, type the administrator password. If the administrator password is blank, press ENTER.

5. At the Windows Recovery Console command prompt, run the following commands. (These commands assume that Windows XP is installed to the C:\Windows folder. Make sure to change C:\Windows to the appropriate folder if Windows XP is in a different location.)

   ❑ **md tmp**

   ❑ **copy c:\windows\system32\config\system c:\windows\tmp\ system.bak**

   ❑ **copy c:\windows\system32\config\software c:\windows\tmp\ software.bak**

   ❑ **copy c:\windows\system32\config\sam c:\windows\tmp\sam.bak**

   ❑ **copy c:\windows\system32\config\security c:\windows\tmp\ security.bak**

   ❑ **copy c:\windows\system32\config\default c:\windows\tmp\ default.bak**

   ❑ **delete c:\windows\system32\config\system**

   ❑ **delete c:\windows\system32\config\software**

❏ delete c:\windows\system32\config\sam

❏ delete c:\windows\system32\config\security

❏ delete c:\windows\system32\config\default

❏ copy c:\windows\repair\system c:\windows\system32\config\ system

❏ copy c:\windows\repair\software c:\windows\system32\config\ software

❏ copy c:\windows\repair\sam c:\windows\system32\config\sam

❏ copy c:\windows\repair\security c:\windows\system32\config\ security

❏ copy c:\windows\repair\default c:\windows\system32\config\ default

6. Type **exit** to exit the Windows Recovery Console. Your computer will restart.

Note Make sure to replace all five of the registry hives. It can cause potential issues if you only replace a single hive or two because software and hardware might have settings in multiple locations in the registry.

Step 2

To complete the instructions described in this section, you must be logged on as an administrator or as an administrative user (a user who has an account in the Administrators group). With Windows XP Home Edition, you must start the computer in safe mode, as described earlier in this chapter.

In step 2, you use System Restore to copy the registry files from their backed-up location. This folder is not available in the Windows Recovery Console and is generally not visible during typical usage. Before you start this procedure, you must change several settings to make the folder visible:

1. Start Windows Explorer.

2. On the Tools menu, click Folder Options.

3. Click the View tab.

4. Under Hidden Files And Folders, click to select Show Hidden Files And Folders, and then click to clear the Hide Protected Operating System Files (Recommended) check box.

5. When the dialog box that confirms that you want to display these files appears, click Yes.

6. If it is important to click the correct drive, double-click the drive where you installed Windows XP to display a list of the folders.

7. Open the System Volume Information folder. This folder is unavailable and appears dimmed because it is set as a super-hidden folder.

> **Note**   For more information about the System Volume Information folder, see Chapter 3, "Backing Up the Registry." You might receive the following error message: "C:\System Volume Information is not accessible. Access is denied." If you receive this message, follow the instructions in article 309531, "How to Gain Access to the System Volume Information Folder," at *http://support .microsoft.com* or Chapter 3, "Backing Up the Registry," to access it.

8. Open a folder with a time stamp that does not match the current time. You might have to click Details on the View menu to see when these folders were created. Under this folder, there might be one or more folders starting with "RPx." These are restore points.

9. Open one of these folders to locate a Snapshot subfolder. The following path is an example of a folder path to the Snapshot folder: C:\System Volume Information_restore{D86480E3-73EF-47BC-A0EB-A81BE6EE3ED8}\RP1\Snapshot.

10. From the Snapshot folder, copy the following files to the C:\Windows\Tmp folder:

    ❏ _REGISTRY_USER_.DEFAULT

    ❏ _REGISTRY_MACHINE_SECURITY

    ❏ _REGISTRY_MACHINE_SOFTWARE

    ❏ _REGISTRY_MACHINE_SYSTEM

    ❏ _REGISTRY_MACHINE_SAM

11. Rename the files in the C:\Windows\Tmp folder as follows:

    ❏ Rename _REGISTRY_USER_.DEFAULT to DEFAULT.

    ❏ Rename _REGISTRY_MACHINE_SECURITY to SECURITY.

    ❏ Rename _REGISTRY_MACHINE_SOFTWARE to SOFTWARE.

    ❏ Rename _REGISTRY_MACHINE_SYSTEM to SYSTEM.

    ❏ Rename _REGISTRY_MACHINE_SAM to SAM.

These files are the backed-up registry files from System Restore. Because you used the registry file that the Setup program created, this registry does not know that these restore points are available. Under System Volume Information, a new folder is created with a new GUID, and a restore point is created that includes a copy of the registry files that were copied during part one. Therefore, it is important not to use the most current folder, especially if the time stamp on the folder is the same as the current time.

The current system configuration is not aware of the previous restore points. You must have a previous copy of the registry from a previous restore point to make the previous restore points available again.

The registry files that were copied to the Tmp folder in the C:\Windows folder are moved to ensure that the files are available within the Windows Recovery Console. You must use these files to replace the registry files currently in the C:\Windows\System32\Config folder. By default, the Windows Recovery Console has limited folder access and cannot copy files from the System Volume folder.

Step 3

In step 3, you delete the existing registry files and then copy the System Restore registry files to the C:\Windows\System32\Config folder:

1. Start the Windows Recovery Console.

2. At the command prompt, type the following lines, pressing ENTER after you type each line. (These steps assume that Windows XP is installed to the C:\Windows folder. Make sure to change C:\Windows to the appropriate folder if Windows XP is in a different location.)

    ❏   **del c:\windows\system32\config\sam**

    ❏   **del c:\windows\system32\config\security**

    ❏   **del c:\windows\system32\config\software**

    ❏   **del c:\windows\system32\config\default**

    ❏   **del c:\windows\system32\config\system**

    ❏   **copy c:\windows\tmp\software c:\windows\system32\config\ software**

❑   copy c:\windows\tmp\system c:\windows\system32\config\system

❑   copy c:\windows\tmp\sam c:\windows\system32\config\sam

❑   copy c:\windows\tmp\security c:\windows\system32\config\security

❑   copy c:\windows\tmp\default c:\windows\system32\config\default

3. Type **exit** to quit Windows Recovery Console. Your computer restarts.

Step 4

Use the following steps to restore your computer to a previous RestorePoint:

1. Click Start, and then click All Programs.

2. Click Accessories, and then click System Tools.

3. Click System Restore, and then click Restore To A Previous RestorePoint.

Chapter 10
Finding Registry Settings

This chapter shows you how to relate a setting in the user interface to a value in the registry. Power users can use this information to find their own registry hacks. IT professionals will find registry information even more useful because they can use the information to locate settings in the registry for a variety of purposes. For example, after they've found settings, they can build administrative templates for them and deploy the settings on their network. They can write scripts that automatically apply the settings they found. They can even use this information to help build and deploy better default user profiles.

Three basic techniques are available for tracking down settings. The first, and often most effective, method is comparing two snapshots of the registry. Take one snapshot before changing a setting and the second after you've made a change. The second method is monitoring the registry to detect changes that a program makes. Monitoring is often difficult because of the way Microsoft Windows XP, Windows Server 2003, and other programs do a lot in the registry. Nonetheless, with a good tool and the tips in this chapter, it is an occasionally useful method. The last method for tracking down registry settings is auditing, which is the most difficult to use effectively and causes performance degradation. Because the first method is often most effective, that's where I start.

Comparing REG Files

Comparing two REG files is often the easiest way to discover where in the registry Windows XP or Windows Server 2003 (Windows) stores a setting. Create these REG files before and after changing a setting that is in the user interface and that you know is somewhere in the registry. This is how I found the location of the settings that Tweak UI includes and that I documented in Chapter 5, "Mapping Tweak UI." First I exported HKCU to a REG file. I changed a setting in Tweak UI and exported the same branch to a second REG file. Then I compared the two files to figure out which value changed when I changed the setting in Tweak UI. You can use this method to trace just about any setting that has a user interface to its location in the registry.

The only disadvantage to comparing two registry files is that the process requires a file-comparison tool. Windows comes with such a tool, which I'll tell you about later in this section. The advantages of this method are many. First, it's quick and easy. Second, its results are dead-on accurate. If you don't let a lot of time pass between each snapshot, the differences between the two should include only those settings you changed. Also, REG files are easy to read, so you won't have any problems deciphering the results.

Now for some details. Recall that Registry Editor (Regedit) can export all or part of the registry to text files that have the .reg extension (REG files). A REG file looks similar to an INI file. It contains one or more sections; the name of each section is the path of a registry key. Each section contains the key's values. The format of each value is *name=value*. If the value is a string containing spaces, *value* must be quoted. Each key's default value looks like @=*value*. Chapter 11, "Scripting Registry Changes," describes REG files in all their glory, including how to interpret the different types of values in them. To export the registry to a REG file, click the key that you want to export. Then on the File menu, click Export. In the Export Registry File dialog box, select Win9x/NT4 Registration Files (*.reg) from the Save As Type drop-down list to export to a version 4 ANSI REG file. Remember from Chapter 2, "Using Registry Editor," that Regedit supports REG files in two different file formats: ANSI and Unicode. Many file-comparison tools work only with the first format, so you must create version 4 ANSI REG files for them. The tools that I talk about in this chapter support Unicode text files, though. If you're not familiar with ANSI and Unicode character encoding, see Chapter 1, "Learning the Basics."

The sections following this one describe tools that you can use to compare two REG files. My personal favorite is WinDiff, which is one of the Windows Support Tools included on the Windows installation CD. I like this tool so much because of its simple user interface and, more importantly, the speed at which it compares very large text files. Another choice is probably already installed on your computer: Microsoft Office Word 2003. It's slower than WinDiff, but you're probably already familiar with how to use this word processor. In any case, the overall process is the same:

1. Export the registry to a REG file. Name the file Before.reg, or something similar. If you have a general idea where the setting is in the registry, export that branch; otherwise, export the entire registry, including HKCU and HKLM.

2. Change a setting in the user interface, or perform some other action that you're trying to trace to the registry. For example, if you want to see where a program stores its settings during installation, install the program.

3. Export the registry to a second REG file. Name it After.reg. Make sure you export the same branch using the same file format as you did in step 1. If you don't duplicate the process exactly, the files won't match, and finding the difference will be difficult.

4. Compare Before.reg and After.reg using your favorite file-comparison utility. The differences between the two files are your changes. The file-comparison tool points out only the values that changed, because only the values under each section heading change; but if you look a little higher in the file, you'll see the key that contains the values.

All-in-One Solutions

LastBit Software produces a program named RegSnap that performs the process described in this section. You don't have to create any REG files or compare two REG files with a file-comparison tool. RegSnap does the whole process for you, making it a handy program to have around if you do comparisons on a regular basis. You can download the shareware version of RegSnap from *http://www.webdon.com*. Give it a try; if you like it, it's very inexpensive. It comes in a standard edition and a professional edition. The professional edition enables you to work with remote registries; otherwise, the standard edition is sufficient to locate a setting in the registry. The only problem I have with Reg-Snap is that its user interface is very clunky.

That leads me to RegView, from Vincent Chiu. This program is available at *http://www.regview.com*. I like this program because it has a cleaner user interface than RegSnap has. You can use RegView to edit and search the registry and to compare different versions of it. RegView doesn't have a setup program, but it really doesn't need one. Figure 10-1 shows the result in RegView of comparing a snapshot to the current registry. RegView's output is a little easier to read than RegSnap's output, but RegView is quite a bit slower at producing it.

Figure 10-1 RegView is an enhanced registry editor.

If turn-around time is important to you, use RegSnap. If you're after an enhanced registry editor that can do a search-and-replace as well as compare snapshots of the registry, you should consider RegView. Both shareware programs are inexpensive, but if you don't want to spend the money, stick with the methods that you learn in this chapter.

There are a few ways to make this process more efficient. Comparing two large REG files can take a while, even using WinDiff. If you're fairly certain that you know the general vicinity of a setting in the registry, export just that branch. For example, if you know a setting is a per-user setting, export only HKCU. If you suspect it's somewhere in HKLM\SOFTWARE\Microsoft, search only that branch. You can always export the entire registry if your hunch isn't correct. Another way to streamline the process is to ignore differences that are irrelevant. Some settings change whether or not you doing anything. For example, Plug and Play values change frequently, as does the configuration of some services. The easiest way to eliminate the confusion that these inherent changes cause is to exclude HKLM\SYSTEM in your REG files. Also, the less time that elapses between snapshots, the less clutter you'll have in your comparison results.

Using WinDiff

WinDiff is the ultimate tool for comparing two versions of a text file. Its roots are as a developer tool for comparing different versions of source files to see changes before checking them into version control. It was also useful as a debugging tool to figure out which changes in a source file might have introduced a problem. WinDiff was originally available in the Windows Software Development Kit (SDK). Microsoft included it in the last several Windows resource kits. It comes with Windows as part of Windows Support Tools. Install the tools from \Support\Tools on your Windows CD. Type **windiff** in the Run dialog box to start it.

After starting WinDiff, here's how to compare two REG files with it:

1.   On the File menu, click Compare Files.

2.   Type the path and name of the first file, and click Open.

3.   Type the path and name of the second file, and click Open.

4.   On the View menu, click Expand, or double-click the files in the list.

After comparing the two files, you see results similar to Figure 10-2. WinDiff combines both files and highlights the differences in red and yellow. Differences are relative to the second file, which is why I had you open the second file after the first one. Deleted lines, present in the first file but not in the second, are red. Inserted lines, absent in the first file but present in the second, are yellow. White lines are the same in both files. You also see arrows that indicate whether a line is deleted or inserted. A left arrow (<!) indicates a line deleted from the second file, and a right arrow(!>) indicates a line inserted into the second file. WinDiff represents changed lines as deletions followed by insertions, as shown in Figure 10-2. Because WinDiff compares files line by line instead of character by character, you have to judge for yourself whether a deleted line followed by an inserted line represents a changed line of text. Press F8 to move to the next block of differences that WinDiff found; press F7 to move to the previous block of differences.

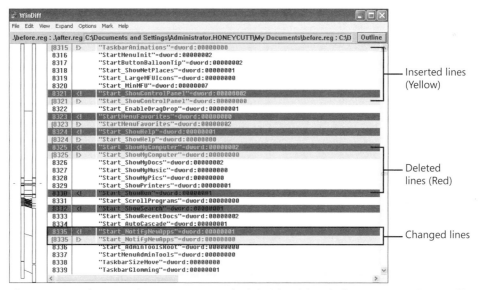

Figure 10-2   The two columns you see on the left side of the window represent the two files that you're comparing. These columns are a roadmap of the files' differences.

Using Word 2003

If WinDiff isn't available to you (for example, if you're not free to install the support tools on a customer's computer), you can use the comparison features of Word to compare REG files. You might also prefer using Word if you're already familiar with this program and don't want to install or learn how to use WinDiff. The only drawback is that using Word to compare REG files is often a slow and tedious process because it's not designed for this purpose.

When using Word to compare REG files, open the second REG file first, and compare it to the first REG file. This order ensures that Word indicates insertions and deletions properly. Here's how to compare two REG files using Word:

1. On the File menu, click Open, type the path and name of the first REG file in the File Name box, and click Open.

2. If the File Conversion dialog box appears, select the encoding method that makes the text in the Preview area readable, and then click OK.

   You can choose between Windows (Default), MS-DOS, and Other Encoding. The option Windows (Default) corresponds to ANSI, which is what version 4 REG files use. If the file is a version 5 REG file, select the Other Encoding option, and then click Unicode in the list.

3. On the Tools menu, click Compare And Merge Documents, type the path and name of the second REG file, and then click Merge.

4. If the File Conversion dialog box appears, select the encoding method that makes the text in the Preview area readable.

Word displays the results as shown in Figure 10-3. To see the next change, click the Next button on the Reviewing toolbar. To see the previous change, click the Previous button. Word displays the results differently depending on the view:

■ **Normal view.** To switch to the normal view, click Normal on the View menu. This is the view shown in Figure 10-3. By default, insertions are underlined. Deletions are crossed out.

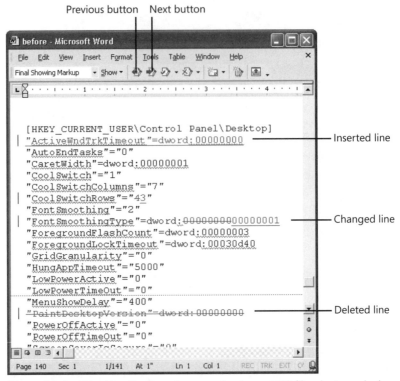

Figure 10-3 Word is effective at comparing large REG files, but much slower than WinDiff.

■ **Print Layout view.** To switch to Print Layout view, click Print Layout on the View menu. In this view, you see bubbles in the right column that describe the differences between the two files. This view is often the easiest to read.

Tip   When comparing two REG files in Word, make sure that you disable grammar and spelling checking. Word isn't likely to find many correctly spelled words in a REG file, so it burns up a lot of resources checking them. To disable both features, on the Tools menu, click Options. In the Options dialog box, click the Spelling & Grammar tab, and clear the Check Spelling As You Type and Check Grammar As You Type check boxes.

Comparing with Reg.exe

The Windows Support Tools, which include WinDiff, as you've already learned, also installs the Console Registry Tool for Windows (Reg.exe). This program can compare two branches of the registry and has a useful feature that helps you track down settings in the registry. Copy the branch that you think contains the value to the temporary key (this is your first snapshot), change the setting you're tracking, and then compare the current key to the temporary key. Using Reg.exe this way has the advantage of being quite straightforward. It has the disadvantage of relying on a command line rather than a graphical user interface, and if you don't remove the temporary keys from the registry, you can end up with an oversized registry that contains a bunch of data that you don't need.

Chapter 11, "Scripting Registry Changes," describes all the command-line options available in Reg.exe. For now, here are the steps necessary to locate a setting in the registry:

1. In a command prompt window, type **reg copy *source destination* /s /f**, where *source* is the key that you want to copy to the temporary key *destination*.

    Make sure the destination doesn't exist first; otherwise, you'll end up with a lot of differences when you compare the two keys. Also, if the name of either key contains spaces, enclose the entire key in quotation marks. Don't use the full names of root keys; use HKCU and HKLM instead.

2. Make changes to the setting.

3. In a command prompt window, type **reg compare *key temp* /s**, where *key* is the current key and *temp* is the temporary key.

The following listing is a sample of the output that Reg.exe generates. Reg.exe indicates lines that are missing from the current key with a right arrow (>) and indicates lines that were added or changed in the current key with a left arrow (<). In other words, you see > next to deleted values and < next to new or changed values.

```
< Value:   HKEY_CURRENT_USER\control panel\desktop  ActiveWndTrkTimeout  REG_DWORD  0x0
> Value:   HKEY_CURRENT_USER\backup  ActiveWndTrkTimeout  REG_DWORD  0x400
< Value:   HKEY_CURRENT_USER\control panel\desktop  DragFullWindows  REG_SZ  1
> Value:   HKEY_CURRENT_USER\backup  DragFullWindows  REG_SZ  0
< Value:   HKEY_CURRENT_USER\control panel\desktop  DragHeight  REG_SZ  4
< Value:   HKEY_CURRENT_USER\control panel\desktop  DragWidth  REG_SZ  4

Result Compared:  Different

The operation completed successfully
```

After you're done with the temporary key, make sure that you delete it; otherwise, you're going to fill up the registry with junk, and you won't be able to use the same temporary key for future comparisons. To quickly remove the temporary key, in a command prompt window, type **reg delete** *key* /*f*, where *key* is the name of the temporary key. The command-line option /f prevents Reg.exe from prompting you to confirm that you want to remove the key.

> **Tip**   An alternative method is to save a branch as a hive file, and then load the hive file into HKU. Then change a setting in the user interface, and compare the original branch to the hive file that you loaded in HKU. Don't forget to unload the hive file when you are finished. This method has the advantage of not cluttering the registry with temporary keys. Chapter 11, "Scripting Registry Changes," shows you the Reg.exe commands that enable you to save, load, and unload hive files.

Auditing the Registry

As I mentioned earlier, comparing snapshots of the registry is just one method of finding a setting; monitoring is another. The first method of monitoring the registry that I'm going to show you is built into Windows: auditing. Use auditing only if you don't have other comparison tools available to you, however, because its disadvantages far outweigh its advantages for the purpose of tracing settings. The first drawback is that auditing the registry for changes requires that you know in advance the general vicinity where a setting is located because auditing the entire registry isn't practical. Second, deciphering the results of an audit is rather cumbersome. It relies on viewing security events in Event Viewer, and the output isn't intuitive.

Auditing the registry for changes is a three-step process. First you must enable Audit Policy. You do this by editing Local Security Policy. After that, you audit branches in the registry where you think the setting is located. You can't just audit the entire registry because doing so would bring even the fastest computer running Windows to a grinding halt. On average, the operating system and the applications access the registry thousands of times during a session, so recording the details of every one of these hits just isn't practical. Last, after changing the setting or performing the action that you're tracking, look at the log files in Event Viewer to see which values changed. The following sections describe each step.

Setting Audit Policy

The first step in auditing the registry is to enable Audit Policy:

1.   From the Administrative Tools folder, launch Local Security Policy.

2.   In the left pane, under Local Policy, click Audit Policy.

3.   In the right pane, double-click Audit Object Access, and then select both the Success and Failure check boxes.

Auditing Registry Keys

After enabling Audit Policy, audit the specific keys in which you think you're going to find the setting:

1.   In Regedit, click the key that you want to audit.

2.   On the Edit menu, point to Permission, and then click Advanced.

3.   On the Auditing tab of the Advanced Security Settings dialog box, shown in Figure 10-4, click Add.

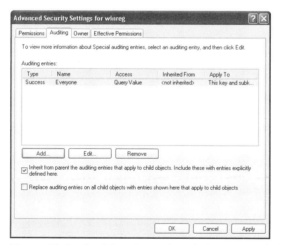

Figure 10-4   Auditing the registry helps you track down settings in the registry.

4. In the Select Users, Computers, Or Group dialog box, click Locations. Then click the computer, domain, or organizational unit in which you want to look for the user or the group that you want to audit.

5. In the Enter The Object Name To Select box, type the name of the user or the group that you want to add to the key's audit list, and then click OK.

6. In the Auditing Entry dialog box, in the Access list, select the Successful and Failed check boxes next to the activities that you want to audit. The following list of permissions corresponds to the permissions that you learned about in Chapter 8, "Configuring Windows Security."

    ❑   Full Control

    ❑   Query Value

    ❑   Set Value

    ❑   Create Subkey

    ❑   Enumerate Subkeys

    ❑   Notify

    ❑   Create Link

    ❑   Delete

    ❑   Write DAC

    ❑   Write Owner

    ❑   Read Control

Tip   Audit carefully to avoid too much of a performance penalty. For example, if you're trying to find the location where an application saves a setting, audit for Set Value, change the value in the user interface, and then check your results.

Analyzing the Results

The final step after enabling Audit Policy and auditing specific keys is checking the results using Event Viewer. To open Event Viewer, click Start, Control Panel, Performance And Maintenance, Administrative Tools, and Event Viewer. In Event Viewer's left pane, click Security. You see each hit in the right pane, and the most recent hits are at the top of the list. Double-click any entry to see more details. The Event Properties dialog box tells you the type of access that Windows detected, the object type, and the process that accessed the key or the value.

Monitoring the Registry

Monitoring the registry for changes is different from comparing snapshots in that you're watching registry access as it happens. Thus, you can change a setting in the user interface and then look at the monitor to see what value Windows wrote to the registry. I tend to monitor the registry instead of compare snapshots when I'm looking for a large number of settings. When doing this, it's helpful to eliminate distractions. I'll show you how to do that in the section "Filtering for Better Results," later in this chapter.

My favorite monitoring tool is Regmon from Winternals. You can download a freeware version of this tool from *http://www.sysinternals.com*. Regmon Enterprise Edition is available at *http://www.winternals.com* and is inexpensive. The difference between the two is that the enterprise edition enables you to monitor a remote registry, which makes the process a little easier if you can work on one computer and see the results on a different computer. Although the freeware version of Regmon contains the enterprise edition's other features, I purchased Regmon Enterprise Edition for the convenience of remote monitoring.

Download either version of Regmon. The freeware version doesn't have a setup program, so you just run it from the directory in which you unzip it. Regmon Enterprise Edition comes with a setup program that adds a shortcut for Regmon to the Start menu. The following sections show you how to use this useful product.

Using Winternals Regmon

Figure 10-5 shows the freeware version of Regmon. Every time that Windows or programs access the registry, Regmon adds a row to the window. The first two columns are the line number and the time. The next column displays the name of the process that accessed the registry, which is usually the program's file name. Next you see the type of access, followed by the path and the result. The last column gives you additional information, such as the contents of a value. The most interesting information here is the type of access, the path of the key, and the Other column. Any time a column is too narrow to display the entire contents of a row, you can point to the data, and Regmon displays its full contents in a balloon—a nifty feature.

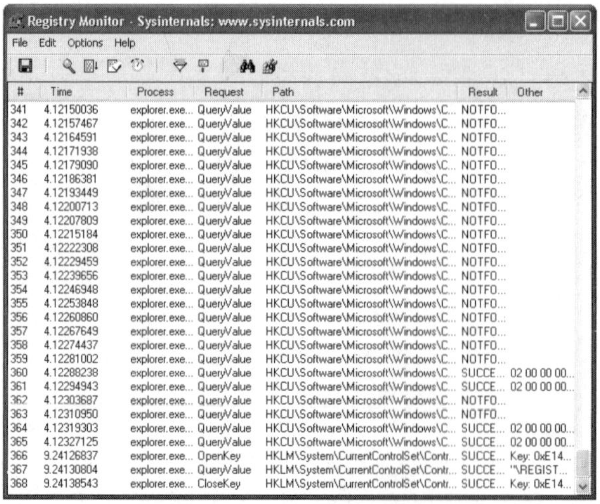

Figure 10-5   Regmon's window quickly fills up with unimportant information. This is Regmon's window seconds after starting it.

Two columns, Request and Other, need more attention. Request tells you what Windows or a program was trying to do. The requests you see in the Request column are different registry application programming interface (API) functions and are shown in Table 10-1. The most interesting type of request is SetValue, of course. The Other column contains a variety of information, depending on the type of request. Again, see Table 10-1. For example, if the request is QueryValue, the Other column contains the data in the value. If the request is OpenKey, the Other column contains the key's handle.

Table 10-1   Regmon Request Types and Data

Request Type	Data in the Other Column
CloseKey	Handle of closed key
CreateKey	Handle of new key
CreateKeyEx	Handle of new key
DeleteKey	None
DeleteValue	None
DeleteValueKey	None
EnumerateKey	Name of next subkey
EnumKeyEx	Name of next subkey
EnumerateValue	None
FlushKey	None
OpenKey	Handle of open key

Table 10-1   Regmon Request Types and Data

Request Type	Data in the Other Column
OpenKeyEx	Handle of open key
QueryKey	Name of key
QueryValue	Value's data
QueryValueEx	Value's data
SetValue	Data stored in value
SetValueEx	Data stored in value

Filtering for Better Results

If you start Regmon and change some settings in the Windows user interface, you won't have a lot of luck sifting through Regmon's output to find the setting. For example, opening Windows Explorer accesses the registry approximately 5000 times. Clicking Options on Windows Explorer's Tools menu accesses the registry a few hundred times. Sorting through all that output isn't practical. Your experience improves dramatically if you learn how to use filtering.

The first step that you can take, particularly if you're interested in finding the value in which Windows stores a setting, is to filter out everything except write requests. On Regmon's Edit menu, click Filter/Highlight. Then clear all the check boxes except Log Successes and Log Writes. Regmon will report only successful writes to the registry. This alone significantly reduces the amount of output that you see. Get more specific, though, and Regmon will all but hand you the setting for which you're looking. The asterisk (*) in the Include box is a wildcard that matches everything; this is the default filter.

To get more specific, limit Regmon to certain processes. For example, if you're searching for a setting in Windows Explorer, look only for registry access by the process *explorer.exe*. If you're searching for settings in Tweak UI, look only for registry access by the process *Tweakui.exe*. On Regmon's Edit menu, click Filter/Highlight. In the Include box, type the name of the process that you want Regmon to display in the window. Include multiple processes separated by a semicolon. The easiest way to figure out the name of a process is to look in Windows Task Manager. Press CTRL+SHIFT+ESC, and then look at the Processes tab. If in doubt, you can also look in Regmon's output for the process name, which is how I usually find it. You might see the process Rundll32.exe. This is a special program that executes APIs in Dynamic Link Libraries (DLL). Because you might have many different instances of this process running at any time, filtering this process is more difficult.

My last tip for how you can limit the output of Regmon is to filter for specific keys. If you have general knowledge of where Windows stores a setting in the registry, filter the output to display only lines that contain that key. For example, if you know that a setting is somewhere in HKLM\SOFTWARE\Microsoft, filter Regmon's output so that it shows only SetValue requests on that key. You'll see very little output in Regmon's window when you change that value in the user interface, and one of the lines is likely to be the value for which you're searching.

Tip   You can combine subkeys and process names in your filter. Separate each with a semicolon. Regmon compares your criteria to all the columns you see in the window so that you can filter multiple columns at one time. You can filter results by process, request type, and key at the same time, for instance.

Chapter 11
Scripting Registry Changes

Think of what life would be like for an IT professional without automation. Each time you needed to change settings, you'd have to get up from your desk and find the right user's computer in a maze of cubicles.

Scripting is a more efficient way to deploy and change settings. Notice that I didn't use the word "manage," which applies more to policies than it does to scripting. If you need to manage settings, see Chapter 7, "Using Registry-Based Policy." Scripting is useful on many levels. You can write a script that changes a group of settings and then test the script in the lab before deploying it. If you need to update the script, you can easily use a regression-test to assess how your changes affect the results. I like scripting registry changes because settings can be made on countless computers without introducing the potential for human error each time. Also, you can deploy scripts without visiting desktops. To deploy scripts without having to interrupt users' work, you can use your software management infrastructure (or a more unreliable methodology if you don't have an infrastructure).

This chapter describes five of my favorite scripting methods. The first is using INF files. I like the simplicity of INF files and the fact that there's no registry setting that they can't edit. The second scripting method is using REG files, which you can easily create by exporting settings from Registry Editor (Regedit). I describe how to use Console Registry Tool for Windows (Reg.exe), which is a terrific tool for changing settings from batch files, to edit the registry from a command prompt window. I also describe how to write scripts that change settings. Microsoft Windows XP and Windows Server 2003 (Windows) come with Windows Script Host, and this chapter shows you how to write scripts using the JScript and Microsoft Visual Basic, Scripting Edition (VBScript) languages. Finally, I describe how to build a Windows Installer package file to deploy settings. This technique is great because you can deploy those settings through Active Directory and Group Policy. Because I cover so many different techniques, the first section, "Choosing a Technique," helps you choose the scripting method that's best for you.

Choosing a Technique

Table 11-1 compares the scripting methods covered in this chapter. Each column represents one of the five scripting methods that I describe. For example, the Batch column describes using Reg.exe in a batch file. The MSI column describes Windows Installer package files that include registry settings. The similarities of all five methods are that they all enable you to change values as well as to add keys or values, and Windows supports all five methods without installing third-party tools or any resource kits.

Table 11-1   **Comparison of Scripting Methods**

Features	INF	REG	Batch	Script	MSI
Difficulty	Medium	Low	Medium	High	Medium
OS access	Basic	None	Full	Full	Basic
Built-in support	Yes	Yes	Yes	Yes	Yes
Change values	Yes	Yes	Yes	Yes	Yes
Add keys/values	Yes	Yes	Yes	Yes	Yes
Delete keys/values	Yes	Keys only	Yes	Yes	Yes
Querying values	No	No	Yes	Yes	No
Support for value types	High	Medium	Medium	Low	Medium
Bitwise support	Yes	No	No	Yes	No

I almost always prefer to write an INF file. You'll notice that most of the scripts in this book are INF files. I chose this method because I'm familiar with INF files, and they're easy to create and to read. I use scripts only when I have to query values from the registry. The advantage of using INF files is that they offer the flexibility to do anything that you want to do in the registry, but they don't require you to be a programmer. Choose whatever methods are most appropriate for you, but rely more heavily on INF files and scripts. You won't end up using just one of these techniques: you'll find that you'll use a combination of these methods, depending on the scenario. After you start using the scripting methods that I describe in this chapter, you'll master them in no time.

Now I'll describe the differences among these scripting methods. As the table shows, using REG files is the easiest method, and using scripts and Windows Installer package files is the most difficult. No matter which method you choose, they all become rather easy after you learn how to use them. Access to the operating system is important only if you're trying to do more than just edit the registry—for example, if you want to read values from the registry and then dump them to a text file. The most important difference to notice among these scripting methods is that only INF files and scripts provide high support for the many different types of values that you can store in the registry. The remaining methods support the basic value types, though, and that's often all you need. If you need to edit more esoteric types, you're better off writing an INF file or a script. INF files and scripts are also the only two methods that you can use to set and clear bits in values. For example, the bits in the value `UserPreferencesMask` indicate different user interface settings, and you enable or disable them by setting or clearing the corresponding bit. If this is your requirement, INF files or scripts are your best methods.

Installing INF Files

Setup Information files have the *.inf* extension; I call them INF files. The Windows setup application programming interface (API) uses INF files to script installations. Most people associate INF files with device-driver installation, but applications often use them, too. Most actions that you associate with installing device drivers and applications are available through INF files. You can copy, remove, and rename files. You can add, change, and delete registry values. You can install and start services. You can install almost anything using INF files. One obvious example is that you can use them to customize registry settings. You can also create INF files that users can uninstall using Add Or Remove Programs.

INF files look similar to INI and REG files. They're text files that contain sections that look like this: `[Section]`. Each section contains items, sometimes called properties, that look like this: `Name=Value`. Windows happens to come with the perfect INF-file editor: Notepad. When you use Notepad to create a new INF file, make sure that you enclose the file name in quotation marks or choose All Files in the Save As Type drop-down list in the Save As dialog box. That way, your file will have the *.inf* extension instead of the *.txt* extension. Installing an INF file is straightforward: right-click the INF file, and then click Install. To deploy an INF file using your existing software-deployment infrastructure, while preventing users from having to install it manually, use the following command, replacing *Filename* with the name of your INF file. (This is the command line that Windows associates with the *.inf* file extension in the registry.)

```
rundll32.exe setupapi,InstallHinfSection DefaultInstall 132 Filename.inf
```

Listing 11-1 shows a simple INF file. The first section, `[Version]`, is required. The name of the second section is arbitrary but is usually `[DefaultInstall]` so that users can right-click the file to install it. The linkage to this section is through the command line that you saw just before this paragraph. The command is `rundll32.exe`, which executes the API in Setupapi.dll called `InstallHinfSection`. The next item on the command line, `DefaultInstall`, is the name of the section to install. The `132` you see before the file name tells the setup API to prompt the user before rebooting the computer, if necessary. The last item on the command line is the name of the INF file to install. As I mentioned, because this is the command that Windows associates with the `.inf` file extension, you should usually name this section `[DefaultInstall]`. Within this section, you see two directives, `AddReg` and `DelReg`. The directive `AddReg=Add.Settings` adds the settings contained in the section `[Add.Settings]`. The directive `DelReg=Del.Settings` deletes the settings listed in the section `[Del.Settings]`. The names of these sections are arbitrary; you should adopt names that make sense to you, and stick with them so you don't confuse yourself later on.

Listing 11-1   Example.inf

```
[Version]
Signature=$CHICAGO$

[DefaultInstall]
AddReg=Add.Settings
DelReg=Del.Settings

[Add.Settings]
HKCR,regfile\shell,,0,"edit"

[Del.Settings]
HKCU,Software\Microsoft\Windows\CurrentVersion\Applets\Regedit
```

Now you've had my brief tour of an INF file. The sections that follow describe how to write the different parts of an INF file. I'm focusing on using INF files to edit the registry, but you can do much more with them. The ultimate resource for writing INF files is *http://msdn.microsoft.com/library/en-us/install/hh/install/inf-format_0a6b2b92-442b-4295-ab95-5011ab9d8dbb.xml.asp* on Microsoft's Web site. This is the "INF File Sections and Directives" section of the Windows Driver Development Kit (DDK). Don't let the fact that this information is in the DDK scare you; it's very straightforward and useful for much more than installing device drivers.

Starting with a Template

I never start INF files from scratch. I can't be bothered to remember the format of the sections and directives, so I use a template. I'm lazy enough (or efficient enough) that I add the template you see in Listing 11-2 to the Templates folder in my user profile so that I can right-click in a folder, and then click New, Setup Information File. The easiest way is to first create the file Setup Information File.inf with the contents of Listing 11-2. Then use Tweak UI, which you learn about in Chapter 5, "Mapping Tweak UI," to add the template. It's a real timesaver.

The reason that this template makes creating INF files so easy is because I've added comments to it. Comments begin with the semicolon (;) and add descriptive information to the file. In this case, for each section, I described the format of the different directives. In the `[Reg.Settings]` section, for example, you see the syntax for adding values to the registry. In the [Bits.Set] section, you see the format for setting individual bits in a number. I often write INF files that users can uninstall using Add Or Remove Programs; the template in Listing 11-2 shows you how to do that. If you don't want users to uninstall the file and its settings, remove the [DefaultUninstall], [Reg.Uninstall], [Inf.Copy], [DestinationDirs], [SourceDisksNames], and [SourceDisksFiles] sections and any linkages to those sections. In this template, words that appear in all capital letters are placeholders that I replace when I create an INF file. For example, I replace FILENAME with the INF file's actual name.

Listing 11-2   Setup Information File.inf

```
[Version]
Signature=$CHICAGO$

[DefaultInstall]
BitReg=Bits.Set
AddReg=Reg.Settings
AddReg=Reg.Uninstall
CopyFiles=Inf.Copy

[DefaultUninstall]
BitReg=Bits.Clear
DelReg=Reg.Settings
DelReg=Reg.Uninstall
DelFiles=Inf.Copy

[Reg.Settings]

; ROOT,SUBKEY[,NAME[,FLAG[,DATA]]]
;
; FLAG:
;
;0x00000 - REG_SZ
;0x00001 - REG_BINARY
;0x10000 - REG_MULTI_SZ
;0x20000 - REG_EXPAND_SZ
;0x10001 - REG_DWORD
;0x20001 - REG_NONE

[Bits.Set]

; ROOT,SUBKEY,NAME,FLAG,MASK,BYTE
;
; FLAG:
;
;0x00000 - Clear bits in mask
;0x00001 - Set bits in mask

[Bits.Clear]

; ROOT,SUBKEY,NAME,FLAG,MASK,BYTE
;
; FLAG:
;
```

```
;0x00000 - Clear bits in mask
;0x00001 - Set bits in mask

[Reg.Uninstall]
HKCU,Software\Microsoft\Windows\CurrentVersion\Uninstall\%NAME%
HKCU,Software\Microsoft\Windows\CurrentVersion\Uninstall\%NAME%,DisplayName\
,,"%NAME%"
HKCU,Software\Microsoft\Windows\CurrentVersion\Uninstall\%NAME%,UninstallString\
,,"Rundll32.exe setupapi.dll,InstallHinfSection DefaultUninstall 132"\
" %53%\Application Data\Custom\FILENAME"

; ROOT:
;
;HKCU
;HKLM

[Inf.Copy]
FILENAME

[DestinationDirs]
Inf.Copy=53,Application Data\Custom

; DIRID:
;
; 10 - %SystemRoot%
; 11 - %SystemRoot%\System32
; 17 - %SystemRoot%\Inf
; 53 - %UserProfile%
; 54 - %SystemDrive%
; -1 - Absolute path

[SourceDisksNames]
55=%DISKNAME%

[SourceDisksFiles]
FILENAME=55

[Strings]
NAME     = "Jerry's NAME"
DISKNAME = "Setup Files"
```

The first two lines in Listing 11-2 are the only ones required. The [Version] section and the signature property identify the file as a valid INF file. You must include these two lines at the top of all your INF files. Incidentally, "Chicago" was Microsoft's code name for Windows 95, so version=$CHICAGO$ identifies the file as a Windows 95 INF file. These days, $CHICAGO$ indicates that an INF file is compatible with all versions of Windows. Use $Windows 95$ if you want to indicate that your INF file is compatible with 16-bit versions of Windows only. Use $Windows NT$ to indicate that your INF file is compatible with 32-bit versions of Windows only. Generally, I leave signature set to $CHICAGO$.

Linking Sections Together

The [DefaultInstall] section usually comes after the [Version] section. As I said earlier, the name of this section is arbitrary, but you should use [DefaultInstall] if you want users to be able to install your INF file by right-clicking it. The command associated with the .*inf* file extension references this section by name. This is the section that links together your INF file. You fill it with directives that tell the Setup API which sections in the INF file to process and what to do with them.

You saw this section in Listing 11-2. Each line in this section is a directive. The Setup API supports a number of different directives, but the ones that we care about in this book are AddReg, DelReg, and BitReg. In the listing, you see a line that says AddReg=Reg.Settings. This adds the settings listed in the [Reg.Settings] section. The line BitReg=Bits.Set sets the bit masks listed in the section [Bits.Set]. As well, you can list more than one section for each directive. You can duplicate a directive on multiple lines, for example, or you can assign multiple sections to it: AddReg=Section1,Section2,SectionN. For an example, see Listing 11-3.

Listing 11-3   Example.inf

```
[Version]
Signature=$CHICAGO$

[DefaultInstall]
AddReg=Reg.Settings1,Reg.Settings2,Reg.Settings3
AddReg=Reg.Settings4
AddReg=Reg.Settings5
DelReg=Reg.Settings6

[Reg.Settings1]
; Registry settings to add or change

[Reg.Settings2]
; Registry settings to add or change

[Reg.Settings3]
; Registry settings to add or change

[Reg.Settings4]
; Registry settings to add or change

[Reg.Settings5]
; Registry settings to add or change

[Reg.Settings6]
; Registry keys and values to remove
```

> **Note**   The order of the AddReg and DelReg directives doesn't matter. The Setup API processes all DelReg directives first, followed by the AddReg sections.

Adding Keys and Values

As you just saw, the AddReg directive in [DefaultInstall] indicates the names of sections that contain settings that you want to add to the registry. These are [add-registry-section] sections. You can add new keys, set default values, create new values, or modify existing values using an [add-registry-section] section. And each section can contain multiple entries. Each [add-registry-section] name must be unique in the INF file.

Syntax

[*add-registry-section*] *rootkey*, [*subkey*], [*value*], [*flags*], [*data*]

rootkey	This is the root key containing the key or value that you're modifying. Use the abbreviations HKCR, HKCU, HKLM, or HKU.
subkey	This is the subkey to create or the subkey in which to add or change a value. This is optional. If missing, all operations are on the root key.
value	This is the name of the value to create or modify if it exists. This value is optional. If *value* is omitted and the *flags* and *data* parameters are given, operations are on the key's default value. If *value*, *flags*, and *data* are omitted, you're adding a subkey.
flags	**0x00000000.** *Value* is REG_SZ. This is the default if you omit *flags*.
	0x00000001. *Value* is REG_BINARY.
	0x00010000. *Value* is REG_MULTI_SZ.
	0x00020000. *Value* is REG_EXPAND_SZ.
	0x00010001. *Value* is REG_DWORD.
	0x00020001. *Value* is REG_NONE.
	0x00000002. Don't overwrite existing keys and values. Combine this flag with others by ORing them together.
	0x00000004. Delete *subkey* from the registry, or delete *value* from *subkey*. Combine this flag with others by ORing them together.
	0x00000008. Append *data* to *value*. This flag is valid only if *value* is REG_MULTI_SZ. The string *data* is not appended if it already exists. Combine this flag with 0x00010000 by ORing them together.
	0x00000010. Create *subkey*, but ignore *value* and *data* if specified. Combine this flag with others by ORing them together.
	0x00000020. Set *value* only if it already exists. Combine this flag with others by ORing them together.
	0x00001000. Make the specified change in the 64-bit registry. If not specified, the change is made to the native registry. Combine this flag with others by ORing them together.
	0x00004000. Make the specified change in the 32-bit registry. If not specified, the change is made to the native registry. Combine this flag with others by ORing them together.

data	This is the data to write to *value*. If the value doesn't exist, the Setup API creates it; if the value exists, the API overwrites it; if the value is REG_MULTI_SZ and you set the 0x00010008 flag, the API adds the value to the existing string list. If you omit *data*, the Setup API creates the value without setting it. See the following example to learn how to format each type of value.

Example

```
[Version]
Signature=$CHICAGO$

[DefaultInstall]
AddReg=Reg.Settings

[Reg.Settings]
; Sets the default value of HKCU\Software\Sample
HKCU,Software\Sample,,,"Default"

; Creates a REG_SZ value called Sample
HKCU,Software\Sample,String,0x00000,"String"

; Creates a REG_BINARY value called Binary
HKCU,Software\Sample,Binary,0x00001,00,01,30,05

; Creates a REG_MULTI_SZ value called Multisz
HKCU,Software\Sample,Multisz,0x10000,"String list"

; Creates a REG_DWORD value called Dword
HKCU,Software\Sample,Dword,0x10001,0x01010102

; Creates a REG_SZ value called Hello
HKLM,SOFTWARE\Sample,Hello,,"World"

; Creates a REG_DWORD value and sets it to 0x0000
HKLM,SOFTWARE\Sample,Nothing,0x10001
```

Deleting Keys and Values

The [DefaultInstall] section's DelReg directive specifies sections containing registry keys and values to delete. These are [del-registry-section] sections. They are much simpler than the [add-registry-section] sections but have similar rules: each section can contain multiple entries, and the name of each section must be unique.

Syntax

[del-registry-section] rootkey, [*subkey*], [*value*], [*flags*], [*data*]

rootkey	This is the root key containing the key or value that you're deleting. Use the abbreviations HKCR, HKCU, HKLM, or HKU.
subkey	This is the subkey to delete or the subkey from which to delete a value. This is optional. If missing, all operations are on the root key.

value	This is the name of the value to delete. This value is optional. If *value* is omitted, you're deleting *subkey*.
flags	**0x00002000**. Delete the entire subkey.
	0x00004000. Make the specified change in the 32-bit registry. If not specified, the change is made to the native registry. Combine this flag with others by ORing them together.
	0x00018002. If *value* is REG_MULTI_SZ, remove all strings matching the string indicated by *data*.
data	This is used only when the value of *flags* is 0x00018002. This specifies the string to remove from a REG_MULTI_SZ value.

Example

```
[Version]
Signature=$CHICAGO$

[DefaultInstall]
DelReg=Reg.Settings

[Reg.Settings]
; Removes the key HKCU\Software\Sample
HKCU,Software\Sample

; Removes the value Hello from HKCU\Software\Sample
HKCU,Software\Sample,Hello

; Removes the string "World" from the REG_MULTI_SZ value Hello
HKCU,Software\Sample,Hello,0x00018002,"World"
```

Setting and Clearing Bits

The BitReg directive is similar to the AddReg directive. You add it to the [DefaultInstall] section to indicate the names of sections that contain bits that you want to set and clear. These are [bit-registry-section] sections. Use the BitReg directive when you want to work with bit masks in the registry. For example, use this directive if you want to enable certain user-interface features in the value UserPreferencesMask. As in the other directives you learned about, each section can contain multiple entries, and the name of each section must be unique.

In the following description of the syntax, notice the differences between the [bit-registry-section] and [add-registry-section] sections. The parameter *value* is not optional. Also, the parameters *mask* and *byte* replace the value *data*. The parameter *mask* is 8 bits long and indicates the bit that you want to enable or disable. The parameter *byte* indicates the byte in the binary value that you want to modify. This indicates bytes left to right starting from 0. This is straightforward when working with REG_BINARY values but is less so when you are working with REG_DWORD values. As discussed in Chapter 1, "Learning the Basics," Windows stores REG_DWORD values in the registry in reverse-byte order (little-endian architecture). To make sure you're masking the bits you think you're masking, test your INF files carefully. Figure 11-1 shows the relationship between *value*, *mask*, and *byte*. The value to which I'm applying the mask is a REG_DWORD value stored in the registry in reverse-byte notation: 0x0180C000. Set the mask in byte 0, and the result is 0x0180C080. Clear the mask in byte 1, and the result is 0x0140C080.

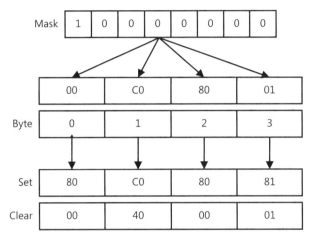

Figure 11-1   The parameter *byte* indicates to which of a number's bytes you want to apply *mask*.

Syntax

[*bit-registry-section*] *rootkey*, [*subkey*], *value*, [*flags*], *mask*, *byte*

rootkey	This is the root key containing the value that you're modifying. Use the abbreviations HKCR, HKCU, HKLM, or HKU.
subkey	This is the subkey in which you change a value. This is optional. If missing, all operations are on the root key.
value	This is the name of the value to modify. This value is *not* optional and should be a REG_DWORD or REG_BINARY value.
flags	0x00000000. Clear the bits specified by *mask*.
	0x00000001. Set the bits specified by *mask*.
	0x00040000. Make the specified change in the 32-bit registry. If not specified, the change is made to the native registry. Combine this flag with others by ORing them together.
mask	This is the byte-sized mask specifying the bits to set or to clear in the specified byte of *value*. Specify this value in hexadecimal notation. Bits that are 1 will be set or cleared, depending on *flags*, and bits that are 0 will be ignored.
byte	This specifies the byte in *value* to which you want to apply *mask*. The leftmost byte is 0, the next is 1, and so on. Keep in mind that Windows stores REG_DWORD values in reverse-byte order when specifying the byte on which you apply *mask*. Thus, in REG_DWORD values, the rightmost byte is stored first in memory.

Example

```
[Version]
Signature=$CHICAGO$

[DefaultInstall]
BitReg=Bit.Settings

[Bit.Settings]
; Changes 50,00,10,00 to 31,00,10,00
HKCU,Software\Sample,Mask,0x0001,0x01,0

; Changes 50,00,F0,00 to 30,00,70,00
HKU,Software\Sample,Mask,0x0000,0x80,2
```

Using Strings in INF Files

You can make your INF files far easier to read if you use the [Strings] section. Each line in this section is a string in the format name="string". You can then use that string elsewhere in the INF file by referencing it as %name%. This makes INF files easier to read in numerous ways. (See Listing 11-4, which is also a good example of using the BitReg directive.)

- The [Strings] section collects strings at the bottom of your INF file so that you can see them in one place.

- The [Strings] section enables you to type a string one time and then use that string in numerous places. The string is consistent throughout your INF file.

- The [Strings] section makes translating INF files easier because localizable strings are at the bottom of the file.

Listing 11-4   Strings.inf

```
[Version]
Signature=$CHICAGO$

[DefaultInstall]
BitReg=Bits.Set
AddReg=Add.Settings
DelReg=Del.Settings

[Add.Settings]
HKCU,%HK_DESKTOP%,ActiveWndTrkTimeout,0x10001,1000
HKLM,%HK_SETUP%,RegisteredOwner,,%OWNER%

[Del.Settings]
HKCU,%HK_EXPLORER%\MenuOrder
HKCU,%HK_EXPLORER%\RunMRU
HKCU,%HK_EXPLORER%\RecentDocs
HKCU,%HK_EXPLORER%\ComDlg32\LastVisitedMRU
HKCU,%HK_SEARCH%\ACMru
HKCU,%HK_INTERNET%\TypedURLs
```

```
[Bits.Set]
HKCU,%HK_DESKTOP%,UserPreferencesMask,1,0x01,0
HKCU,%HK_DESKTOP%,UserPreferencesMask,1,0x40,0

[Strings]
HK_DESKTOP="Control Panel\Desktop"
HK_EXPLORER="Software\Microsoft\Windows\CurrentVersion\Explorer"
HK_SEARCH="Software\Microsoft\Search Assistant"
HK_INTERNET="Software\Microsoft\Internet Explorer"
HK_SETUP="SOFTWARE\Microsoft\Windows NT\CurrentVersion"
OWNER="Fuzzy Wuzzy Was a Bear"
```

Note   To be honest, I seldom use strings because I don't often localize INF files. I use strings only when doing so really does make the INF file easier to read. In particular, when a line becomes so long that it wraps, I use a string to shorten it. Alternatively, you can use the line-continuation character, a backslash (\), to split lines. I also use strings for values that change frequently, particularly in template INF files. Strings make using templates easier.

Setting Values with REG Files

You learned how to use Regedit to create REG files in Chapter 2, "Using Registry Editor." REG files are the classic method for adding and changing values in the registry, but as I said in the section "Choosing a Technique," they're not as powerful as the other methods that you learn about in this chapter. The big weakness of REG files is that you can't use them to remove values; you can only add or modify values, or remove keys.

After you've created a REG file, which has the *.reg* file extension, you import it into the registry by double-clicking the file. This method is great if you want users to manually import the file, but you need the command regedit /s filename.reg if you want to import a REG file by using your software management infrastructure or by providing a link to it on the intranet. Replace filename.reg with the path and name of your REG file. The /s command-line option imports the file into the registry without prompting the user, which is what you want to do most of the time. To edit a REG file, right-click it, and then click Edit. Don't accidentally double-click a REG file thinking that you're going to open it in Notepad, because double-clicking a REG file imports it into the registry.

Remember that Regedit supports two different file formats for REG files. Version 4 REG files are ANSI. ANSI character encoding uses one byte to represent each character. Also, Regedit uses ANSI character encoding to write REG_EXPAND_SZ and REG_MULTI_SZ strings to REG files, so each character is a single byte. Version 5 REG files are Unicode. Unicode character encoding uses two bytes for each character, and when you create a Unicode REG file, Regedit uses the two-byte Unicode encoding scheme to write REG_EXPAND_SZ and REG_MULTI_SZ strings to the file. Chapter 1, "Learning the Basics," tells you more about the differences between the two encoding standards. Chapter 2, "Using Registry Editor," describes the differences between the two different types of REG files. What you need to know is that choosing to create a version 4 REG file means that the file and the values in the file use ANSI; likewise, creating a version 5 REG file means that the file and the values in the file use Unicode. I tend to use version 4, ANSI REG files, except when I know that the registry data contains localized text that requires Unicode to represent it. If in doubt, always create version 5, Unicode files.

Listing 11-5 shows a sample REG file. The first line in this file is the header, which identifies the file's version. The header `Windows Registry Editor Version 5.00` indicates that this is a version 5, Unicode REG file. The header `REGEDIT4` would indicate a version 4, ANSI REG file. A blank line usually follows the header, but the file works fine without it. Notice how similar the remainder of this file looks to INF and INI files. Each section contains the fully qualified name of a key. Each section also uses the full names of root keys, rather than the abbreviations for them. Listing 11-5 is importing settings into three keys: `HKCU\Control Panel\Desktop`, `HKCU\Control Panel\Desktop\WindowMetrics`, and `HKCU\Control Panel\Mouse`. The lines below each section are values that Regedit will add to that key when Regedit imports the file into the registry. The format is `"name"=value`. The value named @ represents the key's default value. Some of the values in Listing 11-5 contain `dword` and `hex`, whereas others are enclosed in quotation marks. Values enclosed in quotation marks are strings. Values in the form `dword:value` are `REG_DWORD` values. Values in the form `hex:values` are `REG_BINARY` values. This gets more complicated when you add subtypes, such as `hex(type):value`, and I'll explain those later.

Listing 11-5 Example.reg

```
Windows Registry Editor Version 5.00

[HKEY_CURRENT_USER\Control Panel\Desktop]
"ActiveWndTrkTimeout"=dword:00000000
"ForegroundFlashCount"=dword:00000003
"ForegroundLockTimeout"=dword:00030d40
"MenuShowDelay"="400"
"PaintDesktopVersion"=dword:00000000
"UserPreferencesMask"=hex:9e,3e,07,80

[HKEY_CURRENT_USER\Control Panel\Desktop\WindowMetrics]
"Shell Icon BPP"="16"
"Shell Icon Size"="32"
"MinAnimate"="1"

[HKEY_CURRENT_USER\Control Panel\Mouse]
@="Rodent"
"ActiveWindowTracking"=dword:00000000
"DoubleClickHeight"="4"
"DoubleClickSpeed"="500"
"DoubleClickWidth"="4"
"MouseSensitivity"="10"
"MouseSpeed"="1"
```

```
"MouseThreshold1"="6"
"MouseThreshold2"="10"
"SnapToDefaultButton"="0"
"SwapMouseButtons"="0"
```

Exporting Settings to REG Files

The easiest way to create a REG file is by using Regedit to export keys to REG files. Follow these steps to export branches of the registry to files:

1. Click the key at the top of the branch that you want to export.

2. On the File menu, click Export.

   The Export Registry File dialog box appears, shown in Figure 11-2.

3. In the File Name box, enter a name for the file you're creating.

4. Select the option for the export range that you want:

   ❑ To back up the entire registry, select the All option.

   ❑ To back up the selected branch, select the Selected Branch option.

5. In the Save As Type drop-down list, click the type of file that you want to create: Registration (*.reg) or Win9x/NT4 Registration (*.reg).

6. Click Save.

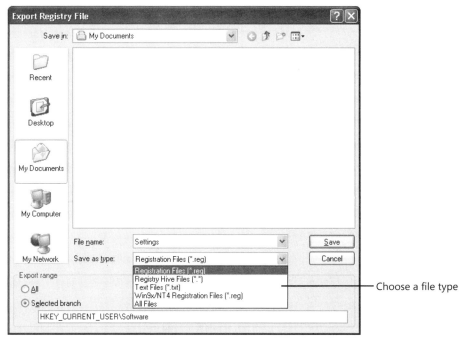

Choose a file type

Figure 11-2   The only two types of files that create REG files are Registration files (*.reg) and Win9x/NT4 Registration files (*.reg).

The REG file that you create contains all the subkeys and values under the key that you exported. It's not likely that you want all the key's subkeys and values, so right-click the file and click Edit to open it in Notepad, and then remove any keys and values that you don't want to keep in the file. You can also change any of the values in the REG file. For example, you can export a key from your own computer, just to get started, and then edit it to suit your requirements, removing keys, changing values, and so on.

> **Caution** If you're creating a REG file for versions of Windows that don't support version 5, Unicode REG files, then use version 4, ANSI REG files. Microsoft Windows 95, Windows 98, and Windows Me do not support Unicode REG files, and any attempt to import Unicode REG files into their registries could yield results that you won't like.

Creating REG Files Manually

Creating REG files by hand is an error-prone process that I don't recommend. Nonetheless, many people do it anyway, so I'm going to show you how. First decide whether you're going to create an ANSI or Unicode REG file, and then follow these instructions to create it:

1. Create a new file in Notepad.

2. At the top of the file, add one of the following, followed by a blank line:

   ❑ To create a version 4 REG file, add `REGEDIT4`.

   ❑ To create a version 5 REG file, add `Windows Registry Editor Version 5.00`.

3. For each key into which you want to import values, add a section to the file in the format `[key]`, where *key* is the fully qualified name of the key. Don't use the root-key abbreviations; use their full names: `HKEY_CURRENT_USER`.

4. For each value that you want to import into the registry, add the value in the format `"name"=value` to the key's section. Use `@` for a key's default value. See Table 11-2 for information about how to format the different types of values in a REG file. You can use the line-continuation character, a backslash (\), to continue an entry from one line to the next.

5. Click File, Save As, and type the name of the file in File Name box, including the extension *.reg*. (Enclose the file name in quotation marks so that Notepad doesn't use the *.txt* extension). Then, from the Encoding drop-down list, choose one of the following, and then click Save:

   ❑ To create a version 4 REG file, choose ANSI.

   ❑ To create a version 5 REG file, choose Unicode.

Table 11-2   Value Formats in REG Files

Type	Version 4	Version 5
REG_SZ	"String"	"String"
REG_DWORD	dword:00007734	dword:00007734
REG_BINARY	hex:00,00,01,03	hex:00,00,01,03
REG_EXPAND_SZ	hex(2):25,53,59,53, 54,45,4d,52,4f,4f, 54,25,00	hex(2):25,00,53,00,59,00,53,00, 54,00,45,00,4d,00,52,00,4f,00, 4f,00,54,00,25,00,00,00
REG_MULTI_SZ	hex(7):48,65,6c,6c, 6f,20,57,6f,72,6c,64, 00,4a,65,72,72,79,20, 77,61,73,20,68,65,72, 65,00,00	hex(7):48,00,65,00,6c,00,6c,00, 6f,00,20,00,57,00,6f,00,72,00, 6c,00,64,00,00,00,4a,00,65,00, 72,00,72,00,79,00,20,00,77,00, 61,00,73,00,20,00,68,00,65,00, 72,00,65,00,00,00,00,00

Encoding Special Characters

Within REG files, certain characters have special meaning. Quotation marks begin and end strings. The backslash character is a line-continuation character. So how do you include these characters in your values? You use *escaping*, which is a very old method for prefixing special characters with a backslash. For example, the string \n represents a newline character, and the string \" represents a quotation mark. Table 11-3 describes the special characters that you can use and shows you examples.

Table 11-3   Special Characters in REG Files

Escape	Expanded	Example
\\	\	C:\\Documents and Settings\\Jerry
\"	"	A \"quoted\" string
\n	newline	This is on \n two lines
\r	return	This is on \r two lines

Deleting Keys Using a REG File

You can't use a REG file to remove individual values, but you can certainly use one to delete entire keys. This is an undocumented feature of REG files: just prefix a key's name with a minus (–) sign: [-key]. Here's a brief example that removes the key HKCU\Software\Honeycutt when you import the REG file into the registry:

```
Windows Registry Editor Version 5.00

[-HKEY_CURRENT_USER\Software\Honeycutt]
```

Rather than manually creating a REG file to remove keys, I prefer to export a key to a REG file and then edit it. After exporting the key to a REG file, remove all the values and keys that you don't want to delete. Then add the minus sign to the names of the keys that you want to delete. Then you can remove those keys quickly and easily by double-clicking the REG file or using the command `regedit /s filename.reg`.

Editing from the Command Prompt

Windows comes with Console Registry Tool for Windows (Reg.exe). This tool is marvelous. You use it to edit the registry from a command prompt window. With Reg.exe, you can do just about anything that you can do with Regedit—and more. The best part is that you can use Reg.exe to write simple scripts in the form of batch files that change the registry. And unlike in earlier versions of Windows, you don't have to install Reg.exe. It's installed by default and combines the numerous registry tools that came with the resource kits for earlier versions of Windows.

I can explain how great this tool is just by starting with an example. Listing 11-6 is a simple batch file that installs Microsoft Office 2003 Editions the first time that the batch file runs. (Think of it as a logon script). After installing Office 2003 Editions, the batch file calls Reg.exe to add the `REG_DWORD` value `Flag` to `HKCU\Software\Example`. Each time that the file runs, the batch file checks for this value's presence and skips the installation if it exists. Thus, the batch file installs the application only one time. This is a method that you can use to deploy software through users' logon scripts. Instead of checking for a value that you add, as Listing 11-6 does, you can check for a value that the application stores in the registry. For example, the second line in the batch file could just as easily have been `Reg QUERY HKCU\Software\Microsoft\Office\11.0 >nul`, which checks to see if Office 2003 Editions is installed for the user.

Listing 11-6   Login.bat

```
@Echo Off

Reg QUERY HKCU\Software\Example /v Flag >nul

goto %ERRORLEVEL%

:1

    Echo Installing software the first time this runs
    \\Camelot\Office\Setup.exe /settings setup.ini

    Reg ADD HKCU\Software\Example /v Flag /t REG_DWORD /d "1"
    goto CONTINUE

:0

    Echo Software is already installed, skipping this section

:CONTINUE

Set HKMS=HKCU\Software\Microsoft
Set HKCV=HKCU\Software\Microsoft\Windows\CurrentVersion

REM Clear the history lists
```

```
Reg DELETE %HKCV%\Explorer\MenuOrder /f
Reg DELETE %HKCV%\Explorer\RunMRU /f
Reg DELETE %HKCV%\Explorer\RecentDocs /f
Reg DELETE %HKCV%\Explorer\ComDlg32\LastVisitedMRU /f
Reg DELETE "%HKMS%\Search Assistant\ACMru" /f
Reg DELETE "%HKMS%\Internet Explorer\TypedURLs" /f
```

The syntax of the Reg.exe command line is straightforward: reg *command options*. *Command* is one of many commands that Reg.exe supports, including ADD, QUERY, and DELETE. *Options* are the options that the command requires. Options usually include the name of a key, and sometimes a value's name and data. If any key or value name contains spaces, you must enclose the name in quotation marks. It gets more complicated with each of the different commands that you can use with it, however, and I cover each of those in the sections following this one. If you're without this book and need a quick reminder, just type **reg /?** in a command prompt window to see a list of commands that Reg.exe supports.

Adding Keys and Values

Use the ADD command to add keys and values to the registry.

Syntax

REG ADD [*computer*\]*key* [/v *value* | /ve] [/t *type*] [/s *separator*] [/d *data*] [/f]

computer	If omitted, Reg.exe connects to the local computer; otherwise, Reg.exe connects to the remote computer.
key	This is the key's path, beginning with the root key. Use the root-key abbreviations HKCR, HKCU, HKLM, and HKU. Only HKLM and HKU are available when connecting to remote computers.
/v *value*	This will add or change *value*.
/ve	This will change the key's default value.
/t *type*	This is the value's type: REG_BINARY, REG_DWORD, REG_DWORD_LITTLE_ENDIAN, REG_DWORD_BIG_ENDIAN, REG_EXPAND_SZ, REG_MULTI_SZ, or REG_SZ. The default is REG_SZ.
/s *separator*	This specifies the character used to separate strings when creating REG_MULTI_SZ values. The default is \0, or null.
/d *data*	This is the data to assign to new or existing values.
/f	This forces Reg.exe to overwrite existing values with prompting.

Example

```
REG ADD \\JERRY1\HKLM\Software\Honeycutt
REG ADD HKLM\Software\Honeycutt /v Data /t REG_BINARY /d CCFEF0BC
REG ADD HKLM\Software\Honeycutt /v List /t REG_MULTI_SZ /d Hello\0World
REG ADD HKLM\Software\Honeycutt /v Path /t REG_EXPAND_SZ /d %%SYSTEMROOT%%
```

> **Note**   The percent sign (%) has a special purpose at a command prompt and within batch files. You enclose environment variables in percent signs to expand them in place. Thus, to use them on the Reg.exe command line and elsewhere, you must use double percent signs (%%). In the previous example, if you had used single percent signs, the command prompt would have expanded the environment variable before running the command. Using double percent signs prevents the command prompt from expanding the environment variable.

Querying Values

The QUERY command works in three ways. First it can display the data in a specific value. Second it can display all of a key's values. Third it can list all the subkeys and values in a key by adding the /s command-line option. How it works depends on the options you use.

Syntax

REG QUERY [*computer*\\]*key* [/v *value* | /ve] [/s]

computer	If omitted, Reg.exe connects to the local computer; otherwise, Reg.exe connects to the remote computer.
key	This is the key's path, beginning with the root key. Use the root-key abbreviations HKCR, HKCU, HKLM, and HKU. Only HKLM and HKU are available when connecting to remote computers.
/v *value*	This will query *value* in *key*. If you omit /v, Reg.exe queries all values in the key.
/ve	This will query the key's default value.
/s	This will query all the key's subkeys and values.

Example

```
REG QUERY HKLM\SOFTWARE\Microsoft\Windows\CurrentVersion /s
REG QUERY HKLM\SOFTWARE\Microsoft\Windows NT\CurrentVersion /v CurrentVersion
```

> **Note**   Reg.exe sets ERRORLEVEL to 0 if the command succeeds and to 1 if it doesn't. Thus, you can test ERRORLEVEL in a batch file to determine whether a value exists. You saw an example of this in Listing 11-6 earlier in this chapter. Although you can use the If statement to test ERRORLEVEL, I prefer creating labels in my batch file, one for each level, as shown in Listing 11-6. Then I can just write statements that look like Goto %ERRORLEVEL% or Goto QUERY%ERRORLEVEL%, which branches to the label QUERY1 if ERRORLEVEL is 1.

Deleting Keys and Values

Use the DELETE command to remove keys and values from the registry.

Syntax

```
REG DELETE [\\computer\]key [/v value | /ve | /va] [/f]
```

\\computer	If omitted, Reg.exe connects to the local computer; otherwise, Reg.exe connects to the remote computer.
key	This is the key's path, beginning with the root key. Use the root-key abbreviations HKCR, HKCU, HKLM, and HKU. Only HKLM and HKU are available when connecting to remote computers.
/v value	This will delete value from key.
/ve	This will delete the key's default value.
/va	This will delete all values from key.
/f	This will force Reg.exe to delete values with prompting.

Example

```
REG DELETE \\JERRY1\HKLM\Software\Honeycutt
REG DELETE HKLM\Software\Honeycutt /v Data /f
REG DELETE HKLM\Software\Honeycutt /va
```

Comparing Keys and Values

Use the COMPARE command to compare two registry keys. Those keys can be on the same computer or on different computers, making this a useful troubleshooting tool.

The /on command-line option seems odd at first. Why would you compare keys or values and not show the differences? Reg.exe sets ERRORLEVEL according to the comparison's result, and you can use the result in your batch files to execute different code depending on whether the two are the same or different—without displaying any results. Here's the meaning of ERRORLEVEL:

- 0. The command was successful, and the keys or values are identical.

- 1. The command failed.

- 2. The command was successful, and the keys or values are different.

Syntax

```
REG COMPARE [\\computer1\]key1 [\\computer2\]key2 [/v value | /ve]
[/oa|/od|/os|/on] [/s]
```

\\computer1	If omitted, Reg.exe connects to the local computer; otherwise, Reg.exe connects to the remote computer.
\\computer2	If omitted, Reg.exe connects to the local computer; otherwise, Reg.exe connects to the remote computer.
key1	This is the key's path, beginning with the root key. Use the root-key abbreviations HKCR, HKCU, HKLM, and HKU. Only HKLM and HKU are available when connecting to remote computers.
key2	This is the key's path, beginning with the root key. Use the root-key abbreviations HKCR, HKCU, HKLM, and HKU. Only HKLM and HKU are available when connecting to remote computers.
/v value	This compares value.
/ve	This compares the key's default value.
/oa	This shows all differences and matches.
/od	This shows only differences.
/os	This shows only matches.
/on	This shows nothing.
/s	This compares all the key's subkeys and values.

Example

```
REG COMPARE HKCR\txtfile HKR\docfile /ve
REG COMPARE \\JERRY1\HKCR \\JERRY2\HKCR /od /s
REG COMPARE HKCU\Software \\JERRY2\HKCU\Software /s
```

Copying Keys and Values

The COPY command copies a subkey to another key. This command is useful to back up subkeys, as you learned in Chapter 3, "Backing Up the Registry."

Syntax

```
REG COPY [\\computer1\]key1 [\\computer2\]key2 [/s] [/f]
```

\\computer1	If omitted, Reg.exe connects to the local computer; otherwise, Reg.exe connects to the remote computer.
\\computer2	If omitted, Reg.exe connects to the local computer; otherwise, Reg.exe connects to the remote computer.
key1	This is the key's path, beginning with the root key. Use the root-key abbreviations HKCR, HKCU, HKLM, and HKU. Only HKLM and HKU are available when connecting to remote computers.
key2	This is the key's path, beginning with the root key. Use the root-key abbreviations HKCR, HKCU, HKLM, and HKU. Only HKLM and HKU are available when connecting to remote computers.
/s	This copies all the key's subkeys and values.
/f	This forces Reg.exe to copy with prompting.

Example

```
REG COPY HKCU\Software\Microsoft\Office HKCU\Backup\Office /s
REG COPY HKCR\regfile HKCU\Backup\regfile /s /f
```

Exporting Keys to REG Files

Use the EXPORT command to export all or part of the registry to REG files. This command has a few limitations, though. First it works only with the local computer. You can't create a REG file from a remote computer's registry. Second it creates only version 5, Unicode REG files. There's no option available to create ANSI REG files. The EXPORT command is the same as clicking File, Export in Regedit.

Syntax

```
REG EXPORT key filename
```

key	This is the key's path, beginning with the root key. Use the root-key abbreviations HKCR, HKCU, HKLM, and HKU. This is the key you want to export to a REG file.
filename	This is the path and name of the REG file to create.

Example

```
REG EXPORT "HKCU\Control Panel" Preferences.reg
```

Importing REG Files

Use the IMPORT command to import a REG file into the registry. This command does the same thing as running `regedit /s filename`. It imports a REG file silently. This command can handle both version 4 and version 5 REG files, but it works only on the local computer.

Syntax

```
REG IMPORT filename
```

filename	This is the path and name of the REG file to import.

Example

```
REG IMPORT Settings.reg
```

Saving Keys to Hive Files

The SAVE command saves a key as a hive file. This command is similar to clicking File, Export in Regedit, and then changing the file type to Registry Hive Files (*.*). It's a convenient method for backing up the registry before making substantial changes. Chapter 3, "Backing Up the Registry," describes this technique. This command works only on the local computer.

Syntax

`REG SAVE key filename`

key	This is the key's path, beginning with the root key. Use the root-key abbreviations HKCR, HKCU, HKLM, and HKU. This is the key that you want to save as a hive file.
filename	This is the path and name of the hive file to create.

Example

`REG SAVE HKU Backup.dat`

Restoring Hive Files to Keys

The RESTORE command overwrites a key and all its contents with the contents of a hive file. This is similar to importing a hive file in Regedit. The difference between this command and loading a hive file is that this command overwrites any existing key, whereas loading a hive file creates a new temporary key to contain the hive file's contents. Use this command to restore a backup hive file. This command works only on the local computer.

Syntax

`REG RESTORE key filename`

key	This is the key's path, beginning with the root key. Use the root-key abbreviations HKCR, HKCU, HKLM, and HKU. This is the key that you want to overwrite with the contents of the hive file.
filename	This is the path and name of the hive file to restore.

Example

`REG RESTORE HKCU Backup.dat`

Loading Hive Files

The LOAD command loads a hive file into a temporary key. You reference the hive file's keys and values through the temporary key that you specify on the command line. This command is similar to loading hive files in Regedit. This command works only on the local computer.

Syntax

```
REG LOAD key filename
```

key	This is the key's path, beginning with the root key. Use the root-key abbreviations HKCR, HKCU, HKLM, and HKU. This is the new temporary key into which you want to load the hive file.
filename	This is the path and name of the hive file to load.

Example

```
REG LOAD HKU\Temporary Settings.dat
```

Unloading Hive Files

The UNLOAD command removes a hive file that you've loaded using the LOAD command. It simply unhooks the hive file from the registry. You must remember to unload a hive file that you've loaded before trying to copy or do anything else with the hive file because Windows locks the file while it's in use.

Syntax

```
REG UNLOAD key
```

key	This is the key's path, beginning with the root key. Use the root-key abbreviations HKCR, HKCU, HKLM, and HKU. This is the name of the key containing the hive file that you want to unload.

Example

```
REG UNLOAD HKU\Temporary
```

Scripting Using Windows Script Host

Scripts give IT professionals the ultimate ability to control and automate Windows. These aren't batch files; they're full-fledged administrative programs that, considering the wealth of power that they enable, are surprisingly easy to create. You can write a script that inventories a computer and writes the result to a file on the network, for example. You can automate an application to perform redundant steps automatically. The possibilities are endless, really, but I'm here to tell you how to use scripts to edit the registry, so I'm confining the discussion a bit.

The scripting technology in Windows is Windows Script Host. The current version is 5.6 and is far more technologically advanced than what was provided by Microsoft Windows 2000. Windows Script Host is called a *host* because it's not aware of a script's language, or as Microsoft says, it is *language agnostic*. Windows Script Host uses different scripting engines to parse the different languages in which you might write a script. Windows provides two scripting engines: VBScript and JScript. If you've ever used the C or C++ languages, you'll be more comfortable using JScript to write scripts. If you've ever used Visual Basic in any of its incarnations, you're going to be more comfortable using VBScript to write scripts.

Focusing this chapter on how to use scripts to edit the registry assumes that you're already familiar with Windows Script Host. If that's not true, I suggest that you find a good book about scripts. If you don't want a book about it, see *http:// msdn.microsoft.com/library/en-us/dnanchor/html/scriptinga.asp* or *http:// www.microsoft.com/technet/scriptcenter/default.mspx*. These are Microsoft's Scripting Web sites, and they contain everything that you need to know about writing scripts for Windows, including accessing WMI (Windows Management Instrumentation) through scripts. After you've mastered the languages, which aren't difficult, you'll appreciate the Web sites' reference content. The content describes the object model and how to use it—which is the most difficult part of writing scripts for Windows.

Note   Using WMI to edit the registry is an alternative to using pure VBScript. WMI enables you to manage remote computer's registries. For complete samples of WMI scripts that edit the registry, see *http://www.microsoft.com/technet/scriptcenter/ scripts/os/registry/default.mspx*. This is the Registry section of the Script Repository in the TechNet Script Center. It includes sample WMI scripts for adding, changing, listing, and removing various types of registry settings. It also includes scripts for monitoring registry settings.

Tweakomatic

Chapter 5, "Mapping Tweak UI," describes one of the most popular utilities for customizing Windows registry settings. The problem with Tweak UI is that you must log on to the computer and run the utility locally. You can of course write your own scripts to change the same settings that Tweak UI changes, because Chapter 5 documents almost every setting and its registry value for you.

> However, the Scripting Guys, the fellows who write all that interesting content in the TechNet Script Center, have created Tweakomatic to automatically create these scripts for you. Tweakomatic writes scripts that retrieve and configure Windows and Microsoft Internet Explorer settings on remote computers. It doesn't support every setting that Tweak UI supports, but you can easily modify the scripts that it creates to change just about any setting you want.
>
> For more information about downloading and using Tweakomatic, see *http://www.microsoft.com/technet/scriptcenter/tools/twkmatic.mspx*.

Creating Script Files

Script files can have two file extensions, and the script's file extension indicates which language the file contains. Use the *.js* extension for files that contain JScript. Use the *.vbs* extension for files that contain VBScript. Regardless, script files are nothing more than text files that contain the language's keywords, so you can use your favorite text editor, Notepad, to create them. When you save a script file using Notepad, make sure that you enclose the file's name in quotation marks, or choose All Files from the Save As Type drop-down list, so that Notepad doesn't add the *.txt* extension to the file.

You access the registry through the **Shell** object. This object contains the methods that you call to add, remove, and update values in the registry. You'll add one of the statements in the following code to every script in which you want to access the registry. The first line shows you how to create the **Shell** object using VBScript, and the second shows you how to do it using JScript. It's very easy to create a script: open Notepad, and type the contents of Listing 11-7. The JScript language is case sensitive, so type carefully. VBScript has the benefit of not being case sensitive. Save the file using the *.js* extension, and then double-click the file to run it. You'll see a message from me. Because double-clicking the script file runs it, you must right-click the file and then click Edit to edit the file.

```
set WshShell = WScript.CreateObject("WScript.Shell")
var WshShell = WScript.CreateObject("WScript.Shell");
```

Listing 11-7   Example.js

```
var WshShell = WScript.CreateObject("WScript.Shell");

WshShell.Popup("Hello from Jerry Honeycutt" );
```

Why Write Scripts When INF Files Are Easier?

I usually write INF files to edit the registry. If I'm not using INF files, I write batch files and use Reg.exe. I like the simplicity of these methods. There are times when writing a script is the only suitable method, however.

Writing a script is necessary in a number of cases. The first is when you must have a user interface. If you want to display settings to or collect settings from users, scripting is the best choice. Also, scripting is the only method that provides rather full access to Windows. For example, you can use a script to inventory the computer and dump the information to a text file on the network. You can use a script to configure users' computers using logic, if-this-then-that, which isn't possible with the other methods. So if you're doing anything more complicated than just adding, changing, or removing values, you're going to end up writing scripts. I've seen some fairly complicated scripts. For example, one fellow I worked with wrote a script that searched the registry for services that Sysprep disabled, and then permanently removed them from the registry. This is a great example of scripting.

Combined with WMI, scripting is amazing. The following script shows you how to use VBScript and WMI to inventory a computer's configuration. It displays the amount of physical memory installed on the computer, the name of the computer, the BIOS version, the type of processor, and more. This script and many more like it are available on Microsoft's TechNet Script Center, which is a large library of scripts that you can download, modify, and use. All these scripts are at *http://www.microsoft.com/technet/scriptcenter/default.mspx*.

```
strComputer = "."
Set objWMIService = GetObject("winmgmts: " _
    & "{impersonationLevel=impersonate}!\\" & strComputer & "\root\cimv2")
Set colSettings = objWMIService.ExecQuery _
    ("Select * from Win32_OperatingSystem")
For Each objOperatingSystem in colSettings
    Wscript.Echo "OS Name: " & objOperatingSystem.Name
    Wscript.Echo "Version: " & objOperatingSystem.Version
    Wscript.Echo "Service Pack: " & _
        objOperatingSystem.ServicePackMajorVersion _
            & "." & objOperatingSystem.ServicePackMinorVersion
    Wscript.Echo "OS Manufacturer: " & objOperatingSystem.Manufacturer
    Wscript.Echo "Windows Directory: " & _
        objOperatingSystem.WindowsDirectory
    Wscript.Echo "Locale: " & objOperatingSystem.Locale
    Wscript.Echo "Available Physical Memory: " & _
        objOperatingSystem.FreePhysicalMemory
    Wscript.Echo "Total Virtual Memory: " & _
        objOperatingSystem.TotalVirtualMemorySize
    Wscript.Echo "Available Virtual Memory: " & _
        objOperatingSystem.FreeVirtualMemory
    Wscript.Echo "OS Name: " & objOperatingSystem.SizeStoredInPagingFiles
```

```
Next
Set colSettings = objWMIService.ExecQuery _
    ("Select * from Win32_ComputerSystem")
For Each objComputer in colSettings
    Wscript.Echo "System Name: " & objComputer.Name
    Wscript.Echo "System Manufacturer: " & objComputer.Manufacturer
    Wscript.Echo "System Model: " & objComputer.Model
    Wscript.Echo "Time Zone: " & objComputer.CurrentTimeZone
    Wscript.Echo "Total Physical Memory: " & _
        objComputer.TotalPhysicalMemory
Next
Set colSettings = objWMIService.ExecQuery _
    ("Select * from Win32_Processor")
For Each objProcessor in colSettings
    Wscript.Echo "System Type: " & objProcessor.Architecture
    Wscript.Echo "Processor: " & objProcessor.Description
Next
Set colSettings = objWMIService.ExecQuery _
    ("Select * from Win32_BIOS")
For Each objBIOS in colSettings
    Wscript.Echo "BIOS Version: " & objBIOS.Version
Next
```

Running Script Files

Windows provides two scripting hosts. The Windows-based version runs scripts when you double-click a script file. The script engine is Wscript.exe. You can also use the command-line version, which is handy when the script outputs data similar to the way in which most command-line programs do. The example given in Listing 11-7 in the section "Why Write Scripts When INF Files Are Easier?" is one script that's better run from the command-line. The command-line scripting engine is Cscript.exe.

Syntax

cscript *script* [//B|//I] [//D] [//E:*engine*] [//H:cscript|//H:wscript]
[//Job:*name*] [//Logo|//Nologo] [//S] [//T:*time*] [//X] [//?]

//B	This specifies batch mode, which does not display alerts, scripting errors, or input prompts.
//I	This specifies interactive mode, which displays alerts, scripting errors, and input prompts. This is the default and the opposite of //B.
//D	This turns on the debugger.
//E:*engine*	This specifies the scripting language that is used to run the script.

`//H:cscript |` `//H:wscript`	This registers either Cscript.exe or Wscript.exe as the default script host for running scripts. If neither is specified, the installation default is Wscript.exe.
`//Job:name`	This runs the job identified by *name* in a *.wsf* script file.
`//Logo`	This specifies that the Windows Script Host banner is displayed in the console window before the script runs. This is the default and the opposite of `//Nologo`.
`//Nologo`	This specifies that the Windows Script Host banner is not displayed before the script runs.
`//S`	This saves the current command-line options for the current user.
`//T:time`	This specifies the maximum time the script can run (in seconds). You can specify up to 32,767 seconds. The default is no time limit.
`//X`	This starts the script in the debugger.
`//?`	This displays available command parameters and provides help for using them. (This is the same as typing **Cscript.exe** with no parameters and no script.)

You can specify some of the same options when using the Windows-based scripting host. Right-click the script file, and then click Properties. You'll see the dialog box shown in Figure 11-3. You can set the amount of time that the script is allowed to run and whether or not the host displays a log. The result is a file (a shortcut to the actual script file) with the *.wsh* extension that contains these settings. It looks like your average INI file. You then execute the script by double-clicking the WSH file.

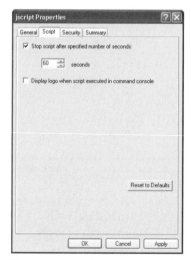

Figure 11-3   You create a WSH file, which contains a script file's settings, by right-clicking the script, clicking Properties, and then clicking the Script tab.

Formatting Key and Value Names

Before I show you how to edit the registry with a script, there's one more detail: how to format the names of keys and values in a script. Unlike other scripting methods I've described in this chapter, the Windows Script Host object model doesn't have separate parameters for the key and value names. Thus, you distinguish key names from value names by how you format them. The rule is simple: if a string ends with a backslash, it's a key name; if a string doesn't end with a backslash, it's a value name. Also, the JScript language reserves the backslash character (\) as the escape character: \n is a newline character, and \t is a tab, for example. That means that you must escape the backslashes in your keys. Thus, any time you have a backslash in a key, you must use two backslashes (\\). For information that can help you keep these clear, see Table 11-4.

Table 11-4   **Key and Value Formatting**

Object	VBScript	JScript
Value	"HKLM\Subkey\Value"	"HKLM\\Subkey\\Value"
Key	"HKLM\Subkey\"	"HKLM\\Subkey\\"

Adding and Updating Values

The Shell object's RegWrite method adds keys and values or changes existing values. If you want to change a key's default value, set *strName* to the name of the key, including the trailing backslash, and then assign a value to it.

> **Tip**   One of the RegWrite method's biggest weaknesses is that it writes only four bytes of REG_BINARY values. It can't handle larger binary values. If you want to change longer binary values or change types of values that this method doesn't support, use the Shell object's Run method to import a REG file. For example, you can put your settings in a REG file called Settings.reg. Then import that REG file using the statement WshShell.Run("Settings.reg").

Syntax

object.RegWrite(*strName*, *anyValue* [,*strType*])

object	This is the Shell object.
strName	This is the string indicating the name of the key or value. You can add keys. You can add or change values. This string must be a fully-qualified path to a key or value and begin with one of the root keys: HKCR, HKCU, HKLM, or HKU.
anyValue	This is the data to assign to new or existing values. Use the format that is appropriate for the value's type.
strType	This is the type of value to create: REG_SZ, REG_EXPAND_SZ, REG_DWORD, or REG_BINARY. The RegWrite method doesn't support the REG_MULTI_SZ value type. Also, this method writes only four-byte REG_BINARY values.

Example (VBScript)

```
Set WshShell = WScript.CreateObject("WScript.Shell" )

WshShell.RegWrite "HKCU\Software\Sample\", 1, "REG_BINARY"
WshShell.RegWrite "HKCU\Software\Sample\Howdy", "World!", "REG_SZ"
```

Example (JScript)

```
var WshShell = WScript.CreateObject("WScript.Shell" );

WshShell.RegWrite("HKCU\\Software\\Sample\\", 1, "REG_BINARY" );
WshShell.RegWrite("HKCU\\Software\\Sample\\Howdy", "World!", "REG_SZ");
```

Removing Keys and Values

The shell object's RegDelete method removes keys and values from the registry. Be careful, however, because removing an entire branch is easy; there's no confirmation. To remove a key, end *strName* with a backslash; otherwise, you're removing a value.

Syntax

object.RegDelete(*strName*)

object	This is the shell object.
strName	This is the string indicating the name of the key or value to delete. This string must be a fully qualified path to a key or value and must begin with one of the root keys: HKCR, HKCU, HKLM, or HKU.

Example (VBScript)

```
Set WshShell = WScript.CreateObject("WScript.Shell" )

WshShell.RegDelete "HKCU\Software\Honeycutt\Howdy"
WshShell.RegDelete "HKCU\Software\Honeycutt\"
```

Example (JScript)

```
var WshShell = WScript.CreateObject("WScript.Shell" );

WshShell.RegDelete ("HKCU\\Software\\Honeycutt\\Howdy" );
WshShell.RegDelete ("HKCU\\Software\\Honeycutt\\" );
```

Querying Registry Values

The shell object's RegRead method returns a value's data. To read a key's default value, end *strName* with a backslash; otherwise, you're reading a value.

Syntax

object.RegRead(*strName*)

object	This is the shell object.
strName	This is the string indicating the name of the value to read. strName must be a fully qualified path to a key or value and begin with one of the root keys: HKCR, HKCU, HKLM, or HKU.

Example (VBScript)

```
Dim WshShell, dwFlag, strValue
Set WshShell = WScript.CreateObject("WScript.Shell" )

dwFlag = WshShell.RegRead("HKCU\Software\Honeycutt\" )
strValue = WshShell.RegRead("HKCU\Software\Honeycutt\Howdy" )
```

Example (JScript)

```
var WshShell = WScript.CreateObject("WScript.Shell" );

var dwFlag = WshShell.RegRead("HKCU\\Software\\Honeycutt\\" );
var strValue = WshShell.RegRead("HKCU\\Software\\Honeycutt\\Howdy" );
```

Creating Windows Installer Packages

The last method of deploying registry settings is creating Windows Installer package files. You've undoubtedly encountered package files by now. Microsoft Office 2000, Office XP, and Office 2003 Editions all ship as package files, which are databases of files and settings that Windows Installer installs on the computer. Creating a package file for a large application is an intense process, but creating package files that contain registry settings is straightforward.

To create a package file, you need an editor. One of the most popular package editors is VERITAS WinINSTALL, and you can learn more about this enterprise-class tool at *www.veritas.com*. If you don't want to spend the money necessary to purchase a full version of WinINSTALL, you can get a free version if you still have your Windows 2000 Professional CD lying around. Look in the Valueadd\3rdparty\Mgmt\Winstle folder. This is an older, limited-edition version of WinINSTALL. It's clunky and short on features when compared to recent versions of WinINSTALL, but it's suitable for creating package files to deploy registry settings. Install the program by double-clicking Swiadmle.msi. This installs WinINSTALL and adds a program group to the Start menu. Click Start, All Programs, VERITAS Software, VERITAS Software Console to run it.

Package files contain features, and features contain components. To deploy registry settings in a package file, you must create all of the above. Follow these steps to create a new package file and to add registry settings to it:

1. In the left pane of Veritas Software Console, right-click Windows Installer Package Editor, and then click New. In the Filename box, type the path and name of the package file, and then click OK.

2. In the left pane, right-click the package file that you created, and then click Add Feature. In the Name box in the right pane, type a new name for the feature.

   The name is likely to be the only feature that you add to the package file, because all you're doing is deploying registry settings. You can create multiple features, though, and each feature can contain different registry settings. That way, users can choose whether or not to install individual features.

3. In the left pane, right-click the feature that you created in step 1, and then click Add Component.

   The package editor automatically gives the component a GUID. Components typically contain all the files and settings required to implement a program unit, so applications often have multiple components. When using a package file to deploy settings, creating multiple components doesn't make a lot of sense.

4. In the left pane, select the component you added, and click Registry.

5. In the right pane, right-click the root key that you want to edit, and click New Key. Continue creating subkeys by right-clicking a key and clicking New Key until you've created the full path of the key that you want to edit.

6. In the right pane, click the key in which you want to add or change a value, and then click New Value. In the Value Name box, type the name of the value. In the Data Type list, select the value's type, and click OK. In the *Type* Editor dialog box, type the value's data, and then click OK.

7. Click File, Save to save your package file.

After you've created a package file, you can deploy it as you would deploy any other package file. For example, users can simply double-click the package file to install it. If the package file contains settings that users don't have permission to change, you can deploy it through Active Directory and Group Policy, which installs package files with elevated privileges. You can also execute the command that installs a package file, which is `msiexec.exe" /i filename.msi`.

Part III
Registry in Deployment

There are two ways to deploy Windows XP and other applications: throw them out there and see what sticks, or carefully plan and design configurations. I prefer the second option, and that's the point of this part. You learn how the registry fits into the deployment of Windows XP.

This part begins with building and deploying user profiles. Then it moves into the registry settings for Windows Installer and how to remove errant Windows Installer–based settings from the registry. Three chapters in this part are about how to deploy settings with Windows XP and Office XP. And the last chapter describes how to fix a variety of IT problems that have solutions in the registry. This part of the book is primarily for IT professionals.

Chapter 12
Deploying User Profiles

Microsoft Windows XP and Microsoft Windows Server 2003 (Windows) store user settings separate from computer settings. The computer's settings affect every user who logs on to Windows. Computer settings include hardware configuration, network configuration, and so on. Typically, only the Administrators group can change computer settings, but some settings are within reach of the Power Users group. On the other hand, a user profile contains settings for a specific user. Users customize the operating system to their liking, and their settings don't affect other users. Users have full control of their own profiles, which contain more than just settings. They also contain files and folders specific to each user.

Deploying and managing user profiles are two of the most significant issues facing IT professionals. Properly deploying and managing user profiles can save companies money. That's because most of the behaviors that users experience in Windows have settings in user profiles, and IT professionals can deploy user profiles that contain defaults for these settings, starting users off correctly. For example, they can populate the Favorites folder with links to the intranet so that users don't have to find those links for themselves. They can add printer connections to a default user profile so that users can print right away without having to figure out how to add a printer. Notice that most of the useful policies that manage operating system and application settings are in user profiles. IT professionals manage the settings in user profiles by applying policies to them.

Mastering user profiles isn't just for IT professionals; power users, particularly those who use multiple accounts on their computers or who work on a home network, can create user profiles to simplify their experience. They can customize a default user profile. Then whenever they reinstall Windows or create a new account, they start with familiar settings and don't have to spend an hour customizing the operating system to suit their tastes. User profiles aren't that complicated, and power users should use them to their full advantage.

I've written this chapter primarily for the IT professional; power users need master only portions of it. First you learn about the contents of a user profile. Then you learn how to use roaming user profiles on a business network. The most compelling part of this chapter shows you how to build and deploy default user profiles. In that part, I show you two techniques for building default user profiles. The first is traditional but rather messy. I prefer the second method, which is a more precise (and tidy) method of building default user profiles. I wrap up this chapter with a discussion of the Microsoft User State Migration Tool, which can help overcome the difficulties involved with migrating users' settings from earlier versions of Windows.

Exploring User Profiles

Windows loads users' profiles when they log on to a computer and unloads their profiles when they log off. A user profile contains a registry hive with per-user settings and folders, which contain documents and data files. The next section, "Profile Hives," describes the registry hive that the operating system loads. The section "Profile Folders" describes the folders in a user profile.

Before delving into the contents of user profiles, knowing their location on the file system is useful. The default location is different than it was in Microsoft Windows NT 4.0 or other operating systems of that era. Remember that Windows NT 4.0 stored user profiles in %SystemRoot%\Profiles, but this location made it difficult to secure the operating system files while allowing access to users' data. Windows 2000, Windows XP, and Windows Server 2003 store user profiles in a different location, which enables you to pull user data out from under an operating system folder: %SystemDrive%\Documents and Settings, C:\Documents and Settings on most computers. This is the case only with a clean installation of Windows, however.

If you upgrade from a version of Windows earlier than Windows 2000, the profiles remain where they were in the previous operating system. For example, if you upgrade from Windows NT 4.0 to Windows XP or Windows Server 2003, the profiles remain in %SystemRoot%\Profiles. The location of user profiles after upgrading from Windows 2000 to Windows XP or Windows Server 2003 depends on whether you installed Windows 2000 cleanly or upgraded from an earlier version of Windows. In other words, the setup program never moves user profiles during an upgrade.

Windows creates and stores a list of user profiles. Table 12-1 shows the locations of user profiles depending on the scenario. The key HKLM\SOFTWARE\Microsoft\Windows NT\CurrentVersion\ProfileList corresponds to the list you see in the User Profiles dialog box. To open the User Profiles dialog box, from Control Panel, launch System, and in the System Properties dialog box, on the Advanced tab, click Settings in the User Profiles frame. Each subkey is a user profile, and the subkey's name is the Security Identifier (SID) of the account that owns the profile. Each profile in `ProfileList` contains the `REG_SZ` value `ProfileImagePath` that points to a user profile folder in %SystemRoot%\Documents and Settings. Figure 12-1 illustrates the relationship between the `ProfileList` key and the user profile folders. This relationship is the reason that you shouldn't just remove a user profile from the file system. Instead, use the User Profiles dialog box to remove user profiles, which cleans the user profile out of the `ProfileList` key as well as off the file system.

Table 12-1   Location of User Profiles

Scenario	Location
Clean installation	%SystemDrive%\Documents and Settings
Upgrade from Windows 2000	%SystemDrive%\Documents and Settings
Upgrade from Windows NT 4.0	%SystemRoot%\Profiles
Upgrade from Windows 98	%SystemDrive%\Documents and Settings

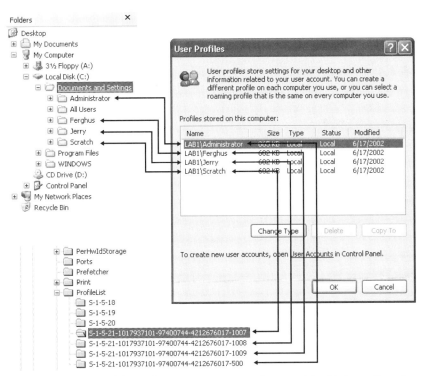

Figure 12-1   The subkeys of `ProfileList` contain a wealth of information about the user profiles that Windows has created, including their paths on the file system.

> **Note**   In enterprises that use Windows NT 4.0, IT professionals sometimes move profiles to %SystemRoot%\Profiles when deploying Windows because managing the profiles is often easier if they are in the same location regardless of the platform. Windows answer files offer a setting that enables you to do that. The setting is ProfilesDir, and it's in the [GuiUnattended] section. Set ProfilesDir to the path of the folder in which you want to store profiles. You should begin the path with either %SystemRoot% or %SystemDrive%; otherwise, the setup program ignores it.

Advantages of User Profiles

The primary goal of user profiles is to keep each user's settings and data distinct from that of other users as well as from the computer's settings. This separation has several advantages for enterprise environments and makes Windows more convenient to use at home, too. User profiles enable *stateless* computing. A company can configure Windows to store key user settings and data separately from the computer. This makes backing up and replacing computers much easier because users' data is stored on the network and maintained separately from the computer's configuration. The first time users log on to a replacement computer, the operating system copies their settings from the network, allowing them to get back to work more quickly.

Roaming user profiles also allow users' settings to follow them from computer to computer. They don't have to reconfigure settings at each computer. When they log on to a network that supports roaming user profiles, the operating system downloads their settings from the network. When they log off the computer, the operating system copies users' settings back to the network. Roaming user profiles make sharing computers more feasible because each user has his or her personalized configuration. Roaming user profiles are a must-have in environments such as call centers, where users aren't guaranteed to sit down at the same computer twice. You learn about roaming user profiles in the section "Using Roaming User Profiles," later in this chapter.

Profile Hives

The first half of a user profile is the profile hive: NTUSER.DAT. You learn about the second half in the next section, "Profile Folders." This profile hive is in the root of users' profile folders. Chapter 1, "Learning the Basics," and Chapter 2, "Using Registry Editor," describe hive files and how to work with them. Users' operating system and application settings are stored in profile hives. For example, you find all the per-user settings for Windows Explorer and persistent network connections in profile hives. Profile hives also contain per-user taskbar, printer, and Control Panel settings. Accessories that come with Windows store per-user settings in the profile hive.

When Windows loads a user profile, the operating system loads the hive file NTUSER.DAT into the subkey HKU*SID*, where SID is the user's SID. (See Chapter 1, "Learning the Basics," for more information about SIDs.) Then Windows links the root key HKCU to HKU*SID*. Figure 12-2 shows this relationship. Windows and most applications reference users' settings through HKCU, not HKU*SID*, because HKCU resolves which subkey of HKU contains the console user's settings. HKU contains a second hive file, HKU*SID*_Classes, which contains per-user file associations and class registrations. You learn about this in Appendix A, "File Associations."

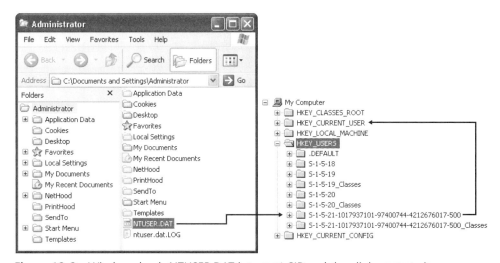

Figure 12-2   Windows loads NTUSER.DAT into HKU*SID* and then links HKCU to it.

The list of profile hives is in the key ProfileList, which you learned about in the previous section. It contains one subkey for each user profile. The subkey's name is the name of the hive in HKU or the account's SID. The REG_SZ value ProfileImagePath is the path of the profile hive file NTUSER.DAT for that user profile. ProfileList does not contain a value for the *SID*_Classes hives, however. HKLM\SYSTEM\CurrentControlSet\Control\hivelist contains one REG_SZ value for each hive in HKLM and HKU that the operating system is currently using. The difference between the values ProfileList and hivelist is that ProfileList contains a list of all user profiles that Windows knows about, loaded or not, and hivelist contains a list of all currently loaded hive files.

> **Tip**   You can load and edit profile hives in Registry Editor (Regedit) without logging on to the computer using the account that owns that user profile. This is one of the techniques that you use later in this chapter to build default user profiles.

Profile Folders

The folders in a user profile contain per-user application files. For example, Microsoft Office 2003 Editions installs templates and custom dictionaries in the user profile. Microsoft Internet Explorer stores its cookies and shortcuts in the user profile. The most interesting folder in a user profile is the Application Data folder. Figure 12-3 shows a user profile in Windows Explorer. Some of the folders are hidden; show the hidden files in Windows Explorer if you want to see the following folders for yourself:

- **Application Data.**   This folder contains application files, such as mail files, shortcuts, templates, and so on. Each application's vendor chooses what files to store here. You can redirect this folder to a network location using Group Policy.

- **Cookies.**   This folder contains Internet Explorer cookies.

- **Desktop.**   This folder contains files, folders, and shortcuts on the desktop. Users see the contents of this folder on the Windows desktop. You can redirect this folder to a network location using Group Policy.

- **Favorites.**   This folder contains Internet Explorer favorite shortcuts. Users see the contents of this folder on Internet Explorer's Favorites menu. Group Policy doesn't support redirecting this folder, but you can redirect it manually as shown in Chapter 18, "Fixing Common IT Problems."

- **Local Settings.**   This folder contains application files that do not roam with the profile. The files you find in this folder are either per-computer or too large to copy to the network. This folder contains four interesting subfolders:

  - ❑ **Application Data.**   This subfolder contains computer-specific application data.

  - ❑ **History.**   This subfolder contains Internet Explorer history.

  - ❑ **Temp.**   This subfolder contains per-user temporary files.

  - ❑ **Temporary Internet Files.**   This subfolder contains Internet Explorer offline files.

- **My Documents.**   This folder contains the default location for users' documents. Applications should save users' documents to this folder by default, and this is the location to which the common dialog boxes open by default. This folder also contains the My Pictures folder, which is the default location for users' pictures, and optionally the My Music folder, which is the default location for users' music files. You can redirect this folder to a network location using Group Policy.

- **NetHood.**   This folder contains shortcuts to objects on the network. Users can browse the folders to which these shortcuts are linked in the My Network Places folder.

- **PrintHood.**   This folder contains shortcuts to printer objects. Users see the contents of this folder in the Printers folder.

- **Recent.**   This folder contains shortcuts to the most recently used documents. Users see these shortcuts on the My Recent Documents menu, which is on the Start menu.

- **SendTo.**   This folder contains shortcuts to drives, folders, and applications that are copy targets. Users see the contents of this folder when they right-click an object and then click Send To.

- **Start Menu.**   This folder contains shortcuts to program items. Users see the contents of this folder on the Start menu and on the Start menu's All Programs menu. IT professionals can redirect this folder to a network location using Group Policy.

- **Templates.**   This folder contains template files. Users see the contents of this folder when they right-click in a folder and then click New.

Figure 12-3   The user profile folders that you see in this figure are the default folders in a clean installation of Windows.

`HKCU\Software\Microsoft\Windows\CurrentVersion\Explorer\User Shell Folders` is the key where Windows stores the location of each folder that's part of a user profile. Each value in this key represents a folder, as shown in Table 12-2. These are `REG_EXPAND_SZ` values, so you can use environment variables in them. Use %UserProfile% to direct the folder somewhere inside users' profile folders and %UserName% to include users' names, particularly when you want to redirect a profile folder to a network location. Redirect users' Favorites folders to the network by setting `Favorites` to *Server**Share*\\%UserName%\\`Favorites`, where *Server**Share* is the server and share containing the folders, for example. Windows does not use the similar key `Shell Folders`.

Table 12-2   User Profile Folders

Name	Default Path
AppData	%UserProfile%\Application Data
Cache	%UserProfile%\Local Settings\Temporary Internet Files
Cookies	%UserProfile%\Cookies
Desktop	%UserProfile%\Desktop
Favorites	%UserProfile%\Favorites

Table 12-2   **User Profile Folders**

Name	Default Path
History	%UserProfile%\Local Settings\History
Local AppData	%UserProfile%\Local Settings\Application Data
Local Settings	%UserProfile%\Local Settings
My Pictures	%UserProfile%\My Documents\My Pictures
NetHood	%UserProfile%\NetHood
Personal	%UserProfile%\My Documents
PrintHood	%UserProfile%\PrintHood
Programs	%UserProfile%\Start Menu\Programs
Recent	%UserProfile%\Recent
SendTo	%UserProfile%\SendTo
Start Menu	%UserProfile%\Start Menu
Startup	%UserProfile%\Start Menu\Programs\Startup
Templates	%UserProfile%\Templates

Special Profiles

The profile folders you saw in Figure 12-1 contain more than the standard user profiles that Windows creates when users log on to the operating system. The following describes four special user profiles about which any IT professional should learn:

- **All Users.**   This profile folder contains settings that apply to all users who log on to the computer. This profile folder contains a profile hive, NTUSER.DAT, which the operating system doesn't load. Also, this profile folder contains the shared documents and music folders, shared Start menu shortcuts, and so on. The key User Shell Folders in HKLM\SOFTWARE\Microsoft\Windows\CurrentVersion\ Explorer contains the linkages to the subfolders in the All Users profile folder.

- **Default User.**   This profile folder contains the default user profile that Windows copies when it creates new user profiles. It contains most of the files and folders that you learned about in the previous section. Customizing this folder is a good way to start each user who logs on to the computer with the same settings. Windows first checks for a Default User folder on the NETLOGON share of the server and uses the local Default User folder only if the network copy isn't available. Customizing this folder is a good way to deploy settings that you don't want to manage. You learn how to customize it in the section "Deploying Default User Profiles," later in this chapter.

- **LocalService.**   This profile folder is for the built-in LocalService account, which Service Control Manager uses to host services that don't need to run under the LocalSystem account. This is a normal user profile with limited data. You don't see it in the User Profiles dialog box, and the LocalService folder is super-hidden.

- **NetworkService.** This profile folder is for the built-in NetworkService account, which the Service Control Manager uses to host network services that don't need to run under the LocalSystem account. This is a normal user profile. You don't see it in the User Profiles dialog box, and the NetworkService folder is super-hidden.

In the previous list, the first two profile folders are far more interesting than the last two. IT professionals often customize the All Users profile folder on disk images. The customization, such as a shortcut on the Start menu, affects all users who log on to the computer. However, IT professionals more frequently customize the Default User folder. Doing so is a great way to create custom settings that you don't want to manage. In other words, it's one method for deploying common user preferences while still allowing users to change those preferences if necessary. As you'll learn throughout this chapter, customizing the Default User folder on a disk image isn't necessarily the most efficient means to deploy default user settings. Instead, create a customized Default User folder on the server's NETLOGON share. See the section "Deploying Default User Profiles," later in this chapter.

> **Tip** Many programs install themselves for use by a single user when you really want all users who share the computer to use them. You can tell when a program is installed per-user because its shortcut is in the profile folder belonging to the account you used to install it. If the program re-creates missing settings as it starts, you can change the program from per-user to per-computer by simply moving its shortcut from the user profile folder in which it installed the shortcut to the All Users profile folder. This works the other way, too. You can move a shortcut from the All Users profile folder to a specific user's profile folder so that only a single user sees the shortcut.

Improvements to User Profiles

In Windows 2000, poorly written applications and services that keep registry keys open during logoff prevent Windows 2000 from unloading the user's registry hive. When this occurs, changes that a user made to his or her profile are not saved to the server. This has three symptoms:

- The user experience is affected because changes are not saved when users log on to another computer.

- Because *locked* profiles never get unloaded, they end up using a lot of memory on a terminal server that has many users logging on to it.

- If a profile is marked for deletion at logoff (to clean up the machine or for temporary profiles), profiles do not get deleted.

> The three symptoms are solved as follows:
>
> ■ In Windows, when a user logs off and the profile is locked, the operating system polls the profile for 60 seconds before giving up. Windows then saves the user's profile hive and roams the profile correctly.
>
> ■ When the application or service closes the registry key and unlocks the profile, Windows unloads the user's profile hive, freeing memory used by the profile.
>
> ■ If a profile is marked for deletion, when the reference count drops to zero, Windows unloads and deletes it. In the event that the application never releases the registry key, Windows deletes all profiles marked for deletion at the next machine boot.

Getting User Profiles

How users get their profiles depends on the type of profile you've configured their accounts to use:

■ **Local user profile.**   This profile is created the first time users log on to their computers. Local user profiles are stored on the local hard disk. Changes that users make to their profiles don't follow them from computer to computer.

■ **Roaming user profile.**   This profile is available to users from any computer on the network, and changes that users make to their profiles follow them from computer to computer.

■ **Mandatory user profile.**   This profile is similar to roaming user profiles. Administrators assign mandatory user profiles to users, and Windows throws away users' changes when they log off the operating system. In other words, users start with the same settings every time they log on to the operating system. Microsoft provides mandatory user profiles to provide compatibility with Windows NT 4.0, but you should consider using Group Policy instead.

The following sections describe how Windows creates a profile when users log on to the operating system. The section "Using Roaming User Profiles" describes how to create and manage roaming user profiles. Also, the section "Managing Roaming User Profiles" shows you how to prevent Windows from merging the local copy of a profile with the server copy by using Group Policy.

Local Profiles

Here's an overview of how Windows creates and uses a local user profile for users the first time they log on to their computers:

1.   The user logs on to Windows.

2. Windows checks the list of user profiles in the key `ProfileList` to determine if a local profile exists for the user. If an entry exists, the operating system uses it; otherwise, the operating system does one of the following:

    ❑   If the computer is a domain member, Windows checks the NETLOGON share on the domain controller for a default user profile in a subfolder named Default User. If it exists, the operating system copies NETLOGON\Default User to %SystemDrive%\Documents and Settings*Username*, where *Username* is the name of the user's account.

    ❑   If the computer is not a domain member or if Windows doesn't find a default user profile on the NETLOGON share, it uses the local default user profile. It copies %SystemDrive%\Documents and Settings\Default User to %SystemDrive%\Documents and Settings*Username*.

3. Windows loads the profile hive NTUSER.DAT into HKU and links the root key HKCU to it.

When the user logs off Windows, the operating system saves any changes to the profile in the user profile folder. It doesn't copy the profile folder to the network. It also unloads the profile hive from the registry.

Roaming Profiles

Here's an overview of how Windows creates and uses a roaming user profile for users the first time they log on to their computers:

1. The user logs on to Windows.

2. Windows checks the list of user profiles in the `ProfileList` key to determine whether a local profile exists for the user. If an entry exists, the operating system merges the network copy of the profile into the local profile folder; otherwise, the operating system does one of the following:

    ❑   Windows checks the NETLOGON share on the domain controller for the Default User folder. If the folder exists, the operating system copies the Default User folder to %SystemDrive%\Documents and Settings*Username*, where *Username* is the name of the user's account.

    ❑   If Windows doesn't find a default user profile on the NETLOGON share, it copies %SystemDrive%\Documents and Settings\Default User to %SystemDrive%\Documents and Settings*Username*.

3. Windows loads the profile hive NTUSER.DAT into HKU and links the root key HKCU to it.

When users log off Windows, the operating system saves their changes to the local profile folders and then unloads the profile hives from HKU. Afterward, the operating system copies their profile folders to the network location specified by the administrator.

If the profile folder already exists on the network, the operating system merges the local copy into the network copy. For more information, see "Understanding the New Merge," later in this chapter.

> **Note**   There are two differences between roaming and mandatory user profiles. First, you create the mandatory profile and copy it to the user's profile folder instead of allowing Windows to create it when the user logs on to the computer. Second, you rename the NTUSER.DAT to NTUSER.MAN. Windows uses the *.MAN* file extension to make the profile mandatory. Windows doesn't merge mandatory user profiles to the network when the user logs off the computer.

Using Roaming User Profiles

You configure roaming user profiles on the server, so the user must be a member of and log on to the domain to use a roaming user profile. Both Microsoft Windows NT Server 4.0 and Microsoft Windows 2000 Server support roaming user profiles, as do Microsoft Windows XP and Windows Server 2003. The following instructions show you how to configure roaming user profiles in Active Directory on Windows Server 2003:

1. Create a folder on the server where you want to store user profiles. This is the top-level folder that will contain individual user profile folders.

2. Share the folder, giving all users full control. (I sometimes reduce users' permissions to read and execute in this folder and then give them full control of their individual profile folders.)

3. In the Active Directory Users and Computers console, double-click the account that you want to configure to use a roaming user profile.

4. On the Profile tab of the *Name* Properties dialog box, shown in Figure 12-4, type the path where you want to store the user's profile in the Profile Path text box. The path is *Server**Share**Username*, where *Server* is the name of the server, *Share* is the share you created in step 2, and *Username* is the name of the account. Optionally, use %UserName% for *Username*, and Active Directory will automatically substitute the current account's name in its place.

If you want to configure a lot of accounts to use roaming user profiles, doing the job by hand is a monumental task. Instead, use a third-party tool or write an Active Directory Scripting Interface (ADSI) script to do the job. You access ADSI through Windows Script Host using Microsoft Visual Basic Scripting Edition (VBScript) or JScript.

> **More Info**   This subject is beyond the scope of this book, but you can find more information about ADSI scripting at *http://www.microsoft.com/resources/documentation/ windows/2000/server/scriptguide/en-us/sas_ads_overview.mspx*.

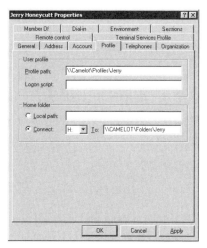

Figure 12-4   Typing a path in the Profile Path box is all that it takes to enable roaming user profiles.

Folder Redirection is a great complement to user profiles, particularly the roaming variety. It enables an IT professional to redirect the location of some profile folders to the network. There's nothing magical about Folder Redirection. Group Policy simply changes the folder's location in the User Shell Folders key so that applications automatically look for the folder on the network. From users' perspectives, redirected folders are similar to roaming user profiles because their documents follow them from computer to computer. Unlike roaming user profiles, however, redirected folders always remain in the same place. You can use redirected folders with or without roaming user profiles. If you use them with roaming user profiles, you can reduce the amount of data that Windows transfers when users log on to and off from the operating system. Furthermore, redirected folders are often useful even when you don't intend to use roaming user profiles; you can allow users' documents to follow them without the complexity and sometimes difficulty of using roaming user profiles. You learn about roaming user profiles in the earlier section "Getting User Profiles." Table 12-3 indicates for each profile folder whether the folder can roam and whether you can redirect it.

Table 12-3   Roaming and Redirecting Folders

Folder	Can Roam?	Can Redirect?
Application Data	Yes	Yes
Cookies	Yes	No
Desktop	Yes	Yes
Favorites	Yes	No
Local Settings	No	No
My Documents	Yes	Yes
My Recent Documents	Yes	No

Table 12-3   **Roaming and Redirecting Folders**

Folder	Can Roam?	Can Redirect?
NetHood	Yes	No
PrintHood	Yes	No
SendTo	Yes	No
Start Menu	Yes	Yes
Templates	Yes	No

Best Practices for Roaming User Profiles

The following are best practices for roaming user profiles:

- Redirect the My Documents folder outside of roaming user profiles. Doing so decreases logon time. Folder Redirection is the best way to do this, but you can redirect the My Documents folder manually, as Chapter 18, "Fixing Common IT Problems," describes.

- Don't use Encrypted File System (EFS) on files in a roaming user profile. EFS is not compatible with roaming user profiles. Encrypting a roaming user profile prevents the user profile from roaming.

- Don't make disk quotas for roaming user profiles too restrictive. If they're too low, roaming user profile synchronization might fail. The server debits the user's quota for temporary files that Windows creates during the synchronization process, so ensure that enough disk space is available on the server. Also, make sure enough disk space is available on the workstation to create temporary duplicate copies of the profile.

- Don't make folders in roaming user profiles available offline. If you use Offline Folders with roaming user profile folders, synchronization problems occur because both Offline Folders and roaming user profiles try to synchronize at the same time. However, you can use Offline Folders with folders that you redirect, such as My Documents.

- Use Group Policy loopback policy processing in moderation if you're also using roaming user profiles. Loopback processing enables you to apply different per-user Group Policy settings to users based on the computer they're using.

- When redirecting the My Documents folder outside of a roaming user profile, set the home folder to the redirected My Documents folder for compatibility with applications that aren't compatible with folder redirection.

- Disable fast network logon using Group Policy if you're using roaming user profiles. This prevents conflicts that occur when user profiles change from local to roaming. For more information, see "Understanding Fast Network Logon," later in this chapter.

> **More Info**   You can get a detailed explanation of loopback processing at *http:// support.microsoft.com/default.aspx?scid=kb;en-us;231287*.

Managing Roaming User Profiles

Group Policy provides a number of policies that you can use to manage how Windows handles user profiles. You can configure these policies in a local Group Policy Object (GPO) or in a network GPO. Chapter 7, "Using Registry-Based Policy," gives more information. For now, here's a description of policies for user profiles:

- **Connect home directory to root of the share.**   This policy restores the definitions of the %HomeShare% and %HomePath% environment variables to those used in Windows NT 4.0 and earlier.

- **Limit profile size.**   This policy sets the maximum size of each roaming user profile and determines the system's response when a roaming user profile reaches the maximum size. If user profiles become excessively large, consider redirecting the My Documents folder to a location outside of the profile.

- **Exclude directories in a roaming profile.**   This policy enables you to add to the list of folders excluded from the user's roaming profile.

- **Delete cached copies of roaming profiles.**   This policy determines whether the system saves a copy of a user's roaming profile on the local computer's hard disk when the user logs off.

- **Do not detect slow network connections.**   This policy disables the slow link detection feature.

- **Slow network connection timeout for user profiles.**   This policy defines a slow connection for roaming user profiles.

- **Wait for remote user profile.**   This policy directs the system to wait for the remote copy of the roaming user profile to load, even when loading is slow. Also, the system waits for the remote copy when the user is notified about a slow connection, but the user does not respond in the time allowed.

- **Prompt user when slow link is detected.**   This policy notifies users when their roaming profile is slow to load. Users can then decide whether to use a local copy or to wait for the roaming user profile.

- **Timeout for dialog boxes.**   This policy determines how long the system waits for a user response before it uses a default value.

- **Log users off when roaming profile fails.**   This policy logs a user off automatically when the system cannot load the user's roaming user profile.

- **`Maximum retries to unload and update user profile.`**   This policy determines how many times the system will try to unload and update the profile hive. When the number of trials specified by this setting is exhausted, the system stops trying. As a result, the user profile might not be current, and local and roaming user profiles might not match.

- **`Add the Administrators security group to roaming user profiles.`**   This policy adds the Administrators security group to the roaming user profile share. The default behavior prevents administrators from managing individual profile folders without taking ownership of them.

- **`Prevent Roaming Profile changes from propagating to the server.`**   This policy determines if the changes a user makes to his or her roaming profile are merged with the server copy of their profile. This is a policy-based method for implementing mandatory user profiles.

- **`Only allow local user profiles.`**   This policy determines if roaming user profiles are available on a particular computer. By default, when roaming-profile users log on to a computer, their roaming profile is copied to the local computer. If they have already logged on to this computer in the past, the roaming profile is merged with the local profile. Similarly, when the users log off this computer, the local copy of their profile, including any changes they have made, is merged with the server copy of their profile.

The first three policies in this list are per-user and the remaining are per-computer policies; Figure 12-5 shows them in Group Policy Editor. All of the policies are administrative policies in System\User Profiles under User Configuration and Computer Configuration.

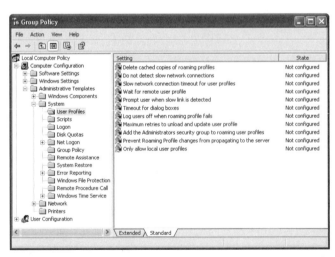

Figure 12-5   These policies give you management control of how Windows uses profiles.

Understanding Fast Network Logon

Windows doesn't wait for the network to start before displaying the Logon To Windows dialog box. This substantially improves start time over Windows 2000. Users who've previously logged on to the computer get to their desktops faster because the operating system uses cached credentials and loads Group Policy in the background after the network becomes available. Although fast network logon improves perceived performance, it has effects that you should understand. The most important fact to understand in this section is that Windows doesn't use fast network logon if you use roaming user profiles.

Because background refresh is the default behavior, users might have to log on to Windows up to three times for Group Policy extensions such as Software Installation and Folder Redirection to take effect. Windows must process these types of extensions in the background without any users logged on to it. Also, because advanced Folder Redirection is based on group membership, users must log on to Windows three times: once to update the cached user object and group membership, a second time to detect the change in group membership and require a foreground policy application, and a third time to apply folder redirection policy in the foreground. The operating system might require users to log on two times to update the properties of other Group Policy objects.

Another thing to keep in mind is the effect that fast network logon has on Windows when users' profiles change from local to roaming. When the operating system uses fast network logon, it always uses the locally cached copy of the profile. By the time the operating system detects that the user has a roaming user profile, it's already loaded the local profile hive and changed its time stamp. The result is that if users log on to multiple computers, the operating system can replace newer profile hives with older ones. To handle this scenario, Windows treats the change from local to roaming as a special case. First the operating system checks the following conditions:

- Is the user changing from a local to a roaming profile?
- Is a copy of the user profile on the server?

If both these conditions are true, then Windows merges the contents of the local user profile with the server copy, without the profile hive NTUSER.DAT. Then the operating system copies the server copy of the profile to the local copy, regardless of the profile hives' time stamps. After the user's profile becomes a roaming profile, Windows always waits for the network so that it can download the user profile. In other words, fast network logon and roaming user profiles don't work together.

Caution   Considering the changes that Windows makes to roaming user profiles, if you remove the roaming profile path from a user in Active Directory, you should remove the profile folder from the server. If you reconfigure the user to use roaming user profiles and you use the same path, the user will receive the older server copy of the user profile.

Understanding the New Merge

Many IT professionals are reluctant to use roaming user profiles because they have experience with the merge algorithm that Windows NT 4.0 uses. That algorithm assumes that there is a single master copy of the user profile. When the user logs on to the computer, the operating system assumes that the master profile is on the local computer, and when the user logs off the computer, it assumes that the master profile is on the server. It mirrors the entire profile from the local computer to the server and vice versa, completely replacing the profile at the target location. This works perfectly well when people use a single computer, but it creates havoc when they use multiple computers.

The merge algorithm in Windows is more advanced; it merges user profiles at the file level. In other words, it's a real merge, not a wipe-and-load. The merged profile then becomes a superset of the files in the local and server copies of the user profile, and when a file exists in both copies, the operating system uses the most recent version of the file. New files don't turn up missing, and updated files are not replaced—both of which are symptoms that occur with the merge algorithm in Windows NT 4.0. In the case of the Windows NT 4.0 merge, if a profile changes on two computers, only the last profile copied to the network persists.

Behind the new and improved merge algorithm is the time stamp that Windows saves in the `ProfileList` key. When a user logs on to the computer, the operating system saves the current time in `ProfileList`. When the user logs off the computer, the operating system uses the time stamp to determine which files have been added or removed from the server's copy of the user profile. For example, if a file named Example.doc is in the server copy of the user profile but not in the local copy, the time stamp helps Windows determine whether the file was added to the server copy or removed from the local copy. If the time stamp of the file is later than the time stamp of the local user profile, the file was added to the server copy. The result is that Windows doesn't touch the file when it merges the local profile into the server copy. If the time stamp of the file is earlier than the time stamp of the local user profile, the file was removed from the local user profile. The result is that Windows removes the file from the server copy of the profile when the operating system merges the local copy into it. With Windows, if a profile changes on two computers, both of them are merged file by file into the server copy.

Note   There is another issue that keeps many IT professionals from using roaming user profiles. Roaming user profiles are terrific when configurations are similar from desktop to desktop. When users log on to different computers with different sets of applications, screen sizes, power management requirements, and so on, roaming user profiles are cumbersome and users' experiences aren't very good. Roaming user profiles are great in scenarios such as call centers and other environments in which configurations are standardized, but they are not very useful when configurations are not standardized in an organization.

Deploying Default User Profiles

Deploying default user profiles is one of the easiest ways to deploy settings to new users. You can't use default user profiles to deploy settings to existing users, however, because they already have user profiles. These aren't settings that you want to manage. They're defaults that you want to establish for users while allowing users to change them when necessary. Essentially, deploying default user profiles is like modifying the default settings in Windows. If you want to define a setting that users *can't* change, use policies. Chapter 7, "Using Registry-Based Policy," contains more information about managing settings.

To deploy a default user profile, follow these steps:

1. Create a template account.

    You can use a local or a domain account, but the user profile is generally cleaner if you use a local account on a computer that's not joined to a domain. (Because I include network shortcuts in my profiles, I usually use a domain account to create default user profiles.) Also, for the template account, choose a name that you're sure is unique in the registry and is shorter than eight characters. You'll learn why using a unique name is important a bit later in this chapter.

2. Log on to the computer using the template account, and customize its settings. The section "Customizing User Settings," later in this chapter, describes settings that I usually customize.

3. Clean up the user profile to remove artifacts that you don't want to deploy. The section "Cleaning User Profiles," later in this chapter, describes how to clean the profile.

4. Copy the template account's user profile folder to a new location, and name it Default User.

    Don't replace %SystemDrive%\Documents and Settings\Default User, however, because you might need to repeat the process a few times to get it right and you'll want the original default user profile handy. In the section "Creating Default User Folders," later in this chapter, I describe an alternative method for building the Default User folder that I think is more precise because it yields a cleaner default user profile.

5. Deploy the default user profile.

    You can put the Default User folder in %SystemDrive%\Documents and Settings on disk images and then deploy them, or you can put the Default User folder on the NETLOGON share of the server. I prefer the second method because it separates settings from the disk images, which allows me to update settings much more easily.

> ### Alternatives to Default User Profiles
>
> An alternative to customizing a bunch of settings in default user profiles is scripting. Create a script that configures Windows user settings per your company's requirements. This assumes that you have a specification, or at the very least, a list of settings that you want to customize for users. Then edit the NTUSER.DAT hive file in the disk image's Default User folder, adding the command that executes the script to the key `HKCU\Software\Microsoft\Windows\CurrentVersion\RunOnce`. The NTUSER.DAT hive file in the Default User folder doesn't contain the `RunOnce` key by default, so you must add it. Then add a `REG_SZ` value to this key—the name is arbitrary—and put the command line that you want to execute in it. Each time Windows creates a new user profile, it executes the script to customize the user's settings.
>
> Also, you can add a script that customizes the current user profile to `HKLM\Software\Microsoft\Windows\CurrentVersion\Run`. Windows runs this script every time a user logs on to the computer. If you want to configure settings only the first time the user logs on to the computer, add code to the script that checks for a value in `HKCU` and runs only if that value doesn't exist. Then end the script with code that creates the missing value so that the script doesn't run the next time the user logs on to the computer. Chapter 11, "Scripting Registry Changes," shows you how to write scripts using Windows Script Host, and these are ideal for this scenario.

Customizing User Settings

Log on to the template account that you created in step 1 of the previous section and customize the account's settings. When customizing settings for a default user profile, less is more. Preferably, you'll work from a list of settings that you've examined with other members of the deployment planning team. The following list gives you an idea of the settings that I frequently target with default user profiles:

- Quick Launch toolbar
- Start menu
- Windows Explorer
- Internet Explorer
- My Network Places
- Search Assistant

- Tweak UI
- Control Panel, in particular:
  - ❑ Display
  - ❑ Folder Options
  - ❑ Mouse
  - ❑ Power Options
  - ❑ Printers and Faxes
  - ❑ Sounds and Audio Devices
  - ❑ Taskbar and Start Menu

You want to customize per-user settings because those are the only settings that are in the user profile. How do you know that a setting is per-user when you're customizing a user profile? You don't necessarily. That's why you must test the settings in your list ahead of time. Sitting down to construct a default user profile isn't the time to begin wondering whether a particular setting is per-user or per-computer. The easiest way to find out is to log on to a new account and customize the settings in your list. Then copy that user profile to a clean installation of Windows, and see which settings made it. The settings that didn't make it are per-computer settings, and you'll want to scratch them off your list. There are a small number of settings that are per-user but still don't work well in default user profiles, and there's generally little you can do about it except edit the profile to make them work. The most prominent example is desktop wallpaper. Including wallpaper in a default user profile requires you to include the wallpaper graphic file inside the profile folder and then edit the profile hive to point to the new location.

You might also want to include settings for applications that you're deploying, whether you include them on your disk images or deploy them using other methods.

> **Note** Before you begin, here's a caveat: don't include settings for Windows Installer–based applications in a default user profile. Windows Installer provides superior methods for deploying settings. That means you shouldn't deploy settings for Office 2003 Editions using default user profiles. Instead, use tools such as Custom Installation Wizard and Office Profile Wizard. Both tools come with the Office 2003 Editions Resource Kit, and Chapter 17, "Deploying Office 2003 Settings," describes how to use them. Install other types of applications and customize their settings to your requirements just as you would customize Windows settings.

This last step is optional but I recommend it: remove artifacts from the user profile that you don't want to deploy. Artifacts include history lists and similar items. I have a preset route that I use to clean up a user profile. First I clear the Start menu and Internet Explorer's history lists. To do this:

- In Control Panel, launch Taskbar And Start Menu. On the Start Menu tab, click Customize. On the Customize Start Menu dialog box's Advanced tab, click the Clear List button.

- In Control Panel, launch Internet Options. In the Internet Options dialog box, click Clear History to remove Internet Explorer's history lists.

You don't need to worry about removing temporary Internet files because these are in the profile's Local Settings folder, and Windows doesn't copy them with the profile. If you opened Internet Explorer to customize it, however, you might clear out the cookies and AutoComplete lists. In the Internet Options dialog box, on the General tab, click Delete Cookies, and then on the Content tab, click AutoComplete, followed by Clear Forms and Clear Passwords.

After you're finished customizing and cleaning the account's settings, log off Windows. My last word of advice is to be cautious; don't open dialog boxes and programs that you don't intend to customize. Doing so keeps their settings out of the default user profile. For example, if you don't intend to customize Microsoft Windows Media Player, don't open the program.

Cleaning User Profiles

You cleaned the user profile a little bit in the previous section, but only to remove some artifacts from the profile hive. The next major step is to open the profile hive in Regedit and scour it for settings that you don't want to deploy or that you must change before deploying.

The most significant example is paths. User profiles contain references to the profile folder: %SystemDrive%\Documents and Settings*Name*. If you deploy the user profile to countless users, they'll all have different profile folders. When they try accessing the profile folder *Name*, Windows and programs will fail because the user doesn't have access to that folder. A more concrete example will make this clear. Assume you created a user profile using a template account named DefUser and deployed that profile to a user named Jerry. The user Jerry has access to %SystemDrive%\Documents and Settings\Jerry, but the folder %SystemDrive%\Documents and Settings\DefUser doesn't even exist. When the user Jerry runs a program that uses a setting containing the path to the DefUser user profile folder, the program causes an error. To correct this situation, follow these steps:

1. Log on to the computer containing the template user profile as Administrator.

2. In Regedit, load the NTUSER.DAT hive file from the template user profile folder. (See Chapter 2, "Using Registry Editor," to learn about using hive files.)

3. Search the hive file for references to the template user profile folder. If the name of the folder is longer than eight characters, search for the long and short versions of the folder's name.

4. Remove values that contain the path of the template user profile folder.

5. Unload the hive file, and restart the computer.

   Restarting the computer is often necessary because Windows locks the file and you can't copy it. Restarting the computer is the quickest way to force it to let go of the file.

When you remove values that contain the path of the template user profile folder in step 4, you're assuming that Windows and other programs re-create missing settings. This isn't always true. Some of my favorite applications fail to re-create missing settings. You'll learn which do and which don't through trial and error. You can handle the problem easily, though. Rather than removing the value permanently, replace a REG_SZ value with a REG_EXPAND_SZ value of the same name. Then set the value to the original path, substituting %USERPROFILE% for the portion that is the user profile folder. For example, if you see a REG_SZ value named Templates that contains C:\Documents and Settings\Jerry\Templates, remove the value; then add the value Templates back as a REG_EXPAND_SZ value, and set it to %USERPROFILE%\Templates. Test these changes in your lab to make sure they work properly.

In the previous section, you cleared some of the history lists using the Windows user interface. Take this opportunity to further neaten your work by removing the keys listed in Table 12-4. These correspond to most of the history lists that Windows keeps, including the Search Assistant and common dialog boxes.

Table 12-4   History Lists to Remove

History List	Key
Internet Explorer's address bar	HKCU\Software\Microsoft\Internet Explorer\TypedURLs
Run dialog box	HKCU\Software\Microsoft\Windows\CurrentVersion\Explorer \RunMRU
Documents menu	HKCU\Software\Microsoft\Windows\CurrentVersion\Explorer \RecentDocs
Common dialog boxes	HKCU\Software\Microsoft\Windows\CurrentVersion\Explorer \ComDlg32\LastVisitedMRU
Search Assistant	HKCU\Software\Microsoft\Search Assistant\ACMru

Creating Default User Folders

The template user profile is ready to go. All you have to do now is copy it. To open the User Profiles dialog box, in Control Panel, launch System. On the Advanced tab, click Settings in the User Profiles frame. In the User Profiles dialog box, click the template user profile and then click Copy To. In the Copy Profile To text box, shown in Figure 12-6, type the path to which you want to copy the profile. To keep things simple, I usually copy the profile folder to C:\Default User. Just make sure that the folder doesn't already exist. Also, give the Everyone group permission to use the profile, which is appropriate for a default user profile: click Change, type **Everyone**, and then click OK. The default user profile is ready to deploy, which you learn how to do in the next section.

Figure 12-6   Copy the template user profile using this dialog box; don't copy the folder using Windows Explorer because doing so copies artifacts that you don't want in the profile.

The method that I just described is common for creating a default user profile from a template user profile. I don't like it because user profiles expand greatly in size and complexity after Windows loads and uses them. A default user profile created using the method that I just described contains more files and folders than necessary. To use the more precise method that I prefer, follow these steps:

1. Copy %SystemDrive%\Documents and Settings\Default User to another location, such as C:\Default User. You want to keep the original Default User folder, just in case you have to start over again.

2. Copy the NTUSER.DAT hive file from the template user profile to your copy of the Default User folder, C:\Default User.

3. Copy other files from the template user profile folder to your copy of the Default User folder, C:\Default User. I tend to copy files from the following folders, assuming they contain files that I want to deploy:

    ❑   \Application Data\Microsoft\Internet Explorer\Quick Launch

    ❑   \Desktop

    ❑   \Favorites

- ❑ \NetHood
- ❑ \PrintHood
- ❑ \SendTo
- ❑ \Templates

Deploying Default User Folders

After completing the steps in the preceding section, you have a default user profile that's ready for deployment. You have two choices. If you're deploying Windows using disk-imaging techniques, you can include the default user profile on the disk image. Replace %SystemDrive%\Documents and Settings\Default User with your own Default User folder. After replacing the Default User folder with your own, clone and deploy the disk image. When new users log on to the computer, they'll receive your default user profile and thus your settings.

I don't like customizing the local Default User folder as my sole means of deploying default settings, however. I prefer to separate settings from configurations. What if I need to update a setting down the line? I don't want to update the Default User folder on each computer in the organization.

The alternative is to copy the customized Default User folder to the NETLOGON share of the server. As you learned earlier in the chapter, Windows looks first for the network version of the Default User folder and then the local version. The first time users log on to a computer, Windows gets my default user profile from the network. Of course, the benefit is that I can always update it later. The primary problem with this method is that if users log on to their computers locally, they still get the local default user profile. That's the reason that I prefer doing both at the same time. I replace the Default User folder on disk images and also copy the same folder to the NETLOGON share of the server.

> **Note**   An alternative to copying a default user profile to the NETLOGON share is keeping a user profile handy on the network and then copying it to users' network profile folders when you create new accounts. For example, stash away a default user profile somewhere on your server. Assuming that you're using roaming user profiles, copy the default user profile into new accounts' profile folders. The first time those users log on to Windows, the operating system downloads their roaming user profile, which you've already preconfigured. This is useful in one-off scenarios when you want users to have a profile other than the default. It's also useful in a heterogeneous environment, which often requires different user profiles for different versions of Windows.

Coexisting with Earlier Versions of Windows

Coexistence is an issue that affects roaming user profiles only. If you're not using roaming user profiles on your network, coexistence isn't an issue because you won't be deploying user profiles to different versions of Windows. In general, though, roaming user profiles are compatible between Windows 2000, Windows XP, and Windows Server 2003. Here are a few precautions that you can take to minimize problems:

- Try to ensure that users with roaming user profiles are logging on to the same version of Windows on each computer. That means you should choose your rollout units so that you're picking up all the computers that users can access.

- At the very least, make sure the same application versions are on each computer and that you've installed applications to the same path on each computer.

- If you're using roaming user profiles with Windows 2000, Windows XP, and Windows Server 2003, make sure that your %SystemDrive% and %System-Root% are the same. Also, make sure that profiles are stored in the same path. If you're using roaming user profiles with Windows NT 4.0 and Windows XP, you should move the location of user profiles that Windows XP uses by setting the `ProfilesDir` property in the `[GuiUnattended]` section of your answer file.

There's nothing in the documentation that says user profiles don't roam between Windows NT and Windows XP. However, I suspect that this scenario isn't workable. First, Windows XP converts Windows NT–based profiles. Second, having knowledge of both versions of the registry, I suspect that subtle differences between the two are likely to cause configuration problems in the long run. If anybody suggests that you can use roaming user profiles with any combination other than Windows 2000, Windows XP, and Windows Server 2003, ask for more information and test these scenarios carefully in a lab.

Migrating User Settings to Windows

Default user profiles give settings to new users, but what do you do about users who already have user profiles? You can let Windows migrate the user profile. Throw disk imaging into the mix, and you have a whole different bag of problems. One of the drawbacks of using disk imaging to deploy the operating system is that users lose their documents and settings. This doesn't have to be a barrier to deployment, though. A variety of third-party utilities are available to migrate users' settings. Also, Microsoft provides two tools, one for the user and one for the IT professional:

- **Files And Settings Transfer Wizard.**   This tool is designed for the user. This wizard is also useful in enterprise environments when employees want to migrate their own documents and settings without the IT department's help.

■ **User State Migration Tool (USMT).**   This tool is designed for IT professionals performing large-scale deployments of Windows in an enterprise. USMT provides the same functionality as the File And Settings Transfer Wizard, but on a larger scale. USMT gives IT professionals precise control over the documents and settings that it migrates.

All these tools work roughly the same way. First you copy users' documents and settings off their computers and store them on the network. You install a new disk image to their computers, and then you reapply their settings. Users get to keep their documents and settings.

Files And Settings Transfer Wizard

Files And Settings Transfer Wizard is a fast and easy way for you to copy all your documents and settings from your previous configuration to Windows XP or Windows Server 2003. To start it, click Start, All Programs, Accessories, System Tools, Files And Settings Transfer Wizard. It migrates settings in four major groups:

■ **Action.**   This group includes settings such as the key repeat rate, whether double-clicking a folder opens it in a new window or the same window, and whether you need to double-click or single-click an object to open it.

■ **Internet.**   This group includes settings that enable you to connect to the Internet and control how Internet Explorer works. They include settings such as your home page URL, favorites, Internet shortcuts, cookies, security settings, dial-up connections, and so on.

■ **Mail.**   This group includes settings for connecting to your mail server, your signature file, views, mail rules, local mail, and contacts. The wizard supports only Microsoft Outlook and Outlook Express.

■ **Application.**   This group includes application settings such as Microsoft Office. The wizard migrates only application settings, not the applications. You must reinstall each after upgrading to Windows XP or Windows Server 2003.

Files And Settings Transfer Wizard also migrates your documents. It does so by type (*.doc), folder (C:\Documents and Settings*username*\My Documents), or name (C:\Documents and Settings*username*\My Documents\Jerry.doc). The wizard is preconfigured to copy the most common types of files and the most useful folders. It also gives you the option to change the folders, the file types, and the file lists.

User State Migration Tool

User State Migration Tool (USMT) is similar to the Files And Settings Transfer Wizard, but it also allows you to fully customize exactly what the tool migrates. USMT is designed for IT professionals only; individual users do not need to use USMT. The tool is designed for large-scale migrations, and it requires a domain controller on which to store settings during migration.

USMT consists of two programs, ScanState.exe and LoadState.exe, and four migration rule information files: Migapp.inf, Migsys.inf, Miguser.inf, and Sysfiles.inf. Scan-State.exe collects users' documents and settings based on the information contained in Migapp.inf, Migsys.inf, Miguser.inf, and Sysfiles.inf. LoadState.exe deposits this user state data on a computer running a clean installation of Windows. Both of these tools are on the Windows CD in the \Valueadd\Msft\Usmt folder. The shared set of INF files drive USMT. IT professionals can modify these files to customize the documents and settings that the tool migrates. In fact, during any real deployment project, you'll most likely have to modify the INF files to handle your unique requirements.

More Info   The white paper "Step-by-Step Guide to Migrating Files and Settings" is a good guide for learning how to use USMT. This white paper is available on the Web at *http://www.microsoft.com/technet/prodtechnol/winxppro/deploy/mgrtfset.mspx.*

Chapter 13
Mapping Windows Installer

Windows Installer is a component of Microsoft Windows XP and Microsoft Windows Server 2003 (Windows) that simplifies application deployment, management, and removal. It manages installation by applying the setup rules contained by a package file. These rules define which files to install and the configuration of the application. After installing Windows Installer–based applications, you can change, repair, or remove them with a high degree of reliability—much greater than with applications that use legacy setup programs. In Windows, Windows Installer is an operating system service.

Windows Installer is a big subject. Component management, customization with transforms, deployment through Active Directory, and resiliency are some of the topics in the vast list of things that you should learn about Windows Installer before deploying applications based on the technology. This is a book about the registry, however, so I must focus on how Windows Installer interacts with the registry. However, you don't necessarily need to run out and buy a book to learn how to deploy Windows Installer–based applications. Microsoft posted incredibly useful documentation on the company's Web site. I suggest that you start with the white paper "Windows Installer: Benefits and Implementation for System Administrators" at *http://www.microsoft.com/windows2000/techinfo/administration/management/ wininstaller.asp*. Also, the *Microsoft Office 2003 Editions Resource Kit*, at *http:// www.microsoft.com/office/ork*, is the ultimate resource for learning how to deploy big Windows Installer–based applications like Office 2003 Editions. From this point forward, I'm assuming that you're familiar with Windows Installer and that you want to know more about how it interacts with the registry.

In this chapter, I describe Windows Installer registry settings. First I describe how to repair a Windows Installer–based application's user and computer settings. One of the really great things about Windows Installer is that it heads off help desk calls by repairing applications automatically when it detects a problem (missing or corrupt files, for example) and by enabling users to repair an application's user and computer settings manually. This chapter also describes the policies that IT professionals use to manage Windows Installer and the applications that use it. Some policies are more useful than others, so I'll describe the ones that offer solutions to common deployment problems. Finally, I describe the tools that you can use to remove an application's Windows Installer settings from the registry. These tools are sometimes essential because when an application's Windows Installer settings become corrupt, you can't remove the application using Add Or Remove Programs, and you can't reinstall or repair it.

> **Note**   Chapter 11, "Scripting Registry Changes," describes how to use Windows Installer to deploy registry settings. For example, you can build a Windows Installer package file that configures computer and user settings; then you can deploy that package file by using Group Policy, logon scripts, and so on.

Repairing Registry Settings

One of the most common activities that you'll do with a Windows Installer–based application's registry settings is repairing them. The most common scenario is when a user's settings are so misconfigured that the only choice is to restore them to their original values. This goes for computer settings, too. After the help desk call has exceeded a reasonable amount of time, the technician can put a quick end to the call by repairing the application. The most straightforward ways to repair a Windows Installer–based application are in the user interface:

- On the application's Help menu, click Detect And Repair.

- In Add Or Remove Programs, select the application that you want to repair, click Change, and then follow the directions that you see on the screen.

Some applications don't provide a user interface for repairing them, so you must use the command line. The syntax of the command that you use to repair an application follows this paragraph. The variable *package* is the path and name of the package file from which you installed the application. To repair user settings, type **msiexec /fu** *package*. To repair computer settings, type **msiexec /fm** *package*. The command **msiexec /fmu** *package* repairs both types of settings at the same time. These commands work rather well, which you can witness for yourself. Install Office 2003 Editions. Remove its settings, which are in HKCU\Software\Microsoft\Office, from the registry, and then repair the user settings. Windows Installer rebuilds the missing settings.

```
msiexec /f[p|o|e|d|c|a|u|m|v|s] package
```

p	Reinstall missing files, but don't check version.
o	Reinstall missing files or files that are from an earlier version.
e	Reinstall missing files or files that are from the same or an earlier version.

d	Reinstall missing files or files that aren't from the same version.
c	Reinstall missing files or files that are corrupt. This option only repairs files that have a checksum in the package file. Checksum is a bit-level error-checking scheme.
a	Reinstall all files regardless of their versions or checksums.
u	Rewrite the essential registry values described in the package file. This includes values in the per-user branches HKU and HKCU.
m	Rewrite essential registry values described in the package file. This includes values in the per-computer branches HKLM and HKCR.
v	Recache the source package locally.
s	Reinstall all shortcuts, and overwrite existing icons.

Note Repairing an application using Windows Installer is a bit extreme, considering that you have System Restore at your disposal. Chapter 3, "Backing Up the Registry," describes how to use this invaluable feature to protect configurations. If users' settings get misconfigured, going back to an earlier restore point will likely fix the problem. IT professionals can easily script this operation, too, which enables the help desk to automatically go back to the most recent restore point.

Managing Windows Installer with Policies

Windows Installer provides a number of policies for managing how it installs applications and interacts with users. Some policies are more important and more useful than others; I'll get to that in just a bit. First here's the complete list of policies provided by Windows Installer. (The parentheses contain the policies' registry values.)

- User Configuration\Administrative Templates\Windows Components\Windows Installer (HKCU\Software\Policies\Microsoft\Windows\Installer)

  - **Always install with elevated privileges (AlwaysInstallElevated).** Directs Windows Installer to use system permissions when it installs any program on the system. For this policy to work, you must also set its per-computer version.

  - **Search order (SearchOrder).** Specifies the order in which Windows Installer searches for installation files. In other words, you can specify the order in which it checks network, local media, and Web locations for installation files.

  - **Prohibit rollback (DisableRollback).** Prohibits Windows Installer from generating and saving the files that it needs to reverse an interrupted or unsuccessful installation. This is useful when you know that the disks won't have enough space to hold the rollback files. However, it's also dangerous because if the installation fails, Windows Installer won't be able to restore the computer.

❑ **Prevent removable media source for any install (Disable-Media).** Prevents users from installing programs from removable media. Using this policy is a great way to prevent users from circumventing IT policies and installing applications themselves. This controls only Windows Installer–based applications, though.

■ Computer Configuration\Administrative Templates\Windows Components\ Windows Installer (HKLM\Software\Policies\Microsoft\Windows\Installer)

❑ **Disable Windows Installer (DisableMSI).** Disables or restricts the use of Windows Installer. Use this policy to limit Windows Installer to only managed applications. Your choices are to allow users to install Windows Installer–based applications, never to allow users to install, or to allow them to install only managed applications.

❑ **Always install with elevated privileges (AlwaysInstallElevated).** Directs Windows Installer to use system permissions when it installs any program on the system. For this policy to work, you must also set its per-user version.

❑ **Prohibit rollback (DisableRollback).** Prohibits Windows Installer from generating and saving the files that it needs in order to reverse an interrupted or unsuccessful installation. This is useful when you know that the user's hard disk doesn't have enough space to hold the rollback files. However, it's also dangerous because if the installation fails, Windows Installer won't be able to restore the installation.

❑ **Remove browse dialog box for new source (DisableBrowse).** Prevents users from searching for installation files when they add features or components to an installed program. By default, if Windows Installer can't find the application's source files, it displays a dialog box allowing users to browse for the files.

❑ **Prohibit patching (DisablePatch).** Prevents users from using Windows Installer to install patches. You prevent users from patching their applications to protect them from malicious code.

❑ **Disable IE security prompt for Windows Installer scripts (SafeForScripting).** Allows Web-based programs to install software on the computer without notifying the user.

❑ **Enable user control over installs (EnableUserControl).** Permits users to change installation options that typically are available to system administrators only. Use this policy only in environments that don't lock down and carefully control configurations because it bypasses some of the security features built into Windows Installer.

❑ **Enable user to browse for source while elevated (AllowLockdown-Browse).** Allows users to search for installation files during privileged installations. By default, when it's running with elevated privileges, Windows Installer doesn't allow users to browse for installation source files.

❑ **Enable user to use media source while elevated (`AllowLockdown-Media`).** Allows users to install programs from removable media, such as floppy disks and CD-ROMs, during privileged installations. By default, when it's running with elevated privileges, Windows Installer doesn't allow users to install applications from local media.

❑ **Enable user to patch elevated products (`AllowLockdown-Patch`).** Allows users to upgrade programs during privileged installations. By default, when the installation program is running with elevated privileges, Windows Installer doesn't allow users to patch applications.

❑ **Allow admin to install from `Terminal Services` session (`Enable-AdminTSRemote`).** Allows Terminal Services administrators to install and configure programs remotely. Windows Installer allows administrators to install applications only when they are console users. This policy allows users to install applications using Terminal Services.

❑ **Cache transforms in secure location on workstation (`Transforms-Secure`).** Saves copies of transform files in a secure location on the local computer. Windows Installer stores transforms in users' profile folders so that transforms follow users from computer to computer. Users can change the transforms, however. This policy causes Windows Installer to store transforms in a secure location, preventing users from changing them, but the transforms don't follow users.

❑ **Logging (`Logging`).** Specifies the types of events that Windows Installer records in its transaction log for each installation. The log, Msi.log, appears in the Temp directory of the system volume.

❑ **Prohibit user installs (`DisableUserInstalls`).** Allows IT professionals to prevent user installs. This policy has three choices. You can allow per-user installations, which is the default, and Windows Installer favors per-user installations over per-computer installations. You can hide per-user installations, and Windows Installer favors per-computer installations over per-user installations. You can prohibit user installations, and Windows Installer prevents applications from performing per-user installations. The last option is desirable to ensure a standard configuration that's available to all users on all computers.

❑ **Turn off creation of `System Restore` checkpoints (`LimitSystem-RestoreCheckpointing`).** Prevents Windows Installer from creating System Restore checkpoints. In the event of a problem, System Restore enables users to restore their computers to a previous state without losing personal data files. By default, Windows Installer automatically creates a System Restore checkpoint each time an application is installed, so that users can restore their computer to the state that it was in before installing the application.

Of all these policies, the most useful are `AlwaysInstallElevated`, which loosens up security enough to allow restricted users to install applications; `TransformsSecure`, which stores transforms to prevent tampering; and the other policies that you can use to significantly restrict use of Windows Installer. Both ends of the spectrum–low and high security–are available to you.

Installing with Elevated Privileges

The policy `InstallAlwaysElevated` installs Windows Installer–based applications with elevated privileges. Microsoft documentation often calls this a *privileged installation*. This policy is one way to enable users to install applications that they couldn't otherwise install either because they're in restricted groups or you've locked down the desktops in your enterprise. Using Active Directory or something like Microsoft SMS (Systems Management Server) is a better way to deploy those applications. If neither product is available to you, consider using this policy, but keep in mind that the consequences of doing so can be severe.

These consequences can potentially result from the fact that users can take advantage of this policy to gain full control of their computers. Users could permanently change their privileges and circumvent your ability to manage their accounts and computers. In addition, using this policy can be an opportunity for viruses disguised as Windows Installer package files. For these reasons, this isn't a setting that I recommend in any but the most dire situations, in which there's no method available other than placing users into the local Administrators group.

For this policy to be effective, you must enable both the per-computer and per-user versions of it at the same time. In other words, enable it in Computer Configuration as well as in User Configuration.

Tip   Deploying applications to locked-down desktops is a common and tricky scenario. Using the `AlwaysInstallElevated` policy isn't the best solution, either. Other than the typical fare, such as Active Directory and SMS, elegant solutions do exist for this problem. Chapter 8, "Configuring Windows Security," describes many of these solutions, including using Security Templates and Security Configuration And Analysis to mitigate security just enough to allow legacy programs to run in Windows. Chapter 18, "Fixing Common IT Problems," shows you a few techniques for launching setup programs with elevated privileges.

Caching Transforms in a Secure Location

Transforms are essentially answer files for Windows Installer–based applications. Chapter 17, "Deploying Office 2003 Settings," describes transforms, but chances are good that you already know all about them. Transforms, which you can build using the Custom Installation Wizard in the *Microsoft Office 2003 Editions Resource Kit*, customize the way in which an application installs.

When you install an application using a transform, Windows Installer stores the transform with an *.mst* extension in the Application Data folder of the user profile. Windows Installer needs this file to reinstall, remove, or repair the application. Keeping this file in the user profile ensures that the file is always available. For example, if users have roaming user profiles, the transform follows them from computer to computer. This is not secure, however. When you set the `TransformsSecure` policy, Windows Installer instead saves transforms in %SystemRoot%, where users don't have permissions to change files. But because Windows Installer requires access to the transform used to install an application, the user must use the same computer on which he or she installed the application or must have access to the original installation source to install, remove, or repair the software. The idea behind this policy is to secure transforms in enterprises when IT professionals can't risk users maliciously changing the files.

Locking Down Windows Installer

Table 13-1 describes the policies that provide the most security for Windows Installer–based applications and for Windows in general. The first part of the table contains per-user policies, and the second part contains per-computer policies. In the Setting column, "Not Configured" means that you don't define the policy. "Enabled" is self-explanatory.

Table 13-1   Secure Windows Installer Settings

Policy	Setting
User Configuration	
`Always install with elevated privileges`	Not Configured
`Prevent removable media source for any install`	Enabled
Computer Configuration	
`Always install with elevated privileges`	Not Configured
`Enable user to browse for source while elevated`	Not Configured
`Enable user to use media source while elevated`	Not Configured
`Enable user to patch elevated products`	Not Configured
`Remove browse dialog box for new source`	Enabled
`Disable Windows Installer`	Enabled for non-managed apps only
`Prohibit patching`	Enabled
`Enable user control over installs`	Not Configured
`Disable IE security prompt for Windows Installer scripts`	Not Configured
`Cache transforms in secure location on workstation`	Enabled

You can configure these policies directly in the registry. I gave you the key and value names earlier in this chapter. To enable a policy, add it to the appropriate key as a REG_DWORD value, and set it to 0x01. To disable the policy, set it to 0x00. Delete the value to remove the policy. These policies are typical of enterprise-style deployments, however, so I don't configure them in the registry, which is totally unmanaged. Instead, configure them using Group Policy locally or on the network so that you can manage them properly.

Removing Windows Installer Data

If you thought manually removing legacy applications was difficult, try removing a Windows Installer–based application manually. More than once I've broken Windows Installer–based applications so badly that I couldn't remove them, repair them, or reinstall them. In these cases, I either had to manually remove the application's Windows Installer data from the registry or reinstall Windows. Tools are available to automate this process, and you learn about them in this chapter. Removing Windows Installer data without these tools is akin to replacing transistors on your computer's mainboard—it's not really possible.

Before I introduce the tools, I'm going to point you to the location in the registry where Windows Installer stores data about the applications that it installs. Don't modify these settings using Registry Editor (Regedit) because doing so will likely cause problems. Understanding the relationships among all the different bits of data that Windows Installer stores in the registry is difficult. This is just good information to have available:

- HKCU\Software\Microsoft\Installer.   This branch contains per-user Windows Installer data for applications that you install per user.
- HKLM\SOFTWARE\Microsoft\Windows\CurrentVersion\Installer.   This branch contains Windows Installer data for per-computer applications and for managed applications.
- HKLM\SOFTWARE\Microsoft\Windows\CurrentVersion\Uninstall.   This branch contains removal information for Windows Installer–based programs.
- HKCR\Installer.   This branch contains information similar to the Installer key under HKLM.

The tools that you learn about in the next two sections come with Windows Support Tools. You install the tools from \Support\Tools on your Windows CD.

Msizap.exe

Msizap is a tool that removes most of the data that Windows Installer maintains for an application. It doesn't remove the application's files or settings from the hard disk, however; you have to remove those yourself. You can focus this utility on a single application, or you can make sweeping changes to the Windows Installer data. I've had good luck using Msizap to remove a single application's Windows Installer data from the registry, but I don't trust it to make huge changes, such as removing all the Windows Installer folders and registry keys.

The following examples show the different forms of the Msizap program's command line. The first two forms in the example are the most useful. In the first form, you specify the product code, which is the product's unique GUID. You're not likely to know the product code, so you'll want to use the second form. In the second form, you specify the path and the name of the package file. Then Msizap will look up the product code for you. For example, if you installed Office 2003 Editions and couldn't remove it using Add Or Remove Programs, you'd type **msizap T!** *path***proplus.msi** in the Run dialog box. *Path* is the path containing the package file Proplus.msi. After Msizap finishes removing the application's Windows Installer data from the registry, you'll still have to remove plenty of files. You'll want to get rid of the application's files and other settings that it might have stored in the registry. For example, you'll still see the application's shortcut on the Start menu, but when you click it, you'll see an error message telling you that the application isn't installed. Chapter 3, "Backing Up the Registry," describes how to manually remove a program after you've got it to this step.

```
msizap T[A!] productcode
msizap T[A!] packagefile
msizap *[A!] ALLPRODUCTS
msizap PSA?!
```

*	Remove all Windows Installer folders and registry keys, adjusting shared DLL counts and stopping the service.
T	Remove all Windows Installer information for a product.
P	Remove the in-progress key.
S	Remove rollback information.
A	Give administrators full control of targeted folders and keys instead of removing them.
W	Apply changes for all users instead of just the current user.
G	Remove cached Windows Installer files that are orphaned.
!	Automatically respond *Yes* to all prompts.
?	Display help.

> **Tip**   I'm not comfortable with manually removing a program's files and registry settings after using Msizap. Most large applications store settings in the registry beyond the typical HKU\Software*Vendor**Product**Version keys*. For example, they register components in HKCR, and you might not get rid of them all. My solution seems odd, but it works well. Zapping a program's Windows Installer data from the registry should enable me to reinstall it. So I reinstall the application and then use Add Or Remove Programs to remove it. Windows Installer is likely to do a much cleaner job of removing the application than I am.

Msicuu.exe

Windows Installer Clean Up (Msicuu.exe in the Windows Support Tools) puts a graphical user interface on Msizap.exe. If you're sitting at the computer, use this tool instead of using Msizap at the command prompt. It's less error-prone.

1. In the Run dialog box, type **Msicuu**, and click OK.

2. In the Windows Installer Clean Up dialog box, shown in Figure 13-1, click the application for which you want to remove Windows Installer data from the registry, and then click Remove.

3. Confirm that you want to remove the application's Windows Installer data from the registry by clicking OK.

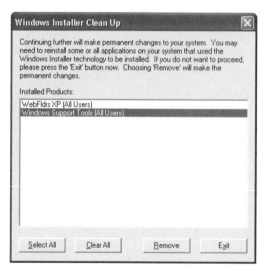

Figure 13-1   Windows Installer Clean Up is the graphical version of Msizap.

Inventorying Applications

One of the most common requests that I receive regarding Windows Installer–based applications is about inventorying the applications and features installed on users' computers. If you have a software management infrastructure already in place, you should use the tools that it provides. Also, the Application Compatibility Toolkit provides tools for collecting an application inventory. For more information about these tools, see *http://www.microsoft.com/windows/appcompatibility/default.mspx*. Otherwise, see Microsoft's TechNet Script Center (*http://www.microsoft.com/technet/scriptcenter/default.mspx*), which contains an awesome collection of useful scripts and has a few scripts that suit the purpose very well.

Listing 13-1 is a script that inventories the software installed on a computer running Windows XP. Listing 13-2 is a script that inventories the features for all software installed on a computer running Windows XP. These only inventory Windows Installer–based applications, though. Using Notepad, type each script and save it as a text file with the *.vbs* extension. In the **CreateTextFile** method (second line of Listing 13-1), you can change the path where the script creates the inventory. Make sure that the path exists; the script will create the file. To run each script, double-click the file.

Listing 13-1   Inventory.vbs

```
Set objFSO = CreateObject("Scripting.FileSystemObject")
Set objTextFile = objFSO.CreateTextFile("c:\software.tsv", True)
strComputer = "."
Set objWMIService = GetObject("winmgmts:" _
    & "{impersonationLevel=impersonate}!\\" & strComputer & "\root\cimv2")
Set colSoftware = objWMIService.ExecQuery _
    ("Select * from Win32_Product")
objTextFile.WriteLine "Caption" & vbtab & _
    "Description" & vbtab & "Identifying Number" & vbtab & _
    "Install Date" & vbtab & "Install Location" & vbtab & _
    "Install State" & vbtab & "Name" & vbtab & _
    "Package Cache" & vbtab & "SKU Number" & vbtab & "Vendor" & vbtab & _
    "Version"
For Each objSoftware in colSoftware
    objTextFile.WriteLine objSoftware.Caption & vbtab & _
    objSoftware.Description & vbtab & _
    objSoftware.IdentifyingNumber & vbtab & _
    objSoftware.InstallDate2 & vbtab & _
    objSoftware.InstallLocation & vbtab & _
    objSoftware.InstallState & vbtab & _
    objSoftware.Name & vbtab & _
    objSoftware.PackageCache & vbtab & _
    objSoftware.SKUNumber & vbtab & _
    objSoftware.Vendor & vbtab & _
    objSoftware.Version
Next
objTextFile.Close

Wscript.Quit
```

Listing 13-2   Software.vbs

```
strComputer = "."
Set objWMIService = GetObject("winmgmts:" _
    & "{impersonationLevel=impersonate}!\\" & strComputer & "\root\cimv2")
Set colFeatures = objWMIService.ExecQuery _
    ("Select * from Win32_SoftwareFeature")
For each objFeature in colfeatures
    Wscript.Echo "Accesses: " & objFeature.Accesses
    Wscript.Echo "Attributes: " & objFeature.Attributes
    Wscript.Echo "Caption: " & objFeature.Caption
    Wscript.Echo "Description: " & objFeature.Description
    Wscript.Echo "Identifying Number: " & objFeature.IdentifyingNumber
    Wscript.Echo "Install Date: " & objFeature.InstallDate
    Wscript.Echo "Install State: " & objFeature.InstallState
    Wscript.Echo "LastUse: " & objFeature.LastUse
    Wscript.Echo "Name: " & objFeature.Name
    Wscript.Echo "ProductName: " & objFeature.ProductName
    Wscript.Echo "Vendor: " & objFeature.Vendor
    Wscript.Echo "Version: " & objFeature.Version
Next

Wscript.Quit
```

Updating Source Lists

After the question of inventorying Windows Installer–based applications, the next most common request I receive is about updating an application's source list. When you deploy a Windows Installer–based application, you specify a list of alternative locations from which Windows Installer can install files. This supports multiple installation locations from a single set of configuration files. If you deployed an application with an incorrect source list or you moved your administration installations, you must update the source lists on each client computer.

With earlier versions of Windows Installer, updating source lists was a difficult task. You had to deploy a registry hack. With the current versions, you can use the Custom Maintenance Wizard to deploy an updated source list. This is a far more elegant solution than deploying a registry hack. Chapter 17, "Deploying Office 2003 Settings," tells you more about using the Custom Maintenance Wizard.

Chapter 14
Deploying with Answer Files

Users installing Microsoft Windows on their own computers don't often worry about automating the setup program. Instead, they drop the CD into the drive, the setup program starts, and they answer the setup program's prompts. But that won't work in a business because most business users don't know the answers to all the setup program's questions. Automating the setup program prevents users from having to fumble with the installation. Furthermore, as an IT professional, you want to ensure that users have a positive experience.

You should still consider automating Windows installations even if you are a power user. It makes installing Windows more convenient, and setup options are available to you through answer files that just aren't available through the setup program's user interface.

Microsoft provides several tools that help you to deploy automated and customized Windows XP and Microsoft Windows Server 2003 (Windows) installations. Each tool has purposes, strengths, and weaknesses that are different from those of the other tools in various deployment scenarios. Examples of deployment tools include Microsoft Sysprep, for disk imaging, and Microsoft Remote Installation Services (RIS), both of which come with Windows 2000 and Windows Server 2003. Every deployment method and tool has unattended answer files, which you use to automate the setup program so that it runs with little or no user interaction. Rather than prompting users for information, the operating system's setup program uses the information contained in the answer files.

Answer files are text files that look like INI files. Answer files have many sections, and each section contains settings. Because this book is about the Windows registry and user settings rather than desktop deployment, I only introduce you to answer files. After you learn the basics, I'll describe two answer file features that specifically enable you to deploy user settings as part of the Windows setup process.

> **More Info**   If you're interested in learning more about deploying Windows, see the following resources:
>
> ■ *Microsoft Windows Desktop Deployment Resource Kit* (Microsoft Press, 2004). This book describes how to deploy Windows XP in detail. It covers answer files, disk imaging, Microsoft Windows Preinstallation Environment (PE), and so on.
>
> ■ Microsoft Windows Corporate Deployment Tools User's Guide. You find it in Deploy.chm, which is in the Deploy.cab cabinet file in the Support\Tools folder of your Windows CD.
>
> ■ *Microsoft Windows Server 2003 Resource Kit* (Microsoft Press, 2005). The resource kit, of which this book is a part, contains a deployment kit for deploying Windows Server 2003 in enterprise environments.

You start this chapter by learning how to add files to Windows distribution files (the i386 folder).

Creating Distribution Folders

To add files to the Windows distribution folder, you start by making a copy of the CD's i386 folder onto your hard disk because you can't modify the CD. You don't need the rest of the files or folders on the CD—just the i386 folder. In a corporate deployment, you'll eventually replicate the customized i386 folder on distribution servers and then deploy the command that installs Windows from them. If you're a power user, you'll likely burn a custom CD that contains your files. You add files to the distribution folder by creating the structure shown in Figure 14-1.

Figure 14-1   In addition to creating this folder structure, you must set OEMPreinstall=Yes in your Windows answer file.

Here's a description of the most important files and folders in Figure 14-1:

■ **i386 folder.**   This is the i386 folder from the Windows CD, including all of its subfolders and files.

■ **OEM.**   This is the OEM distribution folder that contains the additional vendor files that you want to deploy and that are required to install Windows. If you use the OemFilesPath setting in the [Unattended] section of the answer file, you can create the OEM folder outside the i386 folder. I often create multiple OEM folders (one for each different configuration) and deploy each along with a single i386 folder. To do that, for each configuration, I create an answer file that points to a unique OEM folder. You must include `OemPreinstall=Yes` in the [`Unattended`] section of the answer file if you are using the OEM folder to add files to the system or if you are using Cmdlines.txt to run other programs during installation.

■ **Cmdlines.txt.**   This file contains optional commands that the setup program runs during installation. The file format is similar to an INI file. You create this file in the OEM folder, adding each command to the [`Commands`] section. For more information about using Cmdlines.txt, particularly for deploying user settings with Windows, see the section "Cmdlines.txt" later in this chapter.

■ **$$Rename.txt.**   This is an optional file that Setup uses during installations and is started from MS-DOS to convert short file names to long file names. You can create a $$Rename.txt file for each folder that contains short file names that you want to rename, or you can use one $$Rename.txt file for an entire folder tree. I often use this file when deploying third-party device drivers that use long file names.

■ **OEM\Textmode.**   This folder contains hardware-dependent files that Setup Loader and the text-mode setup program install on the target computer during text-mode setup. These files include OEM hardware abstraction layers (HALs), mass storage controller device drivers, and the Txtsetup.oem file, which describes how to load and install these components. List these files in the [OEMBootFiles] section of your answer file. This folder isn't as necessary as it was when hardware configurations varied more widely.

■ **OEM\$$.**   This is the folder into which you add files and subfolders that you want the setup program to copy to the target computer's %SystemRoot% folder. This is how to customize Windows system folders. To add a file called Sample.dll to %SystemRoot%\System32, add it to OEM\$$\System32. The setup program creates subfolders that don't exist on the target computer. Therefore, to deploy third-party device drivers with Windows, you can create a new subfolder called Drivers in %SystemRoot%. `OemPnPDriversPath` must indicate the location of the third-party device drivers on the target computer—in this case, `OemPnPDriversPath=%SYSTEMROOT%\Drivers`.

■ **OEM\$1.**   This folder enables you to add files and folders to %SystemDrive% on the target computer. It works in a similar way to OEM\$$, except that you use OEM\$1 to add files to the root of the drive on which you're installing Windows. A typical example is creating a folder on %SystemDrive% called OEM\$1\Sysprep, which automatically adds the Sysprep folder and files necessary to prepare the target computer's drive for duplication. (See Chapter 15, "Cloning Disks with Sysprep," for more information about disk imaging.)

> **Tip** You can use Setup Manager to create the i386 distribution folder for Sysprep, Remote Installation Services, or an unattended installation using an answer file. Setup Manager is in Deploy.cab, which is located in \Support\Tools on the Windows CD. Open Deploy.cab in Windows Explorer, and extract its contents to a folder on your hard disk. I prefer to create the distribution folder manually because many options aren't available through Setup Manager's user interface. For more information, see the section "Setup Manager" later in this chapter.

Customizing Default Settings

Windows doesn't invent its settings automatically. It uses four INF files in the i386 distribution folder to create the registry's hive files when you install the operating system. These INF files use the same syntax as the one I described in Chapter 11, "Scripting Registry Changes," and you should be able to customize them easily. Here are those four INF files:

- **Hivecls.inf.** This INF file creates the settings in HKLM\SOFTWARE\Classes (HKCR).

- **Hivedef.inf.** This INF file creates the settings in HKU\.DEFAULT. It also creates the settings for the default user profile.

- **Hivesft.inf.** This INF file creates the settings in HKLM\SOFTWARE.

- **Hivesys.inf.** This INF file creates the settings in HKLM\SYSTEM.

You can change any of the Windows default settings by changing the setting in the hive files listed. For example, if you want to deploy some of the per-user hacks shown in Chapter 4, "Hacking the Registry," change those values in the file Hivedef.inf in lieu of creating a default user profile for Windows. If you want to change file associations for every computer in the organization, change them in the file Hivecls.inf. Of course, this method isn't officially supported, so carefully test your changes before deploying in an enterprise environment.

Customizing Answer Files

As you have already learned, an answer file is a script that looks much like an INI file. The script drives the setup program, rather than the setup program prompting the user for information. Not only does an answer file automate the setup program's user interface, but it also enables you to configure Windows in ways that aren't possible through the user interface. I use an answer file to change the location of user profiles from %SystemDrive%\Documents and Settings to %SystemDrive%\Profiles, for example, because I much prefer the shorter path to typing C:\Documents and Settings over and over again.

Unattend.txt is the traditional name for answer files, but I prefer to give answer files names that make it easy to decipher their purpose. Just make sure to limit their names to eight characters so that you can read their names when installing Windows using MS-DOS. (MS-DOS is an antiquated method of installing Windows. Using Microsoft Windows PE is a better way, as described in Chapter 16, "Configuring Windows PE.") Also, I don't like to use the *.txt* extension for answer files. I prefer to use *.sif*, which is the file extension for Setup Information Files, so that I can easily differentiate a text file from an answer file. For example, I might have an answer file to install Windows on a lab computer called Labprep.sif. You might create different answer files for different departments called Sales.sif, Legal.sif, and so on. Regardless, use descriptive names that help you discern the differences between answer files, because you'll grow a collection.

Listing 14-1 shows a sample answer file. (Most tend to be neither this complicated nor this well-documented with comments.)

Listing 14-1   Unattend.txt

```
[Unattended]
UnattendMode = FullUnattended
TargetPath = Windows
FileSystem = LeaveAlone
OemPreinstall = Yes
OemSkipEula = Yes


[GuiUnattended]
; Set the TimeZone. For example, to set the TimeZone for the
; Pacific Northwest, use a value of "004." Be sure to use the
; numeric value that represents your own time zone. To look up
; a numeric value, see the Deploy.chm file on the Windows CD.
; The Deploy.cab file is in the \Support\Tools folder.
TimeZone = "YourTimeZone"
OemSkipWelcome = 1
; The OemSkipRegional key allows Unattended Installation to skip
; RegionalSettings when the final location of the computer is unknown.
OemSkipRegional = 1


[UserData]
; Tip: Avoid using spaces in the ComputerName value.
ComputerName = "YourComputerName"
; To ensure a fully unattended installation, you must provide a value
; for the ProductKey key.
ProductKey = "Your product key"
[LicenseFilePrintData]
; This section is used for server installs.
AutoMode = "PerServer"
AutoUsers = "50"
[Display]
BitsPerPel = 16
XResolution = 800
YResolution = 600
VRefresh = 60
```

```
[Components]
; This section contains keys for installing the components of
; Windows. A value of On installs the component, and a
; value of Off prevents the component from being installed.
iis_common = On
iis_inetmgr = Off
iis_www = Off
iis_ftp = Off
iis_doc = Off
iis_smtp = On
; The Fp_extensions key installs Front Page Server Extensions.
Fp_extensions = On
; If you set the TSEnabled key to On, Terminal Services is installed on
; a current version of Windows Server.
TSEnabled = On
; If you set the TSClients key to On, the files required to create
; Terminal Services client disks are installed. If you set this key
; to On, you must also set the TSEnabled key to On.
TSClients = On
Indexsrv_system = On
Accessopt = On
Calc = On
Charmap = On
Chat = Off
Clipbook = On
Deskpaper = On
Dialer = On
Freecell = Off
Hypertrm = On
Media_clips = On
Media_utopia = On
Minesweeper = Off
Mousepoint = Off
Mplay = On
Mswordpad = On
Paint = On
Pinball = Off
Rec = On
Solitaire = Off
Templates = On
Vol = On

[TapiLocation]
CountryCode = "1"
Dialing = Pulse
; Indicates the area code for your telephone. This value must
; be a 3-digit number.
AreaCode = "Your telephone area code"
LongDistanceAccess = 9

[Networking]

[Identification]
JoinDomain = YourCorpNet
```

```
DomainAdmin = YourCorpAdmin
DomainAdminPassword = YourAdminPassword

[NetOptionalComponents]
; Section contains a list of optional network components to install.
Snmp = Off
Lpdsvc = Off
Simptcp = Off

[Branding]
; This section brands Microsoft® Internet Explorer with custom
; properties from the Unattended answer file.
BrandIEUsingUnattended = Yes

[URL]
; This section contains custom URL settings for Microsoft
; Internet Explorer. If these settings are not present, the
; default settings are used. Specifies the URL for the
; browser's default home page. For example, you might use the
; following: Home_Page = www.microsoft.com.
Home_Page = YourHomePageURL
; Specifies the URL for the default search page. For example, you might
; use the following: Search Page = www.msn.com
Search_Page = YourSearchPageURL
; Specifies a shortcut name in the link folder of Favorites.
; For example, you might use the following: Quick_Link_1_Name =
; "Microsoft Product Support Services"
Quick_Link_1_Name = "Your Quick Link Name"
; Specifies a shortcut URL in the link folder of Favorites. For example,
; you might use this: Quick_Link_1 = http://support.microsoft.com/.
Quick_Link_1 = YourQuickLinkURL

[Proxy]
; This section contains custom proxy settings for Microsoft
; Internet Explorer. If these settings are not present, the default
; settings are used. If proxysrv:80 is not accurate for your
; configuration, be sure to replace the proxy server and port number
; with your own values.
HTTP_Proxy_Server = proxysrv:80
Use_Same_Proxy = 1
```

You tell the setup program about your answer file using the **/unattend** command-line option. You can shorten this to **/u**. (We all know that technology professionals and enthusiasts have a limited number of keystrokes in their lifetime.) You also must use the setup program's **/source** command-line option, which you can shorten to **/s**, to tell it where to find the Windows source files. The setup program's command line has many other options that control how it works. For more information about them, see Deploy.chm in Deploy.cab in the Support\Tools folder of the Windows CD. The following sample commands run the MS-DOS–based setup program from \\camelot\wxppro:

```
net use w: \\camelot\wxppro
w:\i386\winnt /s:w:\i386 /u:w:\winnt.sif
```

The following sample commands run the setup program from \\camelot\wxppro from Windows PE or another 32-bit version of Windows:

```
net use w: \\camelot\wxppro
w:\i386\winnt32 /source:w:\i386 /unattend:w:\winnt.sif
```

Setup Manager

You can use Setup Manager to create answer files for unattended Windows installations, automated installations using Sysprep, or automated installations using Remote Installation Services. Setup Manager is on the Windows CD in the Deploy.cab file of the Support\Tools folder. Setup Manager is a wizard that helps you create and modify answer files by prompting you for the information required to create answer files. Setup Manager can create new answer files, import existing answer files, and create new answer files based on a computer's current configuration. The last option is useful when you want to configure network settings in an answer file and you don't understand all the settings available or you don't want to risk errors, which are likely, considering how complex these sections sometimes are.

To install and run Setup Manager, double-click Deploy.cab in the Windows CD's Support\Tools folder, copy the cabinet file's contents to a folder on your disk, and double-click Setupmgr.exe to run Setup Manager, as shown in Figure 14-2. The result of the wizard is an answer file. Table 14-1 describes some of Setup Manager's different pages in the order that you see them.

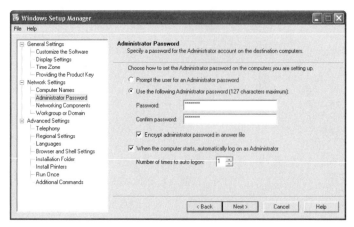

Figure 14-2   The Windows Setup Manager has greatly improved since the version in Windows 2000. Most of the changes are in the user interface, but encrypting the local administrator password is also a new feature.

Table 14-1 Setup Manager Pages

Page	Description
User Interaction	Use this page to set the level of user interaction during the setup process. Select Provide Defaults to display the configurable values supplied in the answer file, or select Fully Automated to create a setup process that requires no user interaction.
Customize The Software	Use this page to specify an organization and a user name.
Display Settings	Use this page to configure the display color depth, screen resolution, and refresh frequency display settings. I prefer to allow Windows to automatically adjust these settings to the best available, and you should generally avoid setting a refresh frequency if you're not 100 percent sure that all the monitors in use by your organization can support that frequency. Generally, 70 hertz (Hz) is a safe bet, and LCD monitors perform best with 60 Hz.
Time Zone	Use this page to set the time zone.
Product Key	Use this page to specify a product key, which is required for a fully automated installation.
Computer Names	Use this page to tell Setup Manager to generate a Uniqueness Database File (UDF), which the setup program will use to give each computer a unique name. If you import names from a text file, Setup Manager converts them into UDF files. You can also set an option to generate unique computer names.
Administrator Password	Use this page to tell Setup Manager to encrypt the local administrator password in the answer file so that users can't gain unauthorized access to the local administrator account. You can also configure the answer file to prompt users for the local administrator password during installation. If the Administrator Password box is blank, you can use the AutoLogon feature to automatically log on to the client computer as an administrator. For more information about using the AutoLogon feature with [GuiRunOnce] to deploy user settings with Windows, see "[GuiRunOnce]," later in this chapter.
Networking Components	Use this page to configure any network setting in Setup Manager that you can configure on the desktop. The interface for setting network settings in Setup Manager is the same as the one that you see in Windows.
Workgroup Or Domain	Use this page to join computers to a domain or a workgroup. You can also automatically create accounts in the domain.
Telephony	Use this page to set telephony properties, such as area codes and dialing rules.
Regional Settings	Use this page to set regional options, such as date, time, and currency formats.
Languages	Use this page to add support for other language groups.

Table 14-1   Setup Manager Pages

Page	Description
Browser And Shell Settings	Use this page to configure Internet connections, including proxy server settings. If you need to customize the browser, you can use Setup Manager to access the Microsoft Internet Explorer Administration Kit (IEAK), available from *http://www.microsoft.com/ windows/ieak/downloads/default.mspx*.
Installation Folder	Use this page to specify the default Windows folder, generate a unique folder during setup, or install Windows in a custom folder. For example, if you plan to keep Microsoft Windows 2000 in parts of your company or you are upgrading to Windows from Windows 2000, you can move Windows from the Windows folder to the Winnt folder so that you have a consistent folder structure throughout the organization.
Install Printers	Use this page to install printers as part of the installation process.
Run Once	Use this page to add commands that run automatically the first time a user logs on to the computer. Setup Manager adds these commands to the answer file's [GuiRunOnce] section. For example, you can start Microsoft Office 2003 Editions setup program from here. For more information about using this feature to deploy user settings, see "[GuiRunOnce]," later in this chapter.
Additional Commands	Use this page to add commands that run at the end of the setup process and before users log on to the system, such as starting a setup program or adding user settings. For more information, see "Cmdlines.txt," later in this chapter.

Notepad and Other Text Editors

Even with all of Setup Manager's features, I prefer to create answer files manually. Now, before you think I'm silly and just making work for myself, let me add that I have a library of answer-file templates that I call on when required. After you've created your first answer file, and you've got it just right, you can reuse it over and over again because little changes from job to job. I've got another surprise for you at the end of this section.

You can use a text editor, Notepad for example, to create answer files. They look just like INI files; both have sections, and their sections contain settings. You don't have to use all the sections or values available in the answer file if you don't need them. In fact, a typical answer file for a computer that you're joining to a Microsoft-based network is only about 20 lines long. If you add errors to an answer file, the setup program reports the line number containing the syntax error.

The answer file in Listing 14-2 is one that I use frequently. Notice that I've commented out the AdminPassword and FullName values by preceding them with a semicolon (;), so the setup program prompts the user for both values. You must provide your own product key for this sample. Also notice that I don't use the [Display] section in this answer file, but Windows automatically optimizes the display settings when the user logs on to the computer. Last, I've commented out the `DomainAdmin` and `DomainAdmin-Password` values in this answer file so that the setup program will prompt the user for the credentials necessary to join the domain. I do this to avoid putting my domain administrator's credentials in an answer file. This isn't a problem, though, because I delegate ownership of each computer object to users so that they can use their own accounts to join their own computers to the domain.

Listing 14-2   Unattend.txt

```
[Unattended]
    FileSystem=ConvertNTFS
    OemPreinstall=Yes
    OemSkipEula=Yes
    TargetPath=\Windows
    UnattendMode=ReadOnly

[GuiUnattended]
;   AdminPassword=
    OEMSkipRegional=1
    OEMSkipWelcome=1
    ProfilesDir=%SYSTEMDRIVE%\Profiles
    TimeZone=020

[UserData]
    ComputerName=*
;   FullName=
    OrgName="Jerry Honeycutt"
    ProductID="Your Product ID"

[TapiLocation]
    AreaCode=972
    CountryCode=1
    Dialing=Tone

[Identification]
;   DomainAdmin=
;   DomainAdminPassword=
    JoinDomain=HONEYCUTT

[Networking]
    InstallDefaultComponents=Yes

;end
```

This answer file is just one example. I built this answer file to do a clean installation of Windows from MS-DOS. I also have answer files that upgrade Windows XP or Windows Server 2003. I have answer files that build disk images for deployment. I have still other answer files for deploying Windows through Remote Installation Services, building lab computers, installing Windows on mobile computers, installing Windows on Novell networks, and so on.

Jerry's Answer File Editor

Here's the surprise that I mentioned. I don't use Notepad to edit answer files. I use Microsoft Office Word 2003. Here's why:

■ Word includes built-in version control, enabling me to manage the different versions of an answer file over time. I can refer back to an earlier version of an answer file to see what I've changed.

■ Word includes revision tracking, which enables me to see the changes that I've made to the current version of my answer file. This is a great feature for documenting answer files as well as for sending answer files out for review.

■ Word enables reviewers to comment on answer files without actually changing them. This is another great feature for sending answer files out for review.

■ Word enables me to build custom dictionaries. I build custom dictionaries that include answer file section names and value names, which ensures that I don't add errors to answer files with something as silly as a typo.

I'm willing to bet that these four features are enough to convince you to start using Word to edit answer files. Doing so will make you a much more productive IT professional. The process requires one bit of explanation, though. I edit and review answer files as document files (DOC files). Only when I'm ready to build a distribution share do I export the answer file from Word to a text file. Enjoy!

Adding Settings to Unattend.txt

Now you know how to build answer files and how to use them. It's time to get to the main point, which is how to deploy user settings with your answer file. To deploy settings with Windows, you need a mechanism for running a program during the setup process. The Windows setup program provides two different mechanisms, but first, think of all the different ways to add settings to the registry (and this is only a partial list):

■ **REG files.**   For more information about creating REG files, see Chapter 2, "Using Registry Editor," and Chapter 11, "Scripting Registry Changes." You import a REG file using the command `regedit` *filename*`.reg /s`.

■ **INF files.**   For more information about building and installing INF files, see Chapter 11, "Scripting Registry Changes." You install an INF file by running the command `rundll32.exe setupapi,InstallHinfSection DefaultInstall 132` *filename*`.inf`.

- **Scripts.**   For more information about writing scripts for Windows Script Host, see Chapter 11, "Scripting Registry Changes." You run a script using the command `wscript` *filename.ext*, where *ext* is either `vbs` or `js`.

- **OPS files.**   For more information about creating and installing OPS files, see Chapter 17, "Deploying Office 2003 Settings." You import an OPS file into the user's profile using the command `proflwiz /r` *filename*`.ops /q`.

- **Console Registry Tool for Windows (Reg.exe).**   For more information about using Reg.exe to edit the registry, see Chapter 2, "Using Registry Editor," and Chapter 11, "Scripting Registry Changes." Reg.exe has a robust command-line interface that enables you to edit the registry using batch files.

- **Windows Installer package files (MSI files).**   For more information about package files, see Chapter 13, "Mapping Windows Installer." To learn how to build MSI files that install registry settings, see Chapter 11, "Scripting Registry Changes."

Now that I've reminded you of the many tools and commands that I describe in this book for installing registry settings, see the following two sections, "[GuiRunOnce]" and "Cmdlines.txt," to learn how to deploy those commands with Windows.

[GuiRunOnce]

The `[GuiRunOnce]` section contains a list of commands that run the first time that a user logs on to the computer after the Windows setup program runs. Enclose each command in quotation marks. The commands in the `[GuiRunOnce]` section run in the context of the console user, so you must ensure that the user has the privileges necessary to run each command. You can use this feature to install a REG file when a user logs on to the computer. For example, add the following lines to your answer file to import Settings.reg into the registry the first time that a user logs on to the computer:

```
[GuiRunOnce]
"regedit %SYSTEMROOT%\Settings.reg /s"
```

You must provide any programs and data files that you want to use, though, and you do that by deploying them through the OEM distribution folders that you learned about in "Creating Distribution Folders," earlier in this chapter. In the previous example of a `[GuiRunOnce]` section, I put Settings.reg in i386\$OEM$\$$ to make sure that the setup program copied it to %SystemRoot% on the target computer. Also, make sure that a program that you run from `[GuiRunOnce]` has a command-line option to run quietly; you don't want to display a user interface while installing registry settings. All the commands that I listed in the section "Adding Settings to Unattend.txt" include the command-line option for running without displaying a user interface.

Another method for deploying settings is running Profile Wizard from the *Microsoft Office 2003 Editions Resource Kit*. Add the following lines to your answer file. You must also make sure that the Windows setup program copies Proflwiz.exe and Settings.ops to the target computer. In this case, I put both files in i386\$OEM$\$$:

```
[GuiRunOnce]
"%SYSTEMROOT%\Proflwiz.exe /r %SYSTEMROOT%\Settings.ops /q"
```

Here are three things to consider when using [GuiRunOnce]:

- You can't run programs from [GuiRunOnce] that force Windows to restart. That's because when Windows restarts, it loses any entries remaining in [GuiRunOnce], and those commands will not run. If you can't prevent the program from restarting the computer, try repackaging it as a Windows Installer package file, or add it as the last command in [GuiRunOnce]. You won't experience this issue with any of the commands that add registry settings.

- When you use [GuiRunOnce], any program that relies on Windows Explorer will not work properly because Windows Explorer is not running when the commands in the [GuiRunOnce] section are. Again, you can consider repackaging these applications.

- If you want to install Windows Installer package files from [GuiRunOnce], you must use the /wait command-line option in order to ensure that two packages don't try to install at the same time. Otherwise, both packages fail. This is an issue only when using Setup.exe to install Windows Installer packages, however, because Setup.exe launches Windows Installer and then returns, allowing the next package to begin installing immediately. If you instead use Msiexec (the Windows Installer command-line interface) to install Windows Installer packages, you won't experience this issue.

> **Tip**   The commands in the [GuiRunOnce] section run asynchronously, which means that they can potentially all run at the same time. If you'd rather run commands synchronously—one at a time—create a batch file that runs the program using the Start command's /wait command-line option. The syntax is Start /wait *program*, where *program* is the path and the name of the program file. The /wait command-line option prevents the Start program from returning control to the batch file until *program* finishes. Then run this batch file from [GuiRunOnce].

Cmdlines.txt

The file Cmdlines.txt contains commands that the GUI-mode portion of the setup program runs when installing optional components, including applications that the setup program must install immediately after installing Windows. The commands in Cmdlines.txt run as a system service, so they run with elevated privileges. You put

Cmdlines.txt in the OEM subfolder of the Windows distribution folder. You put into Cmdlines.txt the same kinds of commands that you'd put into [GuiRunOnce]. You also must use the OEM folder to copy data files, such as REG files, INF files, and scripts, to the target computer.

The format of Cmdlines.txt is simple. It has a single section called [Commands], followed by zero or more commands. If the command contains spaces, then it's a good idea to enclose each command in quotation marks. The following sample imports a REG file called Settings.reg and installs an INF file called Config.inf. (It assumes that I added both files to OEM\$$ in the distribution folder.)

```
[Commands]
"regedit.exe %SYSTEMROOT%\Settings.reg /s"
"rundll32.exe setupapi,InstallHinfSection DefaultInstall 132 \Windows\Config.inf"
```

In some important aspects, though, using Cmdlines.txt is different from using [GuiRunOnce]:

- Environment variables are not available.

- When using Cmdlines.txt, you must create the OEM distribution folders, and you must set OEMPreinstall=Yes in your answer file.

- When the setup program runs the command in Cmdlines.txt, no user is logged on to Windows, and no network connection is guaranteed. The result is that Windows stores settings in the default user hive file so that all users receive the same settings.

- You can't use Cmdlines.txt to install Windows Installer packages.

Adding Multiple Settings with One Script

Rather than listing each REG or script file in the [GuiRunOnce] section, I prefer to put one command in the section that runs all of the REG and script files in a single folder. That way, I can update my distribution point by simply adding the appropriate file to the folder; I don't have to add a command to the answer file that runs the file.

Listing 14-3 shows the script runinst.vbs, which I use to run files (REG, INF, and MSI files, for example) in a given folder. The script accepts a single command-line option: the folder containing the files that you want to run. This script launches all of the files that the folder contains, and it can launch different types of files, including files with the extensions EXE, MSI, BAT, JS, VBS, REG, and INF. If Windows Installer is already running, then it waits to launch a Windows Installer setup database because you can only install one setup database at a time. These files run the gamut from setup programs and Windows Installer databases to scripts and registry settings deployed via files with the REG extension.

Listing 14-3 runinst.vbs

```vbs
' runinst.vbs: run commands in the given folder
'
' USAGE
'
'   runinst.vbs FOLDER
'
'   FOLDER  Path of folder containing installations to run
'
' NOTES
'
'   This script supports files with the extensions EXE,
'   MSI, BAT, CMD, JS, VBS, REG, and INF.
'
'   If the folder doesn't exist, this script displays an error
'   message that times out in 10 seconds, since it's for use during
'   the Windows setup process and the folder doesn't always exist.
'

Option Explicit

Main()

Sub Main()

  ' Check the command-line argument (which must be the path of
  ' a folder that contains installations to run); then, call
  ' LaunchInstallations to silently run each installation contained
  ' in the folder.
  '
  Dim intRC
  Dim objArguments
  Dim objFileSystem
  Dim objShell

  Set objArguments = WScript.Arguments
  Set objFilesystem = CreateObject( "Scripting.FileSystemObject" )
  Set objShell = CreateObject( "WScript.Shell" )

  If objArguments.Count > 0 Then
    If objFileSystem.FolderExists( objArguments(0) ) Then
      LaunchInstallations( objArguments(0) )
    Else

      ' The folder doesn't exist

      intRC = objShell.Popup( "The folder " & objArguments(0) & _
                " doesn't exist.", 10, "Folder Missing", 0 )

    End If

  Else

    ' No folder was given on the command line
```

```
        WScript.Echo "Usage: runinst.vbs FOLDER"

    End If

End Sub

Sub LaunchInstallations( strPath )

  ' Execute each installation file contained in strPath silently:
  '
  '    strPath Path of the folder containing installations
  '

  Dim objFileSystem
  Dim objShell

  Set objFileSystem = CreateObject( "Scripting.FileSystemObject" )
  Set objShell = CreateObject( "WScript.Shell" )

  ' Build a list of files in the given subfolder

  Dim intRC
  Dim objFolder
  Dim colFiles
  Dim objFile

  Set objFolder = objFileSystem.GetFolder( strPath )
  Set colFiles = objFolder.Files

  ' Launch each file in the list using the appropriate command

  For Each objFile in colFiles
    Select Case UCase( objFileSystem.GetExtensionName( objFile ))

      Case "EXE"
        intRC = objShell.Run( objFile, 1, True )

      case "MSI"

        Dim objWMIService
        Dim strProcessName

      ' Wait for any current MSI processes to finish

        strProcessName = "msiexec.exe"
        Set objWMIService = GetObject("winmgmts:\\.\root\cimv2")

        Do While objWMIService.ExecQuery( "Select Name from _
          Win32_Process where Name='" & strProcessName & "'").Count > 1
          WScript.Sleep 5000
        Loop

        intRC = objShell.Run( "msiexec.exe /qb /i " & _
                            objFile & " ALLUSERS=2", 1, True )
```

```
         Case "BAT"
           intRC = objShell.Run( "cmd.exe /c " & objFile, 1, True )

         Case "CMD"
           intRC = objShell.Run( "cmd.exe /c " & objFile, 1, True )

         Case "JS"
           intRC = objShell.Run( "wscript.exe //e:jscript " & _
                               objFile, 1, True )

         Case "VBS"
           intRC = objShell.Run( "wscript.exe //e:vbscript " & objFile, 1, True )

         Case "REG"
           intRC = objShell.Run( "regedit.exe /s " & objFile, 1, True )

         Case "INF"
           intRC = objShell.Run( _
           "rundll32.exe setupapi,InstallHinfSection DefaultInstall 132 " _
           & objFile, 1, True )

       End Select
     Next

   End Sub
```

This script prevents you from having to edit Cmdlines.txt or the [GuiRunOnce] section of your unattended-setup answer file just to add a setting to the target computer's registry or install a Windows Installer database. Run this script from Cmdlines.txt or from [GuiRunOnce], and you'll never again have to change either just to run a batch script or install a program. Instead, you'll just drop the file into the appropriate folder, and the script will automatically run the file at the appropriate point in the installation process. For example, I can drop the files settings.reg and config.vbs into the folder, and without changing any other files, runinst.vbs automatically loads settings.reg into the registry and uses Windows Script Host to run config.vbs.

In the distribution point, I put this script into OEM\$$\APPS so that it's easy to access from unattended-setup answer files. (You must create the folder APPS in OEM\$$.) The path on the target computer is %SystemRoot%\APPS\runinst.vbs. Then I create a subfolder called GUI for the files that will run from [GuiRunOnce] and a subfolder called CMD for the files that will run from Cmdlines.txt. The following list describes each in more detail:

- **Cmdlines.txt in the OEM directory.**   Add the following line to Cmdlines.txt. Then create the folder OEM\$$\APPS\CMD in your distribution point, and copy to it each file that you want runinst.vbs to launch during installation.

  ```
  [Commands]
  "wscript.exe //e:vbscript \WINDOWS\APPS\runinst.vbs \WINDOWS\APPS\CMD"
  ```

■ **[GuiRunOnce] in the unattended-setup answer file.**   Add the following line to the [GuiRunOnce] section of your unattended-setup answer file. Then create the folder OEM\$$\APPS\GUI in your distribution point, and copy to it each file that you want runinst.vbs to launch after installation is complete:

```
[GuiRunOnce]
"%SYSTEMROOT%\APPS\runinst.vbs %SYSTEMROOT%\APPS\GUI"
```

Logging On Automatically After Installation

If you're using the [GuiRunOnce] section to deploy settings or to run programs after installing Windows, you'll want to automatically log on to the operating system immediately after the Windows installation is finished. You'll also likely want to log on as local Administrator to install applications that require elevated privileges or to change settings in HKLM that restricted users can't change. For the latter task, use the AutoLogon setting in the [GuiUnattended] section of your answer file. Set AutoLogon=Yes. This sets the value AutoAdminLogon in the key HKLM\Software\Microsoft\Windows NT\CurrentVersion\WinLogon, which you learn about in Chapter 18, "Fixing Common IT Problems."

You must also set AutoLogonCount in the [GuiUnattended] section. This setting specifies the number of times that you want to automatically log on to Windows as local Administrator. This sets the value AutoLogonCount in the key HKLM\Software\Microsoft\Windows\CurrentVersion\WinLogon. Normally, you'd log on to Windows only one time by setting AutoLogonCount=1. However, you can log on to the operating system as many times as necessary, such as when a setup program restarts the computer in the middle of the installation process. The following lines show you the settings necessary to use this feature:

```
[GuiUnattended]
AutoLogon=Yes
AutoLogonCount=1

[GuiRunOnce]
"regedit %SYSTEMROOT%\Settings.reg /s"
```

When you set a password using the AdminPassword setting in the [GuiUnattended] section, Windows uses that password to log the local Administrator on to it. However, if you encrypt the password and set EncryptedAdminPassword=Yes, Windows disables this feature. You trade between security and deployment convenience. Don't panic, though; when Windows finishes installing, it removes the password from any local copies of the answer file, such as %SystemRoot%\System32\$winnt$.sif.

Configuring Windows Firewall

Windows XP Service Pack 2 (SP2) and Windows Server 2003 Service Pack 1 (SP1) include the new Windows Firewall. Most companies and many enthusiasts will want to customize Windows Firewall during installation. Microsoft provides three methods of doing this. In a business environment, the best way to manage Windows Firewall settings is to use the new Windows Firewall Group Policy settings. This requires using Active Directory with either Windows 2000 or Windows Server 2003 domain controllers. For more information, see *http://www.microsoft.com/technet/prodtechnol/winxppro/deploy/depfwset/wfsp2wgp.mspx.*

The following list describes customization methods that don't require Group Policy:

- **Unattended-setup answer file.**   The unattended-setup answer file for Windows XP SP2 has options for configuring Windows Firewall settings when running an unattended setup of Windows XP SP2.

- **Netfw.inf.**   The Netfw.inf file for Windows XP SP2 configures Windows Firewall. It specifies a set of registry settings that are equivalent to the options available through both the Windows Firewall component in Control Panel and the Windows Firewall Group Policy settings.

- **Netsh script.**   To configure computers running Windows XP with SP2 after SP2 has been installed, have your users run a script file, such as a BAT or a CMD file, that contains the series of Netsh commands that configure the Windows Firewall operational mode, allowed programs, allowed ports, and so on.

- **Custom configuration programs.**   To configure a computer running Windows XP with SP2 after SP2 has been installed, have your users run a custom configuration program that uses the new Windows Firewall configuration APIs to configure the Windows Firewall for operation mode, allowed programs, allowed ports, and other settings.

For more information about using these options, see *http://www.microsoft.com/technet/prodtechnol/winxppro/deploy/depfwset/wfsp2ngp.mspx.*

Chapter 15
Cloning Disks with Sysprep

Disk imaging entails taking a snapshot of a computer's configuration, which includes Microsoft Windows XP or Microsoft Windows Server 2003 (Windows) and applications such as those in Microsoft Office 2003 Editions, and then deploying that snapshot to other computers in the organization. It's essentially like installing Windows on a computer's hard disk and then copying that hard disk to other computers. Use disk imaging to deploy clean Windows installations in large organizations when hundreds of computers require the same configuration. Disk imaging is more effective when organizations have standard hardware configurations, but with a tweak here and there, it is a method that can be used in companies that tend to purchase whatever computer is popular at the time.

Even though I say that disk imaging is for large organizations, I use it in my small 25-PC shop. It's more convenient and much quicker to install Windows from a disk image than by running the setup program from scratch. This is a major productivity boost for me because I install Windows in my lab a few dozen times a week.

Disk imaging has two sides: good and bad. First the good: disk imaging is the fastest way to deploy Windows. Rather than installing the operating system from the CD, which can take 45 minutes or longer, a disk image installs in less than 10 minutes And with multicasting technologies, you can deploy disk images to many computers at the same time. Possibly the biggest benefit of disk imaging is that you can include third-party applications and custom settings to standardize desktop computers throughout the enterprise, and you do all that without requiring user interaction. Now for the bad: you can't use disk imaging to upgrade from an earlier version of Windows because you're replacing the hard disk's contents. That means users' documents, settings, and applications are lost unless you use the User State Migration

Tool (USMT) that's on the Windows CD in the ValueAdd directory. Also, disk imaging requires somewhat compatible sample and target hardware configurations, although you can mitigate this issue a bit by using the techniques you learn in this chapter. An additional concern is that multicasting can bring a network to its knees, so you must manage the rollout so that it doesn't affect the productivity of users. The last problem is that deploying disk images to remote computers is difficult—but it's not impossible if you can fit the images on CDs.

The benefits of disk imaging far outweigh the potential problems, particularly in large enterprises. Disk imaging got better with Windows than it was with Windows 2000; new Windows disk-imaging tools significantly reduce the number of disk images that you maintain now. The Microsoft Web site is full of case studies of companies that have reduced their image count by 60 percent. One company reduced its image count from 50 with Windows 2000 to one with Windows. That's impressive! This chapter shows you how to reap those benefits for yourself. After I briefly introduce you to disk imaging, I'll focus on how the registry fits into the disk-imaging process.

More Info If you're interested in learning more about disk imaging, see the following resources:

- *Microsoft Windows Desktop Deployment Resource Kit* (Microsoft Press, 2004). This book describes how to deploy Windows XP in detail. It covers answer files, disk imaging, Windows Preinstallation Environment (Windows PE), and so on.

- *Microsoft Windows Corporate Deployment Tools User's Guide.* You find it in Deploy.chm, which is in the Deploy.cab cabinet file in the Support\Tools folder of your Windows CD.

- *Microsoft Windows Server 2003 Resource Kit* (Microsoft Press, 2005). The resource kit, of which this book is a part, contains a deployment kit for deploying Windows Server 2003 in enterprise environments.

Cloning Windows

The best way to understand disk imaging is to walk through the entire process; you'll learn more about this process later in this chapter, though. (See Figure 15-1 as you're working through the following steps.)

1. Install Windows on the sample computer.

   Install the operating system from a fully customized distribution folder, as you learned in Chapter 14, "Deploying with Answer Files." Doing so ensures that you can regression test your disk images after fixing problems. Do not join the computer to a domain; just join a workgroup.

2. Log on to the computer as Administrator, and do any of the following:

    ❑   Install and customize each application you want to include in the disk
        image. For example, install Office 2003 Editions. As a rule, don't custom-
        ize per-user settings on a disk image; save those for a network-based
        default user profile. (See Chapter 12, "Deploying User Profiles.")

    ❑   Install any third-party device drivers that are not included in Drivers.cab,
        the file in which Microsoft distributes the Windows device drivers, and
        that you didn't add to your distribution folders.

3. Customize the %SystemDrive%\Sysprep folder.

    Copy Sysprep.exe and Setupcl.exe to this folder. Also, copy the Sysprep.inf file,
    which you build ahead of time. Sysprep.inf automates Mini-Setup Wizard, a
    stripped-down version of the full setup program that runs when users start a
    computer to which you've deployed the disk image. I'll tell you where to get
    these files in the next section.

4. Run Sysprep.exe, select the Mini-Setup check box, and then click Reseal.

    If the computer is ACPI-compliant, Sysprep automatically shuts down the PC;
    otherwise, turn off the computer when you see a message that says that it's safe
    to shut down the computer.

5. Clone the disk to an image file.

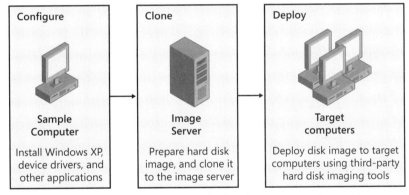

Figure 15 1   Using disk imaging, you deploy the contents of a sample computer's hard disk
to many other computers' hard disks. It's an effective way to deploy many desktops.

After you deploy the disk image to users' computers and they turn their computers
on, Mini-Setup Wizard starts. First the wizard detects the computers' Plug and Play
devices. Then the wizard prompts users to accept the license agreement, type their
name and organization, join a domain or a workgroup, specify regional options, configure TAPI, and choose the networking protocols and services to install. The wizard
can skip some or all of these settings if you configure them in Sysprep.inf (the answer

file). Last, Mini-Setup Wizard removes %SystemDrive%\Sysprep and restarts the computer. The whole process takes less than five minutes.

Before we move on to actual techniques, I'm going to introduce you to the tools necessary for doing the job. You'll find everything you need for preparing disk images on the Windows CD. The following sections describe these tools, their limitations, and a list of third-party disk-imaging suites to evaluate. (Third-party tools are necessary to duplicate disk images after you prepare them.)

Windows Tools

Disk imaging has two phases: preparing the disk image and cloning the disk image. All the tools you need for preparing a disk image are on the Windows CD in the Deploy.cab file. This file is in the Support\Tools folder; extract its contents by opening the file in Windows Explorer. The disk-imaging tools in Deploy.cab include:

- **Sysprep.exe.**   Prepares the disk for duplication by configuring Windows so that Setupcl.exe runs the next time it starts.

- **Setupcl.exe.**   Regenerates the computer's security identifier (SID) because every computer on the network must have a unique SID. It also starts Mini-Setup Wizard to configure Windows on the computer.

- **Sysprep.inf.**   Automates Mini-Setup Wizard by providing settings for users.

The tools are a given, but I'm excited about the documentation in the file Deploy.cab— it's a huge improvement over the deployment documentation for Windows 2000. First Ref.chm describes how to build answer files and includes a reference that describes all the settings that you can use. Second Deploy.chm describes how to use the disk-imaging tools in Deploy.cab. Deploy.chm also contains a complete reference for all the settings you can use in answer files. This is the resource from which you're going to learn the most about disk imaging.

 Note   Ensure that you're using the correct version of Sysprep for the version of Windows that you're deploying. Windows XP Service Pack 2 (SP2) contains an updated version of the deployment tools, so you'll need to update your images with them after slipstreaming the service pack into your distribution points.

Sysprep Limitations

Due to the nature of disk imaging—copying a hard disk's image to other computers— Sysprep has a few requirements (call them limitations, if you like):

- The sample and target computers must have the identical hardware abstraction layers (HALs). For example, a disk image created on a computer using a single processor HAL is not compatible with one that uses a multiprocessor HAL.

- The sample and target computers must have compatible BIOS types. For example, a disk image created on a computer with an ACPI BIOS is not compatible with a computer that has an APM BIOS. However, a disk image created using an APM BIOS is often compatible with a computer that has an ACPI BIOS.

- The target computer's hard disk must be the same size or larger than the sample computer's hard disk. If the target computer's hard disk is larger, you can set ExtendOEMPartition in Sysprep.inf to extend the disk image to the end of the disk. The Sysprep.inf sample in Listing 15-1 shows an example of using this setting to extend a partition.

- Sysprep only prepares the disk image; it doesn't clone the disk. Thus, to deploy the disk image, you'll have to use a third-party disk-imaging product. The sidebar "Third-Party Disk-Imaging Suites," on the following page, gives you choices to evaluate. My preference is Symantec Ghost, but there are many good products.

The Windows documentation also says that the mass-storage controllers (IDE, SCSI, and the like) must be identical on the sample and target computers. This isn't required if you tell Sysprep in advance about the mass-storage controllers that you're anticipating. For more information, see the section titled "Reducing Image Count," later in this chapter. I've had good results from building images using one mass-storage controller and deploying to computers with completely different mass-storage controllers.

The sample and target computers' remaining devices do not have to be the same. That includes Plug and Play devices, such as modems, sound cards, network cards, video adapters, and so on. If you anticipate devices for which Windows doesn't include native support—that is, the device doesn't have a driver in Drivers.cab—you should include those device drivers in your image so that Mini-Setup Wizard can detect and install them during installation. This usually includes devices that come to market after Windows. Chapter 14, "Deploying with Answer Files," describes how to deploy third-party device drivers with Windows.

Tip   Often, device drivers that you download from a vendor's Web site aren't suitable for deployment. They install from package files, so you can't easily extract the device driver files and then figure out which files are necessary and which aren't. You can almost always get the latest device drivers from Windows Update, however, and these device drivers are in a suitable format for deployment through an answer file and on a disk image. The trick is to use the Windows Update Catalog. In Microsoft Internet Explorer, click Tools, Windows Update. In the Web page's left pane, click Administrator Options. In the right pane, Windows Update Catalog. Now you can search for and download device drivers that are packaged and ready for deployment.

> **Third-Party Disk-Imaging Suites**
>
> Sysprep only prepares disks for duplication; it doesn't clone them. Thus, you're going to need a third-party tool to deploy disk images. A small selection of the tools with which I'm familiar includes the following:
>
> - **Symantec Ghost.**   *http://www.symantec.com*
> - **Altiris eXpress 5.**   *http://www.altiris.com*
> - **Phoenix ImageCast.**   *http://www.phoenix.com*
>
> Symantec Ghost is at the top of my list because it's the tool that I know best and the one that I use most often. It's a robust disk-imaging tool that does much more than just clone disk images. For example, you can deploy a disk image to a remote computer without ever getting up from your desk. You can use it to manage configurations, too, not just disk images. When I talk to administrators around the world, this is the tool that 90 percent of them use, whereas the other tools in the list tend to have a small but loyal following. Regardless, the disk-imaging process is roughly the same with all these tools, and most of them are high quality.

Building a Disk Image

You got the overview earlier in this chapter. Now it's time for some detail.

The first step is to configure a sample computer, and you start by installing Windows. Don't just drop the Windows CD in the drive and install the operating system manually, however. If you find an error in your disk image, you're likely to repeat it or introduce different errors because you're using a manual process. Instead, install Windows from a fully customized distribution folder. Chapter 14, "Deploying with Answer Files," describes how to customize the distribution folders so that Windows installs without any user interaction. Just make sure that your answer file joins a workgroup and not a domain because Sysprep will remove the computer from the domain anyway and you don't want the extra configuration information in the registry.

Next install the applications you want to include in your disk image. Include only the applications that you want to install on every computer to which you deploy the disk image. For example, include Office 2003 Editions and your antivirus software, but don't include line of business applications that only one department uses if you want to use that disk image for other departments. I don't like to install applications manually for the same reasons that I don't like to install Windows manually: regression testing. Instead, install Windows Installer–based applications from fully customized administrative installations. Install other applications using any quiet mode switches that those programs provide, or consider repackaging them as Windows Installer packages, which you can install without interaction. After you automate each application's installation, you can easily install each from your Windows answer file.

> **Tip**   Whether it's superstition or has some basis in fact, I usually build custom computers for the express purpose of building disk images. I use the most generic hardware I can find and I leave out any unnecessary devices (sound cards, and so on). My thinking, and what I want to pass on to you, is that by using generic hardware, I have a better chance of producing a disk image that works on many different configurations. The goal, of course, is to manage fewer disk images.

Customizing Mini-Setup

Sysprep.inf automates Mini-Setup Wizard. In other words, the wizard avoids prompting users for settings that you provide in Sysprep.inf. If your goal is a 100-percent automated installation, you'll want to create a robust Sysprep.inf. Completely automating Mini-Setup Wizard can be difficult in the following three cases, however:

- **User name.**   You can provide a user name, such as *Valued Microsoft Employee* in Sysprep.inf, or you can allow the wizard to prompt users for their names.

- **Computer name.**   This is the toughest of all to automate. You can accept the random computer names that Mini-Setup Wizard generates when you set `ComputerName=*` in Sysprep.inf, or you can allow the wizard to prompt users for a computer name. This is one of the reasons that many organizations send technicians to desktops to install Windows. Alternatively, you can accept the random computer name and then change the name after installation using scripts. The TechNet Script Center provides Windows Script Host scripts for renaming computers and joining them to domains, and you can run these scripts from Sysprep.inf. See Chapter 14, "Deploying with Answer Files," to learn how to run programs after Windows finishes installation. The Script Center is at *http://www.microsoft.com/technet/scriptcenter/default.mspx*.

- **Joining a domain.**   To automatically join a domain, you must provide domain administrator credentials in your answer file. But, annoyingly, they are in plain text. (Documentation that says you can encrypt the domain Administrator password is inaccurate.) One solution is to create a domain account with just enough rights and permissions to join computers to the domain and then use those credentials in the answer file. Otherwise, you can delegate ownership of computers to users so that they can join their own computers to the domain. You can also use the scripts from the TechNet Script Center to automatically join computers to domains after Windows finishes installing.

The remaining settings in a typical Sysprep.inf file will be easy to understand because you already learned about answer files in Chapter 14. The ultimate reference is Ref.chm in Deploy.cab, however. Microsoft's documentation is full of sample answer files, but Listing 15-1 shows you one that I typically use. A few notes about this listing:

- ■ `ExtendOemPartition` causes Mini-Setup Wizard to extend the partition to the end of the disk, which is necessary if the target computer's hard disk is bigger than that of the sample computer.

- ■ `InstallFilesPath` tells Mini-Setup Wizard where to find additional installation files, including the OEM folder, which contains a Cmdlines.txt file (more on that later).

- ■ `OemPnPDriversPath` tells Mini-Setup Wizard where to find the third-party device drivers that I've included in the disk image (which helps reduce image count).

- ■ `ComputerName` and `Username` are missing from this Sysprep.inf file, so Mini-Setup Wizard prompts users for both values.

- ■ `DomainAdmin` and `DomainAdminPassword` are absent from this Sysprep.inf file, so Mini-Setup Wizard prompts users for the credentials necessary to join the computer to the domain.

- ■ `[Sysprep]` and `[SysprepMassStorage]` help to reduce the number of disk images that you must maintain. I discuss these two sections in "Reducing Image Count," later in this chapter.

Listing 15-1   Sysprep.inf

```
[Unattended]
    ExtendOemPartition=1
    InstallFilesPath=\Sysprep\i386
    OemPnPDriversPath=\Windows\Drivers
    OemPreinstall=Yes
    OemSkipEula=Yes

[GuiUnattended]
    OemSkipRegional=1
    OemSkipWelcome=1
    TimeZone=020

[UserData]
    OrgName="Jerry Honeycutt"
    ProductID=#####-#####-#####-#####-#####

[TapiLocation]
    AreaCode=972
    CountryCode=1
    Dialing=Tone

[Identification]
    JoinDomain=HONEYCUTT
```

```
[Networking]
    InstallDefaultComponents=Yes

[Sysprep]
    BuildMassStorageSection=Yes

[SysprepMassStorage]

;end
```

The easiest way to build your own Sysprep.inf file is to use a template and then edit it in Notepad. You can use the preceding listing with very little modification. If you prefer, you can use Windows Setup Manager. Chapter 14, "Deploying with Answer Files," introduced Windows Setup Manager to you. There are a few more settings available to you in Windows Setup Manager that this listing doesn't show, such as installing printers; thus, you might build a Sysprep.inf file using Windows Setup Manager and then use that as your template for future jobs.

 Note Chapter 14 describes how to deploy settings in an answer file. It shows how to use REG files, INF files, and so on from an answer file. You can use those same methods in the Sysprep.inf file, too. Just like in any normal answer file, you can run a command in the [GuiRunOnce] section or run a command from the Cmdlines.txt file that edits the registry. Because Chapter 14 covers these topics thoroughly, I won't duplicate them here.

Preparing for Duplication

You're almost done; now you must prepare the sample computer's hard disk for duplication. On the surface, this is the easy part but, as I sometimes do, I'm going to complicate matters. To prepare for duplication, create %SystemDrive%\Sysprep and copy Sysprep.exe, Setupcl.exe, and the Sysprep.inf file you created to it.

That's it—now for the complication: fully automated disk image production is the ideal. It enables regression testing. If you can (and you can with a good bit of work), you'll want to modify your Windows answer file (Unattend.txt, or whatever you've named it) so that it runs Sysprep after it installs all the applications. Here's how:

1. Create a Sysprep folder in the Windows distribution folder under OEM\\$1 so that the setup program creates %SystemDrive%\Sysprep for you during installation. This prevents you from having to interact with the disk image at all.

2. Add the following lines of code to the answer file you're using to build the disk image. This installs each application. The placeholders *setup1* and *setup2* are the commands necessary to install the applications you want to include on the disk image. If you prefer, you can run a batch file from the [GuiRunOnce] section and install all the applications from that batch file. Running each setup program with no user interaction is preferable. This script quietly runs

Sysprep configured to use Mini-Setup Wizard, which prepares the disk for duplication:

```
[GuiRunOnce]
"setup1"
"setup2"
"%SYSTEMDRIVE%\Sysprep\Sysprep.exe -mini -quiet -reseal -forceshutdown"
```

3. Add the following code to the answer file you're using to build the disk image. This automatically logs the local Administrator on to Windows to run the programs in [GuiRunOnce]. (Set AutoLogonCount to the number of times you need to log on to Windows to complete the installation process in [GuiRunOnce].)

```
[GuiUnattended]
    AutoLogon=Yes
    AutoLogonCount=1
```

4. In the answer file you're using to install Windows on the sample computer, leave the local Administrator password null: AdminPassword=*. Doing so ensures that you can change the local Administrator password in Sysprep.inf.

Cloning the Disk Image

The last step is to run Sysprep and clone the disk to an image file. If you're fully automating disk image production, this occurs automatically. Otherwise, run Sysprep manually. The following steps describe how to run Sysprep so that it prepares the disk for duplication and configures it to automate Mini-Setup Wizard:

1. Run %SystemDrive%\Sysprep.exe.

   You see the Sysprep window shown in Figure 15-2.

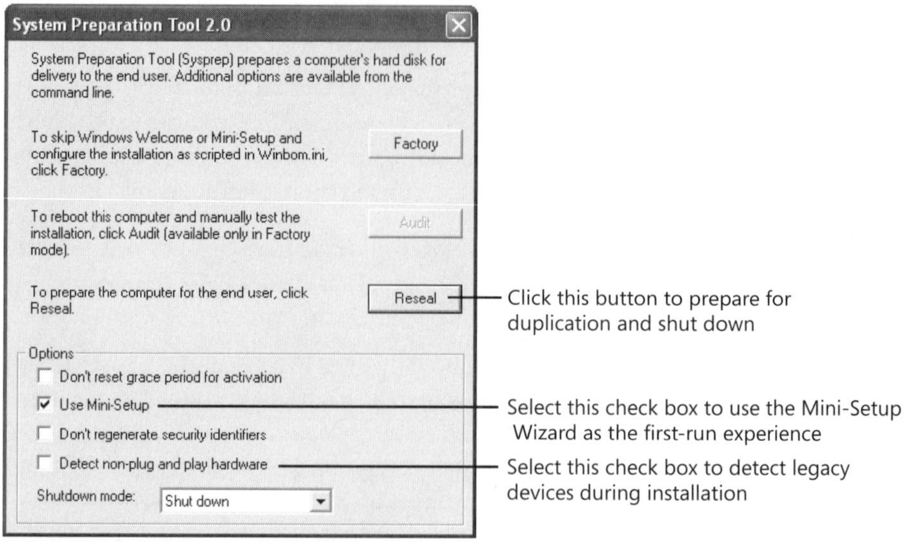

Figure 15-2   Earlier versions of Sysprep had no user interface, so this look and feel is truly new.

2. Select the MiniSetup check box.

    This causes Sysprep to use Mini-Setup Wizard as the first-run experience instead of Windows Welcome, which is the default. Mini-Setup Wizard is the first-run experience that you customize with Sysprep.inf.

3. Optionally, select the Detect Non-Plug And Play Hardware check box.

    Do this only if you want Mini-Setup Wizard to detect legacy devices during hardware detection, which adds about 10 minutes to the installation process.

4. Click Reseal to prepare the disk for duplication, and shut down the computer.

I'm not a fan of graphical user interfaces when there is a perfectly good command that I can type in the command prompt window. As a result, I almost always use Sysprep's command-line options instead:

```
sysprep {[-clean] | [-activated] [-audit] [-factory] [-forceshutdown] [-mini]
[-noreboot] [-nosidgen] [-pnp] [-quiet] [-reboot] [-reseal]}
```

Table 15-1   Sysprep Command-Line Options

`-activated`	Does not reset the grace period for Windows Product Activation. Use this option only if you have activated Windows in Factory mode. The product key that you use to activate Windows must match the product key located on the COA sticker attached to that particular computer.
`-audit`	Reboots the computer into Factory mode without generating new SIDs or processing any items in the `[OEMRunOnce]` section of Winbom.ini. Use this command-line option only if the computer is already in Factory mode.
`-clean`	Clears the critical devices database used by the `[SysprepMass-Storage]` section in Sysprep.inf. You learn about this setting in the section titled "Reducing Image Count," later in this chapter.
`-factory`	Restarts the computer without displaying Windows Welcome or Mini-Setup Wizard. This option is useful for updating drivers, running Plug and Play enumeration, installing applications, testing, configuring the computer with customer data, and making other configuration changes in your factory environment. For companies that use disk imaging, Factory mode can reduce the number of images required. When you have finished your desired set of tasks in Factory mode, run Sysprep with the `-reseal` option selected to prepare the computer for end-user delivery.
`-forceshutdown`	Shuts down the computer after Sysprep is complete. Use this option with a computer that has ACPI BIOS and that does not shut down properly with Sysprep's default behavior.
`-mini`	Configures Windows Professional to use Mini-Setup Wizard rather than Windows Welcome. This option has no effect on Windows XP Home Edition, in which the first-run experience is always Windows Welcome.

Table 15-1   Sysprep Command-Line Options

-noreboot	Modifies registry keys (SID, OemDuplicatorString, and so on) without the system rebooting or preparing for duplication. This option is used mainly for testing, specifically to see if the registry is modified properly. This option is not recommended because making changes to a computer after Sysprep has run can invalidate the preparation done by Sysprep. Do not use this option in a production environment.
-nosidgen	Runs Sysprep without generating new SIDs. You must use this option if you are not duplicating the computer on which you are running Sysprep or if you are pre-installing domain controllers.
-pnp	Runs the full Plug and Play device enumeration and installation during Mini-Setup Wizard. This command-line option has no effect if the first-run experience is Windows Welcome. Use -pnp only when you need to detect and install legacy, non–Plug and Play devices. Do not use sysprep -pnp on computer systems that use only Plug and Play devices. If you do, you will increase the time required for the first-run experience without providing any additional benefit to the user.
-quiet	Runs Sysprep without displaying onscreen confirmation messages. This option is useful if you are automating Sysprep. Select -quiet if you plan to run Sysprep immediately following installation, for example.
-reboot	Forces the computer to automatically reboot and then start Windows Welcome, Mini-Setup Wizard, or Factory mode. This is useful when you want to audit the system and verify that the first-run experience is operating correctly.
-reseal	Clears the Event Viewer logs and prepares the computer for delivery to the customer. Windows Welcome or Mini-Setup Wizard is set to start at the next boot. If you run the command sysprep -factory, you must seal the installation as the last step in your pre-installation process, either by running the command sysprep -reseal or by clicking Reseal in the Sysprep window.

After you've prepared the disk for duplication, use your third-party disk-imaging product to clone the disk to an image file. For example, with Symantec Ghost, the product I know and love, you run the Ghost Multicast client on the sample computer to transfer the disk image to the Ghost Multicast server. This is the simplistic way to clone a disk image, though. The product gets more complicated when you configure disk images so that you can deploy them remotely. In the case of Symantec Ghost, you use the Ghost Enterprise Console to manage and deploy images. For more information, see your vendor's documentation.

Tip   Sysprep doesn't always shut down the computer properly. Sometimes it just reboots the computer. If Mini-Setup Wizard starts, however, you can't use the image. To prevent a surprise reboot, stick a blank floppy disk in drive A before running Sysprep so that if the computer does restart, the computer will boot from the floppy disk and Mini-Setup Wizard won't run.

Reducing Image Count

In this section, I get to the point: how to reduce the number of images that you manage, and how the registry fits into that process. To reduce image count, you have to make sure that Windows can start on each hardware configuration because Windows must start before Mini-Setup Wizard can. Without additional effort on your part, this isn't always possible. Windows only knows about the devices installed on the sample computer, and if the target computer has different boot hardware (mass-storage controllers and system devices), it won't start.

The secret is to tell Windows about the other boot hardware that you expect it to encounter when you deploy the operating system. I'll show you the hard way first, which is to manually customize the Sysprep.inf file's [SysprepMassStorage] section, and then I'll show you the easy way, which is to allow Sysprep to build this section for you automatically. The manual method is what you used for Windows 2000, and you must use it with Windows if the operating system doesn't include native support for all the boot hardware in your organization. In either case, customizing [SysprepMassStorage] allows for the following combinations:

- **IDE to IDE.**   The sample computer uses a different IDE controller than the target computers.

- **IDE to SCSI.**   The sample computer uses an IDE controller, and the target computers use SCSI controllers.

- **SCSI to SCSI.**   The sample computer uses a different SCSI controller than the target computers.

- **SCSI to IDE.**   The sample computer uses a SCSI controller, and the target computers use IDE controllers.

> **Note**   When deploying disk images to computers that use SCSI controllers, the target computers' hard disks must support the extended INT13 BIOS functions. They must be able to start using a Boot.ini file that uses the `multi()` syntax in lieu of the `scsi()` or `signature()` syntax. To ensure the use of the `multi()` syntax, add `AddBiosToBoot` to your answer file.

Filling SysprepMassStorage Manually

To fill the [SysprepMassStorage] section, you need to dig up the Plug and Play ID for each boot device on the target computers. There are a few ways to get this ID. One is to look for it in the INF files that come with Windows. Search %SystemRoot%\Inf for the name of the device, look in the INF file that you find, and record the device's ID as well as the name of the INF file in which you found it. For example, if I'm deploying a disk image to computers that have the Intel 82801BA Bus Master IDE Controller, I'd look in Mshdc.inf to get its Plug and Play ID, which is `PCI\VEN_8086&DEV_244A`. All your hits will be in Machine.inf, Scsi.inf, Pnpscsi.inf, and Mshdc.inf.

After you've identified boot devices, add them to your Sysprep.inf file in the [Sysprep-MassStorage] section. The following code shows the format. *PNPID* is the device's Plug and Play ID, and *INF* is the path and file name of the INF file that contains the Plug and Play ID of the device.

```
[SysprepMassStorage]
PNPID = INF
```

Here's an excerpt from a Sysprep.inf file that I used recently:

```
[SysprepMassStorage]
Primary_IDE_Channel=%SYSTEMROOT%\Inf\Mshdc.inf
Secondary_IDE_Channel=%SYSTEMROOT%\Inf\Mshdc.inf
PCI\VEN_8086&DEV_1222=%SYSTEMROOT%\Inf\Mshdc.inf
PCI\VEN_8086&DEV_1230=%SYSTEMROOT%\Inf\Mshdc.inf
PCI\VEN_8086&DEV_7010=%SYSTEMROOT%\Inf\Mshdc.inf
PCI\VEN_8086&DEV_7111=%SYSTEMROOT%\Inf\Mshdc.inf
PCI\VEN_8086&DEV_2411=%SYSTEMROOT%\Inf\Mshdc.inf
PCI\VEN_8086&DEV_2421=%SYSTEMROOT%\Inf\Mshdc.inf
PCI\VEN_8086&DEV_2441=%SYSTEMROOT%\Inf\Mshdc.inf
PCI\VEN_8086&DEV_244A=%SYSTEMROOT%\Inf\Mshdc.inf
```

If Windows doesn't provide native support for a boot device, you use a different format. First copy the device driver's files to a folder on the disk image. The easiest way is to add them to the Windows distribution folder OEM\$$\Drivers so that the setup program automatically copies them to %SystemRoot%\Drivers on the sample computer. Then add lines to the [SysprepMassStorage] section that look like the following line of code. *PNPID* is the Plug and Play ID of the device. *INF* is the path and file name of the INF file that contains the Plug and Play ID, such as %SystemRoot%\Drivers*Filename*.inf. *DIR* is the name of the directory on the floppy disk that contains the device driver. *DESC* is a description of the disk as specified in the Txtsetup.oem file, and *TAG* is the disk tag as specified in the Txtsetup.oem file. The last three items are optional.

```
PNPID = INF[, DIR[, DESC[, TAG]]]
```

Filling SysprepMassStorage Automatically

New for Windows is the ability to automatically build the Sysprep.inf file's [Sysprep-MassStorage] section. By adding the lines that you see in the following code to your Sysprep.inf file, Sysprep extracts all the Plug and Play IDs from Machine.inf, Scsi.inf, Pnpscsi.inf, and Mshdc.inf and adds the appropriate entries. Make sure that you leave the [SysprepMassStorage] section empty, and double-check your spelling of `BuildMassStorageSection`. (I've spent hours troubleshooting a file in which I misspelled the name of this setting.)

```
[Sysprep]
    BuildMassStorageSection=Yes

[SysprepMassStorage]
```

> **Note**   When you build the `[SysprepMassStorage]` section automatically, Sysprep takes much longer to run. Rather than shutting down the computer after a few seconds, which is Sysprep's typical behavior, Sysprep grinds away for about 15 minutes while it builds this section. Be patient as long as you see hard disk activity and a spinning hourglass. Reducing image count is worth the wait.

Cleaning Up After Sysprep

You're not finished yet. Sysprep adds the devices in the `[SysprepMassStorage]` section to the Windows critical device's database. This database is in the registry at `HKLM\SYSTEM\CurrentControlSet\Control\CriticalDeviceDatabase`. Each subkey corresponds to a device you added to `[SysprepMassStorage]` and contains a link to the actual device driver in the registry. Windows tries to start each device in the database every time it boots. The problem is that this increases boot time significantly—something you don't want to inflict on users.

Don't I always have a solution? On each target computer, run `sysprep.exe -clean -quiet`. This command disables all the devices that Windows didn't find when it started. The next time the operating system starts, it doesn't try to start device drivers for those devices that it didn't find. The trick is when to run this command. You don't do it when you build the image. Instead, you run the command during Mini-Setup Wizard. Add the command to the Cmdlines.txt file that you create in %SystemDrive%\Sysprep\i386\OEM. The file looks like the following code. Make sure that `InstallFilesPath` points to the folder containing the OEM folder, which is usually %SystemDrive%\Sysprep\i386, and that you set `OemPreinstall=Yes`.

```
[Commands]
"%SYSTEMDRTVF%\Sysprep\Sysprep.exe -clean  quiet"
```

Removing the Paging File

By using the registry, you can remove the Windows paging file before running Sysprep. Simply change the `REG_MULTI_SZ` value `PagingFiles` to `C:\pagefile.sys 0 0` immediately before running Sysprep. This value is in `HKLM\SYSTEM\CurrentControlSet\Control\Session Manager\Memory Management`. The easiest way to change this value is to export the setting to a REG file (remove all settings but the `PagingFiles` setting from the

REG file), and then add it to a batch file that also starts Sysprep with the command-line options that you need for creating the image. For example, you can add the command %SystemDrive%\Sysprep\Sysprep.cmd to the [GuiRunOnce] section of the Sysprep.inf file, and then add the following lines of code to the Sysprep.cmd file:

```
Regedit /s %SYSTEMDRIVE%\Sysprep\pagefile.reg
%SYSTEMDRIVE%\Sysprep\Sysprep.exe -mini -quiet -reseal -forceshutdown
```

Mapping Sysprep Settings

When you run Sysprep, it modifies hundreds if not thousands of registry settings to prepare the computer's hard disk for duplication. Table 15-2 on the next page describes the registry settings that relate directly to Sysprep. These are settings that prepare Mini-Setup Wizard to run the next time Windows starts. I tracked these down by comparing snapshots of the registry before and after running Sysprep. I divided the table into sections, with each key in a different section.

Sysprep changes other settings that I don't describe in Table 15-2. The settings that it changes depend on the computer's configuration. For example, Sysprep disables Remote Desktop and Remote Assistance. It configures System Restore to create an initial system checkpoint the next time that Windows starts. Sysprep also resets the computer's digital ID and resets the Windows Product Activation timer. Last, if you're using [SysprepMassStorage], Sysprep fills the critical devices database and configures the device drivers for each device. The changes that Sysprep makes to the registry are numerous, but the following list summarizes some of the most significant differences that I found from comparing the registry snapshots:

- Sysprep resets the event system. These settings are in HKLM\SOFTWARE\ Microsoft\EventSystem.

- Sysprep removes certificate templates and certificates from the following keys: HKLM\SOFTWARE\Microsoft\Cryptography HKLM\SOFTWARE\Microsoft\ EnterpriseCertificates

- Sysprep resets the configuration of Group Policy in the key HKLM\SOFTWARE\ Microsoft\Windows\CurrentVersion\Group Policy.

- Sysprep removes the computer from the domain, if it's a domain member, by deleting the appropriate values from the following keys, and elsewhere: HKLM\SOFTWARE\Microsoft\Windows NT\CurrentVersion\Winlogon HKLM\ SOFTWARE\Microsoft\Windows NT\CurrentVersion\Winlogon\DomainCache

- Sysprep removes policies from the key HKLM\SOFTWARE\Policies.

- Sysprep removes networking components from the following keys: HKLM\ SYSTEM\CurrentControlSet\Control HKLM\SYSTEM\CurrentControlSet\Enum HKLM\SYSTEM\CurrentControlSet\Services.

- Sysprep resets the application compatibility data in HKLM\SYSTEM\Current-ControlSet\Control\Session Manager\AppCompatibility.

- Sysprep resets power management settings in the key HKLM\SYSTEM\ControlSet001\Control\Session Manager\Power.

- Sysprep configures the Netlogon service to load on demand instead of automatically in HKLM\SYSTEM\CurrentControlSet\Services\Netlogon.

- Sysprep adds the devices specified in [SysprepMassStorage] to the critical devices database. This database is in the key HKLM\SYSTEM\CurrentControlSet\Control\CriticalDeviceDatabase.

- Sysprep installs and configures device drivers for the devices listed in the [SysprepMassStorage] section. It configures these device drivers in the key HKLM\SYSTEM\CurrentControlSet\Services.

Table 15-2   Sysprep Registry Settings

Value	Type	Description
HKLM\SOFTWARE\Microsoft\Sysprep		
SidsGenerated	REG_DWORD	Sysprep sets this value to 0x01, indicating that it removed the computer's SID and Setupcl.exe will regenerate it.
CriticalDevices-Installed	REG_DWORD	Sysprep sets this value to 0x01, indicating that it created the critical devices database.
HKLM\SOFTWARE\Microsoft\Windows\CurrentVersion\Setup		
SourcePath	REG_DWORD	Sysprep sets this to the value of Install-FilesPath in Sysprep.inf, which indicates to the setup program where to find installation files.
HKLM\SOFTWARE\Microsoft\Windows\CurrentVersion\Setup\OOBE		
RunWelcomeProcess	REG_DWORD	Sysprep sets this value to 0x00, which disables the Windows Welcome out-of-box experience.
HKLM\SYSTEM\CurrentControlSet\Control\Lsa\Kerberos\SidCache		
MachineSid	REG_BINARY	Sysprep deletes this value to remove the computer's SID.
HKLM\SYSTEM\CurrentControlSet\Control\Session Manager		
SetupExecute	REG_MULTI_SZ	Setup adds Setupcl.exe to this value. This runs Setupcl.exe when Windows restarts so that Setupcl.exe can regenerate the computer's SID and run Mini-Setup Wizard.

Table 15-2   Sysprep Registry Settings

Value	Type	Description
HKLM\SYSTEM\Setup		
BootDiskSig	REG_DWORD	Sysprep stores the signature of the boot disk in this value.
CloneTag	REG_MULTI_SZ	Sysprep stores the date and time that you ran the prepared disk in this value.
Cmdline	REG_SZ	Sysprep stores the setup command line setup -newsetup -mini in this value. This is the command that runs Mini-Setup Wizard.
MiniSetupInProgress	REG_DWORD	Sysprep sets this value to 0x01, indicating that Mini-Setup Wizard is in the process of running.
SetupType	REG_DWORD	Sysprep sets this value to 0x01.
SystemSetupInProgress	REG_DWORD	Sysprep sets this value to 0x01.

Keeping Perspective

In this chapter, I've given you enough information to start testing Sysprep in your lab right away. Sysprep is even a great tool for those power users who install Windows over and over again. But I haven't told you enough about Sysprep for you to build an image and start deploying it on an enterprise's desktops.

There's much more to Sysprep than just writing a few answer files and running Sysprep.exe. Considerations include everything from defining preferred configurations to licensing to whether you've configured your routers for multicast. Disk imaging is a part of an overall deployment plan, which includes hardware and software inventories, migration plans, configuration plans, and much more.

More Info   Microsoft has several resources available to help you plan large-scale deployments using disk-imaging techniques. To learn more about these important resources, contact your Microsoft account manager, who'd be happy to tell you about them. The ultimate resource for online deployment information is *http://www.microsoft.com/technet/desktopdeployment/default.mspx*.

## Chapter 16

Configuring Windows PE

Half the job of installing Microsoft Windows XP and Microsoft Windows Server 2003 (Windows) or building disk images is starting the computer. Microsoft Windows Preinstallation Environment (Windows PE or WinPE) is just another way to start computers, similar to using MS-DOS, only better. It allows you to more fully automate the installation process than using MS-DOS does. This chapter describes how to use, customize, and automate Windows PE for the purpose of installing Windows in enterprise environments.

 Note Do you have Windows PE? Windows PE is a benefit of Microsoft Software Assurance. For more information, see *http://www.microsoft.com/licensing/programs /sa/support/winpe.mspx*.

Exploring Windows PE

Windows PE is a supercharged replacement for MS-DOS in your deployment processes. Windows PE is a minimal Windows system that provides limited services based on the Windows XP or Windows Server 2003 kernel, depending on which version of Windows you used to build Windows PE. Windows PE also provides the minimal set of features required to run Windows Setup, install Windows from networks, script basic repetitive tasks, and validate hardware. For example, with Windows PE, you can use more powerful batch scripts, Windows Scripting Host (WSH), and HTML Applications (HTA) to fully automate computer preparation and Windows installation, rather than the limited batch commands in MS-DOS. Here are examples of what you can do with Windows PE:

- Create and format disk partitions, including NTFS file-system partitions, without rebooting the computer before installing Windows on them. Formatting disks with NTFS by using an MS-DOS-bootable disk required third-party utilities. Windows PE replaces the MS-DOS-bootable disk in this scenario, allowing you to format disks with NTFS without using third-party utilities. Also, the file-system utilities that Windows PE provides are scriptable, so you can completely automate the setup-preparation process.

- Access network shares to run preparation tools or install Windows. Windows PE provides network access comparable to Windows. In fact, Windows PE provides the same network drivers that come with Windows, allowing you to access the network quickly and easily. Customizing MS-DOS-bootable disks to access network shares was a time-consuming and tedious process—now it isn't.

- Use all the mass-storage devices that rely on Windows device drivers. Windows PE includes the same mass-storage device drivers that Windows provides, which means that you no longer have to customize MS-DOS-bootable disks for use with specialized mass-storage devices. Once again, Windows PE allows you to focus on important jobs rather than on maintaining MS-DOS-bootable disks.

- Customize Windows PE by using techniques and technologies that are already familiar to you. Windows PE is based on Windows, so you are already familiar with the techniques and tools used to customize Windows PE. You can customize Windows PE for a variety of scenarios, which this chapter goes into in greater detail.

The following sections provide more detail about the features and limitations of using Windows PE. They focus specifically on using it in enterprise deployment scenarios, rather than in manufacturing environments.

Capabilities

Windows PE is a bootable CD that replaces the MS-DOS-bootable disk in most deployment scenarios. (You can start it using Remote Installation Services, too.) It's a lightweight, 32-bit environment that supports the same set of networking and mass-storage device drivers that Windows XP or Windows Server 2003 supports, and it provides access to similar features, including NTFS file system (NTFS) and stand-alone Distributed File System (DFS). Windows PE includes the following features:

- **Hardware independence.**   Windows PE is a hardware-independent Windows environment for both x86 and Itanium architectures. You can use the same preinstallation environment on all the desktop computers and servers in your company, without creating and maintaining different bootable disks for different hardware configurations. Say goodbye to that collection of MS-DOS disks.

- **APIs and scripting capabilities.**   Windows PE contains a subset of the Win32 APIs; a command interpreter capable of running batch scripts; and support for adding WSH, HTML Applications, and Microsoft ActiveX Data Objects (ADO) to create custom tools or scripts. The scripting capabilities in Windows PE far exceed the capabilities of MS-DOS-bootable disks. For example, the command interpreter in Windows PE supports a more robust batch-scripting language than does MS-DOS, allowing you to create more advanced scripts.

- **Network access.**   Windows PE uses Transmission Control Protocol/Internet Protocol (TCP/IP) to provide network access and supports standard network drivers for running Windows Setup and copying source files from the network to the computer. You can easily add or remove network drivers from a customized version of Windows PE. In contrast, customizing MS-DOS-bootable disks to access network shares is frustrating, mostly due to the need to build and maintain numerous disks. Windows PE alleviates this frustration by supporting the network drivers that Windows supports, and Windows PE is easier to customize with additional network drivers.

- **Mass-storage devices.**   Windows PE includes support for all mass-storage devices that Windows supports. As new devices become available, you can easily add drivers into or remove them from a customized version of Windows PE. Customizing an MS-DOS-bootable disk to access atypical mass-storage devices requires tracking down and installing the 16-bit device drivers. However, Windows PE supports many of these mass-storage devices out of the box. Also, customizing Windows PE to support additional mass-storage devices is easier because it uses standard Windows device drivers that are readily available.

- **Disk management.**   Windows PE includes native support for creating, deleting, formatting, and managing NTFS file system partitions. Also, Windows PE provides full, unrestricted access to NTFS file systems. With Windows PE, you don't have to restart the computer after formatting a disk.

- **Support for Preboot Execution Environment (PXE) protocol.**   If the computer supports PXE, you can start it automatically from a Windows PE image located on a Remote Installation Services (RIS) server—and RIS doesn't install the Windows PE image on the computer's hard disk. Starting Windows PE from the network makes it a convenient tool to use in deployment scenarios, and you can easily customize Windows PE directly on the RIS server.

> **Note**   You must build a custom Windows PE CD from the Windows PE source files as described in "Customizing Windows PE," later in this chapter.

Limitations

Windows PE has the following limitations:

- Windows PE doesn't fit on floppy disks, although you can write a custom Windows PE image to a bootable CD.

- Windows PE supports TCP/IP and NetBIOS over TCP/IP for network connectivity, but it doesn't support other protocols, such as Internetwork Packet Exchange/ Sequenced Packet Exchange (IPX/SPX).

- The Windows on Windows 32 (WOW32) subsystem allows 16-bit applications to run on the 32-bit Windows platform. The WOW32 subsystem isn't available in Windows PE, so 16-bit applications won't run in 32-bit versions of Windows PE. Similarly, in the Itanium version of Windows PE, the WOW64 subsystem is not available, so applications must be fully 64-bit compliant.

- To reduce its size, Windows PE includes only a subset of the available Win32 APIs. Included are I/O (disk and network) and core Win32 APIs. The following categories of Win32 APIs aren't available in Windows PE (applications that require these APIs do not run in Windows PE):

    - ☐ Active Directory Services Interfaces (ADSI)
    - ☐ DirectX
    - ☐ Microsoft .NET Framework
    - ☐ OpenGL
    - ☐ Power Options
    - ☐ Printing and Print Spooler
    - ☐ Still Image
    - ☐ Tape Backup
    - ☐ Terminal Services
    - ☐ User Profile
    - ☐ Window Station and Desktop
    - ☐ Windows Management Instrumentation (WMI)
    - ☐ Windows Multimedia
    - ☐ Windows Shell

- Drive letter assignments aren't persistent between sessions. After you restart Windows PE, the drive letter assignments will be in the default order.

- Windows PE supports the distributed file system (DFS) name resolution to stand-alone DFS roots only.

- You can't access files or folders on a computer running Windows PE from another computer.

- Windows PE requires a Video Electronics Standards Association (VESA)–compatible display device and will use the highest screen resolution that it can determine is supported. If the operating system can't detect video settings, it uses a resolution of 640 x 480 pixels.

- You can build custom versions of Windows PE from Windows XP Professional and Windows Server 2003 products, but not from Windows XP Home Edition.

- To prevent its use as a pirated operating system, Windows PE automatically reboots after 24 hours.

- Windows PE doesn't support the .NET Framework.

Using Windows PE as an Installation Platform

You probably used MS-DOS-bootable disks to handle system configuration, prepare computers for installation, and then install the operating system on the computer. MS-DOS-bootable disks are difficult to configure and maintain for this purpose because you must first track down the 16-bit device drivers required and then customize the disks to connect to the network. Each type of network adapter requires a unique disk, too, escalating the amount of work involved in maintaining these MS-DOS-bootable disks. Add to that the computer systems with atypical mass-storage devices that require you to customize disks with mass-storage device drivers, and the number of combinations that you must maintain grows quickly. Even after all the time you spend building and maintaining MS-DOS-bootable disks, they are barely adequate to get the job done because MS-DOS provides minimal scripting capabilities and memory resources—and the utilities it provides are the bare essentials. For example, after you start computers with an MS-DOS-bootable disk, you must usually perform many tasks manually before starting the Windows installation instead of moving on to the next computer to install Windows. After formatting a hard disk, you must usually restart the computer before installing Windows.

Microsoft developed Windows PE specifically for deployment scenarios. Windows PE provides a lightweight, 32-bit environment that leverages the same device drivers as Windows. You have access to a similar set of basic features that Windows provides, including the NTFS file system and DFS shares. Windows PE supports long file names, too. In addition, you can fully automate the installation process, so you can move on to the next computer or the next disk image faster. In deployment scenarios, there are a variety of ways you can use Windows PE, including the following examples:

- You can use the Windows PE bootable CD as-is—that is, without customizations—to start computers. (You must still build a Windows PE CD from Windows XP or

Windows Server 2003 source files, however.) Then you can connect to the network and install an operating system from a customized network share. Without customizations, the Windows PE bootable CD doesn't support WSH, HTA, or ADO.

- You can customize Windows PE in a variety of ways—such as adding device drivers, optional components, and other utilities—and then create a new Windows PE CD. You use the Windows PE CD to connect to the network and install an operating system from a customized network share. In this scenario, the user or technician starts the computer using the CD. Windows PE starts and then processes Startnet.cmd, which starts the networking connection. You can also customize this batch script to map a drive letter to the network share that contains the Windows source files, verifies that the computer's configuration matches the require configuration, backs up the user's data to the network, runs Diskpart to partition the hard disk, formats the hard disk with the NTFS file system, and then runs Windows Setup fully unattended. Alternatively, the script can run a third-party disk-imaging utility to restore an operating-system image from the network share to the hard disk. (See Chapter 15, "Cloning Disks with Sysprep," for a list of disk-imaging products that support Windows PE.)

- You can create a Windows PE CD that contains both Windows PE and the operating system that you're installing and then customize the CD so that it automatically installs the operating system when the CD starts. Because more powerful scripting capabilities are available with Windows PE than with MS-DOS, you're more able to completely automate the process. You can then distribute the CD to users or technicians so that they can automatically install the operating system. This scenario is much like the previous one, except that the CD contains the Windows source files, so a network connection isn't necessary.

- In an Active Directory environment, you can customize and install Windows PE using RIS. Rather than starting computers with a CD, you can start Windows PE remotely by using RIS. This scenario is similar to using a Windows PE CD to start the computer and connect to the network, except that the user or technician starts the computer from the Windows PE image on the RIS server. Then the custom scripts you add to Windows PE connect to the network, verify the computer's configuration, prepare the disk for installation, and then start Windows Setup. No floppy disks or CDs are required.

The following sections describe how Windows PE and your customizations enable these scenarios. They start with the basics, starting the computer. Then they describe how to verify that the computer's configuration meets requirements, how to configure the computer's hard disk, and how to install Windows.

Starting the Computer

To start the computer using a Windows PE CD, insert the CD into the computer's CD-ROM, configure the computer's BIOS to boot from the CD before booting from the local hard disk (only if necessary), and then restart the computer. When prompted, press any key to boot the computer from the CD. Windows PE loads and then runs the all-important Startnet.cmd batch script to configure the environment. (Startnet.cmd serves a similar purpose to Autoexec.bat in MS-DOS.) Windows PE runs Startnet.cmd every time it starts, making this file the central location from which to customize Windows PE for your scenarios.

There are two versions of Startnet.cmd that you might encounter, depending on when and from where you received Windows PE. The first version contains the line `factory -winpe`. This version relies entirely on Factory to configure the network connection. The second version contains the line `factory -minint` followed by several other lines that configure the network connection. The first version is the default in newer versions of Windows PE, beginning with version 1.2. The second version is the default in older versions. I prefer the first version because it's much cleaner. You should use it, too. Listing 16-1 shows a slightly customized version of Startnet.cmd, and the following steps describe how it works:

1. `if exist oc.bat call oc.bat.`   This command installs optional components only if they exist. See the section "Optional Components," later in this chapter.

2. `factory -winpe.`   This command detects, installs, and configures network support for Windows PE. It first looks for the Winbom.ini file, as described in the sidebar "Finding Winbom.ini," later in this chapter. When Factory finds a Winbom.ini, it looks in the file's `[Factory]` section for the `WinbomType` entry and checks that it is `winPE`. If not, it continues looking for another Winbom.ini file. After locating the Winbom.ini file, Factory configures the network connection as specified in the `[WinPE.Net]` section. Factory uses Plug and Play to install the network interface card and then configures the networking services and binds the network protocols.

3. `if exist a:\floppy.cmd a:\floppy.cmd.`   This command runs the batch script called Floppy.cmd located on drive A, only if it exists. It provides an easy way to further customize Windows PE for different scenarios without requiring a separate copy of Windows PE for each. Instead, simply create a separate floppy for each scenario.

Listing 16-1   Startnet.cmd

```
@echo off
@rem startnet.cmd: configure Windows PE networking, etc.

    echo Installing optional components...
```

```
if exist oc.bat call oc.bat

echo Configuring network components...

factory -winpe

cls
if exist a:\floppy.cmd a:\floppy.cmd

:end
```

More Info   Using Windows PE, you can accomplish many tasks by using three methods: answer files, batch scripts, or Winbom.ini. Winbom.ini is a simple configuration settings file that Windows PE uses when the command `factory -winpe` runs in Startnet.cmd. Using Winbom.ini to partition and format disks is often easier than using Diskpart, for example. Winbom.ini also gives you a moderate amount of control over how Windows PE starts.

Note   "Windows Preinstallation Environment User's Guide," which is Winpe.chm in the Docs folder on the Windows PE CD, contains a complete reference for the Factory command and for Winbom.ini. I typically use batch scripts because they give me more control of the installation process than Winbom.ini does.

Finding Winbom.ini

When you run the command `factory -winpe` in Startnet.cmd, Factory searches for Winbom.ini in the following order:

1. The path and file name specified by the registry key HKLM\SOFTWARE\Microsoft\Factory\Winbom

2. The root of all removable media drives that are not CD-ROM drives, such as a floppy disk drive

3. The root of all CD-ROM drives

4. The location of Factory.exe, usually the %SystemRoot%\System32 or %SystemRoot%\Sysprep folders

5. The root of %SystemDrive%

Configuring the Hard Disks

There are two ways to configure the target computer's hard disk using native Windows PE tools. The first is using Diskpart to partition the disk and using Format to format it. This method provides the greatest amount of flexibility for scenarios in which you want to support various computer configurations from a single Windows PE CD or RIS image.

The second method is using the [`DiskConfig`] section in Winbom.ini. Using this section, you describe the disk layout using settings such as `SizeN`, `PartitionTypeN`, and `FileSystemN`.

> **More Info**   Winbom.ini is predominately an Original Equipment Manufacturer (OEM) tool, and I prefer the flexibility of using batch scripts and Diskpart, so I'll refer you to "Windows Preinstallation Environment User's Guide," which is Winpe.chm on the Windows PE CD in the Docs folder, for more information about using Winbom.ini to configure hard disks.

Listings 16-2 and 16-3 show how to use the first method. Listing 16-2 is Diskpart.txt (similar to an answer file). This file is a script for Diskpart.exe that automatically configures the disk. It selects the first disk installed on the computer, removes its current partitions, creates a new primary partition using all the available space, assigns the drive letter C, and then marks the partition as active so that it will boot.

Listing 16-3 shows the command necessary to run Diskpart.exe with Diskpart.txt as the script and then format the disk. The batch script setup32.cmd contains these commands. The command to use diskpart.txt in Windows PE is `diskpart.exe /s diskpart.txt`. Diskpart does not format the disk, so you must format the disk after partitioning it. The command `format c: /q /fs:ntfs /y` quickly formats the newly partitioned disk with the NTFS file system and without a volume label. The command-line option `/y` runs Format without prompting for input. You can run both commands within a batch script to automatically partition and format a disk, which is what you see happening in setup32.cmd in the next section, Listing 16-3.

Listing 16-2   diskpart.txt

```
select disk=0
clean
create partition primary
assign letter=c
active
```

Listing 16-3   setup32.cmd

```
diskpart /s diskpart.txt
format c: /q /fs:ntfs /y
```

Installing Windows

After configuring the computer's hard disk and performing any other preinstallation tasks you've planned, you run Winnt32 (not Winnt) to start Windows Setup. Listing 16-4 shows setup32.cmd, updated with the commands to run Winnt32 from Windows PE and restart the computer.

The important takeaway from Listing 16-4 is the command-line option `/syspart:c:`. If you partition the disk using Diskpart and then format it using Format, Windows Setup fails without using the `/syspart` command-line option. This option changes Windows Setup so that it simply copies the source files to the target computer and then prepares the disk so that Windows Setup continues after the computer restarts.

So how do you restart the computer in Windows PE from a batch script? I'm embarrassed to say that it took a few tries for me to figure this out. I first tried the Shutdown utility. Then I tried some third-party utilities. None of them worked. I tried a script. That didn't work. Then, out of frustration, I typed **exit** at the command prompt and, low and behold, Windows PE restarted the computer. So, that's the trick and that's why you see the line **exit** in the listing.

Listing 16-4   setup32.cmd
```
diskpart /s diskpart.txt
format c: /q /fs:ntfs /y
@..\i386\winnt32 /unattended:winnt.sif /syspart:c:
exit
```

Customizing Windows PE

The uncustomized version of Windows PE is useful for preparing computers for installation, but you don't realize its full power until you customize it. You can add your own 32-bit command-line tools, scripts, optional components, and so on. To do that, you need the Windows PE source files and, *possibly but not always*, a Windows product CD, both of which must have matching build numbers. You also need access to any command-line tools, scripts, and device drivers that you want to add to Windows PE. The Windows PE source files you received from Microsoft contain the following folders:

- ****   The root folder of the source files contains four files: Win51, Win51ip, Win51ip.sp1, and Winbom.ini. When you build a customized Windows PE CD, you must place these files at the root of the CD; otherwise, Windows PE will not start properly. For example, if Winbom.ini is missing, Windows PE hangs.

- **\Docs**   This folder contains the Windows PE documentation. In particular, "Windows Preinstallation Environment User's Guide," which is Winpe.chm on the Windows PE CD in the Docs folder, contains reference information that this chapter doesn't.

- **\I386**   This folder contains the Windows system files. You can usually use these files when customizing a Windows PE CD rather than starting from scratch. If you want to start from scratch, however, you can rebuild the I386 folder.

- **\Winpe**   This folder contains scripts and other files necessary to build an I386 folder and customized Windows PE CDs.

The first step in customizing Windows PE is simply to copy the Windows PE source files to your hard disk. If you received Windows PE on a CD, copy them from the CD. If you downloaded the files from Microsoft, keep the original files intact by making another copy. Make sure you copy the root folder that contains Win51, Win51ip, sp1, and Winbom.ini, as well as the three subfolders, Docs, I386, and Winpe. If you want to, you can rebuild the I386 folder using the following steps:

1. Delete the existing I386 folder.

2. Turn off the read-only attribute of all files in the Winpe folder.

   The scripts in the Winpe folder overwrite certain files and can't do so with the read-only attribute set on those files.

3. Put the Windows product CD in the CD-ROM drive, or make sure that a folder containing the Windows source files is available on your local hard disk or on the network.

   If the files are on the network, map a drive to the share containing them, because it simplifies the command line.

4. Run the command **mkimg.cmd** *source destination [isoimage]* in the folder containing the Windows PE tools.

   ❏ *Source* is the path of the Windows product CD or the folder containing the I386 folder. Don't use a trailing slash (\). C:\Winxp is good, but C:\Winxp\ is bad.

   ❏ *Destination* is the folder in which Mkimg.cmd will create the custom version of Windows PE. Mkimg.cmd will create this folder if it doesn't already exist.

   ❏ *Isoimage* is the path and file name of the International Organization for Standardization (ISO) image you want to create. You typically will *not* use *isoimage* because you want to create the ISO image after you've made other customizations. For example, if the Windows PE source files are in C:\MyWinpe, and the Windows CD is in drive D, run the command **mkimg D: C:\MyWinpe\I386**

The process completes after several minutes. The result is the Windows PE files in the destination directory and optionally an ISO image that you can burn to a CD. If you're using Windows PE from RIS or from a hard disk image, you probably don't care about the ISO image. Keep in mind that you should wait to create the ISO image if you have additional customizations you want to make.

Note   You can create a custom version of Windows PE from any version of Windows XP or Windows Server 2003 except for Windows XP Home Edition or Windows Datacenter Server 2003.

The size of the 32-bit Windows PE image is about 120 megabytes (MB). Your customizations will use additional space. Adding languages to the image also uses additional space. Regardless, there is usually enough room to copy the Windows source files to the Windows PE CD so that you can more fully automate the Windows installation process for users or technicians. If the Windows source files don't fit on the CD with your custom version of Windows PE, you can reduce the size of Windows PE considerably.

More Info   "Windows Preinstallation Environment User's Guide," which you find on the Windows PE CD in the file Winpe.chm, describes which files you can remove to reduce the size of Windows PE.

Tip   To configure Windows PE so that it starts from the CD every time without requiring the user to press a key, remove the file bootfix.bin from the I386 folder of the Windows PE directory structure before you create an ISO image. Bootfix.bin provides the "Press any key to boot from CD-ROM" message.

Command-Line Tools

The following command-line tools are available when preinstalling an operating system or using Windows PE:

- **Diskpart.exe**   Diskpart is a text-mode command interpreter that enables you to manage objects (disks, partitions, or volumes) by using scripts or direct input from a command prompt. With Diskpart, you can create and remove volumes, assign drive letters, and so on.

- **Factory.exe**   Use Factory to update drivers, run Plug and Play enumeration, install applications, test, configure the computer with customer data, or make other configuration changes in your factory environment. For companies that use disk imaging (or cloning) software, efficient use of Factory can reduce the number of images that you require.

- **Mkimg.cmd**   This command builds the file set for Windows PE from any Windows XP or Windows Server 2003 product CD except Windows XP Home Edition and Windows Server 2003 Datacenter Edition. It optionally creates an ISO image of the files. You can then burn that ISO file to a CD by using any CD-burning software that supports ISO-9660. The CD image-creation process takes several minutes, and then the files are placed in the same location as where you run the Mkimg command.

- **Netcfg.exe**   The network configuration tool configures network access. When you preinstall Windows, it is most commonly used in a script that runs when Windows PE boots. You don't need to use this tool if you're starting the network with the command `factory -winpe` in Startnet.cmd, which is the default.

- **Oscdimg.exe**   This is a command-line tool that creates an ISO image file of a customized, 32-bit or 64-bit version of Windows PE. You can then burn that ISO image file to a CD.

> **More Info**   See "Windows Preinstallation Environment User's Guide," which is Winpe.chm on the Windows PE CD in the Docs folder, for more information about these tools. Winpe.chm includes detailed documentation for each command-line option that these tools support. You find examples of using these tools in this chapter.

There are additional tools that would be useful to add to your Windows PE image, including the scripts that you create to automate redundant processes such as partitioning and formatting disks. You can place them anywhere within your Windows PE CD, but I recommend a subfolder in the I386 folder so that the tools will be available if you install Windows PE from a RIS server. Also, the following list describes tools that I like to include in a Windows PE image for installation preparation:

- Windiff.exe from the Windows Support Tools

- Depends.exe from the Windows Support Tools

- File Monitor (FileMon from Sysinternals at *http://www.sysinternals.com*)

- Registry Monitor (RegMon from Sysinternals at *http://www.sysinternals.com*)

Optional Components

You can add the following components to a customized Windows PE image:

- **ActiveX Data Objects**   ADO enables your client applications to access and manipulate data from a Microsoft SQL Server database through an OLE DB provider. Its primary benefits are ease of use, high speed, low memory overhead, and a small disk footprint. ADO supports key features for building client/server and Web-based applications. Windows PE doesn't support ADO access to Microsoft Access or Active Directory, however.

- **HTML Applications**   HTAs are full-fledged applications that are trusted and display only the menus, icons, toolbars, and title information that the Web developer creates. In short, HTAs pack all the power of Microsoft Internet Explorer—its object model, performance, rendering power, protocol support, and channel-download technology—without enforcing the strict security model and user interface of the browser. You can use the HTML and Dynamic HTML (DHTML) that you already know to create HTAs.

- **Windows Script Host**   WSH is a language-independent host that allows you to run any script engine on the Windows operating system. WSH is useful for scripting complex tasks that you can't easily do by using batch scripts.

> **Tip**   If you intend to automate installations, you almost always want to include WSH and HTA in Windows PE. Size isn't a concern if you're installing Windows from the network.

BuildOptionalComponents.vbs is the script you use to add support for optional components packages. This script is in the Windows PE Winpe folder. If you run this script without any command-line options, it creates a folder containing all the optional components. If you run this script with specific command-line options, the folder that it creates contains only those components. After the script finishes, you simply copy the folder that it creates over the I386 folder for your Windows PE image. The following line of code describes the syntax of BuildOptionalComponents.vbs, and Table 16-1 describes each command-line option:

```
BuildOptionalComponents [/S: location] [/D: location] /ADO /HTA /WSH /64 /Q /E
```

Table 16-1   BuildOptionalComponents.vbs Command-Line Options

/S:*location*	Specifies the source location of the Windows source files
/D:*location*	Specifies the destination location for the component files
/ADO	Specifies to build ADO for SQL Server connectivity
/HTA	Specifies to build HTA
/WSH	Specifies to build WSH
/64	Specifies to build and check 64-bit version of Windows PE (requires Windows XP 64-Bit Edition)
/Q	Runs the script without prompting for inputs; returns any errors
/E	Explores the resulting folder automatically when complete

After you add optional components to Windows PE, customize Startnet.cmd to install them when Windows PE starts. BuildOptionalComponents.vbs creates the batch script oc.bat in %SystemRoot%\System32, which installs the optional components. Call this batch script from Startnet.cmd, as shown in Listing 16-1.

Network Drivers

Although Windows PE supports network and mass-storage drivers, other types of device drivers don't function in Windows PE. Even if they appear to function, they're likely to be missing key dependencies that prevent them from working properly.

Windows PE supports all the network drivers included on the Windows product CD. When customizing a Windows PE image, you can add, remove, or replace network drivers as necessary. For example, you can remove unnecessary network drivers to reduce the size of the image and the time required to boot. After completing the following three steps, executing the Factory command in Startnet.cmd automatically identifies the network drivers that you add:

1. Copy the driver's INF files to %SystemRoot%\Inf (the matching catalog file isn't necessary).

2. Copy the driver's SYS files to %SystemRoot%\System32\drivers.

3. Copy related DLL, EXE, or other files to %SystemRoot%\system32.

In addition to adding, removing, and replacing network drivers, you can limit the number of network adapters that the factory command scans by using the [`netcards`] section of the Winbom.ini file. When this command runs from the Startnet.cmd batch file, it scans only for the network adapters in this section, resulting in a faster boot time. To add network adapters to this section, you must know the adapter's Plug and Play ID and the path of its INF file. The following example shows the values necessary to specify the adapter's specific Plug and Play ID as well as its more generic ID, which ensures that it matches any network adapter supported by the driver:

```
[NetCards]
PCI\VEN_10B7&DEV_9200&SUBSYS_100010B7&REV_78\3&61AAA01&0&78=%systemroot%\
nic\netel90b.inf
PCI\VEN_10B7&DEV_9200&SUBSYS_100010B7=%systemroot%\nic\netel90b.inf
```

Mass-Storage Drivers

Configuring a limited set of mass-storage drivers can reduce the boot time of Windows PE. Instead of loading the entire set of mass-storage drivers that the Windows product CD natively supports, Windows PE just loads the drivers that you specify in the Winpeoem.sif file, which is in %SystemRoot%\System32. You can also configure this file to support additional mass-storage drivers that the Windows product CD doesn't natively support. The Winpeoem.sif file has the following three sections for controlling mass-storage drivers:

■   [`MassStorageDrivers.Append`]   Specifies one or more third-party mass-storage drivers that a custom version of Windows PE loads in addition to the entire set of drivers that the Windows product CD supports. You copy the driver files to the %SystemRoot%\System32\Drivers folder and copy supporting files to the appropriate locations as specified in the driver's INF file.

■   [`MassStorageDrivers.Replace`]   Specifies one or more third-party mass-storage drivers that a custom version of Windows PE loads instead of the entire set of drivers that the Windows product CD supports. You copy the driver files to the %SystemRoot%\System32\Drivers folder and copy supporting files to the appropriate locations as specified in the driver's INF file.

■   [`OEMDriverParams`]   Specifies non–Plug and Play drivers for Windows PE to load in addition to the drivers that Windows natively supports.

> **More Info**   See "Windows Preinstallation Environment User's Guide," which is Winpe.chm in the Docs folder on the Windows PE CD, for detailed instructions about using this section.

> **Note**   Similar to booting to a Windows CD, the F6 option to add mass-storage drivers still works when starting Windows PE.

Languages

Windows PE doesn't support multilanguage builds—only individual-language localized builds. Still, you can build Windows PE images in various languages without needing localized Windows PE tools for each language. In other words, you can use a single set of tools to build multiple localized Windows PE images.

You use the [RegionalSettings] section in the Config.inf file to add support for multiple languages. You must always match the Language value to the language of the Windows product CD that you're using to build the Windows PE image. Then you use the LanguageGroup value to specify the languages of both the Windows PE tools and the Windows product CD. For a list of the specific languages that correspond to particular language groups, see the Microsoft Global Software Development Web site at *http://www.microsoft.com/globaldev/default.mspx*.

For example, to create a Japanese Windows PE image by using a Japanese Windows product CD, set LanguageGroup=1,7 and Language=0x0411 in the [RegionalSettings] section of Config.inf. The language group ID for Western Europe and United States is 1, and 7 is the language group ID for Japanese. The local ID (LCID) for Japanese is 0x0411, which matches the local of the Windows product CD. Adding 1 to the LanguageGroup value ensures that you can use the English preinstallation tools.

Starting Windows PE

Table 16-2 summarizes the three ways that you can start Windows PE. You can create a bootable Windows PE CD or DVD, for example. You can also start Windows PE from a RIS server. You can even install Windows PE on a computer's hard disk so that the next time the computer starts, it logs on to the network, installs Windows, and then deploys an image of that hard disk. The sections following this one describe how to create each of these three scenarios.

> **More Info**   Notice the entry for 64-bit Windows in Table 16-2. You can create a 64-bit version of Windows PE from 64-bit Windows XP. The steps for creating this version of Windows PE are only slightly different from creating the 32-bit version, and they're well documented in the "Windows Preinstallation Environment User's Guide," which you find on the Windows PE CD in the file Winpe.chm.

Table 16-2   Starting Windows PE

	Removable Media (CDs)	RIS	Non-Removable Media (Hard Disks)
Disconnected PCs	Yes	No	Yes
Networked PCs	Not recommended	Yes	Not recommended
Active Directory	Not required	Required by RIS	Not required
64-bit Windows	Yes	No	Yes
Third-Party Tools	Not required	Not required	Useful

CD-Based Installation

When you build a custom Windows PE image (which you learned about in the section "Customizing Windows PE," earlier in this chapter), the result is an ISO image that you can burn to a CD using most of the popular CD-burning programs, such as Ahead Nero Burning ROM (*http://www.nero.com*). However, you might want to create an ISO image after customizing Windows PE further. In the folder that contains the Windows PE customization tools, Winpe, run the command **oscdimg.exe −n −b etfsboot.com** *winpedestdir imagename*. *Winpedestdir* is the path of the customized version of Windows PE (the folder containing the I386 folder, Win51, Win51iP, Win51ip.sp1, and Winbom.ini). *Imagename* is the path and file name of the ISO image file that you want to create.

Customizing Product CDs

You can use Oscdimg.exe to create customized CD's from the original Windows XP or Windows Server 2003 CDs without Windows PE, too. For example, you can replace the file Winnt.sif in the product CDs' I386 folder to customize installation. Here's an example using Windows:

1. Copy a Windows CD to a folder on your hard disk. For example, copy the entire CD to C:\Winxp.

2. Replace Winnt.sif in the I386 folder with a customized version that installs Windows per your requirements.

3. In the Winpe folder, run the command **oscdimg.exe -n −b etfsboot.com −l** *Label Path Isopath*. The placeholder *Label* is the volume label of the original Windows CD. The placeholder *Path* is the path of the folder containing the copy of the Windows CD (C:\Winxp in step 1). The placeholder *Isopath* is the path and file name of the ISO image you want to create.

4. Burn the ISO image you created in step 3 to a new CD.

You can boot the computer using the customized Windows product CD, and Windows Setup will use your customized Winnt.sif to install the operating system.

RIS-Based Installation

To speed the deployment process, you can start the target computer with Windows PE by using RIS. The benefit of starting Windows PE from the network is that you don't need to start the computer manually by using a bootable CD. This method is available for the 32-bit versions of Windows PE, but not for the 64-bit version.

To install a Windows PE image on a RIS server, you need either a Windows product CD or an existing Windows CD–based image. The Windows product CD or existing Windows CD–based image must be the same build number as Windows PE. (Otherwise, Windows PE might not start properly.) You also need a properly configured RIS server, either Windows 2000 Service Pack 2 (SP2) or Windows Server 2003.

Finally, the client computer must support booting with PXE, or the RIS boot disk must support the NIC installed in the computer. With these requirements met, the following steps show how to install a Windows PE image on a RIS server:

1. Do one of the following:

   ❑ Copy an existing Windows CD-based image.

   ❑ Create a new CD-based image using a Windows product CD.

2. Copy the I386 folder from the CD or the folder containing the Windows PE files over the I386 folder of the Windows CD–based image you created in step 1. If Windows Explorer prompts you to overwrite folders or files, click Yes.

3. If your Windows PE files don't include a Winbom.ini file in %SystemRoot%\ System32, copy Winbom.ini from the root folder containing the files to the RIS image's I386\System32 folder.

   If Factory doesn't find a Winbom.ini file that contains the setting `Restart=No` in the `[winpe]` section, it prompts the user to restart the computer, shut down the computer, or quit. The default Winbom.ini file that comes with Windows PE contains this setting, but you must copy the file to the image's System32 folder for Factory to find it when starting Windows PE from RIS.

4. In the CD-based image's Templates folder, open Ristndrd.sif in a text editor. Then, add the option `/minint` to the line that begins with `OSLoadOptions`.

   Also change the description and help in the `[OSChooser]` section.

5. Start the RIS client and choose the operating system image that you created in the first step.

   This starts Windows PE from the network.

Disk-Based Installation

You can install a customized version of Windows PE on a hard disk, which is useful for preinstalling an operating system or creating a hard disk–based recovery solution, particularly for laptop computers. For example, you can install Windows PE on a small partition and the operating system on another partition. This configuration supports disaster-recovery scenarios by preventing the need for boot media to start the PC and source files for reinstalling the operating system, recovering data from the computer, or repairing the configuration. Here are the steps for installing Windows PE on a hard disk:

1. Boot the destination computer into Windows PE using a Windows PE CD.

2. Partition and format the computer's hard disk.

   You can use Diskpart to quickly partition the disk and then use Format to format it. Don't forget to mark the disk as active.

3. On the active hard disk, create the directory C:\Minint and then copy the contents of the Windows PE CD's I386 folder to C:\Minint.

   For example, use the command **xcopy d:\i386 c:\minint /s**.

4. Copy Ntdetect.com from the CD to the root of the hard disk.

5. Copy C:\Minint\setupldr.bin to C:\ntldr.

6. Restart the computer; it starts using Windows PE.

Automating Installations

So far in this chapter, you've learned how to customize Windows PE. You can add optional components such as WSH and HTA. You can add your own batch scripts and utilities to it. After you complete your customizations, you can create a new CD or copy them to a RIS server. With a customized Windows PE CD, you can start each target computer in fine detail but you still have to manually configure disks, start Windows Setup, and so on. The power of Windows PE is its automation features. You can script most of the installation tasks that you might need to perform. And when you do need to collect information from the user or technician, you can use HTA.

> **More Info**   For more information about creating HTAs, see HTML Goodies at *http://www.htmlgoodies.com/beyond/hta.html* and Microsoft MSDN at *http://msdn.microsoft.com/workshop/author/hta/hta_node_entry.asp*. For more information about customizing Windows PE, see *http://www.microsoft.com/whdc/system/winpreinst/WindowsPE_tech.mspx*.

Chapter 17

Deploying Office 2003 Settings

Microsoft Office 2003 Editions is extremely flexible and highly customizable. Users can customize Office 2003 Editions through its settings, custom templates, tools, and much more. For example, an accounting department can create custom templates for expense reports, and IT professionals can create custom dictionaries that contain computer terminology and product names. Users can customize everything from how their toolbars look to the file formats for saving documents. Almost all these settings are in the registry.

IT professionals can customize user settings and distribute standard Office 2003 Editions configurations to all users. First install Office 2003 Editions on a sample computer, and then customize the toolbars, settings, templates, dictionaries, and any other options for each program. Run the Microsoft Office 2003 Profile Wizard to create an Office Profile Settings (OPS) file that contains all these settings. If you add the OPS file to a transform (MST) file, your customized settings are included when you install Office 2003 Editions on client computers. The Microsoft Office 2003 Custom Installation Wizard is the tool that you use to build MST files. It enables you to customize settings directly in the MST file without using an OPS file. You can also use the Custom Installation Wizard to set user options and to edit registry entries.

The Profile Wizard and the Custom Installation Wizard are part of the *Microsoft Office 2003 Editions Resource Kit*, which you can find in the ORK folder on any Office 2003 Editions Enterprise Edition CD. You can also download it from *http://www.microsoft.com/office/ork*. Because the resource kit's tools are covered comprehensively in the resource kit book, I won't go into detail about them. Instead, I'll focus on how to use these tools to deploy user settings, which are essentially registry settings. And if you're interested in learning about specific Office 2003 Editions settings, including Office 2003 Editions policies and where to find them in the registry, see Part IV, "Appendixes."

 Tip Most of the tools in the *Microsoft Office 2003 Editions Resource Kit* are useful for more than just deploying Office 2003 Editions. For example, you can use the Profile Wizard to deploy settings for any program, and with the Custom Installation Wizard, you can customize other Microsoft Windows Installer–based applications. You can even use the Profile Wizard to customize Windows XP or Windows Server 2003 (Windows) if you're prone to frequent reinstallation.

Profile Wizard

The Profile Wizard saves and restores Office 2003 Editions user settings, which are in the Office 2003 Editions portion of users' profiles. (See Chapter 12, "Deploying User Profiles.") When you run the Profile Wizard to save a user profile, you create an OPS file that you can use later to restore those settings. The *Microsoft Office 2003 Editions Resource Kit* installs the Profile Wizard on the Start menu. Click Start, All Programs, Microsoft Office, Microsoft Office Tools, Microsoft Office 2003 Resource Kit, and then click Profile Wizard. The program file Proflwiz.exe is in C:\Program Files\ORK-Tools\ORK11\Tools\Profile Wizard.

By default, the Profile Wizard uses the file OPW11adm.ini to decide which settings and files to include in an OPS file. This file is essentially a big list of settings and files. This file also indicates which settings and files will be purposely excluded from an OPS file. The default OPW11adm.ini file is for Office 2003 Editions; it nabs most Office 2003 Editions settings from the registry and takes files from the user profile folder. It excludes settings that shouldn't be deployed, like user names, lists of recently used files, and so on. You can use the Profile Wizard with the default OPW11adm.ini file to capture and apply Office 2003 Editions settings, or you can customize it to capture and deploy any settings, including settings for applications other than Office 2003 Editions.

The following sections describe how to capture, apply, and customize settings with the Profile Wizard. The following list describes the Profile Wizard's command-line options:

```
proflwiz.exe [/a] [/u] [/q] [/e] [/p] [/f] [/i filename.ini] /s filename.ops |
/r filename.ops
```

/a	Starts the wizard in administrator mode (Profile Wizard). Uses the OPW11adm.ini file by default. This is the default setting if neither /a nor /u is on the command line.
/u	Starts the wizard in user mode (The Save My Settings Wizard). Proflwiz.exe uses the OPW11usr.ini file if /u is present on the command line. OPW11usr.ini is available only with Office 2003 Editions and not with the *Microsoft Office 2003 Editions Resource Kit.*
/q	Runs the wizard in quiet mode and displays no progress indicators or error messages. Use this option with either the /s option or the /r option but not with the /p or the /e options. You do not need to specify a mode of operation (/a or /u) when using the quiet mode option.
/e	Displays only error messages and no progress indicators while the wizard is running. Use this option with either the /s or the /r option but not with the /q option.
/p	Displays only progress indicators and no error messages while the wizard is running. Use this option with either the /s or the /r option, but not with the /q option.
/f	Displays a completion message at the end of the restore or the save process. Use this option with either the /s or the /r option but not with the /q option. The options /e, /p, and /f are additive. Including /e and /f in the command line displays only error messages and finish messages.
/i filename.ini	Specifies the INI file to use. Instructs the Profile Wizard not to use the default INI file (OPW11adm.ini or OPW11usr.ini). Instead, it uses the INI file *filename*.ini to determine which settings and files to store in the OPS file.
/s filename.ops	Saves user configuration settings from the current computer to the OPS file *filename*.ops. The wizard displays progress indicators and error messages while it is running.
/r *filename*.ops	Restores the application settings from the specified OPS file *filename*.ops to the computer. The wizard displays progress indicators and error messages while it is running.

Note   The Save My Settings Wizard in Office 2003 Editions is based on the Profile Wizard. It uses an INI file that saves and restores users' settings. That INI file is OPW11usr.ini. The OPS file that it creates includes personal settings and information, though, which makes it inappropriate for deployment to other users.

Customizing the Wizard

You do not need to edit the Profile Wizard's INI file to include or exclude entire Office 2003 Editions applications in your OPS file. On the wizard's Save Or Restore Settings page, select the check boxes next to the applications for which you want to save settings. If a setting that you want to capture from Office 2003 Editions (or another program) isn't in OPW11adm.ini, you must customize OPW11adm.ini or build a new INI file to capture it in an OPS file.

Edit OPW11adm.ini in Notepad or another text editor, and then add or delete references to settings and files that you want to include or exclude. You can also run the Profile Wizard from the command line with no loss in functionality. Every option available in the wizard has a corresponding command-line switch. Listing 17-1 shows the default OPW11adm.ini file. You'll notice that it contains thorough instructions on how to customize the file. If you're capturing settings for Office 2003 Editions, start with this file. If you're capturing user settings for Windows or for another application, consider creating a new INI file using OPW11adm.ini as a reference. Make sure that your new INI file contains the [Header] section shown in Listing 17-1; otherwise, the Profile Wizard won't let you save the settings defined in your INI file to an OPS file. Here's an overview of what each section contains:

- **[IncludeFolderTrees].**   List the folder trees that you want to include in the OPS file. The Profile Wizard captures all the subfolders and files in each tree. All entries in this section must begin with one of the following tokens, each of which represents a subfolder in the user's profile folder: <AppData>, <Desktop>, <Favorites>, <NetHood>, <Personal>, <PrintHood>, <ProgramsMenu>, <Recent-Files>, <SendTo>, <StartMenu>, <StartupMenu>, <UserProfile>.

- **[IncludeIndividualFolders].**   List individual folders that you want to include in the OPS file; the format is the same as that of [IncludeFolderTrees].

- **[IncludeIndividualFiles].**   List individual files that you want to include in the OPS file. The format is the same as that of [IncludeFolderTrees].

- **[ExcludeFiles].**   List files that you don't want to include in the OPS file. The format is the same as that of [IncludeFolderTrees] except that you can use wildcards to specify all files of a certain type.

- **[FolderTreesToRemoveToResetToDefaults].**   List the folder trees that you want the Profile Wizard to remove prior to restoring the settings in the OPS file. This essentially resets the application. The format is the same as that of [IncludeFolderTrees].

- **[IndividualFilesToRemoveToResetToDefaults].**   List individual files that you want the Profile Wizard to remove prior to restoring the settings in the OPS file. The format is the same as that of [IncludeFolderTrees].

- **[ExcludeFilesToRemoveToResetToDefaults].**   List the individual files that you *don't* want the Profile Wizard to remove, regardless of where they exist in the profile folder. This enables you to keep certain files within folders that you're removing through **[FolderTreesToRemoveToResetToDefaults]**. You can use a wildcard only as the first character of a file name, and you cannot specify a path: *.doc.

- **[IncludeRegistryTrees].**   List the registry branches that you want to include in the OPS file. The Profile Wizard captures all the subkeys and values in each branch. Include one branch per line.

- **[IncludeIndividualRegistryKeys].**   List individual registry keys that you want to include in the OPS file.

- **[IncludeIndividualRegistryValues].**   List individual registry values that you want to include in the OPS files. For the default value, use a trailing backslash: HKCU\Software\. Otherwise, include the value name in each line: HKCU \Software\Value.

- **[ExcludeRegistryTrees].**   List the registry branches that you want to exclude from the OPS file.

- **[ExcludeIndividualRegistryKeys].**   List the individual registry keys that you want to exclude from the OPS file.

- **[ExcludeIndividualRegistryValues].**   List the individual values that you want to exclude from the OPS file. The format is the same as that of **[Include-IndividualRegistryValues]**.

- **[RegistryTreesToRemoveToResetToDefaults].**   List the registry branches you want the Profile Wizard to remove prior to applying the OPS file.

- **[IndividualRegistryValuesToRemoveToResetToDefaults].**   List individual values that you want the Profile Wizard to remove prior to applying the OPS file. The format is the same as that of **[IncludeIndividualRegistryValues]**.

- **[RegistryTreesToExcludeToResetToDefaults].**   List the individual registry branches that you *don't* want the Profile Wizard to remove when applying an OPS file. You cannot use this section if you're embedding the OPS file in an MST file. This overwrites **[RegistryTreesToRemoveToResetToDefaults]**.

- **[RegistryKeysToExcludeToResetToDefaults].**   List the individual registry keys that you *don't* want the Profile Wizard to remove when applying the OPS file. You cannot use this section if you're embedding the OPS file in an MST file. This overwrites **[RegistryTreesToRemoveToResetToDefaults]**.

- **[RegistryValuesToExcludeToResetToDefaults].**   List the individual values that you *don't* want the Profile Wizard to remove when applying the OPS file. You cannot use this section if you're embedding the OPS file in an MST file. This overwrites **[RegistryTreesToRemoveToResetToDefaults]**.

Listing 17-1   OPW11adm.ini

```
# Microsoft Office Save My Settings/Profile Wizard INI file

# Edit this file to change which files and registry keys are included into
# the OPS file, and/or to change what gets deleted when using the
# 'Reset to defaults before restoring settings' option.

# Syntax is documented in each section.
# All include and exclude strings are case insensitive.
# Comments are denoted with # at the beginning of the line.

# At the end of a line is a '#' followed by one or more of the following
# possible terminal symbols:
#   word, xl, access, ppt, ol, pub, fp, inf, visio, project, onenote, ic, common, al
l
# Terminal symbols indicate which applications the line of settings belongs to.
#   "all"     indicates settings to be saved for any application.
#   "common"  indicates settings that are common among all applications.


[Header]
Version = 11.0
Product = Microsoft Office 11.0


# *************************** File/Folder Sections ******************************


[IncludeFolderTrees]
# List folder trees to be included into the OPS file.
# Syntax is one folder per line; no trailing backslash.
# Includes all subfolders in specified tree.
# Wildcards are not supported.
# Entries must begin with one of the following Folder tokens:
#   <AppData>, <Desktop>, <Favorites>, <NetHood>, <Personal>,
#   <PrintHood>, <ProgramsMenu>, <RecentFiles>, <SendTo>,
#   <StartMenu>, <StartupMenu>, <UserProfile>.
# Subfolder tokens of format <SubFolder_$$$$> can be embedded in lines
#   and are replaced at SAVE time by the registry data found in the $$$$
#   value of HKCU\Software\Microsoft\Office\11.0\Common\General.
<AppData>\Microsoft\<SubFolder_AddIns>                      # xl word
<AppData>\Microsoft\ClipGallery                             # ppt
<AppData>\Microsoft\Excel                                   # xl
<AppData>\Microsoft\FrontPage                               # fp
<AppData>\Microsoft\Graph                                   # all
<AppData>\Microsoft\Office                                  # common
<AppData>\Microsoft\Outlook                                 # ol
<AppData>\Microsoft\PowerPoint                              # ppt
<AppData>\Microsoft\InfoPath                                # inf
<AppData>\Microsoft\OneNote                                 # onenote
<AppData>\Microsoft\InterConnect                            # ic
<AppData>\Microsoft\<SubFolder_Proof>                       # common all
<AppData>\Microsoft\<SubFolder_Queries>                     # xl access
<AppData>\Microsoft\<SubFolder_Signatures>                  # ol
<AppData>\Microsoft\<SubFolder_Stationery>                  # ol
<AppData>\Microsoft\<SubFolder_Templates>                   # word ppt xl
<AppData>\Microsoft\<SubFolder_Themes>                      # ppt
<AppData>\Microsoft\Word                                    # word
```

```
# Use the following two lines for Outlook 98:
#    <AppData>\Microsoft\Shared\<SubFolder_Signatures>       # ol
#    <AppData>\Microsoft\Shared\<SubFolder_Stationery>       # ol
# Use the following line for Web Server Locations:
#    <NetHood>                                                # fp


[IncludeIndividualFolders]
# List individual folders to be included into the OPS file.
# Syntax same as [IncludeFolderTrees] but does not include subfolders.
# Wildcards are not supported.

[IncludeIndividualFiles]
# List individual files to be included into the OPS file.
# Syntax is one path\filename per line.
# Entries must begin with one of the Folder tokens listed under
#    [IncludeFolderTrees].
# Wildcards are not supported.
#
# Example for including Normal.dot:
#    <AppData>\Microsoft\<SubFolder_Templates>\Normal.dot   # word

[ExcludeFiles]
# List files to not include into the OPS file.
# Syntax is one filename or path\filename per line.
# Folder-token (e.g. <AppData>) is optional.
# Path relative to folder-token is optional.
# Wildcards are supported in the filename.
# Wildcards are not supported in the path.
#
# Examples for excluding Normal.dot:
#    Normal.dot
#    Normal.*
#    Norm??.dot
#    <AppData>\Microsoft\<SubFolder_Templates>\Normal.dot
*.OST
*.PAB
*.PST
*.TMP
*.RWZ
*.NICK
*.NK2
EXTEND.DAT
OutlPrnt
<AppData>\Microsoft\Outlook\*.FAV
<AppData>\Microsoft\Word\*.ASD
<AppData>\Microsoft\Word\*.WBK

[FolderTreesToRemoveToResetToDefaults]
# List folder trees to be deleted prior to restoring data from OPS file.
# Syntax is same as [IncludeFolderTrees].
# Wildcards are not supported.
# Every file in the folder and all subfolders will be deleted.
# Use this section with caution; it might delete more than you intend.
# Terminal Symbols are ignored and treated as "all".
```

```
<AppData>\Microsoft\Office\Shortcut Bar
<AppData>\Microsoft\FrontPage

[IndividualFilesToRemoveToResetToDefaults]
# List files to be deleted prior to restoring data from OPS file.
# Syntax is one path\filename per line.
# Specify all subfolders explicitly.
# Entries must begin with one of the Folder tokens listed under
#    [IncludeFolderTrees].
# Wildcards are supported in the filename.
# Wildcards are not supported in the path.
# Terminal Symbols are ignored and treated as "all".
<AppData>\Microsoft\<SubFolder_AddIns>\*.*
<AppData>\Microsoft\ClipGallery\*.*
<AppData>\Microsoft\Excel\*.*
<AppData>\Microsoft\InfoPath\*.*
<AppData>\Microsoft\OneNote\*.*
<AppData>\Microsoft\Excel\<SubFolder_Xlstart>\*.*
<AppData>\Microsoft\Graph\*.*
<AppData>\Microsoft\Office\*.*
<AppData>\Microsoft\Office\<SubFolder_Actors>\*.*
#    <AppData>\Microsoft\Office\<SubFolder_RecentFiles>\*.*
<AppData>\Microsoft\PowerPoint\*.*
<AppData>\Microsoft\<SubFolder_Proof>\*.*
<AppData>\Microsoft\<SubFolder_Queries>\*.*
<AppData>\Microsoft\<SubFolder_Signatures>\*.*
<AppData>\Microsoft\<SubFolder_Stationery>\*.*
<AppData>\Microsoft\<SubFolder_Templates>\*.*
<AppData>\Microsoft\<SubFolder_Themes>\*.*
<AppData>\Microsoft\Word\*.*
<AppData>\Microsoft\Word\<SubFolder_Startup>\*.*

[ExcludeFilesToRemoveToResetToDefaults]
# List of files NOT to be removed regardless of where they live when
#    resetting to defaults prior to restoring data from OPS file.
#
# Syntax is one filename per line; no preceeding path.
# Wildcards "*" and "?" are supported as the first character only.
# The following are allowed:*.DIC
#    NORMAL.DOC
#    ?FOO.FIL
#    *FILE.FOO
#    *.DIC
# Terminal Symbols are ignored and treated as "all".
# Your files must not be preceeded by a path.
*.PST
*.DIC
*.OST

# ***************************** Registry Sections *****************************

[SubstituteEnvironmentVariables]
# List environment variables to substitute in registry values
#    that take the data type REG_EXPAND_SZ.
# Syntax is one environment variable per line.
```

```
# Wildcards are not supported.
%USERPROFILE%
%USERNAME%

[IncludeRegistryTrees]
# List registry trees to include.
# All values and subkeys within the specified tree are included.
# Syntax is one key per line.
# Wildcards are not supported.
HKCU\Software\Microsoft\Office\11.0\Access            # access
HKCU\Software\Microsoft\Office\11.0\Common            # common
HKCU\Software\Microsoft\Office\11.0\Excel             # xl
HKCU\Software\Microsoft\Office\11.0\Graph             # all
HKCU\Software\Microsoft\Office\11.0\MS Project        # all
HKCU\Software\Microsoft\Office\11.0\NetFolder         # common
HKCU\Software\Microsoft\Office\11.0\Osa               # common
HKCU\Software\Microsoft\Office\11.0\Outlook           # ol
HKCU\Software\Microsoft\Office\11.0\PowerPoint        # ppt
HKCU\Software\Microsoft\Office\11.0\Shortcut Bar      # common
HKCU\Software\Microsoft\Office\11.0\Web Server        # fp
HKCU\Software\Microsoft\Office\11.0\Word              # word
HKCU\Software\Microsoft\Office\11.0\Publisher         # pub
HKCU\Software\Microsoft\Office\11.0\ClipGallery       # common
HKCU\Software\Microsoft\Office\11.0\InfoPath          # inf
HKCU\Software\Microsoft\Office\11.0\OneNote           # onenote
HKCU\Software\Microsoft\Office\11.0\InterConnect      # ic
HKCU\Software\Microsoft\Office\11.0\Visio             # visio
HKCU\Software\Microsoft\Visio                         # visio
HKCU\Software\Microsoft\Office\11.0\MS Project        # project
HKCU\Software\Microsoft\Office\Access                 # access
HKCU\Software\Microsoft\Office\Common                 # common
HKCU\Software\Microsoft\Office\Excel                  # xl
HKCU\Software\Microsoft\Office\Outlook                # ol
HKCU\Software\Microsoft\Office\PowerPoint             # ppt
HKCU\Software\Microsoft\Office\Word                   # word
HKCU\Software\Microsoft\FrontPage                     # fp
HKCU\Software\Microsoft\Shared Tools\Font Mapping     # all
HKCU\Software\Microsoft\Shared Tools\Proofing Tools   # all
HKCU\Software\Microsoft\Shared Tools\Outlook\Journaling  # ol
HKCU\Software\Microsoft\VBA\Office                    # all
HKCU\ControlPanel\International\NumShape              # common
HKCU\ControlPanel\International\Calendars\TwoDigitYearMax  # common
HKCU\AppEvents\Schemes\Apps\Office97                  # ol

[IncludeIndividualRegistryKeys]
# List individual registry keys to include.
# Syntax is same as [IncludeRegistryTrees] but includes only values
#   in the specified key, not subkeys.
# Wildcards are not supported.
HKCU\Software\Microsoft\Exchange\Client\Options        # ol
HKCU\Software\Microsoft\Office\11.0\Common\LanguageResources  # common
HKCU\Software\Microsoft\VBA\Trusted                    # common

[IncludeIndividualRegistryValues]
# List individual registry values to include.
# Same as [IncludeIndividualRegistryKeys] but includes only specific named
```

```
#    value, not subkeys.
# Syntax is key\valuename.
# Wildcards are not supported.
# Name can be blank to denote the default value (use a trailing backslash).

[ExcludeRegistryTrees]
# List registry trees to exclude.
# All values and subkeys within the specified tree are excluded.
# Syntax is one key per line.
# Wildcards are not supported.
HKCU\Software\Microsoft\Office\11.0\Common\Migration              # all

[ExcludeIndividualRegistryKeys]
# List individual registry keys to exclude.
# Syntax is same as [ExcludeRegistryTrees] but excludes only values
#    in the specified key, not subkeys.
# Wildcards are not supported.
HKCU\Software\Microsoft\Office\11.0\PowerPoint\Tips               # all
HKCU\Software\Microsoft\Office\11.0\Common\UserInfo               # all
HKCU\Software\Microsoft\Office\11.0\Excel\Recent Files            # all
HKCU\Software\Microsoft\Office\11.0\PowerPoint\Recent File List   # all
HKCU\Software\Microsoft\Office\Outlook\OMI Account Manager\Accounts  # all
HKCU\Software\Microsoft\FrontPage\Explorer\FrontPage Explorer\Recent File List  # al
l
HKCU\Software\Microsoft\FrontPage\Explorer\FrontPage Explorer\Recent Page List  # al
l
HKCU\Software\Microsoft\FrontPage\Explorer\FrontPage Explorer\Recent Web List   # al
l
HKCU\Software\Microsoft\Office\11.0\PhotoDraw\Recent File List                  # al
l
HKCU\Software\Microsoft\Office\11.0\Common\Licensing              # all

[ExcludeIndividualRegistryValues]
# List individual registry values to exclude.
# Same as [ExcludeIndividualRegistryKeys] but excludes only specific named
#    value, not subkeys.
# Syntax is key\valuename.
# Wildcards are not supported.
# Name can be blank to denote the default value (use a trailing backslash).
HKCU\Software\Microsoft\Office\11.0\Access\MRU1
HKCU\Software\Microsoft\Office\11.0\Access\MRUFlags1
HKCU\Software\Microsoft\Office\11.0\Access\MRU2
HKCU\Software\Microsoft\Office\11.0\Access\MRUFlags2
HKCU\Software\Microsoft\Office\11.0\Access\MRU3
HKCU\Software\Microsoft\Office\11.0\Access\MRUFlags3
HKCU\Software\Microsoft\Office\11.0\Access\MRU4
HKCU\Software\Microsoft\Office\11.0\Access\MRUFlags4
HKCU\Software\Microsoft\Office\11.0\Access\MRU5
HKCU\Software\Microsoft\Office\11.0\Access\MRUFlags5
HKCU\Software\Microsoft\Office\11.0\Access\MRU6
HKCU\Software\Microsoft\Office\11.0\Access\MRUFlags6
HKCU\Software\Microsoft\Office\11.0\Access\MRU7
HKCU\Software\Microsoft\Office\11.0\Access\MRUFlags7
HKCU\Software\Microsoft\Office\11.0\Access\MRU8
HKCU\Software\Microsoft\Office\11.0\Access\MRUFlags8
```

```
HKCU\Software\Microsoft\Office\11.0\Access\MRU9
HKCU\Software\Microsoft\Office\11.0\Access\MRUFlags9
HKCU\Software\Microsoft\Office\11.0\Access\Settings\Prefs Migrated
HKCU\Software\Microsoft\Office\11.0\Access\UserData
HKCU\Software\Microsoft\Office\11.0\Common\General\FirstRun
HKCU\Software\Microsoft\Office\11.0\Common\UserData
HKCU\Software\Microsoft\Office\11.0\Excel\Options\FirstRun
HKCU\Software\Microsoft\Office\11.0\Excel\Options\TipShown
HKCU\Software\Microsoft\Office\11.0\Excel\UserData
HKCU\Software\Microsoft\Office\11.0\Outlook\Setup\First-Run
HKCU\Software\Microsoft\Office\11.0\Outlook\Setup\MailSupport
HKCU\Software\Microsoft\Office\11.0\Outlook\UserData
HKCU\Software\Microsoft\office\11.0\Outlook\Journal\Item Log File
HKCU\Software\Microsoft\office\11.0\Outlook\Journal\Outlook Item Log File
HKCU\Software\Microsoft\Office\11.0\PowerPoint\First Run\FirstRun
HKCU\Software\Microsoft\Office\11.0\PowerPoint\UserData
HKCU\Software\Microsoft\Office\11.0\Word\Options\FirstRun
HKCU\Software\Microsoft\Office\11.0\Word\Options\ReplyMessageComment
HKCU\Software\Microsoft\Office\11.0\Word\UserData
HKCU\Software\Microsoft\Office\11.0\Outlook\Preferences\AnnotationText
HKCU\Software\Microsoft\Office\11.0\Shortcut Bar\LocalPath
HKCU\Software\Microsoft\office\11.0\Word\Options\PROGRAMDIR
HKCU\Software\Microsoft\Office\Common\Assistant\AsstFile
HKCU\Software\Microsoft\Office\Common\Assistant\CurrAsstFile
HKCU\Software\Microsoft\Office\11.0\Common\General\InstalledonWin2K
HKCU\Software\Microsoft\Office\11.0\Common\General\InstalledonWinME
HKCU\Software\Microsoft\Office\11.0\Publisher\FirstRun
HKCU\Software\Microsoft\Office\11.0\InfoPath\FirstBoot
HKCU\Software\Microsoft\Office\11.0\OneNote\FirstBoot
HKCU\Software\Microsoft\Office\11.0\InterConnect\General\FirstRun
HKCU\Software\Microsoft\Office\11.0\InterConnect\Bizcard\OfficeBizcardDesign
HKCU\Software\Microsoft\Office\11.0\InterConnect\Bizcard\HomeBizcardDesign
HKCU\Software\Microsoft\Office\11.0\InterConnect\Bizcard\UtilityBizcardDesign
HKCU\Software\Microsoft\Office\11.0\InterConnect\Bizcard\FakeBizcardDesign
HKCU\Software\Microsoft\Office\11.0\InterConnect\Bizcard\ActiveDigitalSignature

[RegistryTreesToRemoveToResetToDefaults]
# List registry trees to be removed prior to writing custom values.
# All values and subkeys within the specified tree will be removed.
# wildcards are not supported.
# Terminal Symbols are ignored and treated as "all".
HKCU\Software\Microsoft\Office\11.0
HKCU\Software\Microsoft\Office\Access
HKCU\Software\Microsoft\Office\Common
HKCU\Software\Microsoft\Office\Excel
HKCU\Software\Microsoft\Office\Outlook
HKCU\Software\Microsoft\Office\PowerPoint
HKCU\Software\Microsoft\Office\Word
HKCU\Software\Microsoft\Visio
HKCU\Software\Microsoft\FrontPage
HKCU\Software\Microsoft\Shared Tools\Proofing Tools
HKCU\Software\Microsoft\VBA\Office
#   HKCU\Software\Microsoft\Windows NT\CurrentVersion\Windows Messaging Subsystem\Pr
ofiles
```

```
HKCU\Software\Microsoft\VBA\Trusted
```

```
[IndividualRegistryValuesToRemoveToResetToDefaults]
# List individual registry values to be removed prior to writing custom values.
# Syntax is key\valuename.
# Wildcards are not supported.
# Valuename can be blank to denote the default value (use a trailing backslash).
# Terminal Symbols are ignored and treated as "all".

[RegistryTreesToExcludeToResetToDefaults]
# List individual registry trees that will not be removed when resetting to defaults
.
# All values and subkeys within the specified tree will be ignored.
# Wildcards are not supported.
# Terminal symbols are ignored and treated as "all".
# This section cannot be used if the OPS file is used for custom setup in a transfor
m.

[RegistryKeysToExcludeToResetToDefaults]
# List individual registry keys that will not be removed when resetting to defaults.
# All values within the specified tree will be ignored.
# Wildcards are not supported.
# Terminal symbols are ignored and treated as "all".
# This section cannot be used if the OPS file is used for custom setup in a transfor
m.

[RegistryValuesToExcludeToResetToDefaults]
# List individual registry values that will not be removed when resetting to default
s.
# Wildcards are not supported.
# Only excludes only specific values, not subkeys.
# Terminal symbols are ignored and treated as "all".
# Syntax is key\valuename.
# Name can be blank to denote the default value (use a trailing backslash).
# This section cannot be used if the OPS file is used for custom setup in a transfor
m.
```

Capturing Settings

Before creating an OPS file, you must start each Office 2003 Editions program on a sample computer and set all the options that you want to capture in the file. The most interesting settings are on each program's Tools menu. To customize toolbars and menus, click Customize on the Tools menu. To configure user settings, click Options on the Tools menu. After you've customized each program, run the Profile Wizard to save the settings to an OPS file. If you're creating an OPS file based on an INI file that you created for a different application, customize that application, instead.

There are two ways to capture the settings defined in your INI file. First, you can run the Profile Wizard from the Start menu. This is interactive and sometimes a bit confusing if you're using this tool for an application other than Office 2003 Editions. You can also run the Profile Wizard from the command prompt window:

```
proflwiz /i filename.ini /s filename.ops /q
```

Replace *filename.ini* with the name of the INI file that you customized. If you're using the default OPW11adm.ini file, you don't need to specify an INI file. (Just make sure it's in the same folder as Proflwiz.exe.) Replace *filename*.ops with the name of the OPS file in which you want to store settings from the current profile. To save settings to an OPS file, perform the following steps:

1. Run the Profile Wizard, and then click Next.

2. On the Save Or Restore Settings page, shown in Figure 17-1, select the Save The Settings From This Machine option. Then, in the Settings File text box, type the name and path for the OPS file.

3. Select the check boxes next to each Office 2003 Editions program that you want to include in your OPS file. Clear the check boxes next to each program that you want to exclude. If you're using an OPS file that you've customized for another program, skip this step.

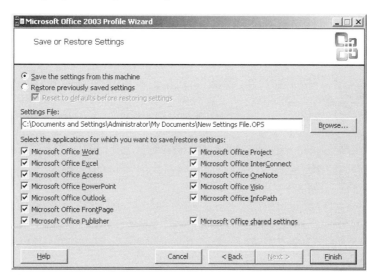

Figure 17-1 The Profile Wizard enables you to exclude settings for some Office 2003 Editions programs and to include settings for others. Clear the check boxes next to the settings that you want to exclude.

Deploying Settings

The primary purpose of OPS files is to deploy settings with Office 2003 Editions. However, they're more useful than that. You can also use them to restore a program's default configuration, as a help desk tool to deploy settings to users' desktops, and as a convenient way to configure a computer after installing a fresh copy of Windows and applications.

Just as there are many different ways to use OPS files, there are also different ways of deploying them. The most common method is embedding them in MST files that you create with the Custom Installation Wizard. You learn about this in the next section. If you want to apply settings outside the setup program in Office 2003 Editions, you must run the Profile Wizard separately, though. This is much more flexible than including OPS files in MST files is, because it enables you to deploy different settings to different groups of users. To restore the settings from an OPS file to a user's profile, run the following command while logged on to Windows as that user:

```
proflwiz /r filename.ops /q
```

Replace *filename*.ops with the name of the OPS file that you want to restore to the user's profile. The Profile Wizard must be available for users to run, so copy Proflwiz.exe from C:\Program Files\ORKTools\ORK11\Tools\Profile Wizard to a share that's available to all users, perhaps the Office 2003 Editions administrative installation.

Custom Installation Wizard

You use the Custom Installation Wizard to customize Office 2003 Editions. You can use it to configure everything from the Office 2003 Editions installation folder to the security settings. It's the one tool you'll always use when deploying Office 2003 Editions. The result of running the Custom Installation Wizard is a transform (MST) file. You associate this MST file with the Office 2003 Editions package file using the TRANSFORMS=*filename*.mst property or the MST1 setting in the Office 2003 Editions Setup.ini file, in the MST section.

> ## Order of Precedence
>
> Most of the Office 2003 Editions settings are in the registry. Office 2003 Editions has rules that determine which setting it uses if you define conflicting values for the same setting. Usually, the later in the process you apply a setting, the more precedence it has. Office 2003 Editions applies settings in the following order:
>
> - Settings in an OPS file included in the transform.
>
> - Settings on the Change Office User Settings, Specify Office Security Settings, and Outlook: Custom Default Settings pages of the Custom Installation Wizard.
>
> - Registry values specified in the transform.
>
> - Settings applied by running the Profile Wizard during installation.
>
> - Settings that migrate from a previous version of Office 2003 Editions.
>
> - Settings applied by using the Profile Wizard or the Custom Maintenance Wizard after installing Office 2003 Editions. This precedence assumes that users have already started each Office 2003 Editions application and that any migrated settings have already been applied.
>
> - Settings managed through policies.

Four of the Custom Installation Wizard's pages enable you to deploy settings with your MST file. You learn more about each page in the following sections: "Adding and Removing Registry Entries," "Customizing Default Application Settings," "Changing Office User Settings," and "Adding Installations and Running Programs."

Adding and Removing Registry Entries

Because most Office 2003 Editions settings are in the registry, you can customize them by adding and changing registry values within MST files. The setup program applies your settings when users install Office 2003 Editions. You can apply settings once per user by adding settings to HKCU, or you can apply settings once per computer by adding settings to HKLM. You can also add values to the registry that customize settings that aren't accessible through the Office 2003 Editions user interface and that the Profile Wizard doesn't capture in OPS files. For example, you can include settings for other programs. To add registry values to a transform, perform the following steps:

1. On the Add Registry Entry page, shown in Figure 17-2, click Add.

2. In the Root box, select the portion of the registry that you want to modify.

3. In the Data type box, select a data type for the new entry.

4. In the remaining boxes, type the full path for the registry value that you want to add, enter the value name and data, and click OK.

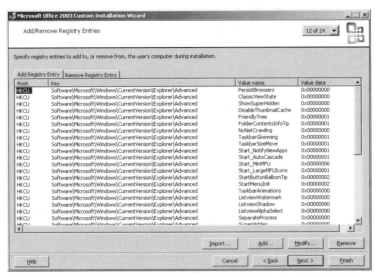

Figure 17-2   The Custom Installation Wizard is the primary tool that you use for customizing Office 2003 Editions.

Typing values on the Add Registry Entries page of the Custom Installation Wizard is an error-prone and tedious process. It's better to export the settings to a REG file and then import that REG file into your MST file. For more information about creating REG files, see Chapter 2, "Using Registry Editor," and Chapter 11, "Scripting Registry Changes." Of course, this assumes that the values that you want to add to the transform already exist in your computer's registry. If the values aren't already present, you can add them with the benefit of Registry Editor's user interface, and then export them to a REG file. To import a registry file to a transform, perform the following steps:

1. On the Custom Installation Wizard's Add Registry Entries page, click Import.

2. In the File Name text box, type the path and file name of the REG file, and then click Open.

    The Custom Installation Wizard adds the values from the REG file to the list on the Add Registry Entries page. If the wizard encounters an entry in the REG file that is a duplicate, and each version contains different value data, the wizard prompts you to select the entry that you want to keep. To remove any values that you don't want to keep, click the value, and then click Remove.

After Windows Installer finishes installing Office 2003 Editions, it copies the values that you added to the Add/ Remove Registry Entries screen to users' computers.

Options that you set by adding or modifying registry values overwrite duplicate values that you set on other pages of the Custom Installation Wizard, including the following options:

- Settings in an OPS file added to a transform
- Settings on the Change Office User Settings page
- Options on the Outlook: Customize Default Settings page
- Settings on the Specify Office Security Settings page

Customizing Default Application Settings

Adding an OPS file to an MST file is an easy way to deploy a bunch of settings throughout the organization. You learned how to create an OPS file earlier in this chapter. Now you need to learn how to embed that OPS file into your MST file. The problem to watch out for here is that any settings in your OPS file will have lower precedence than settings that you define elsewhere in your MST file. That means that settings in the Change Office User Settings page overwrite settings in your OPS file, for example, and so do settings defined on the Add Registry Entries page.

You embed an OPS file into your MST file on the Custom Installation Wizard's Customize Default Application Settings page. Select the Get Values From An Existing Settings Profile check box, and type the file name and path of the OPS file. The Custom Installation Wizard creates a transform that contains your OPS file and any other customizations that you have made.

 Note   Adding an OPS file to the MST file increases the size of the transform and requires you to re-create the MST file any time that you change the OPS file. You can store the OPS file on the network and run the Profile Wizard with your OPS file during the Office 2003 Editions installation, instead. See "Adding Installations and Running Programs," later in this chapter, for more information.

If an earlier version of Office is installed on a user's computer, Windows Installer migrates the previous version's settings to Office 2003 Editions the first time the user starts an Office 2003 Editions program. Users' migrated settings overwrite duplicate settings in an OPS file or MST file. On the Customize Default Application Settings page of the Custom Installation Wizard, shown in Figure 17-3, you can change this behavior. If you are not including an OPS file in the MST file, the wizard selects the Migrate User Settings check box by default. When users install Office 2003 Editions with your transform, Setup migrates settings from an earlier version of Office. If you add an OPS file to the transform, the wizard clears the Migrate User Settings check box and uses the values in your OPS file instead.

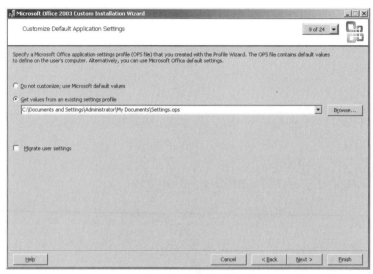

Figure 17-3   The Custom Installation Wizard clears the Migrate User Settings check box if you include an OPS file in your MST file.

If you add an OPS file to an MST file and select the Migrate User Settings check box, the settings from your OPS file are applied during the initial installation. The first time that a user runs one of the Office 2003 Editions programs, Windows Installer migrates settings from an earlier version of Office and overwrites any corresponding settings previously applied.

Changing Office User Settings

On the Custom Installation Wizard's Change Office User Settings page, you can set most of the options that you capture with the Profile Wizard. That includes any REG_DWORD and REG_SZ values, but not REG_BINARY values. This is useful for customizing a small number of settings or for changing a default configuration without rebuilding an OPS file that's already in the MST file.

To configure settings on the Change Office User Settings page, shown in Figure 17-4, click a category in the left pane. In the right pane, double-click the settings that you want to configure and to include in your MST file.

When users install Office 2003 Editions using your transform, the settings that you configure on the Change Office User Settings page apply to every user on that computer. However, Windows Installer applies only the settings that differ from existing default settings. Settings that you configure on this page of the wizard overwrite the same settings in the OPS file that you've included in the transform.

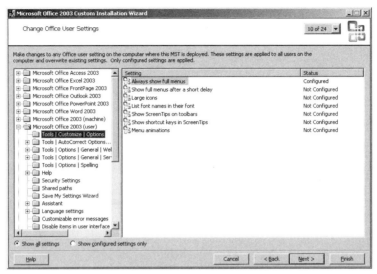

Figure 17-4 The Custom Installation Wizard's Change Office User Settings page is very similar to System Policy Editor when the Office 2003 Editions policy templates (ADM files) loaded.

> **Tip** The Change Office User Settings page uses templates for the settings it displays, just as Group Policy and system policies use templates. These templates are in C:\Program Files \ORKTools\ORK11\Tools\Shared and have the OPA file extension.

Adding Installations and Running Programs

The Custom Installation Wizard enables you to run programs during the Office 2003 Editions installation. You can run the Profile Wizard (Proflwiz.exe) to distribute custom settings at the end of the Office 2003 Editions installation, for example. You cannot use the Custom Installation Wizard's Add Installations And Run Programs page to install other Windows Installer packages, however. If Windows Installer starts installing a second package before it's finished installing the first, the entire process fails. To add the Profile Wizard to the Add Installations And Run Programs page, perform the following steps:

1. On the Add Installations And Run Programs page, click Add.

2. In the Target text box, type the path and file name of Profile Wizard, which is typically **C:\Program Files\ORKTools\ORK11\Tools\Profile Wizard \Proflwiz.exe**.

3. To apply the OPS file to the user's computer, in the Arguments text box, add command-line options which are usually **/r** filename.ops /q.

4. Do either of the following, as shown in Figure 17-5:

   ❑ To apply your settings the first time that a user logs on, click Run This Program Once Per Machine.

   ❑ To apply your default settings to every user on that computer, click Run This Program Once Per User. This option requires an active network connection to the network the first time that a user logs on to the computer.

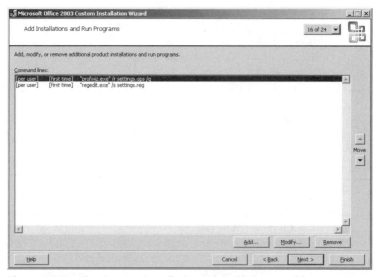

Figure 17-5   The Custom Installation Wizard lets you add programs to your installation by customizing the Office 2003 Editions Setup.ini file.

Custom Maintenance Wizard

You get one chance to apply an MST file to Office 2003 Editions, and that's during installation. If you want to change settings after installing Office 2003 Editions, you can use the Custom Maintenance Wizard to modify almost everything that you can configure in the Custom Installation Wizard, including user settings, security levels, Microsoft Outlook profile settings, and so on. The Custom Maintenance Wizard is one of the biggest improvements in the *Microsoft Office 2003 Editions Resource Kit* from the Office 2000 version.

The resource kit installs the Custom Maintenance Wizard on the Start menu. Click Start, All Programs, Microsoft Office, Microsoft Office Tools, Microsoft Office 2003 Resource Kit, and then click Custom Maintenance Wizard. The program file Maintwiz.exe is in C:\Program Files \ORKTools\ORK11\Tools\Custom Maintenance Wizard. The result of running the wizard is a Custom Maintenance Wizard (CMW) file that contains your configuration changes. For users to be able to apply the CMW files that the wizard creates, you must copy Maintwiz.exe and the CMW files to the Office 2003 Editions administrative share, which gives the Custom Maintenance Wizard elevated privileges by proxy. Alternatively, you can use the policy `Allow CMW files at any location to be applied`.

The user interfaces of both wizards are almost identical, so I won't describe how to use the Custom Maintenance Wizard here. You specify new settings using the Custom Maintenance Wizard's Change Office User Settings page, for instance. You can't use the Custom Maintenance Wizard to deploy a new OPS file, however, so you have to run the Profile Wizard separately. (Think logon script, and so on.) Chapter 18, "Fixing Common IT Problems," has recommendations for pushing command lines to users' computers.

Group and System Policy

Everything I've presented up until this point helps you deploy user settings for Office 2003 Editions and sometimes for other programs. If you want to manage settings, however, you must use Group Policy or system policies. Group Policy is a feature of Windows 2003 and of Active Directory. System policies is a legacy policy-based management technology that's still available if you haven't yet deployed Active Directory.

Chapter 7, "Using Registry-Based Policy," describes policies in detail. Part IV, "Appendixes," describes many of the policies in Office 2003 Editions and tells you where to find them in the registry. The *Microsoft Office 2003 Editions Resource Kit* provides policy templates (ADM files) that you can use with either Group Policy or system policies. It installs several ADM files in %SystemRoot%\Inf, such as OFFICE11.ADM, which contains policy settings that are common to all Office 2003 Editions programs.

> ## When to Use Which Tools
> Table 17-1 describes common Office 2003 Editions configuration scenarios and which methods and tools to use for each scenario.
>
> Table 17-1   **Office Configuration Scenarios**
>
> | Scenario | Method | Tool |
> |---|---|---|
> | Distribute a standard default Office 2003 Editions configuration. | Add an OPS file to a transform. | The Profile Wizard and the Custom Installation Wizard (Customize Default Application Settings page) |
> | Configure a few options, or overwrite the OPS file's settings without rebuilding it. | Add user settings to a transform. | The Custom Installation Wizard (Change Office User Settings page) |

Table 17-1   Office Configuration Scenarios

Scenario	Method	Tool
Set default security levels, and customize trusted sources list.	Specify security settings in a transform.	The Custom Installation Wizard (Specify Office Security Settings page)
Set migration and e-mail options for Outlook.	Specify Outlook settings in a transform.	The Custom Installation Wizard (Outlook: Custom Default Settings page)
Specify settings that are not captured in an OPS file.	Add registry values to a transform.	The Custom Installation Wizard (Add/Remove Registry Entries page)
Distribute a default Office 2003 Editions configuration but store one or more OPS files separately from the MST file.	Run the Profile Wizard during Setup.	The Profile Wizard and the Custom Installation Wizard (Add Installations and Run Programs page)
Preserve users' custom settings from a previous version instead of specifying new default settings.	Enable Setup to migrate settings from a previous version of Office.	Default behavior
Set unique options for Office 2003 Editions Multilingual User Interface Packs or for other chained packages.	Specify settings in the transform applied to the chained package.	The Custom Installation Wizard and Setup.ini
Distribute a default Office 2003 Editions configuration that overwrites individual users' settings.	Run the Profile Wizard as a stand-alone tool after installing Office 2003 Editions.	The Profile Wizard
Modify user settings after installing Office 2003 Editions.	Distribute a CMW file after installing Office 2003 Editions.	The Custom Maintenance Wizard
Prevent users from modifying settings.	Set policies	System Policy Editor or Windows 2003 Group Policy

Chapter 18

Fixing Common IT Problems

IT professionals often have to struggle with getting configurations just right before *and* after deployment. They try to play by the rules, but they sometimes must bend them to get things to work well in their environments. Bending the rules often means using the registry to achieve a goal that's not usually possible. Chapter 4, "Hacking the Registry," showed good examples of bending the rules. If you want to use Folder Redirection without Active Directory, for example, you have to hack the registry. This chapter follows that example with many more.

I could fill an entire book (I'd sure like to try) with the tricks that IT professionals use to get things to work the way they want them to. I've focused this chapter on the topics that I'm asked about most frequently, though. For example, I don't know many professionals who aren't frustrated with the Microsoft Outlook Express icons that keep popping up on users' desktops. This chapter shows you how to get rid of them. I also know that many professionals want to permanently remove some components from Microsoft Windows XP and Windows Server 2003 (Windows), and of course, this chapter shows you how to do that as well. Last, this chapter shows you how to run processes with elevated privileges, which is necessary if you want to distribute applications without the benefit of a software management infrastructure, and how to customize the logon process.

> **Note**   With the release of Windows XP Service Pack 2 (SP2), many IT professionals are looking for information about configuring Windows Security Center and other service pack features by using the registry. Chapter 8, "Configuring Windows Security," covers this topic in detail.

Controlling Just-in-Time Setup

Every IT professional I've spoken with, particularly desktop-deployment types, have the same problem: they want to know how to prevent Windows from creating icons for Outlook Express on the Quick Launch toolbar and Start menu when users log on to the computer the first time. More specifically, Windows creates these icons when it creates user profiles for new users. These icons aren't in the default user profile, which you learned about in Chapter 12, "Deploying User Profiles," so you can't just remove them from it to avoid creating them.

At this point, you might be asking why you can't just remove those components from Windows. Well, the operating system doesn't provide a user interface for doing that. However, in the section "Removing Components," later in this chapter, I show you how to limit which components the setup program installs. Still, other components are required for the operating system to work properly. For example, Windows requires access to Microsoft Internet Explorer. If you're deploying Microsoft Outlook 2002, you must install Outlook Express, because Outlook 2002 depends on many of the components in Outlook Express. The best you can do is not advertise these programs so users don't get sidetracked while using their computers.

Windows actually creates these icons as part of its *just-in-time* setup process for user profiles. The operating system creates a user profile for a new user, and then runs this just-in-time setup process to finish configuring it. Another way to think of the process is that the setup program defers configuring per-user settings until Windows creates user profiles, when decisions about those settings are better made. This just-in-time setup process is what you need to control to prevent the pesky Outlook Express icons from showing up on the desktop.

The key `HKLM\SOFTWARE\Microsoft\Active Setup\Installed Components` drives the just-in-time setup process. Each subkey is a component. For example, the subkey `{2179C5D3-EBFF-11CF-B6FD-00AA00B4E220}` is for NetShow. Within each subkey, you might see the `REG_EXPAND_SZ` value `StubPath`. If this value exists, Windows executes the command that it contains when the operating system creates a new user profile. If you don't see this value or the value is empty, Windows does nothing. So, to keep Windows from running a component's just-in-time setup process, remove the value `StubPath` from that component's subkey under `Installed Components`. The next several sections describe how to use this hack to control different components. You should include changes to `Installed Components` on disk images. Chapter 15, "Cloning Disks with Sysprep," describes how to deploy settings on your disk images.

> **Note**   Why should you care if Outlook Express has an icon on the Quick Launch toolbar? It's distracting and keeps users from their work. Specifically, your enterprise isn't likely to use Outlook Express as its mail client; you probably deployed a full-featured client such as Microsoft Office Outlook 2003 or a similar program. If you advertise Outlook Express on the desktop, users are going to have two mail clients. If that doesn't confuse them and cause problems, it'll certainly tease them into playing with Outlook Express. This applies to many of the other programs that come with Windows, including Windows Media Player, NetMeeting, and so on.

Outlook Express

When Windows creates a new user profile, it executes the command in the REG_EXPAND_SZ value `HKLM\SOFTWARE\Microsoft\Active Setup\Installed Components\{44BBA840-CC51-11CF-AAFA-00AA00B6015C}\StubPath` to create the Outlook Express icon in the Start menu and on the Quick Launch toolbar. This command is `"%ProgramFiles%\Outlook Express\setup50.exe" /APP:OE /CALLER:WINNT /user / install`. To prevent this command from running, remove the `StubPath` value or, alternatively, change its name to `HideStubPath`, as shown in Figure 18-1.

Name	Type	Data
(Default)	REG_SZ	Microsoft Outlook Express 6
CloneUser	REG_DWORD	0x00000001 (1)
ComponentID	REG_SZ	MailNews
HideStubPath	REG_EXPAND_SZ	"%ProgramFiles%\Outlook Express\setup50.exe" /APP:OE /C...
IsInstalled	REG_DWORD	0x00000001 (1)
Locale	REG_SZ	EN
Version	REG_SZ	6,0,2600,0000

Figure 18-1   Prevent Windows from creating Outlook Express shortcuts by hiding `Stub-Path`.

This customization is common on disk images, so I'm providing you with a script to do it. Save the script shown in Listing 18-1 to a text file with the *.inf* extension. Right-click it, and then click Install. Keep this script handy as a disk-image customization tool.

Listing 18-1   Outlook.inf

```
[Version]
Signature=$CHICAGO$

[DefaultInstall]
DelReg=Reg.Settings

[Reg.Settings]
HKLM,SOFTWARE\Microsoft\Active Setup\Installed Components\{44BBA840-\
CC51-11CF-AAFA-00AA00B6015C},StubPath
```

> **Tip** An alternative to hiding the Outlook Express icon is making Outlook Express a newsreader client only. Add the option /outnews to the target of each icon (placing this command-line option outside of the quotation marks). When users choose the shortcut, Outlook Express opens with all its news-client features working, but its mail-client features don't work. This is useful in scenarios when you must provide news-group access to users, such as developers, who usually require access to Microsoft and developer newsgroups. To easily deploy this customized Outlook Express shortcut, add it to the default user profile. Alternatively, because this hack usually accompanies an Outlook 2002 deployment, you can add this shortcut to your Microsoft Office 2003 Editions transform.

Windows Media Player

Windows Media Player has two subkeys in `HKLM\SOFTWARE\Microsoft\ Active Setup\Installed Components`:

- {22d6f312-b0f6-11d0-94ab-0080c74c7e95} is for version 6.4 and the value `StubPath` is `rundll32.exe advpack.dll,LaunchINFSection C:\WIN-DOWS\INF\mplayer2.inf,PerUserStub.NT`.

- {6BF52A52-394A-11d3-B153-00C04F79FAA6} is for version 8 and the value `Stub-Path` is `rundll32.exe advpack.dll,LaunchINFSection C:\WIN-DOWS\INF\wmp.inf,PerUserStub`

These values are responsible for the numerous Windows Media Player shortcuts. Remove both `StubPath` values to prevent Windows from adding the Windows Media Player shortcut to the Quick Launch toolbar. Also, if you want to keep the Windows Media Player shortcut off the top of the Start menu, remove it from the default user profile. (See Chapter 12, "Deploying User Profiles," for more information.) You also find Windows Media Player shortcuts in the All Users profile folder in %SystemDrive%\Documents and Settings\All Users\Start Menu\Programs\Accessories\Entertainment. Ideally, remove the shortcut from your network-based Default User profile, and then remove the shortcut from the All Users profile folder on your disk images.

Desktop Themes

Preventing Windows from configuring desktop themes when it creates a user profile is an easy way to revert to the classic user interface. (See Figure 18-2.) Remove or hide the `REG_EXPAND_SZ` value `StubPath` from the key `HKLM\SOFTWARE\Microsoft\Active Setup\Installed Components\{2C7339CF-2B09-4501-B3F3-F3508C9228ED}`. The command that this value contains is `%SystemRoot%\system32\regsvr32.exe /s /n /i:/ UserInstall%SystemRoot%\system32\themeui.dll`.

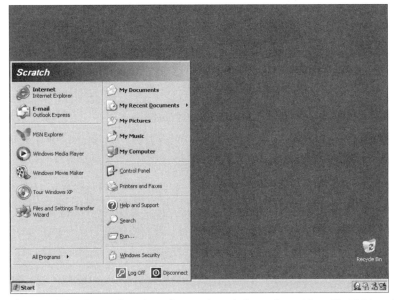

Figure 18-2   Removing the value `StubPath` from the subkey `{2C7339CF-2B09-4501-B3F3-F3508C9228ED}` prevents Windows from configuring the new user interface.

Other Shortcuts

The key `HKLM\SOFTWARE\Microsoft\Active Setup\Installed Components` contains many other components with `StubPath` values that I haven't mentioned yet. You can prevent Windows from configuring any of the components when the operating system creates a user profile by removing or hiding the `StubPath` value in the corresponding subkey. Table 18-1 lists all the components that I've already described plus some of the ones that I haven't.

Table 18-1   Components in Installed Components

Component	Subkey	StubPath
Address Book 6	{7790769C-0471-11d2-AF11-00C04FA35D02}	"%ProgramFiles%\Outlook Express\setup50.exe" /APP:WAB /CALLER:WINNT /user /install
Internet Explorer 6	{89820200-ECBD-11cf-8B85-00AA005B4383}	%SystemRoot%\system32\ie4uinit.exe
Internet Explorer Access	{ACC563BC-4266-43f0-B6ED-9D38C4202C7E}	rundll32 iesetup.dll, IEAccessUserInst
Microsoft Outlook Express 6	{44BBA840-CC51-11CF-AAFA-00AA00B6015C}	"%ProgramFiles%\Outlook Express\setup50.exe" /APP:OE /CALLER:WINNT /user /install

Table 18-1   Components in Installed Components

Component	Subkey	StubPath
Microsoft Windows Media Player 6.4	{22d6f312-b0f6-11d0-94ab-0080c74c7e95}	`rundll32.exe adv-pack.dll,LaunchINFSection C:\WINDOWS\INF \mplayer2.inf,Pe-rUserStub.NT`
Microsoft Windows Media Player 8	{6BF52A52-394A-11d3-B153-00C04F79FAA6}	`rundll32.exe advpack.dll, LaunchINFSection C:\WINDOWS\INF \wmp.inf,PerUserStub`
NetMeeting 3.01	{44BBA842-CC51-11CF-AAFA-00AA00B6015B}	`rundll32.exe adv-pack.dll,LaunchINFSection C:\WINDOWS\INF \msnetmtg.inf, NetMtg.Install.PerUser.NT`
Theme Component	{2C7339CF-2B09-4501-B3F3-F3508C9228ED}	`%System-Root%\system32\regsvr32.exe /s /n /i: /UserInstall %SystemRoot% \system32 \themeui.dll`
Windows Desktop Update	{89820200-ECBD-11cf-8B85-00AA005B4340}	`regsvr32.exe /s /n /i:U shell32.dll`
Windows Messenger 4.0	{5945c046-1e7d-11d1-bc44-00c04fd912be}	`rundll32.exe adv-pack.dll,LaunchINFSection C:\WINDOWS\INF \msmsgs.inf,BLC.Install.PerUser`

Keep in mind that even if you prevent Windows from configuring every component that I list in the preceding table, you might still have unwanted icons. These icons come from the Default User and All User profile folders. Remove the shortcuts that you don't want from any default user profile you've deployed. Remove the shortcuts that you don't want from the All Users folder on your disk images.

> **Caution**   Be wary of preventing Windows from configuring the Windows Desktop Update component. This component is necessary to provide resiliency for Windows Installer–based applications. For example, when a user opens the shortcut of a Windows Installer–based application, the Windows Desktop Update component passes it on to Windows Installer so that Windows Installer can check and repair the application if necessary. If you prevent the operating system from configuring the Windows Desktop Update component, you remove Windows Installer from the process. Even though this prevents Windows Installer from repairing broken shortcuts, it doesn't prevent Windows Installer from repairing components within an application.

Removing Components

Whereas the previous section showed you how to prevent Windows from configuring components when it creates a user profile, this section shows you how to prevent Windows from installing certain components altogether. Be careful when you prevent the operating system from installing components, though, because doing so could cripple some features and applications. For example, Office 2003 Editions requires Internet Explorer, Outlook Express, and NetMeeting for a lot of its features, particularly its collaboration features. The moral is to test your configurations in a lab before deploying them to unsuspecting users.

The Windows setup program doesn't provide a user interface for removing components during installation. You can use an answer file to remove components, however; Chapter 14, "Deploying with Answer Files," shows you what the [Components] section looks like in an answer file, and I summarize that information in this chapter. The operating system does allow users to add or remove components using the Windows Components Wizard, though: in Control Panel launch Add Or Remove Programs, Add/Remove Windows Components. Still, the wizard and answer files do not allow you to remove and disable some of the features that enterprises would rather not install. There's no option to remove Windows Movie Maker, for example, nor is there an option to remove Windows Messenger.

This section shows you some alternative ways to get rid of components, if possible, or to hide them. The most common requests that I get are to remove the Tour Windows, Movie Maker, Outlook Express, and Files And Settings Transfer Wizard components. Interestingly, I'm not often asked about removing the games, but you can do that easily enough through your Windows answer file.

Answer File [Components] Section

Chapter 14, "Deploying with Answer Files," describes how to build an answer file. If you're an IT professional deploying Windows, you're probably already familiar with answer files. The [Components] section of answer files enables you to prevent the operating system from installing certain components. Table 18-2 describes all the components that Windows answer files support. The names of each component are self-explanatory. To install a component, set it to on. To prevent its installation, set it to off. In the listing, I've set each component to its default installation value.

Microsoft doesn't document a way to prevent the setup program from installing Windows Messenger—a common request. I've added the component msmsgs to Table 18-2, however, which prevents the setup program from installing it. The file Sysoc.inf, which you learn about in the next section, hides this component in the Windows Components Wizard. You can edit that file to show Windows Messenger in the wizard, but doing so relies on users to remove Windows Messenger. Instead, you can add the component to the [Components] section of your answer file to prevent the setup program from installing it.

Table 18-2   [Components] Section

Setting	Default Value	Description
AccessOpt	On	Specifies whether to install the Accessibility Wizard
appsrv_console	Off	Specifies whether to install the Application Server Console
aspnet	Off	Specifies whether to install the ASP.NET Web development platform
AutoUpdate		See the AutomaticUpdates entry in the [Data] section of Unattend.txt
BitsServerExtensionsISAPI	Off	Specifies whether to install Internet Server Application Programming Interface (ISAPI) for Background Intelligent Transfer Service (BITS) server extensions on client computers
BitsServerExtensionsManager	Off	Specifies whether to install the Microsoft Management Console (MMC) snap-in, administrative Application Programming Interfaces (APIs), and Active Directory Service Interfaces (ADSI) extensions for Background Intelligent Transfer Service (BITS) server extensions
Calc	On	Specifies whether to install the Calculator feature
certsrv	Off	Specifies whether to install the Certificate Services components
certsrv_client	Off	Specifies whether to install the Web client components of Certificate Services
certsrv_server	Off	Specifies whether to install the server components of the Certificate Services feature for the Windows Server 2003 family only
charmap	On	Specifies whether to install the Character Map feature that inserts symbols and characters into documents
chat	Off	Specifies whether to install the Chat feature
clipbook	On	Specifies whether to install the clipboard viewer
cluster	Off	Specifies whether to install the Cluster service (for Windows 2000 Advanced or Datacenter Server only)
complusnetwork	Off	Specifies whether to enable network COM+ access

Table 18-2   [Components] Section

Setting	Default Value	Description
deskpaper	On	Specifies whether to install a desktop background on the computer desktop
dialer	On	Specifies whether to install the Phone Dialer feature
dtcnetwork	Off	Specifies whether to enable Microsoft Distributed Transaction Coordinator (DTC) network access
fax	Off	Specifies whether to install the Fax feature
fp_extensions	Off	Specifies whether to install Microsoft FrontPage server extensions
fp_vdir_deploy	Off	Specifies whether to install Microsoft Visual InterDev RAD Remote Deployment Support
freecell	On	Specifies whether to install the Freecell game (not available in the Windows Server 2003 family)
hearts	On	Specifies whether to install the Hearts game (not available in the Windows Server 2003 family)
hypertrm	On	Specifies whether to install the HyperTerminal feature (Windows XP)
IEAccess	On	Specifies whether to install visible entry points to Internet Explorer
IEHardenAdmin	On	Applies the Enhanced Security Configuration to members of the Administrators and Power Users groups
IEHardenUser	On	Applies the Enhanced Security Configuration to members of the Restricted Users and Guests groups
iis_asp	Off	Specifies whether to install Active Server Pages (ASP) for Internet Information Services (IIS)
iis_common	On	Specifies whether to install the common set of files required by IIS
iis_ftp	Off	Specifies whether to install the FTP service
iis_inetmgr	On	Specifies whether to install the Microsoft Management Console (MMC)–based administration tools for IIS
iis_internetdataconnector	Off	Specifies whether to install the Internet Data Connector
iis_nntp	Off	Specifies whether to install the Network News Transfer Protocol (NNTP) service for the Windows Server 2003 family

Table 18-2   [Components] Section

Setting	Default Value	Description
iis_serversideincludes	Off	Specifies whether to install the Server-Side Includes
iis_smtp	On	Specifies whether to install the Simple Mail Transfer Protocol (SMTP)
iis_webdav	Off	Specifies whether to install WebDAV Publishing
iis_www	On	Specifies whether to install the World Wide Web (WWW) service
indexsrv_system	On	Specifies whether to install the Indexing Service files
inetprint	Off	Specifies whether to install Internet Printing
licenseserver	Off	Specifies whether to turn Terminal Services licensing on
media_clips	On	Specifies whether to install sample sound clips on the computer (Windows XP)
media_utopia	Off	Specifies whether to install the Utopia Sound Scheme on the computer
minesweeper	On	Specifies whether to install the Minesweeper game on the computer (not available in the Windows Server 2003 family)
mousepoint	On	Specifies whether to install all the available mouse pointers distributed with Windows XP or Windows Server 2003 family
msmq_ADIntegrated	Off	Specifies whether to integrate Message Queuing (also known as *MSMQ*) with Active Directory if the computer belongs to a domain
msmq_Core	Off	Specifies whether to set up the Message Queuing components and provide functionality for any dependent clients
msmq_HTTPSupport	Off	Specifies whether to enable the sending and receiving of messages using the HTTP protocol
msmq_LocalStorage	Off	Specifies whether to store messages locally, so the computer can send and receive messages even when not connected to a network
msmq_MQDSService	Off	Specifies whether to provide access to Active Directory and site recognition for downstream clients
msmq_RoutingSupport	Off	Specifies whether to provide efficient routing

Table 18-2   `[Components]` **Section**

Setting	Default Value	Description
msmq_TriggersService	Off	Specifies whether to associate the arrival of incoming messages at a queue with functionality in a Component Object Model (COM) component or a stand-alone executable program
msnexplr	On	Specifies whether to install MSN Explorer
mswordpad	On	Specifies whether to install the WordPad feature on the computer
netcis	Off	Specifies whether to install Microsoft Component Object Model (COM) Internet Services
netoc	On	Specifies whether to install additional optional networking components
objectpkg	On	Specifies whether to install the Object Packager feature (Packager.exe) on the computer
OEAccess	On	Specifies whether to install visible entry points to Outlook Express
paint	On	Specifies whether to install the Microsoft Paint feature on the computer
pinball	On	Specifies whether to install the Pinball game on the computer (not available in the Windows Server 2003 family)
Pop3Admin	Off	Specifies whether to install the optional POP Web UI for the Remote Administration Tools on the computer
Pop3Service	On	Specifies whether to install the main POP3 service on the computer
Pop3Srv	On	Specifies whether to install the root POP3 component on the computer
rec	On	Specifies whether to install the Sound Recorder feature on the computer
reminst	Off	Specifies whether to install Remote Installation Services (RIS), which enables you to install an operating system remotely onto a computer with either a new PXE-based remote boot read-only memory (ROM) or a network card supported by the remote installation boot floppy disk
rootautoupdate	On	Specifies whether to turn on the Optional Components Manager (OCM) Update Root Certificates

Table 18-2   [Components] Section

Setting	Default Value	Description
rstorage	Off	Specifies whether to install the Remote Storage feature that enables the use of tape libraries as extensions of NTFS file system volumes
sakit_web	Off	Specifies whether to install the Remote Administration Tools (formerly known as the Server Administration Kit)
solitaire	On	Specifies whether to install the Solitaire game on the computer (not available in the Windows Server 2003 family)
spider	On	Specifies whether to install the Spider Solitaire game on the computer (not available in the Windows Server 2003 family)
templates	On	Specifies whether to install Document Templates on the computer
TerminalServer	Off	Specifies whether to install Terminal Server (Terminal Services for multiple users) on the computer
TSWebClient	Off	Specifies whether to install the ActiveX control and sample pages for hosting Terminal Services client connections over the Web
vol	On	Specifies whether to install the Volume Control feature on the computer
WbemCrrl	On	Specifies whether to install the Windows Management Instrumentation (WMI) event correlation component
WbemFwrd	On	Specifies whether to install the Windows Management Instrumentation (WMI) event forwarding components
WbemMSI	On	Specifies whether to install the WMI Windows installer provider
WMAccess	On	Specifies whether to install visible entry points to Windows Messenger
WMPOCM	On	Specifies whether to install visible entry points to Windows Media Player
wms	Off	Specifies whether to install the core Windows Media Server components
wms_admin_asp	Off	Specifies whether to install the Windows Media Services Web-based administrative components

Table 18-2 [Components] Section

Setting	Default Value	Description
wms_admin_mmc	Off	Specifies whether to install the Windows Media Services Microsoft Management Console (MMC)–based administrative components
wms_isapi	Off	Specifies whether to install the Windows Media Services Multicast and Advertisement Logging Agent components
wms_server	Off	Specifies whether to install the Windows Media Services server components
zonegames	On	Specifies whether to install the Microsoft Gaming Zone Internet games on the computer (not available in the Windows Server 2003 family)

This is a great technique for preventing the operating system from installing things such as the games, but it doesn't prevent the installation of components such as Movie Maker, because the [Components] section doesn't include settings for those components. You can use it to prevent the installation of Windows Media Player and Windows Messenger, though, which strikes two components off of my checklist.

Extending Windows Components Wizard

Just because you don't see a component in the Windows Components Wizard doesn't mean that Windows isn't prepared to remove it. The file Sysoc.inf controls which components appear in the wizard. This file is in %SystemRoot%\Inf, and Listing 18-2 shows its default contents. You must display super-hidden files to see the Inf folder: in Windows Explorer, click Tools, Folder Options. On the View tab, select the Show Hidden Files And Folders check box.

In Listing 18-2, the important section in this file is [Components]. Each line in this section is either a specific component or a category of components. If you see the word hide, Windows doesn't display the component or category in the Windows Components Wizard. To allow users to remove the component, or the components in the category, remove the word hide. For example, to allow users to remove Windows Messenger, change the line msmsgs=msgrocm.dll,OcEntry,msmsgs.inf, hide,7 to msmsgs=msgrocm.dll,OcEntry,msmsgs.inf,,7.

Listing 18-2 Sysoc.inf

```
[Version]
Signature = "$Windows NT$"
DriverVer=07/01/2001,5.1.2600.2180
```

```
[Components]
NtComponents=ntoc.dll,NtOcSetupProc,,4
WBEM=ocgen.dll,OcEntry,wbemoc.inf,hide,7
Display=desk.cpl,DisplayOcSetupProc,,7
Fax=fxsocm.dll,FaxOcmSetupProc,fxsocm.inf,,7
NetOC=netoc.dll,NetOcSetupProc,netoc.inf,,7
iis=iis.dll,OcEntry,iis.inf,,7
com=comsetup.dll,OcEntry,comnt5.inf,hide,7
dtc=msdtcstp.dll,OcEntry,dtcnt5.inf,hide,7
IndexSrv_System = setupqry.dll,IndexSrv,setupqry.inf,,7
TerminalServer=TsOc.dll, HydraOc, TsOc.inf,hide,2
msmq=msmqocm.dll,MsmqOcm,msmqocm.inf,,6
ims=imsinsnt.dll,OcEntry,ims.inf,,7
fp_extensions=fp40ext.dll,FrontPage4Extensions,fp40ext.inf,,7
msmsgs=msgrocm.dll,OcEntry,msmsgs.inf,hide,7
WMAccess=ocgen.dll,OcEntry,wmaccess.inf,,7
RootAutoUpdate=ocgen.dll,OcEntry,rootau.inf,,7
IEAccess=ocgen.dll,OcEntry,ieaccess.inf,,7
OEAccess=ocgen.dll,OcEntry,oeaccess.inf,,7
WMPOCM=ocgen.dll,OcEntry,wmpocm.inf,,7
Games=ocgen.dll,OcEntry,games.inf,,7
AccessUtil=ocgen.dll,OcEntry,accessor.inf,,7
CommApps=ocgen.dll,OcEntry,communic.inf,HIDE,7
MultiM=ocgen.dll,OcEntry,multimed.inf,HIDE,7
AccessOpt=ocgen.dll,OcEntry,optional.inf,HIDE,7
Pinball=ocgen.dll,OcEntry,pinball.inf,HIDE,7
MSWordPad=ocgen.dll,OcEntry,wordpad.inf,HIDE,7
ZoneGames=zoneoc.dll,ZoneSetupProc,igames.inf,,7
TabletPC=tabletoc.dll,TabletSetupProc,Tabletpc.inf,HIDE,7
Freestyle=medctroc.dll,MedCtrOCISetupProc,medctroc.inf,HIDE,7
netfx=netfxocm.dll,UrtOcmProc,netfxocm.inf,hide,7

[Global]
WindowTitle=%WindowTitle%
WindowTitle.StandAlone="*"

[Components]
msnexplr=ocmsn.dll,OcEntry,msnmsn.inf,,7

[Strings]
WindowTitle="Windows Professional Setup"
WindowTitle_Standalone="Windows Components Wizard"Removing Components After Installa
tion
```

The first option that I gave you enables you to prevent the Windows setup program from installing components during installation. The second option enables you to expose additional components in the Windows Components Wizard. This last option is for scenarios in which you want to remove a component without exposing it in the Windows Components Wizard. This option is also useful when you want to script the removal so that you don't have to visit the desktop.

The first step is to find the component's INF file in %SystemRoot%\Inf. Remember that this is a super-hidden folder, and I gave you instructions for showing it earlier in this chapter. The easiest way to find the component's INF file is to use Search Assistant.

Look for all files with the .*inf* extension that contain the name of the component. For example, to find the INF file for Windows Messenger, search for all files with the .*inf* extension in %SystemRoot%\Inf that contain *Windows Messenger*. You should come up with the file Msmsgs.inf as shown in Figure 18-3. Then look in the file for a section with the words *remove* or *uninstall* in it. In this case, the section is named [`BLC.Remove`]. Then execute the following command, whether in a script or in the Run dialog box, where *Filename.inf* is the name of the INF file and *Section* is the name of the uninstall section:

```
rundll32 advpack.dll,LaunchINFSection %systemroot%\Inf\Filename.inf,Section
```

Thus, to remove Windows Messenger, run the command:

```
rundll32 advpack.dll,LaunchINFSection %systemroot%\Inf\Msmsgs.inf,BLC.Remove.
```

Alas, many components don't have uninstall sections in their INF files, and that leaves you looking for other ways to remove them. You can use this method for many device drivers, programs, and components that do provide INF files, however.

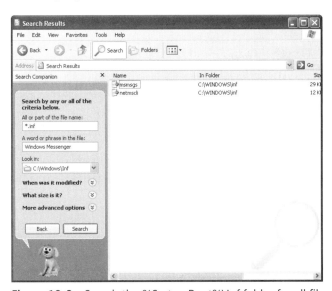

Figure 18-3   Search the %SystemRoot%\Inf folder for all files with the .*inf* extension that contain the name of the component you want to remove.

Hiding Non-Removable Components

None of the methods I've shown will help you get rid of certain components, including Tour Windows XP, Movie Maker, Outlook Express, and the Files And Settings Transfer Wizard, which is what started me on this rampage in the first place. To prevent users from accessing these applications, you're going to have to get creative. Tour Windows XP is easy to hide, if not get rid of altogether. Create a new subkey in

HKLM\Software\Microsoft\Windows\CurrentVersion\Applets\Tour named Tour. Then create the REG_DWORD value RunCount and set it to 0x00. Do this on your disk images so that users aren't accosted by Tour Windows XP the first time they log on to the operating system; they can run the tour from the Start menu.

The remaining bits aren't as easy. You can't just remove the program files because Windows File Protection (WFP) immediately restores them. You could disable Windows File Protection, but I don't recommend doing so because it protects users' configurations from accidents and misbehaved applications that like to replace files that they have no business replacing. Instead, on your disk images, hide the shortcuts, and use Software Restriction Policies to prevent users from running the programs by opening the program files:

1. Prevent Windows from creating new shortcuts by removing the appropriate StubPath values from HKLM\SOFTWARE\Microsoft\Active Setup\Installed Components. See the section "Controlling Just-in-Time Setup," earlier in this chapter, for more information.

2. Hide existing shortcuts to the program (do this on your disk images):

   ❑ Search %SystemDrive%\Documents and Settings\All Users for shortcuts to the program, and remove them.

   ❑ Search %SystemDrive%\Documents and Settings\Default User for shortcuts to the program, and remove them.

   ❑ Search the Default User folder in *Server*\NETLOGON\Default User share for the program's shortcuts, and remove them.

3. Create a new Group Policy object (GPO) in Active Directory or locally on your disk images that prevents users from running the program.

That last step requires more explanation. Chapter 7, "Using Registry-Based Policy," contains more information about Group Policy, but I'll get you started. The following instructions assume that you're defining Software Restriction Policies in the local GPO, but the steps transfer to network-based Group Policy:

1. In Group Policy Editor's left pane, click Software Restriction Policies.

   To start Group Policy Editor, type **gpedit.msc** in the Run dialog box. Software Restriction Policies is under Computer Configuration\Windows Settings\Security Settings.

2. Right-click Software Restriction Policies, and then click Create New Policies.

3. Under Software Restrictions Policies, right-click Additional Rules, and then click New Hash Rule.

4. Click Browse, and select the file that you want to prevent users from executing. For example to prevent users from running the Files And Settings Migration Wizard, select %SystemRoot%\system32\usmt\migwiz.exe.

After you select the file that you want to prevent users from running, Group Policy Editor creates a hash for the file. Figure 18-4 shows an example that prevents users from running Files And Settings Transfer Wizard. Users won't be able to run any program that matches that hash value. That way, users can't trick the system by copying the file to a different location (because some users can be clever). After you save the policy, you must log off of Windows for the change to take effect. When users try to run the program, they see an error message that reads, *Windows cannot open this program because it has been prevented by a software restriction policy.* So between hiding the advertisements and preventing the program file from executing, you can prevent programs such as Movie Maker and the Files And Settings Transfer Wizard from being run.

Figure 18-4   Without a Files And Settings Transfer Wizard shortcut on the Start menu, users will not usually try to run the wizard. Those who do will see an error message.

Removing Policy Tattoos

Tattoos are a significant problem with System Policy, which versions of Windows before Windows 2000 supported. Tattooing means that policies make permanent changes to the registry. The administrator must explicitly remove those policies. For example, if you create a policy file, which has the *.pol* extension, and Windows applies its settings to the registry, when you remove the policy file, the settings remain. To remove those policies, you must remove the settings from the registry or edit the policy file to remove the settings.

Tattoos become more problematic when you upgrade to Windows from an earlier version of Windows. It's also a problem when you deploy Windows on a network that doesn't have Active Directory but uses System Policy, and then you deploy Active Directory down the line. The upgrade process doesn't remove System Policy settings from the registry during an upgrade, so those settings remain. The shotgun approach is to remove the following keys from each computer's registry and each user's profile hive before upgrading to Windows; the surgical approach is to remove individual policies, but that's too tedious:

- `HKLM\SOFTWARE\Policies`

- `HKLM\SOFTWARE\Microsoft\Windows\CurrentVersion\Policies`

- `HKCU\Software\Policies`

- `HKCU\Software\Microsoft\Windows\CurrentVersion\Policies`

How you remove these keys during the upgrade is the question. This isn't an issue for disk images because the problem occurs only during an upgrade. If technicians are visiting desktops during the upgrade, and I hope they aren't doing that, they can remove these keys manually. Otherwise, run the Windows setup program from a batch file or a script. Then you can precede the command that starts the setup program with the commands that remove these keys. Listing 18-3 is an example of an INF file that removes them. To run this INF file from a batch file, save it in a file named Tattos.inf; then add the command `%SystemRoot%\System32\rundll32.exe setupapi, InstallHinfSection DefaultInstall 132 Tattoos.inf` to the batch file that starts the Windows installation. You can also script this edit using Windows Script Host (WSH), which Chapter 11, "Scripting Registry Changes," describes how to do.

Listing 18-3   Tattoos.inf

```
[Version]
Signature=$CHICAGO$

[DefaultInstall]
DelReg=Reg.Settings

[Reg.Settings]
HKLM,SOFTWARE\Policies
HKLM,SOFTWARE\Microsoft\Windows\CurrentVersion\Policies
```

There a few major issues with this script, however. The first is that the user must be an administrator to remove the policy branches from the registry. You can use the techniques described in the next section, "Elevating Privileges of Processes," to take care of this issue or rely on your software management infrastructure. The second issue is that it removes only the per-computer policies. It doesn't remove policies from users' profile hives. You won't be able to use a script like this from a logon script or allow the user to run it because they don't have the privileges required to remove the policy branches from the registry. This is true unless you've dumped all users into the local Administrators group, which I hope you haven't done. The only reasonable solution is to load each user's profile hive in Registry Editor (Regedit), and then remove the two policy branches from it. You can more or less automate this process by writing a script that connects to a remote computer, loads each profile hive file that exists in `HKLM\SOFTWARE\Microsoft\Windows NT\CurrentVersion\ProfileList`, removes the policy branches, and then unloads the hive file.

Elevating Privileges of Processes

Privileges are a nasty little paradox. On one hand, you don't want to add users to the local Administrators group. Restricting users is a best practice that prevents human error, senseless distractions, opportunistic viruses, and so on. On the other hand, deploying software to restricted users is difficult. They don't have the privileges necessary to install most applications, such as Office 2003 Editions. Chapter 8, "Configuring Windows Security," shows you a variety of features that you can use to reach a happy medium between unbridled access and totally locked-down desktops. What I want to show you in this chapter is how to run processes elevated so that you can perform many of the tasks I've described in locked-down environments.

The sections following this one go from elegant to dodgy. Group Policy, specifically the `InstallAlwaysElevated` policy, is one way to allow restricted users to install Windows Installer–based applications. You can also use the Secondary Logon feature or Scheduled Tasks. The section "AutoLogon," later in this chapter, describes a method that Microsoft Systems Management Server (SMS) uses, and I tend to like this solution. The last two methods that I describe in this section are very risky and can be used against you if you're not careful.

Group Policy

The policy `InstallAlwaysElevated` installs Windows Installer–based applications with elevated privileges. This policy is one way to allow users to install Windows Installer–based applications that they couldn't otherwise install because their accounts are in restricted groups or you've locked down the desktops.

Keep in mind the consequences of using this policy. Users can take advantage of this policy to gain full control of their computers. Potentially, users can even permanently change their privileges and circumvent your ability to manage their accounts and computers. Not only that, this policy opens the door to viruses disguised as Windows Installer package files. For these reasons, this isn't a setting that I recommend in any but the most necessary scenarios when there's no other method available other than to toss users into the local Administrators group.

For this policy to be effective, you must enable both the per-computer and per-user versions of it at the same time. In other words, enable it in Computer Configuration as well as User Configuration. If you're going to use this policy, I recommend that you enable it for each rollout unit prior to deploying software to it. Deploy your package, and then immediately remove the policy for that unit. You can at least limit your exposure to the perils that this policy creates.

> **Note**   If you have Active Directory and Group Policy, you shouldn't consider using the `InstallAlwaysElevated` policy. The only reason you'd use this policy is in lieu of a software management infrastructure. If you have Active Directory and Group Policy, however, you have at your disposal an elegant solution for small and medium businesses: Software Installation And Maintenance. This feature enables you to deploy software through GPOs. The best part is that you can deploy Windows Installer–based software to restricted users and locked-down desktops because applications you deploy through Group Policy install with elevated privileges. The white paper "Understanding Software Installation" is an excellent walkthrough for the subject. You can find this document at *http://www.microsoft.com/resources/documentation/windows/xp/all/proddocs/en-us/sag_adeconcepts_01.mspx.*

Secondary Logon

Secondary Logon, also called Run As, enables users to run programs in the context of accounts other than their own. For example, if I'm logged on to the computer using the account Jerry, which is in the Power Users group, but I need to run a program as an administrator, I hold down the SHIFT key, right-click the program's shortcut icon, click Run As, and then type the Administrator account's name and password. The program runs under the Administrator account. Because Secondary Logon relies on users knowing the credentials (which they won't know), it's not a really useful tool for software deployment. I include it here to answer the inevitable question about whether you can use it for that purpose.

You can use Secondary Logon from a command prompt window, too. The following shows you the syntax for this command:

```
RUNAS [ [/noprofile | /profile] [/env] [/netonly] ] /user:Username Program
RUNAS [ [/noprofile | /profile] [/env] [/netonly] ] /smartcard [/
user:Username] Program
```

Table 18-3   Runas Command-Line Options

`/noprofile`	Specifies that Runas should not load the user profile. Programs load faster but often don't work properly.
`/profile`	Specifies that Runas should load the user profile.
`/env`	Uses the current environment instead of the user's environment.
`/netonly`	Specifies that the credentials are for remote access only.
`/savecred`	Uses the credentials previously saved by the user.
`/smartcard`	Specifies that the credentials are provided by a smartcard.
`/user Username`	Specifies the account name to use. This should be in the form of *user@domain* or *domain\user*.
Program	Specifies the command to execute.

Scheduled Tasks

One thing I like about Scheduled Tasks is that you have remote access to the Scheduled Tasks folder on each computer. Also, you can include an account name and a password in each task. You're not relying on users to provide the credentials necessary to run a job, such as installing software. For this reason, Scheduled Tasks beats Secondary Logon. In My Network Places, find the computer on which you want to add a task. Open the computer's Scheduled Tasks folder, right-click the within folder, point to New, click Scheduled Task, and then rename the task. Configure the task as follows (shown in Figure 18-5).

- In the Task tab's Run text box, type the command that you want to execute. Remember to keep the command's path relative to the computer on which you're running it.

- In the Task tab's Run As text box, type the account in which you want to run the task, and then click Set Password to set the matching password. As shown in Figure 18-5, type the account in the form domain\username.

- On the Schedule tab, configure the task's schedule. In the scenarios that I've described (deploying software and settings), you'd want to schedule the task to run once.

- On the Settings tab, configure Windows to remove the task from the Scheduled Tasks folder after it runs. There is no reason to leave behind artifacts.

Figure 18-5   Scheduled Tasks is a useful way to run programs on remote computers with elevated privileges, particularly in one-off scenarios.

> **Note**   Be careful not to schedule tasks that require user interaction. Users won't see the task running unless they look in Windows Task Manager and view tasks for all users. For example, if you schedule a task to run on a computer as the local administrator and the user Jerry is the current console user, Jerry won't be able to interact with the task. If the task requires user interaction, it'll hang. Many programs, particularly setup programs, have command-line options that run them quietly. Install Office 2003 Editions with no user interaction, for example, using the /qn command-line option. Also, use this method to install software or run programs that don't interact with the current console user's profile, because this method will affect only the profile of the user you typed in the Run As box. In other words, install applications that support per-computer installations or run programs that interact with HKLM.

AutoLogon

This is my favorite method when I don't have a software management infrastructure available for deploying software: I use AutoLogon. This is the same capability that you can configure in answer files, as described in Chapter 14, "Deploying with Answer Files," but you can use it after deployment. Table 18-4 describes the settings you need to configure for AutoLogon. To enable this feature, you must set the REG_SZ value AutoAdminLogon to 1. Then you set the REG_SZ value DefaultUserName to the account that you want to use, and the REG_SZ value DefaultPassword to the account's password. If the user name doesn't include the domain, set the REG_SZ value DefaultDomainName to the name of the domain authenticating the account. Just remember that you must add the account to one of the local groups to log on to Windows using that account. The domain administrator is already a member of the local Administrators group, but I don't recommend using the domain administrator account with this technique. Instead, you can use the local Administrator account, which is always available. The last value you set is the REG_DWORD value AutoLogonCount. Set this value to the number of times that you want to automatically log on to Windows.

Here's how it works. If the AutoAdminLogon value is 1 and the AutoLogonCount value is not 0, Windows automatically logs on to the computer using the credentials provided in the values DefaultUserName, DefaultDomainName, and DefaultPassword. The operating system then decrements the value in AutoLogonCount. When AutoLogonCount reaches zero, Windows removes the values AutoLogonCount and DefaultPassword from the registry and no longer logs the user on to it automatically.

The last step is to put the command you want to run in HKLM\SOFTWARE\Microsoft\Windows\CurrentVersion\RunOnce. Because you're putting this command in the RunOnce key, Windows runs this command one time and then removes the value from the registry. Each value in RunOnce is a command. The name of each REG_SZ value doesn't matter, but you store the command line you want to execute in it.

Table 18-4   Configuring Autologon

Setting	Name	Type	Data
HKLM\SOFTWARE\Microsoft\Windows NT\CurrentVersion\Winlogon			
Enable Autologon	AutoAdminLogon	REG_SZ	0 | 1
User name	DefaultUserName	REG_SZ	*Name*
User domain	DefaultDomainName	REG_SZ	*Domain*
User password	DefaultPassword	REG_SZ	*Password*
Number of times to log on to Windows	AutoLogonCount	REG_DWORD	*N*
HKLM\SOFTWARE\Microsoft\Windows\CurrentVersion\RunOnce			
Program to run	*Name*	REG_SZ	*Command*

An example will tie everything together for you. I want to deploy an application to a computer but the users in my organization are restricted and can't install it. I configure the values described in Table 18-4 so that when the current user logs off or when Windows restarts, the operating system automatically logs the local Administrator on to the computer. I know that the application reboots the computer one time during the installation process, so I have to set AutoLogonCount to 2. The first time Windows logs the user on to it starts the setup program, and the second logon continues the setup program. The script shown in Listing 18-4 shows a way to automatically configure Windows for this scenario.

Listing 18-4   Install.inf

```
[Version]
Signature=$CHICAGO$

[DefaultInstall]
AddReg=Reg.Settings

[Reg.Settings]
HKLM,SOFTWARE\Microsoft\Windows NT\CurrentVersion\Winlogon,AutoAdminLogon,0,"1"
HKLM,SOFTWARE\Microsoft\Windows NT\CurrentVersion\Winlogon,DefaultUserName,0\
,"Administrator"
HKLM,SOFTWARE\Microsoft\Windows NT\CurrentVersion\Winlogon,DefaultDomainName,0\
,"HONEYCUTT"
HKLM,SOFTWARE\Microsoft\Windows NT\CurrentVersion\Winlogon,DefaultPassword,0\
,"PASSWORD"
HKLM,SOFTWARE\Microsoft\Windows NT\CurrentVersion\Winlogon,AutoLogonCount\
,0x10001,0x02
HKLM,SOFTWARE\Microsoft\Windows\CurrentVersion\RunOnce,Setup,0\
,"\\Server\Share\Setup.exe"
```

The last thing that you should know about this technique is that after Windows automatically logs the user on and the task completes, you're going to want to log the account off of the computer. Otherwise, you leave Windows vulnerable because anybody wandering by the computer has access to the account that you used. The Windows Support Tools, which you install from the Windows CD in the Support\Tools folder, contain a utility named Shutdown. After installing the application, run the command `shutdown -1` to log the user off of Windows. To restart the computer, run `shutdown -r`. To chain the application's setup program to the Shutdown command, use a batch file and the Start command with the `/wait` command-line option, which enables you to run programs synchronously, one after the other. To see the command-line options for the Shutdown command, type **shutdown /?** in a command prompt window. Type **start /?** to see the options for the Start command.

Severing File Associations

There are two scenarios in which severing the default file associations is useful to IT professionals. The first is when you're concerned about users accidentally running scripts that they receive as e-mail attachments. If you don't have a virus filter on your mail server and you're not using a mail client such as Office Outlook 2003, which blocks dangerous attachments, you can break the associations between the script files' extensions and the program class that opens them. Appendix A, "File Associations," describes how Windows associates file extensions with program classes. In the first scenario, you'd break the file association between the *.vbs* and *.js* file extensions and WSH. To do that, clear the default values of HKCR\\.vbs and HKCR\\.js. This isn't foolproof, however, because you can't break other dangerous file associations without affecting users' ability to use the operating system.

The second common scenario is when deploying Office 2003 Editions in coexistence scenarios. For example, if you need to keep Microsoft Access 97 in the field until after you migrate those databases to Office Access 2003, you might consider blocking the installation of Access 2003 until later. However, some businesses deploy Access 2003 so that it coexists with Access 97. Technically, this scenario works, but you have to consider your license agreement. The problem with this scenario is that the default file association for the *.mdb* extension will be with Access 2003, which isn't usually appropriate. Instead, you'll want to restore the association with Access 97. Better yet, to prevent confusion, don't associate the *.mdb* file extension with any program class. To do this, clear the default value of HKCR\\.mdb, and then teach users to use one of the following methods to ensure that they're opening each database in the appropriate version of Access:

- Open either version of Access first, and then open the database through the File menu.

- Create a shortcut for each database file that opens the file in the right version of Access.

Note   In the second scenario, you'll want to prevent Access 2003 users from accidentally converting down-level databases to the Access 2003 file format. You accomplish this by using the policies that come with the Office 2003 Editions Resource Kit. The kit installs these policy templates in %SystemRoot%\Inf, and you must load them into a GPO to use them. Be sure to enable the policy Do Not Prompt To Convert Older Databases, which prevents accidental database conversions.

Deploying Office Trusted Sources

Odds are good that you're concerned about security. Rightfully so, too. The security best practices that Microsoft prescribes will protect your business from most macro viruses. Those best practices are first to set the security level to high for all Office programs, which means that users can run only signed macros from trusted sources, and then to lock the list of trusted sources so users can't add to it. But how are users going to work if they can't run unsigned macros and they can't add sources to the list of trusted sources?

When a user opens a document that contains signed code, enables those macros, and then adds the source to the list of trusted sources, HKCU\Software\Microsoft\VBA\Trusted is where Office stores those certificates. To enable user to add sources to the list of trusted sources, distribute the list of trusted sources along with Office. The Office 2003 Editions Custom Installation Wizard provides a user interface for doing this. However, the deployment tools for earlier versions don't provide a user interface, so here's my solution:

1. Create a document that contains code, and then sign the code using a certificate you want to deploy. Repeat this for each certificate.

2. Install Office on a lab computer, and set the security levels to high.

3. Open each document containing a certificate that you want to deploy. Enable the document's macros, and then add the source to the list of trusted sources. Figure 18-6 shows you an example.

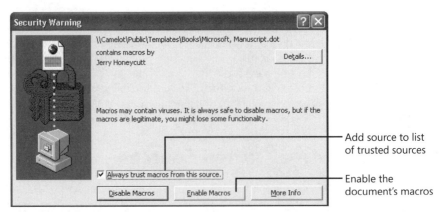

Add source to list of trusted sources

Enable the document's macros

Figure 18-6   High security in combination with code signing protects your business from viruses.

4. Export the key `HKCU\Software\Microsoft\VBA\Trusted` to a REG file, and include this REG file in your deployment. Chapter 17, "Deploying Office 2003 Settings," describes how to deploy registry settings with Office.

Enabling Remote Desktop Remotely

Remote Desktop is one of my all-time favorite Windows features. I've raved about it numerous times throughout this book because it enables me to use several computers from the comfort of a single screen and keyboard. In an enterprise environment, Remote Desktop enables users to connect to their desktop computers from any other computer in the organization. It also enables administrators to manage computers remotely and even install software on remote computers.

As a security measure, Windows doesn't enable Remote Desktop by default. As a result, you must enable it on your disk image or enable it using the System Properties dialog box. In Control Panel, launch System. On the Remote tab, select the Allow Users To Connect Remotely To This Computer check box.

I've got a better solution. Use Regedit to edit the remote computer's registry. Change the `REG_DWORD` value `fDenyTSConnections` in the key `HKLM\SYSTEM\CurrentControlSet\Control\Terminal Server` to `0x00`. Setting this value to `0x01` disables Remote Desktop. After you change this value, you'll be able to log on to the computer using Remote Desktop. The account you use to edit this setting must belong to the remote computer's local Administrators group.

Customizing the Windows Logon

I'll end this chapter by showing you how to customize the logon process in Windows. The first thing I want to show you is how to customize the screen saver that Windows uses when it's displaying the Log On To Windows dialog box. There's no user interface for configuring this screen saver. However, you can change it in the key HKU\.DEFAULT\Control Panel\Desktop. Set the value of SCRNSAVE.EXE to the name of the screen saver file that you want to use. The default value is Logon.scr, which is the logon screen saver. If you want to use the Starfield screen saver instead, set SCRN-SAVE.EXE to Ssstars.scr.

The second customization is a bit more serious. Companies often want to display an acceptable usage policy when users log on to their computers. You can do that by setting the REG_SZ value LegalNoticeCaption to the caption that you want to display in the window's title bar, and the REG_SZ value LegalNoticeText to the text that you want to display in the window. Both values are in the key HKLM\SOFT-WARE\Microsoft\Windows NT\CurrentVersion\Winlogon. For example, you can set LegalNoticeCaption to Corporate Policy and LegalNoticeText to Corporate policy prohibits the use of this computer for actual work.

Restoring Administrative Shares

By default, Windows automatically creates special hidden administrative shares that administrators, programs, and services can use to manage the computer environment or network. These special shared resources are not visible in Windows Explorer or My Computer, but you can view them by using the Shared Folders node in the Computer Management console. Depending on the configuration of your computer, you might see some or all of the following special shared resources listed in the Shares folder under Shared Folders:

- **DriveLetter$.** Root partitions and volumes are shared as the drive letter name appended with the $ character. For example, drive letters C and D are shared as C$ and D$.
- **ADMIN$.** A resource that is used during remote administration of a computer.
- **IPC$.** A resource that shares the named pipes that are necessary for communication between programs. Remember that this resource cannot be deleted.
- **NETLOGON.** A resource that is used on domain controllers.
- **SYSVOL.** A resource that is used on Active Directory domain controllers.
- **PRINT$.** A resource that is used during the remote administration of printers.
- **FAX$.** A shared folder on a server that is used by fax clients during fax transmissions.

Microsoft recommends that you not delete or modify these special shared resources. If the default administrative shares were removed or if the automatic creation of these shares is turned off, you can edit the registry to restore the shares so that they are automatically created in Windows. To restore administrative shares so that they are automatically created in Windows, use the following steps:

1. Start Regedit.

2. Delete the REG_DWORD value AutoShareServer or set it to 0x01. This value is in HKLM\SYSTEM\CurrentControlSet\Services\LanmanServer\Parameters. When this value is set to 0x01 or if it doesn't exist, Windows automatically creates the administrative shares.

3. Restart the Server service. To do so, run the following commands:

    net stop server

    net start server

Changing Source Location

If you build a Windows-based disk image in a lab and then install it on a production computer, Windows looks for the installation source files in their original location when users add or remove components. This isn't a huge problem, because Windows prompts users to specify a different path for the source files; however, will users know this path? Do you want to bother users with this step?

A better solution is to change the source file in the registry. Set the REG_SZ value SourcePath to the path of the Windows source files. This value is in HKLM\Software \Microsoft\Windows\CurrentVersion\Setup\SourcePath. While you're at it, you should go ahead and reset the path of the service pack source files. This is the REG_SZ value ServicePackSourcePath in the same key.

Tip   You can automatically reset the source path when you deploy disk images. Set the value ResetSourcePath in the [Unattended] section of Sysprep.inf. If the path specified in this value doesn't exist, Windows automatically resets the source path to the first CD-ROM drive.

Part IV
Appendixes

The appendixes in this part describe how Microsoft Windows XP and Windows Server 2003 organize the registry. They also describe some of the more interesting settings in the registry. They don't describe every key and every setting, but they give you the information you'll need to find your way. Both power users and IT professionals can use this information as a road map to navigate the thousands of settings that the registry contains.

Appendix A
File Associations

The bulk of the registry's content is in HKCR, which is where Microsoft Windows XP and Windows Server 2003 (Windows) store file associations and class registrations. These settings associate different types of files with the programs that can open, edit, and print them. They also register different program classes so that Windows can create objects using them.

A large number of the customizations I make on a regular basis are simple ones in HKCR. For example, I like to add commands to the file association for folders so that I can open a command prompt window with the selected folder set as the current working directory. I've also added commands to the My Computer object so that I can quickly access Registry Editor (Regedit) and Tweak UI. If you master the contents of HKCR, the opportunities for tweaking Windows so that it looks and feels the way you want are boundless.

The root key HKCR is many times more complex than it was back in the days of Microsoft Windows 95, when I wrote my first registry book. I won't even attempt to describe all the different values you find in HKCR. Instead, I'm going to describe the most useful subkeys and values so that you can customize Windows using the same techniques that I use.

Merge Algorithm

Recall from Chapter 1, "Learning the Basics," that HKCR was a link to the key HKLM\SOFTWARE\Classes before Microsoft Windows 2000, but it is more complicated now. Windows merges HKLM\SOFTWARE\Classes and HKCU\Software\Classes. The data in HKLM is default file associations and class registrations, whereas the data in HKCU is per-user file associations and class registrations. HKCU\Software\Classes is really a link to HKU*SID*_Classes, which Windows loads when it loads the profile hive in HKU*SID*. If the same value appears in both branches, the value in HKCU\Software\Classes has higher precedence and wins over the value in HKLM \SOFTWARE\Classes.

Chapter 1 described the benefits of this merge algorithm, but in short, it enables users to install applications and use file associations that don't affect other users. Thus, two users who share a computer can use two different programs to edit the same types of files.

When you create a new key in the root of HKCR, Windows actually creates it in HKLM\SOFTWARE\Classes. Windows doesn't provide a user interface other than Registry Editor to add class registrations to HKCU\Software\Classes because the intention is to allow programs to register per-user program classes. When you edit an existing program class, however, the change is reflected in HKLM or HKCU, depending on where the program class already exists. If the program class exists in both places, Windows updates only the version in HKCU.

File Extension Keys

Files containing particular types of data usually have the same file extension. For example, Microsoft Office Word 2003 documents have the *.doc* file extension. Although three-character extensions are the norm, extensions can be longer. Files with the same extension are members of a *file class*. File classes define behaviors common to all files that share that file name extension. By customizing file associations, you can specify which application opens a file, add commands to the shortcut menu, or even specify a custom icon that Windows Explorer will use for that type of file.

File associations have two parts. The first is a file extension key, HKCR*.ext*. When Windows needs information about a file type, it looks up this key. The default value of the file extension key contains the name of the program class associated with it, which is the second part. Program classes are in HKCR*progid*, where *progid* is the program ID of the application. The default value of progid contains the friendly name of the application. For example, the file extension key HKCR\.txt has a default value of txtfile. If you look in HKCR\txtfile to find the program class associated with it, you'll find the description *Text File*. Figure A-1 illustrates this relationship with the *.ani* file extension.

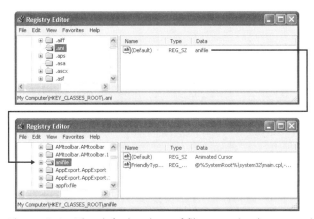

Figure A-1   The default values of file extension keys associate these keys with program classes.

File extension keys can have a variety of subkeys and values. The following list describes the most common:

- **OpenWithList.**   This subkey contains one or more keys bearing the names of the applications to appear in the Recommended Programs list in the Open With dialog box. See the "OpenWithList" section that follows for more information.

- **PerceivedType.**   This REG_SZ value indicates the file's perceived type. Windows XP and Windows Server 2003 are the only versions of Windows that use this key. See the "PerceivedType" section that follows for more information.

- **ShellNew.**   This subkey defines a template from which Windows creates a new file when users choose this file type on the New menu. See the "ShellNew" section that follows for more information.

- **Content Type.**   This REG_SZ value indicates the MIME type.

- **OpenWithProgids.**   This subkey contains a list of alternate program classes associated with the file extension. Windows displays these programs in the Other Programs list in the Open With dialog box.

OpenWithList

Sometimes users want to open files with applications that aren't associated with the file class. For example, a user might want to open a document in WordPad instead of Microsoft Office Word 2003. In other cases, users might want to open files that have no file associations. The Open With dialog box allows both scenarios.

The applications you see in the Open With dialog box are registered in HKCR \Applications. This key contains one subkey for each application, and the subkey bears the name of the program's executable file. You can prevent Windows from displaying an application in the Open With dialog box by adding the REG_SZ value NoOpenWith to HKCR\Applications*program*.exe.

PerceivedType

Perceived types are similar to file types, except perceived types refer to broad catego-ries of file format types, rather than to specific types of files. Think of them as super types. Perceived types include images, text files, audio files, and compressed files. In Windows, you can associate a perceived type with each file type. For example, the file extensions *.bmp*, *.png*, *.jpg*, and *.gif* are perceived as image files. Windows defines sev-eral perceived file types. In the file extension key, you set the REG_SZ value Perceived-Type to one of the following:

- Image
- Text
- Audio
- Video
- Compressed
- System

ShellNew

When users right-click in a folder and click New, they see a list of template files that they can create in the folder. You can extend the New menu with additional file tem-plates. First make sure that HKCR contains a file extension key for the type of file you're creating. Then create the ShellNew subkey under the file extension key. For example, to define a template for files with the *.inf* extension, create the key HKCR\.inf\ShellNew. Then in ShellNew, create one of the following values:

- **Command.** Executes an application. This is a REG_SZ value command to execute. For example, you use a command to launch a wizard.

- **Data.** Creates a file containing specified data. This is a REG_BINARY value that contains the file's data. Windows ignores this value if either NullFile or File-Name exists.

- **FileName.** Creates a file that is a copy of a specified file. This is a REG_SZ value that contains the path and name of the file to copy. If the file is in the user pro-file's Templates folder, you can leave off the path.

- **NullFile.** Creates an empty file. This is a REG_SZ value that contains no data. If the value NullFile exists, Windows ignores Data and FileName.

Program Class Keys

Program classes define a program and the behaviors associated with it. Program classes are in HKCR\progid, where *progid* is a program identifier. For example, HKCR\txtfile is a program class. Windows associates file extension keys with pro-gram classes through the file extension keys' default values. The default value of the program class contains the class's friendly name. The proper format of a program ID is *application.component.version*. For example, Word.Document.6 is a proper program ID. This format isn't always used, though, not even by Windows.

Program classes contain the following values and subkeys:

- **AlwaysShowExt.**   This empty REG_SZ value indicates that Windows Explorer should always show the file extension, even if the user has hidden it.

- **CurVer.**   The default value of this subkey contains the program ID of the most current version.

- **DefaultIcon.**   The default value of this subkey is the default icon that Windows displays for files associated with this program class. This value can be either a REG_SZ or a REG_EXPAND_SZ string, but it must use the format *file,index*, where *file* is the path and name of the file containing the icon, and *index* is the index of the icon in the file. Optionally, if you know the exact resource ID, you can use the format *file,- resource*. See the "DefaultIcon" section that follows for more information.

- **EditFlags.**   This is a REG_DWORD value that controls how Windows handles file classes linked to this program class. You can also use the EditFlags value to control users' ability to modify certain aspects of these file classes. See the "EditFlags" section that follows for more information.

- **FriendlyTypeName.**   This REG_SZ value is the friendly name for the program class. You see this value in Windows Explorer. In Windows, this value supercedes the program class's default value, which earlier versions of Windows still use and Windows maintains for backward compatibility. Still, the default value of the program class and this value should remain the same for consistency. Windows commonly specifies a resource instead of a string in this value. The format is *@file,index* or *@file,-resource*.

- **InfoTip.**   This REG_SZ value contains a brief message that Windows displays for this program class when users position the mouse pointer over a file or folder linked to it. This value can be a string or a resource as described for the FriendlyTypeName value.

- **IsShortcut.**   This empty REG_SZ values indicates that the file is a shortcut. Windows Explorer displays the shortcut overlay on top of the file's icon.

- **NeverShowExt.**   This empty REG_SZ value indicates that Windows Explorer should never show the file extension, even if the user has configured Windows Explorer to show file extensions for known types.

- **Shell.**   This subkey contains commands (called *verbs*) defined for the program class. For example, the txtfile program class defines the commands for opening and printing text files. See the "Shell" section, later in this appendix, for more information. This subkey is the heart of most customizations you'll do in HKCR.

> ## Special Program Classes
>
> The program classes `Directory`, `Drive`, and `Folder` are specialized program classes that are useful to customize. The organization of these program classes is just like any other. They contain `Shell` subkeys that you can customize to add, change, and remove the commands you see on their shortcut menus. The trick is knowing which program classes apply to which types of objects:
>
> - **`Directory`.**   This program class applies to any normal folder that you can view in Windows Explorer.
>
> - **`Drive`.**   This program class applies only to drives that you see in My Computer.
>
> - **`Folder`.**   This program class applies to all system folders, drives, and other folders that you can view in Windows Explorer.
>
> The program class `Folder` is the most inclusive. It includes all folders and all special system folders, such as Control Panel, My Computer, and so on. As such, this is typically the program class that you want to customize unless you need to restrict your customization to specific drives or non-system folders.

DefaultIcon

Windows provides default icons for every type of object you see in Windows Explorer. That includes files, drives, and so on. You can customize these icons as described in Chapter 4, "Hacking the Registry." Each file class's `DefaultIcon` value contains the path and name of the file containing the icon. You can assign an icon file, which has the *.ico* extension, to this value, or you can assign an icon from program files using the formats *file,index* or *file,-resource*. *Index* is an incremental index number of a resource, and *resource* is a specific resource ID. Doing this requires that you know either the relative location of an icon in a file or the icon's exact resource ID. To find this value, you can use a third-party resource editor. Many third-party resource editors are shareware tools you can download from your favorite shareware Web site.

EditFlags

The `REG_DWORD` value `EditFlags` gives you some control of a program class's behavior. You can also use it to limit the ways in which users can change a program class. Each bit in this value represents a different setting, and Table A-1 describes the bit mask of each. See Chapter 1, "Learning the Basics," to refresh your memory on how to use bit masks.

Table A-1   **Bits in EditFlags**

Bit mask	Description
0x00000001	Excludes the file class.
0x00000002	Shows file classes, such as folders, that aren't associated with a file extension.
0x00000004	Denotes that the file class has a file extension.
0x00000008	Prevents users from editing the registry entries associated with this file class. They can't add new entries or change existing entries.
0x00000010	Prevents users from deleting the registry entries associated with this file class.
0x00000020	Prevents users from adding new verbs to the file class.
0x00000040	Prevents users from changing verbs.
0x00000080	Prevents users from deleting verbs.
0x00000100	Prevents users from changing the description of the file class.
0x00000200	Prevents users from changing the icon assigned to the file class.
0x00000400	Prevents users from changing the default verb.
0x00000800	Prevents users from changing the commands associated with verbs.
0x00001000	Prevents users from modifying or deleting verbs.
0x00002000	Prevents users from changing or deleting DDE-related values.
0x00008000	Prevents users from changing the content type associate with this file class.
0x00010000	Allows users to safely use the file class's open verb for downloaded files.
0x00020000	Disables the Never Ask Me check box.
0x00040000	Denotes that the file class's file name extension is always shown, even if the user hides known file extensions in the Folder Options dialog box.
0x00100000	Denotes that members of this file class are not added to the Recent Documents folder.

Shell

File classes contain verbs, which are commands that Windows executes to complete certain actions. Verbs are related to the shortcut menus that you see when you right-click a file. Each item on the shortcut menu is a verb. A program class's verbs are in HKCR\progid\shell, which contains one subkey for each verb. For example, HKCR\txtfile\shell contains the subkeys open and print, which are the Open and Print verbs. The default value of the shell key indicates the name of the default verb. For example, if the default value of shell is edit, the subkey edit is the default verb. If the default value of shell is empty, Windows uses the verb open. If that verb is missing, it uses the first verb as the default. Figure A-2 shows an example that relates the shell key to shortcut menus.

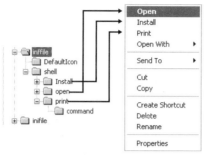

Figure A-2   This figure shows the relationship of a program class's verbs to the shortcut menu.

Canonical verbs are built into the operating system. Examples of canonical verbs are Open, Edit, and Print. One thing that makes canonical verbs special is that Windows automatically translates them to different languages as necessary. The following list shows typical canonical verbs, some of which are special verbs that users don't see on menus:

- **Edit.**   This verb is usually the same as Open, but it enables the user to edit the file's contents.

- **Explore.**   This verb opens the selected folder in Windows Explorer.

- **Find.**   This verb opens Search Assistant with the selected folder as the default search location.

- **Open.**   This verb is typically the default verb, which opens a file in the associated application.

- **Open As.**   This verb opens the Open With dialog box.

- **Play.**   This verb indicates that the contents of the file will be opened and played, rather than just opening the file and waiting for the user to play it.

- **Preview.**   This verb enables users to preview files without opening or editing them. An example is previewing images, rather than opening to edit them.

- **Print.**   This verb causes the application to print the file's contents and exit. Applications should display as little user interface as possible.

- **PrintTo.**   This verb is a special verb that supports performing drag-and-drop operations to printers. Users don't see this verb on shortcut menus.

- **Properties.**   This verb opens the *Name* Properties dialog box.

- **RunAs.**   This is a special verb that enables users to open a file or run an application in the context of a different user. Users can see this verb on shortcut menus by holding down the SHIFT key while right-clicking the file.

You can add supplemental verbs to any program class. For example, you can add the verb Edit in WordPad to the `txtfile` program class to have the option of editing text files in WordPad without changing the default verbs. To add verbs to a program class, create a new subkey for it in the `Shell` key. The new subkey is `HKCR\`*`progid`*`\Shell\verb`. Then set the default value of the verb to the text you want to see on the shortcut menu. You can make any character in the description a hotkey by prefixing it with an ampersand (&). For example, `Open in &WordPad` makes the letter *W* a hotkey for that the verb. Add the subkey command to the verb, and set its default value to the command you want to execute when you choose that verb. Figure A-3 shows an example.

Figure A-3   Add supplemental verbs to a program class by creating new subkeys in `Shell`.

The default value of the command needs a bit more explanation. First, if the path and name of the program file contain spaces, you should enclose the command in quotation marks. Second, you use `%1` as a placeholder for the file name that you right-clicked. For example, assume the command is *Notepad "%1"*. If you right-click `C:\Sample\Text.txt`, the command is *Notepad "C:\Sample\Text.txt"*. Note that you should always enclose `%1` in quotation marks so that the command works with long file names.

You see extended verbs only when you press the SHIFT key while right-clicking a file. Creating extended verbs is a handy way to remove clutter from shortcut menus. For example, you can add extended verbs that you don't use often to shortcut menus, hiding them behind the SHIFT key. To make a verb an extended verb, add the empty `REG_SZ` value extended to the verb's subkey, `Shell\`*`verb`*.

Specialized Keys

When Windows queries a file association, it checks the following keys in the order shown; that is, locations further down the list have a higher order of precedence than locations higher in the list:

- `HKCR\`*`progid`*.   This is the program class associated with the file extension key through the file extension key's default value.

- `HKCR\SystemFileAssociations`.   This key defines perceived file types and associates commands with each. See the "SystemFileAssociations" section that follows for more information.

- HKCR*.   This is the base class for files of all types. You see the commands in this key on the shortcut menus of all files.

- HKCR\AllFileSystemObjects.   This key defines commands for all files and folders. By default, this key just adds the Send To item on shortcut menus.

The following sections describe some keys in the previous list as well as others that are useful for customizing Windows. Notably, the section "SystemFileAssociations" describes how to customize the commands you see on files perceived as a certain type. The section "Applications" describes how to customize the Open With dialog box and more.

Applications

To display an application in the Open With dialog box, that application must register in HKCR\Applications. Each subkey in Applications bears the name of the program file. For example, Notepad is in HKCR\Applications\Notepad.exe. You must also add the OpenWithList key to the file extension key, as described earlier in this appendix. You find combinations of the following values and subkeys in the program's subkeys:

- FriendlyAppName.   This REG_SZ value contains the application's friendly name. This value can contain a string, but it more likely contains a value in the format *@file,- resource*, where *file* is the name of the program file containing the string resource identified by *resource*.

- NoOpenWith.   This empty REG_SZ value indicates that Windows should not add the program to the Open With list.

- SupportedTypes.   This subkey contains a list of file extensions, including the leading period, which indicates which type of files the program can open. For example, HKCR \Applications\mplayer2.exe\SupportedTypes contains the empty REG_SZ values *.asf* and *.mp3*, indicating that the program can open files that have these file extensions. This list filters the Open With list.

SystemFileAssociations

The key HKCR\SystemFileAssociations is a cool way to customize the shortcut menus of files by their perceived purposes. For example, you can customize the verbs you see for all files you perceive as text files or all files you perceive as image files.

HKCR\SystemFileAssociations contains subkeys for the different perceived types you can set in the value PerceivedType. You learned about this value in the "Perceived-Type" section earlier in this appendix. Thus, setting PerceivedType in a file extension key associates that file name extension with the commands in this key. For example, if you set the value `PerceivedType` in `HKCR\.inf` to `text`, you'll see the commands in `HKCR\SystemFileAssociations\text` on the shortcut menu of any file that has the *.inf* extension. Perceived types in `SystemFileAssociations` include `audio`, `image`, `system`, `text`, and `video`. You can add additional perceived types to `SystemFileAssociations`, though. The organization of `HKCR\SystemFileAssociations\type` is the same as program classes, which you learned about in the "Program Class Keys" section earlier in this appendix.

Unknown

When users try opening files that have an extension not registered in `HKCR`, Windows looks in `HKCR\Unknown`. By default, the only verb in `Unknown\Shell` is Open As. Windows displays the Open With dialog box for unknown types of files.

COM Class Keys

The key `HKCR\CLSID` contains COM class registrations. `HKCR\CLSID\clsid` is an individual class registration, where *clsid* is the class's class ID, which is a GUID. See Chapter 1, "Learning the Basics," to learn more about GUIDs. The default value of each class registration contains the class's name, but it's not all that friendly. There's not a lot to customize in `HKCR\CLSID`. Programs register these classes when you install them so that they can create objects from these classes.

Class registrations sometimes contain the same subkeys as program classes in `HKCR`. For example, class registrations support the `DefaultIcon` and `InfoTip` values. They also contain many more subkeys and values that program classes don't support. Listing them here is senseless because they are in the programmer's domain and not useful for a power user or IT professional customizing Windows. However, knowing the class ID of certain COM classes is useful when customizing other parts of the registry. For example, adding some classes to the desktop's namespace enables you to customize the objects you see on it. You can use this same information to hide icons that you see in My Network Places. Chapter 4, "Hacking the Registry," describes how to show and hide desktop icons using these class IDs. Thus, Table A-2 lists the most interesting COM classes that are in `HKCR\CLSID`.

Table A-2   Special Classes in HKCR\CLSID

Object	Class identifier
Shell folders	
ActiveX Cache	{88C6C381-2E85-11D0-94DE-444553540000}
Computer Search Results	{1F4DE370-D627-11D1-BA4F-00A0C91EEDBA}
History	{FF393560-C2A7-11CF-BFF4-444553540000}
Internet Explorer	{871C5380-42A0-1069-A2EA-08002B30309D}
My Computer	{20D04FE0-3AEA-1069-A2D8-08002B30309D}
My Documents	{450D8FBA-AD25-11D0-98A8-0800361B1103}
My Network Places	{208D2C60-3AEA-1069-A2D7-08002B30309D}
Offline Files	{AFDB1F70-2A4C-11D2-9039-00C04F8EEB3E}
Programs	{7BE9D83C-A729-4D97-B5A7-1B7313C39E0A}
Recycle Bin	{645FF040-5081-101B-9F08-00AA002F954E}
Search Results	{E17D4FC0-5564-11D1-83F2-00A0C90DC849}
Shared Documents	{59031A47-3F72-44A7-89C5-5595FE6B30EE}
Start Menu	{48E7CAAB-B918-4E58-A94D-505519C795DC}
Temporary Internet Files	{7BD29E00-76C1-11CF-9DD0-00A0C9034933}
Web	{BDEADF00-C265-11D0-BCED-00A0C90AB50F}
Control Panel folders	
Administrative Tools	{D20EA4E1-3957-11D2-A40B-0C5020524153}
Fonts	{D20EA4E1-3957-11D2-A40B-0C5020524152}
Network Connections	{7007ACC7-3202-11D1-AAD2-00805FC1270E}
Printers And Faxes	{2227A280-3AEA-1069-A2DE-08002B30309D}
Scanners And Cameras	{E211B736-43FD-11D1-9EFB-0000F8757FCD}
Scheduled Tasks	{D6277990-4C6A-11CF-8D87-00AA0060F5BF}
Control Panel icons	
Folder Options	{6DFD7C5C-2451-11D3-A299-00C04F8EF6AF}
Taskbar And Start Menu	{0DF44EAA-FF21-4412-828E-260A8728E7F1}
User Accounts	{7A9D77BD-5403-11D2-8785-2E0420524153}
Other	
Add Network Places	{D4480A50-BA28-11D1-8E75-00C04FA31A86}
Briefcase	{85BBD920-42A0-1069-A2E4-08002B30309D}
E-mail	{2559A1F5-21D7-11D4-BDAF-00C04F60B9F0}
Help And Support	{2559A1F1-21D7-11D4-BDAF-00C04F60B9F0}
Internet	{2559A1F4-21D7-11D4-BDAF-00C04F60B9F0}
Network Setup Wizard	{2728520D-1EC8-4C68-A551-316B684C4EA7}
Run	{2559A1F3-21D7-11D4-BDAF-00C04F60B9F0}
Search	{2559A1F0-21D7-11D4-BDAF-00C04F60B9F0}
Windows Security	{2559A1F2-21D7-11D4-BDAF-00C04F60B9F0}

Appendix B
Network Settings

This appendix describes some core network settings in Microsoft Windows XP and Windows Server 2003 (Windows). This includes client, server, and TCP/IP service settings. This appendix is not comprehensive. (A comprehensive description of network settings would fill half this book.) The Windows Resource Kit Registry Reference, available at *http://go.microsoft.com/fwlink/?linkid=4543*, contains a more thorough description of the many network settings.

HKCU\Network

The Network key stores information about mapped network drives. Each subkey in Network represents a drive that is connected to the computer and that will be reconnected when the user logs on again. The subkeys are named for the drive letter to which the drive is mapped. The system adds a *Driveletter* subkey to the registry when a drive is mapped and Reconnect at Logon is selected. The entries in the *Driveletter* subkeys store data that is used to reconnect the drive. Table B-1 describes some of these entries.

Table B-1 HKCU\Network*Drive Letter*

Name	Type	Values	Default	Description
Connection-Type	REG_DWORD	0x01—Drive redirection 0x02—Print redirection	0x01	Specifies how the drive is connected to the local computer.
ProviderName	REG_SZ	*Network name*	Microsoft Windows Network	Specifies the network provider used to map this particular network drive.

Table B-1   HKCU\Network*Drive Letter*

Name	Type	Values	Default	Description
ProviderType	REG_DWORD	*Provider-number*		Specifies a constant that identifies the provider used to map this network drive. The value for the Microsoft LanMan provider is 0x20000. Other values are assigned by Microsoft to third-party providers.

HKLM\SYSTEM\CurrentControlSet\Services

The Services subkeys contain entries for standard and optional Windows services, such as network drivers and services. Although the values of the entries differ for each service, most Services subkeys have the same subkeys and entries.

Each Services subkey bears the name of the service that uses it. Often, this is also the name of the file from which the service is loaded. Some services and devices represented by subkeys in the Services subkey are installed on the computer, but some subkeys represent services that are not installed or not enabled. To determine which services are installed on the computer, click Services in the Computer Management console. To determine which devices are installed on the computer, use Device Manager.

For more information about the Services key, see Appendix D, "Per-Computer Settings."

LanmanServer

The LanmanServer subkey stores configuration data for the LAN Manager 2.x Server service. The following list describes the settings in the Parameters subkey of LanmanServer:

- **AlertSchedule.**   This REG_DWORD value specifies how often the Server service checks alert conditions and sends alert messages. This entry also defines the time interval used in calculating the general error rate (ErrorThreshold) and the rate of network errors (NetworkErrorThreshold). This entry does not exist in the registry by default. You can add it by using the registry editor Regedit.exe. Valid values range from 0x01 to 0xFFFF. The default value is 0x05.

- **ConnectionNoSessionTimeout.**   This REG_DWORD value specifies how long the Server service maintains an unused virtual circuit. If the time specified in the value of this entry expires and the client has not established a session, the Server service closes the virtual circuit. Decreasing this value can conserve server resources, but it might impair performance by requiring more virtual circuits to be re-established. This entry does not exist in the registry by default. You can add it by using the registry editor Regedit.exe. Values range from 0x01 through 0xFFFFFFFF, and the default value is 0x02.

- **DiskSpaceThreshold.**   This REG_DWORD value specifies the percentage of disk space that must remain free for use. If the percentage of free space falls below the value of this entry, the Server service records the following event in the System Log in Event Viewer:

  "The *<disk-letter>* disk is at or near capacity. You might need to delete some files." (Srv Event ID 2013)

  If the value of this entry is zero, the system does not check the percentage of free space on the disk; it also does not check for free space in megabytes as specified by LowDiskSpaceMinimum. Values range from 0 through 99. The default value is 10. This entry does not exist in the registry by default. You can add it by using the registry editor Regedit.exe.

- **EnableWFW311DirectIpx.**   This REG_DWORD value specifies whether older, direct-hosted Internetwork Packet Exchange (IPX) clients can connect to this server. Clients running earlier versions of Windows for Workgroups provide inadequate support for named pipes when running over direct-hosted IPX, causing named-pipe applications to stop responding. You can prevent these clients from connecting to the server by setting the value of this entry to 0.

- **hidden.**   This REG_DWORD value specifies whether the server's computer name is displayed to other computers in the domain. If the value of this entry is 0, or if this entry is absent from the registry, users can see the server's computer name in the following displays:

  - ❑ In the Network Connection Wizard

  - ❑ In the Browse for Network Connections dialog box. (In the Map Network Drive dialog box, click Browse, or in My Network Places, click Add Network Place)

  - ❑ In My Network Places, by clicking Entire Network or Computers Near Me

  To omit this computer's name from the display, add this entry to the registry and change its value to 1.

  This entry does not exist in the registry by default. You can add it by using the registry editor Regedit.exe.

- **IRPstackSize.**   This REG_DWORD value specifies how many stack locations the Server service establishes for I/O Request Packets (IRPs). It might be necessary to increase this number for certain transports or if you have many file system drivers installed on the system. Each stack uses 36 bytes of memory for each receive buffer (also known as a *work item*). This entry does not exist in the registry by default. You can add it by using the registry editor Regedit.exe. Values range from 11 through 50, and the default is 15.

■ **LowDiskSpaceMinimum.**   This REG_DWORD value specifies the amount of disk space that must remain free for use. If the amount of free space falls below the value of this entry and below the percentage specified by the value of the DiskSpaceThreshhold entry, the Server service records the following event in the System Log in Event Viewer:

"The *<disk-letter>* disk is at or near capacity. You might need to delete some files." (Srv Event ID 2013)

If the value of this entry is 0, the system does not check whether free disk space has decreased below a specific number of megabytes. However, unlike DiskSpaceThreshhold (which when equal to zero prevents both checks of free space), the value of this entry has no effect on the check specified by DiskSpaceThreshhold. This entry does not exist in the registry by default. You can add it by using the registry editor Regedit.exe. Values range from 0x00 through 0xFFFFFFFF, and the default value is 400.

■ **RestrictNullSessAccess.**   This REG_DWORD value specifies whether the Server service limits access to the system by clients that are logged on to the system account without username and password authentication. Setting this value to 0x01 restricts access to Null sessions. Unauthenticated users can access only the server pipes listed in the value of the NullSessionPipes entry and the shared directories listed in the value of the NullSessionShares entry. This entry does not exist in the registry by default. You can add it by using the registry editor Regedit.exe.

■ **SessConns.**   This REG_DWORD value specifies the maximum number of connections to network shares (tree connects) that are permitted for a single network connection. If the client requests more connections, the Server service returns an error message. Values range from 1 through 2048 seconds, and the default value is 2048. This entry does not exist in the registry by default. You can add it by using the registry editor Regedit.exe.

■ **SessOpens.**   This REG_DWORD value specifies the maximum number of open files permitted for each connection. It is possible to have multiple sessions on a single connection. Values range from 1 through 16384, and the default is 16384. This entry does not exist in the registry by default. You can add it by using the registry editor Regedit.exe.

■ **SessUsers.**   This REG_DWORD value specifies the maximum number of users who can be logged on to each virtual circuit. Values range from 1 through 2048, and the default is 2048. This entry does not exist in the registry by default. You can add it by using the registry editor Regedit.exe.

- **SharingViolationDelay.** This REG_DWORD value specifies how often the Server service repeats a file operation when the initial request resulted in a sharing violation error. The value of this entry specifies the minimum time that must elapse between repeated attempts to open, rename, or delete a file. This entry does not exist in the registry by default. You can add it by using the registry editor Regedit.exe. Values range from 1 through 1000 milliseconds, and the default is 200.

- **SharingViolationRetries.** This REG_DWORD value specifies the maximum number of times the Server service repeats an attempted file operation when the request results in a sharing violation error. The Server service repeats the operation, at a rate determined by the value of the **SharingViolationDelay** entry, until either the operation is successful or the value of this entry is reached. If a client requests more attempts than the value of this entry permits, the Server service returns an error. This entry applies to open, rename, and delete file operations. This entry does not exist in the registry by default. You can add it by using the registry editor Regedit.exe. Values range from 1 through 1000 attempts, and the default value is 5.

- **SizReqBuf.** This REG_DWORD value specifies the size of the request buffers that the Server service uses. Small buffers use less memory, but large buffers can improve performance. For computers running Windows Server 2003 and with 512 MB or more of physical memory, the default size of the request buffers is 16,644 bytes; for servers with less physical memory, the default size is 4,356 bytes. If this entry is present in the registry, its value overrides the default value. This entry does not exist in the registry by default. You can add it by using the registry editor Regedit.exe. Values range from 512 through 65,536 bytes.

- **srvcomment.** This REG_SZ value specifies the text that appears in the Comment field next to the name of this computer in My Network Places. To view the comment text, in My Network Places, double-click Entire Network or Computers Near Me. From the View menu, either click Details or double-click the name of any computer. Or, in My Network Places, double-click Add Network Place, and view the comment text in the Browse for Network Resource dialog box. This entry does not exist in the registry by default.

- **ThreadPriority.** This REG_DWORD value specifies the priority of all Server service threads in relation to the base priority of the Server service process. Table B-2 describes the valid values. This entry does not exist in the registry by default. You can add it by using the registry editor Regedit.exe.

Table B-2   ThreadPriority

Value	Description
0	Run at the same priority as the process.
1	Run at one priority level higher than the process. This is equivalent to a process running in the foreground, where it interacts with users.

Table B-2 `ThreadPriority`

Value	Description
2	Run at two priority levels higher than the process.
15	Run at real-time priority. Threads running in real time can exclude all other threads, including essential system threads and threads that process mouse and keyboard commands.

- **Users.**   This REG_DWORD value specifies whether a limit exists for the number of users that can be logged on to the Server service simultaneously, and if so, specifies what the limit is. Values range from 0x01 through 0xFFFFFFFF users, and the default value is 0xFFFFFFFF. If the value is 0xFFFFFFFF, there is no limit to the number of users that can log on to the Server service simultaneously. This entry does not exist in the registry by default. You can add it by using the registry editor Regedit.exe.

LanmanWorkstation

The LanmanWorkstation subkey stores configuration data for the Workstation service. The Workstation service provides network connections and communications on computers running Windows XP Professional and Windows Server 2003. The following list describes the settings in this key's Parameters subkey:

- **BufNamedPipes.**   This REG_DWORD value specifies whether the redirector caches character-mode named pipes. If named pipes are not stored in the cache, they are flushed to the server immediately, and read-ahead is disabled on these named pipes. Set this value to 0x01 to permit the Workstation service to cache character-mode named pipes. This entry does not exist in the registry by default. You can add it by using the registry editor Regedit.exe.

- **KeepConn.**   This REG_DWORD value specifies the maximum amount of time that an idle connection can remain open. If the idle time for a connection reaches the value of this entry, the connection is closed. Increase the value of this entry if your application closes and opens Universal Naming Convention (UNC) files on a server less frequently than every 10 minutes. This decreases the number of reconnections to a server. Values range from 1 through 65,536 seconds, and the default value is 600 seconds.

- **LockIncrement.**   This REG_DWORD value specifies how long an OS/2-based application can wait when a request for a lock fails. If the lock request cannot be granted before the time specified in the value of this entry expires, the redirector rejects the lock request. This entry is used either if OS/2-based applications running on servers (except servers using LAN Manager version 2.0 and later) request that a lock operation wait indefinitely or if the lock cannot be granted immediately. Do not change this value unless you are running an OS/2-based application that requests lock operations that might fail. This entry does not affect Windows 32-bit applications. Values range from 0x00 through 0xFFFFFFFF, and the default value is 0x0A milliseconds.

- **LockMaximum.** This REG_DWORD value is used to configure the lock backoff package. This entry prevents an application from consuming server time by issuing nonblocking requests when no data is available for the application. Values range from 0x00 through 0xFFFFFFFF milliseconds, and the default is 0x01F4.

- **LockQuota.** This REG_DWORD value specifies the maximum amount of data that can be read from a file when the value of the UseLockReadUnlock entry is 1. Consider increasing the value of this entry if your application performs a significant number of lock-and-read operations. These are operations in which an application locks data and then immediately reads the data. This entry does not exist in the registry by default. You can add it by using the registry editor Regedit.exe. Increasing the value of this entry to more than 2 MB and using an application that locks megabtyes of data can cause the system to deplete its paged pool. Values range from 0x00 through 0xFFFFFFFF, and the default is 0x1800 bytes.

- **MaxCmds.** This REG_DWORD value specifies the maximum number of network control blocks that the redirector can reserve. The value of this entry coincides with the number of execution threads that can be outstanding simultaneously. Increase this value to improve network throughput, especially if you are running applications that perform more than 15 operations simultaneously. However, because this entry also limits the number of outstanding execution threads, your network performance might not improve. Each additional execution thread uses a margin of 1 KB of nonpaged pool when the network is at capacity. However, these resources are not consumed until the user references data in the network control block. Values range from 50 through 65,536 network control blocks, and the default value is 50.

- **MaxCollectionCount.** This REG_DWORD value specifies the amount of data that must be present in the character-mode buffer of a named pipe to trigger a write operation. If the amount of data in the buffer meets or exceeds this value, it is written immediately. Otherwise, it is retained in the buffer until either more data is added or the value of the CollectionTime entry expires. Increasing the value of this entry can improve the performance of named-pipe applications, but it does not affect applications that do their own buffering, such as Microsoft SQL Server applications. This entry does not exist in the registry by default. You can add it by using the registry editor Regedit.exe. Values range from 0x00 through 0xFFFF, and the default value is 0x10 bytes.

- **SizCharBuf.** This REG_DWORD value specifies the size of the character buffers for a named pipe. The redirector maintains a read-ahead buffer and a write-behind buffer for each pipe. This entry establishes the size of both buffers. The buffer size determines the amount of data the redirector reads and writes. When reading, the redirector attempts to read enough data to fill the read buffer. If the data it is reading is smaller than the buffer, the redirector reads ahead until the buffer is full. If the data is larger than the buffer, the redirector bypasses the character-mode buffer and reads the data directly into the user buffer. When writing, the redirector collects data in the character-mode buffer until it meets or exceeds the size specified by the value of the MaxCollectionCount entry, or until the time specified by the value of the CollectionTime entry expires. Increasing the value of this entry can improve the performance of named-pipe applications, but it does not affect applications that do their own buffering, such as SQL Server applications. This entry does not exist in the registry by default. You can add it by using the registry editor Regedit.exe. Values range from 64 through 4096 bytes. The default value is 512.

- **UseLockReadUnlock.** Specifies whether the lock-and-read and write-and-unlock performance enhancements are enabled. These features improve performance when an application locks data and then immediately reads the data, or writes data and then immediately unlocks it. Setting this value to 0x01 enables lock-and-read and write-and-unlock features. Setting this value to 1 usually improves performance significantly. However, it degrades the performance of database applications that lock a range of data and do not allow data within that range to be read. This entry does not exist in the registry by default. You can add it by using the registry editor Regedit.exe.

- **UseOpportunisticLocking.** This REG_DWORD value specifies whether the opportunistic-locking (oplock) performance enhancement is enabled. If it is enabled, the redirector requests an opportunistic lock on any file opened in "Deny None" mode. As a result, the server performs automatic read-ahead and write-behind caching on behalf of the redirector. Setting this value to 0x01 enables opportunistic locking. This is the default value. This entry does not exist in the registry by default. You can add it by using the registry editor Regedit.exe.

- **UseUnlockBehind.** This REG_DWORD value specifies whether the unlock-behind optimization feature is enabled. If it is enabled, the redirector unlocks data immediately in response to an unlock request. It does not wait for confirmation from the server that the unlock operation is complete. Setting this value to 0x01 enables unlock-behind optimization. This entry does not exist in the registry by default. You can add it by using the registry editor Regedit.exe.

Tcpip\Parameters

The Tcpip subkey stores configuration data for the Microsoft implementation of TCP/IP (Transmission Control Protocol/Internet Protocol). TCP/IP is a suite of networking protocols that enable communication over diverse, interconnected networks.

This subkey stores some of the configuration data for TCP/IP, primarily the settings for the TCP/IP service. Other subkeys also store entries that affect the operation of the

TCP/IP implementation on your computer. These other subkeys include those for network components and for services related to TCP/IP, such as the Dynamic Host Configuration Protocol (DHCP), NetBIOS over TCP/IP (NetBT), and Windows Sockets (Winsock).

The `Parameters` subkey stores configuration data that applies to the TCP/IP service as a whole. This data can be overridden by settings specific to a network component using TCP/IP, such as a network adapter driver, or by settings specific to a service using TCP/IP, such as the Dynamic Host Configuration Protocol (DHCP) or Windows Sockets (Winsock). These component-specific entries reside in subkeys representing the component. The following list describes the settings in the `Parameters` subkey:

- **`KeepAliveInterval`.**   This `REG_DWORD` value specifies how often TCP repeats keep-alive transmissions when no response is received. TCP sends keep-alive transmissions to verify that idle connections are still active. This prevents TCP from inadvertently disconnecting active lines. Windows Server 2003 does not add this entry to the registry. You can add it by using the registry editor Regedit.exe. Values range from 0x01 through 0xFFFFFFFF milliseconds. The default is 0x03E8.

- **`KeepAliveTime`.**   This `REG_DWORD` value specifies how often TCP sends keep-alive transmissions. TCP sends keep-alive transmissions to verify that an idle connection is still active. This entry is used when the remote system is responding to TCP. Otherwise, the interval between transmissions is determined by the value of the `KeepAliveInterval` entry. By default, keep-alive transmissions are not sent. The TCP keep-alive feature must be enabled by a program (such as Telnet), or by an Internet browser (such as Internet Explorer). Windows does not add this entry to the registry. You can add it by using the registry editor Regedit.exe. Values range from 0x01 through 0xFFFFFFFF, and the default value is 0x6DDD00 milliseconds.

- **`MaxUserPort`.**   This `REG_DWORD` value specifies the highest port number that TCP can assign when an application requests an available user port from the system. Typically, ephemeral ports (those used briefly) are allocated to port numbers 1024 through 5000. Windows does not add this entry to the registry. You can add it by using the registry editor Regedit.exe. Values range from 5000 through 65,534. The default value is 5000.

- **`NumTcbTablePartitions`.**   This `REG_DWORD` value specifies the number of partitions in the Transport Control Block table. Partitioning the Transport Control Block table minimizes contention for table access. This is especially useful on multiprocessor systems. This entry does not exist in the registry by default. You can add it by using the registry editor Regedit.exe. Do not change the value of this entry before carefully studying the effect of different values in a test environment. When testing, do not enter a value greater than two times the number of processors on the computer. Values range from 0x01 through 0xFFFF TCB table partitions. The default value is 0x01.

- **PPTPTcpMaxDataRetransmissions.** This REG_DWORD value specifies how many times an unacknowledged Point-to-Point Tunneling Protocol (PPTP) packet is retransmitted before the connection is dropped. This entry lets you configure a limit on PPTP retransmissions separately from the limit for regular TCP retransmissions, which is stored in the value of the TCPMaxDataRetransmissions entry. You can then adjust the TCP setting to prevent denial-of-service attacks (also known as SYN flooding) without affecting PPTP traffic. To prevent the TCP dead gateway detection feature from inadvertently disconnecting a congested Internet link, set this value higher than the default value of the TCPMaxDataRetransmissions entry. Values range from 0x00 through 0xFF, and the default value is 0x05.

- **PrioritizeRecordData.** This REG_DWORD value specifies whether the Domain Name System (DNS) client, upon receiving an answer to a DNS query, looks for the address most similar to its own when there are multiple addresses in the answer to its query. By choosing the address most like its own, the client connects to the server nearest to it on the network, which reduces network traffic. When the value of this entry is 1, the client prioritizes for the nearest address; when the value is zero, the client attempts to connect to the first address in the answer. Values are 0x00 and 0x01; the default value is 0x01.

- **SackOpts.** This REG_DWORD value enables and disables the Selective Acknowledgment (SACK) feature of Windows TCP/IP. SACK is specified in RFC 2018, TCP Selective Acknowledgement Options. SACK is an optimizing feature that lets you acknowledge receipt of individual blocks of data in a continuous sequence, rather than just the last sequence number. The recipient can tell the sender that one or more data blocks are missing from the middle of a sequence, and the sender can retransmit only the missing data. Set this value to 0x01 to enable SACK.

- **SynAttackProtect.** This REG_DWORD value specifies whether the SYN flooding attack protection feature of TCP/IP is enabled. SYN flooding attack protection is enabled when the value of this entry is 1 and the value of the TcpMaxConnectResponseRetransmissions entry is at least 2. The SYN flooding attack protection feature of TCP detects symptoms of denial-of-service attacks (also known as SYN flooding), and it responds by reducing the time that the server spends on connection requests that it cannot acknowledge. Set this value to 0x01 to enable SYN flooding attack protection. The default is 0x00.

- **Tcp1323Opts.** This REG_DWORD value specifies whether TCP uses the timestamping and window-scaling features described in RFC 1323, TCP Extensions for High Performance. Window scaling permits TCP to negotiate a scaling factor for the TCP receive window size, allowing for a very large TCP receive window of up to 1 GB. The TCP receive window is the amount of data that the sending host can send at one time on a connection. Timestamps help TCP measure round-trip time (RTT) accurately in order to adjust retransmission timeouts. The Time-stamps option provides two timestamp fields of 4 bytes each in the TCP header, one to record the time the initial transmission is sent and one to record the time on the remote host. This entry is a 2-bit bitmask. The lower bit determines whether scaling is enabled; the higher bit determines whether timestamps are enabled. To enable a feature, set the bit representing the feature to 1. To disable a feature, set its bit to 0. Table B-3 describes the possible values.

Table B-3   Tcp1323Opts

Value	Description
0	Timestamps and window scaling are disabled.
1	Window scaling is enabled.
2	Timestamps are enabled.
3	Timestamps and window scaling are enabled.

- **TcpMaxConnectRetransmissions.**   This REG_DWORD value specifies how many times TCP retransmits an unanswered request for a new connection. TCP retransmits new connection requests until they are answered or until this value expires. TCP/IP adjusts the frequency of retransmissions over time. The delay between the original transmission and the first retransmission for each interface is determined by the value of the TcpInitialRTT entry. By default, it is three sec-onds. This delay doubles after each attempt. After the final attempt, TCP/IP waits for an interval equal to double the last delay, and then it abandons the con-nection request. This entry determines how many times TCP retransmits requests for new connections. When sending data on existing connections, the maximum number of retransmissions is determined by the value of the TcpMax-DataRetransmissions entry. Windows does not add this entry to the registry. You can add it by using the registry editor Regedit.exe. Values range from 0 through 255, and the default value is 2 retransmission attempts.

- **TcpMaxDataRetransmissions.**   This REG_DWORD value specifies how many times TCP retransmits an unacknowledged data segment on an existing connection. TCP retransmits data segments until they are acknowledged or until this value expires. TCP/IP adjusts the frequency of retransmissions over time. TCP estab-lishes an initial retransmission interval by measuring the round-trip time on the connection. The interval doubles with each successive retransmission on a con-nection, and it is reset to the initial value when responses resume. This entry is also used in the Windows algorithm for defining nonoperational (dead) gate-ways. A given connection defines a gateway as dead (and switches to the next gateway in the list stored in the value of the DefaultGateway or DhcpDefault-Gateway entries) when a packet sent to the gateway must be retransmitted more than half of the number of times specified in the value of this entry. The system defines a gateway as dead when more than 25 percent of its connections have switched to the next default gateway in the list. This entry determines how many times TCP retransmits data segments. The maximum number of retransmissions of requests for new connections is determined by the value of the Tcp-MaxConnectRetransmissions entry. Windows does not add this entry to the registry. You can add it by using the registry editor Regedit.exe. Values range from 0x00 through 0xFFFFFFFF retransmission attempts, and the default value is 0x05.

- **TcpMaxDupAcks.**   This REG_DWORD value specifies how many duplicate ACKs (ACKs for the same sequence numbers) constitute a signal to retransmit a segment. If you set the value of this entry to 1, the system retransmits a segment when it receives an ACK for a segment with a sequence number that is less than the number of the segment currently being sent. When data arrives with a sequence number that is greater than expected, the receiver assumes that data with the expected number was dropped, and it immediately sends an ACK with the ACK number set to the expected sequence number. The receiver sends ACKs set to the same missing number each time it receives a TCP segment that has a sequence number greater than expected. The sender recognizes the duplicate ACKs and sends the missing segment. Values range from 1 through 3, and 2 is the default.

- **TcpMaxHalfOpen.**   This REG_DWORD value specifies how many connections the server can maintain in the half-open (SYN-RCVD) state before TCP/IP initiates SYN flooding attack protection. This entry is used only when SYN flooding attack protection is enabled on this server—that is, when the value of the SynAttackProtect entry is 1 and the value of the TcpMaxConnectResponseRetransmissionsentry is at least 2. This entry establishes one of three configurable thresholds that, if exceeded, trigger TCP's SYN attack flooding protection feature. Because SYN flooding often results in many half-open connections, TCP interprets an elevated number of half-open connections to be a symptom of SYN flooding. The other two thresholds are:

  - ❏ The number of connections that remain in the half-open (SYN-RCVD) state even after a connection request has been retransmitted exceeds the value of the TcpMaxHalfOpenRetried entry.

  - ❏ The number of connection requests that the system refuses exceeds the value of the TcpMaxPortsExhausted entry. The system must refuse all connection requests when its reserve of open connection ports runs out.

The value of this entry should be greater than the value of the TCPMaxHalfOpenRetried entry. Windows does not add this entry to the registry. You can add it by using the registry editor Regedit.exe. Values range from 0x01 through

0xFFFFFFFF. In Windows Server 2003, the default value 0x1F4, and in Windows XP, the default value is 0x64.

■ **TCPMaxHalfOpenRetired.**   This REG_DWORD value specifies how many connections the server can maintain in the half-open (SYN-RCVD) state even after a connection request has been retransmitted. If the number of connections exceeds the value of this entry, TCP/IP initiates SYN flooding attack protection. This entry is used only when SYN flooding attack protection is enabled on this server—that is, when the value of the SynAttackProtect entry is 1 and the value of the TcpMaxConnectResponseRetransmissions entry is at least 2. This entry establishes one of three configurable thresholds that, if exceeded, trigger TCP's SYN attack flooding protection feature. Because SYN flooding often results in many half-open connections, TCP interprets an elevated number of half-open connections to be a symptom of SYN flooding. The other two thresholds are:

❑ The total number of connections in the half-open (SYN-RCVD) state exceeds the value of the TcpMaxHalfOpen entry.

❑ The number of connection requests that the system refuses exceeds the value of the TcpMaxPortsExhausted entry. The system must refuse all connection requests when its reserve of open connection ports runs out.

The value of this entry should be less than the value of the TCPMaxHalfOpen entry. Windows does not add this entry to the registry. You can add it by using the registry editor Regedit.exe. Values range from 0x00 through 0xFFFFFFF. In Windows Server 2003, the default value is 0x190. In Windows XP, the default value is 0x50.

■ **TcpMaxSendFree.**   This REG_DWORD value sets the size limit of the TCP header resource. On computers with ample RAM, increasing this limit can improve responsiveness during a SYN flood denial-of-service attack. Values range from 0 through 65,535, and the default value is 5000.

■ **TcpNumConnections.**   This REG_DWORD value specifies the maximum number of connections that TCP can have open simultaneously. If the value of this entry is 0, you cannot establish any connections. Values range from 0x40000 through 0xFFFFFe, and the default value is 0xFFFFE.

■ **TcpTimedWaitDelay.**   This REG_DWORD value specifies the time that must elapse before TCP can release a closed connection and reuse its resources. This interval between closure and release is known as the TIME_WAIT state or 2MSL state. During this time, the connection can be reopened at much less cost to the client and server than establishing a new connection. RFC 793 requires that TCP maintains a closed connection for an interval at least equal to twice the maximum segment lifetime (2MSL) of the network. When a connection is released, its socket pair and TCP control block can be used to support another connection. By default, the maximum segment lifetime is defined to be 120 seconds, and the value of this entry is equal to twice that, or 4 minutes. However, you can use this entry to customize the interval. Reducing the value of this entry allows TCP to release closed connections faster, providing more resources for new connections. However, if the value is too low, TCP might release connection resources before the connection is complete, requiring the server to use additional resources to reestablish the connection. Normally, TCP does not release closed connections until the value of this entry expires. However, TCP can release connections before this value expires if it is running out of TCP control blocks. The number of TCP control blocks that the system creates is specified by the value of the MaxFreeTcbs entry. Windows does not add this entry to the registry. You can add it by using the registry editor Regedit.exe. Values range from 0x00 through 0x12C seconds, and the default value is 0x78.

- **TcpUseRFC1122UrgentPointer.**   This REG_DWORD value specifies which mode TCP uses for urgent data. The two modes interpret the urgent pointer in the TCP header and the length of the urgent data differently. The two modes do not interoperate. Set this value to 0x01 to use the specification in RFC 1122, Requirements for Internet Hosts—Communication Layers, for urgent data. Set this value to 0x00 to use the mode used by systems derived from Berkeley Software Distribution (BSD). The default value is 0x00.

- **TcpWindowSize.**   This REG_DWORD value sets the maximum size of the TCP receive window. The receive window specifies the number of bytes that a sender can transmit without receiving an acknowledgment. In general, larger receive windows improve performance over high-latency, high-bandwidth networks. For greatest efficiency, the receive window should be an even multiple of the TCP Maximum Segment Size (MSS). The TCP/IP stack of Windows was designed to tune itself in most environments. Instead of using a fixed size for the receive window, TCP negotiates for and adjusts to an even increment of the MSS. Matching the receive window to even increments of the maximum segment size increases the percentage of full-sized TCP segments used during bulk data transmission. (Sizes larger than 64 KB can be achieved only when connecting to other systems that support RFC 1323 Window Scaling.) The default value is the smaller of the following numbers:

  - ❑   65,535

  - ❑   Value of registry entry GlobalMaxTcpWindowSize

  - ❑   Four times the MSS on the network

  - ❑   Even multiple of the MSS larger than 16,384

This entry does not exist in the registry by default. You can add it by using the registry editor Regedit.exe.

The default window size can start at 17,520 for Ethernet, but it might shrink slightly when a connection to another computer is established that supports extended TCP options (such as SACK and TIMESTAMPS) because these options increase the TCP header beyond the usual 20 bytes, which decreases room for data.

When an entry with the name of this entry is in `HKLM\SYSTEM\CurrentControlSet\Services\Tcpip\Parameters`, it sets the receive window size globally for all TCP interfaces. However, an entry with this name in `HKLM\SYSTEM\CurrentControlSet\Services\Tcpip\Parameters\Interfaces\`*interface-name* has precedence for the interface named in its registry path, and its value, rather than whatever value might be set globally, is used for that interface.

- **DisableDynamicUpdate.**   This `REG_DWORD` value disables the Domain Name System (DNS) dynamic update registration for all interfaces on the system. The default value is zero. With dynamic update, DNS client computers automatically register and update their resource records whenever address changes occur. Set this value to 0x01 to disable dynamic registration. The default value is 0x00.

- **DisableReplaceAddressInConflicts.**   This `REG_DWORD` value prevents the Domain Name System (DNS) client from overwriting an existing resource record when it discovers an address conflict during dynamic update. An address conflict occurs when the DNS client discovers that an existing A (address) record associates its DNS name with the IP address of a different computer. By default, the DNS client tries to replace the original registration with a record associating the DNS name to its own IP address. However, you can use this entry to direct DNS to back out of the registration process and to record an error in the Event Viewer log instead. This entry is designed for zones that do not use secure dynamic update. It prevents unauthorized users from changing the IP address registration of a client computer. Setting this value to 0x00 allows the DNS client to overwrite the existing A record with an A record for its own IP address. Setting this value to 0x01 allows the DNS client to back out of the registration process and write an error to the Event Viewer log.

- **DisableRevserAddressRegistrations.**   This `REG_DWORD` value disables the Domain Name System (DNS) dynamic update registration of PTR (pointer) records by this DNS client. PTR records associate an IP address with a computer name. This entry is designed for enterprises in which the primary DNS server that is authoritative for the reverse lookup zone cannot or is not configured to perform dynamic updates. It reduces unnecessary network traffic and eliminates event log errors that record failed attempts to register PTR records. Set this value to 0x01 to prevent registration of PTR records. Setting this value to 0x00 allows registration of PTR records.

- **DisableUserTOSSetting.**   This REG_DWORD value specifies whether individual applications can alter the type of service (TOS) bits in the header of outgoing IP packets. In general, individual applications should not be allowed to manipulate TOS bits, because this can defeat system policy mechanisms. You must restart the computer for this setting to take effect.

- **EnableICMPRedirect.**   This REG_DWORD value controls whether Windows alters its routing table in response to Internet Control Message Protocol (ICMP) messages that instruct it to direct datagrams for the recipient along a different route. You must restart the computer for this setting to take effect.

- **IGMPLevel.**   This REG_DWORD value specifies the extent to which the system supports IP multicasting and participates in the Internet Group Management Protocol. Table B-4 describes this value's settings.

Table B-4   IGMPLevel

Value	Description
0	Only send IP multicast packets. Treated the same as a value of 1.
1	Only send IP multicast packets.
2	Send and receive IP multicast packets (participate in IGMP).

Tcpip\Interfaces

The Interfaces subkey stores configuration data specific to a TCP/IP communications interface. This subkey stores TCP/IP configuration data that can be configured differently for each interface that the system uses. It contains one or more subkeys, called *interface-name* (represented by a GUID), each of which represents one interface. The entries in the interface-name subkeys apply only to the interface that the subkey represents, and they take precedence over any conflicting settings in the Parameters subkey.

The *interface-name* subkeys represent TCP\IP communication interfaces, and they are named for the network name of the interface. Each subkey represents a particular interface, and it stores configuration data that applies only to that interface. Most of the entries in the interface-name subkey described here can appear in any of the subkeys in the Interfaces subkey. Some entries can appear in the Parameters subkey, in an *interface-name* subkey, or in both. If an entry appears in the Parameters subkey, it applies to all interfaces by default. If it appears in an *interface-name* subkey, it applies only to the interface that the subkey represents, and it takes precedence over the entry in the Parameters subkey when configuring that interface.

The following list describes the values for each interface-name subkey:

- **EnableDHCP.** This REG_DWORD value determines whether the Dynamic Host Configuration Protocol (DHCP) service is enabled. If the value of this entry is 1, the DHCP client service is used to configure this interface.

- **IPAutoconfigurationAddress.** This REG_DWORD value stores the IP address that the IP autoconfiguration feature assigns to this interface. Autoconfiguration allows TCP/IP to configure an interface even when it cannot locate a Dynamic Host Configuration Protocol (DHCP) server. If TCP/IP cannot locate a DHCP server, it configures the interface by using IP addresses from the Microsoft reserved Class B network (169.254.0.0), subnet mask 255.255.0.0. During auto-configuration, TCP/IP continues trying to locate a DHCP server, and it abandons autoconfiguration if it finds one. This entry is used only when IP autoconfiguration is enabled—that is, when the value of the IPAutoconfigurationEnabled entry is 1.

- **IPAutoconfigurationEnabled.** This REG_DWORD value specifies whether the IP autoconfiguration feature is enabled for this interface. If the value of this entry is 1, autoconfiguration is enabled; if the value of this entry is 0 or if this entry is absent from the registry, autoconfiguration is not enabled. Autoconfiguration allows TCP/IP to configure an interface even when it cannot locate a Dynamic Host Configuration Protocol (DHCP) server. If TCP/IP cannot locate a DHCP server, it configures the interface by using IP addresses from the Microsoft reserved Class B network (169.254.0.0), subnet mask 255.255.0.0. During auto-configuration, TCP/IP continues trying to locate a DHCP server, and it abandons autoconfiguration if it finds one. IPAutoconfigurationEnabled also appears in the **Parameters** subkey, and its value applies, by default, to all interfaces. However, if this entry appears in any subkey of the Interfaces subkey, it takes precedence over the entry in the **Parameters** subkey when configuring the interface. Windows does not add this entry to the registry. You can add it by using the registry editor Regedit.exe.

- **SubnetMask.** This REG_DWORD value specifies the subnet mask for the IP address specified in the value of the IPAddress entry or the DhcpIPAddress entry. This entry, which can be changed by the user, overrides the DHCP-configured values for the subnet mask. The subnet mask is determined by two entries, DhcpSubnetMask (which is configured by DHCP) and SubnetMask (which you can configure). If the value of SubnetMask is not 0.0.0.0, it overrides the value of DhcpSubnetMask.

Appendix C
Per-User Settings

Chapter 4, "Hacking the Registry," and Chapter 18, "Fixing Common IT Problems," described numerous useful registry settings. This appendix continues by describing the most interesting settings in the Microsoft Windows XP and Windows Server 2003 (Windows) registries.

The settings in this appendix are per user; they're in HKCU. The root key HKLM contains similar settings, but the settings in HKCU are more interesting because these are often useful for deployment and customization. Also, many of my favorite IT hacks are in HKCU rather than HKLM because they affect per-user behaviors instead of the overall computer configuration. I'm not able to describe every setting in HKCU, incidentally. Even if I could figure out every setting, documenting them all would require hundreds of pages. Instead, I'm focusing on the most interesting and useful settings in the registry with a dab of just-plain-cool settings thrown into the mix.

The resources that I used to discover these settings vary. Many times I just know what a setting does from experience. Other times, I used Microsoft's Developer Network (MSDN), Knowledge Base, or resource kits. If I get really desperate to figure out a setting, I'll install the Windows Software Development Kit (SDK) and then search for the setting in the header files, which yields surprisingly good results.

The headings in this appendix follow the organization of HKCU to make finding information easier. Thus, you'll see top-level headings for HKCU\Control Panel, and so on. This appendix doesn't describe the relationship of HKCU to HKU and the profile hives that the operating system loads, though. For more information about this relationship, see Chapter 1, "Learning the Basics."

AppEvents

Windows associates sounds with certain events. The most notable are the sounds you hear when you log on to or off of the operating system. You assign sounds to different events—including minimizing windows, opening menus, and so on—in the Sounds And Audio Devices Properties dialog box shown in Figure C-1. To open this dialog box, in Control Panel click Sounds And Audio Devices. Figure C-1 shows which subkeys of AppEvents provide this dialog box's values. Many applications also associate sounds with certain events. For example, you can download and install sounds for use with Microsoft Office 2003 Editions. These sounds provide great feedback that I've missed when they're not available. If you don't like the sound that a particular event produces, you can change the sound file associated with it. For example, you can create your own recording that says "You've got spam!" and associate that sound file with Windows Messenger's New Mail event.

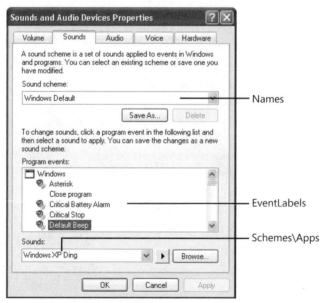

Figure C-1   Associate sounds with events using the Sounds And Audio Devices Properties dialog box.

These events and the sounds associated with them are in HKCU\AppEvents. There are two subkeys in AppEvents. The first is EventLabels, which contains one subkey for each event, and the subkey's default value is the name of the event as you see it in Control Panel. The second is Schemes. This is the more interesting subkey because it actually associates sound files with each event. You can customize AppEvents, but doing so isn't worth the extra effort. Configuring sounds is far easier through Control Panel. My suggestion is that you configure your sounds the way you like them, and then export AppEvents to a REG file that you can use to configure sounds down the line. Just make sure the sound files are available if you're using the REG file on a different computer. Most times, you'll find all these sound files in %SystemRoot%\media.

Note Windows XP Service Pack 2 and Windows Server 2003 Service Pack 1 add a small number of new events to the AppEvents key. For example, the new security features of Internet Explorer have sound events for blocked popup windows, automatic file downloads, and so on.

Console

The key HKCU\Console contains the default configuration for a command-prompt window (console subsystem). This is the environment that hosts all character-mode applications. To change console settings, click the System icon (top-left corner of the window), and then click Properties. After changing the properties, Windows prompts you to change the default settings or save the settings for console windows that have the same title:

- If you change the default settings, the operating system stores those settings in HKCU\Console.

- If you save the settings for console windows with the same title, the operating system creates the subkey HKCU\Console*Title*, where *Title* is the window's title, and stores the custom settings in it. (See Figure C-2.)

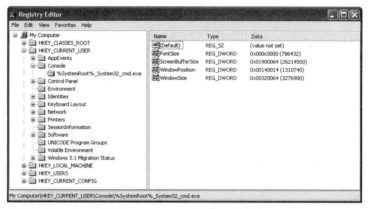

Figure C-2   Each subkey in `Console` is the title of a customized console window. You typically see this key only after starting a command prompt window from the Run dialog box.

As with `AppEvents`, there's seldom a good reason to customize these settings directly. It's not really a cool hack, and a user interface is available for all these settings. What is cool is that after you've configured your console windows just the way you want them, you can export `Console` to a REG file. Then, the next time you install Windows, import the REG file to restore your console settings. You'll never configure a command prompt again.

Control Panel

The key `HKCU\Control Panel` has a wealth of customization possibilities. This is the key where Windows stores most of the settings you configure in Control Panel. The most interesting subkeys are `Desktop` and `Mouse`. The following list gives you an overview of what's in most of the subkeys, and I describe the `Desktop` and `Mouse` subkeys in more detail in the sections following this one:

- **`Accessibility`.**   This subkey stores accessibility settings you set using the Accessibility Options dialog box. To open this dialog box, in Control Panel, launch Accessibility Options. The values' names are self-explanatory, and you can easily map them to the user interface.

- **`Appearance`.**   This subkey contains values for each scheme you see on the Appearance tab of the Display Properties dialog box. To open this dialog box, in Control Panel, launch Display, and then click the Appearance tab. Customizing themes in the registry is too cumbersome to do reliably, so stick with the user interface.

- **Colors.** This subkey defines the color of each element in the Windows user interface. `ActiveBorder` defines the color of each active window's border, for instance. Each value is a `\CONSOLE` value that contains three decimal numbers that correspond to the RGB color notation.

- **Current.** Windows does not use this subkey.

- **Cursors.** This subkey contains values that associate the name of a mouse pointer with a file containing the mouse pointer. The file has the *.cur* extension, or if the pointer is animated, the *.ani* extension. The value's name is the name of the pointer. This key's default value contains the name of the current pointer scheme. You don't see values in this key unless you've customized your pointers in the Mouse Pointers dialog box. To open the Mouse Pointers dialog box, in Control Panel launch Mouse.

- **Custom Colors.** This subkey defines the custom colors in the color palette. The values in the `Custom Colors` subkey are named `ColorA` through `ColorP`, and all have a default value of `0xFFFFFF`.

- **Desktop.** See the "Desktop" section later in this appendix.

- **don't load.** This subkey indicates which Control Panel files to load. Windows consults the values in don't load to decide whether to display the option in Control Panel. The operating system looks for a value whose name is the same as the file. If the `\CONSOLE` value is `Yes`, the operating system displays the file's icon in Control Panel; otherwise, it doesn't display the icon.

- **International.** This subkey contains a value called `Locale` that contains the ID of the user's locale. See Intl.inf in %SystemRoot%\Inf for a list of the locale IDs available. Configure this setting in the Regional And Language Options dialog box. To see this dialog box, in Control Panel launch Regional And Language Options. You see many other values in this subkey, which define settings such as the currency symbol, date format, list separator, and so on.

- **Keyboard.** This subkey stores options configured in the Keyboard Properties dialog box. To display the Keyboard Properties dialog box, in Control Panel launch Keyboard. The most interesting value in this subkey is the `\CONSOLE` value `InitialKeyboardIndicators`. If the value is `0`, Windows turns NUMLOCK off when it starts. If the value is `2`, the operating system turns on NUMLOCK. The operating system stores the current state of NUMLOCK in this value when users log off or restart the computer.

- **Mouse.** See the "Mouse" section later in this appendix.

- **PowerCfg.**   This subkey defines the schemes that you see in the Power Options dialog box. To open the Power Options dialog box, in Control Panel launch Power Options. The \CONSOLE value **CurrentPowerPolicy** indicates the current power scheme. You find that scheme in **PowerCfg\PowerPolicies**.

- **Screen Saver.Name.**   These subkeys contain settings unique to each screen saver. *Name* is the name of the screen saver.

- **Sound.**   This subkey contains the \CONSOLE value **Beep**, which indicates whether Windows beeps on errors. The operating system beeps on errors if this value is **Yes**.

Desktop

The values in HKCU\Control Panel\Desktop control many aspects of the Windows user interface. A good number of them don't have a user interface for configuring them, however, so there's a lot of potential in this subkey for customizing the operating system. The following list describes these values:

- **ActiveWndTrkTimeout.**   This REG_DWORD value indicates the time in milliseconds that the mouse pointer must remain over a window before Windows activates the window. The default value is **0**.

- **AutoEndTasks.**   This \CONSOLE value determines whether the operating system ends tasks automatically when users log off or shut down Windows. If the value is **0**, the operating system doesn't end processes automatically; instead, it waits until the timeout in **HungAppTimeout** expires and then displays the End Task dialog box. If the value is **1**, the operating system automatically ends processes.

- **CaretWidth.**   This REG_DWORD value specifies the width of the blinking caret. The default value is **1**. This value is not in the registry by default.

- **CoolSwitch.**   Windows doesn't use this value.

- **CoolSwitchColumns.**   This \CONSOLE value determines how many columns of icons you see in Task Switcher (ALT+TAB). The default value is **7**.

- **CoolSwitchRows.**   This \CONSOLE value determines how many rows of icons you see in Task Switcher (ALT+TAB). The default value is **3**.

- **CursorBlinkRate.**   This \CONSOLE value determines the amount of time in milliseconds that elapses between each blink of the selection cursor. The default value is **530**, which is a little more than a half a second.

- **DragFullWindows.**   This \CONSOLE value determines whether users see windows' contents when they drag them. The default value is **1**, which means users see full window contents when dragging. Set this value to **0** to see window outlines only.

- **DragHeight.** This \CONSOLE value indicates the height of the rectangle that determines the start of a drag operation. The default value is 4.

- **DragWidth.** This \CONSOLE value indicates the width of the rectangle that determines the start of a drag operation. The default value is 4.

- **FontSmoothing.** This \CONSOLE value determines whether Windows smoothes the edges of large fonts using anti-aliasing techniques. The default value is 0, which disables font smoothing. To enable font smoothing, set the value to 2.

- **ForegroundFlashcount.** This REG_DWORD value indicates the number of times that a taskbar button flashes to get the user's attention. The default value is 3. If the timeout value in ForegroundLockTimeout expires without user input, Windows automatically brings the window to the foreground.

- **ForegroundLockTimeout.** This REG_DWORD value specifies the time in milliseconds that must elapse since the last user input before Windows allows windows to come to the foreground. The default value is 200,000 (200 seconds).

- **GridGranularity.** Windows doesn't use this value.

- **HungAppTimeout.** This \CONSOLE value controls how long Windows waits for processes to end in response to users' clicking the End Task button in Task Manager. If the timeout expires, Windows displays the End Task dialog box, which tells the user that the process did not respond to the request. The default value is 5000, or five seconds.

- **LowPowerActive.** This \CONSOLE value indicates the status of the low-power alarm. If this value is 0, no alarm activates when battery power is low. This is the default value. If this value is 1, an alarm activates when battery power is low. This value affects only computers that use Advanced Power Management (APM).

- **LowPowerTimeOut.** This \CONSOLE value determines whether a lower-power timeout is set. If this value is 0, the timeout is not set. This is the default value. If this value is 1, the timeout is set. This value affects only computers that use Advanced Power Management (APM).

- **MenuShowDelay.** This \CONSOLE value determines the time in milliseconds that elapses between when the user points to a menu and when Windows displays it. The default value is 400, which is almost half a second.

- **PaintDesktopVersion.** This REG_DWORD value determines whether Windows displays its version and build number on the desktop. The default value is 0, which doesn't display the version. Set this value to 1 to display the version of Windows on the desktop.

- **Pattern.** This \CONSOLE value defines a two-color, 8-pixel-by-8-pixel bitmap used for the background. The default value is an empty string. To define a bit-map, set this value to B1 B2 B3 B4 B5 B6 B7 B8. *BN* is an 8-bit binary number that represents a row of 8 pixels. Bits that are 0 show the background color, whereas bits that are 1 show the foreground color.

- **ScreenSaveActive.** This \CONSOLE value determines whether the user has selected a screen saver. The default value is 1, indicating that a screen saver is active. Set this value to 0 to indicate that a screen saver is not active.

- **ScreenSaverIsSecure.** This \CONSOLE value has a default value of 0. This value indicates whether or not the screen saver is password-protected. The value 1 indicates the screen saver is password-protected; 0 indicates that it's not protected.

- **ScreenSaveTimeOut.** This \CONSOLE value specifies the time in seconds that the computer must remain idle before the screen saver starts. The default is 600, which is 10 minutes.

- **SCRNSAVE.EXE.** This \CONSOLE value has no default value. This value specifies the path and name of the screen-saver executable file. If the screen-saver file is in %SystemRoot%\System32, no path is necessary.

- **TileWallpaper.** This \CONSOLE value indicates how to format wallpaper on the screen. If the value is 0, Windows centers the wallpaper. This is the default value. If the value is 1, Windows tiles the wallpaper.

- **WaitToKillAppTimeout.** This \CONSOLE value indicates the time in milliseconds that Windows waits for processes to end after users log off or shut down Windows. If the timeout expires and processes are still running, Windows displays the End Task dialog box, unless you've set the value AutoEndTasks to end processes automatically. The default value is 20,000, which is 20 seconds.

- **Wallpaper.** This \CONSOLE value is the path and file name of the image to use for wallpaper. The default value is an empty string. You don't need to include the path if the file is in %SystemRoot% or %SystemRoot%\System32. If you want to include wallpaper in a default user profile, copy the image file to the user profile folder and then specify the full path in this value.

- **WallpaperStyle.** This \CONSOLE value determines how to display the wallpaper on the desktop. The default value is 0, which centers the bitmap on the desktop. Set this value to 2 to stretch the wallpaper.

- **WheelScrollLines.** This \CONSOLE value specifies the number of lines to scroll for each one-notch rotation of the mouse wheel when users don't use modifier keys such as CTRL or ALT. The default value is 3. To turn off wheel scrolling, set this value to 0.

I left the value `UserPreferencesMask` out of the list because this value represents some of the most interesting and most useful ways to customize Windows. It's also more complicated than other values in the list because it's a bit mask that contains a large number of settings in one value. Lately, Microsoft has stayed away from using large bit masks like this one, favoring `REG_DWORD` values that you set to `0x00` to disable a feature and `0x01` to enable a feature. This value is a holdover from earlier versions of Windows, however. It's a 4-byte `REG_BINARY` value that might as well be a `REG_DWORD` value. The default value is `0x80003E9E`, which will make more sense after you know what the different bits in this value represent.

Table C-1 describes each bit. Because this is a `REG_BINARY` value, count the bits from left to right, beginning with 0. If this were a `REG_DWORD` value, you'd count the bits from right to left instead. The table indicates each setting's bit number, describes the feature that it controls, and shows the bit mask. For any feature you see in the table, setting the bit to 0 disables the feature and setting it to 1 enables the feature. If you'd like to see an example of writing a script that changes settings in `UserPreferencesMask`, see Chapter 4, "Hacking the Registry." Chapter 4 contains a script that updates this value to cause Windows to raise windows to the foreground when you point at them. For more information about doing bitwise math, see Chapter 1, "Learning the Basics."

Table C-1   Bits in `UserPreferencesMask`

Bit	Bit Mask	Default	Description
0	0x00000001	0	Active window tracking. Windows get focus when the user positions the mouse pointer over them.
1	0x00000002	1	Menu animation. This depends on the value of bit 9.
2	0x00000004	1	Combo box animation. The combo boxes slide open.
3	0x00000008	1	List box smooth scrolling. The list boxes scroll smoothly.
4	0x00000010	1	Gradient captions. The title bars display a gradient.
5	0x00000020	0	Keyboard cues. Menu hotkeys are underlined only when accessed from the keyboard.
6	0x00000040	0	Active window tracking Z order. Windows that gain focus through active window tracking are brought to the foreground.
7	0x00000080	1	Mouse hot tracking.
8	0x00000100	0	Reserved for future use.
9	0x00000200	1	Menu fade animation. Menus fade when closed; otherwise, menus use slide animation.
10	0x00000400	1	Selection fade animation. Lists fade after users make a selection.
11	0x00000800	1	ToolTip animation. This depends on bit 12.

Table C-1   Bits in UserPreferencesMask

Bit	Bit Mask	Default	Description
12	0x00001000	1	ToolTip fade animation. ToolTips fade when they close. When the bit is set to 0, ToolTips use slide animation.
13	0x00002000	1	Cursor shadow. This requires more than 256 colors.
31	0x80000000	1	All user-interface effects. This enables combo box animation, cursor shadow, gradient captions, hot tracking, list box smooth scrolling, menu animation, menu hotkey underlining, selection fade, and ToolTip animation.

Desktop\WindowMetrics

The key HKCU\Control Panel\Desktop\WindowMetrics contains settings that govern the dimensions of the elements you see on the screen. Some of these settings represent dimensions in pixels, whereas others are actually coordinates. The following list describes the settings in WindowMetrics, which you define by clicking Advanced on the Display Properties dialog box's Appearance tab, as shown in Figure C-3.

Figure C-3   After you've configured the settings in this dialog box, consider exporting them to a REG file so that you can use the same settings on other computers.

- **BorderWidth.**   This \CONSOLE value determines the width of the borders for all windows that users can't resize. The default is -15, which is 15 twips. (The minus sign indicates a twip, which is 1/1440th of an inch.) Valid values are 0 through -750.

- **CaptionFont.** This REG_BINARY value contains the name of the font to use in window captions. The default is Trebuchet MS.

- **CaptionHeight.** This \CONSOLE value specifies the height of caption buttons. This value is measured in twips, and the default value is –375.

- **CaptionWidth.** This \CONSOLE value specifies the width of caption buttons. This value is measured in twips, and the default value is –270.

- **IconFont.** This REG_BINARY value contains the name of the font used to display icon text. The default value is Tahoma.

- **IconSpacing.** This \CONSOLE value specifies the width of the grid cell used to display the large view of an icon. This value is measured in twips, and the default is –1125.

- **IconTitleWrap.** This \CONSOLE value determines whether icon text wraps or truncates when it's too long to fit on one line. The default value is 1, which causes icon text to wrap; 0 causes icon text to truncate.

- **IconVerticalSpacing.** This \CONSOLE value specifies the vertical space between icons. This value is measured in twips, and the default is –1125.

- **MenuFont.** This REG_BINARY value specifies the font to use in menu bars. The default value is Tahoma.

- **MenuHeight.** This \CONSOLE value specifies the height of menu bars. This value is measured in twips, and the default is –285.

- **MenuWidth.** This \CONSOLE value specifies the width of buttons on menu bars. This value is measured in twips, and the default is –270.

- **MessageFont.** This REG_BINARY value contains the name of the font to use in message boxes. The default value is Tahoma.

- **MinAnimate.** This \CONSOLE value determines whether Windows uses animation for minimizing and restoring windows. The default value is 1, which uses animation. Set this value to 0 to prevent window animation.

- **ScrollHeight.** This \CONSOLE value specifies the height of horizontal scroll bars. The default value, measured in twips, is –255.

- **ScrollWidth.** This \CONSOLE value specifies the width of vertical scroll bars. The default value, measured in twips, is –255.

- **Shell Icon BPP.** This \CONSOLE value determines the color depth of icons on the desktop. The default value is 4, but valid values include 4 (16 colors), 8 (256 colors), 16 (65,536 colors), 24 (16,777,216 colors), and 32 (4,294,967,296 colors).

- **Shell Icon Size.** This \CONSOLE value specifies the size in pixels of icons that Windows Explorer displays. The default value is 32. Valid values range from 16 to 48 pixels.

- **SmCaptionFont.** This REG_BINARY value specifies the font to use for small captions. The default value is Tahoma.

- **SmCaptionHeight.** This \CONSOLE value specifies the height of small captions. This value is measured in twips, and the default is –255.

- **SmCaptionWidth.** This \CONSOLE value specifies the width of small captions. This value is measured in twips, and the default is –255.

- **StatusFont.** This REG_BINARY value specifies the font to use in status bars. The default value is Tahoma.

Mouse

The values in HKCU\Control Panel\Mouse configure the mouse. The following list describes these values, including their types and default values:

- **DoubleClickHeight.** This \CONSOLE value specifies the height of the rectangle that Windows uses to detect double-clicks. If two clicks are within the rectangle and within the time specified by the value DoubleClickSpeed, the clicks are combined into a double-click. The default value is 4.

- **DoubleClickSpeed.** This \CONSOLE value specifies the amount of time that can elapse between two mouse clicks for Windows to consider them a double-click. If the amount of time between clicks is greater than this timeout, the operating system considers them separate clicks. The default value is 500, which is half a second, and the valid range is 100 through 900.

- **DoubleClickWidth.** This \CONSOLE value specifies the width of the rectangle that Windows uses to detect double-clicks. If two clicks are within the rectangle and within the time specified by the value DoubleClickSpeed, the clicks are combined into a double-click. The default value is 4.

- **MouseSpeed.** This \CONSOLE value determines how fast the pointer moves in response to mouse movements. Valid values are 0, 1, and 2. The default value is 1. When this value is 0, Windows doesn't accelerate the mouse. When this value is 1, Windows doubles the mouse speed when it exceeds the value in MouseThreshold1. When this value is 2, Windows doubles the mouse speed when it exceeds the value in MouseThreshold1 and quadruples the mouse speed when it exceeds the value in MouseThreshold2.

- **MouseThreshold1.** This \CONSOLE value, measured in pixels, specifies the mouse speed that triggers mouse acceleration. The default value is 6.

- **MouseThreshold2.**   This \CONSOLE value, measured in pixels, specifies the mouse speed that triggers quadruple mouse acceleration. The default is 10.

- **MouseTrails.**   This \CONSOLE value specifies whether mouse trails are enabled or disabled. Setting this value to 0 disables mouse trails; setting it to 1 enables them.

- **SnapToDefaultButton.**   This \CONSOLE value determines whether the mouse snaps to the default button when you open a dialog box. The default value is 0, which turns off this feature. To enable this feature, set the default value to 1.

- **SwapMouseButtons.**   This \CONSOLE value determines whether Windows swaps the left and right mouse buttons. The default value is 0, which disables this feature. To swap the mouse buttons, set this value to 1.

Environment

The key HKCU\Environment defines per-user environment variables. Normally, all you see in this key are two values: TEMP and TMP. Both are REG_EXPAND_SZ values. You can add environment variables to Environment, however, and then use those from within batch files, REG_EXPAND_SZ values, and so on. Of course, you can also rely on the user interface to add environment variables. In Control Panel launch System, and then, on the Advanced tab, click Environment Variables. Per-user environment variables are at the top of the dialog box, and per-computer environment variables are at the bottom.

Keyboard Layout

The key HKCU\Keyboard Layout defines the keyboard layouts that you configure using the Regional And Language Options dialog box. In essence, a keyboard layout maps the physical keys on your keyboard to the characters they generate. Keyboard layouts enable you to write German text using a U.S. English keyboard, for example. This key sometimes contains a single REG_DWORD value, Attributes, which determines which key to use for CAPS LOCK. If this value is 0, Windows uses the CAPS LOCK key. If this value is 0x10000, the operating system uses the SHIFT key. You sometimes see three subkeys in HKCU\Keyboard Layout:

- **Preload.**   This subkey contains the ID of each keyboard layout the user chooses through the Regional And Language Options dialog box. Windows uses this data to restore the keyboard layout when the user logs back on. The first value is 1, the second is 2, and so on. The value 1 is the default keyboard layout.

- **Substitutes.**   This subkey stores the IDs of alternate keyboard layouts. Windows checks this subkey when loading a keyboard layout, and if it finds a substitute, it uses that instead of the default layout. This key is usually empty until the user chooses substitute keyboard layouts.

■ **Toggle.**   This subkey specifies the key sequences that toggle between input locales. It contains the \CONSOLE value Hotkey, which can have one of four values. The value 1 specifies that LEFT ALT+SHIFT switches locales. The value 2 specifies CTRL+SHIFT, 3 disables the key sequence altogether, and 4 specifies the accent grave key when the default locale is Thai.

Network

The key HKCU\Network contains data about the user's mapped network drives. Each subkey represents a mapped drive that Windows restores the next time the user logs on to the computer. The name of the subkey is HKCU\Network*Drive*, where *drive* is the drive letter mapped to the network path. The following values are in each mapped drive's subkey:

■ **ConnectionType.**   This REG_DWORD value specifies how to connect the drive to the local computer. A value of 1 means drive redirection and 2 means print redirection. The default value is 1.

■ **ProviderName.**   This \CONSOLE value specifies the connection's network provider. The default value is Microsoft Windows Network.

■ **ProviderType.**   This REG_DWORD value identifies the provider that makes the network connection. The value for the Microsoft LanMan provider is 0x20000. Other network providers use different values.

■ **RemotePath.**   This \CONSOLE value contains the network connection's UNC path using the notation *Computer**Share*.

■ **UserName.**   This \CONSOLE value contains the user's name, including the domain. It identifies the user who made the network connection, and Windows uses it to fill the Connect As box in the Map Network Drive dialog box.

Printers

The key HKCU\Printers defines the user's printer connections. The following list describes the three subkeys you find in this key:

■ **Connections.**   This subkey contains one subkey for each printer connection. The name of the key defines the printer connection: ,,*Server*,*Printer*. Also, values in this subkey define the print provider and server.

■ **DevModePerUser.**   This subkey contains per-user printer settings.

■ **Settings.**   This subkey contains settings for Add Printer Wizard, including the users' preferences from the last time they used the wizard to add a printer.

SessionInformation

The itty-bitty key HKCU\SessionInformation contains a single value. The REG_DWORD value ProgramCount indicates how many programs are running in the foreground. Each time you open a program on the desktop, Windows increments this value. Each time you close a foreground program, Windows decrements this value.

Software

The key HKCU\Software contains per-user program settings. Windows stores much of its own configuration in this key, too. Microsoft standardized this key's organization, which makes finding settings easier because you generally know where in the registry to look for a program's settings. Applications store their settings in HKCU\Software *Vendor**Program**Version*\. *Vendor* is the name of the program's publisher, *Program* is the name of the program, and *Version* is the program's version number. Often, *Version* is simply CurrentVersion. Figure C-4 shows an example of a program that stores its settings in this key.

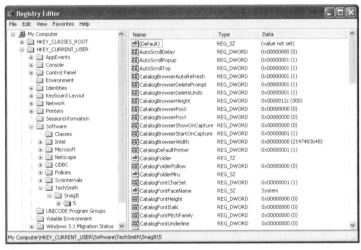

Figure C-4   TechSmith SnagIt stores its settings in HKCU\Software\TechSmith\SnagIt\5.

By far, the most interesting subkey is Microsoft because it contains most of the Windows per-user settings. This subkey is discussed in detail in "Software\Microsoft \Windows*CurrentVersion*," later in this appendix. Other interesting subkeys are Classes and Policies, which I describe in the following sections.

Classes

The key HKCU\Software\Classes contains per-user file associations and class registrations. It's really a link to HKU\SID_Classes, which you learned about in Chapter 1, "Learning the Basics." File associations in HKCU have precedence over file associations in HKLM. Per-user file associations began with Microsoft Windows 2000, and they enable users to install applications without affecting the file associations of other users who share the same computer. They also enable users' file associations to follow them when roaming user profiles are enabled. The contents of this key are the same as HKCR, so see Appendix A, "File Associations," for more information.

Microsoft\Command Processor

Command-prompt windows support file and folder name completion, as well as a few other features. You can configure these features using Tweak UI, as described in Chapter 5, "Mapping Tweak UI," or you can hack them directly in the registry. These are settings that I apply to just about every computer I use, so I keep them handy in a script. The following list describes the settings in the subkey Command Processor, which configure the command-prompt window:

- **AutoRun.** This \CONSOLE value, which has no default, contains a list of commands that run automatically when you start a command-prompt window.

- **CompletionChar.** This REG_DWORD value specifies the ASCII character code of the key to use for file name completion. You can set this value to 0x00, 0x01 through 0x1F, 0x20, or 0x40. The Tab key is 0x09 and is the default.

- **DefaultColor.** This REG_DWORD value specifies the default background and foreground color for a command prompt window. The first hexadecimal digit specifies the background color, and the second digit specifies the foreground color. Valid values range from 0x00 through 0xFE; the default is 0.The digits correspond to the colors shown in Table C-2.

Table C-2   Values for DefaultColor

Value	Color
0	Black
1	Blue
2	Green
3	Aqua
4	Red
5	Purple
6	Yellow
7	White

Table C-2 Values for DefaultColor

Value	Color
8	Gray
9	Light Blue
A	Light Green
B	Light Aqua
C	Light Red
D	Light Purple
E	Light Yellow
F	Bright White

- **DelayedExpansion.** This REG_DWORD value specifies whether the command prompt delays environment variable expansion. If the value is 0x01, the command prompt interprets the exclamation point (!) as an environment variable that expands only when used. The default is 0x00.

- **EnableExtensions.** This REG_DWORD value determines whether command-processor extensions are enabled or not. Setting this value to 0x00 disables extensions. You need to disable extensions only when they interfere with a script language with which they aren't compatible. The default value is 0x01.

- **PathCompletionChar.** This REG_DWORD value specifies the ASCII character code of the key to use for path completion. Set this value to 0x00, 0x01 through 0x1F, 0x20, or 0x40. The Tab key is 0x09. You can use the same key that you use for file name completion, which expands both.

Microsoft\Internet Connection Wizard

The key HKCU\Software\Microsoft\Internet Connection Wizard contains a single value that indicates whether users have run the wizard. Unlike earlier versions of Windows, the wizard doesn't run automatically when users first open Internet Explorer, so this value is only interesting for inventorying. If the REG_BINARY value Completed is 0x0000, the user has not run the wizard. If the value is 0x0001, the user has run the wizard.

Microsoft\Internet Explorer

The key HKCU\Software\Microsoft\Internet Explorer contains per-user settings for Internet Explorer. Many subkeys in Internet Explorer are difficult to understand or uninteresting. Many of the changes that Windows XP Service Pack 2 and Windows Server 2003 Service Pack 1 make to HKCU are in this branch, though. There are settings in this key that are very useful to customize:

- **Download.**   By default, this subkey contains a single REG_SZ value called Check-ExeSignatures. If this value is Yes, Internet Explorer checks programs you download for valid signatures. This value is new for Windows XP Service Pack 2.

- **Help_Menu_URLs.**   This subkey is used to redirect Internet Explorer's online support feature to an intranet location, instead of Microsoft's Web site. To do that, add the \CONSOLE value Online_Support to this subkey, and then set its value to the URL of your Internet Explorer support page. After customizing this setting, when users click Help, Online Support, Internet Explorer opens your support page. As far as I can discover, this is the only choice that you can redirect.

- **IntelliForms.**   This subkey contains the REG_DWORD value AskUser that indicates whether Internet Explorer should ask users whether they want to use the AutoComplete feature. You can set this value to 0x00 to prevent the prompt, but in a business environment where you're more likely to disable this feature, you should disable it using Group Policy.

- **Main.**   This subkey contains many settings for Internet Explorer. For example, you can configure whether Internet Explorer shows its status bar and toolbar.

- **Settings.**   This subkey contains five values that specify the colors used in Internet Explorer: Anchor Color, Anchor Color Visited, Background Color, Text Color, and Use Anchor Color Hover. Each is a \CONSOLE value in the format *R,G,B*, where you specify each color component—red, green, and blue—using decimal numbers *0* through *255*.

- **Toolbar.**   This subkey contains information about the Internet Explorer toolbars. The REG_DWORD value Locked indicates whether the toolbars are locked. The \CONSOLE value LinksFolderName contains the name of the annoying Links folder, which you can rename if you like so that it better matches the contents of your Favorites folder. You can also create the \CONSOLE value BackBitmap to customize the bitmap that you see on the toolbar.

- **TypedURLs.**   This subkey contains a list of the URLs that users type in the address bar. You can quickly clear this history list by removing this subkey.

The subkey Internet Explorer contains two other subkeys that enable some pretty cool customizations. The first subkey is MenuExt. This subkey enables you to extend Internet Explorer's menus with your own scripts. The second subkey is SearchURL, which makes searching the Internet a snap. You add custom search URLs to this subkey, and then search the Internet by typing one of their names in the address bar. It's a real timesaver and one of my all-time favorite customizations, which I also describe in Chapter 4, "Hacking the Registry."

Microsoft\Internet Explorer\MenuExt

Right-click a Web page, and Internet Explorer displays a shortcut menu. You can customize this shortcut menu by adding commands to it that you link to scripts in an HTML file. For example, you can add a command to the shortcut menu that opens the current Web page in a new window or highlights the selected text on it.

Internet Explorer looks for extensions in HKCU\Software\Microsoft\Internet Explorer\MenuExt. Add this key if it doesn't exist, and then add a subkey for each command that you want to add. Then set that subkey's default value to the path and name of the HTML file containing the script that carries out the command. For example, to add the command Magnify to the shortcut menu that runs the script in the HTML file C:\Windows\Web\Magnify.htm, add the subkey Magnify and set its default value to C:\Windows\Web\Magnify.htm. When you choose this command on Internet Explorer's shortcut menu, it executes the script that the file contains. Then you need to create Magnify.htm. Listing C-1 is Magnify.htm. The property external.menuArguments contains the window object in which you executed the command. Because you have access to the window object, you can do almost anything in that window, such as reformatting its contents, and so on.

Listing C-1   Magnify.htm

```
<HTML>
<SCRIPT LANGUAGE="JavaScript" defer>
var objWin = external.menuArguments;
var objDoc = objWin.document;
var objSel = objDoc.selection;
var objRange = objSel.createRange();
objRange.execCommand( "FontSize", 0, "+2" );
</SCRIPT>
</HTML>
```

You can choose the shortcut menus to which Internet Explorer adds your command. In the subkey you created for the extension, add the REG_DWORD value Contexts, and apply the bit masks shown in Table C-3 to it. For example, to limit the previous example so that Internet Explorer displays it only for text selections, add the REG_DWORD value Contexts to Magnify, and set it to 0x10.

Table C-3   Internet Explorer Menu Extensions

Bit Mask	Menu
0x01	Default
0x02	Image
0x04	Control
0x08	Table
0x10	Text Selection

Table C-3   Internet Explorer Menu Extensions

Bit Mask	Menu
0x11	Anchor
0x12	Unknown

Microsoft\Internet Explorer\SearchURL

Search URLs are a convenient way to use different Internet search engines. For example, you might have a search URL called *shop* that searches eBay. As shown in Figure C-5, type **shop casino chip** (yes, I collect them) in the address bar to automatically search eBay for all items that contain the words *casino* and *chip*.

Figure C-5   Customizing the key `SearchURL` is the ultimate shortcut for searching the Internet.

`HKCU\Software\Microsoft\Internet Explorer\SearchURL` is where you create search URLs. If you don't see this subkey, create it. Then add a subkey for each search prefix you want to use. To use the example I just gave you, create the subkey **shop**. Set the default value of the prefix's subkey to the URL of the search engine. Use **%s** as a placeholder for the search string. Internet Explorer replaces the **%s** with any text you type to the right of the prefix. In my example, set it to `http://search.ebay.com/search /search.dll?MfcISAPICommand=GetResult&ht=1&SortProperty=MetaEndSort& query=%s`.

Add the `\CONSOLE` values shown in Table C-4 to the prefix key you created. These values describe what to substitute for special characters in your search string, including a space, percent sign (%), ampersand (&), and plus sign (+). These characters have special meaning when submitting forms to Web sites, so you must substitute a plus sign for a space, for example, or %26 for an ampersand. Thus, the browser translates the string *casino & chip* to *casino+%26+chip*.

Finding the URL to use is easy. Open the search engine that you want to add to Internet Explorer's search URLs, and then search for something. When the browser displays the results, copy the URL from the address bar to the default value of the search URL you're creating, replacing your search word with a **%s**. For example, after searching eBay for *sample*, the resulting URL is *http://search.ebay.com/search /search.dll?MfcISAPICommand=GetResult&ht=1&SortProperty=MetaEndSort&query= sample*. Replace *sample* with **%s** to get `http://search.ebay.com/search /search.dll?MfcISAPICommand=GetResult&ht=1&SortProperty= MetaEndSort&query=%s`.

Table C-4 **Values in** SearchURLs

Name	Data
<space>	+
%	%25
&	%26
+	%2B

Microsoft\MessengerService

The key HKCU\Software\Microsoft\MessengerService contains the settings for Windows Messenger:

- **AlwaysOnTop.** This REG_BINARY value is 0x01 when you've configured Windows Messenger to appear on top of other windows; otherwise, it's 0x00.

- **DSBkgndMode.** The first time users close Windows Messenger, this REG_BINARY value displays a prompt that tells them it's running in the background. Setting this REG_BINARY value to 0x01 disables that prompt.

- **FirstTimeUser.** This REG_BINARY value is 0x01 for first-time users, and it's 0x00 for old-timers. That's the best explanation I've got.

- **FtReceiveFolder.** This REG_BINARY value contains the folder into which Windows Messenger downloads files it receives. The default value is the My Received Files folder in the user's My Documents folder.

- **PassportBallon.** This REG_BINARY value indicates the number of times that Windows Messenger has displayed its prompt to sign up for a Passport. To prevent it from prompting to create a Passport, set this value to 0x0a. (Remember to reverse the bits because this is a REG_BINARY value.)

- **PassportWizard.** This REG_BINARY value indicates whether the user has run .NET Passport Wizard. If this value is 0x01, the user has run the wizard.

- **Server.** This value specifies the server to which Windows Messenger connects. messenger.hotmail.com;64.4.13.143:1863 is the default value.

- **StatusBar.** This REG_BINARY value indicates whether to display the status bar. If this value is 0x01, you see the status bar.

- **TabsShowHide.** This REG_BINARY value indicates which tabs to show or hide.

- **Toolbar.** This REG_BINARY value is 0x01 if Windows Messenger displays its toolbar; otherwise, it's 0x00.

- **WindowMax.**   This REG_BINARY value is 0x01 when the Windows Messenger window is maximized; otherwise, it's 0x00.

- **WindowRect.**   This REG_BINARY value indicates the coordinates of the normal Windows Messenger window.

Microsoft\Office

This is where Office 2003 Editions stores its per-user settings. In reality, most IT professionals will use the tools outlined in Chapter 17, "Deploying Office 2003 Settings," instead of customizing these settings for deployment. However, a brief tour of these settings is useful, and a handful of settings are important enough to explain a bit more about them here.

First I'll describe what's in HKCU\Software\Microsoft\Office. At the top of this key, you'll see one subkey for each version of Office that's installed on the computer. For example, you'll see the subkeys 11.0, 10.0, and 9.0. Version 11.0 is Office 2003 Editions. Note that installing Office 2003 Editions creates the keys 8.0, 9.0, 10.0, and 11.0, even though you don't have Office XP or an earlier version of Office on the computer. You'll also see a subkey for the different programs in Office at the top of Office. Although user settings are in HKCU\Software\Microsoft\Office*version*, information about add-ins is in HKCU\Software\Microsoft\Office*program*, and all Office applications share this information.

The subkey 11.0 contains the majority of the Office 2003 Editions settings, whereas the remaining subkeys contain only a handful of settings. For example, in the key 10.0, you see subkeys for each application—Excel, FrontPage, Outlook, Word, and so on. You also see the subkey Common, which contains settings that are common to all the programs in Office 2003 Editions. Some of these settings are important to know about for two reasons. First, the more you understand about them, the more successful you'll be at customizing Office 2003 Editions. Second, you can deploy some Office 2003 Editions settings only as registry values in Custom Installation Wizard. Simply put, the only way to customize a REG_BINARY value in Custom Installation Wizard is by using the Add/Remove Registry Entries screen. You can't customize these settings on the Change Office User Settings screen. Here's a description of these and other important settings:

- **First-run settings.**   The first time a user starts one of the Office 2003 Editions programs, Office 2003 Editions goes through its first-run process to configure the computer for the user. It prompts the user for his or her name and initials, for example, and it customizes settings in HKCU\Software\Microsoft \Office. A handful of values prevent the first-run process from starting a second time. These values are in HKCU\Software\Microsoft\Office\10.0. The value UserData in the subkey Common is 0x01 after the first-run process. You'll find this value in each program's subkey, too. A second, related setting is FirstRun. This value indicates whether the first-run process is complete or not. You find this value in different subkeys of HKCU\Software\Microsoft\Office*version*.

  ❏   HKCU\Software\Microsoft\Office\10.0\Common\General

  ❏   HKCU\Software\Microsoft\Office\10.0\Excel\Options

  ❏   HKCU\Software\Microsoft\Office\10.0\Outlook\Setup

  ❏   HKCU\Software\Microsoft\Office\10.0\PowerPoint\First Run

  ❏   HKCU\Software\Microsoft\Office\10.0\Word\Options

- **Toolbar settings.**   Office 2003 Editions stores most programs' toolbar settings in REG_BINARY values. This means that you can't customize them using the Change Office User Settings screen in Custom Installation Wizard. You can capture those toolbar settings using Profile Wizard, as described in Chapter 17, but what if you don't want to deploy an OPS file? The solution is to customize the toolbars and then export HKCU\Software\Microsoft\Office\10.0\Common \Toolbars to a REG file. Import that REG file into your transform using the Add/Remove Registry Entries screen of Custom Installation Wizard. Office 2003 Editions maintains a number of other REG_BINARY values that you can deploy the same way. If you don't find a setting in the Change Office User Settings screen, track down the setting using the techniques you learn about in Chapter 10, "Finding Registry Settings." The setting is likely a REG_BINARY value.

Microsoft\Search Assistant

The key HKCU\Software\Microsoft\Search Assistant contains the configuration for the Windows Explorer and Internet Explorer Search Assistant. The \CONSOLE value Actor contains the file name of the character that the assistant uses. The REG_DWORD value UseAdvancedSearchAlways is 0x01 if you've configured the assistant to always display its advanced search features. You don't see the REG_DWORD value SocialUI unless you've turned off the animated character. If this value is 0x01, you'll see the animated character. If this value is 0x00, you won't. Most folks don't like the new search interface, and they can restore it to a user interface more similar to the one in Windows 2000 by setting `SocialUI` to `0x00` and `UseAdvancedSearchAlways` to `0x01`. I admit that I like the little dog, so I usually leave `SocialUI` set to `0x01` but use the advanced search features.

Search Assistant's history list is in the subkey `ACMru`. This subkey contains a variety of subkeys, depending on the types of things for which you've searched. For example, if you search for files and folders, you'll see the subkey `5603`, and that subkey contains a list of the different search strings. If you search the Internet using Search Assistant, you'll see the subkey `5001`. You can remove each subkey individually to clear a specific type of query's history list, or you can remove the key `ACMru` to clear all of Search Assistant's history lists. Table C-5 contains a list of the subkeys that I've found in `ACMru`.

Table C-5   History Lists in Search Assistant

Subkey	Description
5001	Internet
5603	Files and folders
5604	Pictures, music, and video
5647	Printers, computers, and people

Microsoft\VBA\Trusted

The key `HKCU\Software\Microsoft\VBA\Trusted` is an important subkey if you're deploying Office 2003 Editions. This is where Office 2003 Editions stores its list of trusted sources. When users open a document that contains signed code, enable those macros, and then add the source to the list of trusted sources, Office 2003 Editions stores those certificates in this key. The reason this key is important is that most businesses should lock the list of trusted sources so that users can't add to it, and then set the security level to high. This prevents users from accidentally running malicious code.

The problem with this scenario is that only Office 2003 Editions provides a tool (the Custom Installation Wizard) to customize this list. With earlier versions of Office, no tool is available to distribute trusted sources. Users can't run legitimate macros that they require to do their jobs. The solution is to distribute the list of trusted sources along with earlier versions of Office by using the registry. So here's my solution:

1. Create a document that contains code and then sign the code using a certificate you want to deploy. Repeat this for each certificate.

2. Install Office on a lab computer, and set the security levels to high.

3. Open each document containing a certificate you want to deploy. Enable the document's macros and then add the source to the list of trusted sources. Figure C-6 shows you an example.

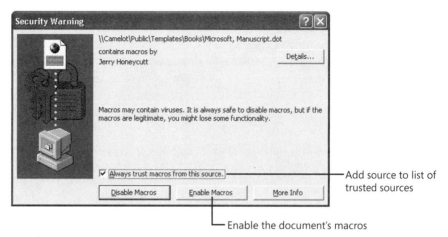

Figure C-6   High security in combination with code signing protects your business from viruses.

4. Export the key HKCU\Software\Microsoft\VBA\Trusted to a REG file, and include this REG file in your deployment. Chapter 17, "Deploying Office 2003 Settings," describes how to deploy registry settings with Office.

Policies

Windows stores policies in the key HKCU\Software\Policies, the preferred branch for registry-based policies. These are per-user policies, so they are in the HKCU branch of the registry. Restricted users don't have permission to change the Policies subkey, which prevents them from circumventing policies by editing the registry. Windows supports hundreds of policies that enable IT professionals to control users' experiences, lock down the desktop, and so on. Chapter 7, "Using Registry-Based Policy," shows you how to customize policies by building custom administrative templates.

Very often, using policies is the best and most interesting way to customize Windows. For example, many customizations you learn about in Chapter 4, "Hacking the Registry," rely on policy settings in the registry to change behaviors. Some of the most interesting policies you learn about in Chapter 4 change how the Start menu and taskbar look and feel. Still other policies enable you to obliterate annoying behavior. Ever wanted to prevent Windows Messenger from running? You can set a policy in this subkey that does that.

Although editing the registry directly is one way to customize these policies, there are better ways. The first way is to use Group Policy Editor to edit the local Group Policy Object (GPO). This provides a user interface for the policies, limiting your settings to valid choices. Chapter 7 describes how to create a local GPO. In short, type **gpedit.msc** in the Run dialog box, and then edit the policies under Computer Configuration and User Configuration in Administrative Templates. The second way is to write scripts that change policies. I use scripts when I want to repeat the same setting many times, such as when I'm configuring my user profile on multiple computers or when I reinstall Windows on computers repeatedly. Chapter 11, "Scripting Registry Changes," shows you how to write scripts to edit the registry. Personally, my favorite method is writing INF files.

Software\Microsoft\Windows\CurrentVersion

This branch of HKCU is one of the most interesting because this is where you find most of the Windows per-user settings. The following list describes some of the more interesting subkeys, and the sections following this one go into more detail:

- **Applets.**   This subkey contains subkeys for many of the different programs that come with Windows. For example, it contains the subkeys Regedit, SysTray, Tour, and Volume Control. If you don't want to see the tour when you create a new user profile, set the REG_DWORD value RunCount in the subkey Tour to 0x00, for example.

- **Internet Settings.**   This subkey contains Internet Explorer settings. A large number of these settings are security settings, such as security zones.

- **NetCache.**   This subkey contains settings for the Windows Offline Files feature. It contains the subkey AssignedOfflineFolders, which is a list of the offline folders assigned to that user through Group Policy.

- **Policies.**   This subkey is the per-user policy branch that Windows inherits from earlier versions of Windows. You learn about policies in Chapter 7, "Using Registry-Based Policy."

- **Run.**   This subkey contains programs that run after the user logs on to the computer. The name of each \CONSOLE value is arbitrary. The value's data contains the command to execute after the user logs on to the computer.

- **RunOnce.**   This subkey contains programs that run after the user logs on to the computer. The name of each \CONSOLE value is arbitrary, and the value's data contains the command to execute after the user logs on to the computer. The difference between this key and Run is that Windows removes commands from this key after they've run, so they only run one time.

HKCU\Software\Microsoft\Windows\CurrentVersion\Explorer is one of the most interesting branches in the registry. For that reason, the remaining sections in this appendix discuss this branch, beginning with the Advanced subkey.

Explorer\Advanced

HKCU\Software\Microsoft\Windows\CurrentVersion\Explorer\Advanced contains settings for Windows Explorer and the Start menu. You configure these settings in two places. The first is the Folder Options dialog box. The second is the Taskbar And Start Menu Properties dialog box. Table C-6 describes these settings.

Table C-6   Start Menu Settings

Name	Data
Folder Options dialog box	
ClassicViewState	0x00—Use the classic folder view
	0x01—Don't use the classic folder view
SeparateProcess	0x00—Don't run folders in separate processes
	0x01—Launch folders in separate processes
DisableThumbnailCache	0x00—Cache thumbnails
	0x01—Do not cache thumbnails
FolderContentsInfoTip	0x00—Do not display file sizes in folder tips
	0x01—Display file sizes in folder tips
FriendlyTree	0x00—Don't display simple folder tree
	0x01—Display simple folder tree in Folders list
Hidden	0x01—Don't show hidden files and folders
	0x02—Show hidden files and folders
HideFileExt	0x00—Show known file extensions
	0x01—Don't show known file extensions
NoNetCrawling	0x00—Don't search for network folders, printers
	0x01—Search for network folders, printers
PersistBrowsers	0x00—Don't restore previous folders
	0x01—Restore previous folders at logon
ShowCompColor	0x00—Don't display compressed files in color
	0x01—Display compressed files in color
ShowInfoTip	0x00—Don't display tips for folders, desktop items
	0x01—Display tips for folders, desktop items

Table C-6   **Start Menu Settings**

Name	Data
ShowSuperHidden	0x00—Don't show protected operating system files
	0x01—Show protected operating system files
WebViewBarricade	0x00—Don't display contents of system folders
	0x01—Display contents of system folders
Customize Classic Start Menu dialog box	
StartMenuAdminTools	NO—Hide Administrative Tools
	YES—Display Administrative Tools
CascadeControlPanel	NO—Display Control Panel as link
	YES—Display Control Panel as menu
CascadeMyDocuments	NO—Display My Documents as link
	YES—Display My Documents as menu
CascadeMyPictures	NO—Display My Pictures as link
	YES—Display My Pictures as menu
CascadePrinters	NO—Display Printers as link
	YES—Display Printers as menu
IntelliMenus	0x00—Don't use personalized menus
	0x01—Use personalized menus
CascadeNetworkConnections	NO—Display Network Connections as link
	YES—Display Network Connections as menu
Start_LargeMFUIcons	0x00—Show small icons on Start menu
	0x01—Show large icons on Start menu
StartMenuChange	0x00—Disable dragging and dropping
	0x01—Enable dragging and dropping
StartMenuFavorites	0x00—Hide Favorites
	0x01—Display Favorites
StartMenuLogoff	0x00—Hide Log Off
	0x01—Display Log Off
StartMenuRun	0x00—Hide Run command
	0x01—Display Run command
StartMenuScrollPrograms	NO—Don't scroll Programs menu
	YES—Scroll Programs menu

Table C-6 **Start Menu Settings**

Name	Data
Customize Start Menu dialog box	
Start_ShowControlPanel	0x00—Hide Control Panel
	0x01—Show Control Panel as link
	0x02—Show Control Panel as menu
Start_EnableDragDrop	0x00—Disable dragging and dropping
	0x01—Enable dragging and dropping
StartMenuFavorites	0x00—Hide Favorites menu
	0x01—Show the Favorites menu
Start_ShowMyComputer	0x00—Hide My Computer
	0x01—Show My Computer as link
	0x02—Show My Computer as menu
Start_ShowMyDocs	0x00—Hide My Documents
	0x01—Show My Documents as link
	0x02—Show My Documents as menu
Start_ShowMyMusic	0x00—Hide My Music
	0x01—Show My Music as link
	0x02—Show My Music as menu
Start_ShowMyPics	0x00—Hide My Pictures
	0x01—Show My Pictures as link
	0x02—Show My Pictures as menu
Start_ShowNetConn	0x00—Hide Network Connections
	0x01—Show Network Connections as link
	0x02—Show Network Connections as menu
Start_AdminToolsTemp	0x00—Hide Administrative Tools
	0x01—Show on All Programs menu
	0x02—Show on All Programs menu and Start menu
Start_ShowHelp	0x00—Hide Help and Support
	0x01—Show Help and Support
Start_ShowNetPlaces	0x00—Hide My Network Places
	0x01—Show My Network Places
Start_ShowOEMLink	0x00—Hide Manufacturer Link
	0x01—Show Manufacturer Link

Table C-6   **Start Menu Settings**

Name	Data
`Start_ShowPrinters`	0x00—Hide Printers and Faxes
	0x01—Show Printers and Faxes
`Start_ShowRun`	0x00—Hide Run command
	0x01—Show Run command
`Start_ShowSearch`	0x00—Hide Search command
	0x01—Show Search command
`Start_ScrollPrograms`	0x00—Don't scroll Programs menu
	0x01—Scroll Programs menu

Windows defines templates, similar to the policy templates that define how to collect and store policies, for these settings. You find these templates in the following places:

- `HKEY_LOCAL_MACHINE\SOFTWARE\Microsoft\Windows\CurrentVersion\Explorer` `\StartMenu\StartMenu` contains templates for the settings in the Advanced Start Menu Options area of the Customize Classic Start Menu dialog box. To open this dialog box, in Control Panel launch Taskbar And Start Menu. Then on the Start Menu tab, select the Classic Start Menu option, and click Customize.

- `HKEY_LOCAL_MACHINE\SOFTWARE\Microsoft\Windows\CurrentVersion\Explorer` `\StartMenu\StartPanel` contains templates for the settings on the Advanced tab of the Customize Start Menu dialog box. To open this dialog box, in Control Panel launch Taskbar And Start Menu. Then on the Start Menu tab, select the Start Menu option, and click Customize.

- `HKLM\SOFTWARE\Microsoft\Windows\CurrentVersion\Explorer\Advanced` `\Folder` contains templates for the settings in the Folder Options dialog box, most of which are on the View tab. To open this dialog box, in Control Panel launch Folder Options.

Explorer\AutoComplete

The subkey `AutoComplete` contains a single value that controls the `AutoComplete` feature in Windows Explorer. If the `\CONSOLE` value `AutoComplete` is `Yes`, Windows Explorer uses `AutoComplete`; otherwise, it doesn't.

Explorer\ComDlg32

The subkey ComDlg32 contains two subkeys. Both are history lists. To clear the history list that the common dialog boxes use, delete both subkeys. The first is LastVisitedMRU, which contains a list of folders that you've opened.

The second is OpenSaveMRU, which is a little more complicated. Within the key Open-SaveMRU are subkeys for different types of files. For example, you see the subkey doc in OpenSaveMRU that lists all the files with the *.doc* extension that you've opened. The sub-key * contains all the files you've opened in the common dialog boxes, regardless of their extensions. Thus, the common dialog boxes can display a history list by type or display all the files in the history.

Explorer\HideDesktopIcons

In HideDesktopIcons, you see two subkeys: ClassicStartMenu and NewStartPanel. The first subkey determines which icons to hide when Windows is using the classic Start menu. The second determines which icons to hide when Windows is using the new Start menu. Add a REG_DWORD value named for the icon's class ID to either subkey to hide it in that view. Set the value to 0x01. Hide the Recycle Bin icon by creating a REG_DWORD value called {645FF040-5081-101B-9F08- 00AA002F954E} in the subkey HideDesktopIcons\NewStartPanel, for example, and then set it to 0x01. Click the desktop and then press F5 to refresh. Appendix A, "File Associations," lists the class IDs you might want to hide.

Explorer\HideMyComputerIcons

The key HideMyComputerIcons enables you to hide icons in My Computer. To hide icons in My Computer, add a REG_DWORD value to HideMyComputerIcons—the name is the class ID of the icon you want to hide—and set it to 0x01. See Appendix A, "File Associations," for a list of class IDs. Refresh Windows Explorer to see your changes.

Explorer\MenuOrder

HKCU\Software\Microsoft\Windows\CurrentVersion\Explorer\MenuOrder contains the sort order of the Favorites menu and Start menu. The subkey Favorites contains the sort order of the Favorites menu. The subkey Start Menu contains the sort order of the classic Start menu, and the subkey Start Menu2 contains the sort order of the new Start menu. Deciphering the contents of these three keys is next to ridiculous, but you can remove any of them to re-sort the corresponding menu in alphabetical order. For example, to restore the All Programs menu to alphabetical order, remove the subkey Start Menu2. To restore the Favorites menu in both Windows Explorer and Internet Explorer, remove the subkey Favorites.

Explorer\RecentDocs

The subkey RecentDocs is the list of recent documents that you see on the Start menu. Within this key are subkeys for different types of files and folders. For example, you see the subkey txt that lists all the files with the .txt extension that you've opened. To clear your list of recent documents, remove this subkey. Along with this subkey, you must remove the documents shortcuts that Windows creates in your profile folder, %UserProfile%\Recent.

Explorer\RunMRU

The subkey RunMRU contains a list of programs that you've run using the Run dialog box. You can remove individual programs from this list or delete the RunMRU subkey to clear the list of programs.

Explorer\User Shell Folders

Special folders include the My Documents, My Pictures, and Favorites folders, among many others. Table C-7 shows the special folders that Windows creates after a fresh installation and their default paths. The first column contains each folder's internal name as Windows and other programs know it. The second column contains each folder's default path, which almost always starts with %UserProfile%, making these folders part of each user's profile folder. Chapter 12, "Deploying User Profiles," describes these user profile folders in depth.

Table C-7   Special Folders

Name	Default Path
AppData	%UserProfile%\Application Data
Cache	%UserProfile%\Local Settings\Temporary Internet Files
Cookies	%UserProfile%\Cookies
Desktop	%UserProfile%\Desktop
Favorites	%UserProfile%\Favorites
History	%UserProfile%\Local Settings\History
Local AppData	%UserProfile%\Local Settings\Application Data
Local Settings	%UserProfile%\Local Settings
My Pictures	%UserProfile%\My Documents\My Pictures

Table C-7   **Special Folders**

Name	Default Path
NetHood	%UserProfile%\NetHood
Personal	%UserProfile%\My Documents
PrintHood	%UserProfile%\PrintHood
Programs	%UserProfile%\Start Menu\Programs
Recent	%UserProfile%\Recent
SendTo	%UserProfile%\SendTo
Start Menu	%UserProfile%\Start Menu
Startup	%UserProfile%\Start Menu\Programs\Startup
Templates	%UserProfile%\Templates

HKCU\Software\Microsoft\Windows\CurrentVersion\Explorer\User Shell Folders is the key where Windows stores the location of per-user special folders. Each value in this key is a special folder, as shown in Table C-7. These are REG_EXPAND_SZ values, so you can use environment variables in them. Use %UserProfile% in a path to direct the folder somewhere inside users' profile folders or %UserName% in a path to include users' names. To redirect users' Favorites folders to the network, set the value Favorites, which you can look up in Table C-7, to *Server**Share*\%USERNAME%\Favorites, where *Server**Share* is the server and share containing the folders. Windows updates a second key, HKCU\Software\Microsoft\Windows\CurrentVersion\Explorer\Shell Folders, with the paths from User Shell Folders the next time the user logs on to the operating system, so you don't have to update it. In fact, Microsoft's documentation says Windows doesn't use Shell Folders.

Appendix D
Per-Computer Settings

In Appendix C, "Per-User Settings," you learned about many of the settings that Microsoft Windows XP and Windows Server 2003 Server (Windows) create for users in the registry. These settings are in HKCU. This appendix is about the per-computer settings in HKLM.

The branch HKLM\SOFTWARE is similar to HKCU\Software. In fact, the organization of this key is almost identical. The difference is that these settings are computer-oriented; they affect every user who logs on to the computer. However, you find some settings in both places, HKLM\SOFTWARE and HKCU\Software. This is common with Microsoft Office 2003 Editions and many of the policies in Windows, for example. Most often, when a setting is in both places, the version in HKLM has precedence over the same setting in HKCU. Only when an administrator removes the setting from HKLM (restricted users don't usually have permission to change settings in HKLM) do users' own preferences mean anything. The only exception to this rule is the file associations in SOFTWARE\Classes in both root keys. File associations in HKCU have precedence over file associations in HKLM. This order of precedence is necessary to enable users to have custom file associations.

Other branches in HKLM are unique, though. Windows stores the computer's configuration in HKLM\SYSTEM. The operating system's lower-level settings are in this branch, too. Lower-level settings include the configuration of the computer's network connections, device drivers, services, and so on. Windows also stores local security data in HKLM. Something else unique in HKLM is that it contains more links than HKCU does.

Recall that links are aliases for other subkeys, and Windows uses links in HKLM to support features such as hardware profiles and configuration sets. This appendix describes these links so that you can better understand how different parts of the registry relate to each other.

This appendix outlines the organization of HKLM, describing its interesting and useful subkeys. But by no means do I cover this root key's entire contents. Instead, I've focused on settings that you're most likely to customize or need to understand as a power user or IT professional. Also, I don't describe the hive files or how Windows loads them into HKLM because Chapter 1, "Learning the Basics," already covers this.

HARDWARE

Windows re-creates HKLM\HARDWARE every time the operating system starts. This key contains configuration data that the operating system detects when it starts. This branch contains few values to customize because the branch's contents are volatile. Some values in it are useful for inventorying the computer's hardware, though. For example, you can read its settings to inventory the computer's processor. You find this value and similar ones in HKLM\HARDWARE\DESCRIPTION, and they're easy-to-read REG_SZ values.

The following list is an overview of the HARDWARE key's subkeys, and the sections following this one give more details about some of them:

- **ACPI.** This subkey describes the computer's ACPI BIOS. The values in this subkey are a bit cryptic.

- **DESCRIPTION.** This is the most interesting subkey in HARDWARE. It describes the computer's BIOS, processors, and buses. (See the "DESCRIPTION" section.)

- **DEVICEMAP.** This subkey maps the devices that the hardware recognizer detects to their device drivers in the SYSTEM branch of HKLM.

- **RESOURCEMAP.** This subkey maps the computer's resources to the devices that use them. Like the ACPI subkey, this subkey is difficult to understand. Resources that the RESOURCEMAP subkey maps include bus number, DMA channels, interrupt vectors, memory ranges, and I/O ports.

Tip You can use System Information to see the computer's hardware configuration and how Windows has been spending its resources. To use this feature, in the Run dialog box, type **msinfo32**. The data that System Information displays is comprehensive. Especially helpful is that you can use it to look at remote computers' configurations. And it sure beats scrounging around the registry for the same information.

DESCRIPTION

Each time Windows boots, its hardware recognizer collects information about the computer's hardware and stores it in HKLM\HARDWARE\DESCRIPTION\System. In this branch, you find three subkeys:

- **CentralProcessor.** This subkey contains one subkey for each CPU that the hardware recognizer finds on the computer. CentralProcessor\0 is the subkey for the first processor, CentralProcessor\1 is the second, and so on. Each subkey contains values that describe the processor. For example, the value ~MHz describes the approximate speed of the processor.

- **FloatingPointProcessor.** This subkey contains one subkey for each FPU that the hardware recognizer finds on the computer. The organization is similar to that of CentralProcessor. Because Pentium-compatible processors contain onboard FPUs, this subkey usually corresponds to CentralProcessor.

- **MultifunctionAdapter.** This subkey contains one subkey for each bus that the hardware recognizer detects. The subkeys are 0, 1, and so on. Each subkey contains the REG_SZ value Identifier, which is a description of the bus: PCI and ISA. Below each bus's subkey are subkeys that describe the devices attached to the bus. This key describes only essential devices; it's not all-inclusive.

DEVICEMAP

The DEVICEMAP subkey is another interesting subkey of HKLM\HARDWARE. It maps the devices that the hardware recognizer detects to the services that drive them. Different device classes have different subkeys in DEVICEMAP. For example, this subkey typically contains the subkeys KeyboardClass and PointerClass. You don't find subkeys for every device in the computer, though. It contains subkeys only for those devices that Windows requires to start the computer. Thus, you don't find subkeys for sound cards and the like.

These subkeys contain one or more values. The values' names are the devices' names. The values' data points to the subkeys that define the services associated with those devices. For example, the subkey DEVICEMAP\KeyboardClass contains the value \Device\KeyboardClass0, and its value is \REGISTRY\MACHINE\SYSTEM\ControlSet001\Services\Kbdclass. This indicates that the service driving the keyboard is in the registry, in HKLM, and in the branch SYSTEM\ControlSet001\Services\Kbdclass.

SAM

The key HKLM\SAM\SAM is a link to HKLM\SECURITY\SAM. You learn about the SECURITY subkey in the next section. This key is where the Security Accounts Manager (SAM) creates the local computer's security database. Examining the contents of this key is interesting, but you can't customize it. You're better off managing local security using the User Accounts dialog box.

Windows protects the SAM key by preventing access to it. The key's access control list (ACL) doesn't even allow the Administrators group to read its contents, much less members of the Users or Power Users group. You can give yourself Read permission to view the key, however, if you're a member of the Administrators group, because this group owns the SAM key. If you want to tour this key, do it on a lab computer. Don't tamper with the SAM key on a production computer. To give yourself Read permission, select HKLM\SAM\SAM; click Edit, Permissions; select the Administrators group; and then select the Read check box in the Allow column. If you don't have a lab computer available, just look at Figure D-1, which shows the contents of this key.

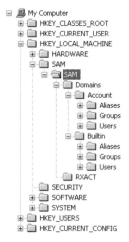

Figure D-1   You can't normally see the contents of the SAM key, but this figure shows what you do see if you give the Administrators group permission to read it.

The key HKLM\SAM\SAM\Domains contains two subkeys. The first subkey, Account, describes local computer accounts, user accounts, and groups. The second subkey, Builtin, describes built-in accounts and groups. You manage these subkeys using the User Accounts dialog box. Both subkeys contain the same three subkeys: Aliases, Groups, and Users. These subkeys define the computer's local accounts and membership in the computer's local groups.

SECURITY

The key HKLM\SECURITY contains Windows security data. You normally can't see the contents of this key, but you can give the Administrators group permission to read it so that you can examine it. The preceding section "SAM" shows you how to do that. The SECURITY key contains the subkey SAM. It also contains the subkey Policies. This subkey defines local, non–registry-based policies for the computer. The key Policies\Accounts has one subkey for each SID in the local security database. Each SID contains four subkeys:

- **ActSysAc.** This subkey defines the SID's operating system access allowed.
- **Privilgs.** This subkey defines the SID's privileges.
- **SecDesc.** This subkey contains the SID's security descriptor.
- **Sid.** This subkey defines the groups to which the SID belongs.

SOFTWARE

The key HKLM\SOFTWARE is second in interest only to HKCU\Software. It contains per-computer software settings, including many Windows settings. Because Windows and most applications store settings as per-user settings, this branch is a bit slimmer than HKCU\Software, but it still contains numerous settings that are useful for customization. The types of settings you find in HKLM\SOFTWARE are typically those that an administrator defines. Because HKLM\SOFTWARE contains per-computer settings, any changes you make here affect all users who log on to the computer. Also, restricted users don't have permission to change settings in HKLM.

The key HKLM\SOFTWARE is organized similarly to the way HKCU\Software is organized. Applications store settings in HKLM\SOFTWARE\Vendor\Program\Version\. *Vendor* is the name of the program's publisher, *Program* is the name of the program, and *Version* is the program's version number. Often, *Version* is CurrentVersion. This branch also contains a handful of subkeys that don't follow this organization. For example, HKLM\SOFTWARE\Policies contains per-computer policies. The sections following this one describe the most interesting and useful parts of HKLM\SOFTWARE.

Classes

The key HKLM\CLASSES contains per-computer file associations. This key contains the vast majority of file associations, as opposed to HKCU\Classes, which contains per-user file associations. Windows merges both subkeys to form HKCR. Appendix A, "File Associations," describes HKCR in detail.

Clients

The key HKLM\SOFTWARE\Clients defines the client programs that Internet Explorer associates with different Internet services. You configure these clients on the Programs tab of the Internet Properties dialog box, shown in Figure D-2. For example, you can choose the mail client that Internet Explorer uses when you click a mailto link, or you can choose the news client to use when you click a news link. These choices also determine the programs that Internet Explorer launches when you choose one of the tools on the Tools menu.

Figure D-2   You associate client programs with Internet services by using the Programs tab.

The Clients key contains six subkeys by default: Contacts, Internet Call, Mail, Media, News, and StartMenuInternet. The default value of each subkey specifies the name of the application that is the default tool for that category. For example, if the default value of HKLM\SOFTWARE\Clients\Mail is Outlook Express, then Outlook Express is the default mail client that Internet Explorer starts when you click a mailto link.

Drill down a bit further and you find one subkey for each client program. For example, Clients\Mail contains the Hotmail, MSN Explorer, and Outlook Express subkeys. The organization of these subkeys is almost the same as the organization of the subkeys in HKCR. Typically, you find the subkeys Protocols and shell under each client program's subkey. The subkey Protocols defines the protocols associated with the application. For example, the key HKLM\SOFTWARE\Clients\Mail\Outlook Express\Protocols describes the command to run when users click a mailto link on a Web page. The subkey `shell` defines the command to run when users choose an option on Internet Explorer's Tools menu. The subkey `HKLM\SOFTWARE\Clients` `\Mail\Outlook Express\shell` describes the command to run when users click Tools, Mail And News, Read Mail in Internet Explorer.

Microsoft\Active Setup

A variety of Windows components, notably Internet Explorer components, still use Active Setup. The key `HKLM\SOFTWARE\Microsoft\Active Setup` contains these components' registrations. The subkey `FeatureComponentID` is sometimes useful for mapping a GUID to a component. Look for the GUID in this subkey; then look at the `REG_SZ` value to determine the component's name.

The key `HKLM\SOFTWARE\Microsoft\Active Setup\Installed Components` is each component's registration. Each subkey is a component. For example, the subkey `{2179C5D3-EBFF-11CF-B6FD-00AA00B4E220}` is for NetShow. Within each subkey, you see several values, some more interesting than others. First the `REG_BINARY` value `IsInstalled` indicates whether the component is installed or not. The value is `0x0001` if the component is installed; if not, the value is `0x0000`. The `REG_SZ` value `Version` contains the component's version.

The most interesting value is the `REG_EXPAND_SZ` value `StubPath`. If this value exists, Windows executes the command it contains after the operating system creates a new user profile. If you don't see this value, nothing happens. To keep Windows from running the command, remove the value `StubPath` from that component's subkey in `Installed Components`.

Microsoft\Command Processor

The command-prompt window supports file and folder name completion, as well as a few other features. You can configure these features using Tweak UI, as described in Chapter 5, "Mapping Tweak UI," or you can hack them directly in the registry. This key is similar to `HKCU\Software\Microsoft\Command Processor`. The difference is that this key applies to all users, whereas the key in `HKCU` applies only to the current console user. The following list describes the settings in the subkey `Command Processor`, which configure the command-prompt window:

- **AutoRun.** This `REG_SZ` value, which has no default, contains a list of commands that run automatically when you start a command-prompt window.

- **CompletionChar.** This is a `REG_DWORD` value. It specifies the ASCII character code of the key to use for file name completion. You can set this value to `0x00`, `0x01` through `0x1F`, `0x20`, or `0x40`. The Tab key is `0x09` and is the default.

- **DefaultColor.**   This REG_DWORD value defaults to 0. Valid values range from 0x00 through 0xFE. It specifies the default background and foreground color of a command-prompt window. The first hexadecimal digit specifies the background color, and the second digit specifies the foreground color. The digits correspond to the colors shown in Table D-1.

- **DelayedExpansion.**   This is a REG_DWORD value with a default of 0x00. It specifies whether the command prompt delays environment variable expansion. If the value is 0x01, the command prompt interprets the exclamation point (!) as an environment variable that expands only when used.

- **EnableExtensions.**   This REG_DWORD value has a default value of 0x01. It determines whether command-processor extensions are enabled or not. Setting this value to 0x00 disables extensions. You need to disable extensions only when they interfere with a script language with which they aren't compatible.

- **PathCompletionChar.**   This is a REG_DWORD value that specifies the ASCII character code of the key to use for path completion. Set this value to 0x00, 0x01 through 0x1F, 0x20, or 0x40. The Tab key is 0x09. You can use the same key that you use for file name completion, which expands both.

Table D-1   **Values for** DefaultColor

Value	Color
0	Black
1	Blue
2	Green
3	Aqua
4	Red
5	Purple
6	Yellow
7	White
8	Gray
9	Light Blue
A	Light Green
B	Light Aqua
C	Light Red
D	Light Purple
E	Light Yellow
F	Bright White

Microsoft\Driver Signing

The key HKLM\SOFTWARE\Microsoft\Driver Signing contains values that configure the Windows driver-signing feature. Microsoft digitally signs driver files so that Windows can verify that Microsoft tested the driver file and that the file hasn't changed since Microsoft tested it. This key's only value, Policy, controls how Windows handles driver files that aren't signed. Here are the possible values:

- **0x00.** Windows installs unsigned device drivers (Ignore).
- **0x01.** Windows warns the user that the device driver is unsigned and enables the user to choose whether or not to install it (Warn).
- **0x02.** Windows does not install unsigned device drivers (Block).

This setting comes from the Driver Signing Options dialog box, shown in Figure D-3. It applies to all users, unless you clear the Make This Action The System Default check box. The figure shows the values associated with each option.

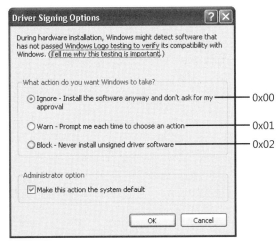

Figure D-3   In an enterprise environment, blocking unsigned device drivers is the safest option.

Microsoft\DrWatson

The DrWatson subkey stores configuration settings for Dr. Watson for Windows (Drwtsn32.exe), the application error debugger. These entries specify how Dr. Watson for Windows notifies the user of an application error, and how its log file and crash dump file are configured. Dr. Watson adds these entries the first time it starts:

- **AppendToLogFile.**   Specifies whether Dr. Watson for Windows overwrites the existing log file with new data or appends new data to the end of the existing log file. By default, the log file is named Drwtsn32.log and is stored in the system root directory. If this REG_DWORD value is 0x00, Dr. Watson overwrites the file; if it's 0x01, it appends the new error information to the file.

■ **CrashDumpFile.**   Specifies the location of the crash dump file for Dr. Watson for Windows. The crash dump file is a binary file that is created when a program stops abnormally. The crash dump file can be interpreted by the Windows Debugger. All users must have permission to read and write to the crash dump file. By default, the crash dump file is named user.dmp and resides in the root of the system directory. Set this REG_SZ value to the path and file name of the crash dump file.

■ **CreateCrashDump.**   Specifies whether Dr. Watson for Windows creates a binary crash dump file when a program stops abnormally. The crash dump file can be interpreted by the Windows Debugger. If the value of this REG_DWORD value is 0x01, the location of the crash dump file must appear in the value of the Crash-DumpFile entry. By default, the crash dump file is named user.dmp and is in the system root directory.

■ **DumpAllThreads.**   Specifies which application threads are included in the log file that Dr. Watson for Windows creates when an application error occurs. By default, the log file is named Drwtsn32.log and is in the system root directory. If this REG_DWORD value is 0x01, Dr. Watson includes all threads.

■ **DumpSymbols.**   Specifies whether Dr. Watson for Windows includes the symbol table for each application module in its log file. The symbol table consists of the name and memory address of each symbol. By default, because it can be very large, the symbol table is not included in the log file. If this REG_DWORD value is 0x01, Dr. Watson includes the debug symbols.

■ **Instructions.**   This REG_DWORD value specifies how many instructions preceding and following the faulty instruction are included in the instruction disassembly portion of Drwtsn32.log, the log file for Dr. Watson for Windows. The default value is 10.

■ **LogFilePath.**   This REG_SZ value specifies the location of Drwtsn32.log, the log file for Dr. Watson for Windows. The log file contains diagnostic data about application errors that occur. All users must have permission to read and write to the log file.

■ **MaximumCrashes.**   This REG_DWORD value specifies how many errors Dr. Watson for Windows maintains at any given time in its application error viewer and in the Event Viewer application log. When the number of recorded errors reaches the value of this entry, Dr. Watson operates normally and adds new errors to its log and crash dump file, but it does not add any new errors to its application log viewer or to the Event Viewer application log until it is reset. The user is not notified that the number of crashes has reached the maximum. To reset Dr. Watson for Windows, run Drwtsn32.exe. You can either click Clear or increase the value in the Number Of Errors To Save box. When you click Clear, you delete all errors from the application error viewer in Dr. Watson for Windows, and you delete all events from the Event Viewer application log, even those not generated by Dr. Watson for Windows. However, records of the application errors remain in the Drwtsn32.log and in the crash dump file, user.dmp, if one has been selected. The default value is 10.

- **NumberOfCrashes.**   This REG_DWORD value counts the number of application errors Dr. Watson for Windows is maintaining in its application error viewer and in the Event Viewer application log. When this value reaches the value of MaximumCrashes, Dr. Watson for Windows operates normally and adds new errors to its log and crash dump file, but it does not add any new errors to its application log viewer or to the Event Viewer application log until it is reset. The user is not notified that the number of crashes has reached the maximum. To reset Dr. Watson for Windows, run Drwtsn32.exe. You can either click Clear or increase the value in the Number Of Errors To Save box. When you click Clear, you delete all errors from the application error viewer in Dr. Watson for Windows, and you delete all events from the Event Viewer application log, even those not generated by Dr. Watson for Windows. However, records of the application errors remain in the Drwtsn32.log and in the crash dump file, user.dmp, if one has been selected.

- **SoundNotification.**   This REG_DWORD value specifies whether Dr. Watson for Windows generates a sound when it detects an application error. If the value of this entry is 0x01, you can enter the name of a wave file (.wav) in the value of the WaveFile entry. Otherwise, Dr. Watson generates two standard beeps.

- **VisualNotification.**   This REG_DWORD value specifies whether Dr. Watson for Windows displays a message box when it detects an application error. While the message box is displayed, no new messages or windows can be displayed, but background processes are not affected. If the buttons on the message box are not clicked within five minutes, the message box is removed.

- **WaveFile.**   This REG_SZ value specifies the file containing the sound that Dr. Watson for Windows plays when it detects an application error. This entry is used only when the computer has a sound card and the value of the SoundNotification entry is 0x01.

Microsoft\Internet Explorer

The key HKLM\SOFTWARE\Microsoft\Internet Explorer contains Internet Explorer settings that apply to every user who logs on to the computer. For example, the subkey AboutURLs contains the URLs of Web pages that Internet Explorer displays in special scenarios. The subkey AdvancedOptions defines templates for the options on the Internet Options dialog box's Advanced tab.

Microsoft\Sysprep

You won't see HKLM\SOFTWARE\Microsoft\Sysprep on your computer unless you installed Windows from a disk image that you prepared with Sysprep. Chapter 15, "Cloning Disks with Sysprep," describes how to use this tool. The values in this subkey are useful for understanding what Sysprep has done:

- **CriticalDevicesInstalled.** This value is 0x01 if Sysprep installed the critical devices. See Chapter 15 for more information.

- **SidsGenerated.** This value is 0x01 if Sysprep regenerated the computer's SID.

Microsoft\Windows NT\CurrentVersion

The key HKLM\SOFTWARE\Microsoft\Windows NT\CurrentVersion contains useful subkeys for learning more about Windows but not customizing it. The values in this subkey describe the current version of Windows, the registered owner, and the path in which you installed the operating system. For IT professionals, the three most useful subkeys are in the following list:

- **HotFix.** This key contains one subkey for each hotfix installed on the computer. The value Installed is 0x01 if the hotfix is installed; it's 0x00 otherwise. The HotFix key fills up quickly when you use Windows Update or Automatic Updates to download and install hotfixes. IT professionals can inventory the hotfixes installed on different computers by writing scripts that extract the contents of this key and dump them to text files on the network.

- **ProfileList.** This key contains one subkey for each user profile you see in the User Profiles dialog box.

- **Winlogon.** This key contains values that define the logon process, as well as the last user who logged on to the computer. There are two interesting customizations in this key, both of which you learn in Chapter 18, "Fixing Common IT Problems." The first is that you can display a legal notice when users log on to the operating system. The second is that you can use this key to automatically log on to the computer using a specific account. You can do that a specific number of times. For example, you can configure this key to automatically log on as Administrator, install an application, and then log off of the operating system. See Chapter 18 for more information about this useful IT trick.

Microsoft\Windows NT\CurrentVersion\Winlogon

The `Winlogon` subkey stores configuration data for the Winlogon service. `Winlogon` provides support for interactive logon to Windows. This subkey stores data that applies to all users of the computer. The `Winlogon` subkey in HKCU stores data that applies to a specific user. The following list describes settings in the `Winlogon` key:

- **AutoRestartShell.**   Specifies whether the Windows user interface (typically, Explorer.exe) restarts automatically if it stops unexpectedly. Set this REG_DWORD value to 0x01 (the default value) to restart the user interface.

- **DCacheMinInterval.**   This REG_SZ value specifies how often the list of domains in the Unlock Workstation dialog box is updated. The list of domains is updated before it is displayed to the user if its age exceeds the value of this entry. A memory cache on the local computer stores the domain list. When the value of this entry is set to the default of two minutes and a user unlocks a workstation or server, the system retrieves domain data and updates the list. The short update interval ensures that the domain list is current. However, refreshing the list can cause a noticeable delay. You can use this entry to increase the time between domain list updates, eliminating some of the delay. However, if the domain list changes between updates, users still will not see the most current list of domains. This value doesn't exist in the registry by default. Add it if required.

- **DCacheUpdate.**   This REG_BINARY value stores domain names in binary form for internal Winlogon programming code to use.

- **DefaultDomainName.**   This REG_SZ value stores the name of the domain to which the user most recently logged on successfully. The value of this entry appears in the Log On To Windows dialog box the next time the dialog box is displayed.

- **DefaultUserName.**   This REG_SZ value stores the last user name entered in the Log On To Windows dialog box. The value of this entry appears in the Log On To Windows dialog box the next time the dialog box is displayed. It is also used in automated logons and unattended setup.

- **DontDisplayLastUserName.**   This REG_DWORD value specifies whether a user name appears in the Log On To Windows dialog box. By default, Windows displays the user name of the last user who logged on successfully (as stored in the value of **DefaultUserName**) in the Log On To Windows dialog box. If the value of this entry is 0x01, the User Name box in the Log On To Windows dialog box is blank.

- **KeepRasConnection.** This REG_DWORD value specifies whether Windows closes all open dial-up (Routing and Remote Access) connections when a user logs off.

- **LogonPrompt.** This REG_SZ value specifies a message for the Log On To Windows dialog box. By default, there is no logon prompt message. This value doesn't exist by default. Add it if required.

- **ProfileDlgTimeOut.** This REG_DWORD value defines the starting time for the User Environment Countdown Timer. (The default is 30 seconds.) This timer determines how long the system waits for a user response before it uses a default value. The value of this entry is used when either of the following events occur:

  - ❏ The system detects a slow link between the client and the server that stores the client's profile.

  - ❏ The system cannot access or update a server-based profile when the user logs on or off.

- **RasForce.** This REG_SZ value specifies whether the Log On Using Dial-Up Connection check box is selected by default when the system starts. This check box appears on the Log On To Windows dialog box that is displayed when the user logs on to Windows. The system uses the value of this entry only when you have created a dial-up connection by using Network and Dial-up Connections and the computer is a member of a domain.

- **RemoteBootOk.** This REG_SZ value specifies whether Winlogon declares startup to be successful. If you change the value of this entry to 0, you must use another program (such as Bootok.exe or Bootvrfy.exe) to declare the startup successful.

- **RemoteControllerMissing.** Stores the computer setting for the domain controller message. (The user setting is stored in the value of the ReportDC entry.) This entry determines, in part, whether the system displays the following message when it cannot contact the domain controller that stores a user's roaming user profile:

  "A domain controller for your domain could not be contacted. You have been logged on using cached account information. Changes made to your profile since you last logged on might not be available."

  When the value of this entry is equal to TRUE, the system displays the message. When the value is any other string and when this value is absent from the registry, the system does not display the message. Two entries manage the display of the domain controller message: ReportDC and ReportControllerMissing. The system displays this message only when both entries are set to the display setting—that is, when ReportDC is either set to 1 or does not appear in the registry, and when ReportDomainController appears in the registry with a value of TRUE. By default, the message does not display.

- **RunLogonScriptSync.**   This REG_DWORD value specifies whether the system waits for the logon script to finish running before it starts Windows Explorer and creates the desktop. If this value is 0x01, Windows Explorer does not start until the logon script is finished.

- **ScreenSaverGracePeriod.**   This REG_DWORD value specifies when password protection of a screen saver becomes effective. This entry specifies the delay between the appearance of a password-protected screen saver and the enforcement of the password requirement. Password protection of a screen saver is not effective immediately. By default, a brief period elapses within which the user can use the mouse or the keyboard to stop the screen saver without entering the password. This delay is designed to minimize the disruption that results when the screen saver starts while the user is working. You can add this entry to the registry to adjust the length of the delay. To make password protection effective immediately, set the value of this entry to 0x0. The default value is 0x05.

- **SFCDIICacheDir.**   This REG_EXPAND_SZ value specifies an alternate location for the Windows File Protection cache.

- **SfcScan.**   Specifies when Windows File Protection scans protected files for changes. By default, it scans protected files only during setup. The possible settings are as follows:

    - ❑   **0.** Windows File Protection scans files only during setup.

    - ❑   **1.** Windows File Protection scans files at setup and each time you start Windows. This setting delays each startup.

    - ❑   **2.** Windows File Protection scans files the next time you start the system.

- **SfcShowProgress.**   This REG_DWORD value hides the file scan progress window. This window provides status information that might be helpful to advanced users, but it might confuse novices. If this value is 0x01, users see the file scan progress window.

- **Shell.**   This REG_SZ value specifies the programs that provide the user interface to the operating system. By default, Winlogon starts the programs specified in the value of Userinit, including Userinit.exe. Userinit.exe starts the user interface program. However, if Winlogon cannot start the programs specified in the value of Userinit, Winlogon directly runs the programs specified in the value of this entry.

- **ShowLogonOptions.**   This REG_DWORD value specifies whether logon options are displayed in the Log On To Windows dialog box when the dialog box opens. The Log On To Windows dialog box has an Options button that alternately hides and displays the Domain box and the Log On Using Dial-Up Connection options. If this value is **0x01**, the options are displayed; otherwise, they are hidden.

- **SlowLinkProfileDefault.**   This REG_DWORD value directs the system to wait for the remote copy of the roaming user profile to load, even if the profile is loading slowly. Also, the system waits for the remote copy when the user is notified about a slow connection but does not respond in the time allowed.

- **SlowLinkTimeOut.**   Defines which connections Winlogon considers to be slow. If the server storing a user's profile does not respond before the time specified in the value of this entry, Winlogon considers the link to the server to be slow, and it offers the user the option of using a profile stored on the local computer instead of waiting for the server. This entry is used only when the value of Slow-LinkDetectEnabled is 1. You can increase the value of SlowLinkTimeOut to favor the server-based profile. This is particularly useful for clients using addresses assigned by Dynamic Host Configuration Protocol (DHCP), or for computers accessing server-based profiles over slow wide area network (WAN) connections, such as dial-up connections.

- **Welcome.**   This REG_SZ value specifies the text that appears in the caption bar beside the title of the Log On To Windows, Windows Security, Computer Locked, and Unlock Computer dialog boxes. This value doesn't exist by default. Add it to customize the caption of the previous dialog boxes.

Policies

Windows stores per-computer policies in the key HKLM\SOFTWARE\Policies, the preferred branch for registry-based policies. Restricted users don't have permission to change the Policies subkey, which prevents them from circumventing policies by editing the registry. Windows supports hundreds of policies that enable IT professionals to control the computer's configuration. Chapter 7, "Using Registry-Based Policy," shows you how to customize policies by building custom administrative templates.

Very often, using policies is the best and most interesting way to customize Windows. For example, many of the customizations you learn about in Chapter 4, "Hacking the Registry," rely on policy settings in the registry to change behaviors. Some policies enable you to change behavior that annoys you. In this regard, the per-user policies in HKCU\Software\Policies offer more customization possibilities that the policies that you find in HKLM\SOFTWARE\Policies.

Although editing the registry directly is certainly one way to customize policies, there are better ways. The first is to use Group Policy Editor to edit the local Group Policy Object (GPO). This provides a user interface for the policies, limiting your settings to valid choices. Chapter 7, "Using Registry-Based Policy," describes how to edit the local GPO. In short, type **gpedit.msc** in the Run dialog box, and then edit the policies under Computer Configuration and User Configuration in Administrative Templates. The second way is to write scripts that change policies. I use scripts when I need to repeat the same setting many times, such as when I'm configuring multiple computers or when I reinstall Windows on computers often. Chapter 11, "Scripting Registry Changes," shows you how to write scripts to edit the registry.

SOFTWARE\Microsoft\Windows\CurrentVersion

The key HKLM\SOFTWARE\Microsoft\Windows\CurrentVersion, and all its subkeys, contains some of the most interesting settings in HKLM. First, this key has a number of REG_SZ and REG_EXPAND_SZ values that are interesting:

- **CommonFilesDir.**   This value contains the path of Windows common files. The default location is C:\Program Files\Common Files.

- **DevicePath.**   This value defines the locations where Windows finds device-driver INF files. %SystemRoot%\inf;%SystemDrive%\Windows\Drivers is the default for this value.

- **MediaPath.**   This value defines the default location for media files. The default value is C:\Windows\Media.

- **MediaPathUnexpanded.**   This value is the same as MediaPath, except that it's a REG_EXPAND_SZ value that includes environment variables.

- **PF_AccessoriesName.**   This value defines the name of the Accessories group on the Program Files menu. The default value is Accessories.

- **ProductId.**   This value contains the Windows product ID. This is not the product key that you typed when you registered Windows.

- **ProgramFilesDir.**   This value contains the location of profile files. The default value is C:\Program Files.

- **ProgramFilesPath.**   This value is the same as ProgramFilesDir, except that it uses environment variables. The default value is %ProgramFiles%.

- **SM_AccessoriesName.**   This value contains the name of the Accessories group on the Start menu. The default value is Accessories.

- **SM_GamesName.**   This value contains the name of the Games group on the Start menu. The default value is Games.

- **WallPaperDir.**   This value contains the default location for Windows wallpaper. The default value is %SystemRoot%\web\wallpaper.

App Paths

The subkey `App Paths` specifies the paths of specific program files. It enables you to run a program from the Run dialog box or a command-prompt window without specifying its path. For example, you can type **Wordpad.exe** in the Run dialog box, and Windows looks up the program's path in the `App Paths` key.

The default value for `App Paths`\filename, where *filename* is the program file's name including the *.exe* file extension, contains the command that executes the program. For example, the default value of `App Paths\Wordpad.exe` contains `%ProgramFiles%` `\Windows NT\Accessories\WORDPAD.EXE`. You can add other programs to the `App Paths` subkey so that you can run them without typing their paths. The value `Path` is optional, and it specifies the working path for the program, which is the path where the program finds additional program files. This path is usually to the folder containing the program file.

Applets

The `Applets` subkey contains per-computer settings for Windows accessories. By default, you find a single subkey, `DeluxeCD`, but other accessories store per-computer settings here after you run them. The more interesting accessory settings are in `HKCU\Software\Microsoft\Windows\CurrentVersion\Applets`, though.

Explorer

The key `Explorer` contains Windows Explorer settings. These are per-computer settings, and they're not as interesting to customize as the same subkey in `HKCU`. The subkey `Advanced` defines the settings you see in Explorer's Folder Options dialog box. There's not a lot to customize here because they're templates, but it's interesting to see how Windows Explorer defines and collects these settings.

Explorer\AutoplayHandlers

`HKLM\SOFTWARE\Microsoft\Windows\CurrentVersion\Explorer\AutoplayHandlers` `\EventHandlers` is the key where you find associations between different types of media and the applications that handle them. When Windows detects that you've inserted a CD, DVD, or removable disk, it automatically runs the program that it associates with the type of content on that disk. In Table D-2, look up the type of content you want to customize. Then open the subkey shown in the Subkey column for `EventHandlers`. In that subkey, add any of the following handlers as an empty `REG_SZ` value:

- `MSCDBurningOnArrival`

- `MSGenericVolumeArrival`

- `MSOpenFolder`

- `MSPlayCDAudioOnArrival`

- `MSPlayDVDMovieOnArrival`

- `MSPlayMediaOnArrival`

- `MSPlayMusicFilesOnArrival`

- `MSPlayVideoFilesOnArrival`

- `MSPrintPicturesOnArrival`

- `MSPromptEachTime`

- `MSPromptEachTimeNoContent`

- `MSShowPicturesOnArrival`

- `MSTakeNoAction`

- `MSVideoCameraArrival`

- `MSWiaEventHandler`

Table D-2   Values in `AutoplayHandlers`

Media	Subkey
Generic	`GenericVolumeArrival`
Blank CDR	`HandleCDBurningOnArrival`
Mixed content	`MixedContentOnArrival`
CD audio	`PlayCDAudioOnArrival`
DVD	`PlayDVDMovieOnArrival`
Music files	`PlayMusicFilesOnArrival`
Video files	`PlayVideoFilesOnArrival`
Digital images	`ShowPicturesOnArrival`
Video camera	`VideoCameraArrival`

Explorer\Desktop\NameSpace

The subkey Desktop\Namespace defines the objects you see on the Windows desktop. It contains one subkey for each object, and the name is the class ID of the object's class registration in HKCR. Appendix A, "File Associations," contains more information about HKCR. Don't remove subkeys to hide desktop icons, though. The best way is to use HideDesktopIcons, which you learn about later in this appendix.

Explorer\FindExtensions

The subkey FindExtensions defines the different extensions that you can use to search. The subkey Static contains three subkeys: ShellSearch, WabFind, and WebSearch. The subkey ShellSearch defines the extensions that enable you to search for files, computers, and printers. The subkey WabFind defines the extensions that enable you to search address books. Last, the subkey WebSearch defines the extensions that enable you to search the Internet.

Explorer\HideDesktopIcons

The subkey HideDesktopIcons specifies which icons to show or hide on the desktop. You see two subkeys below the key HideDesktopIcons. The first is ClassicStartMenu. It affects the classic Start menu. This subkey contains REG_DWORD values. The names of these values are the GUID of the object's class registration. The value is either 0x01, which indicates that Windows should hide the icon, or 0x00, which indicates that Windows shouldn't hide the icon. The subkey NewStartPanel affects the new Start menu. Its organization is similar to the subkey ClassicStartMenu.

Explorer\HideMyComputerIcons

The subkey HideMyComputerIcons specifies which icons to show or hide in the My Computer folder. This subkey contains REG_DWORD values. The names of these values are the GUID of the object's class registration. The value is either 0x01, which indicates that Windows should hide the icon, or 0x00, which indicates that Windows shouldn't hide the icon.

Explorer\MyComputer

The MyComputer subkey specifies the path and file name of the special tools you see when you right-click a drive in My Computer and then click Properties. The following subkeys define these paths:

- **BackupPath.** The default value of this subkey contains the command to run when users right-click a drive in My Computer, click Properties, and then click Backup Now on the Tools tab.

- **CleanupPath.** The default value of this subkey contains the command to run when users right-click a drive in My Computer, click Properties, and then click Disk Cleanup on the General tab.

- **DefragPath.** The default value of this subkey contains the command to run when users right-click a drive in My Computer, click Properties, and then click Defragment Now on the Tools tab.

The subkey MyComputer\NameSpace also serves a similar purpose to the subkey Desktop\NameSpace. It defines the objects you see in My Computer. By default, this subkey doesn't contain any GUIDs. You can add subkeys to this subkey named for the object's GUID to add objects to My Computer, though.

Explorer\NetworkNeighborhood\NameSpace

The subkey NetworkNeighborhood\Namespace defines the objects you see in the My Network Places folder. It contains one subkey for each object, and the name is the class ID of the object's class registration in HKCR. By default, you see icons for Network Setup Wizard and Add Network Place.

Explorer\RemoteComputer\NameSpace

The subkey RemoteComputer\NameSpace defines the objects you see when you browse remote computers in the My Network Places folder. It contains one subkey for each object, and the name is the class ID of the object's class registration in HKCR. You see icons for the Printers and Scheduled Tasks folders on remote computers. If browsing remote computers is a slow process, you can remove the subkeys in the RemoteComputer\NameSpace key. This prevents Windows from looking up the remote printers and scheduled tasks on remote computers and could speed up browsing a bit.

Explorer\StartMenu

The subkey StartMenu defines templates for the settings you see in the Taskbar And Start Menu Properties dialog box. Because these are templates, they aren't often useful to customize. Their usefulness to you as a power user or IT professional is in sorting out where Windows stores settings and each setting's values in the registry.

Explorer\User Shell Folders

Windows maintains a set of shared folders in the All Users profile folder, which is in %SystemRoot%\Documents and Settings. The operating system specifies the paths of these folders in User Shell Folders under HKLM. Table D-3 describes each value you find in User Shell Folders and the default path. The first column is the folder's internal name, and the second is the default path. You can redirect these folders to different locations by changing the path in User Shell Folders.

The values in Table D-3 are REG_EXPAND_SZ values, so you can use environment variables in them. Use %AllUsersProfile% in a path to direct the folder somewhere inside the All Users profile folder. To redirect the Common Favorites folder to the network, set the value Common Favorites to \\Server\Share. The next time the operating system starts, Windows updates a second key, HKLM\SOFTWARE\Microsoft\Windows\Current-Version\Explorer\Shell Folders, with the paths from User Shell Folders. Windows doesn't actually use the values in Shell Folders.

Table D-3 Special Folders

Name	Default Path
Common AppData	%AllUsersProfile%\Application Data
Common Desktop	%AllUsersProfile%\Desktop
Common Documents	%AllUsersProfile%\Documents
Common Favorites	%AllUsersProfile%\Favorites
Common Programs	%AllUsersProfile%\Start Menu\Programs
Common Start Menu	%AllUsersProfile%\Start Menu
Common Startup	%AllUsersProfile%\Start Menu\Programs\Startup
Common Templates	%AllUsersProfile%\Templates

Explorer\VisualEffects

The subkey VisualEffects contains templates for the settings you see in the Performance Options dialog box. They aren't useful for customizing Windows, but they are handy to map specific settings to their corresponding registry settings.

Policies

The key HKLM\SOFTWARE\Microsoft\Windows\CurrentVersion\Policies is the policy branch that Windows inherits from earlier versions of Windows. Windows still stores many policies in this branch, although the new, preferred policy branch is HKLM \SOFTWARE\Policies. Often, the settings you find in this key are leftovers from old-style policy files that have tattooed the registry.

Run

Windows runs the commands in the subkey Run for every user who logs on to the computer every time they log on. The name of each value in this subkey is arbitrary. The operating system runs the command in each REG_SZ value, though. So if you don't want to use the Start Up group in the Program Files menu to run programs when you log on to the computer, you can add the command to the Run subkey. Although this subkey affects all users because it's in HKLM, the commands in HKCU\Software \Microsoft\Windows\CurrentVersion\Run are per-user commands. Chapter 18, "Fixing Common IT Problems," describes a useful workaround using this subkey.

RunOnce

The RunOnce subkey is similar to the Run subkey. The difference is that Windows removes commands from the RunOnce subkey after running them. Thus, commands in the RunOnce subkey execute only one time.

Uninstall

The Uninstall key describes how to remove applications using the Add Or Remove Programs dialog box. Each subkey, Uninstall\Name, describes how to remove the program. For example, the Add Or Remove Programs dialog box uses the REG_SZ value DisplayName to display the program's name in the list, and the REG_SZ value UninstallString contains the command that it uses to uninstall the program.

Some programs store more information in the Uninstall key. For example, in Uninstall\SnagIt5, TechSmith SnagIt stores the location in which you installed the program so that it can find the program files to remove. Some programs store the location of any shortcuts they create in Uninstall\Name so that they can remove those when you remove the program.

SYSTEM

The subkeys in HKLM\SYSTEM are ControlSet*N*, where *N* is a number beginning with 001. These are control sets, and they describe the computer's configuration. Of all the configuration data stored in the registry, this is by far the most important. Windows maintains at least two control sets to make sure that the operating system can always start. If the first fails, you can start with the second by choosing Last Known Good Configuration from the boot options menu.

The subkey CurrentControlSet is a link to the current control set ControlSet*N*. Windows identifies the current control set using the key HKLM\SYSTEM\Select. The REG_DWORD value Current contains the number of the current control set. The REG_DWORD value LastKnownGood contains the number of the last control set that worked properly. This is the control set that Windows loads when users choose Last Known Good Configuration.

All the control sets have a similar organization and similar contents. The sections following this one describe the contents of CurrentControlSet, which is a link to one of the numbered control sets.

> **Note**   The following sections provide an overview of the contents of control sets. The *Windows Resource Kit Registry Reference*, available at *http://go.microsoft.com/ fwlink/?linkid=4543*, provides detailed descriptions of the many settings contained in them.

CurrentControlSet\Control

The subkey CurrentControlSet\Control contains values that control how Windows starts. It defines the components to load and their configurations. The following list describes many of the interesting subkeys of Control:

- **BackupRestore.**   This subkey contains subkeys that specify the files and registry keys that Windows won't back up or restore. You learn about this subkey in Chapter 3, "Backing Up the Registry."

- **Class.**   This subkey stores configuration data for classes of hardware devices.

- **CrashControl.**   This subkey contains values that specify what happens when Windows locks, fails, or terminates abnormally.

- **CriticalDeviceDatabase.**   This subkey contains the critical device database, which you learn about in Chapter 15, "Cloning Disks with Sysprep." It contains configuration data for new devices that Windows must install and start before the components that the operating system normally installs are started.

- **FileSystem.**   This subkey contains file system configurations.

- **GraphicsDrivers.**   This subkey contains DirectX and graphics drivers settings.

- **GroupOrderList.**   This subkey contains the order in which Windows loads services in a service group when the operating system starts.

- **hivelist.**   This subkey defines the locations of hive files that are loaded in the registry. You learned about this subkey in Chapter 1, "Learning the Basics."

- **IDConfigDB.**   This subkey contains settings that identify the current hardware configuration for Windows.

- **Lsa.**   This subkey contains configuration data for the Local Security Authority (LSA).

- **Network.**   This subkey contains network settings.

- **NetworkProvider.**   This subkey contains network provider settings.

- **Print.**   This subkey contains printer settings that apply to all users.

- **PriorityControl.**   This subkey specifies the relative priority of foreground applications to background applications.

- **SafeBoot.**   This subkey contains data about the computer's safe-mode settings. See Chapter 3, "Backing Up the Registry," to learn about boot options.

- **SecurePipeServers.**   This subkey contains the winreg subkey, which controls remote access to the registry. See Chapter 8, "Configuring Windows Security," to learn how to use this subkey to secure remote access to the registry.

- **ServiceGroupOrder.**   This subkey contains a list of all service groups in the order in which Windows loaded them.

- **ServiceProvider.**   This subkey contains data about the installed service providers.

- **Session Manager.**   This subkey contains Session Manager data.

- **Update.**   This subkey contains configuration data for System Policy. Chapter 7, "Using Registry-Based Policy," describes how to use this subkey.

- **VirtualDeviceDrivers.**   This subkey contains data for virtual device drivers.

- **Windows.**   This subkey contains data for the Win32 subsystem.

- **WOW.**   This subkey contains settings that control MS-DOS-based applications and applications created for 16-bit versions of Windows.

CurrentControlSet\Enum

The subkey `CurrentControlSet\Enum` is a database of all the computer's devices that Windows recognized. This database stores configuration data for hardware devices separately from the device drivers they use. This database is an important part of Plug and Play in Windows.

> **Tip**   The most common reason to hack `CurrentControlSet\Enum` is to remove devices that don't appear in Device Manager. Windows provides a better, safer alternative. In Device Manager, click View, Show Hidden Devices; and then remove the devices you want to remove from the `Enum` subkey.

CurrentControlSet\Hardware Profiles

The subkey `CurrentControlSet\Hardware Profiles` stores hardware profiles, which are usually created for laptop computers that have configurations for their docked and undocked states. A hardware profile contains changes to the original hardware profile configured in `HKLM\SOFTWARE` and `HKLM\SYSTEM` keys. Windows doesn't change the original value, so it can change hardware profiles easily. You use the Hardware Profiles dialog box to create and choose hardware profiles. Also, Windows automatically creates hardware profiles when it finds scenarios that require them.

Each hardware profile is in the subkey `Hardware Profiles\N`, where N is an incremental number beginning with `0000`. These subkeys look like stripped-down versions of `HKLM\SOFTWARE` and `HKLM\SYSTEM` keys. They contain only those values that the hardware profile changes, though. In other words, when Windows uses a hardware profile, the settings in the profile overwrite the settings in `SOFTWARE` and `SYSTEM`. They represent a powerful way to customize the operating system for different hardware scenarios, which is particularly important to laptop users.

The subkey `HKLM\SYSTEM\CurrentControlSet\Hardware Profiles\Current` is a link to the current hardware profile. `HKCC` is also a link to the current hardware profile (which explains why you don't find a separate section for `HKCC` in this appendix). Changing a value in any of these three locations changes the same value in the remaining two locations.

Windows maintains information about all its hardware profiles in the key `HKLM\SYSTEM\CurrentControlSet\Control\IDConfigDB`. This key contains the `REG_DWORD` value `CurrentConfig`, which indicates the number of the current hardware profile. The subkey `Hardware Profiles` in `IDConfigDB` defines each hardware profile in further detail. For example, each subkey in `Hardware Profiles` defines the friendly name of the hardware profile.

CurrentControlSet\Services

The subkey `CurrentControlSet\Services` defines services, such as device drivers, file system drivers, and Win32 services. The settings differ for each service. Each subkey in the `Services` key has the name of the service that uses it. This is frequently the name of the file from which Windows loads the service. Some of the subkeys in `Services` represent devices and services that are actually installed and running on the computer. Others aren't installed or aren't enabled. While different services might have unique values and subkeys, they all have the following values and subkeys in common:

- **DependOnGroup.**   This REG_MULTI_SZ value specifies the service groups that Windows must load before loading this service. This value ensures that all of a service's prerequisites are met.

- **DependOnService.**   This REG_MULTI_SZ value specifies the services that Windows must load before loading this service. This value ensures that all of a service's prerequisites are met.

- **Enum.**   You see this subkey in services that store values for device drivers and other services that control devices. It stores information about the hardware associated with this service.

- **ErrorControl.**   This REG_DWORD value specifies how to continue if the device driver fails to load or initialize properly. The following values are possible:

    - ❏   0x00 (Ignore). Ignore the error and continue starting Windows.

    - ❏   0x01 (Normal). Display a warning and continue starting Windows.

    - ❏   0x02 (Severe). Restart using the last known good configuration, and if that fails, continue starting Windows.

    - ❏   0x03 (Critical). Restart using the last known good configuration, and if that fails, do not continue starting Windows.

- **Group.**   This REG_DWORD value specifies the service group to which the service belongs. If this value doesn't exist, the service doesn't belong to a group, and the service loads after all service groups load.

- **ImagePath.**   This REG_EXPAND_SZ value specifies the path and name of the service's executable file. Network adapters don't use this value.

- **Linkage.**   This subkey contains data for binding network components. They associate network services with protocols and devices that support them.

- **NetworkProvider.**   This subkey contains the name of the device, the provider, and the provider order for a network service.

- **ObjectName.**   This `REG_SZ` value specifies the name of a driver object that the I/O Manager uses to load the device driver. This value exists in services that are kernel-mode or file system drivers.

- **Parameters.**   This subkey contains entries specific to each service.

- **Performance.**   This subkey contains data for the service's performance counter.

- **Security.**   This subkey contains information about a driver's or service's permissions.

- **Start.**   This `REG_DWORD` value specifies how Windows loads or starts the service. The following values are possible:

    - ❏   0x00 (Boot). The kernel loader loads the driver when Windows boots.

    - ❏   0x01 (System). The I/O Subsystem loads the driver during kernel initialization.

    - ❏   0x02 (Automatic). The Session Control Manager starts the service automatically.

    - ❏   0x03 (Manual). The service must be started manually.

    - ❏   0x04 (Disabled). The service is never started.

- **Tag.**   This `REG_DWORD` value specifies the services tag number, which is a unique number within the service group.

- **Type.**   This `REG_DWORD` value indicates the service's type. The following values are possible:

    - ❏   0x01. Kernel-mode device drivers

    - ❏   0x02. File system drivers

    - ❏   0x04. Arguments for an adapter

    - ❏   0x08. File system driver services

    - ❏   0x10. Win32 programs that run their own processes

    - ❏   0x20. Win32 programs that share processes

    - ❏   0x110. Win32 programs that run in processes by themselves

    - ❏   0x120. Win32 programs that share processes and interact with users

Index

About the Author

Jerry Honeycutt empowers people to work more productively by helping them deploy and use popular technologies, including the Microsoft Windows and Microsoft Office product families. He reaches out through his frequent writings, talks, and consulting practice (specializing in business desktop deployment).

Jerry is intimately involved in Microsoft's desktop-deployment initiatives. He was the documentation lead for the Microsoft Solution Accelerator for Business Desktop Deployment (BDD) 2.0. Following this project, Jerry developed Microsoft's courseware for BDD. Currently, he is the development lead for two market-focused versions of BDD.

As a best-selling author, Jerry has written more than 25 books. His most recent includes *Microsoft Windows Desktop Deployment Resource Kit* (Microsoft Press, 2004). Most of his books are sold internationally and are available in a variety of languages.

Jerry is also a columnist for Microsoft's Windows XP Expert Zone, a Web site for Windows XP enthusiasts, and for Microsoft TechNet, focusing on desktop deployment and management. He makes frequent contributions to a variety of other content areas on Microsoft's Web site. For example, Jerry has written more than 20 white papers on topics ranging from wireless networking to desktop deployment.

Jerry is a frequent speaker at assorted public events, such as COMDEX, Developer Days, the Microsoft Exchange Conference, and Microsoft Global Briefing. He occasionally gives webcasts on Microsoft's TechNet Web site.

In addition to writing and speaking, Jerry has a long history of using his skills for more practical purposes—providing technical leadership to business. He specializes in desktop deployment, management, and networking—particularly using the Windows product family. Companies like Sunbeam Products, Capital One, Travelers, IBM, Nielsen North America, IRM, Howard Systems International, and NCR have all leveraged his expertise. He continues writing, training, and consulting to serve the business community.

Jerry graduated from University of Texas at Dallas in 1992 with a Bachelor of Science in Computer Science. He also studied at Texas Tech University in Lubbock, Texas. In his spare time, Jerry plays golf, is an avid amateur photographer, and travels. Jerry lives in the Dallas suburb of Frisco.

For more information about Jerry and how he can help you deploy the business desktop, see his Web site at *http://www.honeycutt.com* or send mail to *jerry@honeycutt.com*.

What do you think of this book?
We want to hear from you!

Do you have a few minutes to participate in a brief online survey? Microsoft is interested in hearing your feedback about this publication so that we can continually improve our books and learning resources for you.

To participate in our survey, please visit:

www.microsoft.com/learning/booksurvey

And enter this book's ISBN, 0-7356-2218-3. As a thank-you to survey participants in the United States and Canada, each month we'll randomly select five respondents to win one of five $100 gift certificates from a leading online merchant.* At the conclusion of the survey, you can enter the drawing by providing your e-mail address, which will be used for prize notification *only*.

Thanks in advance for your input. Your opinion counts!

Sincerely,

Microsoft Learning

Learn More. Go Further.

To see special offers on Microsoft Learning products for developers, IT professionals, and home and office users, visit: *www.microsoft.com/learning/booksurvey*